THE CHURCH'S BIBLE

General Editor
Robert Louis Wilken

• •

The Song of Songs
Richard A. Norris Jr.

Isaiah
Robert Louis Wilken

Romans
J. Patout Burns Jr.

1 Corinthians
Judith L. Kovacs

ROMANS

*Interpreted by
Early Christian Commentators*

Translated and Edited by

J. Patout Burns Jr.

with

Father Constantine Newman

William B. Eerdmans Publishing Company
Grand Rapids, Michigan

Wm. B. Eerdmans Publishing Co.
4035 Park East Court SE, Grand Rapids, Michigan 49546
www.eerdmans.com

© 2012 J. Patout Burns Jr.
All rights reserved

Hardcover edition 2012
Paperback edition 2021

ISBN 978-0-8028-8191-5

Library of Congress Cataloging-in-Publication Data

Romans: interpreted by early Christian commentators /
translated and edited by J. Patout Burns, Jr. with Constantine Newman.
    p.   cm. — (The church's Bible)
ISBN 978-0-8028-8191-5 (pbk.: alk. paper)
1. Bible. N.T. Romans — Commentaries.
I. Burns, J. Patout. II. Newman, Constantine.
BS2665.53.R67 2012
227′.10609 — dc23

                                  2011039489

The Scripture quotations in this publication are from the Revised Standard Version of the Bible, copyrighted 1946, 1952 © 1971, 1973 by the Division of Christian Education of the National Council of Churches of Christ in the U.S.A., and used by permission. All rights reserved.

To Sean Edward McEvenue

Contents

Series Preface	ix
Acknowledgments	xi
Interpreting the New Testament	xiii
An Introduction to Romans	xxiii
Preface to Romans	1
Romans 1	13
Romans 2	37
Romans 3	61
Romans 4	83
Romans 5	102
Romans 6	132
Romans 7	154
Romans 8	182
Romans 9	217
Romans 10	245
Romans 11	260
Romans 12	289
Romans 13	314
Romans 14	334
Romans 15	359
Romans 16	381

CONTENTS

APPENDIX 1: *Authors of Works Excerpted*   394

APPENDIX 2: *Sources of Texts Translated*   396

Index of Names   414

Index of Subjects   417

Index of Scripture References   422

Series Preface

The volumes in The Church's Bible are designed to present the Holy Scriptures as understood and interpreted during the first millennium of Christian history. The Christian Church has a long tradition of commentary on the Bible. In the early Church all discussion of theological topics, of moral issues, and of Christian practice took the biblical text as the starting point. The recitation of the psalms and meditation on books of the Bible, particularly in the context of the liturgy or of private prayer, nurtured the spiritual life. For most of the Church's history theology and scriptural interpretation were one. Theology was called *sacra pagina* (the sacred page), and the task of interpreting the Bible was a spiritual enterprise.

During the first two centuries interpretation of the Bible took the form of exposition of select passages on particular issues. For example, Irenaeus, bishop of Lyons, discussed many passages from the Old and New Testaments in his defense of the apostolic faith against the Gnostics. By the beginning of the third century Christian bishops and scholars had begun to preach regular series of sermons that followed the biblical books verse by verse. Some wrote more scholarly commentaries that examined in greater detail grammatical, literary, and historical questions as well as theological ideas and spiritual teachings found in the texts. From Origen of Alexandria, the first great biblical commentator in the Church's history, we have, among others, a large verse-by-verse commentary on the Gospel of John, a series of homilies on Genesis and Exodus, and a large part of his *Commentary on the Epistle to the Romans*. In the course of the first eight hundred years of Christian history Christian teachers produced a library of biblical commentaries and homilies on the Bible.

Today this ancient tradition of biblical interpretation is known only in bits and pieces, and even where it still shapes our understanding of the Bible, for example, in the selection of readings for Christian worship (e.g., Isaiah 7 and Isaiah 9 read at Christmas), or the interpretation of the Psalms in daily prayer, the spiritual world that gave it birth remains shadowy and indistinct. It is the purpose of this series to make available the richness of the Church's classical tradition of interpretation for clergy, Sunday school and Bible class teachers, men and women living in religious communities, and all serious readers of the Bible.

Anyone who reads the ancient commentaries realizes at once that they are deeply spiritual, insightful, edifying, and, shall we say, "biblical." Early Christian thinkers moved in the world of the Bible, understood its idiom, loved its teaching, and were filled with awe before its mysteries. They believed in the maxim, "Scripture interprets Scripture." They knew something that has largely been forgotten by biblical scholars, and their commentaries are an untapped resource for understanding the Bible as a book about Christ.

The distinctive mark of The Church's Bible is that it draws extensively on the ancient commentaries, not only on random comments drawn from theological treatises, sermons, or devotional works. Its volumes will, in the main, offer fairly lengthy excerpts from the ancient commentaries and from series of sermons on specific books. For example, in the first volume on the Song of Songs, there are long passages from Origen of Alexandria's *Commentary on the Song of Songs,* from Gregory of Nyssa's *Homilies on the Song,* and from Bernard of Clairvaux's sermons on the Song. Some passages will be as brief as a paragraph, but many will be several pages in length, and some longer. We believe that only through a deeper immersion in the ancient sources can contemporary readers enter into the inexhaustible spiritual and theological world of the early Church and hence of the Bible.

It is also hoped that longer passages will be suitable for private devotional reading and for spiritual reading in religious communities, in Bible study groups, and in prayer circles.

ROBERT LOUIS WILKEN
General Editor

Acknowledgments

A book of this scope and size is the work of many scholars. Robert L. Wilken developed the plan for the series and has been involved in each of the many stages of this particular volume. He called attention to textual resources, such as the critical editions of the fragments from the commentaries of Origen and Cyril of Alexandria. He helped choose passages for inclusion (and exclusion); he reviewed each translation to maintain continuity of style and diction across the many volumes in this series. In consultation with Judith Kovacs and myself, he determined the style of presentation used in the volumes dedicated to Isaiah, 1 Corinthians, and Romans.

Kevin Herbert, my colleague in the Classics Department at Washington University, and David Hunter made draft translations for some early chapters. Janet Fairweather contributed a rough translation of Ambrosiaster's commentary on Romans that I used as the base for the present work. Thomas Scheck made his translation of Origen's commentary available for consultation prior to its publication. Fr. Constantine Newman initially joined the project because of his expertise in the work of John Chrysostom; he then assumed responsibility for translating the excerpts of Apollinaris of Laodicea, Cyril of Alexandria, Gennadius of Constantinople, and Theodoret of Cyrrhus.

The selection of passages for inclusion was assisted in many ways. Joseph Fitzmyer's commentary on the Letter to the Romans (Anchor Bible, vol. 33) provided early guidance in the use of patristic materials for the interpretation of Paul's text. My colleagues at Vanderbilt University Divinity School were more direct contributors. Amy-Jill Levine offered principled advice on handling the condemnations of contemporary Jews by early Christian commentators. Eugene TeSelle suggested early anthologies of Augustine's work, such as that of Eugippus, as guides for identifying relevant passages. In addition to the editors of the scholarly texts on which these translations were based, particular gratitude is due to the editors of the electronic database, *Corpus Augustinianum Gissense,* produced by the Zentrum für Augustinus-Forschung in Würzburg. This resource facilitated a review of every quotation of the text of Romans in Augustine's extant writings and thereby the construction of an Augustinian commentary on Romans.

The resources of the divinity collection in Pius XII Memorial Library of St. Louis University, the Thomas P. O'Neill, Jr. Library of Boston College, and the Vanderbilt Divinity Library were essential to this work in its various stages. Milton Essenburg of Eerdmans Publishing Company undertook final preparation of the text for printing. Only the present writer knows how many errors he corrected — and asks the indulgence of the reader for those that remain.

This volume is dedicated to Sean Edward McEvenue, who introduced this writer to the study of Scripture, and to his colleagues who formed the faculty of Regis College in Willowdale, Ontario.

J. PATOUT BURNS, JR.

Interpreting the New Testament

The traditional greeting on Easter morning is "Christ is risen!" To which the response is: "He is risen indeed. Alleluia!" This ancient phrase echoes the greeting of the angel to Mary Magdalene and Mary the mother of James and Joseph as they arrived at the sepulchre to anoint the body of Jesus: "He is not here; for he has risen, as he said" (Matt 28:6). After the two disciples recognized Christ in the breaking of bread on the road to Emmaus, they immediately rose and returned to the others gathered in Jerusalem, announcing: "The Lord has risen indeed, and has appeared to Simon!" (Luke 24:34).

The resurrection of Christ is the ground of Christian belief and the wellspring from which the books of the New Testament flow. The Gospels culminate in the resurrection, at the beginning of the Epistle to the Romans Paul invokes the resurrection as warrant for his apostleship, and he brings 1 Corinthians to a close with a magnificent peroration on the resurrected body. In places 1 Peter reads like an Easter baptismal sermon ("we have been born anew to a living hope through the resurrection of Jesus Christ from the dead" [1 Pet 1:3]), and in the Acts of the Apostles the disciples of Christ are portrayed again and again as "witnesses" to the resurrection (1:22; 2:32; 3:15, et al.).

The New Testament is a collection of books whose authors bore witness in their lives (and some in their deaths) to the living Christ. "It is no longer I who live," writes St. Paul in Galatians, "but Christ who lives in me" (Gal 2:20). Before there was a book, there were persons who handed on Christ's sayings and told of the marvelous things God had worked in him. First came Christ, then the witnesses, then the books. This ordering of things is at the heart of the early interpretation of the New Testament. The goal was to delve more deeply into the mystery of God revealed in Christ, to whom the writings bear witness. In introducing the volumes on the New Testament in this series, it may be helpful to say a few things about how the early Christians approached this task.

We are inclined to begin with the book, with historical context and social setting, words and idioms, grammar and literary forms, religious and theological vocabulary, and the many other topics that command our attention. But the early Christians began with the risen Christ, and long before there was a book the faith was handed on orally. Although St. Paul said that he had received his commission "through a revelation of Jesus Christ" (Gal 1:12), not from a human intermediary, he associated himself with traditions that he had received from others. "For I *delivered* to you as of first importance what I also *received*, that Christ died for our sins in accordance with the scriptures, that he was buried, that he was raised on the third day in accordance with the scriptures, and that he appeared to Cephas, then to the twelve. Then he appeared to more than five hundred brethren at one time, most of whom are still alive, though some have fallen asleep. Then he appeared to James, then to all the apostles. Last of all, as to one untimely born, he appeared to me" (1 Cor 15:3-8).

The memory of Christ centered on his death and resurrection, and the brief narrative of his birth, suffering, death, burial, and resurrection formed the core of early Christian tradition. It was complemented by "sayings" of Jesus, but the sayings were understood in light of the events, as the structure of the Gospels makes plain. The setting of the early confessions of faith was almost certainly Christian worship, and they reflect local catechetical instruction. The details varied from place to place, but the central narrative remained constant. Here, for example, is a somewhat freer (and idiosyncratic) form that appears in 1 Peter: "For Christ also *died for sins once for all*, the righteous for the unrighteous, that he might bring us to God, *being put to death in the flesh but made alive in the spirit;* in which he went and preached to the spirits in prison, who formerly did not obey when God's patience waited in the days of Noah, during the building of the ark, in which few, that is, eight persons, were saved through water. Baptism, which corresponds to this, now saves you, not as a removal of dirt from the body but as an appeal to God for a clear conscience, through the *resurrection of Jesus Christ, who has gone into heaven and is at the right hand of God,* with angels, authorities, and powers subject to him" (1 Pet 3:18-22).

The mention of Baptism indicates that the early tradition also included how one was to understand Christian practices. In 1 Corinthians Paul's language about the Lord's Supper is similar to what he had used about the resurrection: "For I *received* from the Lord what I also *delivered* to you, that the Lord Jesus on the night when he was betrayed took bread, and when he had given thanks, he broke it, and said, 'This is my body which is for you. Do this in remembrance of me.' In the same way also the cup, after supper, saying, 'This cup is the new covenant in my blood. Do this, as often as you drink it, in remembrance of me.' For as often as you eat this bread and drink this cup, you proclaim the Lord's death until he comes" (1 Cor 11:23-26). Though Paul says that he had received the account about the Last Supper directly from the Lord, the terms "received" and "delivered" are the customary words for handing on tradition. Paul is repeating word for word what he has received from others.

Early in the Church's history, then, the living Christ was identified by verbal formulas and practices, notably Baptism and the Eucharist. The purpose of the creedlike summaries of faith was primarily catechetical, but they served as guarantors of the truth of what had taken place during Christ's lifetime and unlocked the Jewish scriptures, what Christians would later call the Old Testament. This is evident in an illuminating testimony from Ignatius, bishop of Antioch, at the end of the first century. The Christians in Philadelphia in western Asia Minor were divided over some aspects of Christian teaching, and Ignatius exhorted them to abandon their contentiousness. Apparently some had argued that the only way the matter could be settled was by appeal to what they called "the archives," that is, the Old Testament. "If I do not find it in the archives, I do not believe it to be in the gospel," they said. Ignatius, however, demurred. "For me," he writes, "the archives are Jesus Christ, the inviolable archives are his cross and death and his resurrection and faith through him...."[1] Although most, if not all, of the books of the New Testament had been written by the time he became bishop, Ignatius makes no mention of Christian writings to settle the dispute. He appeals only to the person of Christ and the brief narrative of his saving deeds, not to written documents.

The time was fast approaching, however, when oral tradition would be complemented by written documents. But not replaced! Even after the writings of the apostles formed the "canon" of writings we call the New Testament, the oral witness of the apostles remained alive. Irenaeus, bishop of Lyons, at the end of the second century still conceived of apostolic tradition in terms of persons first, books second. "The Lord of all gave to his apostles the power of the gospel, and through them we have learned the truth, that is, the teaching of the Son of God.... We have not learned the plan of our salvation from any others than those through whom the gospel came to us. They first proclaimed it, and then later by the will of God handed it down to us in writings...."[2] For St. Irenaeus the most authentic tradition was oral, what "the elders, the disciples of the apostles, have handed on to us."[3]

At the same time Irenaeus is the first writer to draw on the apostolic writings as part of an authoritative collection. He does not use the term "New Testament" but its basic structure of Gospels, the Acts of the Apostles, and epistles is clearly visible in his works. In fact, a large part of his work against the Gnostics is given over to the exegesis of specific passages from the New Testament that were in dispute. But the books did not stand on their own. They needed to be explained and individual passages fitted into the pattern of God's saving work in Christ. For this task the oral tradition confessed in the rule of faith and explained by teachers whose lineage could be traced back to the apostles was indispensable. Without a grasp of the plot that holds the books together, said Irenaeus, the Bible is as vacuous as a mosaic in which the tiny colored stones have been arbitrarily rearranged without reference to the original design. Even the apostolic writings, the Christian scriptures, required a framework of interpretation, a canopy of beliefs and practices to envelop the texts.

The oral tradition took form in a tripartite, that is, trinitarian, rule of faith that identified God by narrating key events recorded in the Scriptures, the creation of the world, the inspiration of the prophets, the coming of Christ in the flesh, his death and resurrection, the outpouring of the Holy Spirit. Though drawn from the New Testament, the rule was distinct from the apostolic writings; it was a brief confession handed on at Baptism that provided a key to the Scriptures. In other words, the Scriptures were read and interpreted in light of the Church's tradition. Or, to put it more precisely, the tradition embodied in the apostolic writings, that is, the New Testament, was complemented by the tradition, equally apostolic, that had been handed on orally (primarily in Christian worship) from one generation to another. The New Testament was the book of the Church, and interpretation took place within a context of shared beliefs and practices.

1. *Philadelphians* 8.
2. *Against Heresies* 3, preface.
3. *Demonstration of the Apostolic Preaching* 3.

For example, during the great debate over the relation of the Son to the Father in the fourth century, Athanasius, bishop of Alexandria, used Irenaeus's principle of interpretation to marshal scriptural support for the decrees of the Council of Nicea. Arius, whose teaching had been condemned at the council, had called attention to the word "therefore" in Phil 2:9, "*Therefore* God has highly exalted him [Christ] and bestowed on him the name which is above every name." In his view the "therefore" implied that the Son had "become" God and was not God from eternity. Athanasius showed that this was an idiosyncratic and "private" interpretation contrary to the "Church's sense of the Scripture" handed on orally and expressed in other texts in the New Testament, for example, John 1:1, "and the Word was God," or Heb 1:6, "Let all God's angels worship him." For good measure he points out that three verses earlier St. Paul had said that Christ, who was "in the form of God, did not count equality with God a thing to be grasped" (Phil 2:6).[4]

By the third century the canon of the New Testament was universally recognized, though certain books remained in dispute, for example, the Apocalypse. Writers such as Tertullian in North Africa and Clement and Origen in Alexandria had at their disposal a Christian Bible composed of two parts, Old Testament and New Testament. But the written Scripture never replaced the living tradition, and its interpretation was guided by the rule of faith and Christian practice. The engine that drove interpretation was the Church's faith in the triune God confessed in the baptismal creed, made present through Christ in the consecrated bread and wine of the Eucharist, whose power and love were confirmed in the lives of the faithful by the searing flame of the Holy Spirit. Once there was a written Scripture, interpretation inevitably entered a new phase. The church fathers did not doubt that the apostolic writings bore witness to the one God, creator of all things, to the Son Jesus Christ the Lord, and to the outpouring of the Holy Spirit to call into one fellowship a new people. But interpretation not only has to do with the big picture but is most decidedly an exercise in particularity, how specific words and passages are to be understood and related to the faith delivered to the apostles. This was a demanding assigment that could be accomplished only through study, prayer, and, let it not be forgotten, argument and debate. Even in the early centuries the New Testament required interpretation, and its readers no less than we had to train their minds and tutor their affections to discern its meaning. All this took time and hard labor, and the number and variety of commentaries and homilies on books and passages of the New Testament during the early centuries of the Church's history is astonishing. Yet the purpose of commentary was always kept in sight. Interpretation was a spiritual voyage of discovery, a way of exploring the luminous world revealed in the coming of Christ.

A good illustration is Gregory of Nyssa's interpretation of the word "righteousness" or "justice" (either a possible translation of a single Greek word), which occurs twice in the Beatitudes: "Blessed are those who hunger and thirst for righteousness (or justice), for they shall be satisfied." And: "Blessed are those who are persecuted for the sake of justice [or righteousness], for theirs is the kingdom of heaven" (Matt 5:6, 10). The same term occurs in the writings of St. Paul, and Gregory of Nyssa, a fourth-century Greek com-

---

4. *Against the Arians* 1.37-44.

mentator, noted in particular its use in 1 Corinthians: "[God] is the source of your life in Christ Jesus, whom God made our wisdom, our *righteousness* [or justice] and sanctification and redemption" (1 Cor 1:30).

In a homily on the fourth beatitude Gregory asks: "What is justice?" to which he gives a traditional philosophical answer: justice is to give to each according to his worth. But then he observes that there is a higher form of justice, not based on merit. This is the justice we are to desire; hence the beatitude speaks of those who "hunger and thirst for justice." Here the homily takes a surprising turn as Gregory offers what he calls a "bolder interpretation": in the beatitude the Lord proposes to his followers that he himself is what they desire, "for he became for us wisdom from God, justice, sanctification, and redemption" (1 Cor 1:30).

By appealing to 1 Corinthians Gregory opens the beatitude to a christological interpretation. In his view it is speaking about hungering and thirsting for the living God, as David said in the psalm, "My soul thirsts for the living God" (Ps 42:2). By interpreting the words of Jesus with the help of St. Paul, a procedure, one might observe, that would be shunned by a modern interpreter, Gregory is able to transform the beatitude into an invitation to seek not only "justice" but the living God, or, better, to find justice by knowing Christ. The one who tastes the Lord "has received God into himself and is filled with him for whom he has thirsted and hungered. He acknowledges that he has been filled with the one he desires when he says, 'Christ lives in me' (Gal 2:20)."[5]

Some texts posed perplexing theological problems, as, for example, the passage at the beginning of the Gospel of John: "No one has ever seen God" (John 1:18). The text is straightforward enough: God has never been seen. 1 Tim 6:16 went further: "no one has ever seen or can see [God]."[6] Yet the prophet Isaiah said explicitly that he had seen God: "In the year that King Uzziah died I *saw* the Lord sitting upon a throne, high and lifted up" (Isa 6:1). How was one to reconcile these passages and relate the words of John to other texts, for example, the report in the book of Genesis that Jacob saw God "face to face" (Gen 32:30)?

For many modern interpreters theological questions — for example, what it means to see God — are quite secondary to the task of interpretation and the unity of the Bible; that is, how one book in the Scriptures is to be understood in relation to other parts of the Bible is peripheral to their exegesis. Isaiah is Isaiah, and John is John. But early Christian commentators believed that the Bible spoke with a single (though nuanced) voice, and they took apparent inconsistencies between biblical authors as an invitation to probe beneath the surface of the inspired words, that is, to penetrate the spiritual reality about which the text spoke, in this case to grasp what it means to see God. "Seeing," they explained, was a form of knowledge, and they claimed that when all the relevant passages are considered, the Scriptures teach that God can be known, although the fullness of his divinity, his ineffable nature or essence, is beyond our comprehension. "It is one thing to see," writes Augustine, "it is another to grasp the whole by seeing."[7] One writer said that

---

5. *Homily 4 on the Beatitudes* (Gregorii Nysseni Opera VII/II.122-23).
6. 1 John 4:12, "No man has ever seen God," was also cited.
7. *Letter* 147.8.21. This letter, a little treatise "on seeing God," discusses the relevant biblical texts.

in the Scriptures "see" means the same as "possess," citing the words of the psalmist: "May you see the good things of Jerusalem" (Ps 128:5), where "see" means "to find." Hence he concludes that one who sees God "possesses all that is good."[8] By drawing on the many uses of the word "see" in the Scriptures (including the beatitude, "Blessed are the pure in heart, for they shall see God" [Matt 5:8]) Christian thinkers were able to explore the place of the vision of God in Christian life and hope.[9]

At times a single biblical word could inspire a preacher to lyrical heights. In a memorable sermon on the phrase "that God may be all in all" (1 Cor 15:28), Augustine asked, "What is the meaning of 'all'? [God] will be for you whatever you desired here on earth, whatever you valued. What did you want here, what did you love? To eat and drink? He himself will be food for you, he himself will be drink. What did you want here? A fragile and transient bodily health? He himself will be immortality for you. What did you look for here? Wealth? Greedy man, what is it that will satisfy you if God himself does not? Well, what did you love? Glory, honors? God will be your glory."[10]

When they listened to the Scriptures read in divine worship or pondered its words in prayer, the early Christians heard the Word of God spoken to their communities and to their lives. In his *Commentary on the Gospel of John* Origen of Alexandria, the first and greatest biblical scholar in the early Church, explained that "a gospel" is a "discourse containing an account of things that have happened which, because of the good they bring, are a source of joy to the hearer." The gospel is a "word that makes present something good for the believer or a word that the promised good is present." Its subject, continues Origen, is the "presence of Jesus Christ, the firstborn of all creation (Col 1:15), among men for their salvation." Accordingly, the Gospels are the "firstfruits" of the Scriptures, and the "firstfruits" of the Gospels is the Gospel according to John, "whose meaning cannot be understood unless one reclines on Jesus' breast (John 13:23) and accepts Mary from Jesus as his own mother."[11]

Anyone who wrote a commentary on the Gospels in this spirit would discover much in the biblical text that a strictly historical approach would miss. And the reader of Origen's *Commentary on John* will not be disappointed. Not only was Origen engaged with the spiritual and theological meaning of the text, but he also assumed that to understand the Gospel one must know Christ, in his words "recline on Jesus' breast." But his commentary is also a work of great scholarship and learning. In the first book he devotes many pages to a single word, "beginning," in the opening sentence, "In the beginning was the Word." Because "beginning" is the first significant term to appear in the Gospel, it sends him off on a discussion of the many uses of "beginning" in the Scriptures. And this in turn allows him to explain why Christ is identified with "beginning." Christ, writes Origen, is the beginning of those "made in the image of God" because he is the "firstborn of all creation" (Col 1:15); he is the beginning of knowledge because he is called "Wisdom" (1 Cor 1:24); he is the beginning of life because he is the "firstborn from the dead"

---

8. Gregory of Nyssa, *Homily on the Beatitudes* (Gregorii Nysseni Opera VII/II.138).

9. Jerome, *Commentary on Isaiah* 6:1 (Corpus Christianorum 73:84-85); Gregory the Great, *Moralia* 18.88.

10. *Sermon* 158.9.

11. *Commentary on John* 1.27.

(Col 1:18); the beginning of creation, that is, the agent of creation, because he is "the beginning of [God's] ways for his work" (Prov 8:22).[12]

Origen is interpreting Scripture by Scripture, an axiom accepted by all early Christian writers. "The entire Scripture is one book and was spoken by the one Holy Spirit," wrote Cyril of Alexandria, another prolific biblical commentator.[13] Accordingly, it was presumed that the interpreter would draw on passages from the entire Bible to illuminate and explain the text under discussion. The technique most often used was word association, seeking words or images that are the same or similar to what is found in the text, as Origen did when he explained "beginning" in his *Commentary on John*. The term could be "life," or "water," or "rock," or "rain," or "man," or "mountain," or a myriad of other words or images. As the expositors sought appropriate texts, they were led to yet more passages, and the commentaries and homilies often read like a pastiche of biblical verses. Yet there was method in their exegetical artistry. As words and phrases were invested with meanings drawn from elsewhere in the Scriptures, they acquired a theological clarity and sonority that only the Bible could give. In effect the words of the Gospel of John become "biblical" rather than simply Johannine; that is, the context of understanding was formed by the Bible as a whole, not just the Gospel of John.

We are so accustomed to think of context as literary or historical that we forget that the words of the Bible have a life that transcends their original setting. Think how a verse from the New Testament can sound when read in Christian worship. It is traditional to read from the book of Titus on Christmas Eve: "For the grace of God has appeared for the salvation of all men, training us to renounce irreligion and worldly passions, and to live sober, upright, and godly lives in this world . . ." (Tit 2:11-13). When this passage is read in the Liturgy for the Nativity of Christ, the word "appear" rings out clearly like the peal of a single bell announcing the birth of Christ, the Incarnation of the divine Word. While this understanding of the verse is certainly implicit within the text, the liturgical setting gives the word "appear" a concreteness and directness that it does not have in the context of the epistle, and the Liturgy, in turn, acquires a word so fitting and right that Tit 2:11 seems composed primarily for the occasion.

Under the tutelage of the church fathers, one learns to read the Bible very closely and to pay particular attention to the subtlety and resonance of its words. As Augustine once remarked: "My heart is exercised by the pounding of the *words* of your Holy Scripture."[14] One also learns to see things whole, to interpret individual texts in light of the central biblical narrative and the Christ confessed in the creeds and celebrated in the Church's worship.

But there is something else to keep in mind while reading the volumes in this series. For the church fathers biblical interpretation had to do with the bearing of the text on the present. The interpreter is not a disinterested observer, a voyeur; rather, he is a participant in the mystery about which he speaks. This can be illustrated by a story told about St. Antony, the monk of the Egyptian desert.

---

12. *Commentary on John* 1.90-108.
13. *Commentary on Isaiah* 29:11-12 (Patrologia Graeca 70:655a).
14. *Confessions* 12.1.

Once some visitors came to Antony and asked him for a good word. He told them that they should heed the Scriptures. When they pressed him for specifics, he said they should follow the word of Jesus in Matthew: "If anyone strikes you on one cheek, turn to him the other also" (Matt 5:39). But they objected, "We can't do that!" So Antony tempered the exhortation: "If you can't do that, at least allow one cheek to be struck." Again they replied, "We cannot do that." So Antony revised the saying another time: "If you are not able to do that, at least do not return evil for evil." But again they protested. Realizing that it was futile to try to teach such folk how to understand the Bible, he instructed his disciples to "Take a little porridge" to them because "they are ill." And to the visitors he said, "If you cannot do this, or that, what can I do for you? What you need is prayers."[15]

The Bible is a book about how to live in the knowledge of God and of oneself. God's Word is not something to be looked at but something to be acted on. St. Bernard said it well: the interpreter must see himself in that which is said. It is not enough, observes Origen, to say, "'Christ was crucified'; one must say with St. Paul, 'I am crucified with Christ' (Gal 2:20). Likewise it is not enough to say, 'Christ is raised'; one who knows Christ says, 'We shall also live with him' (Rom 6:8)."[16] This is why St. Augustine said that anyone who "thinks he has understood the divine scriptures . . . but does not build up the double love of God and neighbor, has not succeeded in understanding them."[17]

The first major commentaries on the New Testament were written by Origen of Alexandria in the early third century. Like many of the biblical commentaries from the early Church, they have come down to us in fragmentary condition. Fortunately, we still possess large sections of his massive *Commentary on the Gospel of John*. It is not certain whether he completed it, but it took him six books just to reach John 1:29. In addition, he authored a *Commentary on the Gospel of Matthew* and delivered series of homilies on the Gospel of Luke. Others followed his example — some writing commentaries, others delivering homilies that went through a book chapter by chapter. For the Fourth Gospel we have homilies by John Chrysostom and Augustine as well as commentaries by Theodore of Mopsuestia and Cyril of Alexandria. On Matthew there are commentaries by Jerome and Cyril and homilies by Ambrose and John Chrysostom, to mention some of the more important. The Gospel of Mark did not receive a commentary until the Venerable Bede in the eighth century.

Origen also expounded the Pauline epistles. From his commentary on Romans we have only fragments in Greek, but a Latin translation of it was made in the early Church. Homilies on the letters to the Corinthians and commentaries on Paul's minor epistles exist only in fragments. The Latin commentator Ambrosiaster wrote a complete commentary on the Pauline epistles, and Jerome also commented on a number of the letters, including Galatians and Ephesians. Theodore of Mopsuestia wrote a commentary on the minor Pauline epistles, John Chrysostom preached homilies on all of Paul's letters (in-

---

15. Patrologia Graeca 65:84c.
16. *Against Celsus* 2.69.
17. *On Christian Doctrine* 1.86.

cluding Hebrews), and Theodoret of Cyrrhus also commented on the entire corpus. Only fragments of Cyril of Alexandria's commentaries on St. Paul remain. John Chrysostom is one of the few who have preached an entire series of homilies on the Acts of Apostles. Augustine delivered a series of sermons on 1 John, and Victorinus and Jerome wrote on the Apocalypse.

Even this partial survey gives some idea of the extent to which the church fathers devoted their energies to expounding the New Testament. Commentaries and homilies, however, are only a small part of the exegetical harvest of the early Church. There are sermons and lengthy letters on particular texts, for example, Gregory of Nyssa on 1 Cor 15:28 and Augustine on Jas 2:10, and homilies on sections of books, for example, the Beatitudes or the Lord's Prayer.[18] In the new English translation of Augustine's sermons, three volumes are devoted to sermons on passages from the New Testament,[19] and Gregory the Great has a series of forty homilies dealing with select texts from the New Testament.[20] There are also works dealing specifically with the infancy narratives of the Gospels and essays that attempt to harmonize the Gospels. Finally, there are wide-ranging discussions of many texts from the New Testament in theological essays, spiritual tracts, and the like.

Given this vast, diffuse, and often formless body of material, it is often difficult to learn how early Christian thinkers interpreted specific passages in the New Testament. In recent years some of the commentaries from the early Church on the New Testament have been translated into English for the first time. For example, Origen's commentaries on the Gospel of John and Romans and his homilies on Luke are now available,[21] as are Ambrose's homilies on Luke,[22] Theodoret of Cyrrhus on the Pauline epistles,[23] and Origen and Jerome on Ephesians.[24] Nevertheless, the great body of commentaries and homilies remain untranslated in English, and may never be translated.

The Church's Bible will provide commentaries on select books of the New Testament drawn from the writings of the church fathers, and in some cases from medieval authors. We have made a selection of passages from the ancient commentaries and homilies that treat books chapter by chapter. In addition, we have included occasional com-

---

18. *St. Gregory of Nyssa: The Lord's Prayer; The Beatitudes,* trans. Hilda C. Graef (New York: Newman, 1954).

19. *The Works of Saint Augustine: A Translation for the 21st Century,* III.3-5, trans. Edmund Hill, O.P. (Brooklyn and New Rochelle, N.Y.: New City Press, 1990-92), 3:3-5.

20. *Gregory the Great: Forty Gospel Homilies,* trans. Dom David Hurst (Kalamazoo: Cistercian Publications, 1990).

21. *Origen: Commentary on the Gospel according to John,* trans. Ronald E. Heine, 2 vols. (Washington, D.C.: Catholic University of America Press, 1989, 1993); *Origen: Homilies on Luke; Fragments on Luke,* trans. Joseph T. Lienhard, S.J. (Washington, D.C.: Catholic University of America Press, 1996); *Origen: Commentary on the Epistle to the Romans,* trans. Thomas P. Schreck, 2 vols. (Washington, D.C.: Catholic University of America Press, 2001, 2002).

22. *Exposition of the Holy Gospel according to Saint Luke: Saint Ambrose of Milan,* trans. Theodosia Tomkinson (Etna, Calif.: Center for Traditionalist Studies, 2003).

23. *Commentary on the Letters of St. Paul by Theodoret of Cyrus,* trans. Robert C. Hill (Brookline, Mass.: Holy Cross Orthodox Press, 2002).

24. Robert E. Heine, *The Commentaries of Origen and Jerome on St. Paul's Epistle to the Ephesians* (New York: Oxford University Press, 2002).

ments on particular verses drawn from theological writings, sermons, and other early Christian writings. Our aim is not a comprehensive survey of early Christian exegesis of the books of the New Testament, but commentaries that we hope will be interesting, theologically significant, and spiritually uplifting to readers of the New Testament today.

In the excerpts the specific text under discussion is printed in bold. When a passage is cited from elsewhere in the Scriptures, it is printed in italics.

The authors and works from which the selections are taken are given in the appendixes.

ROBERT LOUIS WILKEN

An Introduction to Romans

The Letter to the Romans has been placed first in the collection of Paul's writings because of its length rather than its being the first to be written. It was prepared late in Paul's career, and it elaborates on themes that were initially discussed in 1 Corinthians and Galatians. This letter has been and continues to be widely regarded as the most important statement of Paul's thinking. Like Ephesians and Colossians, the Letter to the Romans is broadly expository rather than focused on a narrow range of topics. Over the centuries, it has been treated again and again by Christian theologians and preachers.

Plan and Structure

Like other Pauline letters, Romans has two clearly differentiated parts: doctrinal exposition and exhortation. It then concludes with a statement of plans for future missionary work and a long list of greetings to and from individuals who were associated with Paul's work.[1]

The doctrinal exposition (1:16–11:36) can be divided into three parts. Paul dealt first with the revelation of divine righteousness which justified people through faith. To develop his argument, Paul discussed the roles of the Mosaic law and of faith in response to divine self-disclosure (1:16–3:20). Then he moved to the divine righteousness revealed in Christ and received by faith, demonstrating that justifying faith was already at work in God's dealings with Abraham (3:21–4:25). The second stage in the doctrinal exposition deals with different forms of liberation granted in the salvation achieved by Christ: from sin and death, from sin and self, from the law. The gift of the Holy Spirit then guides and sustains the Christian life (4:26–8:39). In the third section, Paul turns to the status of Israel in the unfolding of the plan of salvation based on faith. God's election of Israel was gratuitous and for this reason was not withdrawn when Jesus was rejected as the fulfillment of the promises made in the Law and the Prophets. Rather, God had foreseen Israel's infidelity and integrated it into a plan for the salvation of the nations as well as the

---

1. This analysis of the text generally follows that of Joseph A. Fitzmyer, S.J., *Romans: A New Translation with Introduction and Commentary,* Anchor Bible 33 (New York: Doubleday, 1993), pp. viii-xii.

redemption of Israel. The Jewish failure, Paul concludes, is partial and temporary; salvation has been offered to all peoples, including the Jews (9:1–11:36).

The letter then turns to exhortation (12:1–15:13). Christian conduct is characterized by worship of God, by the sharing of spiritual gifts for the upbuilding of the whole community, and by mutual love. The community should expect to live within society without conflict (12:1–13:14). Paul insisted that those who are strong in their Christian faith and practice should support the weaker members and must not allow their freedom to hinder their fellows. All must be welcome within their community (14:1–15:13).

Finally, the letter concludes with plans for future missions and a sharing of greetings (15:14–16:27). Paul explains his guiding principle of preaching the gospel only where it had not yet been heard, but he reminds his readers that he must first deliver the gift of the Gentile Christians to the Jerusalem community. Then he can turn to his plan of travel to Spain via Rome (15:14-33). He then commends Phoebe, greets a large number of people, and warns against false teachers (16:1-20). The letter ends with greetings from Paul's companions.

Early Christian Interpretation of Romans

Paul's letter was focused on the unity of the divine plan of salvation. He explained the universal need for salvation, the relation between divine promise and human faith, the roles of Christ and of the law, and the continuing validity of the promises made for Israel. When he spoke of the law, he was primarily concerned with the particular practices enjoined in the Pentateuch rather than with the standards of moral conduct which were more broadly recognized in the Greco-Roman culture of his day. In considering the status of Israel, moreover, he had to address the interaction between divine initiative and human response, and particularly the way in which God had used Israel's infidelity to achieve the salvation of both Jews and Gentiles through Christ.

When Christian commentators took up this book in the centuries that followed, they were faced with religious questions somewhat different from those Paul had addressed. In the second-century conflict with Marcion, interpreters argued that the Jewish Scriptures were authoritative for Christians and developed techniques that allowed them to understand both the Law and the Prophets as stages in a unified process of salvation that had reached its fulfillment in Christ. By a thoroughgoing christological reading, the Jewish Bible became the Christian Old Testament. The rabbinical schools which survived the destruction of Jerusalem and the loss of temple worship also adopted new techniques of interpretation in the context of a new historical situation and changed practices.

Although questions of the status of Israel remained current because of continuing competition between Christians and Jews in some parts of the Roman Empire, the increasing separation of the communities in other regions meant that the issues central to Paul's time attracted significantly less attention. The commentators did not hesitate to adapt Paul's teaching to this new and different context. The plan of divine governance which had integrated the Jewish response to Christ into the process of salvation of the nations could be understood as a paradigm for the interaction of divine initiative and human response in the election and calling of Christians from among many peoples. Most of the commentators followed Origen's lead in upholding human autonomy and free choice — though carefully limited — because they considered this essential for safeguarding the human moral responsibility essential to their understanding of God's justice in condemning sinners and rewarding the faithful. Augustine, and occasionally others, emphasized the sinfulness of humanity and the absolute gratuity of all God's operations which led chosen individuals to that salvation provided in Christ. In a similar way, the various parts and roles of the divine law — natural, Mosaic, and Christian — had to be distinguished and related. Some Christians used allegorical techniques to direct the entire law to the guidance of conduct;[2] others treated the ritual provisions as foreshadowing the work of Christ.[3]

The Text of the Pauline Letters

The textual differences in the Greek manuscripts of the New Testament books are well known, and are noted in any critical edition of the text as well as in translations intended for scholarly use. As the text was copied and transmitted, errors crept in and were amplified as scribes tried to make sense of uncertain readings. The translation of the text into Latin, beginning in the second century, introduced additional variations in its meaning. What is generally referred to as the Old Latin (Vetus Latina or VL) version is evidenced in Africa by the last decades of the second century. The translation of the thirteen Pauline epistles (excluding Hebrews) seems to have been completed by a single translator fairly early in the process.[4] Over the next two centuries, many different Latin translations of the Gospels seem to have been added. At the end of the fourth century and at the request of Pope Damasus, Jerome revised the Old Latin texts of the Gospels; his version gradually displaced the others. Another editor, whose identity has been lost, revised the remainder of the books of the New Testament. Jerome was subsequently responsible for the translation of most of the Old Testament books from the Hebrew, to replace Old Latin versions which had been made from the Greek Septuagint (LXX) version. This became the Vulgate (Vg) version, the standard Latin Bible from the fifth century onward.

The earliest of the commentaries used in this volume — that of Origen — was originally composed in Greek during the first half of the third century. Some fragments of that original Greek text, for chapters 3 through 5 of the letter, have been recovered, but the text as a whole did not survive in Greek. At the end of the fourth century, Rufinus of Aquileia translated the Greek commentary into Latin. Some of Origen's major ideas had been called into question during the intervening century and a half. Rufinus had to adapt his version not only to the Latin version of the letter familiar to his

---

2. This is already evident in 1 Tim 5:18 and is fully developed in the *Letter of Barnabas*.
3. As is already evident in Heb 4:14–5:14.
4. The introduction to the text of Romans was published by Hugo S. Eymann in 1996.

readers but to the doctrinal developments formalized in the councils of Nicea and Constantinople. The fullest form of Origen's commentary is now available only through Rufinus's revised version.

The major Latin commentators, Augustine and the Roman scholar known only as Ambrosiaster, generally worked from the Latin text of the letter, though they knew and even used multiple versions of it. Augustine was attentive to differences not only between the Latin texts but occasionally to the Greek version which was available to him. In dealing with the transmission of death and sin from Adam in chapter 5, for example, he considered various versions of the text and attempted to show that his was the appropriate interpretation for all of them.

The Present Text

The division of the text of the Letter to the Romans used in this volume generally follows that of Joseph Fitzmyer's commentary (Anchor Bible, vol. 33). The text of the Revised Standard Version is used between sections of the patristic commentary in order to identify the text being considered. When this translation is substantially the same as that being quoted by the ancient commentator, the RSV is employed in that translation as well. When, however, the ancient explanation depends on a particular wording of the text of Romans or some other biblical text, that text is translated into English. Thus the reader will observe that the ancient commentators were occasionally explaining significantly different versions of Paul's letter than are familiar today. It should be noted, however, that the ancient and medieval copyists who preserved these texts had a tendency to substitute the biblical text familiar to them for that which might have appeared in the manuscript they were reproducing. Thus it cannot be presumed that even modern critical editions of these ancient texts always present the version used by the original author. Differences between the text appearing in these translations and contemporary English translations may also be the consequence of the decisions by these translators to adapt the biblical text to their own — in some instances widely shared but distinctly contemporary — religious sensibilities.

Selection of Passages

Two criteria have been used in selecting the passages from ancient Christian commentaries included in this volume. First, interpretations that have relevance for current living and understanding of Christian life have been preferred to observations and explanations of the text which have only historical value for understanding the ancient Christian church. Second, interpretations representing different perspectives and thereby illustrating the range of ancient Christian understandings of the Letter to the Romans have been included. Sometimes an interpretation was advanced by a single author, but in many instances understandings were shared among several commentators. Thus Chrysostom and Theodoret often agree, while Augustine diverges from a widely held view.

An Introduction to Romans

Paul devotes extended attention to the status of the Jews and of the promises which were made to Israel. He argues that those promises were fulfilled in Christ and that the Jews will share in that gift of God. The ancient commentators in some instances no longer found the original Pauline message plausible; it was contradicted by their experienced separation and antagonism between Christians and Jews. In many instances, therefore, they developed interpretations of the Pauline text which adapted its meaning to their own times and culture. This has occasionally resulted in strongly negative statements about Jews, which are contrary to what now appears as Paul's intention. For the most part, these negative judgments have not been selected for inclusion because they do not contribute to the objectives and goals of this series, which is to make the resources of an earlier and foundational period of Christian life available for the contemporary edification of Christians.

In most cases, the texts which are gathered in this volume are taken from extended commentaries on the Pauline letters. Origen's is the longest commentary, even in the Latin translation prepared by Rufinus of Aquileia. John Chrysostom preached his exposition of the text, and that original homiletic form is still evident in some of the passages. Theodoret of Cyrrhus wrote a commentary on all the letters. Cyril of Alexandria's commentary has survived only in fragments, from which selections have been made. On the Latin side, the most important full commentary is that of "Ambrosiaster," who wrote in Rome at the end of the fourth century. Both Pelagius and an anonymous writer produced short expositions of the text. Although Augustine wrote extensively on Romans throughout his career, his only attempt at a full commentary stopped early in the first chapter. Expositions of Romans in his other works have been selected by use of the electronic database, *Corpus Augustinianum Gissense,* to locate passages in which he explained the meaning of individual sections of Romans.

Other Translations

The full texts of a number of the major ancient commentaries on Paul's Letter to the Romans are available to the interested reader in English. John Chrysostom's homilies appeared in the nineteenth-century British translation series and were subsequently printed in the *Nicene and Post-Nicene Fathers,* series 1, volume 11; as such they are widely available in electronic form. Paul Fredriksen prepared a text and translation of Augustine's two early works on Romans which was published in the Society of Biblical Literature's Texts and Translation series, volume 23, in 1982. Pelagius's commentary was published in 1993 by Oxford University Press in a translation by Theodore de Bruyn, while Origen's commentary was translated by Thomas P. Scheck and published in The Fathers of the Church, volumes 103 and 104, in 2001. That same year, Robert C. Hill's translation of the commentary of Theodoret of Cyrrhus was published by Holy Cross Orthodox Press. A translation of Ambrosiaster's commentaries on the letters of Paul is in preparation. Few of these were available when work began on the current volume in 1996, and its translations were made independently, though not without consultation of these other versions as they became available.

Preface to Romans

In their introductory observations on the Letter to the Romans, Origen and John Chrysostom focus on questions of chronology to place the letter in the sequence of Paul's surviving correspondence. Origen uses indicators of Paul's personal progress in the Christian life to relate the letters to one another; Chrysostom prefers to use the social network manifest in the persons Paul mentions to determine the circumstances of composition. Ambrosiaster, Pelagius, and the Anonymous commentator deal with the conflict between converts from Judaism and the traditional Roman religion within the Christian community in Rome. Ambrosiaster judged that the status of the Mosaic law was the principal cause of friction; Pelagius and the Anonymous commentator — in statements which are not independent of one another — focused on conflicting claims for superiority based on divine election (for the Jews) or acceptance of Christ (for the Gentiles). Augustine's statement is a variation on and refutation of this theme: he stresses the gratuity of divine grace rather than the merits of human works or faith. In Theodoret's view, Paul drew the contrast between the work of Christ and the laws — that embedded in nature by the creator and that revealed by Moses. He also noted that Paul judged his letter as an inadequate tool for settling the problem and had to rely on the work of the Holy Spirit among the Christians at Rome. Most commentators recognize that the scope of the letter and the breadth of issues it treats make it difficult to interpret.

(1) Origen

The letter the Apostle Paul wrote to the Romans is usually considered more difficult to understand than his other letters. There are, I think, two reasons for this. First, Paul uses expressions having more than one meaning. Second, he addresses many different questions, particularly the opinions that heretics use to assert that people's actions are determined by their natural dispositions and that, as a consequence, they are not free to choose for themselves. By focusing attention on a few statements in this letter, these heretics try to subvert the teaching found throughout the whole of Scripture: that God has given human beings freedom of choice. For this reason, we begin our consideration of the letter by invoking God, *who teaches humans knowledge* (Ps 94:10), *who gives through the Spirit the utterance of wisdom* (1 Cor 12:8), and *who enlightens everyone coming into the world* (John 1:9). We pray that God would make us worthy *to understand parables and obscure words, and the sayings and riddles of the wise* (Prov 1:6). In this frame of mind, we begin our exposition of Paul's Letter to the Romans.

First, however, we will focus on what learned expositors usually have observed, that the Apostle was working at a higher level in this letter than in his other ones. When he wrote to the Corinthians for the first time, he had already made great advances. Still, he said something about himself there which would indicate that he was still a bit unsettled: *I wear down my body and subdue it, lest after preaching to others I myself should be rejected* (1 Cor 9:27). Then, writing to the Philippians, he showed that he had not yet attained that perfection which he would later achieve; he said *that he conformed himself to the death of Christ, so that if possible he might attain the resurrection from the dead* (Phil 3:10-11). He would not have said, *if possible*, if things were already fully clear to him at the time. He confirmed this in what follows immediately afterward in the same letter, *Not that I have already obtained it or am already perfect; but I press on to make it my own, as Christ Jesus has made me his own. Brethren, I do not judge that I have already attained it* (Phil 3:12-13). If someone thinks that he said this out of humility, he should notice that in the next sentence he did not hesitate to recall how far he had advanced, *forgetting what is in the past and straining forward to what is still ahead, I press on toward my goal, to the prize of God's heavenly call in Christ Jesus* (Phil 3:13-14). Then he says, *Let those of us who are perfect think this way* (Phil 3:15). In these statements, he distinguishes two types of perfection. He does not claim for himself that perfection which consists in the full measure of all the virtues. Another form is proper to those who have advanced so far that they cannot fall away or even look back, as he said, *Let those of us who are perfect think this way* (Phil 3:15).

Is there reason to say that in his second letter to the Corinthians, Paul is more advanced than in the first? To be sure, as is evident from what he said in that letter, *We are afflicted, but not crushed; perplexed, but not driven to despair; persecuted, but not forsaken; struck down, but not destroyed; always carrying in our body the death of Jesus, so that the life of Jesus may also be manifest in our body* (2 Cor 4:8-10). Anyone who is *always carrying in his body the death of Jesus* is not driven by the lust of the flesh against the spirit. His flesh was subject to the Spirit because it had been put to death in the likeness of the death of Christ.

Someone might find such a great change in him implausible because not much time passed between his writing the first and second letters to the Corinthians. Still, the length of time is evident if one considers the expulsion of the man polluted by the crime of incest. He was *delivered to Satan for the destruction of his flesh, so that his spirit might be saved* (1 Cor 5:5); then, in the second letter, he was readmitted and reunited to the members of the church (2 Cor 2:8). Paul would have allowed that readmission only if enough time had passed for fruits worthy of repentance to appear in the sinner; his flesh must have experienced what the Apostle called its destruction, dying to sin and depravity; he was once again living for God. This incestuous sinner had enough time to undergo the praiseworthy destruction of his flesh and to attain spiritual health. How can we think that the Apostle, who progressed much more quickly, had not himself attained greater perfection?

How much more Paul had advanced, how much higher and more outstanding he had become by the time he wrote to the Romans, can be understood from statements he made in that letter: *Who shall separate us from the love of Christ? Shall tribulation, or distress, or persecution, or famine, or nakedness, or danger, or the sword? As it is written, "For your sake we are being put to death all day long; we are considered sheep to be slaughtered"* (Ps 44:22). *But in all these things we conquer because of him who loved us. For I am sure that neither death, nor life, nor angels, nor principalities, nor powers, nor things present, nor things to come, nor forces, nor height, nor depth, nor anything else in all creation, will be able to separate us from the love of God which is in Christ Jesus our Lord. I am speaking the truth in Christ, I am not lying; my conscience bears me witness in the Holy Spirit* (Rom 8:35–9:1). When he said, *I wear down my body and subdue it, lest after preaching to others I myself should be rejected* (1 Cor 9:27), was he already displaying that same greatness of spirit that he did when he later said, *But in all these we conquer* (Rom 8:37), or, *For I am sure that neither death, nor life, nor angels, nor principalities,* nor all the other things he described, *will be able to separate us from the love of God* (Rom 8:38-39)? With these observations, we have to the best of our ability shown that when he wrote this letter Paul was working at a higher level. From these and many other considerations which are even clearer, it seems reasonable to suggest that he wrote this letter while he was in Corinth. He says, for example, *I commend to you your sister Phoebe, a minister of the church at Cenchreae* (Rom 16:1). Cenchreae is near Corinth; actually, it is the port of Corinth. His saying, *Gaius, who is my host, greets you* (Rom 16:23), also indicates that he wrote from Corinth, since he mentioned this same Gaius in writing to the Corinthians, *I thank God that I baptized none of you except Crispus and Gaius* (1 Cor 1:14). A further indication is given by his saying, *Erastus, the city treasurer, greets you* (Rom 16:23). This is the same Erastus about whom he wrote in the second letter to Timothy, *Erastus remained at Corinth* (2 Tim 4:20). From all this evidence, we can conclude with certainty that the letter was sent from Corinth.

This letter is difficult to understand in no small measure because of the variety of topics which Paul addressed in it. He spoke extensively about the Mosaic law, but he also discussed the call of the nations, the distinction between carnal and spiritual Israel, circumcision of the flesh and of the heart, the spirit and the letter of the law, the laws of the flesh and the bodily members, the laws of the mind and of sin, the inner and the outer person. Any one of these issues could have filled a letter on its own.

Let us then begin the explanation of this letter, following the paths the Lord opens to us.

The first question to arise would seem to be the name of Paul himself: why is the person who was called Saul in the Acts of the Apostles here called Paul? In the divine Scriptures we find names being changed: Abram was renamed Abraham (Gen 17:5), Sarai became Sarah (Gen 17:15), and Jacob became Israel (Gen 35:10). In the Gospels, Simon became Peter (Matt 16:17) and the sons of Zebedee were also called the Sons of Thunder (Mark 3:16-17). These changes were made by divine command, but we find nothing similar in Paul's case. Some think that Paul took this name from the proconsul on Cyprus whom he won over to faith in Christ (Acts 13:6-12). In the way a king can be given a title from a nation he conquers — like "Parthian" or "Goth" — Paul might have earned this name by conquering Sergius Paulus. This particular naming practice, however, can be found nowhere in the Scriptures, and we must limit ourselves to solutions for which Scripture provides some precedent.

In the Scriptures we do find that a single person is sometimes given two or even three names. In the books of Judges and Kingdoms,[1] we find people with multiple names: Solomon is also called Jedidiah (2 Sam 12:24-25); Zedekiah is named Jehoiachin (2 Kgs 25:7, 27); Uzziah is called Azariah (2 Kgs 15:1-7, 32-34). The Evangelists occasionally do the same: Matthew refers to himself in saying, *As Jesus passed on from there, he found a man sitting in the tax office called Matthew* (Matt 9:9); Luke recounts the same event: *as Jesus went out, he saw a tax collector by the name of Levi and said to him, "Follow me"* (Luke 5:27). Similarly, in the list of the apostles, Matthew names, after some others, *Matthew the tax collector, James the son of Alphaeus, Lebbaeus, and Simon the Cananaean* (Matt 10:3-4). The parallel in Mark reads, *Matthew the tax collector, Thomas, James the son of Alphaeus, and Thaddaeus* (Mark 3:18). Mark names Thaddaeus where Matthew has Lebbaeus. Luke lists them as *Matthew, Thomas, James, and Judas the son of James* (Luke 6:15-16). So where Matthew writes Lebbaeus and Mark has Thaddaeus,[2] Luke says Judas the son of James. We must assume that the Evangelists were not mistaken about the names of the apostles. Rather, they give different names because Jewish practice used two or three different names for the same person.

Following this custom, Paul himself apparently used two names. When he was working among his own people, he was called Saul, as more appropriate for his native culture. He was called Paul when he established laws and precepts for the Greeks and the Gentiles. Indeed, the scripture text which we cited above says, *Saul, who is called Paul* (Acts 13:9). This clearly shows that the name Paul was already in use and was not being used for the first time in this text.

(2) John Chrysostom

When I regularly hear the epistles of the blessed Paul read (twice each week and often three and four times when we celebrate the memorials of the holy martyrs), I rejoice and enjoy the spiritual trumpet, and I am aroused and warmed by desire. I recognize the voice I love; I almost feel his presence and see him speaking. Yet, I also suffer and am troubled: not everyone knows this man as one should; some are so ignorant of him that they do not know how many letters he wrote. This results not from some learning disability but because they lack interest in spending time with him regularly. Our knowledge, such as it is, arises not only from natural ability and mental keenness but through regular study and a love of the subject matter. People who love a particular person are always the first to know his deeds, simply because they are interested. The blessed man himself demonstrated this when he said to the Philippians: *Just as it is right for me to think this about you, because I hold you in my heart, even in my chains, and in the defense and assurance of the gospel* (Phil 1:7).

So, if you too are willing and eager to pay attention to the reading, you need nothing else, for the Christ's word is true when he says, *Seek, and you will find; knock, and it*

---

1. The books of Samuel and the books of Kings.
2. The manuscript tradition shows a great deal of variation on these two names.

will be opened to you (Matt 7:7). The majority of those gathered here together with us have committed themselves to raising children, supporting a wife, and caring for a house. For this reason, they would be unwilling to dedicate themselves completely to this task of understanding Paul. Rouse yourselves up, then, to receive what has been collected by others. Be as attentive to hearing what is said as you are in piling up money. Although I am ashamed to demand so little from you, still I do want you to give at least that much.

Ignorance of the Scriptures has given rise to thousands of evils. From this seed the great corruption of heresies has blossomed; from this spring have flowed careless living and wasted labors. Just as anyone deprived of the light of this world cannot walk straight, so those who do not see the rays of the divine Scriptures walk in thick darkness. They regularly and inevitably fall into many sins. To prevent this happening to us, let us open wide our eyes to the brightness of the apostolic words — for Paul's tongue shone more brightly than the sun, and his teaching has surpassed that of all others. Since he *labored more than they* (1 Cor 15:10), he drew down upon himself great graces from the Spirit. I assert this not on the basis of his letters alone, but also from what is written about him in Acts. For whenever public oratory was needed, they always called upon him. He was such a powerful speaker that the non-believers identified him with Hermes (Acts 14:12).

Since we intend to enter upon the study of this epistle, we must consider the time when it was written. It was certainly not written before all the other epistles, as many think. It is earlier than his letters written from Rome but later than most, though not all, of Paul's other letters. Both epistles to the Corinthians, for example, had been sent before this one. This is clear from what is written at the end of this epistle, where he says: *Now I go to Jerusalem in order to serve the saints. For Macedonia and Achaia have seen fit to make some charitable contribution to the poor of the saints who are in Jerusalem* (Rom 15:25-26). But writing to the Corinthians, he said: *If it is right that I also come, they will come with me* (1 Cor 16:4), referring to those who were bringing the money with them from Corinth. This makes clear that when he wrote the Epistle to the Corinthians, he was not yet sure that he would make the trip; when, however, he wrote to the Romans, it had finally been decided. When this evidence has been taken into account, we learn that the Epistle to the Romans was written after the Epistle to the Corinthians. I think that the Epistle to the Thessalonians was written prior to the Epistle to the Corinthians. He wrote to the Thessalonians first and spoke to them about charity when he said: *Concerning love for the brethren we have no need to write to you, for you yourselves are taught by God to love one another, and you do this toward all the brethren* (1 Thess 4:9-10). Afterward he wrote the Epistle to the Corinthians, as is itself clear when he says: *For I know of your zeal, of which I boast to the Macedonians, because Achaia has been prepared since last year; and because your zeal has roused up most people* (2 Cor 9:2).[3] From these things he showed that he had already spoken about this with the Thessalonians.

Therefore the Epistle to the Romans, though prior to those letters written from Rome, is later than these other epistles. He had not yet arrived in the city of the Romans when he wrote this letter, as is clear when he says: *For I desire to see you, in order to convey*

---

3. John Chrysostom does distinguish between the two letters written to the Corinthians in his homilies on them. Here he seems to take the two as written about the same time.

some spiritual grace (Rom 1:11). But he wrote to the Philippians from Rome; as he says, *All the saints greet you, especially those from Caesar's household* (Phil 4:22). He also wrote to the Hebrews from there; for this reason he says that *those from Italy greet* all of them (Heb 13:24). He also sent the Epistle to Timothy from Rome, when he was in chains. This one seems to me to be the last of all the epistles, as is clear from the end: *For I am already poured out like a libation,* he says, *and the appointed time of my dissolution is standing near* (2 Tim 4:6). That he ended his life in Rome is clear to everyone. Also the Epistle to Philemon is among the last of his letters; for he wrote it in extreme old age; for this reason he said: *As Paul an old man and now chained in Christ Jesus* (Philem 9). Nevertheless, this epistle is prior to the Epistle to the Colossians, which is clear from the end. For writing to the Colossians, he says: *Tychicus will relate all things to you; I sent him with Onesimus our faithful and beloved brother* (Col 4:7). Onesimus was the subject of the Epistle to Philemon. That the two references are not to different people having the same name is clear also from the mention of Archippus. For Paul spoke of him as a fellow worker in the Epistle to Philemon when making an appeal for Onesimus (Philem 2), and when he wrote the Epistle to the Colossians Paul encouraged him by saying: *Say to Archippus: "See that you fulfill the ministry which you have received"* (Col 4:17). I think that the Epistle to the Galatians is also earlier than the Epistle to the Romans. It is not surprising that they are in a different order in the Bible; the twelve prophets do not follow one another in chronological order. Although they were far apart in time, they follow one another in the order of the Bible. Indeed, Haggai and Zechariah and others prophesied after Ezekiel and Daniel, and many prophesied after Jonah and Zephaniah and all the rest. In the text, however, they were grouped with those from whom they were separated chronologically.

Let no one consider this wasted labor, nor the investigation itself a sign of idle curiosity. For knowing the chronological sequence of the epistles is of great help in our studying them. I see Paul writing a letter to the Romans and to the Colossians about the same topics, but not speaking about these things in the same way. He is very accommodating with the Romans, as when he says: *Support the person who is weak in faith, not for quarrels or debates; one person believes he can eat everything, but another who is weak eats vegetables* (Rom 14:1-2). In writing to the Colossians about this issue, he does not address them in the same way but with more boldness: *For if with Christ you have died to the elements of the universe, why do you make decisions as if you were living in the world — do not grasp, do not taste, do not touch? All these things perish when used — they have no value in checking the indulgence of the flesh* (Col 2:20-23). I find no reason for this difference other than the circumstance of chronology. For gentleness is necessary in the beginning but not later. We can observe Paul doing the same thing elsewhere. Moreover, both physicians and teachers usually act in this same way. For a physician does not treat a patient at the onset of an illness in the same way he treats one who is about to reach the goal of renewed health. The teacher does not instruct children who are just beginning to learn in the same way as he does those who want more advanced instruction.

And so, Paul wrote the other epistles because of some particular matter or dispute. This is clear in his saying to the Corinthians, *Concerning the things which you have written to me* (1 Cor 7:1). In writing to the Galatians, he launches into a similar argument immediately after the introduction. What were his reason and purpose in writing to the Romans? Apparently, he was congratulating them because they were *full of goodness, filled with all knowledge, able to instruct others* (Rom 15:14). What, then, was the purpose of this letter? *On account of the grace of God*, he says, *which was given to me to be a minister of Jesus Christ* (Rom 15:15-16). He gave the same reason in the beginning: *I am a debtor; the zeal on my part is to announce the good news also to you who are in Rome* (Rom 1:14-15). When he says they were able to correct others, and similar things, it sounds like praise and encouragement. But they also needed correction. Since he had not yet worked among them, he used a two-pronged approach in instructing them: sending them letters and letting them know they could expect a visit.

His was indeed a holy soul: he embraced the whole known world and he bore all peoples within his heart. He thought there was no greater relation among people than being joined together in God. He loved them as though they were all his children; indeed, he displayed a love more tender than that of any father. The grace of the Spirit surpasses the bonds of bodily birth; it shows a more ardent desire. We see this especially in the soul of Paul, whose love makes him act like some bird flying around all peoples, never standing still and being at rest. He had heard about Christ saying, *Peter, do you love me? Shepherd my sheep* (John 21:15), so he realized that this kind of care was the greatest expression of love and he practiced it beyond all measure. Therefore we too follow his example: even if we cannot instruct the whole known world with all its cities and nations, let each of us at least guide our own household, our spouse, children, friends, and neighbors. Let no one offer the excuse, "I am ignorant and untrained." No one was less well educated than Peter or less skilled than Paul. He freely admits this of himself and is not ashamed to say, *Although I am unskilled in speaking, yet not in knowledge* (2 Cor 11:6). This untrained man and that uneducated man, by their own effort and the grace of God, have converted thousands of philosophers and silenced thousands of orators. What excuse shall we offer for ourselves when we fail to influence twenty people, or at least be of some value to those who live with us? Pleading a lack of education or skill is nothing more than an excuse and a pretense. The true obstacles to teaching are not a lack of learning or training but laziness and love of leisure. Once we have roused ourselves from sleep, let us zealously care for our own members. Even here in this life we may enjoy great peace, as we guide those well disposed toward us according to the fear of God. In the next life, we will share in thousands of goods, by the grace and generosity of our Lord Jesus Christ, through whom and with whom be glory to the Father together with the Holy Spirit, now and forever and unto the ages of ages. Amen.

(3) Ambrosiaster

In order to understand something, one must investigate its structural principles. Thus its purpose will be easier to explain if we learn its origin. What we intend will be clear once we have explained the structure and the objectives of this letter.

Paul had four things in mind when he wrote to the Romans; he made his case partly by discussing the natural beginning of the human race and partly from the law.

Because the Romans were the rulers of all the other nations, those peoples would also learn from what Paul said to them. The first step was to introduce himself to them: who he was, whom he represented, what he had been before, and how he combated false teaching. Next, he accused them of refusing to subject themselves to the one God, according to the natural law, and of doing wicked and shameful things to one another. Thus they were despised by God. The believers rejoiced to hear this. His third point was their refusal to obey the law they had been given. On this point, he was able to prefer the Jews to the Greeks. Then in the fourth part he taught that because of their response to Christ, the Jews had been deprived of the Law and the Prophets and become no different from the Gentiles. Thus he reached the conclusion that both Jews and Gentiles were in need of the mercy of God and could hope for salvation through faith in Christ rather than the law.

In the times of the apostles, the Jews were under Roman rule, and as a result some of them lived in Rome. Believers among them had taught the Romans both to believe in Christ and to obey the law. The Romans had heard the reports of the power of Christ and, as prudent people, were ready to believe. They did not waste this opportunity but immediately corrected their evil ways and committed themselves to Christ. Their faith, however, had been formed by what they learned from the Jews. They falsely believed that Christ was not himself the fullness of salvation but that the law also had to be observed.

Paul, therefore, insisted that they had not received the spiritual grace of God. Their teachers were just like those who had subverted the faith of the Galatians, causing them to pull back from the apostolic tradition and follow the Jewish way of life. In that instance, the Apostle blamed the Galatians: they were so easily led astray after being taught well. He had no reason to be angry with the Romans, however, and he was right to praise their faith. Without witnessing any displays of power or meeting any of the apostles, they had accepted faith in Christ — though they had not understood it properly. They had not heard about the mystery of the cross of Christ. As a result, when some Christians who had a true understanding of the faith, such as Aquila and Priscilla, came from Judea to Rome, a dispute arose about eating or not eating meat.

For this reason, then, Paul works so hard for them. He strives to draw them away from the law — *since the Law and the Prophets were until John* (Luke 16:16) — and to establish them solely in the faith of Christ. He tries to free the gospel from the claims of the law, not in order to destroy the law but to give primacy to Christian teaching. He shows that the promise of Christ meant that his coming would bring the rule of the law to an end. The law was not completely abolished; rather, it was summarized so that it would lead to salvation. Because of the hardness of their hearts, the ancients had been weighed down with many observances. Through Christ, the divine mercy focused the law, freeing them from what had gone before. Anyone who preferred to remain under the law, then, was ungrateful for the mercy of God. For Moses had said: *You shall live in fear, O children of Israel* (Lev 15:31). Wherever they turned, they found themselves fenced in by the law; they worried constantly about fulfilling its requirements. Paul wrote this letter, then, to teach them that Christ is Lord of all and to guide them to place their hope for life and salvation in Christ, without being concerned for the law.

(4) Theodoret

Through this writing, the divine Apostle offers a varied and multifaceted teaching. This epistle presents a universal message. For those who sincerely believe, the mystery of the divine Incarnation is honored and worthy of worship. It clearly demonstrates God's love for humanity. Those who shroud themselves in the fog of unbelief and block out the rays of spiritual light, however, ridicule things which even the assemblies of the angels cannot give fitting praise. And the divinely inspired Apostle taught this clearly when he wrote his epistle to the Corinthians, *For the word of the cross is folly for those who are perishing, but for those who are being saved, it is the power of God* (1 Cor 1:18).

When then Paul wrote this proclamation of salvation to the Romans, he showed that it applies to all humanity, and is profitable and beneficial for both Jews and Greeks. He first reproaches the Greeks because they openly transgressed the laws of nature and corrupted that power of discerning good and evil with which the creator had endowed our nature. Then he blamed the Jews because the written instruction in the divine laws they received not only brought them no benefit but made them liable to greater punishments.

Next, the Apostle says that the appearance of our God and Savior was intended not for the judgment and punishment of those who had transgressed the law but for forgiving their sins, promising that death would be destroyed, and announcing the gift of eternal life. Paul knew that the Jews held very firmly to the law, and that those infected by teaching like that of Marcion and Valentinus — as well as the Manicheans — accused him of many errors. He behaved like a brilliant strategist who overcomes the enemies surrounding him on all sides and raises a trophy to his victory. Through God's grace, the divine Apostle destroys the column of the heretics and the phalanx of the Jews. How does he fight? He neither overestimates the law in the response to Jewish attacks, nor does he provide the heretics a basis for their criticisms. Showing himself a teacher of necessary truth, he offers the doctrine of righteousness, though the weakness of those who had received the law prevented him from completing this task. Then he teaches that when faith arrived, the objectives of the law were realized. And so what he intended but was himself unable to complete was accomplished through the grace of the Holy Spirit.

Through all this, we learn that the goal was accomplished by the God who created us and always cares for humanity. First, God endowed our nature with the power to distinguish good from its opposite. Then through the creation, God guided those who longed for it to live devoutly. Although not everyone wanted to understand the truth, those who sought it were not frustrated. In addition, the God of all also taught us that this system of salvation was not some afterthought; from the very beginning, it was announced through the divine prophets.

The Apostle also teaches the reason for the rejection of the Jews and exhorts the believing Gentiles not to look down on them. He urged these Gentiles to surpass the Jews in preaching. He mixed doctrinal exposition with instruction in practical virtue, teaching truth and giving guidance on how to live. This, then, is a general overview of the epistle: the exposition of its individual parts will teach us everything more precisely.

(5) Augustine

Judging from the text itself, the letter which the Apostle Paul wrote to the Romans focuses on the question of whether the gospel of our Lord Jesus Christ was given only to the Jews because of their merits in fulfilling the mandates of the law or whether the justification by faith which is in Christ Jesus was given to all the Gentiles without any prior merits of works. The question, then, is whether people believed because they were already righteous or whether the believing itself made them righteous and only then did they began to live justly. The Apostle's purpose was to teach that the grace of the gospel of our Lord Jesus Christ had come for everyone. He showed that it was called grace because it was given gratuitously rather than paid as something owed in justice.

Some of the Jews who had believed began to agitate against the Gentiles, and against the Apostle Paul in particular, because he extended the grace of the gospel to people who were uncircumcised and unconcerned with the requirements of the old law. He invited them to believe in Christ without imposing on them the yoke of fleshly circumcision.

Paul walks a fine line between the two parties. He neither allows the Jews any ground for pride because they had accomplished the works of the law nor gives the Gentiles any basis for considering themselves superior to the Jews because of the merits of their faith — that they accepted Christ after the Jews had crucified him. As he says in another passage, he was acting as a legate of the Lord himself, for the one who is the cornerstone (Eph 2:20). By the bonds of grace, he joined Jews and Gentiles together in Christ to form a single people. He banished from both all pride in their merits, and he united them to be justified together through the discipline of humility.

(6) Pelagius

The Romans to whom Paul wrote were made up of Jews and Gentiles who had believed. These two groups were proudly engaged in a contest to establish superiority over one another.

The Jews were making this claim. We are the people of God, those he loved and favored from the beginning. We descend from a holy stock; we are the circumcised in the line of Abraham. God is known only among the Jews. We were freed from Egypt by miracles and powerful deeds of God; we crossed through the sea dry-shod, while a great wave swooped down on our enemies. The Lord rained manna down on us in the desert and fed us like children with heavenly food. God led us day and night in a column of cloud and fire, showing us the path in the wilderness. Not to mention the many other favors God bestowed on us, we alone were worthy to receive the law of God, to hear his voice speaking to us and to acknowledge his will. In that same law, God promised Christ to us. Christ confirmed this when he said, *I have come only to the sheep of the house of Israel who have perished* (Matt 15:24); he then called you dogs rather than humans (Matt 15:26). Is it right that you should be made our equals, when you are only now turning away from the idols to which you have devoted yourselves from the beginning? Should you not rather accept the status of proselytes assigned you by both the authority of the law and long practice?

You would not deserve even this unless the great mercy of God had willed to let you imitate us.

The Gentiles responded to this charge. The more you Jews recount the great favors God has bestowed on you, the more you show yourselves guilty criminals. You have always proved yourselves ungrateful for these benefits. The same feet that had crossed the dry sea danced before the idols you had made. The same mouths that had praised the Lord for the destruction of your enemies then demanded that images be made for you. The eyes that worshiped God in the cloud and had seen God in the fire then stared at images. You got tired of eating manna and complained about God the whole time you were in the desert. You wanted to go back to Egypt, from which God's strong hand had delivered you. Why say more? Your fathers wore God out with constant complaining, and as a result they all died in the wilderness. No more than two men out of that whole group of elders actually entered the promised land. But why review all this ancient history? Even if you had done none of those things, no one would find you deserving of the least mercy because of what you have just now done. The Lord Christ, who had always been promised to you by the sayings of the prophets, you not only refused to welcome when he came but you put him to a most cruel death. We, in contrast, believed in him as soon as we heard about him, even though we had been told nothing about him in advance. We can prove that we had served idols out of ignorance rather than obstinacy: those who obeyed him as soon as they learned about him would have followed him earlier if they had only known about him. You brag about your noble lineage, as though anyone becomes a child of the saints by carnal birth rather than imitating their lives. Remember that Esau and Ishmael were both offspring of Abraham; that certainly did not make them his children.

Paul thrust himself between these warring parties. He shattered the arguments of both sides and established that neither had earned salvation by its own righteousness. Both peoples had sinned knowingly and seriously: the Jews had dishonored God by transgressing against the law; the Gentiles had known the creator through the creation; they ought to have worshiped him as God, but they turned his glory onto handmade images. Paul showed that they had both received the same pardon. He proved that they were equal and of the exact same standing, since in the same law it had been foretold that both the Jews and the Gentiles would be called to faith in Christ. By humbling both sides, he drew them into peace and concord.

(7) Anonymous

First we ought to understand to whom the Apostle wrote and for what purpose. No one should believe that he wrote these letters to the various churches for no particular reason. The Gospels are themselves the fullness of the law; in them, the precepts and examples of living were already fully set out for us. But in the initial phase of the church's growth, new situations arose which had to be addressed. The apostles then had to do what the prophets had done before them. The law given by Moses had contained all the commandments; still the prophets had to preach against the new sins of the people, and their messages were preserved for us in books, through which they have reached the end of the ages.

Paul writes in this Letter to the Romans, a community made up of Jewish and Gentile believers who were proudly competing for superiority. The Jews claimed: We are the holy race whom God loved and preferred from the beginning. We come from the line of Abraham and descend from a holy stock. We were freed from Egypt and crossed the sea dry-shod. For our sake, Pharaoh died under the waves and drowned with his whole army. The Lord rained manna on us in the desert and performed other wondrous works so numerous that it would take too long to enumerate them. Our only point is that the Lord himself, in whom even you seem to believe, was promised to us in the law. You, however, are Gentiles whom God never cared about. You never knew God but always served demons. Could it possibly be just that you who are only now turning away from idols should suddenly become our equals rather than being proselytes, as has always been your status under the law? God has been very merciful to you indeed in deciding to lead you to imitating us.

The Gentiles, for their part, responded. The more you recount of the great blessings God bestowed upon you, the more you prove your own guilt for such great crimes. You have always showed yourselves ungrateful for these benefits. After you had heard the voice of God, you built yourselves an idol. Even if you had done none of those things, still you would never have been able to win pardon for your one great crime. The Lord had been promised to you by the voices of the prophets, yet you not only refused to welcome him but even killed him. We accepted him, even though no one ever told us to expect him. The greater value of our faith is clearly evident. We had indeed served idols, but through ignorance rather than malice. When we finally learned the truth, we acted on it immediately. The grace of God, not some carnal birth, made us children of Abraham.

Paul thrust himself between these warring factions. He showed both peoples that neither circumcision nor its absence had any value at all: the only thing that counts is faith which works through love. Throughout the epistle, he humbled each of them in turn; by arguments and proofs he urged them to unity; he showed them that neither had merited anything by its own righteousness, that whatever they had become must be attributed to the mercy of God. The Jews and the Gentiles had both sinned seriously and knowingly: the Jews dishonored God by transgressing the law; the Gentiles exchanged God's truth for a lie.

Romans 1

From the beginning of the epistle, Origen set a pattern of interpretation others follow. To account for differences in God's dealing with individuals, he highlights human merits, either actual or foreseen. Augustine, on the other hand, emphasizes the divine initiative and the gratuity of grace in both the Incarnation of the Son of God and in the humans who become the members of Christ's body, the Church. The commentators elaborate on Paul's argument that humans learn of God through the creation, yet they point out that many refused to worship the one God. Origen specifies the limits of knowledge based on creation; Ambrosiaster shows that it was falsified by the unwillingness to worship God. All agree that the moral corruption of humanity followed from the sin of idolatry. Only Theodoret of Cyrrhus explains the various forms of sin which Paul enumerated in this chapter.

Romans 1:1-7

₁Paul, a servant of Jesus Christ, called to be an apostle, set apart for the gospel of God ₂which he promised beforehand through his prophets in the holy scriptures, ₃the gospel concerning his Son, who was descended from David according to the flesh ₄and designated Son of God in power according to the Spirit of holiness by his resurrection from the dead, Jesus Christ our Lord, ₅through whom we have received grace and apostleship to bring about the obedience of faith for the sake of his name among all the nations, ₆including yourselves who are called to belong to Jesus Christ;

₇To all God's beloved in Rome, who are called to be saints:
Grace to you and peace from God our Father and the Lord Jesus Christ.

(1) John Chrysostom on verses 1-6

Moses wrote five books, but nowhere in them did he record his own name as author; nor did the writers who followed him and narrated the subsequent events. Neither Matthew, John, Mark, nor Luke recorded their names. But the blessed Paul included his own name in every one of his epistles. Why did he do this? Because all the others wrote for people who were actually present. They had no need to identify themselves, since they were already in the presence of their readers. But Paul sent his writings to people who were at a distance in the form of letters. For this reason he had to put down his name.

Paul called himself not simply **a servant** but **of Christ**, because service takes many forms. One type arises from the relationship of a maker to the thing made — the product is the servant of the one who makes it; thus the Scriptures say, *All things are your servants* (Ps 119:91), and, *Nebuchadnezzar, my servant* (Jer 25:9). Another type of servitude derives from faith, as the Scripture says, *Thanks be to God that you, having once been slaves of sin, have become obedient from the heart to the form of teaching to which you were entrusted, and that you, having been set free from sin, have become slaves of righteousness* (Rom 6:17-18). A third kind of servitude is based on a person's relationship to a community, as Scripture says, *My servant Moses is dead* (Josh 1:2). Although all the Jews were servants, Moses was so named because he was an outstanding representative of their nation. Because Paul was a servant according to all three types, he claimed this title as the highest form of honor, **servant of Jesus Christ.** Paul lists the parts of the title in this greeting according to their sequence in the work of salvation. For the angel came from heaven bringing the name *Jesus* when he was born from the Virgin (Matt 1:21; Luke 1:31). The name "Christ" comes from the verb "to anoint," which belongs to his human nature. With what oil was he anointed? He was anointed not with oil but with the Spirit. You should know that Scripture calls those who are anointed "christs," and the Spirit plays the central role in the anointing. For this reason oil (Greek: *chrisma*) is traditionally used to anoint. Where does Scripture refer to people who have been anointed with oil as "christs"? In the place that says, *Do not touch my anointed ones [my "christs"], do my prophets no harm* (Ps 105:15). . . .

Called to be an apostle. Paul always refers to himself as **called**, speaking with his characteristic frankness. He also shows that he was not out searching for what he found; rather, he followed and obeyed when he was called. He refers to the faithful as **called to be saints**, for they were called to that type of fidelity. Paul himself received a different gift, the office of apostle: this comprises thousands of blessings; it includes and surpasses all other gifts. . . . He calls his message the **gospel of God**, and thus brings joy to his hearers at the outset of the letter. He did not come proclaiming a gloomy message — like the charges, accusations, and denunciations of the prophets. Instead, Paul came with good news, the good news of God, with countless treasures of enduring and unchangeable blessings.

Which he promised beforehand through his prophets in the holy scriptures. Since they had charged Paul with introducing novelties, he asserts that his message is, in fact, before the time of the Greeks and was intimated in advance by the prophets. In general, God did not reveal this good news from the beginning because most people were not interested in it; those who were willing to accept it, however, did hear it. *Your ancestor Abraham*, Jesus said, *rejoiced that he would see my day; he saw it and was glad* (John 8:56). How then could Jesus say, *Many prophets and righteous persons longed to see what you see, but did not see it* (Matt 13:17)? He said that they were seeing and hearing it in the flesh, that the signs were actually before their eyes. Yet, consider how many years in advance these things had been announced. For when God prepares great things, these are announced many years ahead of time in order to get people's attention so that the signs will be accepted when they actually occur. The prophets not only spoke but also wrote down their messages; indeed, they even prefigured the future events through their actions. In this way, Abraham led Isaac to be sacrificed (Gen 22:1-13); Moses lifted up the bronze serpent (Num 21:9), spread out his hands against Amalek (Exod 17:11-13), and sacrificed the Paschal Lamb (Exodus 12).

Concerning his Son, who was descended from David according to the flesh. The one who plans to lead people by the hand to heaven must first bring them up from below. So was the economy of salvation arranged. People first saw Jesus as a human on earth; only later did they realize that he was divine. His disciple Paul maps out the road leading to heaven in the same way. First he talks about Jesus' birth **according to the flesh**, not because it happened first but because he was leading his hearers from the earthly up to the heavenly.

Declared to be Son of God with power according to the Spirit of holiness by his resurrection from the dead, Jesus Christ our Lord. Paul's statement is obscure because the words are twisted; we will have to analyze this passage in stages. What, then, is he saying? He says that he preached the one who was born from David. This much is clear. But how is it clear that the one who became flesh was also the Son of God? First, from the prophets, as Paul said, **which he promised beforehand through the prophets in the holy scriptures.** This is a powerful type of demonstration. Second, from the way he was born, as Paul made clear by saying, **from David according to the flesh**, since Christ broke the law of nature in his birth. Third, from the miracles he performed over and over; these provided an indication of his great power. That is what Paul meant by saying, **with power.** Fourth, we know it from the Spirit whom Jesus gave to those who believe in him, through whom he made them all holy. Thus Paul says, **according to the Spirit of holiness.** God alone bestows such gifts. Fifth, we know it from the resurrection of the Lord. For he was the first — indeed, the only one — who raised himself up. Jesus himself asserted that his resurrection was, above all else, a sign sufficient to shut the mouths of the shameless. For he says, *Destroy this temple, and in three days I will raise it up* (John 2:19), and, *When you raise me up from the earth* (John 8:28), and also, *This generation asks for a sign, but no sign will be given to it except the sign of the prophet Jonah* (Matt 12:39). What does he mean by **declared**? He means shown, manifested, judged, confessed in many ways: by the prophets, by the paradox of his birth according to the flesh, by the power manifested in the signs, by his bestowing holiness through the Spirit, by overthrowing the tyranny of death through his resurrection.

Through whom we have received grace and apostleship to bring about the obedience of faith among all the Gentiles for the sake of his name. For we did not make ourselves apostles. Nor did we attain this honor as a recognition of our enduring many labors and undergoing great sufferings. Rather, we received it as a grace, and all our subsequent success is a gift from above. **To bring about the obedience of faith.** Indeed, the apostles did not accomplish things by acting on their own; God's grace prepared the way for them. Their role was to go about preaching; the actual persuasion was the work of God, acting through them. Just as Luke said, *He opened their hearts* (Acts 16:14), and also, *To those to whom it was given to hear the word of God* (cf. Luke 8:10; Acts 19:20).

For obedience. He says that this grace and apostleship were intended not for discussion and debating, but **for obedience.** We were not sent to construct syllogisms but to share what had been entrusted to our hands. When the master makes a declaration, the hearers must not scrutinize it closely or try to specify exactly what was said. They need only accept it. The apostles were sent out in order to repeat what they had been told, and not to add anything of their own.

Notice that Paul did not engage in flattery. He was speaking to the Romans, people who were, one might say, sitting on top of the whole world. Yet he attributed to them nothing more than he did to the other Gentiles. Nor did he proclaim them preeminent in spiritual matters, even though they ruled and controlled the world. Instead, he says: we preach to you just as we do to all the Gentiles — thus lumping them in with the Scythians and the Thracians. Had he not intended to make just this point, he would have omitted, **including yourselves**, as unnecessary. Paul spoke in this way in order to purify the Romans of their arrogance, to destroy their exaggerated self-importance, and to teach them to respect others as their equals.

He did not write to everyone living in Rome but specified his addressees as **all God's beloved.** This is the best way of naming them because it shows the source of their holiness. Whence comes that holiness? From divine love. Paul says, **to all God's beloved**, then he adds **who are called to be saints**, making clear the source of all our blessings. He addresses all the faithful as saints.

How powerful is the love of God! Those who had been enemies and disgraced have suddenly become holy and children! When Paul calls God Father, he makes it clear that they are children. Then in saying "children," he showed them the entire treasury of blessings.

(2) Origen on verse 1

Paul is said to have been **set apart for the gospel** and set apart from his mother's womb because God had seen the reasons and the merits by which Paul deserved to be set apart for that purpose. For God foresaw that Paul *would labor on behalf of the gospel with greater fruit than anyone else* (1 Cor 15:10), that he was to preach the gospel of Christ *in hunger and thirst, in cold and nakedness, in danger from robbers, the sea,* and its waves (2 Cor 11:26-27). Indeed, Paul himself knew that he would not prosper if he did not preach it (1 Cor 9:16); that he would suffer bodily torments and be subjected to slavery so that he himself *might not be rejected even though he had preached to others* (1 Cor 9:27).

And so God, foreseeing this and much else besides, set him apart from his mother's womb for the sake of the gospel. For if, as the heretics think, he was chosen by chance or because he had a higher type of nature than others, Paul would never have feared that he might not have sufficiently restrained his body, that he might be condemned, or that he would not fare well if he ceased to preach the gospel. Paul himself spoke about this divine choice when he said, *Those whom God foreknew he also predestined to be conformed to the image of his Son* (Rom 8:29). Obviously, he meant that those whom God foreknew would conform themselves to Christ in their sufferings, God then predestined to be conformed to Christ's image and to be like him in glory as well. Therefore, the foreknowledge precedes, by which God knows all the labors and virtues that will be completed; then predestination follows on that basis. Nevertheless, the foreknowledge itself should not be considered the cause of the predestination. Humans can only judge a person's merits on the basis of accomplished deeds; God judges on the basis of deeds which are still future. Indeed, it is impious not to recognize that God can see in the future what we humans see only in the past.

(3) Augustine on verse 1

The scene of St. Stephen being stoned is striking because at the same place you see Saul, holding the coats of those hurling the rocks. There is Paul, the **apostle** of Christ Jesus; there is Paul, **the servant of Christ Jesus.** You hear Christ's voice clearly, *Why are you persecuting me?* (Acts 9:4). You, Paul, are knocked flat and then picked up; you are prostrate as a persecutor but upright as a preacher. Let Paul speak then and let us listen, *Paul, the servant of Christ Jesus by the will of God* (2 Cor 1:1). This was certainly not a result of your own choice, was it, Saul? We know what was done in accordance with your preference; we see what you did. By your will, Stephen was killed. We also see what you accomplished by God's will: everywhere you are read; everywhere you are proclaimed; everywhere you turn resisting hearts to Christ; everywhere you gather great flocks like a good shepherd. You reign now with the Christ and the very one you helped kill. Together now, you two see each other; together now, you two hear us speaking; together, you both pray for us. May he who crowned you both now hear you together: first one, then the other, the persecuted and the persecutor. One was a lamb then, the other a wolf; now both are lambs. May these two lambs recognize us and find us in the flock of Christ. May they commend us to him by their prayers; may their prayers obtain a peaceful and undisturbed life for the Church of their Lord.

(4) Augustine on verse 2

He says, **through his prophets**, but then he immediately adds, **in the holy scriptures**, lest false prophets seduce anyone into impiety by accidentally announcing a truth. He intended to indicate clearly that the literature of the nations, filled as it is with superstitious idolatry, should not be considered holy just because a few references to Christ can be found in it.

(5) Ambrosiaster on verse 3

He who was the Son of God in accordance with the Holy Spirit, that is, in accordance with God, because God is a spirit and undoubtedly holy — was **made Son of God according to the flesh** from Mary, as is written, *And the Word became flesh* (John 1:14). As a consequence, the same Christ Jesus is both Son of God and Son of Man, so that just as he is truly divine, he might be truly human as well. He would not be truly human unless he had both flesh and soul, and was thus complete. He was from all eternity Son of God, but was not known by created beings. Yet God wished him to be revealed for humanity's salvation. So God made him visible and corporeal, because God wanted him to be recognized through his mighty power, wanted him to conquer death in the flesh, and wanted him to cleanse humans from their sins by his suffering.

And he is made ... from the seed of David that, just as he was born a king of God before all ages, so too he would take his origin from a king according to the flesh. He was made, that is, born, by the operation of the Holy Spirit from a virgin, so that by this privilege he might be recognized as more than human, because he was set apart from the normal way of human birth, as had been foretold by the prophet Isaiah, *Behold, a virgin shall conceive*, etc. (Isa 7:14). Since this birth would be acknowledged as something altogether new and praiseworthy, in it God's plan for a future visit to the human race would be recognized.

(6) Theodoret on verse 4

Before his cross and passion, the Lord Christ did not seem to be God — not only to the other Jews, but even to the apostles themselves. For they kept stumbling over his human traits: they saw him eating and drinking, tiring and sleeping. Not even his miracles led them to make a true judgment. . . . But after his resurrection, his ascension into heaven, his sending of the Holy Spirit, and the miracles of every sort done by invoking his venerable name, all the believers recognized that he is both God and the only-begotten Son of God. Therefore, the divine Apostle taught here that he who bore the title Son of David according to the flesh was appointed and revealed to be the Son of God through that power exercised by the Holy Spirit after the resurrection from the dead of our Lord Jesus Christ.

(7) Origen on verses 4-5

Although one usually finds the word **predestined** in Latin manuscripts,[1] the better reading is **destined**, not **predestined**. For a person who already exists is "destined," but someone who does not yet exist is "predestined," as is the case for those whom the Apostle had in mind when he said, *Those whom he foreknew he also predestined* (Rom 8:29). Thus, those who do not yet exist can be "foreknown" and "predestined"; but the one who exists, and always exists, is not "predestined" but "destined." We must insist on this point because of those who insult the only-begotten Son of God. Because they do not understand the difference between "predestined" and "destined," they think that he should be ranked

---

1. This and other references to the Latin manuscripts were added by the translator, Rufinus of Aquileia, to alert his readers to the difference between their versions of the New Testament and the one Origen himself used.

among those who have been predestined to exist, since previously they did not exist. But he was never "predestined" to be Son, since he always exists, just as the Father always exists. Therefore, one who always exists is "destined," as we have said, not "predestined." Others are "predestined," if they did not yet exist when they were predestined but had an origin at some later point in time. . . .

Paul says that he received **grace and apostleship** through Christ as a mediator between God and humanity (1 Tim 2:5). **Grace** should be understood as referring to his patient endurance of labor; **apostleship** to his authority to preach, since Christ himself is called an "apostle," that is, one sent by the Father (Heb 3:1). Indeed, Christ says that he had been sent to preach the gospel to the poor (Luke 4:18), and for that reason he gives to his disciples everything that belongs to him. Grace is said to be *poured upon your lips* (Ps 45:2). Christ also gives to his apostles the grace by which they labor, since one of them says, *I worked harder than any of them — though it was not I, but the grace of God that is with me* (1 Cor 15:10). Since it has been said of him, *having Christ, the priest and apostle of our confession* (Heb 3:1), Christ gave to his disciples the dignity of apostleship, so that they might themselves become apostles of God. For the Gentiles, who were *estranged from the covenant of God and from the community of Israel* (Eph 2:12), could have believed in the gospel only through that grace which was given to the apostles. Through that grace the nations accepted the preaching of the apostles in faith, and the sound of the name of Christ *went forth into all the earth* (Ps 19:4; Rom 10:18) because of the grace bestowed on the apostles.

(8) Augustine on verse 4

Jesus was predestined, so that the one who would be the son of David **according to the flesh** would nevertheless be **the Son of God in power according to the Spirit of holiness**, because he was born of the Holy Spirit and the Virgin Mary. In the unique and inexplicable taking on of a human being by the Word of God, he was at once both the Son of God and the Son of Man; the Son of Man because of the human being who was taken up; the Son of God because the one who took up the human was truly and properly called the Only-Begotten God. Thus we believe not in a quaternity but in a trinity. This assumption of human nature was predestined; it was so great, so glorious, so wonderful that humanity could not have been lifted any higher. At the same time, divinity could not have acted more humbly than to lower itself into that assumed human nature, with the weakness of the flesh, even to suffering death on the cross. Just as that one was predestined to be our head, so are we many predestined to be his members. Human merits are here silenced since we have all perished through Adam. Let that reign instead which reigns by the grace of God, through Our Lord Jesus Christ, the only Son of God, the one Lord. If any preceding merits could be found in our head for that unique birth, then we could go looking for merits in ourselves his members for each of our rebirths. That birth was granted rather than paid to Christ, so that he was born of the Holy Spirit and the Virgin, free of any debt of sin. In the same way, to be reborn of water and the Holy Spirit is freely granted to us; it is not a reward for any merit of ours.

(9) Augustine on verses 6-7

Again he highlights God's graciousness rather than their merits. He did not say, "lovers of God," but **God's beloved.** God loved us before any merits, so that by already being loved we might then love God (cf. 1 John 4:19). For the same reason, he adds, **called to be saints.** Although a person might claim credit for responding to God's call, no one can claim credit for being called. **Called to be saints** should be understood to mean not that they had been called because they were already holy but rather that they were made holy because they had been called. . . .

The Apostle says, **Grace to you and peace from God our Father and the Lord Jesus Christ,** without adding the Holy Spirit, so that we might recognize that the Holy Spirit is the gift of God. What else are grace and peace except the gift of God? That grace by which we are freed from sins and that peace by which we are reconciled to God can be given to humans only in the gift of the Holy Spirit. In this way, both the trinity and the unchangeable unity of God are evident in this greeting.

Romans 1:8-9

8First, I thank my God through Jesus Christ for all of you, because your faith is proclaimed in all the world. 9For God is my witness, whom I serve with my spirit in the gospel of his Son, that without ceasing I remember you always in my prayers. . . .

(1) John Chrysostom on verse 8

These words are an appropriate introduction for someone as blessed as Paul. They instruct all people to sacrifice the firstfruits of good works and words to God, and to give thanks not only for their own virtuous actions but also for those of others. Such thanksgiving frees the soul from envy and jealousy, and so draws God to the good intentions of those who give thanks. . . . Paul says, **your faith is proclaimed in all the world.** Had the whole world heard of the faith of the Romans? Yes, Paul says, the whole world. This is not improbable, since the city of Rome was not without distinction but was established, so to speak, on a mountaintop and was famous in every way. Consider the power of the preaching, how through tax collectors and fishermen it took hold of this chief of cities in such a short time. Syrians became teachers and instructors of the Romans. Paul testifies to two excellent traits of the Romans, that they believed and did so boldly. They were so bold that their reputation reached almost to the ends of the world.

(2) Origen on verses 8-9

Paul's first word is one of thanksgiving. Now to give thanks to God is to offer a sacrifice of praise. That is why he adds **through Jesus Christ**, as through a great high priest. For anyone wishing to offer sacrifice to God ought to know that it should be offered through the hands of a priest (Heb 8:3). Moreover, his words **my God** should not be regarded as superfluous. They are similar to the way God is named as the God of certain saints, as in the phrase *the God of Abraham, Isaac, and Jacob* (Exod 3:6). For one cannot call the Lord God one's own if one's god is the stomach (Phil 3:19), or if one's god is avarice, or worldly glory, or earthly glamour, or power over transient goods. For whatever anyone worships above all else is that person's god. . . .

To serve in my spirit seems to me similar or perhaps even greater than "to worship in the spirit." The Lord himself said to the Samaritan woman, *Woman, the hour will come, and it is now here, when the true worshipers will worship the Father in spirit and truth* (John 4:23). Paul not only worships in the spirit; he also **serves in the spirit.** For a person can worship without the affections, but serving implies being moved by strong feelings. Therefore, the Apostle served God not only in the body, not only in the soul, but in the spirit and with his better part.

Romans 1:10-15

10. . . asking that somehow by God's will I may now at last succeed in coming to you. 11For I long to see you, that I may impart to you some spiritual gift to strengthen you, 12that is, that we may be mutually encouraged by each other's faith, both yours and mine. 13I want you to know, brethren, that I have often intended to come to you (but thus far have been prevented), in order that I may reap some harvest among you as well as among the rest of the Gentiles. 14I am under obligation both to Greeks and to barbarians, both to the wise and to the foolish; 15so I am eager to preach the gospel to you also who are in Rome.

(1) John Chrysostom on verses 10-12

Do you notice that even though Paul was in agony to see them, he refused to come to them if it seemed against God's will? His longing for them was mingled with the fear of God. For he loved them and was eager to see them. Since he loved them, he desired to do only what God willed. This is genuine love, and unlike our love; we fail to obey the laws of love on both extremes. Either we do not love anyone or we act contrary to God's will when we do. In both ways, we act against the divine law. If these things are grievous for you to hear, they are more grievous for you to do.

Someone may ask, "How can our love be contrary to God's will?" When we ignore Christ wasting away with hunger but provide more than is necessary for our children, friends, and relatives. Why should I continue the argument further? For if each of us would examine our own conscience, we would notice ourselves acting this way in many situations. That blessed man Paul was not like us. Rather, he knew how to love, as he ought and as was fitting. Although he surpassed all people in loving, he did not exceed the right measure of love. Notice how he excels both in his fear of God and in his desire to see the Romans. Excellent love consists in praying continually for something, and in not giving up when we do not obtain what we ask. Intense reverence is characterized by continuing to love and yet yielding to the will of God. . . . Once Paul had given himself into the hands which govern all things and had submitted himself as clay submits to the potter, he followed wherever God led him.

Paul showed that he himself needed the Romans, not only that they needed him. He put the disciples in Rome in the role of teacher, abdicating his own superior status. He treated the Romans with equal honor, observed a great equality of honor with the Romans, saying that both would benefit from his visit: I need comfort from you, and you need comfort from me. How so? **By each other's faith, both yours and mine.** Just as in the case of fire, a flame grows brighter when many lamps are brought together, so too with the faithful. When we are driven apart from one another and are off by ourselves, how dispirited we are! But when we see one another and throw our arms around one another, we are very happy. Moreover, anyone who infers that Paul's comfort and happiness came when the Romans grew in faith would not be missing Paul's point.

(2) Ambrosiaster on verse 11

When he says, **so that I may share with you some spiritual gift**, he implies that they have been susceptible to carnal thoughts, because they wore the name of Christ but had received not the teaching of Christ but that of the Jews. Thus, he wanted to get to Rome very quickly so that he could draw them away from such teaching and bring them a spiritual gift instead. If he shared a spiritual grace with them, they would be won over for God and might be made perfect in what they believed and in professing that belief. Clearly, then, he had praised them earlier for their promptness and their prayerful devotion to Christ but not for their understanding of the faith. For, while professing to be Christians, they continued naively to observe the law, as they had been taught to do. God's mercy, however, had lifted the burdens of the law — as I have often said. Because of its frailty, God had decreed that the human race should be saved by faith alone, and guided by the law known from nature.

(3) Ambrosiaster on verses 13-14

He calls them **brethren** not only because they had been born again, but because some among them, though only a few, were faithful in their thinking. Thus he says, **called to be saints.** What does **called to be saints** mean? If they are already saints, how are they still *called to be sanctified* (Rom 1:7)? The key here is God's foreknowledge: people whom God knows will be saints in the future are already **saints** before God, and thus are so **called.** However, Paul says that he has **been prevented** — by God no doubt — from coming to them until the time of the letter's composition. Because God knew that the Romans were not yet ready, God directed the Apostle to other cities which were already disposed to receive the truth. Although the Romans were acting in the name of the Savior, still their negligence made them unprepared to learn spiritual things. . . . In saying that he was prevented, Paul is not making excuses: he wants them to understand the reasons for the delay and urges the Romans to get themselves ready. Hearing that a spiritual grace was to be ministered to them, they should then make themselves worthy to receive it. . . .

I am a debtor both to Greeks and to barbarians, both to the wise and to the foolish. He is saying that he is a **debtor** to those he lists because he was sent to preach to all. Thus he implies that all are debtors: to acknowledge God the Creator, by whom and through whom all things exist, is the debt, the honor, and the salvation of the person who confesses it. He says **Greeks** to mean Gentiles, specifically those who are called Romans either by nationality or by adoption; by **barbarians**, he intends those who are not Romans, who are ethnically different and thus not Gentiles. By **the wise**, Paul means those called wise in the secular world because of their expertise in worldly learning: they investigate the stars or they study geometry, arithmetic, grammar, rhetoric, or music. He shows them all that such pursuits are unprofitable and that true wisdom is found only by believing in Christ. Conversely, he calls **foolish** those who avoid such complexities and are untrained in secular studies. Paul claims that he has been sent to preach to all these different kinds of people. He says nothing about the Jews, however, because he is the teacher of the Gentiles.

Romans 1:16-17

16For I am not ashamed of the gospel; it is the power of God for salvation to everyone who has faith, to the Jew first and also to the Greek. 17For in it the righteousness of God is revealed through faith for faith; as it is written, *He who through faith is righteous shall live* (Hab. 2:4).

(1) Ambrosiaster on verses 16-17

For I am not ashamed of the gospel; it is the power of God for salvation to everyone who has faith. This statement is directed at those who had passed on a false understanding of faith to the Romans to whom this letter is addressed. The power of the apostles supported their teaching. Because their preaching seemed beyond belief, the signs and wonders they did served as proof that their teaching ought not be despised — since they had such power at their disposal. No one doubts that demonstrated power outweighs mere words. So, because those who preached to the Romans had worked no miracles, their preaching lacked the power of God. Paul, then, says he is not ashamed of the gospel of God — though those other teachers were now ashamed, because what they had taught was being criticized by Paul: their teaching was not confirmed by signs and was actually contrary to the apostolic teaching. The power of God invites people to faith and then bestows salvation on every believer, remitting sins and justifying them, so that a person marked by the mystery of the cross will not be liable to the second death.[2] For the preaching of the cross of Christ is evidence of the victory over death, as the Apostle John says, *For the Son of God has come to destroy the works of the devil* (1 John 3:8). Therefore no believer may be held fast by death, because the believer bears the sign that death has been conquered.

To the Jew first and also to the Greek. That is, to those from the race of Abraham and to those from the nations. For by **Greek** he means Gentile, and by **Jew** those of the seed of Abraham. . . .

The righteousness of God is revealed in the gospel from faith to faith. He says this because **the righteousness of God** is revealed in one who believes, whether Jew or Greek. He calls it **the righteousness of God** because God freely justifies the impious through faith, without the works of the law, as he says elsewhere, *So that I may be found in him, not having a righteousness of my own that comes from the law, but one which comes through faith, the righteousness which is from God in faith* (Phil 3:9). He says that righteousness is revealed in the gospel, since it gives the faith which justifies: the truth and righteousness of God are manifest in a person who believes in the gospel and professes that belief. It is the **righteousness of <u>God</u>** because God has actually given what God had promised. Therefore, someone who believes that what God had promised through the prophets actually has been granted affirms and bears witness to God's righteousness. What does **from faith to faith** mean? Divine faith consists in God's making a promise; human faith is placed in God who makes this promise. **Thus the righteousness of God is revealed by the fidelity** of God who promises, and **in the faith** of the one who believes the promise. As the righteousness of God is manifest in the believer, so the unbeliever makes God appear unrighteous. To refuse to believe that God has granted what God had promised is to deny that God is faithful. Paul's statement is directed against the Jews, who deny that Jesus is the Christ whom God had promised.

As it is written, *The one who is righteous will live by faith.* Paul appeals to the example of the prophet Habakkuk to declare that the just person has been shown to live by faith rather than the works of the law and that faith rather than the law justifies a person before God. Living by faith is not the same as life in the present world; it belongs to the future. The just lives by faith in the presence of God.

(2) Origen on verse 16

The Greeks believed that every human being could be designated by one of two names: that is, everyone was either a Greek or a barbarian: anyone who was not a Greek they considered a barbarian. Paul employs a more accurate distinction when he says **Jews** first, and then **Greeks**, and lastly *barbarians* (Rom 1:16). The Greeks lived according to laws and thus called all who lived without laws "barbarians." For this very reason, the Apostle set the Jews ahead of the Greeks: they began living under laws even before the Greeks did, and the Jewish laws were issued by God rather than by human beings.

---

2. By the second death, Ambrosiaster means eternal damnation, which could follow bodily death. Christ does not prevent the first death but liberates from the second.

(3) Theodoret on verse 17

He says here not that righteousness is given but that it is **revealed.** For the righteousness hidden long ago becomes manifest to those who believe. **Through faith for faith,** he says. For one must believe the prophets and through them be led to believe in the gospel. This has another meaning as well: the one who believes in the Lord Christ, who receives the grace of holy Baptism and the gift of adoption as a child, is then led through these to believe in the good things which are still to come: the resurrection from the dead, eternal life, and the kingdom of heaven.

(4) John Chrysostom on verse 17

Indeed, the righteous person lives not only for this present life, but also for the life to come. Paul hints at this future life and at its splendor and glory. A person might be spared even while continuing to live in shame, for a king does not punish everyone who deserves it, and thus "saves" them. For that reason, we must then be attentive to the meaning of the word **salvation.** With this in mind, Paul has added, **righteousness.** He is speaking not about your own righteousness, but about the righteousness of God. He also implies that this life is abundant and easy. For you receive this life not through toil and suffering but as a gift from above. From your side, you bring only one thing, which is **faith.** Paul's argument seemed to be incredible: that someone such as the adulterer, the effeminate, the grave robber, and the sorcerer is not only spared punishment, but actually becomes righteous with a righteousness given from above. So Paul confirms his argument by citing the Old Testament. First he uses a short phrase that opens a vast sea of stories, if one is able to understand his meaning. By saying, **through faith for faith,** he sends the hearer back to God's plan at work in the Old Testament. He writes this in the Epistle to the Hebrews[3] as well, where with great wisdom he explains that both the righteous and sinners are made just in this same way even in the Old Testament. There he named both Rahab the harlot and Abraham (Heb 11:31; Josh 2:1-6; 6:17-25).

(5) Augustine on verse 17

You who are just, who are upright, *Rejoice in the Lord. . . . Praise befits* you (Ps 33:1). Let none of you say, "Am I just?" or "When did I become just?" Do not underestimate yourselves; do not give up on yourselves. You are all human, made in the image of God. God, who made you human, became human for your sake. The blood of the Only-Begotten was poured out so that you, as many children, might be adopted into an everlasting inheritance. If you are embarrassed by your earthly weakness, then remind yourselves of the price paid for you. Consider what you eat, what you drink, to what you give your amen. We are not urging this point to make you proud, of course, or to make you claim

---

3. The church fathers considered St. Paul the author of the Epistle to the Hebrews.

some perfection for yourself. Still you must not think that you have once again been deprived of all justice. My objective is not to question you about your own justice, since I fully expect that none of you would dare to claim to be righteous. No, I am asking about your faith. As none of you would dare to claim, "I am righteous," none would dare to say, "I am not a believer." I am not questioning how you live but asking what you believe. You will answer that you believe in Christ. Have you not heard the Apostle say, **the just lives from faith**? Your faith is your justice. If you believe, you will certainly be careful. And in being careful, you will strive. God knows your efforts; God sees your intention; God judges your battle against the flesh. God urges you to fight and helps you to win. God looks forward to your struggling, catches you when you totter, crowns you when you succeed. Therefore, *Let the righteous rejoice in the Lord;* or as I would say, "Let the faithful rejoice in the Lord," because **the just lives from faith.** *Praise befits the upright* (Ps 33:1).

Romans 1:18-23

18For the wrath of God is revealed from heaven against all ungodliness and wickedness of men who by their wickedness suppress the truth. 19For what can be known about God is plain to them, because God has shown it to them. 20Ever since the creation of the world his invisible nature, namely, his eternal power and deity, has been clearly perceived in the things that have been made. So they are without excuse; 21for although they knew God, they did not honor him as God or give thanks to him, but they became futile in their thinking and their senseless minds were darkened. 22Claiming to be wise, they became fools, 23and exchanged the glory of the immortal God for images resembling mortal man or birds or animals or reptiles.

(1) Origen on verses 18-20

The wrath of God is now said to be revealed not generally, but **against all ungodliness and wickedness.** It is revealed not against everyone but only against those who possess the truth of God and in wickedness **suppress the truth.** Paul even says **what is known about God is plain to them**, thereby showing that something of God is known but other things about God remain unknown. Therefore, he says that **the wrath of God is revealed from heaven against those who by their wickedness suppress the truth.** Things that are revealed are brought out of darkness and obscurity into knowledge. Therefore, the wrath of God is said to be **revealed from heaven**, not against those who do not know the truth at all but against those who possess it but act in the wrong way. Paul seems to be saying that the knowledge and understanding of the wrath of God are plain to those who know the truth but stifle it in their wickedness. This at least becomes clear in the following statements about the wise and learned of this world. Or he may refer to philosophers who, though they knew the truth and justice of God, **did not honor him as God or give thanks to him.** Instead, they turned to idols and **became futile in their thinking. Claiming to be wise, they became fools, and they exchanged the glory of the immortal**

God for images resembling a mortal human being or birds or four-footed animals or reptiles. In these sentences the Apostle indicates that even those things attained by the wise of this world through their knowledge of the truth actually come to them through the revelation of God. And yet as long as they pursue empty glory or respect customary errors or remain bound by fear of earthly rulers, they serve as judges of their own damnation. They hide from themselves that truth which they had known through the revelation of God, covering it over by their refusal of freedom or denying it by the wickedness of their deeds. . . .

Against all the godlessness and wickedness of men who by their wickedness suppress the truth. Godlessness is sinning against God; **wickedness** is sinning against human beings. Therefore, those who **by their wickedness suppress the truth** sin against both God and humanity. We must believe that these people knew the truth because of the ideas that are natural and implanted in the soul by God. Sufficient wisdom has been granted for them to know the invisible qualities of God on the basis of what is visible — such knowledge of God as can be inferred from the creation itself. Because of this, God's judgment will be just against those who fell away from the worship of God to the cult of images of human beings and animals, even before the coming of Christ. . . .

For what is known about God is plain to them, because God has shown it to them. We have already pointed to that knowledge of God which we are able to attain by inference from this world or by ideas implanted in the soul by God. The Apostle himself affirmed this by saying that the **invisible qualities of God have been perceived by reflection on what he has made.** We should understand that what remains unknown about God is the actual reality of his substance or nature. In fact, I think that the character proper to God's nature is hidden, not only from us human beings but also from every other creature — unless at some time a rational nature makes such great progress that it can attain even this knowledge of God. . . .

Ever since the creation of the world his eternal power and divine nature, invisible though they are, have been understood and seen through the things he has made. So they are without excuse; for though they knew God, they did not honor him as God or give thanks to him, but they became futile in their thinking, and their senseless minds were darkened. Claiming to be wise, they became fools; and they exchanged the glory of the immortal God for images resembling a mortal human being or birds or four-footed animals or reptiles. . . . It should be noted that Paul sometimes uses the term **invisible** to refer even to created things; for example, in another place the same Apostle writes, *for in him,* that is, in Jesus Christ, *all things in heaven and on earth were created, things visible and invisible* (Col 1:16). That is why he added the words **his eternal power and divine nature** to the term **invisible.** The power and divinity of God, each of which is eternal, are known by reflection on the creation. God rules all things by **power**; God fills all things by the **divine nature.** Thus are they without excuse: although they knew God by God's own revelation, they neither worshiped nor thanked God, as they should have. Instead, through the vanity of their own minds, by insisting on bodily forms and representations for God, they destroyed the image of God within themselves. Thus, those who seemed to exalt themselves as living in the light of wisdom were cast down into the deepest darkness of stupidity.

(2) Augustine on verses 18-23

I suggested to you that the learned people among the nations, the most outstanding of whom are called philosophers, examined nature itself and through these things that had been made recognized their maker. They did not hear the prophets, nor did they receive the law of God, yet God spoke to them silently through the very operation of the world. The spectacle of the world drew them to inquire about the one who had produced all things. They could not accept the notion that heaven and earth had somehow been established without a maker. The blessed Apostle Paul speaks of these people when he says, **the wrath of God is revealed from heaven against all ungodliness.** What does he mean, **against all ungodliness**? Not only against the Jews, who received the law of God and then sinned against the lawgiver. Truly, **the wrath of God is revealed from heaven against all ungodliness** of the nations. To forestall any protest at their not having received the law of God, he added, **and the wickedness of those who by their wickedness suppress the truth.** What truth? you ask. They did not receive the law; they did not hear the prophets. Observe which truth he is speaking about: **For what is known about God is plain to them.** How is it clear? Listen again: **Because God has shown it to them.** If you ask further: how **has God shown it to them** without giving them the law? Hear how: **Ever since the creation of the world God's eternal power and divine nature, invisible though they are, have been understood and seen through the things God has made. The invisible things,** that is, the invisible properties of God; **ever since the creation of the world,** that is, from the time God established the world; **have been understood and seen through the things God has made,** those invisible things have been seen and understood through these visible ones. **The eternal,** I quote the Apostle, **the eternal power and divine nature,** you understand as implied, **have been understood and seen. So they are without excuse.** Why without excuse? **Because even though they knew God, they did not honor God as God or give thanks.** He did not say, "they were ignorant of God," but **they knew God.**

How did they know God? From the things that God made. Ask the beauty of the earth; ask the beauty of the sea; ask the beauty of the swelling, spreading air; ask the beauty of the heavens; ask the order of the stars; ask the sun illumining the day with its brightness; ask the moon tempering the darkness of the following night with its splendor; ask the living things moving in the waters, moving on the earth, flying in the air; ask their observable bodies and hidden souls, the visible guided and the invisible guiding things. Question these, and they will all answer you: "Behold, we are beautiful." Their beauty is itself their confession. Who made all these beautiful, changing things, then, if not the one who is unchangeably beautiful? Finally, in human beings themselves, so that they might understand and recognize God who is the creator of the whole world, I say, the philosophers investigated the twin realities of body and soul in human beings. They investigated the parts of which they were themselves constituted. They saw the body but did not see the soul. Yet they could actually see the body only by the power of the soul. They saw through their eyes, but someone was inside them looking out these windows. When that occupant departs, the house collapses; when the ruler leaves, the realm falls; it is called the remains. The eyes still appear fine; they are open but see nothing. The ears are still there, but the hearer has gone. That musical instrument, the tongue, remains, but its player has taken leave. They investigated these two: the body which they saw and the soul which they did not see. They discovered that what was not seen was better than what was seen, that the hidden soul was higher, the manifest body lower. They knew these two things, they perceived them, they discussed them both and found that both were changeable in human beings. They found the body changeable through age, decay, nourishment, rest, sickness, life, and death. They moved on to consider the soul, which they understood as better, and marveled at its invisibility. Yet they found that it too was changeable: it was accepting and refusing, knowing and ignoring, remembering and forgetting, frightened and brave, growing in wisdom and falling into folly. It too was changeable, they found, and thus passed beyond the human soul as well, in search of some unchanging reality.

Through these things which had been made, they finally came to recognize their maker. **But they did not honor the maker as God or give thanks**, as the Apostle says. **They became futile in their thinking and their senseless minds were darkened.** By claiming as their own what they had actually received, they lost what they had. **Claiming to be wise, they became fools.** Where did they end up? **They exchanged**, he says, **the glory of the incorruptible God for images resembling a corruptible human being.** He refers to idols. Making an idol in human form and attributing the appearance of one of God's works to God who had designed them all was not so terrible. Making a human image of God was not so bad. They did not stop there. **Or birds or four-footed animals or reptiles.** These great, wise ones set up all these mute, irrational animals as gods for themselves. I criticized you for worshiping a human image as God; what will I do with you when you adore the image of a dog, the image of a vulture, the image of a crocodile? They ended up worshiping these things. In their investigations, the higher they mounted, the deeper they plunged when they fell. The higher they rose, the lower they sank.

(3) Anonymous on verse 18

If, as the Manichees assert, the God of the Old Testament is cruel because of taking vengeance on sinners, how can the Apostle here assert that vengeance will be visited on sinful people by the God of the New Testament? This shows that the same God gave both the Old and the New Testaments.

(4) John Chrysostom on verses 19-20

Paul says, **what can be known about God is plain to them.** How was this clear? Did God send them a voice from above? Not at all! Rather, Paul introduced creation itself into the argument, which could draw them to God more effectively than a voice. Through the creation the wise and the ignorant, the Scythians and the barbarians, are able to climb up to God, learning of God through the beauty of visible things. . . . The prophet said, *The heavens declare the glory of God* (Ps 19:1). What will the Greeks say on that day? Might they say to God, "We did not know you"? To this, God could respond, "So did you not hear the voice of the heavens speaking through what could be seen? Did you not hear the voice in the order and harmony of all things blaring out more clearly than a trumpet? Did you not see the laws of night and day in place always without change? Did you not see the good order of winter, spring, and the other seasons, always stable and predictable? Did you not see the steadiness of the sea despite its great turbulence and waves? Did you not see that all things remain well ordered and by their beauty and grandeur proclaim the creator?" Paul brought together all these things, and many more, when he said, **Ever since the creation of the world his eternal power and divine nature, invisible though they are, have been understood and seen though the things he has made. So they are without excuse.** And yet God did not create these things in order to convict them, even though this was one result. God set such a great lesson before the Gentiles so that they might come to know God, not to deprive them of an excuse for their failings.

(5) Pelagius on verse 19

Every creature bears witness that it is not God but was made by something other than itself and that it should conform to God's will. For if God is the highest and the greatest, invisible, incomprehensible, inestimable, and the one over all — that is, the one to whom nothing is superior nor equal in greatness or splendor or power — then God obviously cannot be like any creature that is seen with the eyes, conceptualized by reason, and assessed by judgment. No creature is in every way greater than all others because they all surpass one another in one way or another: some in size, as heaven and earth; some in splendor, as the sun and the moon or the stars; some in depth, as the sea. Obviously, therefore, none of the elements is God. Furthermore, that they are changeable and alien to eternity proves that they were created. . . . In fact, because they change and modify their patterns of action and replace one another, they show that they were created by one maker and that they follow not their own will but that of their master, whose governance they cannot impede.

(6) Ambrosiaster on verses 21-23

For though they knew God, they did not honor God as God or give thanks. They were not deprived of all knowledge of God since they professed that all things in heaven, on earth, and in the world below have one origin, and that God alone determined their properties and functions. Yet, knowing this, they did not give thanks. Paul refers to the people of earlier ages in order to correct those living in his day and who would live in the future. **But they became futile in their thinking.** Seeing the world laid out in wondrous array by God whom they recognized as its creator, they were negligent. Futility consists in knowing the truth — God — but then deciding to worship something that they knew was not true — idols. **And their senseless minds were darkened.** A cloud of error completely covered their hearts. They ought to have given greater and fuller honor to the creator, because of the beauty God had created. By abandoning God, they became stupid, believing they should worship only things they could see. **Claiming to be wise, they be-**

came fools. They considered themselves wise, because they judged that they had thoroughly researched the laws of physics, scrutinizing the courses of the stars and the sizes of the elements. Yet they despise the God of this whole realm. They are foolish: if these things are wonderful, how much more wonderful is their creator! . . .

And they exchanged the glory of the immortal God for images resembling a mortal human being. So blinded were their hearts that they did not substitute human beings but the likeness of human beings for the majesty of the invisible God, although they should have recognized God through the things that were made. This is an even worse, nay an inexcusable offense. They give the title "god" to the form of a corruptible human, to a statue of a human being! They accord divine honors to images of dead humans, though they would not have dared to make offerings to such beings while they were still alive. What foolishness and what stupidity! These people called themselves wise, to their own damnation, when they judged fiction more powerful than truth and the dead more powerful than the living! Abandoning the living God, they preferred the dead, among whom they themselves should be classed, according to a text in the Wisdom of Solomon: *A dead person makes with wicked hands a dead thing* (Wis 15:17). This saying of the Wisdom of Solomon aims at just such people.

Like birds or four-footed animals or reptiles. By these additions Paul builds up the case that their folly deserves punishment; they are beyond silly and stupid. They have so debased the majesty and glory of God that they offer divine worship to the images of the tiniest and least significant creatures. The Babylonians took the lead by giving the name "god" to a statue of Bel, a certain dead man who supposedly ruled over them. They also worshiped a slithering dragon (of whom they had an effigy) killed by Daniel, a man of God (Bel 23-27). Moreover, the Egyptians worship a four-footed animal resembling a cow, named Apis. Imitating their wickedness, Jeroboam set up cows in Samaria to which the Jews made sacrifices (1 Kgs 12:28); birds, too, because the pagans have "raven festivals." The Egyptians worshiped statues of all the things, those I have mentioned and others best passed over in silence. These statues were made by people who considered themselves wise in worldly ways. Although they acknowledged the invisible God, they failed to give God honor. In this way they showed that they were unwise even in managing visible things. The imprudent in important matters will seldom be wise in lesser ones.

(7) **Augustine on verse 22**

Paul's words, **The wrath of God is revealed from heaven upon all impiety** and following, has a different meaning than the statement in the Wisdom of Solomon about the wise of this world, *If they knew so much that they could evaluate the world, why did they not more easily discover the Lord and Creator of this world?* (Wis 13:9). Those whom Solomon accuses failed to recognize the creator through the creature; those whom the Apostle accuses did recognize the creator but did not give thanks; claiming to be wise, they became foolish and fell into the worship of idols. In speaking to the Athenians, the same Apostle clearly shows that the wise among the nations had found the creator. When he said, *For "In him we live and move and have our being,"* he added, *just as some among you* *have said* (Acts 17:28). Paul begins by attacking the impiety of the nations. He can then show that once they are converted they can receive God's grace. It would be unjust for them to be punished for impiety but not be rewarded for faith.

Romans 1:24-27

24Therefore God gave them up in the lusts of their hearts to impurity, to the dishonoring of their bodies among themselves, 25because they exchanged the truth about God for a lie and worshiped and served the creature rather than the Creator, who is blessed forever! Amen.

26For this reason God gave them up to dishonorable passions. Their women exchanged natural relations for unnatural, 27and the men likewise gave up natural relations with women and were consumed with passion for one another, men committing shameless acts with men and receiving in their own persons the due penalty for their error.

(1) Origen on verses 24-26

Therefore God gave them up in the lusts of their hearts to impurity, to inflict insults on one another's bodies, because they exchanged the truth about God for a lie and worshiped and served the creature rather than the Creator, who is blessed forever! These particular verses are best explained according to the faith of the Church. As we have already demonstrated, those who know the truth God has revealed but wickedly stifle it have rightly and deservedly been rejected by God (Rom 1:18). For this reason, they have been delivered over to the cravings of their hearts — which degrade their bodies by impurity. When they exchanged the glory of the incorruptible God for the foul and worthless shapes of human beings and animals, their abuse of divine worship brought a comparable judgment upon themselves: rational human beings began to live like irrational beasts.

(2) Ambrosiaster on verses 24-25

Therefore God gave them up in the lusts of their hearts to impurity, to inflicting insults on one another's bodies. Since, says Paul, they insulted God the creator by deifying figments of God and representations of creatures, they have been handed over to mockery, indeed handed over not to practices they rejected but to carry out what they actually longed to do. Still, God's goodness is operative even in this. It would have been right for them to be enslaved and forced to do what they hated, and so tormented — because even the good is bitter and repulsive when done against one's will. When they turned away from God, they were handed over to the devil. "To hand over" is "to allow"; it does not mean "to force" or "to drive." In that way, they brought forth in action what they had conceived in desire — for such people are incapable of good thoughts. Well, then, they were handed over to impurity, to afflict their own bodies through mutual abuse. While Paul censures past events, he also has in mind those living today: even now they are still being handed over to abuse each other's bodies. For even now, people dishonor each other's bodies in this way. When they plan crimes in their souls, they are accused of dishonoring their bodies. Is not polluting the body evidence of sin in the soul? When the body is stained, can anyone doubt that the soul has sinned?

These people exchanged the truth about God for a lie and reverenced and worshiped the creature rather than the Creator — blessed be he forever! Amen. They exchanged the truth of God for a lie by bestowing the name of the true God upon false gods. They deny the true nature of stones and pieces of wood and other materials, then proceed to make them out to be what they are not. Thus the "truth of God" is turned into a lie by calling a stone "god." Such a lie attacks the true God: when the same name is applied to both the false and true, the true God is made into something false. Truth is changed into falsehood. The material is no longer called "stone" or "wood," but a "god." Thus they serve a creature rather than the creator. Although they do not deny God, they actually serve a creature. If they are not to appear utterly ridiculous in worshiping such things, they must invest them with divine status. Thus their worship becomes an assault on God. Such worship adds to their punishment: though they know God, they dishonor God, who is blessed for evermore. Amen, this is true.

The blessing of God, says Paul, is forever, because God endures forever. But impiety honors idols for only a limited time and so has no lasting truth — which is found only in God.

(3) Augustine on verses 24-27

Pelagius says, "Retribution is itself the source of sin if the sinner becomes so weakened by the punishment that sin follows sin." He judges, then, that the light of truth should not abandon those who have transgressed the law. Once deprived of this light, sinners are blind and necessarily sin even more; sinners are impeded by their prior failure and are unable to escape further dangers. Such sinners then hear the voice of the law warning them to beg for the Savior's grace. Was not the Apostle describing people who were already being punished in just this way when he said, *for though they knew God they did not honor God as God or give thanks, but they became futile in their thinking and their senseless minds were darkened* (Rom 1:21). That darkening was itself a retribution and punishment. When their hearts became blind as they were being punished by the withdrawal of wisdom, they fell into more and greater sins. *Claiming to be wise, they became fools* (Rom 1:22). To understand the seriousness of this punishment, one should consider where it led them. *They exchanged the glory of the immortal God for images resembling a mortal human being or birds or four-footed animals or reptiles* (Rom 1:23). They did these things as punishment for their sin, for *their senseless minds were darkened* (Rom 1:22). Because these sins are themselves punishments, he adds, **Therefore God gave them up in the lusts of their hearts to impurity.** Notice that God condemns them further by **giving them up in the lusts of their hearts to impurity.** Note also what they do as a consequence of this punishment: **to inflicting insults on one another's bodies.** He clearly is speaking here about both wickedness and the punishment of wickedness, **because they exchanged the truth about God for a lie and worshiped and served the creature rather than the Creator, who is blessed forever! Amen. For this reason, God gave them up to degrading passions.** Each time God punishes them, fresh and more serious sins follow from the retribution itself. **Their women exchanged natural intercourse for unnatural, and in the same way also the men, giving up natural intercourse with women, were consumed with passion for one another. Men did depraved things to one another.** To show that these actions were both sins and punishments for sins, he continued: **and received in their own persons the due penalty for their error.** Pay attention: each time God takes revenge, the vengeance itself gives birth to further sins. Read what follows: *And since they did not see fit to acknowledge God, God gave them up to a debased mind and to things that should not be done. They were filled with every kind of wickedness, evil, covetousness, malice. Full of envy, murder, strife, deceit, craftiness, gossipers, slanderers, God-haters, insolent, haughty, boastful, inventors of evil, rebellious toward parents, foolish, faithless, heartless, ruthless* (Rom 1:28-31). Yet he [Pelagius] still pronounces: "Sins should not be punished in a way that leads the sinner to sin even more because of that retribution."

(4) John Chrysostom on verses 26-27

When Paul was discussing their teachings, he explained the world and human intelligence to them. He affirmed that the power of judgment which was given to them by God could lead and guide them through the visible creation to the creator. They did not want to arrive at the creator, however, and this meant they had no excuse. In the present passage, Paul replaces this argument from the visible creation with another one based on the pleasure which is proper to human nature. By enjoying such natural pleasure, they could easily have escaped from shame and attained greater happiness. But they did not want to do this. As a consequence, they are beyond all forgiveness, for they treat even nature itself with contempt. . . .

The two persons (I am talking about the man and the woman) had to become one. Scripture says, *The two will be one flesh* (Gen 2:24). The desire for intercourse led to this union and joined the sexes together. The devil subverted this desire, diverted it to another direction, divided the sexes from each other, and thus split the unity of humanity into two parts contrary to the law of God. For God said, *The two will be one flesh* (Gen 2:24). But the devil divided the one flesh into two, setting them at war. He made these two parts war against themselves and against each other. For women were abusing women and not just men; men opposed one another and the female sex. It was like a night battle in the darkness. You could enumerate a second, third, fourth, and fifth war. Another war, besides those already listed, is their violation of nature itself. Since the devil saw that this desire for intercourse is the main force bringing the sexes together, he was eager to provoke men and women to conflict and discord, to cut the bond so that he might destroy the human race by their refusing to join together according to the law. . . . If Paul had focused on hell and eternal punishment, his assertions would have seemed implausible and ridiculous to the ungodly living in this immoral way. Hence he argued that pleasure itself was its own punishment. Do not be surprised if they still do not understand this and continue to seek that pleasure. For those who are insane and disturbed laugh and revel, even though they harm themselves, provoke pity by their behavior, and move people to weep for them. We do not say that their ignorance will enable them to escape punishment but that they will experience an even more grievous penalty, because they do not recognize that they are already living in punishment. . . . Even if hell did not exist, even if no further punishment were threatened, to live as they do would be worse than any punishment.

Romans 1:28-32

28And since they did not see fit to acknowledge God, God gave them up to a base mind and to improper conduct. 29They were filled with all manner of wickedness, evil, covetousness, malice. Full of envy, murder, strife, deceit, malignity, they are gossips, 30slanderers, haters of God, insolent, haughty, boastful, inventors of evil, disobedient to parents, 31foolish, faithless, heartless, ruthless. 32Though they know God's decree that those who do such things deserve to die, they not only do them but approve others who practice them.

(1) Ambrosiaster on verse 28

Because of their devotion to idols, they were handed over to doing shameful things to one another, as has already been said. They then decided that God was indifferent to such things and could therefore be ignored; they assumed that their behavior would go unpunished. As a result, they became increasingly hardened and prone to all kinds of evil. Although they knew their fellow humans objected to their behavior, still they believed that God would not punish them.

(2) Augustine on verse 28

God can know things that God does not actually bring about. Thus certain sins, although they are sins, are also the punishments of other sins. Thus is it said, **God gave them up to a debased mind and to things that should not be done.** The sin itself is not caused by God, but the punishment is God's work.

(3) Theodoret on verses 29-31

He names **wickedness** or injustice whatever is diametrically opposed to justice, from which everything reprehensible proceeds. **Evil**, a pugnacious attitude. **Covetousness**, desiring to possess more and snatching what is not one's own. **Malice**, the soul's tendency to the worst and plotting harm to one's neighbor. **Envy**, a savage disturbance which cannot bear the happiness of one's neighbor; envy breeds **deceit** and gives birth to **murder.** Cain was wounded by envy; he used deceit to seduce his brother into the field where he murdered him (Gen 4:8). Paul calls **crafty** those who use the power of reason to devise plots and plan harm for their neighbors. **Gossips** whisper in the ear and speak evil of those who are part of the community. **Slanderers** boldly bring false charges against those who are not present. **God haters** are hostile in spirit to God. The **insolent** are always ready to inflict abuse. The **haughty** are carried away by the desire to be placed above others. The **boastful** are puffed up without reason, since they have no basis for thinking well of themselves. **Inventors of evil** think up new and uncommon forms of wrongdoing. **Disobedience to parents** is the greatest and most repulsive vice, one that nature itself denounces. The **foolish** live worthless and thoughtless lives. The **disorderly** embrace an abominable life, opposed to civil society. The **friendless** refuse to practice the customs of friendship. The **faithless** recklessly transgress established agreements. The **ruthless** imitate the cruelty of wild beasts.

(4) Ambrosiaster on verse 32

Some people consider themselves innocent as long as they refrain from evil deeds, even though they approve the evil deeds of others. "To approve" is to be silent when one could condemn or to listen to accounts of evil actions with approval. If impure or mean people whose vices are well known are welcomed rather than shunned, they become self-satisfied. One cannot shame sinners while still offering them respect and welcome — even if their sin is not imitated. People who furnish kindling for the sins of others are just as guilty as those who commit the sins. Another kind of person not only does evil but approves others who do the same: thus they both do and support others who do. In supporting others and sinning themselves, they double their wickedness. Those who do evil themselves but still condemn others for doing the same are not quite as bad, because they do not defend behavior which they know is abominable. The most wicked people of all, then, are those who both do evil and approve others who do it; their desire to see wickedness prevail shuts out all fear of God. Not only do they refuse to punish evil, but they persuade others that evil should not be avoided.

(5) Origen on verses 28-32

I believe two things are clearly asserted in this passage, and that one of them is entailed by the other. Clearly, if God has delivered people over to the cravings of their hearts or to disgraceful passions or to a base mentality — as though sending them to a worthless and horrible land — these persons will reap a harvest of crime. Moreover, if someone knows God but does not worship God as God or give thanks, and if that person becomes like those the Apostle describes here, there is no doubt that such a soul has been abandoned and handed over by God. For it is impossible to have one's dwelling with God and still harbor these evils; for such evils are not welcome in God's dwelling place.

Romans 2

All the commentators picked up Paul's point that God withholds judgment in order to provide an opportunity for sinners to repent. This delay, however, is regularly abused and, as Ambrosiaster points out, leads some to think that God does not care what humans do to each other and will never judge them. It can also lead, Augustine observes, to the false hope that God will forgive everyone indiscriminately. On the Day of Judgment, all affirmed, God will judge both Jews and Gentiles impartially by the two standards of faith and good works. Origen argues that unbelievers who have done good works will not lose all reward, though they may be deprived of eternal life. Ambrosiaster takes a contrary stance: believing in Christ is itself part of fulfilling the law, since the law promises Christ. Both he and Augustine agree that Gentiles who failed to believe because they did not know about Christ will be punished, though in a lesser way. Augustine here introduces his distinctive doctrine that both faith and good works are gifts of God rather than independent human accomplishments; all the other interpreters presume that humans retain the natural power to recognize and accomplish the necessary good works.

Romans 2:1-5

₁Therefore you have no excuse, O man, whoever you are, when you judge another; for in passing judgment upon him you condemn yourself, because you, the judge, are doing the very same things. ₂We know that the judgment of God rightly falls upon those who do such things. ₃Do you suppose, O man, that when you judge those who do such things and yet do them yourself, you will escape the judgment of God? ₄Or do you presume upon the riches of his kindness and forbearance and patience? Do you not know that God's kindness is meant to lead you to repentance? ₅But by your hard and impenitent heart you are storing up wrath for yourself on the day of wrath, when God's righteous judgment will be revealed.

(1) Ambrosiaster on verses 1-5

Therefore you have no excuse, O man, when you judge others; for in passing judgment on another you condemn yourself, because you are doing the very same things you

condemn. Paul clearly states that both the one who does evil things and the one who approves those actions deserve punishment. Still, someone who does evil might try to escape by making a show of condemning evildoers and outwardly pretending to be horrified at such behavior, all the while doing the same things in private. Paul teaches, however, that it is out of the question that someone's deeds would not be justly punished. Hypocrisy about one's evil deeds is actually worse, for it is deceitful to appear honorable while actually deserving punishment. . . .

We know that God's judgment on those who do such things is in accordance with truth. We know that God will in fact pass judgment on these people, since we ourselves also pass judgment on them. For if such conduct displeases us, how much more will it displease God, who is truly just and cares for the creation! When, therefore, Paul says **in accordance with truth**, he means that God will undoubtedly pass judgment on them. For he wishes to strike terror into the Romans. Unbelievers claim that God is not concerned with such matters, but Paul makes clear that God will really pass judgment on the wicked. God will not spare them but will inflict the severest retribution appropriate to the merits of each individual. . . .

Do you think, O man, who judges those who do such things and yet does them yourself, that you will escape the judgment of God? . . . If such people are not going to escape judgment, then all should believe that God will pass judgment, and that justly. Let all recognize that the creator of the world will carefully and exactly examine the merits of each creature. If God were to take no further interest in the creatures after making them, that divine disregard would imply that creatures were not actually made good. Yet no one can deny that God made things good — for it would be unfitting and even impossible for one who is good to have made things evil. So we can be certain that God is concerned for the creatures. To say that God paid no further attention to such good things once they were made would be to insult and slander God. In fact, life itself is governed by God's command and providence, through the natural rhythm of the world, as the Lord says, *He makes his sun rise on the good and on the evil, and sends rain on the righteous and on the unrighteous* (Matt 5:45). . . .

Or do you despise the riches of God's kindness and patience? Do you not realize that God's kindness is meant to lead you to repentance? Paul warns people that they should not think they have escaped God's judgment if God allows them to continue sinning for a long time. They should not abuse God's patience by believing that God is unconcerned with human affairs. Instead, they should understand that God's ways are hidden and that the divine judgment will take place not during this present life but in the future. So in the life to come, they will regret believing that God would not judge. To show the horror of the coming judgment and the necessity of repentance, God says, *I have kept silence. Surely I shall not always keep silence* (Isa 42:14). . . .

But by your hard and impenitent heart you are storing up wrath for yourself on the day of wrath, when God's righteous judgment will be revealed. If people expect that their sins will go unpunished and refuse both correction and direction, they will sin more grievously because they are confident that no vengeance will follow. They have **impenitent hearts**; they do not realize that they are heaping up wrath for themselves **on the day of wrath.** Those who have squandered a long delay not only by refusing to mend their ways but by piling up their sins and thus making themselves more contemptible must inevitably suffer more severe punishment; indeed, they should be tormented in everlasting flames. The **day of wrath** means the day on which sinners are to be punished.

(2) Pelagius on verses 2-4

The kind of people who condemned in others what they did not hesitate to commit themselves will be judged **in accordance with the truth.** For if you, a sinner, pass judgment upon a sinner like yourself, how much more will God, who is just, judge you to be unjust. Otherwise evil would seem pleasing to God and good displeasing. In fact, we read that God showed no favoritism and spared neither friends nor angels when they sinned! Human judgment, however, is compromised in many ways: the integrity of judges is often corrupted by love, hatred, fear, and greed; now and then mercy opposes the standard of justice. . . . Or do you delude yourself about your impunity because God does not punish you immediately; does the passage of time and the abundance of God's goodness lead you to imagine that judgment will never follow? Well, then, listen to the words of Scripture, *The Lord is not slow about the promise, but is patient with you, not wanting any to perish, but all to come to repentance* (2 Pet 3:9). The Lord is good in delaying but just in punishing. Wherefore the prophet warns, *Do not delay to turn back to God, and do not postpone it from day to day; for suddenly the wrath of God will come upon you, and at the time of punishment you will perish* (Eccl 5:7), and again, *Do not say, "I sinned, yet what has happened to me?" for God is slow to anger* (Eccl 5:4). People are led far astray because of God's patience, especially because God decides not to punish sinners immediately. When God delays, they suppose either that God does not care at all about human affairs or that God pardons faults. Many even rail at God, "Why doesn't God punish right away?" They do not realize that, were God to do so, almost no one would have survived, and those who are now righteous would never have crossed over from the ranks of the unrighteous.

(3) Origen on verses 4-5

Or do you despise the riches of God's kindness and forbearance and patience? Do you not realize that God's kindness is meant to lead you to repentance? Here is how to recognize the riches of God's kindness: consider how much evil people do on earth every day, and how almost everyone backslides and acts badly. They walk down the broad and spacious road to perdition, neglecting the narrow way of life. Yet God supplies sun and rain each day to serve them all. And consider how many people each day turn their mouths to heaven and speak blasphemy against God. What should I say about fraud, violence, crime, sacrilege, and wickedness? And yet, according to this passage all these crimes seem to be surpassed in wickedness by those who judge others and yet themselves commit the very same deeds that they punish in their fellows. Therefore, if people despise the kindness, patience, and forbearance of God, they will also fail to grasp that these very divine virtues call them to repentance. Now forbearance seems to differ from patience in this respect: people who sin out of weakness rather than deliberately are treated with **forbearance**; but those who exult in their sins and act with deliberation are met with **patience.**

But just as God has made all things according to measure, both in weight and number, so too there is a definite limit to God's patience. One must recognize that God reached that limit with those who perished in the flood and those who were destroyed at Sodom by fire from heaven. This is why it was said about the Amorites, *For the iniquity of the Amorites is not yet complete* (Gen 15:16). Therefore God waits patiently and watches for each person to repent. This should not make us negligent and slow to convert, however, since God's patience and forbearance have a definite limit.

(4) Augustine on verses 4-5

There are some people who do not perish by despairing. They do not say to themselves, *Our transgressions and our sins are upon us, and we waste away because of them; how then can we live?* (Ezek 33:10). Instead, they deceive themselves in a different way: presuming on God's wonderful mercy, they never submit to correction. They say, "Even if we do evil, even if we commit iniquities, even if we live in a wicked and self-indulgent way, even if we despise the poor and needy, even if we are puffed up with pride, even if our hearts are never weighed down by our bad deeds, is God going to destroy such a great multitude as we are and save only a few?" Two dangers appear then: the one we hear from the prophet, the other the Apostle does not hide. Against those who die in despair, like gladiators destined for the sword, drinking in pleasures and living badly, who scorn their souls as already enslaved, the prophet quotes what these say to themselves: *Our transgressions and our sins are upon us, and we waste away because of them; how then can we live?* (Ezek 33:10). The Apostle marks the other danger: **Or do you despise the riches of God's kindness and mercy and forbearance?** He contradicts those who say, "God is good; God is merciful; God will not condemn so many sinners and save so few. They continue to live only because God allows it. If the way they live and the evil they do really displeased God, they would immediately be wiped off the face of the earth." The Apostle responds to them: **Do you not realize that God's kindness is meant to lead you to repentance? But by your hard and impenitent heart you are storing up wrath for yourself on the day of wrath and the revelation of God's righteous judgment. For God will repay according to each one's deeds.** To whom does Paul say this? To those who say that God is good and will not repay. *God will repay according to each one's deeds* (Rom 2:6). So what are you doing? What are you storing up for yourself? Wrath. Piling wrath on top of wrath, you build the treasure. What you store up will be repaid. Your banker will not defraud you.

(5) John Chrysostom on verse 5

What could be harder than a person neither softened by kindness nor stopped by fear? For after having demonstrated God's love for humanity, Paul then shows the intolerable punishment awaiting those who do not turn back in repentance. Notice how precisely he spoke, **you are storing up wrath for yourself.** He clearly indicates both what is surely being stored up, and that the judge is not the cause of this punishment; rather, the one being judged is. For Paul says, **For you store up for yourself**, not that God stores it up for you. God did everything necessary: God created you with the ability to discern between good and evil; God has been long-suffering; God has called you to repentance; God has threatened you with the fearful Day of Judgment. God has tried every means to draw you to repentance. But if you remain unyielding, then **you are storing up wrath for yourself on the day of wrath, when God's righteous judgment will be revealed.**

Romans 2:6-11

6For he will render to every man according to his works: 7to those who by patience in well-doing seek for glory and honor and immortality, he will give eternal life; 8but for those who are factious and do not obey the truth, but obey wickedness, there will be wrath and fury. 9There will be tribulation and distress for every human being who does evil, the Jew first and also the Greek, 10but glory and honor and peace for everyone who does good, the Jew first and also the Greek. 11For God shows no partiality.

(1) Origen on verses 6-11

Now let us inquire about the just judgment by which God will repay all according to their deeds. First, we must reject the heretics who say that souls have either good or bad natures. They should notice that God will **repay according to each one's deeds**, not "according to each one's nature." Second, the faithful should be taught that faith alone is not sufficient. Rather, they must recognize that the just judgment of **God repays according to each one's deeds.** Moreover, since Paul says that the just judgment of God means that **God will repay according to each one's deeds**, not even the Gentiles would seem to be excluded from this message, as long as they do something good and act in a praiseworthy way. . . .

For those who are quarrelsome and who distrust the truth and believe in wickedness, there will be wrath and fury. There will be anguish and distress. . . . A person who takes these words in a straightforward way will realize that they are best understood as they have just been explained: that **God repays every person according to each one's deeds.** That is to say: just as God bestows **eternal life on those who by patiently doing good seek for glory and honor and immortality,** so too will God render **wrath and fury** and **anguish and distress for those who are quarrelsome and who distrust the truth and believe in wickedness.** Whoever believes that not one dot or dash is superfluous in the letters of the Apostle through which Christ speaks, will hold that the Apostle did not go astray when he said that God will grant **eternal life to those who by patiently doing good seek for glory and honor.** In referring to those who contentiously trust wickedness rather than the truth, however, Paul did not say that God would repay them with **wrath**

and fury, in exact parallel to what he had said about rewarding the good. Rather, he said, **there will be wrath and fury, there will be anguish and distress.** Thus the spiritual person who grasps what the Spirit is saying through Paul will recognize that the Apostle wrote these words on the basis of an experience of God, not in ignorance. Thus, Paul wanted to show that the **eternal life** which is bestowed by God on those who **by patiently doing good strive for glory and immortality** is indeed a reward. But the painful things that come upon those who **contentiously trust wickedness rather than the truth** are not sent by God, all of whose gifts are eternal and worthy of the divine nature. Instead, these are the result of people's own evil actions. **There will be wrath and fury, there will be anguish and distress**, in keeping with the treasure they have stored up for themselves. In the prior clause Paul made the words **eternal life** the direct object of the verb; so in the latter clause, if he had wanted to indicate God as the giver, he would also have made the words **wrath and fury, anguish and distress** the direct objects of the verb. . . .

In order to make this matter even clearer, let us add an illustration. A patient who disobeys a physician's advice and eats inappropriate food will upset the body's equilibrium and bring on a fever or some other illness. If this happens, the ensuing sickness would certainly be brought on not by the physician but by the patient's self-indulgence. When a patient follows the physician's directions and remains in good health, this grace of good health is credited to the physician. In the same way, God repays each one with good according to that person's own deeds. But we understand that bad things derive not from God but from the most wicked food of intemperance and the undigested depravity of human misconduct. . . .

Why then is **wrath and fury** for the Jew first, then for the Greek? Because the glory and honor belong to the Jews first. *For in the first place the Jews were entrusted with the oracles of God* (Rom 3:2). And they themselves say, *Blessed are we, O Israel, for we know what is pleasing to God* (Bar 4:4). Moreover, according to the gospel, the servant who knew the will of the master — the Jew — and did not act accordingly will be severely flogged. But the Greek who did not know it — the Gentile — will be beaten only a little. To know God and the will of God is a great benefit for the Jew. Both God's eternal power and the divine nature can be known even by the Gentiles from the creation of the world through the things that have been made; God's will, however, can be known only through the Law and the Prophets. . . .

Everyone, therefore, who does not acknowledge that the Father of our Lord Jesus Christ is the only true God and that Jesus Christ is God's Son will be deprived of eternal life. Indeed, this recognition and faith are themselves called **eternal life.** Therefore, Christians belong in the first category, to whom eternal life is given when they **seek glory and honor and immortality** through the patience of good conduct. Surely that **eternal life** is none other than the one who said, *I am the way, the truth, and the life* (John 14:6). In the second group belong those who contentiously dispute the truth and submit to wickedness; upon them **wrath and fury, anguish and distress** will fall. This refers to every soul that does evil, **first the Jew, then the Greek.** With the same distinction between Jews and Gentiles, a reward for good behavior is promised to a third class of people. As Paul says, **but glory and honor and peace for everyone who does good, the Jew first and also the Greek.** If I follow Paul's meaning here, he is talking about Jews and Gentiles who do not believe. For a Jew might not believe in Christ but still do what was good, that is, hold fast to justice, love mercy, preserve chastity, and do every good work. Even if such a person does not have eternal life — because of believing only in God and not also in the Son, Jesus Christ, whom God has sent — nevertheless **the glory and peace and honor** of the works cannot be lost. But the Greek — the Gentile — although not having the law, is in possession of a law. For guided by natural reason and performing the works of that law, such a person may hold fast to justice or preserve chastity or cultivate prudence, temperance, and modesty (just as we see some of the Gentiles do). Such a person may seem to be deprived of eternal life, not believing in Christ, not having been *born again of water and the spirit* (John 3:5), and thus being unable to enter the kingdom of heaven. Nevertheless, this kind of person apparently will not perish completely, because of what the Apostle says about the **glory and honor and peace** of good works. As we discussed above, the Apostle appears to condemn the Gentiles because they recognized God by natural intelligence but *did not honor God as God* (Rom 1:21).[1] How, then, could we fail to think that Paul would praise those Gentiles (indeed, he should praise them) who recognize God and actually do honor God as God? No one would doubt, I think, that people who deserve to be condemned for wicked action would be judged worthy of reward had they performed good action instead. See what the Apostle says, *For all of us must appear before the judgment seat of Christ, so that each may give an account of what has been done in the body, whether good or evil* (2 Cor 5:10).

And then he adds these words: **for God shows no partiality.** If you still have any doubt, listen to what Peter said in the Acts of the Apostles, when he had entered the house of the Gentile Cornelius: *I truly understand that God shows no partiality, but in every place and in every nation the person who does God's will is acceptable to God* (Acts 10:34-35). But what the Lord said in the gospel might be posed as a counterargument, *Everyone who believes in me is not judged. Whoever does not believe in me is already judged, since he does not believe in the name of the only-begotten Son of God* (John 3:18). Let us then specify how we who believe in Christ are not judged, so that we might thereby understand exactly how the person who does not believe is already judged. Would we ever consider that a Christian believer who committed murder or adultery or gave false testimony or committed some other offense — which occasionally we see even the faithful committing — will not be judged, just because the one who believes in Christ will not be judged for these actions? Certainly all these deeds will come to judgment. In this light, we should understand the Lord's statement, *Everyone who believes in me is not judged* (John 3:18), in the following way. A person who believes will not be judged as an unbeliever or an infidel. Still, the believer will doubtlessly be judged according to deeds. Thus, anyone who does not believe has already been judged regarding what is not believed. Just as the believer will come to judgment for committing any sin apart from that saving faith, so too the unbeliever will not lose the reward for accomplishing any good work, apart from the unbelief. Someone could, of course, propose the following serious and unacceptable argument: that a person who sins should not be numbered among the believers, since anyone who believed would not sin and, therefore, that by the very fact of sinning, the

---

1. See Origen's discussion of Rom 1:18-20 above.

person is shown not to be a believer. I am convinced that this opinion is too harsh. For how many people on earth manage to live a life totally free from sin?

(2) Ambrosiaster on verses 7-11

To those who by patiently doing good seek for glory and honor and immortality, God will give eternal life. Since Paul preaches the just judgment of God, he says that judgment will also apply to good people who place their trust in the fidelity of God. Such people recognize that the patience of God is prolonged for two reasons, partly in order that God may correct and partly so that God may then take vengeance upon those who do not mend their ways. As a consequence, these good people are moved to repent of their former actions and behave well, lest the length of their life cause them to lose the promised life. God will give these good people **glory and honor.** Paul adds: **and immortality**, lest this should appear nothing particularly great in comparison with the present life, because in this life also, people receive glory and honor. Thus the **glory** and the **honor** may be understood to be different, since they are accompanied by **immortality.** For in the present circumstances **honor and glory** are frequently lost, because the giver, the gift, and the recipient are all subject to corruption. On the day of God's judgment, however, **honor and glory** will be given to those who are uncorrupted so all may be eternal. For their very being will be glorified in a sort of exchange for their merits. The people who seek **eternal life**, then, are those whose life, not just their outward profession, is good.

For those who are quarrelsome and who distrust the truth but obey wickedness — wrath and fury and anguish. These people do not believe that the judgment of God will come through Christ; consequently, they are contemptuous of God's patience and dismiss the judgment as an empty threat, even though it is a true and irrevocable fact. For they believe in **wickedness**, which in this context means denial that what God foretells will happen. Paul adds three other punishments appropriate for unbelief: **wrath and fury and anguish.** The **wrath** is not that of the judge but of the person judged, once found guilty. God is called wrathful only so that people may believe that God will take vengeance; the divine nature is not subject to such emotions. Moreover, to make people believe that God not only becomes wrathful but actually takes vengeance, Paul adds: **and fury**, indicating thereby that God is going to avenge the injury suffered. **Anguish**, on the other hand, is what the condemned will suffer once they are actually sentenced. . . .

But glory and honor and peace for everyone who does good, the Jew first and also the Greek. Just as Paul imposed three painful punishments on unbelievers, so he bestowed three splendid rewards on the faithful: genuine enjoyment of **honor** as children of God, **glory** in their transformation, and **peace** because those who live well will be untroubled by disturbance and at rest in the future, and also because everyone who guards against what is harmful will find the judge **peaceful**. . . .

For God shows no partiality. Paul has clearly asserted that neither Jews nor Greeks are despised by God, provided they believe in Christ, and that justice is conferred on both by having faith. He then explains that Jews and Greeks who do not believe are equally culpable, because being circumcised without faith will confer no good and faith comes to the aid of the uncircumcised. So he teaches that **God shows no partiality** toward persons. Nor does God judge according to ethnic prejudice, either accepting unbelievers for the sake of their ancestors or rejecting a believer because of an unworthy lineage. Instead, God rewards or condemns on the basis of each one's own merits.

(3) Augustine on verses 6, 10

For who indeed has drawn us out of that compacted lump of damnation, who but the one who *came to seek and save what was lost* (Luke 19:10)? Thus the Apostle asks, *Who has separated you?* (1 Cor 4:7). If a person responds, "my faith, my good will, my good works," then the response will be, *What have you that you did not receive? If then you received it, why do you boast as though it were not a gift?* (1 Cor 4:7). This does not prevent all boasting but directs *that whoever boasts should boast of the Lord* (1 Cor 1:31; 2 Cor 10:17). If we have a devout understanding of the words, *Not because of works, lest anyone should boast* (Eph 2:9), then good works are not considered worthless, **for God will repay according to each one's deeds**, and there will be **glory and honor and peace for everyone who does good.** Good works do not earn grace but rather follow from grace. For faith, *which works through love* (Gal 5:6), would accomplish nothing unless *the love of God were spread abroad in our hearts through the Holy Spirit who is given to us* (Rom 5:5). Nor would we have faith itself *unless God assigned to each a measure of faith* (Rom 12:3).

(4) John Chrysostom on verse 11

When Paul says that both the Jew and the Gentile are punished because they are sinners, he does not need further reasons. But when he wants to prove that the Gentile can be honored, he needs a foundation for this assertion. It seemed marvelous and incredible that someone who did not hear either the Law or the Prophets would be rewarded for performing good works. For this reason, he asks his readers to consider the time before the coming of grace, so that he might then more easily win their approval when he deals with faith. In this matter he remains above suspicion, since he is not relying on his own evidence to prove his point. He said, **Glory and honor and peace for everyone who does good, the Jew first and also the Greek,** and he added, **for there is no respect of persons with God.** How wonderful that is! Paul has claimed victory from this outstanding position! By arguing from the absurdity of the alternative, he shows that not acting in this way would be contrary to God's nature. If God did not act in this way, God would be respecting persons, and God does not act in that way. He did not say, "if it were not done in this way, then God would be a respecter of persons." Instead he formulated it more piously, **There is no respect of persons with God.** That is to say, God attends not to the status of their persons but to the differences in their actions. By stating the case this way, Paul clearly showed that the Jew differed from the Gentile not in action but only in personal status. The conclusion of this argument could be expressed in this way: one person is honored and another disgraced not on the basis of being a Jew or a Gentile but because their works differ.

Romans 2:12-16

12All who have sinned without the law will also perish without the law, and all who have sinned under the law will be judged by the law. **13**For it is not the hearers of the law who are righteous before God, but the doers of the law who will be justified. **14**When Gentiles who have not the law do by nature what the law requires, they are a law to themselves, even though they do not have the law. **15**They show that what the law requires is written on their hearts, while their conscience also bears witness and their conflicting thoughts accuse or perhaps excuse them **16**on that day when, according to my gospel, God judges the secrets of men by Christ Jesus.

(1) Ambrosiaster on verses 12-16

All who have sinned without the law will also perish without the law. How can a person sin without the law when everyone is subject to natural law? Because Paul is talking about the law of Moses, to which the Jews are under obligation so long as they do not believe; the Gentiles too were under obligation for a long time, because they were unwilling to adhere to it. Unbelieving Gentiles are doubly culpable, for they neither assented to the law given through Moses nor accepted the grace of Christ. Hence they deserve to perish. Therefore, just as anyone who sins without the law will perish, so too anyone who has obeyed the law — even without the law — will be justified. Anyone who lives justly according to the law of nature is an observer of the law. If *the law is not laid down for righteous people but for the unrighteous* (1 Tim 1:9), then anyone who avoids sin is a follower of the law and needs only faith to become perfect. Abstaining from evil actions, however, brings no benefit in the sight of God unless a person also accepts faith in God and thereby becomes righteous in both ways. To avoid evil is to live justly in this life; to place faith in God is eternal righteousness.

And all who have sinned under the law will be judged through the law. The Gentiles, even if they follow the law of nature, will nevertheless perish unless they have embraced faith in Christ. The most important thing is to acknowledge Christ alone as the Lord, for idolatry is the greatest sin. This sin has to do with God; other sins affect human beings. Similarly, the Jews living under the law will be judged by the law, because they did not accept Christ, who was promised by the law itself....

For it is not the hearers of the law who are righteous in God's sight, but the doers of the law who will be justified. Paul means that people who hear the law are not righteous unless they believe in Christ, by which one fulfills the law because Christ was promised by this same law. How can someone fulfill the law without placing faith in the law and accepting the one to whom the law bears witness? A person uncircumcised in the flesh — and thus apparently outside the law — but who does believe in Christ has fulfilled the law because of that faith. Someone who claims to be under the law — a Jew — **is a hearer** but not a **doer of the law** because assent is not given to its commands. Such a person does not believe in the Christ who is written about in the law: as Philip said to Nathanael, *We have found him about whom Moses in the law and also the prophets wrote — Jesus* (John 1:45)....

When the Gentiles, who do not possess the law, do instinctively what the law requires. Paul calls Christians **Gentiles** because he is the teacher of the Gentiles, as he says elsewhere, *For I am speaking to you Gentiles* (Rom 11:13). Being uncircumcised, these people do not observe the new moons or the Sabbath or the dietary law. Instead, under the guidance of nature they believe in God and in Christ, that is, in the Father and in the Son.[2] So to recognize the God of the law is to observe the law. The first principle of wisdom is to fear God the Father, from whom all things exist, and the Lord Jesus, God's Son, through whom all things exist. Nature itself, then, acknowledges its creator by its own judgment, not through the Mosaic law but through the natural order. The artifact discovers its artificer in its own being.

These, though not having the law, are a law to themselves. They show that what the law requires is written in their hearts. The meaning is the same: believing by the guidance of nature, they display the works of the law by following conscience rather than the written word. Faith is itself the work of the law. Thus those who rely on this natural judgment put their faith in what God says, thereby proving that they are a law unto themselves. They do what the law commands: believe in Christ. . . .

And their conflicting thoughts will accuse or perhaps excuse them on the day when, according to my gospel, God, through Jesus Christ, will judge the secret thoughts of all. Paul has said that the Jews who do not believe will be judged through the law. The law promised them Christ, whom they refused to accept when he came. Hence the law will accuse them. The Gentiles, on the other hand, who clearly do not have the law, will be judged through their own conscience if they refuse to believe. The believing Gentiles will be the first accusers of those Gentiles who do not believe. Similarly, the Lord refers to his own disciples when he says to Jewish unbelievers, *They will be your judges* (Matt 12:27). For the unbelief of the Jews will be judged by the faith of the Apostles who, being Jewish themselves, did believe, while other Jews did not believe. Secondly, if they refused to believe even when they were moved by the creator's fidelity and power, the Gentiles will be accused by their own thoughts. If, however, their dullness prevents their reflecting on and believing in the words and actions of the Lord, then their conscience will defend itself on the Day of Judgment because they did not realize they should believe. That kind of person will be judged as inattentive rather than ill-willed. Because such ignorance is culpable, however, even such an unbeliever will not go unpunished.

(2) John Chrysostom on verses 12-16

In this passage, Paul shows not only the equality with which the Jew and the Gentile are honored but also that the Jew is burdened by the gift of the law. The Greek is judged **apart from the law**, a phrase which in the context indicates that the Gentiles will be judged less severely. The Mosaic law does not accuse the Gentile. The phrase **apart from the law**, that is, without the condemnation coming from the Mosaic law, means that the

---

2. Ambrosiaster's point seems to be that Christ must be accepted as himself divine, like the Father, and not simply as a chosen human.

Gentile is judged solely based on reasoning from nature. But the Jew is **under the law.** Both nature and the Mosaic law accuse the Jew. Thus the greater the divine attention enjoyed by the Jews, the greater the punishment they will suffer. Paul makes this greater demand on the Jews to turn them more quickly to grace. Although the Jews claimed that they were justified through the Mosaic law alone and did not need grace, Paul shows that they need grace even more than the Gentiles, because they would be punished more.

Then Paul introduces a second argument to buttress the previous one, **For it is not the hearers of the law who are righteous in God's sight.** His adding **in God's sight** is important. In human estimation the Jews might appear holy and could boast about great achievements; in God's judgment, however, their status is exactly opposite. **The doers of the law will be justified.** Do you understand what Paul accomplishes by turning this argument around in the opposite direction? If the law makes a person worthy of salvation, then even by this standard of fulfilling what was written in the law, the Gentile will once again outstrip the Jew. **When the Gentiles,** Paul says, **who do not possess the law, do instinctively what the law requires, these, though not having the law, are a law to themselves.** I am not rejecting the law, he says, because I justify the Gentiles on the basis of the law. He undermines the boasting of Judaism without exposing himself to the criticism that he denigrates the Mosaic law. In fact, the result is just the opposite. By praising the law and showing its greatness, he strengthens it. When he says, **by nature,** he is speaking about the directives that can be derived from reasoning on nature. Paul shows that the Gentiles are better than the Jews, precisely because they did not receive the law and thus did not have the very thing which gave the Jews an advantage over them. For, he says, on account of this the Gentiles are admirable: they did not require the law and still they performed all the works of the law. They engraved not the letter but the works of the law on their minds.

Conscience and reason are sufficient to take the place of the law. Through them Paul has shown again that God made human beings responsible for choosing virtue and rejecting evil. Do not be surprised when Paul proves this same point many times over. It was necessary for him to do that because of those who say, "Why in the world did Christ come at this particular time? Where is the evidence of such exceptional divine providence in the time before he came?" In order to defend against these objectors, as a secondary argument he shows that in earlier ages and before the Mosaic law was given, human nature enjoyed fully the divine governance.

(3) Origen on verse 12

Paul has made clear that different laws are referred to in the Scriptures. If anyone so neglects all these laws that even the natural law, which nearly everyone possesses, appears to have been obliterated by the hardness or denseness of the heart, then such a person will **perish without the law.** He says that the person who lives under the law will be judged by the law, for the Apostle has also testified that everyone who is circumcised is required to obey the entire law.

(4) Augustine on verse 12

Those who knew the divine commandments could not claim ignorance as some do. Even those who do not know the law of God will not escape punishment. **All who have sinned without the law will also perish without the law, and all who have sinned under the law will be judged through the law.** I think that the Apostle did not intend to say here that those who did not know the law when they sinned would suffer a worse punishment than those who did know it. Yet to perish does seem to be worse than to be judged. He is speaking here about the Jews, who received a law, and the Gentiles, who were without one. Now, would anyone dare to assert that the Jews, who sinned against the law, are not going to perish, since they did not believe in Christ? Nevertheless, he says of them, that they **will be judged through the law.** No one can be saved without the faith of Christ. So the Jews will be liable to judgment. But if the situation of those who do not know the law of God is worse than of those who know it, how can what the Lord said in the gospel be true, *The servant who did not know the will of the master, and did what deserved a beating, will receive a light beating* (Luke 12:48); *the servant, however, who knew the will of the master, and did what deserved a beating, will receive a severe beating* (Luke 12:47)? Notice that here he shows that a knowledgeable person sins more seriously than an ignorant one. Yet this does not mean that one is excused by hiding in the shadows of ignorance. Not to have known is different from having been unwilling to know. The will itself is accused when Scripture says, *They refused to understand, so that they would act well* (Ps 36:4 LXX). The ignorance which provides some excuse is that of people who simply do not know rather than of those who do not want to know. Even if they had never heard what they should believe, however, this does not exempt them from everlasting fire for failing to believe; it only mitigates their suffering. *Pour your anger on the nations which have not known you* (Ps 79:6) was not said for nothing. Nor was the Apostle's statement, *When he comes in flaming fire to inflict vengeance on those who do not know God* (2 Thess 1:7-8). No one can say, "I did not know, I did not hear, I did not understand," about this kind of knowledge. This ignorance arises from human willing, as it is said, *Be not like a horse or a mule, without understanding* (Ps 32:9).

(5) Anonymous on verse 12

Up to this point, those subject to natural law are being addressed, which includes the Jews as well. The Jews were preferred to the Gentiles because they had the "written law" of Moses in addition to the natural law.

(6) Origen on verses 13-16

When Paul says that **the nations who have not the law do by nature what the law requires,** ... he is clearly not concerned with matters such as the Sabbath, new moons, or the sacrifices specified in the written law. This is not the law written in the hearts of the people of the nations. They can grasp other things by nature, such as not to commit murder or adultery, not to steal or lie, to honor their fathers and mothers, and similar kinds of principles. That God is one and the creator of all else is also written on the hearts of the Gentiles. What seems most plausible to me is that **written on their hearts** refers to principles like the laws of the gospel, which are based on a kind of natural equity. What, for example, is more like a natural instinct than the precept that people should not do to others what they do not wish done to themselves (Matt 7:12)?

The natural law can be correlated with the Mosaic law, then, according to the spirit but not the letter. How could the natural power of understanding include such detailed provisions as performing circumcision for an infant on the eighth day, or not weaving wool and linen together, or not eating leavened food on certain days? We have occasionally discussed these regulations with Jews and asked them to explain their practical value. The only response they have ever offered is that the lawgiver chose these provisions. Our own conclusion is that such rules were meant to be understood spiritually. We reach this judgment by reasoning from our belief that **not the hearers but the doers of the law will be justified.** If the Mosaic law were taken literally, however, no one could possibly do what it requires; it can be fulfilled only if it is understood according to the spirit. These gospel principles, then, are the requirements of the law which the Apostle asserts even the Gentiles can fulfill by nature. When they perform the works of the law, it is manifest that a law has been written on their hearts by God, not with ink but by the Spirit of the living God. When Paul says it is **on their hearts**, however, we must not think that he refers to the bodily organ. How could that bodily heart possibly produce such prudential judgments or contain such storehouses of memory? **Their hearts**, in this context, refers to the rational power of their souls.

The Apostle says that those who have the law **written on their hearts** use **the witness of conscience.** So we have to ask what the Apostle is calling the conscience: is it something different from the heart or the soul? Elsewhere the conscience is described as reproaching but not itself reproached, as judging a person but not itself subject to judgment. Thus John says, *If our conscience does not reproach us, we have confidence before God* (1 John 3:21). In another place, Paul himself says, *For our boasting is this, the witness of our conscience* (2 Cor 1:12). Now I observe the freedom in good works which this conscience always enjoyed and celebrated; that it was not accused of evil deeds but rather that it charged and reproached the soul to which it was bound. From this I conclude that the conscience must be that spirit which the Apostle describes as companion of the soul. As we explained earlier, it acts like a tutor or guide to the soul it accompanies: it urges it to better things; it corrects and accuses the soul when it fails. The Apostle says of this spirit, *No one knows a person's thoughts but that person's own inner spirit* (1 Cor 2:11). And he refers to the spirit of the conscience when he says, *The spirit itself bears witness with our spirit* (Rom 8:16). This might be the same spirit which joins itself to the souls of those just people who have followed its directives in everything they do, so that it is written, *Spirits and souls of the just, praise the Lord* (Dan 3:86 LXX). If the soul has been disobedient and deviated from it, however, that spirit will be separated and cut off from it after death. I think this is the meaning of the statement in the gospel about the evil steward, *The Lord will cut him off and place him with the unfaithful* (Luke 12:46). This might also be the spirit described in Wisdom 12:1, *The immortal spirit is in all things*. Because this spirit is cut off and separated from any sinful soul which is going to be assigned a place with the unfaithful, as we have just suggested, another saying might also be applied to that process, *Two men will be in the field; one is taken and one is left. Two women will be grinding at the mill; one is taken and one is left* (Matt 24:40-41). These are our views on the passage: **their conscience bears witness to them.**

Now let us consider what follows, **and their conflicting thoughts accuse or perhaps excuse them on the day when God will judge the secrets of men, according to my gospel, through Jesus Christ.** Who could doubt that God's judgment is right since it uses accusers, defenders, and witnesses? We humans take the just judging of God as our model, since we think that a right verdict cannot be reached without an accuser, a defender, and witnesses.

Now we must investigate how each person's **thoughts will either accuse or defend** on that day when God will **judge the secrets of all.** Paul refers not to the thoughts that will be in our minds at that time, but to the ones that we have now. The good or bad thoughts that we entertain leave certain marks or tracks on our hearts, like traces on wax tablets. These signs, which are now hidden in our hearts, will be revealed on that day by the one who alone can discern everyone's secrets. Our consciences also bear witness now that the thoughts which make these marks or signs do not escape the sight of God.

(7) Augustine on verses 13-15

We must investigate what the Apostle means when he says, **When the Gentiles who have not the law do by nature what the law requires, they are a law to themselves, even though they do not have the law. They show that what the law requires is written on their hearts.** By saying that the nations **have the law written on their hearts**, Paul does not undercut the distinctive character of the New Testament: that the Lord promises to write his laws on the hearts of his people. This important issue must be addressed. The problem might be stated this way: If God distinguished the New Testament from the Old because in the Old the law was written on tablets while in the New it was written on hearts, then how are the faithful in the New Testament different from the nations, who also have the commandments of the law **written on their hearts**, so that they **do by nature what the law requires**? The Gentiles would then be in a position superior to the older people, for whom the law was written on tablets. They would also be more privileged than the newer people, because nature itself had already given the Gentiles what the New Testament had to provide for Christians.

Might the Apostle be referring in this statement to those Gentiles who belong to the New Testament and thereby have the law written on their hearts? Tracking the development of his argument makes this seem a possible explanation. . . . Paul appears to be using the term "Gentiles" for the same people he had just called Greeks, both in the prior chapter (Rom 1:16-17) and in the immediately preceding passage (Rom 2:8-13). . . . He uses the name "Gentile" for these Greeks when he says that they **do by nature what the law requires** and **have the law written on their hearts**. These Gentiles **who have the law**

written on their hearts would then be the ones who have accepted the gospel. *It is the power of God for salvation to these believers* (Rom 1:16). Furthermore, would Paul have promised *glory and honor and peace* (Rom 2:10) to Gentiles because they were doing good, even though they had not received the grace of the gospel? So, then, since *God shows no partiality* (Rom 2:11), and since **not the hearers of the law but the doers will be justified**, it follows that all who believe will have the same salvation in the gospel, whether Jews or Greeks (by which he intends any of the Gentiles). As he says later, *There is no distinction; since all have sinned and fall short of the glory of God, they are justified by divine grace as a gift* (Rom 3:23-24). How could Paul ever have meant that the Greeks were justified by fulfilling the law but without receiving the grace of the Savior?

Paul says, **the doers of the law will be justified**, which could imply that they would be justified through works rather than by grace. But he does not contradict his teaching that human beings *are justified freely through faith* (Rom 3:24) *without the works of the law* (Rom 3:28). In saying *freely*, he intends us to understand that meritorious works do not precede justification. He expresses this clearly elsewhere, *If it is by grace, it is no longer on the basis of works; otherwise grace would no longer be grace* (Rom 11:6). Thus, we should understand, **the doers of the law will be justified**, to mean that they would not fulfill the law unless they had already been justified. Justification precedes their doing the law; it is not bestowed on those who have already obeyed the law. Think about this. Does justification mean something different from being made just; and that by the one who makes evildoers righteous, so that they stop being evil and become good? If we were to say, "human beings were set free," for example, we would mean that those already human were then liberated. But in saying, "humans were created," we would mean not that those who were already human were then created but that they became human through the creative process itself. In the same way, if we said, "doers of the law were honored," we would properly be understood to mean that only those who had already fulfilled the law subsequently received honors. But applying this interpretation to the statement, **doers of the law will be justified**, would make it mean that those already just — since they had fulfilled the law — were then made just. That makes no sense. Clearly, then, the proper meaning is the one parallel to, "doers of the law will be created." They will not be created because they have already fulfilled the law, but so that they will then do so. Thus Paul's meaning is that the Jews, who were **hearers of the law**, needed the justifying grace of God in order to be able to **do the law.** Otherwise, **will be justified** would have to mean not that they were actually just but only that they were considered or declared righteous — as is said of a certain person in the Gospel, *he, desiring to justify himself* (Luke 10:29). He wanted to be recognized or regarded as righteous. In a more positive sense, we mean one thing when we say that God sanctifies the saints and quite another when we pray, *Hallowed be your name* (Matt 6:9). The first means that God makes holy people who are not already holy; the other that what is always holy in itself is acknowledged as holy by humans, that the divine name is revered because of its holiness.

In referring to Gentiles **who naturally do what belongs to the law** and **have what the law requires written on their hearts**, Paul might have had in mind those Gentiles who have come to believe in Christ, though differently than the Jews who first had the law and then came to faith. In this interpretation, we would not distinguish these

Gentiles from those for whom the Lord, promising a new covenant through the prophet, would write God's laws *on their hearts* (Jer 31:33). Through the process that Paul describes as engrafting the wild olive into the domestic olive (Rom 11:17), these Gentiles belong to the same people of God as the faithful Jews. Thus the testimony of the Apostle would follow that of the prophet: to belong to the new covenant is to have the law of God written not on tablets but on the heart, which means that these Gentiles embrace the justice of the law with their deepest desires, so that their faith works through love. God justifies these Gentiles through faith, which Scripture foresaw and foretold to Abraham: *in your seed all the nations will be blessed* (Gen 22:18). So through the grace of this promise, the wild olive was grafted into the domestic olive and the believing Gentiles became children of Abraham in that *seed of Abraham* who is Christ. They imitate the faith of Abraham, who did not receive a law written on tablets and was not even circumcised when he *believed God, and it was reckoned to him as righteousness* (Gen 15:6; Rom 4:3). Thus when the Apostle states that these Gentiles have **what the law requires written on their hearts**, he means the same thing that he wrote to the Corinthians, *not on tablets of stone but on tablets of fleshly hearts* (2 Cor 3:3). They belong to the house of Israel and, though uncircumcised, they are counted as circumcised, because instead of displaying the righteousness of the law by cutting off their flesh, they maintain its justice by the love in their hearts. *So, if those who are uncircumcised keep the requirements of the law, will not their uncircumcision be regarded as circumcision?* (Rom 2:26). They are among the people of the true Israel, which is free of guile. They share in the new covenant, because God bestows laws on their minds and writes them in their hearts through the Holy Spirit, God's finger, by pouring out charity — the fullness of the law — upon them.

Nor is it significant that Paul says that they **do by nature what the law requires** rather than attributing this to the Spirit of God or faith or grace. The Spirit of grace renews in us the image of God, in which we were made by nature. Vice corrupts nature, while grace heals our nature. Thus we say to God, *Have mercy on me and heal my soul, because I have sinned against you* (Ps 41:4). Human beings actually do what the law requires by their nature. Those who do not fulfill the law fail because of their vice, which erases the law of God from their hearts. When that vice is healed, the law is again written there and they do what the law requires by nature. Nature does not destroy grace; grace restores nature. *Through one man sin came into the world; death entered through sin and thus spread to all human beings, because all sinned in that one* (Rom 5:12). *And therefore there is no distinction; all . . . fall short of the glory of God; they are justified by divine grace as a gift* (Rom 3:22-24). God's renewing grace writes upon a person that justice which sin had erased. This is the mercy bestowed upon the human race through Jesus Christ our Lord. *For there is one God and one mediator between God and human beings, the man Christ Jesus* (1 Tim 2:5).

Some, however, would argue that those who **do by nature what the law requires** are not Gentiles whom the grace of Christ has justified, but are rather people who are evil, who do not rightly and justly worship the true God. Now we do indeed read or know or hear about certain of these people's actions which, according to the standards of justice, we not only cannot condemn but really ought to praise. If we were to push the question further and inquire into their intentions in doing these deeds, however, we would discover that they do not deserve the praise or protection owed to justice.

(8) Theodoret on verses 15-16

They show that what the law requires is written on their hearts, to which their own conscience also bears witness; and their conflicting thoughts will accuse or perhaps excuse them on the day when, according to my gospel, God, through Jesus Christ, will judge the secret thoughts of all. God demonstrated that the law of nature has been written on the human heart, and that this has truly guided each person's conscience in its self-accusations and justifications. I think the argument can be made clear by a certain example. When Joseph, in his cunning, fabricated against Benjamin a charge that the boy had stolen his silver cup and so would be seized as a slave, he was, as it were, testing by fire the dispositions of his brothers. The power of the testimony of the conscience was at once revealed. For although his brothers certainly did not want to recall their crime against Joseph, yet they were all reminded of their actions of two-and-twenty years earlier. Some were saying that *The blood of our younger brother is now traced to our hands* (Gen 42:22). And Reuben recalled the dark memories of those events. Following this pattern we can discern the future standard for the conscience of those who have conducted their affairs apart from the law and will offer a defense, as well as for that conscience which professes ignorance and then acknowledges itself guilty. The justice of the verdict will be manifest. For so Abimelech prayed to God, relying on his witness as a person of conscience, *O Lord, will you destroy a people who have been unenlightened but just? Did he [Abraham] not say to me, "She is my sister?" And did she [Sarah] not say to me, "He is my brother?" With an honest heart I have done this* (Gen 20:4-5).

Romans 2:17-24

17But if you call yourself a Jew and rely upon the law and boast of your relation to God 18and know his will and approve what is excellent, because you are instructed in the law, 19and if you are sure that you are a guide to the blind, a light to those who are in darkness, 20a corrector of the foolish, a teacher of children, having in the law the embodiment of knowledge and truth — 21you then who teach others, will you not teach yourself? While you preach against stealing, do you steal? 22You who say that one must not commit adultery, do you commit adultery? You who abhor idols, do you rob temples? 23You who boast in the law, do you dishonor God by breaking the law? 24For, as it is written, *The name of God is blasphemed among the Gentiles because of you* (Isa 52:5).

(1) Ambrosiaster on verses 17-24

But if you call yourself a Jew. Jew is an ethnic name, a prerogative deriving from their ancestors, just as they are called Israelites. And yet, to understand everything relevant to this matter, we must attend to the three meanings of that name, **Jew**. First, they are children of Abraham, who was named father of all nations as a reward for his faith. Secondly, Jacob is called Israel because through him the number of those who believed increased. Thirdly, they are called **Jews** because of Christ, who was born of the tribe of Judah according to the flesh, even more than because of Judah himself. The name "Judah" indicated what was to be accomplished in Christ. It was said, *Judah will lead you* (Judg 20:18) and *Judah, your brothers will join in praising you* (Gen 49:8). That praise was not given to Judah himself but to Christ, who is praised daily by all proven worthy to be called his fellows. . . .

And you rely on the law and boast of your relation to God and know God's will and determine what is more useful because you are instructed in the law. Paul does not want to exaggerate the greatness of the faith of a Jew, since Jews have been taught through the law. On the contrary, failing to believe is extremely dangerous for Jews, because they have been guided by the law. But Paul gives precedence to believing Jews for the sake of the patriarchs. No matter how much an individual Jew may succeed, however, the shame of their people remains an embarrassment for them.

And if you are sure that you are a guide to the blind, a light to those who are in darkness, a corrector of the foolish, a teacher of children, having in the law the embodiment of knowledge and truth. All this is true. The teaching of the law is given to instruct the ignorant and subject the impious to God. The promises of the law are given in order to move those made evil by worshiping idols toward hope for better things. The teacher of the law is rightly proud, therefore, of handing on an **embodiment of truth.** But if that teacher does not then accept the one promised by the law, if the teacher attacks the law by rejecting the Christ promised in the law, then all that pride is in vain. Such a Jew will not be a **corrector of the foolish**, a **teacher of children**, a **light to those who are in darkness**, but a guide leading them all to perdition. **You, then, that teach others, will you not teach yourself?** In rebuking the Gentiles for ignoring the Mosaic law and God, you are accusing yourself. By refusing to believe in the Christ promised by the Mosaic law, you commit the very offense that you condemn. **While you preach against stealing, do you steal?** You are doing what, according to your own preaching, ought to be avoided. By denying that our Christ was promised in the law and thus undercutting faith in Christ through your perverse interpretation, you are doing what you teach should not be done. **You that forbid adultery, do you commit adultery?** When you replace the truth of Christ with a lie, you are indeed adulterating the law. Hence Paul says in another epistle, *You are adulterers of the word of God* (2 Cor 2:17). **You who abhor idols, are you committing sacrilege?** You are sacrilegious when you deny Christ, to whom the Law and the Prophets point. For Isaiah says, *Because God is in you, and there is no God besides you. For you are God, and we did not know it. The Savior is the God of Israel* (Isa 45:14-15). Surely the Jews were not referring to God the Father when they said, *For you are God, and we did not know it*, since the whole law manifests the authority of the Father, from whom all things have their being. Instead, the Son of God is addressed in that confession, *For you are God, and we did not know it*. Although he could always be perceived, what he was became recognized clearly only after the resurrection. For in the law he was considered one of the angels and the leader of the Lord's army. Thus, once he was finally understood as the Son of God, the passage, *For you are God, and we did not know it,* is addressed to him in thanksgiving. He had appeared to the patriarchs as divine and afterward became incarnate, though he had not been comprehended by all. **You that boast in the law, do you dishonor God by breaking the law?** You transgress the law by ignoring its meaning —

the Incarnation and divinity of Christ. You fail to honor God when you do not accept the testimony God gave concerning the Son, *This is my beloved Son* (Matt 3:17). **The name of God is blasphemed among the Gentiles because of you, as it is written.** The prophet Isaiah declared that *the name of God is blasphemed through you among the Gentiles* (Isa 52:5). The nations did not recognize that the Jews had been handed over to them because of the Jews' own evil deeds. Instead, the nations attributed their victories over the Jews to the glorious achievements of their own idols, whom they thought had triumphed over the God of the Jews. Similarly, in the time of the apostles **the name of God was blasphemed** in Christ: by denying that Christ is God the Jews were blaspheming the Father as well. Thus the Lord says, *One who receives me, receives not me but the one who sent me* (Luke 9:48). God was blasphemed among the Gentiles, therefore, because the Jews tried to convince Gentile believers that Christ must not be acknowledged as God. Thus the blasphemy of the Gentiles was instigated by Jews.

(2) Origen on verses 17-24

We must first note that Paul did not say, "But if you are a Jew." Rather, he said, **But if you call yourself a Jew.** For to be a Jew is not the same as to be called a Jew. Paul himself teaches in later verses that the true Jew is so "in secret," and that he who has been circumcised in the heart keeps the law in the spirit, not in the letter. *His praise comes not from human beings, but from God* (Rom 2:29). But the person who has been circumcised externally in the flesh observes the law as a means of gaining praise from others. Such a person is not truly a Jew but is only called a Jew. . . .

The person who is called a Jew and boasts in the letter of the Mosaic law but does not believe in Christ is condemned as a blasphemer of the law. For those who really believed Moses would also believe in the one about whom Moses wrote. Because of such persons, who are called Jews but are not true Jews, **the name of God is blasphemed among the Gentiles.** They are blasphemers not only because of their wicked deeds but also because of their impoverished and deficient understanding of the Law and the Prophets. When the Jews follow the law literally and say, *Do not handle, do not taste, do not incur defilement; all these things are a corruption according to human precepts and teachings* (Col 2:21), they lead the Gentiles to despise the law. Thus the Apostle speaks to the person who is a Jew in name but not in deed.

But Paul's words can also apply to any person who holds religion and piety in name only and lacks deeds, knowledge, and faith. For this reason, we should attend carefully to this problem among ourselves rather than worrying about those who have not come to faith in Christ. We have become true Jews through faith in Christ and the circumcision we received in Baptism; we have found our place in the law of Christ. Therefore, we must avoid boasting that we have come to know God after rejecting the error of idolatry and that we have come to know the will of God for ourselves. For we know how to test what is good, pleasing, and perfect; we have thereby become leaders and teachers of the church with a duty to illumine those blind in their understanding and to instruct the little ones in Christ. We must not teach a stricter way of life or demand the highest degree of discipline and self-restraint from those whom we instruct, while we ourselves remain afflicted with the vices of intemperance and desire, or are sometimes inflamed with secret lust. The Apostle's words are quite well suited to those who act like this: **You, then, that teach others and do not teach yourself. While you preach against stealing, you steal. You forbid adultery, and you commit adultery.** And if, as occasionally happens, a person takes for private use a gift that was offered to God or a donation that was intended for the support of the poor, then that person is surely being asked, **You abhor idols, and you rob temples?** But if people incur a public condemnation or if their avarice, corrupt judgments, and drunkenness become notorious, then God is also dishonored by their failures. If a teacher of the church acquires such a reputation, then *the name of God is blasphemed among the Gentiles.*

(3) Augustine on verse 17

Here Paul makes clear what he meant by saying, **boast in God.** If such Jews really **boasted in God** in the way appropriate to that grace which is given freely rather than as payment for the merits of works, then their praise would come from God rather than from their fellow human beings. But **they boasted in God** as though they alone had deserved to receive God's law, as the psalm says, *God has not dealt thus with any other nation, and did not make known God's judgments to them* (Ps 147:20). They believe that they then fulfill this law of God through their own righteousness, even though they violate more than observe it. So the abundance of their sin, which they commit knowingly, results in the law bringing down wrath on them. Whoever does what the law commands without the aid of the Spirit of grace acts from fear of punishment rather than love of justice. What their performance displayed to other people was not what God observed in their intention. Thus they were held guilty by God, who knew what they would have preferred to do if they could have done it and still escaped punishment. What Paul calls the circumcision of the heart is an intention free of all illicit desires; this purity is attained not through the letter of the law teaching and threatening but by the Spirit helping and healing. Such persons are honored, therefore, not by human beings but by God, whose grace actually provides that good willing for which they are praised. Of God is it said: *My soul will be praised in the Lord* (Ps 34:3); and to God, *my praise is in your presence* (Ps 22:26). Such people are not like those who want God to be praised for creating them human, while they are praised for making themselves righteous.[3]

Romans 2:25-29

25**Circumcision indeed is of value if you obey the law; but if you break the law, your circumcision has become uncircumcision.** 26**So, if a man who is uncircumcised keeps the**

---

3. Augustine is here attacking Pelagius and his followers, who asserted that human beings retained and could not lose the powers of doing good and avoiding evil with which God had endowed humanity at the creation. He argued that this meant that humans, rather than God, were to be praised for their just deeds.

precepts of the law, will not his uncircumcision be regarded as circumcision? 27Then those who are physically uncircumcised but keep the law will condemn you who have the written code and circumcision but break the law. 28For he is not a real Jew who is one outwardly, nor is true circumcision something external and physical. 29He is a Jew who is one inwardly, and real circumcision is a matter of the heart, spiritual and not literal. His praise is not from men but from God.

(1) Origen on verses 25-27

Which circumcision, according to the Apostle, is valuable? What is the law that must be observed? We must carefully inquire into the words of the Apostle so that once we have understood them we can also be circumcised ourselves. Circumcision has value, as the Apostle suggests when he says, **Circumcision indeed is helpful if you obey the law.** The Apostle himself teaches in what follows, however, that what is helpful is not the **outward circumcision in the flesh**, but rather the **circumcision of the heart.** It is **a thing of the spirit, not of the letter**, that wins **praise not from men but from God.** In another place Paul says, *Behold the circumcision! We are the circumcision, we who serve God in spirit and do not trust in the flesh* (Phil 3:3). In my opinion, the Apostle intends **circumcision of the heart** when he says that it **is helpful if you obey the law.** It is not the law of the letter, whose circumcision in the flesh you do not receive, but the law of the spirit by which you were circumcised in the heart. *For the law kills, but the spirit brings life* (2 Cor 3:6), because the law of God does not refer to something written in ink, but written by the finger of God — God's Spirit — not on tablets of stone but on those of the heart.

The following objection might be made against this interpretation: if the Apostle says that circumcision of the heart has value — and certainly this must be understood only as a cleansing of the soul and the rejection of vices — then why does he go on to specify that this type of circumcision is valuable if you observe the law? For this kind of circumcision happens only by observing the law. Perhaps **circumcision** could here refer to avoiding vices and ceasing to do evil; to **obey the law** would then refer to attempting and actually performing good deeds. Perfection does not consist only in avoiding evil; it requires doing good actions as well. The psalm teaches this clearly when it says, *Turn away from evil,* but goes on to add, *and do good* (Ps 37:27). The Apostle, who was learned in these matters, makes a similar point. He says that the circumcision of the heart and avoidance of evil are valuable only when the law of good works is also observed. For no one can be perfect simply by avoiding evil without also doing good. . . .

But if, Paul says, **you break the law,** that is, as we have just explained, if you fail to do good deeds, **your circumcision has become uncircumcision.** Although you appear to avoid evil deeds, still by failing to perform the works of faith and justice you are relegated to the ranks of the unfaithful. Someone who is physically circumcised cannot, of course, become uncircumcised, since the foreskin cannot grow back once it has been cut off. Therefore, the obvious interpretation of this statement is that the avoidance of evil — signified by the word **circumcision** — will be reckoned as uncleanness unless it is accompanied by works of faith. If someone circumcised by the grace of Baptism in the Church should subsequently become a transgressor of the law of Christ, that baptismal circumcision will be treated as the uncircumcision of infidelity. For faith without works is called dead (Jas 2:17), and those who act like the wicked steward will be ranked among the unfaithful.

So, if those who are uncircumcised keep the requirements of the law, then those who are physically uncircumcised but keep the law will condemn you that have the written code and circumcision but break the law. Earlier we noted that the Apostle discusses two types of Jew and two types of circumcision. Now he is speaking of a physical and a spiritual circumcision. In this passage he appears to use the term **uncircumcised** to refer to Gentiles who have come to faith in Christ while remaining physically uncircumcised. He then compares these Gentiles, who observe a spiritual law, to the Jews who transgress the law by understanding it literally and by physical circumcision. The latter, he says, will be judged by those who lack bodily circumcision but observe the law.

But we can also read this contrast as a warning to those of us in the Church by applying the word **uncircumcised** to catechumens or even pagans, and the word **circumcised** to baptized believers. If a catechumen not yet circumcised through the grace of baptismal washing keeps the law of Christ and observes the precepts of justice, will not such a person stand in judgment over someone ranked among the faithful but who does not keep the commandments and despises the law of Christ and his precepts? Finally, the Lord himself has said, *The queen of the South will rise up at the judgment with this generation and condemn it, because she came from the ends of the earth to listen to the wisdom of Solomon* (Matt 12:42). These words have been spoken to us, for the instruction of the Church.

(2) Theodoret on verse 25

Circumcision indeed is of value if you obey the law; but if you break the law, your circumcision has become uncircumcision. The holy Apostle agreed with the words of prophecy. Through the prophet Jeremiah, God says, *All the nations are uncircumcised in the flesh, but the house of Israel is uncircumcised in its heart* (Jer 9:26). Add to this, *Be circumcised for the Lord* (Jer 4:4), with *Circumcise the foreskin of your heart* (Jer 4:4), and thus specify the type of circumcision that is pleasing to God. So inspired, the holy Apostle asserts that circumcision of the flesh is futile unless it is accompanied by circumcision of the spirit. This is why the practice was established in the first place; nothing is gained by cutting away the flesh if it has no effect on the spirit. Circumcision functions properly only as a sign and seal. When we possess gold, silver, expensive gems, or costly clothing, we usually put our identifying mark on them. But when the locked treasury is empty and contains none of these valuables, trying to use your seal is a meaningless gesture.

(3) Ambrosiaster on verse 25

Paul is saying that the Jew who has not kept the law becomes a Gentile — only he uses the term **circumcision** to stand for "the race of Abraham," because circumcision derives from Abraham. Nor could Paul here affirm what he had already taken apart. He teaches that belonging to the race of Abraham is profitable on condition that its law is obeyed, that is, if a person believes in the Christ who was promised to Abraham. In addition to their own merits, these descendants share the merits of the patriarchs by being justified through faith. Since all salvation received through the law actually derives from Christ, anyone who believes in Christ thereby obeys the law. Conversely, a nonbeliever breaks the law by refusing to accept Christ, whom the law prophesies will come to bring the justification which it cannot provide. Being called a descendant of Abraham confers no advantage on a nonbeliever, therefore, because the true child of Abraham is characterized by the merit which comes from faith, that faith which made Abraham worthy of God.

(4) Ambrosiaster on verses 28-29

Evidently Paul denies that bodily circumcision wins any praise at all from God. Even Abraham was justified not because he was circumcised but because he believed and was circumcised only afterward. Circumcision of the heart wins praise from God because it cuts away error and comes to know the creator. Because this circumcision of heart was still in the future, Moses was the first to say, *You will circumcise the hardness of your heart* (Deut 10:16), and Jeremiah also said to Jews who were worshiping idols, *Circumcise the foreskin of your heart* (Jer 4:4). A covering surrounds the heart. The person who turns to God will cut it away, since faith removes the shadow of error and brings a full recognition of God in the mystery of the Trinity, which was unknown from the beginning of time. Praise for this kind of circumcision derives from God but is not manifest to humans; for God scrutinizes the merit of the heart, not of the flesh. Jews receive praise from humans since they glory in the circumcision of the flesh, which comes from the patriarchs. Hence in another epistle Paul says, among other things, *their glory is in the shame of those who have worldly thoughts* (Phil 3:19), referring to those who consider circumcision of the flesh glorious. For anyone who glories in the flesh follows worldly ways of thinking. But one who glories in the spirit wins praise from God for believing in the spirit, not by the flesh.

(5) Augustine on verse 29

You recognize that you are Israelites according to the seed of Abraham, and heirs of the house of Jacob according to the promise. Realize as well that you have gone out of Egypt, since you have given up hope for this world. You have gone out from a barbarian people, since your confession of faith has segregated you from the blasphemies of the nations. That language is not your own; it belongs to the barbarians who do not care to praise God; but you sing "Alleluia" to God. In you, *Judah became his holy dwelling* (Ps 114:2). **For he is not a real Jew who is one obviously, nor is true circumcision something obvious in the flesh. He is a Jew who is one secretly, and real circumcision is a matter of the heart.** Question your hearts, then. If faith has circumcised them, if confession has purified them, then in you has *Judah become his holy dwelling*; in you *is Israel his power* (Ps 114:2). He has given you the power to become children of God.

Romans 3

In the third chapter, Paul began to address the role of faith in the process of salvation. The commentators offered different explanations of God's fidelity and victory over human rejection. Ambrosiaster identified God's victory as fulfilling promises even when humans had not trusted them. John Chrysostom also noted that God's goodness toward humans is not conditioned by their response. Augustine was most straightforward: God will prove true by denying to sinners what was promised to the saints.

Origen, as he does regularly throughout his commentary, distinguished the Mosaic law from the natural law written in the human heart which, at a certain age, enables an individual to distinguish right from wrong, and thereby to become subject to an imposed law, such as that of Moses. This natural law also made humans responsible for sin prior to the Mosaic law. Within the Mosaic law, Ambrosiaster distinguished the moral precepts of the natural law from the promises of God and from the rituals which were enjoined until those promises were fulfilled. Augustine here introduced his characteristic thesis — echoed by Theodoret — that the law revealed human sinfulness and that humans needed grace to fulfill its precepts.

Both faith and works were taken as necessary for righteousness by all commentators. Origen and Ambrosiaster explained that the promises of God which are fulfilled in Christ were included in the Mosaic law, so that obeying that law requires both following its moral precepts which mirror the natural law and believing that the promises have been fulfilled in Christ. The ritual part of the law, the commentators claim, was intended to be in force only until the promises were fulfilled and was thus no longer binding once Christ had come.

Paul's assertion that righteousness is given apart from the law was explained in different ways. In Origen's view, either faith or works may precede but one usually must be complemented or perfected by the other. Faith, however, would suffice for a person — like the thief crucified with Christ — who does not live long enough to do good deeds after conversion to faith. Ambrosiaster explained that God's righteousness is given for faith in the promises alone because Christ makes the ritual law irrelevant and gives forgiveness for sins against the natural law. Augustine introduced a different explanation: the precepts of the law prepare for faith and forgiveness by convicting a person of sin and demonstrating human inability to fulfill its precepts. Faith in Christ and the righteousness of God given by the indwelling of the Holy Spirit win forgiveness of sins and empower good deeds. Grace precedes faith and its works, which fulfill the law. The teachings of Paul and James are thus shown to be complementary rather than opposed.

In this chapter, the commentators begin to note the role of Christ legitimating the forgiveness of sins either by dealing with the devil or winning the divine mercy.

Romans 3:1-4

₁**Then what advantage has the Jew? Or what is the value of circumcision? ₂Much in every way! To begin with, the Jews were entrusted with the oracles of God. ₃What if some were unfaithful? Does their faithlessness nullify the faithfulness of God? ₄By no means! Let God be true though every man be false, as it is written,** *So that you may be justified in your words, and prevail when you are judged* (Ps 51:4).

(1) Ambrosiaster on verses 1-4

Then what advantage has the Jew? Or what is the value of circumcision? Much in every way. To begin with, the Jews were entrusted with the oracles of God. Although in many ways Paul alludes to the dignity and merit of the people of Abraham, he explicitly affirms that their greatest glory was that they were worthy to receive the law and thereby learned to distinguish right from wrong, and so to judge other matters. He clearly asserts, however, that what is said about their race is of no advantage to individual Jews who are carnal, that is, unbelievers. To avoid the appearance of depreciating all Jews, Paul affirms that being children of Abraham is a great benefit to Jews who believe. **The Jews were entrusted with the oracles of God.** By their sinning, humans had worn away that warning given in the original law and had come to believe that God would not punish them. Because of the merits of their ancestors, the Jews then received a renewed law and became the people of God.

What if some were unfaithful? Will their faithlessness nullify the faithfulness of God? By no means! The unbelief of some Jews has not offended God to such a degree that other, believing Jews will also be deprived of the eternal life which God had promised would come through faith in Christ. The unbelievers made themselves unworthy without prejudice to the believers. In this way, Paul praises believing Jews; they were not harmed by the many Jews who refused to believe.

Although every man is a liar, God is truthful, as it is written. God is truthful and delivers what has been promised. To fail is human: the passage of time and the weakness of the natural order make humans inconstant; they cannot foresee what will happen to them. The future, however, is already present to God, who is always constant, as is proclaimed, *I am, and I will not be changed* (Mal 3:6). . . .

Because they do not trust God's promises, Paul calls humans untruthful. This is directed at the Jews in particular, whom the Apostle is discussing at this point; they were eyewitnesses to Christ, yet they denied that he was the one whom God had promised. For this reason, they are called liars. But God is truthful, sending Christ as was promised. And so God will be victorious at the judgment, because God will indeed provide what some deny will be given. To distrust the divine promises is to judge God untruthful. Thus, when God actually gives what people claim will not be given, God wins a victory by proving true and demonstrating that unbelievers are liars. They will see Christ, whom they denied, in majesty; they will witness the resurrection of the flesh. Then will they realize that unbelief has been defeated by the promise and the truth of God. For Christ also won a victory when he was judged. For when he was unjustly killed, the devil bore the guilt. Christ had first overcome when he did not sin; then he defeated the devil this second time, and the devil lost those who were held prisoners in hell. In all these ways, then, every human is a liar and God alone is truthful.

(2) Origen on verses 2-3

In considering the passage where Paul says, **they were entrusted with the oracles of God**, note that he did not say that they were entrusted with the "letters" of God, but rather with the "**oracles**" of God. His wording suggests the following interpretation to us: those who read but either do not understand or do not believe, have been entrusted with the "letter," specifically that letter which the Apostle described when he said, *the letter kills* (2 Cor 3:6). **The oracles of God**, by contrast, have been entrusted to those who understand and believe what Moses wrote and believe in Christ as well. For the Lord said, *If you had believed in Moses, you would also believe in me, for Moses wrote about me* (John 5:46).

But let us grant that the Jew has an advantage, in respect to both the letter and the oracles of God. Does this mean that those who come to Christ from among the Gentiles are left with nothing? Or do they too have some advantage? Listen to the Lord addressing the centurion who became a believer from among the Gentiles: *Amen, I say to you, not even in Israel have I found such faith* (Matt 8:10). Note that in the case of faith, Gentiles possess a much greater advantage; in another place the Lord says this about them: *They will come from east and west and from the four corners of the earth; and they will recline along with Abraham, Isaac, and Jacob in the kingdom of God; but the sons of the kingdom will be cast into the outer darkness* (Matt 8:11-12). Therefore, when it comes to the laws and to the letters, the Jews have every advantage. When it comes to faith, as my comparison has shown, the Gentiles have the greater advantage. . . .

The oracles of God, therefore, were entrusted first to the Jews, of whom I spoke above. But as Paul says, some of them believed neither in God nor in the oracles of God. Note that those who do not believe are *according to the flesh* (Rom 8:12), as he says of them elsewhere, *The natural person does not perceive those things which belong to the Spirit of God; they are foolishness to such a person* (1 Cor 2:14). Still, their unbelief does not **nullify the faithfulness of God**. By **the faithfulness of God** we understand either that by which God maintains fidelity with those to whom **the oracles have been entrusted** or that by which those who have received **the oracles of God** believe in God. Therefore, those who either do not come to faith or who fall away from the faith might ridicule us when we perform the works of faith: when we fast or do acts of mercy or devote ourselves to the study of God's law, or even when we suffer torture in martyrdom for Christ. We are here admonished to bear in mind always that their infidelity will not nullify that faithfulness of God which is at work in us. . . .

Granted, he says, that some of the Jews did not believe. Still, God alone is entirely truthful, while **every human being is a liar.** Even a person who is righteous necessarily falls short of the truth in some respect, for human nature can hardly preserve the truth in every instance. **Every human being is a liar**; consequently some of the Jews, being mendacious human beings, did not believe. **Every human being is a liar**; consequently on that day when the Lord enters into judgment with them, God alone **will be justified in God's words.** For the Lord's words are true in every way, since they are the words of Truth itself.

(3) Augustine on verse 3

Those who boast about themselves will be put to shame, for they will not be found sinless. Only those who boast in the Lord will not be ashamed. *Since all have sinned and fall short of the glory of God* (Rom 3:23). When he addressed the infidelity of the Jews, he did not say, "Suppose some of them had sinned, would their sin nullify the fidelity of God?" How could he have said, "Suppose some of them had sinned," when he said himself, *Since all have sinned* (Rom 3:23)? Instead he said, **What if some did not believe? Will their unbelief nullify the faithfulness of God?** He spoke this way to specify clearly that one sin which locks up all others, which prevents their being loosed through the grace of God. Through the coming of the Holy Spirit — through the gift of the Spirit's grace to the faithful — the world is condemned for this one sin, as the Lord says, *of sin indeed, because they did not believe in me* (John 16:9).

(4) Augustine on verse 4

The gospel says, *Those who lie speak from what is their own* (John 8:44). Every sin is a lie, since a lie is whatever is opposed to the law and to truth. So what does the gospel say? *Those who lie, speak from what is their own* (John 8:44); thus those who sin, sin from what is their own. Consider the opposite situation: if those who lie speak from their own resources, then those who speak truthfully speak from what is God's. For this reason the Scripture also says, *Only God is true; every man is a liar* (Ps 115:11). This does not permit you to lie with impunity because you are human. Rather, it says that because you are false, you must be human. To be true, drink in the truth, so that what you bring forth comes from God and you are true. Because you cannot have truth from your own selves, you must drink it in from that source whence it flows. In the same way, if you withdraw from the light, you will be in darkness. Just as a stone is hot not by itself but from the sun or a fire, if you take it away from the heat, it will grow cold. Evidently, the stone does not heat itself; it is warmed by the sun or a fire. In the same way, if you withdraw from God, you will grow cold. If you draw near to God, you will be warmed. Thus the Apostle says, *glowing with the Spirit* (Rom 12:11).

Romans 3:5-9

5But if our wickedness serves to show the justice of God, what shall we say? That God is unjust to inflict wrath on us? (I speak in a human way.) 6By no means! For then how could God judge the world? 7But if through my falsehood God's truthfulness abounds to his glory, why am I still being condemned as a sinner? 8And why not do evil that good may come? — as some people slanderously charge us with saying. Their condemnation is just. 9What, then? Are we Jews any better off? No, not at all; for I have already charged that all men, both Jews and Greeks, are under the power of sin.

(1) Ambrosiaster on verses 5-9

By no means, he says, **I speak in a human way.** Paul has in mind something that fits humans, not God, for there is no evil in God, only in humans. Nor does our injustice serve to make God just, as, for example, when God gives us sinners the benefits promised to the saints. Although sinners, we are formed anew through repentance. The result is that we deserve to receive the promise not because we are still sinners but we because have been purified.

The prophet David said, *Against you, you alone, I have sinned, and done what is evil in your sight, so that you are justified in your sentence and blameless when you pass judgment* (Ps 51:4). Now the meaning of this confession is not what evil-minded people perversely claim: that the sins and the wrongdoings of humans promote the righteousness of God; or that our evils make God seem just; or that our unrighteousness proves God righteous. If our sins did actually justify God, then God would be doing evil in punishing them; since God is not evil in calling down wrath, our sins do not make God righteous. **By no means!** God does not want us to sin; God inflicts punishment because God is just.

For then how could God judge this world? The answer is obvious. God could not fairly judge the world if sins helped God; or if people sinned with God's connivance so that divine goodness could then be displayed in giving them forgiveness; or if God could not be acknowledged as just unless people sinned; or if God could not be good unless people sinned so that God would have something to forgive. **By no means!**

But if through my falsehood God's truthfulness abounds to God's glory, why am I still being condemned as a sinner? Here too the meaning is clear. If human deceit were contributing to the divine glory by making God alone appear truthful, then those who sin should not be called evil. Manifestly, they would then sin not by their own initiative but at God's instigation. **By no means!**

And why not do evil that good may come? — as some people slanderously charge us with saying. The Apostle posed this question for that very reason. Perverse people had charged that those who preach the forgiveness of sins intended that people should do evil in order that good might come of it, that they should sin so that God could appear good by forgiving them — as was just discussed. Paul rejects such a construal of the divine teaching as slanderous. Faith does not promote sinning, especially when it warns that the

Lord will come to judge. Rather, it works a cure for those who have failed, so that they might regain their salvation, live according to God's law, and so sin no more.

Their condemnation is just! It is surely just to condemn people whose jealous ill-will misconstrues our teaching. The Jews used to throw up these kinds of objections to vilify the apostolic teaching. By preaching the forgiveness of sins, they claimed, the apostles encouraged sinning; by making people confident of forgiveness, they urged them to sin. However, Paul was speaking to believers. If they continued to sin after accepting faith, that would place them in great danger.

Why, then, do we hold back further? For we have already charged that all, both Jews and Greeks, are under the power of sin. First, Paul showed that the Greeks are guilty under the law of nature and also because they refused to accept the law of Moses. Consequently, their situation is extremely serious, indeed, as bad as it could be. Then he showed that the Jews are also guilty. Although they ostensibly live under the law of God and claim honor for themselves because of their patriarchs' merit, they render the grace of God ineffective by spurning the promise made to the patriarchs.

(2) John Chrysostom on verse 5

Paul refutes one absurd argument by another. Let me explain. What is he saying? God honored the Jews, but they offended God. Since God still honored the Jews as Jews, God gained the victory and demonstrated great love for humanity. Now then, some may say, if we have offended God, and God has the victory, and the righteousness of God is evident, why are we being punished? For by offending God we have assured a divine victory. How, then, does Paul solve this problem? By yet another argument from absurdity. For, he says, if you have become the cause of God's victory, then punishing you afterward would be an unjust act. But if God is not unjust, and you are still punished, then you cannot claim to be the cause of the divine victory. Note the Apostle's reverence: he says, **God is not unrighteous to inflict wrath on us**, and then he adds, **I speak in a human way.** As if, Paul says, the argument was being made according to human reasoning. For the righteous judgments of God far exceed human standards of righteousness; God has different, ineffable reasons.

(3) Origen on verse 5

Every field of knowledge consists in contraries, that is, in positive and negative qualities. Medicine, for example, involves knowledge not only of health but also of sickness. Although it focuses on health, it cannot ignore the various elements of disease. Similarly, the virtue of prudence requires knowledge of both good and evil; temperance encompasses what should be pursued and what should be avoided; courage is not oblivious of the causes of fear; and justice must necessarily know what makes for injustice. If, then, we wish to understand what justice is, then we must also know what injustice is. Thus when we attain full knowledge of injustice, we will also know the very essence of justice: when what is unjust becomes clear, what is just will also be manifest. Now justice exists in God, whose nature is beyond human perception, but injustice finds its place among us human beings and in every rational creature. Thus it follows that the justice of God, which is incomprehensible and beyond us, is made known and attractive to us through our own injustice, just as any contrary is revealed by its opposite.

(4) Anonymous on verse 5

Our injustice does not add to **the justice of God.** When we will be judged by God, those of us who have not observed God's commandments will be deprived of the promised reward. Thus God will be *proved true* (Rom 3:4) by not giving to sinners what was promised to the saints.

(5) Augustine on verse 8

O the depths of the riches and wisdom and knowledge of God! How unsearchable are his judgments and how inscrutable his ways! (Rom 11:33). Perverse humans, who do not consider these judgments inscrutable and these ways unsearchable, are quick to complain and reluctant to understand. They thought and even proclaimed that the Apostle had said, **Let us do evil, so that good may come of it.** Far be it from the Apostle to say such a thing! But in their inability to understand, these people thought he had meant just this when they heard that he had said, *the law came in, to increase the trespass; where sin increased, grace abounded all the more* (Rom 5:20). Grace did not have the effect of making sinners continue in evil deeds and expect to be repaid in good things. Instead the coming of grace changed those who had been doing evil and brought them to do good deeds. Thus they should not say, **Let us do evil, so that good may come of it** but instead, "We did evil, but then good came. So let us do good deeds now, so that in the age to come we may be repaid with good things for those good acts. For in the present age we have been given good things in return for even our evil deeds."

(6) Origen on verse 9

Let us investigate what it means to be **under sin.** For Paul seems to include everyone without exception, both Jew and Gentile. I am reminded of another statement of his: *But where there is no law, there is no transgression* (Rom 4:5). Obviously, the law of Moses is found among the Jews. He confirms that the law of nature exists among the Gentiles, where it accuses those who violate the testimony of their conscience. Where, then, could we find a person who has no law at all and thereby seems not to be trapped in sinful transgression? Now Paul said of himself: *But I once lived without the law* (Rom 7:9). When did Paul live apart from the law, since he also says about himself, *I was circumcised on the eighth day, a Hebrew born of Hebrews* (Phil 3:5)? How, then, can he once have lived apart from the law when on the eighth day after his birth he received the mark of circumcision according to the law? A solution to this apparent contradiction would be that people begin to be **under the law** when they reach the age at which they can understand the law and make a choice about it. They do not take up the yoke of that external law until they have begun to live by the internal, natural law. Thus when Paul said, *I once lived without the law*, he went on to add, *but where the commandment came, sin revived* (Rom 7:9). By this statement, he means that in childhood, before people have the capacity to discern right from wrong, they are said to live *without the law*. Even if they should sin, that sin is not imputed to them because the law is not yet within them. But when they acquire the ability to distinguish right from wrong, the law has come to them and given them the commandments. But whenever the power of the commandment — an accusing conscience — is present in them, then sin, which was previously dead in them, has revived.

Therefore, if at this time people submit to the law of Moses with the intention of observing its precepts according to the letter, they become Jews openly. If they observe it according to the spirit, they become *Jews inwardly* (Rom 2:29). This is what Paul means in saying, **I have already charged that all of us, both Jews and Greeks, are placed under sin.** The word **all** should be taken to include only those whom either the natural or the written law has taught not to sin. And **the Gentiles are placed under sin** should be interpreted as explained above: when they begin to do the deeds of the law naturally and when they begin to be a law unto themselves because their conscience accuses them whenever they act against that law. Thus, I think the right interpretation is to identify the natural law as the law of God and to understand the written law as an imposed law. If, then, Paul had been referring to the written law — the law of Moses — when he said, *Sin is not imputed when there is no law* (Rom 5:13), then sin could not have been imputed to Cain, or to those who perished in the flood, or to those consumed by fire at Sodom. Since we know that sins were not only imputed to them but also that vengeance was taken upon them, however, it is clear that Paul was speaking of the natural law which is present in all human beings, excepting only the very young. He was, therefore, quite right to say, **for I have already charged that all, both Jews and Greeks, are under sin.**

Romans 3:10-20

10 **As it is written,**

> *None is righteous, no, not one;*
> 11 *no one understands, no one seeks for God.*
> 12 *All have turned aside, together they have gone wrong;*
> *no one does good, not even one.* (Ps 14:1-3)
>
> 13 *Their throat is an open grave,*
> *they use their tongues to deceive.* (Ps 5:9)
>
> *The venom of asps is under their lips.* (Ps 140:3)
>
> 14 *Their mouth is full of curses and bitterness.* (Ps 10:7)

15 *Their feet are swift to shed blood,*
16 *in their paths are ruin and misery,*
17 *and the way of peace they do not know.* (Isa 59:7-8)

18 *There is no fear of God before their eyes.* (Ps 36:1)

19 Now we know that whatever the law says, it speaks to those who are under the law, so that every mouth may be stopped, and the whole world may be held accountable to God. 20 For no human being will be justified in his sight by works of the law, since through the law comes the knowledge of sin.

(1) Ambrosiaster on verses 10-20

As it is written: *None is righteous, no, not one.* Paul began to enumerate the Jews' wrongdoings, taking unrighteousness as his starting point and gradually piling on more serious charges. His aim was to show that their only hope was to implore the mercy of Christ, who forgives sins. Next he adds: ***no one understands.*** The point is that anyone who made the effort to understand would not be unrighteous. ***No one seeks for God.*** This is also true, because anyone who understood what was profitable would seek God. ***All have turned aside, together they have gone wrong.*** Doubtless, all who do not seek God grow weak and find comfort in vanity. But this is futile; because vanity is an idol, they become worthless. ***No one does good, not even one.*** Through their neglect of God, they become weak and cannot do good. Already depraved, they get even worse. ***Their throat is an open grave.*** Having been handed over to evil, they would devour the good if they could. Just as a tomb lies open to receive corpses, so are their throats open to swallow the good. ***They use their tongues to deceive.*** They became so habituated to evil that everything they say is false. ***The venom of asps is under their lips.*** Their words are snares; they speak only to deceive. Just as poison is injected through the mouth of a snake, so deceit pours out of their lips. ***Their mouths are full of curses and bitterness.*** Evil people always make malicious and bitter charges against the good; they are always shouting abuse and detraction. ***Their feet are swift to shed blood.*** He refers here to the death of the prophets, whom they were ready to kill. Slow to do good, they are quick to murder. ***In their paths are grief and misery.*** Since they rush toward evil, he calls their ways — or rather running on them — disastrous and calamitous. ***And the way of peace they do not know.*** Preferring the path of hostility, which they travel toward the second death, they despised the road which leads to eternal life. Eternal life is called **peace** because when God is gracious, trouble will not turn up. Those people despise this way; they want no part in that peace which the good will enjoy in the presence of God. ***There is no fear of God before their eyes.*** Deprived of good sense, they have no respect for God. *For the fear of the Lord is the beginning of wisdom,* says Solomon (Prov 1:7). Paul did not say that these people have no fear of God, but, ***There is no fear of God before their eyes.*** These people see the evil of their actions yet feel no revulsion; thus they do not have the fear of God before their eyes. . . .

Now we know that whatever the law says, it speaks to those who are under the

law. Clearly, the law censures those who believed neither their leader, Moses, nor their ancestors, the prophets, whom they persecuted and killed, nor their kin according to the flesh, the apostles, whose blood they shed. They have always been impious, rebels against God. Thus the law, whose authority they despised, condemns them. . . .

So that every mouth may be silenced, and the whole world may be held accountable to God. Because the Jews too were bound by sin, the whole world was accountable to God. No one doubts that the pagans had already been overwhelmed by sins and impieties. Thus the whole world now lay prostrate before God, so that it might then receive forgiveness. . . .

For all flesh *will not be justified in God's sight* by works of the law. Humans are unjustified before God, not because they failed to observe the precepts of the law of righteousness but because they refused to believe the promise of the mystery of God in Christ. God decreed that humanity should be justified through this promise and not through the law, which can justify only in this present earthly life but not **in God's sight**. Therefore those who keep the law are righteous in the present but not **in God's sight**. They do not have that faith which justifies a person **in God's sight**. Faith is greater than the law, because the law has to do with human things but faith concerns God. Thus the law achieves a temporal righteousness, but faith attains eternal righteousness. . . .

For through the law comes the knowledge of sin. But through faith comes the obliteration of sin; so faith is the right course to follow. Which law does Paul say brings the recognition of sin? How is it recognized? We notice that the ancients were not ignorant of sin: Joseph was imprisoned, though on a false accusation (Gen 39:20); Pharaoh's butler and baker were condemned because of sin (Gen 40:1-3). How were sins not recognized? The law is threefold: the first part holds the plan of God's governance; the second part corresponds to the natural law, which forbids sin; the third part, however, consists in rules for rituals: Sabbaths, new moons, circumcision, and the rest. The natural law made sin manifest. It was reformed through Moses and by his authority strengthened to suppress vices. As I have said, it made sin manifest not in the sense that sin had been utterly unknown before but in the sense that it showed that the sins committed would not go unpunished by God. The judgment of God was coming, and no sinner was exempt from punishment, lest anyone think that the law could be disregarded because one could escape it for the present time. The law showed that sin would be brought to account before God.

(2) Origen on verse 19

We should carefully inquire which law **speaks to those who are under the law** and thus deprives them of any excuse that might shelter them from their sins. For this is what Paul says, **so that every mouth may be silenced, and the whole world may be held accountable to God.** If we try to apply this statement to the law of Moses, we are faced with the problem that it speaks only to those who have been circumcised and instructed from their mother's womb. How then would anyone conclude that a law whose commands have been given to only one nation could **silence every mouth and hold the whole world**

accountable to God? Do all nations have this law in common? Does the whole world share some part of it? How could Paul say that the knowledge of sin comes through the law of Moses when obviously many people recognized their own sins even prior to this law? When Cain sinned, for example, he said: *My sin is greater than I can repay* (Gen 4:13). And when the patriarchs had gone down to Egypt and were caught in Joseph's stratagem, they said to one another: *We are being punished for our sins against our brother, because we saw his anguish when he pleaded with us, but we would not listen. That is why this anguish has come upon us* (Gen 42:21). Likewise Job, who certainly lived before the law, says: *But if I have sinned unwillingly, if I have hidden my sin or prevented the multitude from announcing my sin* (Job 31:33). Clearly, all these people had knowledge of their sins. From all this, therefore, we conclude that when the Apostle Paul says, **the law speaks to those who are under the law**, he is referring not to the law of Moses but to the law of nature written on the human heart. Whatever this law says, it **speaks to those who are under the law**. Everyone old enough to have attained the capacity to distinguish right from wrong is under this law. Those who have not yet reached this age of discretion are apart from this law; Paul referred to them in saying, *once I lived without the law* (Rom 7:9). The Apostle said, **every mouth would be silenced, and the whole world would be held accountable to the future judgment of God** through this natural law. For no one is deprived of this law, which exists naturally in human beings, both Jews and Gentiles. Thus is it said, *God is justified in God's words and will be vindicated at the time of judgment* (Ps 51:4).

(3) Origen on verse 20

How is it that **the knowledge of sin comes by means of the law** but not from the law? If one studies the law and understands it by both examining its injunctions and attending to its prohibitions, then one knows that sin occurs both in neglecting what ought to be done and in not avoiding what is forbidden. Therefore, **the knowledge of sin comes through the law**, but sin is not committed by means of the law. For the tree of evil bears sin as its rotten fruit. The law is not a bad tree, however, because the law itself is not evil. Rather, it produces good fruit. Thus that **the knowledge of sin comes through the law** is similar to the diagnosis of disease coming through the art of healing. This is especially true of that illness which sometimes evades discovery by the patient and by a physician only moderately skilled in medical practice. Therefore, just as medical knowledge is good even in detecting disease when the healing art diagnoses the sickness, so also the law is good in revealing and reproving dereliction when the system of law brings recognition of sin.

(4) Augustine on verse 20

Some think that Paul is vilifying the law when he says, **For *no human being will be justified in his sight* by works of the law, for through the law comes the knowledge of sin**, and similar things. Such statements, however, must be carefully interpreted so that the

Apostle is understood neither as attacking the law nor as depriving humans of free choice. For this purpose, we distinguish four stages of human life: before the law, under the law, under grace, and in peace. Before the law, we follow carnal concupiscence; under the law, we are dragged along by it; under grace, we neither follow nor are drawn by it; in peace, we are free of carnal concupiscence. Before the law, therefore, we do not struggle because we not only desire evil and sin but even approve the sins. Under the law, we struggle but are overcome; we confess that our deeds are sinful. In confessing that our actions are evil, we wish that we did not do them but we are overcome by our evil desires because we have not yet received grace. At this stage, we are shown that we have been laid low; we try to rise up but we fall back again and then are even more miserable. *The law entered so that sin might increase* (Rom 5:20) refers to this situation. Similarly, Paul now says, **through the law comes the knowledge of sin**, not the taking away of sin, because sin is taken away only through grace. The law is indeed good because it forbids and commands what should be forbidden and commanded. When people think that they can fulfill the law by their own power rather than by the grace of their Liberator, their presumption not only fails to help but even hurts them. They are swept away by a more vehement sinful desire and their sin also convicts them of transgression: *Where there is no law neither is there transgression* (Rom 4:15). Laid low and realizing that they cannot rise through their own strength, they then implore the help of the Liberator.

(5) Theodoret on verse 20

The law, Paul says, has imposed a more precise knowledge of sin upon humans, and has made the condemnation deriving from it more grievous. The law is not sufficient for individuals to achieve virtue. Thus in showing that the law is only a tutor of right conduct, he makes clear the power of grace.

(6) Anonymous on verse 20

The Apostle does not contradict himself by saying first, *They show that what the law requires is written on their hearts* (Rom 2:15) and then, **no flesh will be justified in his sight by deeds prescribed by the law.** He accuses **the flesh**, whose attitude rejects subjection to the law of God. The law is able to teach what sin is but cannot show how it should itself be followed; it can punish evildoing but does not grant forgiveness to the penitent. Christ, however, gives the forgiveness of sins to believers and teaches them how to cut off the desires and dispositions of the flesh.

Romans 3:21-26

21But now the righteousness of God has been manifested apart from law, although the law and the prophets bear witness to it, 22the righteousness of God through faith in Je-

sus Christ for all who believe. For there is no distinction; 23since all have sinned and fall short of the glory of God, 24they are justified by his grace as a gift, through the redemption which is in Christ Jesus, 25whom God put forward as an expiation by his blood, to be received by faith. This was to show God's righteousness, because in his divine forbearance he had passed over former sins; 26it was to prove at the present time that he himself is righteous and that he justifies him who has faith in Jesus.

(1) Ambrosiaster on verses 21-26

But now the righteousness of God has been manifested apart from law, although the law and the prophets bear witness to it. Clearly the righteousness of God has appeared **without the law**: without the law of Sabbath and circumcision, the new moon and retributive punishment. Not, however, apart from the plan of God's governance, since the righteousness of God comes from the promise of God. When the righteousness of God forgave those whom the law held guilty, it certainly did this **without the law**, since it forgave the sin of those whom the law was going to punish. Lest anyone infer that this was opposed to the law, Paul added that the Law and the Prophets witness to the righteousness of God. The law itself had long ago proclaimed that this justification would be fulfilled, that one would come to save humanity, that one would accomplish the forgiveness of sins which the law had not been empowered to do. Therefore, what seems to be mercy is actually called the **righteousness of God**, because it was based on the promise; the fulfilling of God's promise is called the righteousness of God. To accomplish what one has promised is itself righteousness. Moreover, because to refuse refuge to those fleeing to God would be evil, to grant refuge is also righteousness.

The righteousness of God through faith in Jesus Christ. What could **through faith in Jesus Christ** mean except that the manifestation of Christ is the very righteousness of God? For through faith in the manifestation of Jesus Christ, the gift long promised by God is recognized and accepted. **In all and over all who believe**: the righteousness of God is seen to extend to all the Jews and Greeks who believe.

For there is no distinction, since all have sinned and fall short of the glory of God. Because he had said that the justice — the grace — of God extends to all Jews and Greeks, he added as a proof: **Since all have sinned.** This is to be taken in the most universal sense, as he says, **there is no distinction, since all have sinned.** Both Jews and Greeks. **Since all.** He includes holy people as well, to show that without faith the law accomplished nothing. The law was given so that there might be faith that hoped for the salvation yet to come. Therefore, the death of Christ helps all: he taught what must be believed and observed here in this age, and he rescued everyone from hell.

They are now justified by God's grace as a gift. They have been justified freely because through faith alone they have been sanctified by the gift of God, without performing anything or giving anything in return. **Through the redemption that is in Christ Jesus.** Paul testifies that the grace of God is in Christ: by the will of God we have been redeemed by Christ, so that we might be released from slavery and justified. Thus he says to the Galatians, *Christ has redeemed us, offering himself for us* (Gal 3:13). For he surrendered himself to the devil, who was raging but unwary. Now the devil thought that he would be able to hold onto Christ as easily as he had laid hold of him. But he could not stand up to Christ's power, and he lost not only Christ but all the others whom he had been holding.

Whom God put forward as a propitiator by faith. In Christ God proposed, that is, planned to be gracious toward humans, if they believe. **In his blood,** Paul says, because we were freed by his death, in which God both revealed Christ and condemned death through his suffering. **To show God's righteousness.** God made the promise plain and clear, by which God would free us from sins, as promised beforehand. By fulfilling it, God demonstrated the divine righteousness. **Because of his intention, the sins previously committed were borne in God's patience.** Knowing the gracious dispensation, whereby God proposed to help sinners — both those in this world above and those confined down in hell — God waited for both kinds for a very long time, then set aside the sentence by which all were shown to be justly condemned. In this way, God displayed to us the divine decree established long ago to free the human race through Christ. Thus had God promised through the prophet Jeremiah, saying, *I will forgive their iniquity, and remember their sin no more* (Jer 31:34). Lest this gift appear to have been promised only to the Jews, God said through Isaiah, *My house shall be called a house of prayer for all peoples* (Isa 56:7). The promise had been made to Judaism, but God knew in advance that the impious Jews would reject the gift, and promised to allow the Gentiles to receive the grace, so that envy would then drive the unbelieving Jews to anger. **At the present time.** In our time God actually gave what had been promised, when it had been promised. **That God is righteous and justifies the one who has faith in Jesus.** Paul is correct: God gave what had been promised **so that God may be righteous.** God promised to justify those who believe in Christ. As God said in Habakkuk, *The righteous shall live from my faith* (Hab 2:4). So, by placing faith in God and Christ, a person is righteous.

(2) Augustine on verses 20-24

That human presumption which does not understand the justice of God and wants to establish its own righteousness might agree that the Apostle was right to say, **no one will be justified by the law.** The law showed only what should be done and avoided, so that a person would then choose to fulfill what the law had shown. Thus, a person would be justified not through the command of the law but through free choice. But pay attention to what follows. **But now the righteousness of God has been manifested apart from the law; the law and the prophets bear witness to it.** Is this statement loud enough for these deaf people? **The righteousness of God,** he says, **has been manifested.** Those who want to establish their own righteousness pay no attention to this statement; they refuse to submit to it. **The righteousness of God,** he says, **has been manifested.** He called it neither human righteousness nor the righteousness of one's own free will, but instead **the righteousness of God.** Not the righteousness by which God is righteous but the justice with which God endows humans, when God justifies the impious. **This is attested by the law and the prophets;** the Law and the Prophets bear witness. The law, indeed, because by commanding and threatening but still justifying no one, it clearly shows that people are made righteous by the gift of God, through the assistance of the Spirit. The prophets, because what they had foretold was fulfilled in the coming of Christ. Thus Paul continues and adds, **the righteousness of God through faith in Jesus Christ**, that is, through the faith by which we believe in Christ. Just as what is called **the faith of Christ** refers not to some faith by which Christ himself believed, so the **righteousness of God** means not that justice by which God is righteous. Both of these are ours; they are attributed to God and to Christ because they graciously give them to us. **The righteousness of God** exists **without law** but is not **manifested** apart from the law. How could it be **attested by the law** if it were **manifested** apart from the law? **The righteousness of God without the law** is that justice which God confers on the believer through the Holy Spirit, without the law's help. It is given without the assistance of the law when God shows people their weakness through the law, so that they might take refuge in the divine mercy through faith and thereby be healed. Thus is it said that the divine wisdom *carries law and mercy in its speech* (Prov 3:16 VL): law by which it makes the proud guilty; mercy by which it justifies those who have been humbled. **The righteousness of God through faith in Jesus Christ for all who believe. For there is no distinction, since all have sinned and fall short of the glory of God**, not of their own glory. *What have they that they have not received? If then they received it, why do they boast as though they had not received it* (1 Cor 4:7)? **They fall short of the glory of God**, and notice what follows: **they are justified by God's grace as a gift.** Not, therefore, justified through the law; not justified through their own willing; but **justified by God's grace as a gift.** None of this is accomplished without our willing, but through the law our will is shown to be sick, so that grace may heal a person's will and that healthy will may then fulfill the law, even though it is neither subjected to the law nor needs the law.

(3) Origen on verse 21

As we have often said and have explained more fully in the introduction to this exposition, the Apostle treats a number of different kinds of law in this letter. As he moves from one to another, the most attentive reader can sometimes follow him only with difficulty. In the present passage, he had just said that *through the law comes the knowledge of sin* (Rom 3:20). He said this, realizing that an objector might respond that if the knowledge of sin comes through the natural law, then the knowledge of righteousness would likewise come from it, according to the example taken from the art of healing that both the diagnosis and cure of a disease are arrived at through the same principles. In this way, if the recognition of sin could come through the natural law, so could the attainment of justice. Realizing that this objection could arise from his assertion that *through the law comes the knowledge of sin* (Rom 3:20), he then added, **But now the righteousness of God is manifest without the law.** This then is the purpose of his saying that the righteousness of God has not been disclosed in the same way that the knowledge of sin has come, that is, through the law. Rather, the righteousness of God has been manifest apart from the law. For the law of nature was able to accuse that nature of sinning and to reveal to it a knowledge of sin. But the righteousness of God transcends and surpasses what the human mind can apprehend by its natural faculties alone. For while the human mind can investigate and understand all kinds of human righteousness, it cannot comprehend God's righteousness and the judgments that derive from it, which Scripture has described as a great depth. Indeed, the righteousness of God and God's judgments are so profound that the Apostle exclaims, *How unsearchable are the judgments of God!* (Rom 11:33). . . . The Apostle Paul says the same about Christ: *He has become for us the wisdom of God, and righteousness, sanctification, and redemption* (1 Cor 1:30). The righteousness of God, which is Christ, is disclosed apart from the natural law, but not apart from the law of Moses or the prophets. That law itself gives testimony to him, as he himself observed: *You should search the scriptures, for they bear witness to me* (John 5:39).

(4) John Chrysostom on verses 22-23

The Jews raise an uproar over this statement, since it does not concede them a status above the rest of humanity but ranks them among the others. In order to help them overcome this feeling, Paul humbles them again with fear by adding, **for there is no distinction, since all have sinned.** Do not say to me "some Greek," "some Scythian," "some Thracian," for all of them are in the same plight. If you also received the law, you learned only one thing from it, to know what sin is; you did not learn how to avoid it. Then, in order to keep anyone from saying, "I might also have sinned, but still not like those people," Paul added, **and fall short of the glory of God.** So that, even if you did not commit the same sins as others did, you are still just as bereft of the glory of God. You are among those who have offended, and as an offender you are among the disgraced, not the glorified. Do not be afraid, for I said these things not to thrust you down into despair, but to show you the Lord's love toward humanity.

(5) Origen on verses 24-26

Thus the righteousness of God comes through faith in Jesus Christ to all who believe — Jews or Greeks — cleanses them of their prior sins, justifies them, and makes them ready for the glory of God. All this it does in response neither to their merits nor to their works; it bestows this glory freely on those who believe. **Through the redemption that is in Jesus Christ,** he says. Let us examine carefully what he means by **the redemption that is in Jesus Christ.** The word **redemption** designates something given to enemies in exchange for their captives, whom they then restore to their prior freedom. Sin conquered the human race in battle and held it in captivity as an enemy. Then came the Son of God, whom God made not only *wisdom, righteousness, and sanctification for us, but redemption* (1 Cor 1:30) as well. The Son gave himself as a redemption; he handed himself over to the enemy and poured out his own blood on those thirsting for it. This is the redemption made for those who believe, as Peter writes in his epistle: *You have been redeemed not with perishable silver or gold, but with the precious blood of the only-begotten Son of God* (1 Pet 1:18-19). . . .

Paul had said earlier that Christ gave himself as a redemption for the entire human race because he tasted death for the sake of all who were apart from God, in order to redeem those who were held in the captivity of their sins. Now he adds something even more sublime in saying, **whom God put forward as a sacrifice of atonement by his blood, effective through faith.** Through the sacrifice of his body, Christ made God well disposed toward humans, so that God might then exercise righteousness by forgiving the earlier faults which they had committed in the service of wicked tyrants — even while God was patiently allowing this to happen. God was forbearing and patient in the past, so that divine righteousness might be displayed in this present age. In fact, at the present time, at the very end of the ages, God has manifested righteousness and given as a redemption that one who was made an atoning sacrifice. For if God had sent the intercessor at an earlier time, he would not have restored as many people to himself as he has now, when the world is full of humans. God is righteous, however, and thus could not have justified those who were unrighteous. Instead, God willed the intervention of an intercessor, so that those who could not have been justified through their own works might be justified through their faith in Christ.

(6) Theodoret on verses 24-25

They are now justified by God's grace as a gift, through the redemption that is in Christ Jesus. Since the Lord Christ offered up his own body and life as the ransom price for us, we have received absolution from our sins by offering faith as our sole contribution. **Whom God put forward as a sacrifice of atonement by his blood, effective through faith.** The propitiation was a golden slab that rested on top of the chest or ark. On either side were images of cherubim sculpted in relief. Here the manifest blessings of God appeared to the high priest as he performed the rituals. The holy Apostle teaches that the true propitiation is the Lord Christ. For he was fulfilling the pattern of that ancient model. The title "propitiation" belongs to him as human, not as divine. For as God, he himself made solemn responses through the propitiation on the ark. But as a human among others he receives different names, such as sheep, lamb, sin, and curse. The ancient propitiation had no blood of its own, since it was not living, though it did receive the sprinklings of the blood of the sacrifices. But the Lord Christ — and he is God, and propitiation, and high priest, and sacrificial lamb — was also effecting our salvation in his own blood, requiring only faith from us.

Romans 3:27-31

27 Then what becomes of our boasting? It is excluded. On what principle? On the principle of works? No, but on the principle of faith. 28 For we hold that a man is justified by faith apart from works of law. 29 Or is God the God of Jews only? Is he not the God of Gentiles also? Yes, of Gentiles also, 30 since God is one; and he will justify the circumcised on the ground of their faith and the uncircumcised through their faith. 31 Do we then overthrow the law by this faith? By no means! On the contrary, we uphold the law.

(1) Ambrosiaster on verses 27-31

Then what becomes of your boasting? It is excluded. By what law? By that of works? No, but by the law of faith. Having explained his position, Paul addresses those who live under the law, asserting that they have no reason for boasting. They flatter themselves on having the law and being descendants of Abraham, failing to realize that a person is justified before God only through faith. **For we hold that a person is justified by faith without works of the law.** He argues that the Gentiles — at least — are justified by believing without performing any of the works of the law: without circumcision or new-moon ceremonies or observance of the Sabbath. **Or is God the God of Jews only? Is God not the God of Gentiles also? Yes, of Gentiles also.** Unquestionably, the one God is God of all. For the Jews cannot claim God as theirs alone, asserting that their God is not also God for the Gentiles. They recognize that Adam is the origin of all humans, and they never reject any convert who is prepared to observe the law.

Since God is one, and he will justify the circumcised from faith and the uncircumcised through faith. By **the circumcised** he means Jews, since they have been justified through belief in Christ as the one whom God had promised in the law. By **the uncircumcised** he means Gentiles who are justified before God through faith in Christ. For God has justified both Jews and Gentiles only by faith. Because there is one God for all, God justifies all in the same way. Since only faith makes a person worthy and deserving, how does circumcision of the flesh help, or how does being uncircumcised hinder?

Do we then overthrow the law by this faith? By no means! On the contrary, we uphold the law. Paul says that the law is fulfilled rather than rejected through faith. Faith confirms the status of the law by witnessing that what the law promised has actually been accomplished. This he asserts for the sake of the Jews who misunderstand the meaning of the law and so conclude that faith in Christ is opposed to it. Faith does not annul the law by believing that the law must now cease. Instead, it asserts that the law was rightly given for its proper time but that it should no longer be observed. The law itself contained the provision that it should come to an end once its promise had been fulfilled.

(2) Origen on verses 27-28

Paul says that the righteousness of faith alone is sufficient, so that a person is justified by faith alone, even without doing any good works. Those of us who try to maintain that the writings of the Apostle are coherent and logically consistent are forced to ask: Who has been justified by faith alone without any works? I think that we have an adequate answer in the robber who was crucified with Christ and cried out to him from the cross: *Lord Jesus, remember me when you come into your kingdom* (Luke 23:42). The Gospels ascribe no good work to him but only that faith for whose sake Jesus said to him: *Amen, I say to you, "Today you will be with me in paradise"* (Luke 23:43). Let us apply the example of this robber to the words of the Apostle Paul and say to the Jews: **What, then, has become of your boasting?** It is certainly ruled out, excluded not by the law of works but by the law of faith. For this robber was justified by faith apart from any works of the law, since the Lord did not require of him anything more than he had already done, nor did God expect him to complete any works once he had believed, but took him as his companion into paradise, made righteous by his confession alone.

Similarly, in the Gospel of Luke we have the story of the woman who learned that Jesus was eating in the house of a Pharisee. She brought a jar of ointment, stood behind him at his feet, wept and bathed his feet with her tears, then dried them with her hair. She continued to kiss his feet and anoint them with the ointment. When the Pharisee who had invited Jesus saw what was happening, he said to himself, *If this man were a prophet, he would know who and what kind of woman this is who is touching his feet — that she is a sinner* (Luke 7:37-39). Then Jesus told him the parable of the five hundred and the fifty denarii. Because of her faith alone and not because of any work of the law, he then said to the woman: *Your sins are forgiven*, and then, *Your faith has saved you. Go in peace* (Luke 7:48-50). In many other places of the gospel, we find the Savior saying that the faith of a believer is the cause of salvation.

From these examples it is clear that the Apostle Paul was right in saying that a person is **justified by faith without works of law.** Might someone hearing this then decide to neglect doing good deeds, because faith alone is sufficient for justification? In response to this, we would say that a person who acts unjustly after being justified has clearly rejected that gift of justification. The forgiveness of sins is not the granting of a license to continue sinning. The indulgence is for past sins, not future ones.

To return to our topic, then, a person is justified by faith, and works of the law contribute nothing toward that justification. In the absence of the faith which would justify a believer, a person cannot be justified even by performing works of the law. Since faith is the distinguishing mark of those who are justified by God and since in this case the works are not based on the foundation of faith, it follows that those works cannot justify the person who has done them, even though the actions might seem to be good.

(3) Augustine on verse 28

Paul was preaching that **a person is justified through faith without works.** He was misunderstood by those who thought that once they had believed in Christ, even if they did evil and lived wickedly and disgracefully, they could be saved through faith. The Letter of James (Jas 2:20) explains how the teaching of the Apostle Paul should be understood properly. Since Paul used the example of Abraham to prove that **a person is justified through faith without works of the law**, the Letter of James uses the example of Abraham to show something more: that faith is ineffective if a person does not act well. When the letter [of James] recalls Abraham's good works, which accompanied his faith, it shows clearly that Paul did not use the example of Abraham to teach that a person is justified by faith without works, so that a believer has no need of good works. By the example of Abraham, Paul intended to demonstrate that no one receives the gift of justification which is in faith as a reward for earlier good works. The Jews wanted to consider themselves better than those Gentiles who believed in Christ because, as they said, they had received the grace of the gospel because of the merits of their good works under the law. Many of these believing Jews were shocked when the grace of Christ was extended to uncircumcised Gentiles. In response to this objection, the Apostle Paul says that people can be justified through faith without any preceding works. Once justified through faith, however, how could they then fail to do just works? Before being justified, however, they did nothing just; they arrived at the righteousness of faith not by any merits of their good works but by the gift of God. That grace was not then idle in them, since it worked well through love. Now, if they had happened to die shortly after they had believed, then the righteousness of their faith would have been preserved with neither preceding nor subsequent good works — since they had first come to righteousness by grace rather than merit and then had not been allowed to remain longer in this life. Thus what the Apostle Paul meant to say is clear: **we hold that a person is justified by faith without works.** This must not be taken to mean that people who receive faith and continue to live afterward can be called just even if they acted badly. Both the Apostle Paul and James, then, use the example of Abraham. Paul showed that he was justified through faith, apart from the works of the law, which was not imposed on him. James proved that good works resulted from the faith of Abraham, and thus showed how what Paul had preached should be properly understood.

(4) John Chrysostom on verse 29

It is as if Paul said, "Why do you think it strange that all humans could be saved?" Could God be partial? They outrage the glory of God by insolence toward the Gentiles, refusing to allow God to be the Lord of all. If God is the Lord of all, then God cares for all. If God cares for all, then God saves all alike through faith. This is the reason Paul says, **Is God the God of Jews only? Is God not the God of Gentiles also? Yes, of Gentiles also.** For God is not partial but is shared by every person, unlike the gods in the myths of the Greeks.

(5) Origen on verses 30-31

The same God will justify the circumcised from faith and the uncircumcised through faith. Out of curiosity someone might ask: On what basis are the circumcised justified, **from faith** or, conversely, on what ground are the uncircumcised justified, **through faith**? Even though the inquiry seems to involve impertinent questioning, we can still answer quite consistently. Those who are justified **from faith** complete their justification by performing good works, once they have been established on the ground of faith. Those who are **justified through faith** begin with good works and then attain the summit of perfection through faith. In this way both faith and works are each brought to completion by adding the other to itself. . . .

Do we then overthrow the law by this faith? By no means! On the contrary, we uphold the law. . . . Though Paul said earlier that a person is not justified by works of the law, we can still understand the value he assigns to works when he confirms the law. In the Gospels the Savior says, *because Moses wrote about me* (John 5:46). Whoever, then, does not believe in Christ, about whom Moses wrote in the law, overthrows the law. But whoever believes in Christ, about whom Moses wrote, confirms the law through this faith by believing in Christ. . . . I would add that everyone who believes in Christ acts well and avoids all stain of sin — thereby confirming the law of God through a good life. A person falling headlong into sinful vices, stained by habitual crimes, and never exercising penitential restraint does not uphold the law. That sinner destroys the law, even while appearing to believe in Christ through faith. . . .

Someone might present as an objection that passage from the Second Epistle to the Corinthians: *But if the ministry of death incised in letters on stone was in such splendor that the sons of Israel could not look directly on the face of Moses because of the brightness of his face, even though its brilliance was fading* (2 Cor 3:7). To this we will then reply: to say, "The law's *brilliance was fading*," is not the same as saying, **we dismiss the law.** Paul himself did not have the power to terminate the law. If the law is to fade away, this must be effected by a superior glory, and this cannot be done even by Paul or by any other of the saints but only by that one who declares himself the *Lord of the Sabbath* (Mark 2:28). In comparison to his superior glory, what was glorious in that partial way is no longer glorious. Paul therefore designates the work of Christ as that part of the law which continues. What does not remain indeed fades away: the *law is the instructor* (Gal 3:24) until the *fulfillment of time* (Gal 4:4) comes. And just as I would say that the task of the instructor is necessary until the child is educated, so I would say that the task of the law is completed when the fullness of time comes, *when the child, who in no way differs from a slave, receives the inheritance* (Gal 4:1). According to both Peter and Paul, our present knowledge is brought to an end, but it is not scorned because of that ending, which occurs only when we reach perfection (1 Cor 13:10). In the same way, Paul establishes rather than terminates the law. When the superior glory of Christ is revealed, that glory brings to an end what had previously appeared and was called glorious. These considerations are reflected in the statement, *It is necessary that he increase, and that I decrease* (John 3:30). Thus the relationship between a pupil and the instructor who has been engaged for teaching is brought to an end upon the achievement of the educational objective, not simply by the student's wish. Paul says, **Do we then overthrow the law by this faith? By no means!** He does not say, "Is the law therefore voided?" but, **Do we then overthrow the law?** And likewise, **On the contrary, we uphold the law.**

(6) Anonymous on verse 31

When he says here, **we uphold the law,** the Apostle does not contradict what he had just said, **the boasting** of the law **is excluded, by the law of faith.** This is what he means: I uphold the law because the law itself testifies to me that Abraham was justified not by the works of the law but by faith.

(7) Augustine on verse 31

Knowledge of the law makes for a proud transgressor. Through the gift of charity, however, the person enjoys fulfilling the law. **We do not, therefore, overthrow the law by faith; on the contrary, we uphold the law.** By frightening a sinner, the law leads to faith. The law works wrath, therefore, so that once a person has been terrified and converted, the mercy of God may bestow, through our Lord Jesus Christ, the grace to fulfill the righteousness of the law.

Romans 4

Paul distinguished the righteousness based on faith in God from that based on good behavior. Because all of the commentators held that good behavior is necessary for salvation, they labored to find explanations of God's preference for the righteousness of faith. Origen observed that only God can judge faith; Ambrosiaster noted that faith — certitude about what remains uncertain — cannot be a duty, as good behavior can. John Chrysostom observed that faith relies on divine works which fulfill promises, rather than human actions. Augustine asserted that human works are sinful and cannot justify anyone until God has given both faith and love.

Paul argued that Abraham's faith and its righteousness preceded circumcision and other rituals, which then served as signs or symbols of that righteousness rather than its cause. Origen and Theodoret focused on the justifying faith of Abraham and those who imitated him, explaining that Christ had freed them from the rituals. Ambrosiaster and John Chrysostom explained that for Abraham's descendants, circumcision was a call and commitment to faith. Augustine regarded the ritual as a forerunner to Christian Baptism, especially when given to infants.

All the commentators recognized that the faithful affirm and live by realities which are neither evident to them nor supported by the assumptions of their human societies or cultures. Such behavior affirms the divine truthfulness and fidelity; it thereby gains access to the blessings God has promised.

Romans 4:1-8

₁What then shall we say about Abraham, our forefather according to the flesh? ₂For if Abraham was justified by works, he has something to boast about, but not before God. ₃For what does the scripture say? *Abraham believed God, and it was reckoned to him as righteousness* (Gen 15:6). ₄Now to one who works, his wages are not reckoned as a gift but as his due. ₅And to one who does not work but trusts him who justifies the ungodly, his faith is reckoned as righteousness. ₆So also David pronounces a blessing upon the man to whom God reckons righteousness apart from works:

> ₇*Blessed are those whose iniquities are forgiven, and whose sins are covered;*
> ₈*blessed is the man against whom the Lord will not reckon his sin.* (Ps 32:1-2)

(1) Ambrosiaster on verses 1-8

What then are we to say was found by Abraham, our ancestor according to the flesh? After having explained that no one can be justified in God's eyes through the works of the law, Paul establishes that even Abraham did not deserve anything **according to the flesh**, by which he meant circumcision. Because Abraham had already been justified before he was circumcised, he sought no benefit through circumcision. **For if Abraham was justified by works, he has glory, but not before God.** That is Paul's point as he develops his exposition. Abraham does indeed have something to brag about before God. His boast was about the faith by which he was justified, for the works of the law do not justify in a way that attains glory in the sight of God. Because observance of the law justifies only in the present age, Paul says, **if Abraham was justified by works, he has glory, but not before God.** It is among his fellow humans that he has glory: under the law of the present age he would not be held guilty. In the sight of God, however, only the faithful have a basis for bragging. **For what does the scripture say?** *Abraham believed God, and it was reckoned to him as righteousness* (Gen 15:16). Paul showed that Abraham could boast in God's sight not because he was circumcised, not because he was free of wickedness, but only because he had faith in God. For that reason he was made righteous and would be rewarded with praise in the future. **Now to one who works, wages are not counted as a gift but as something owed.** Anyone subject to the law of works — the law of Moses or the law of nature — gains absolutely no merit, deserves no reward, and has no basis for boasting before God. Instead, a person subject to the law has a duty to fulfill it. The law imposes an obligation; a person must do what it requires, willingly or unwillingly, simply in order to avoid being condemned. As Paul says elsewhere, *Those who are contemptuous bring damnation upon themselves* (Rom 13:2), because they are culpable in the present age. To believe or not to believe, however, is voluntary. A person cannot be obliged to affirm what is not evidently true, but must be convinced; a believer is persuaded, not commanded. For this reason, belief deserves a reward. Belief is about hope, not sight. **But to one who does not perform works** — addicted to sin and not performing the works commanded by the law — **yet trusts him who justifies the ungodly, such faith is counted as righteousness.** Paul asserts that for a believer who is not observant and does not fulfill the works of the law — a Gentile — faith is counted as righteousness, as it was for Abraham. How, therefore, can the Jews think that through the works of the law they achieve that justification proper to Abraham, when they acknowledge that Abraham was justified not by fulfilling the law but by faith alone? The law is unnecessary, then, when on the basis of faith alone God's judgment justifies one who has broken the law. **According to the purpose of God's grace.** Paul says that God has decreed that with the ending of the law, the grace of God would require only faith for salvation.

So also David speaks of the blessedness of the man whom God accepts and gives righteousness without works! Paul corroborates this particular statement by a prophetic precedent. David calls blessed those whom God decreed would be justified in the divine sight without works or observances but by faith alone. He foretells the blessedness of the time when Christ was born. As the Lord himself says, *Many righteous people and prophets longed to see what you see and to hear what you hear, and they did not hear* (Matt

13:17). ***Blessed are those whose iniquities are forgiven, and whose sins are covered; blessed is the man against whom the Lord will not reckon his sin*** (Ps 32:1-2). Clearly, blessed are those whose wrongdoing is forgiven and whose sins are covered because they believe, without their being required to perform any penitential works. Also blessed is ***the man against whom the Lord will not reckon his sin.*** Whether one says ***to forgive*** or ***to cover*** or ***not to reckon,*** all expressions convey the same thought and meaning: sins are either retained or forgiven in only one way. . . .

David distinguished three stages of sin, each having to do with a different kind of transgression: the first was wrongdoing or rebellion, by not acknowledging the creator; the second consisted of grave sins of action; and the third encompassed light sins. By these three categories, he referred to the whole realm of sin. All these, however, are wiped out in Baptism. How, though, could the text be referring to penitents when it says, ***Blessed are they whose sins are covered*** (Ps 32:1), since everyone knows that penitents attain remission of their sins through labor and lament? How could the saying, ***Blessed is the one against whom the Lord will not count sins*** (Ps 32:2), refer to martyrdom, since the glory of martyrdom is obviously attained by sufferings and afflictions? The prophet, foreseeing the blessed time of the Savior's coming, calls those persons ***blessed*** whose sins are ***forgiven*** and ***covered*** and ***not counted,*** by Baptism without any effort or labor on their part. Because of the abundance that came with the *fullness of time* (Gal 4:4) and because more grace was given to the apostles than to the prophets, the Apostle testifies to our receiving even greater things through the gift of Baptism. He proclaims that we not only receive the remission of sins but are justified and become children of God, so that this **blessedness** will include perfect glory and security.

(2) Origen on verses 1-2

Now that he has distinguished two laws, of works and of faith, and asserted that boasting was excluded not by the law of works but by the law of faith, Paul then goes on to state that a person can be justified without the works of the law. . . . Then, speaking of Abraham and showing that he was justified by faith rather than by works, . . . Paul nonetheless affirmed that he still accomplished those works which usually accompany a faith worthy of justification. . . . Through this whole passage he seems to propose two types of righteousness, one from works, the other from faith. . . . But we affirm that the one who is justified by works has a basis for boasting not only in the sight of humans . . . but also in the presence of . . . every rational being that is more excellent than creatures of flesh and blood. Someone who is perfect in goodness would be justified in the sight of God by the faith which God counts for righteousness, and justified in the opinion of humans and higher rational beings by the performance of works. Their fellows declare them justified by their deeds, for works themselves are incapable of justifying a person in any other way than in the eyes of others. . . .

Two forms of righteousness are distinguished: the one from faith justifies before God; the one from works justifies before other rational beings. This is fulfilled in the words *The righteous will live by faith* (Hab 2:4). You can also adapt the following statement to these two types: *The secret things belong to the Lord our God, but the revealed things belong to us and to our children* (Deut 29:29). You might say that the *secret things* visible to the Lord God refer to the faith which justifies before God, and that the *revealed things* visible to humans and other rational beings indicate works that justify. Yet do not think that the faith which God counts for righteousness can exist in a person alongside injustice or any evil. For if *everyone who believes that Jesus is the Christ has been born of God* (1 John 5:1), and if *those who are born of God do not sin* (1 John 5:18), then obviously a person who believes that Jesus is the Christ does not sin, and the person who sins does not believe.

(3) John Chrysostom on verses 1-2

Paul displays his exceptional gifts by turning the objection on its head and showing that the traits characteristic of salvation through works — boasting and speaking boldly — are actually more proper to faith. For people who brag about deeds cite their own works as a model. In contrast, those who take pride in their faith in God offer a better reason for boasting, since they glorify and praise the Lord rather than themselves. For when, through their faith in God, they discover things that cannot be known through the physical world, they show their true love for God and clearly proclaim God's power. The noble soul, the lofty mind, and the lover of true wisdom all share this attribute. While anyone might avoid stealing or killing, to believe that God can accomplish what appears impossible requires an exceptional soul, one that is deeply attached to God; it is a sign of genuine love. The person who fulfills the commandments honors God, but the person who lives virtuously through faith glorifies God even more. The person who fulfills the commandments simply obeys God; the one who has faith in God trusts the word of someone else about God, glorifies God by accepting this testimony, and marvels at God even more than a person who only does good works. For this reason, the person who fulfills the commandments boasts of having done something right, whereas the person who has faith glorifies God and belongs entirely to God, since the believer brags by recounting God's great deeds that redound to the divine glory.

(4) Augustine on verses 1-3

For if Abraham was justified by works, he has glory, but not before God. May God protect us from such boasting. Let us attend instead to, *Let whoever boasts, boast of the Lord* (1 Cor 1:31). Many indeed are proud of their accomplishments. You will find many pagans refusing to become Christians because they are satisfied that they live good lives. "What is important is living a good life," they say; "what is Christ going to teach me? To live well? I live a good life already. Why do I need Christ? I do not murder, steal, or plunder. I do not long for another person's property or get involved in adultery. Point out my faults; then you will make me a Christian." Such a person **has glory, but not before God.** This is not the way our father Abraham acted. This word of Scripture is meant to draw our attention to the grounds for his boasting. Because we recognize and our faith affirms that the holy patriarch was pleasing to God, we know and we assert that he does have grounds for praise from God. The Apostle says that we are certain, for it is clearly evident that Abraham has glory before God. But **if Abraham was justified by works, he has glory, but not before God.** Since he does have glory before God, it necessarily follows that he was justified but not by works. How then was Abraham justified, if not by works? It follows, and Paul shows how: **What does the scripture say?** How does the Scripture say that Abraham was justified? *Abraham believed God, and it was counted for him as righteousness.* Abraham, therefore, was justified by faith.

(5) Theodoret on verse 2

Performing good deeds brings honor to those who do them but does not display God's benevolence toward humanity. Faith makes both obvious, God's love for humanity and the corresponding love of one who believes in the covenant with God. Believers proclaim as Lord the one who is the source of their faith.

(6) Augustine on verses 3-5

Who then are the blessed? Not those God finds free of sin, since God finds sin in everyone. *Since all have sinned and fall short of the glory of God* (Rom 3:23). If sins are found in everyone, the blessed are only those whose sins have been forgiven. This was the Apostle's point in saying: *Abraham believed God, and it was counted for him as righteousness.* **Now to one who** works — that is, one who relies on works and claims that the grace of faith is given in return for those works — **wages are not counted as a gift but as something due.** What then could this mean but that our wages would be called grace? But grace is given freely. What does given freely mean? That it is a gift. You did nothing good and yet your sins were forgiven. Take a close look at your works; you will find all of them evil. If God gave you what was owed for those works, God would condemn you. *The wages of sin is death* (Rom 6:23). What do evil works deserve but condemnation? What do good works deserve? The kingdom of heaven. Your works, however, were judged evil; if you received what you have coming, you would be punished. Yet God does not repay the punishment you deserve; instead God gives you a grace you did not earn. Vengeance was due; indulgence was given. Your faithfulness, therefore, begins through a gratuitous gift. Once that faith is joined to hope and love, it begins to do well. You must not begin at that point to boast and congratulate yourself. Remember who set you on this path; remember that even if your feet were strong and swift, you were already straying; remember that even if you were weak and lying half-dead on the road, you were lifted up onto the pack animal and taken to the inn (Luke 10:33-34). **Now to one who works**, he says, **wages are not counted as a gift but as something due.** If you want to break free of grace, then boast of what you deserve. God, however, sees what is in you and knows what each person deserves. **But to one without works**, he says. Think about some evil sinner, **one without works**. What then? **Who trusts God who justifies the ungodly**. Such people are evil because they do not act well. Even their works that seem to be good cannot be recognized as such because they act without faith. **To one who trusts God who justifies the ungodly, such faith is counted as righteousness. So also David speaks of the blessedness of those to whom God grants righteousness apart from works**. What kind of righteousness, then? The righteousness of faith: although no good works go before it, good works follow from it.

(7) Augustine on verse 4

Paul contrasts the way one human being rewards another to the way God rewards. God gave gratuitously, bestowing grace on sinners so that through faith they would then live justly and do good works. Once we have received grace, therefore, we must not claim our good deeds for ourselves but attribute them to God, who made us righteous through grace before we did anything good. If God had preferred to give the reward we deserved, we would have been punished as sinners.

(8) Augustine on verse 5

This is the work of God, that you believe in him whom God has sent (John 6:29). He did not say, that you trust him or that you believe him but *that you believe in him*. We have heard the prophets speaking; we trust them but we do not believe in them. We have heard the apostles preaching; we trust their preaching but we do not believe in them. We do not believe in Paul but we do believe Paul. When some wanted to place their hope in him and — in this sense — believe in him, he rebuked them. They were not supposed to believe in him but with him to believe in Christ. *Was Paul crucified for you? Or were you baptized in the name of Paul?* (1 Cor 1:13). Along with the apostles and our holy teachers, we ourselves who are unworthy to be compared to them often say: "Trust me." We would never dare to say, "Believe in me." Everyone says, "Trust me." Nobody says, "Believe in me," or at least no one in their right mind. In whom, then, should we believe? Paul answers clearly: **to the one who trusts in him who justifies the ungodly, such faith is counted as righteousness**. Paul, however, does not justify the ungodly. When you trust in the one who does, **your faith is counted as righteousness**. You believe in **him who justifies the ungodly**. But you do not trust in Paul because he does not justify the ungodly. Not Paul, not Elijah, not any angel, but the Just of the just, the Holy of the holy, the one of whom is said, *that he is just and justifies anyone who has faith* (Rom 3:26). You might be called just, but no one would say that you justify anyone. What does it mean to justify: to make just. Just as to vivify is to make alive, and to save is to make safe. Who then makes just? The one who came without sin. Who is this just one? The one who makes just; not one who is made just here but one who comes here already just. This is the one in whom we believe; and by believing in him, we perform the work of God. *This, indeed, is the work of God* (John 6:29), **to believe in him who justifies the ungodly**.

(9) Origen on verses 6-8

So also David speaks of the blessedness of the man to whom God grants righteousness apart from works: *Blessed are those whose iniquities are forgiven, and whose sins are covered; blessed is the man against whom the Lord will not count sins.* From these words one can comprehend how righteousness might be assigned to a person apart from works. Here I see that the Apostle understood that a person who had reached the age of discerning right from wrong must become either righteousness or unrighteousness. At that age, every soul must be one or the other; to be free of evil certainly entails possessing goodness. Any soul *whose iniquities are forgiven, and whose sins are covered,* and *against whom God does not count sins,* is not evil and thus must be good. On the basis of *the forgiveness of iniquities, the covering of sins,* and the Lord's *not counting sins,* the Apostle says that righteousness is attributed to a person — even one who has still done no righteous works — solely on the basis of believing in the one who justifies the impious. The beginning of God's process of justification is the faith which believes in the one who justifies. This faith, once the person has been justified, clings to the soil of the soul like a root which has received rain. Once it has been cultivated by the law of God, branches grow from it and bear the fruit of good works. For the root of righteousness does not come from works; rather, works grow as fruit from the root of righteousness, from that root of righteousness by which God makes a person acceptable even without works. . . .

I am also struck by the order of what he says: first, *Blessed are those whose iniquities are forgiven*; second, *whose sins are covered*; and third, *against whom the Lord will not count sins.* This sequence seems applicable to an individual human soul. The beginning of a soul's conversion is turning away from evil, whereby it becomes worthy of the forgiveness of sins. Once the soul has begun to do good, it covers over each of its prior evil deeds with new good deeds and produces good works more numerous than the preceding evil ones; thus, the soul is said to cover its sins. When it reaches perfection, when every wicked root has been thoroughly eradicated and no trace of evil can be found in it, then the summit of perfect blessedness is promised to the soul against whom the Lord can reckon no sin.

(10) Anonymous on verse 7

Blessed are those whose iniquities are forgiven, and whose sins are covered. **The forgiving of iniquities** can be understood as happening in Baptism, and **the covering of sins** through penance.

Romans 4:9-12

9Is this blessing pronounced only upon the circumcised, or also upon the uncircumcised? We say that faith was reckoned to Abraham as righteousness. 10How then was it reckoned to him? Was it before or after he had been circumcised? It was not after, but before he was circumcised. 11He received circumcision as a sign or seal of the righ-

teousness which he had by faith while he was still uncircumcised. The purpose was to make him the father of all who believe without being circumcised and who thus have righteousness reckoned to them, 12and likewise the father of the circumcised who are not merely circumcised but also follow the example of the faith which our father Abraham had before he was circumcised.

(1) Ambrosiaster on verses 9-12

Has this **blessing** been granted only to the children of Abraham or to the Gentiles as well? If Gentiles were not denied access to the law and to the promise of Abraham at an earlier time, then why should these people be hindered from coming to grace at the time of Christ, once God had fully invited them? **We say** — that is, we express the meaning of the law — **faith was counted as righteousness for Abraham.** He addresses the question at its foundation, to prevent quibbling and subterfuge. Someone blocked at the outset will have no basis for raising an objection later.

    How then was it counted to him? Was it before or after he had been circumcised? It was not after, but before he was circumcised. He received circumcision as a sign or seal of the righteousness which he had by faith while he was still uncircumcised. The purpose was to make him the father of all who believe without being circumcised and thus have righteousness reckoned to them. Abraham believed in God while he was still uncircumcised. What did he believe? That he was going to have offspring, specifically a son, in whom all the nations would be made righteous through faith without circumcision, just as Abraham was himself justified. He then received circumcision as a sign of this righteousness of faith. Believing that he would have a son, he received a sign of the reality he believed, to indicate the believing for which he was justified. Therefore, circumcision confers no particular status in itself but is only a sign. The children of Abraham were given this sign so they would identify themselves as descendants of that man who had himself received this sign for believing in God. Thus the descendants would emulate their forefather's faith and believe in Jesus, who was promised to Abraham and prefigured in Isaac's birth. All the nations are blessed not in Isaac but in Christ, because *no other name has been given beneath heaven, in which we ought to be saved,* as the Apostle Peter says (Acts 4:12).

    And likewise the father of the circumcised who are not only circumcised but who also follow in the footsteps of that faith which our father Abraham had before he was circumcised. Paul says that Abraham became the first father of the circumcised through believing. This circumcision was of the heart, however, so that he became father not only of those who descend from him but also of those among the Gentiles who believe as he did. He is father of the Jews by the flesh but of all believers by faith.

(2) Origen on verses 9-12

When David speaks of **blessing** in the psalm (Ps 32:1-2), he has in mind not the circumcised but the uncircumcised. . . . Even if faith is counted as righteousness, is it attributed to the just person or to the unjust? Obviously, to the unjust. For how would grace be credited for granting righteousness to a person who is already just? But if the reference is not to the just person, then clearly the psalm refers to someone who was unjust prior to faith. Now if the faith that brings righteousness is credited to the unjust, this person becomes blessed and the Lord does not impute sin but absolves those faults that were prior to faith. Paul then asks: Was Abraham still uncircumcised when faith was credited to him for righteousness or had he already been circumcised? He says therefore, **How then was it imputed to him?** After being justified by faith, he received circumcision as a sign and seal of the faith which he had shown in his uncircumcised state. Faith was attributed to him for righteousness while he was still uncircumcised, so that he would bear the name of father of both peoples, the circumcised and the uncircumcised. Thus he became father of those who believe while still in an uncircumcised state. When he begot Isaac, he was already circumcised and thus became the father of those circumcised according to the flesh on the eighth day. The practice of circumcision on the eighth day began with Isaac. After being made righteous by faith, he received the sign of circumcision as a mark affixed like a seal, the sacrament of those justified by faith. Those who were generated by Abraham after his act of faith and thus belong to him through circumcision form a people, distinct from the others who were made righteous by their faith without circumcision. . . . According to Paul, *when the full complement of the nations comes in, then the whole of Israel will be saved* (Rom 11:25-26). That seal was preserved intact, since those who would be faithful but uncircumcised had not yet arrived. When a people made righteous by their faith without circumcision arose, then that seal and its sign were abolished. For the time during which the seal had been preserved had come to fulfillment. Thus anyone wanting to receive this seal after that time could be told: *if you let yourselves be circumcised, Christ will be of no benefit to you* (Gal 5:2). I think that just as he *redeemed us from the curse of the law by becoming a curse for us* (Gal 3:13), so Christ freed us from the requirement of circumcision by taking circumcision upon himself, for *the law and the prophets were until John* (Luke 16:16).

(3) John Chrysostom on verses 9-12

Addressing the Jews, Paul says that if you do not follow in the footsteps of Abraham's faith, you would not be an offspring of Abraham even if you were circumcised ten thousand times. For Abraham received circumcision so that uncircumcised people would not reject you. Do not, then, require it of them, since it works for your benefit, not theirs. **But,** Paul says, **it is a sign of righteousness.** Even this function of circumcision is for your sake, since it no longer signifies righteousness. You needed a bodily sign in the past but no longer now. Someone may say, "Was it not possible to discern the virtue of Abraham's soul from his faith itself?" It certainly was possible. But you needed the help of this sign to learn about his virtue. Since you did not strive to imitate him and were thus incapable of recognizing his soul's virtue, you were given circumcision as a sensible sign. In this way, you would become accustomed to the bodily sign and, little by little, would be led to appreciate the love of wisdom within the soul. Once you became convinced and committed to the love of wisdom as the greatest honor, then you would be taught to imitate and respect your ancestor Abraham. This was God's plan, not for circumcision alone, but also for the other commands of the law, such as sacrifices, Sabbaths, and festivals.

Since Abraham received circumcision for your sake, listen to what follows. After Paul says that Abraham received circumcision as a sign and a seal, he gives the reason: **In order that he might become the ancestor of the circumcision.** Another reason for his receiving bodily circumcision was to become the ancestor of those who would receive a spiritual circumcision, since bodily circumcision alone gives no one an advantage. Circumcision works as a sign only when the reality which it signifies — faith — is also present. In the absence of faith, this sign has no significance. If the reality which is to be sealed does not exist, what does the circumcision signify or seal? It would be like showing me a sealed purse with nothing inside. In the same way, circumcision is ridiculous when a person has no faith. If circumcision is a sign of righteousness and you have no righteousness, then you have a sign of nothing. You received the sign so that you would diligently seek the reality signified by your sign. So, if you fully intended to strive for the reality even without the sign, you would have no need for the sign itself. Circumcision proclaims righteousness in the uncircumcised as well as the circumcised. Therefore, circumcision actually signifies that circumcision itself is unnecessary.

(4) Augustine on verses 9-12

The Apostle says this about Abraham himself: **He received the sign of circumcision as a seal of this righteousness of faith.** He had already believed in his heart, and *it had been reckoned to him as righteousness* (Rom 4:3). Why, then, was he commanded that every one of his male children should be circumcised on the eighth day, a time when they could not yet believe with their hearts and have it credited to them as righteousness? Why else than because the sacrament itself, taken in itself, was of such great value. This was manifest through the action of an angel in the case of Moses' son. As he was being carried by his mother, still uncircumcised, he came into clear and present danger, which required that he be circumcised immediately. Once this was done, he was protected from the danger. In Abraham, the righteousness of faith preceded and circumcision was then added **as a seal of this righteousness of faith.** The case of Cornelius is similar, for spiritual sanctification through the gift of the Holy Spirit came first and the sacrament of regeneration in the baptismal washing followed (Acts 11–12). In the case of Isaac, circumcision was performed as a sign of the righteousness of faith on the eighth day after his birth; he then followed the example of his father's faith. Thus, the sign of righteousness had come first in the infant, and the righteousness itself followed in the growing man. In a similar way, the sacrament of regeneration comes first in baptized infants and, if they later commit themselves to Christian fidelity, then the conversion of heart follows, for which there was an earlier sign in their bodies. Or compare two other cases. The omnipotent goodness of God supplied the effect of the sacrament of Baptism in the robber because it was omitted not by his pride or contempt but by circumstances beyond his control (Luke 23:39-43). So must we believe that the same grace of Almighty God supplies what is missing in infants who die baptized, since their defect arises not from perverse will but from the impotence of their age, when they cannot *believe with their hearts for righteousness or confess with their mouths for salvation* (Rom 10:10). Because they cannot speak for themselves, others speak for them so that the sacrament can be fully celebrated and they be fully consecrated.

(5) Theodoret on verse 12

The purpose was to make him the father of all who believe without being circumcised and who thus have righteousness reckoned to them. Some distinctions are necessary. He shows that the patriarch Abraham is first the father of those who were believers without the mark of circumcision, since he offered the gift of faith to God while he was himself still uncircumcised. Then he was also father of the Jews, who share the rite of circumcision with him. Paul teaches this more clearly in his next statement: **likewise the ancestor of the circumcised who are not only circumcised but who also follow the example of the faith that our father Abraham had before he was circumcised.** If anyone from among the Gentiles without circumcision follows the patriarch's faith, exemplified before his own circumcision, that person will not be excluded from the family of the patriarch. The God of all the nations, who governs all things, will bring together the Gentiles and the Jews to make one people and will offer them both salvation through faith, just as God had earlier selected both to have Abraham as their patriarch. God proclaimed him father of the nations because Abraham possessed righteousness before circumcision, and after that ritual he guided his life by continuing in the path of faith, not by following the Mosaic law. God so arranged that both Jew and Greek would reflect on Abraham and strive to emulate his faith, setting great value neither on circumcision nor its absence. Holy Scripture has declared that neither circumcision nor uncircumcision confers righteousness, only faith. Thus by showing that faith is more venerable and honored than the law, it demonstrates again that the law is of lesser value than the promise to Abraham and that grace takes precedence over the law. The promises made to Abraham, that from his seed would come a blessing to all the nations, rest on faith. And through the Lord Christ the promise has been fulfilled.

Romans 4:13-17

13The promise to Abraham and his descendants, that they should inherit the world, did not come through the law but through the righteousness of faith. 14If it is the adherents of the law who are to be the heirs, faith is null and the promise is void. 15For the law brings wrath, but where there is no law there is no transgression. 16That is why it depends on faith, in order that the promise may rest on grace and be guaranteed to all his descendants — not only to the adherents of the law but also to those who share the faith of Abraham, for he is the father of us all, 17as it is written, *I have made you the father of many nations* **(Gen 17:4) — in the presence of the God in whom he believed, who gives life to the dead and calls into existence the things that do not exist.**

(1) Ambrosiaster on verses 13-17

For the promise that he would inherit the world did not come to Abraham or to his descendants through the law but through the righteousness of faith. Clearly neither the law nor circumcision had yet been given when the promise was made to Abraham and to his offspring — to Christ, who would wash away everyone's sins. For in the Gospel of John, John the Baptist says, *Behold, the Lamb of God, who takes away the sins of the world* (John 1:29). Abraham was made **inheritor of the world**, therefore, not because he had kept the law but in virtue of his faith. **The inheritor of the world** is the inheritor of the earth, which he acquired in his offspring. Moreover, Christ is the inheritor of the Gentiles, as David sings, *I shall give you the Gentiles as your inheritance, and the ends of the earth as your possession* (Ps 2:8). For we shall die in him and live with him. **If it is the adherents of the law who are to be the heirs** — if those who are under the law are heirs because of the **law — faith is null and the promise is void.** If the inheritance comes from the law, the promise made to Abraham on the basis of faith becomes meaningless. The promise, however, was not made through the law; instead, the inheritance comes through the righteousness of faith. The Apostle shows that it is mistaken to hope for the inheritance from the law.

For the law brings wrath. To prove that human beings can neither be justified in God's sight nor the promise fulfilled through the Mosaic law, he says, **the law brings wrath.** The function of the law is to make wrongdoers culpable. Faith, in contrast, is a gift of God's mercy, given to pardon those made guilty through the law. Thus, faith brings joy. Paul is not denigrating the law but is giving precedence to faith: those who could not be saved through the law are saved by the grace of God through faith. Though the law is not wrathful, **it brings wrath** — that is, punishment — on the sinner because it avenges and does not pardon. For wrath is born of sin and grows into punishment. Consequently, Paul wants his readers to abandon the law and take refuge in faith, which pardons sins and brings salvation.

For **where there is no law, neither is there violation.** By being granted forgiveness, the guilty are freed from the power of the law and transgression ceases. Those who had been sinners by violating the law have been justified. The observances of the law have come to an end; observance of Sabbaths, new moons and circumcision, dietary discrimination, expiation for a dead animal, or weasel's blood (Lev 11:29) exists no longer.

For this reason it depends on faith, so that the promise may rest firmly on grace for all his descendants. The promise could not be secure for the whole progeny, for people of all races, unless it was based on faith. Because those who are subject to the law are guilty and the guilty do not secure the promise, this promise had to be based on faith rather than the law. Thus they must be purified through faith, so that they may be made worthy to be called children of God and the promise may be secured. If they call themselves children of God while they remain subject to the law and therefore guilty, then the promise is not secure because only those freed from sin are children of God. If, therefore, those who were under the law had to be rescued from the law in order to become worthy to receive the promise, how much more deserving are those who never had the law. To be cured more quickly from their wounds, they must avoid subjecting themselves to the law.

Not only to the adherent of the law but also to him who shares the faith of Abraham. As he has said previously, **to all the descendants**, consisting both of Jews — coming **from the law** — and of Gentiles — following **the faith of Abraham** which he exercised as a Gentile and which made him righteous. For Abraham came to faith without the law and is thereby strongly identified with the Gentiles. The promise is thus secured for all those who believe in the God in whom Abraham placed his faith.

For he is the father of all of us, as it is written, *I have made you the father of many nations.* By using this argument from the law, Paul confirms that Abraham is the father of all — of all who believe — and that the promise is secured by abandoning the law in favor of faith. Those subject to the law are subject to sin, because all have sinned; yet the kingdom of heaven is promised not to sinners but to the righteous. No one can receive grace, moreover, while remaining under the law, as Paul says to the Galatians: *You who want to be justified by the law have cut yourselves off from Christ; you have fallen away from grace* (Gal 5:4). **In the presence of God in whom you believed.** To show that one God is Lord of all, Paul says to the Gentiles that Abraham believed in and was justified in the sight of the same God in whom the Gentiles also believe for justification. Consequently, faith is not different for Jew and Greek. Once the difference between circumcised and uncircumcised has been set aside, they become one in Christ, because Abraham was still uncircumcised when he believed and was justified.

Who gives life to the dead and calls the things that are not as though they did exist. Paul summons the Gentiles to the faith of Abraham, who was still uncircumcised and yet was brought back to life along with his wife, when he believed in that God whose fidelity is now being proclaimed in Christ. For although they were enfeebled by advanced age, they took on new life. Abraham did not doubt that he would have a son by Sarah, whom he knew had been barren and unable to conceive. They did not give a thought to uncircumcision or circumcision but were resolute in their faith, untroubled because they trusted the God who gives life to the dead and who alone has power to make things that do not exist spring forth into being at once by a divine command. Although not yet a father, Abraham was called the father of many nations and confidently placed his trust in God's power. Then, so that the Father of Christ might be recognized as the same God Abraham had believed, this same sign was given to Zechariah and Elizabeth.[1] When the coming of Christ was imminent, the same promise given to Abraham and Sarah was once again realized in the world. For the signal promise was that bodies already dead with age would bring forth John in the same way Isaac had been born.

(2) Origen on verse 15

Before we provide a fuller explanation, let us respond briefly to those objections that heretics customarily raise about this passage. For they say: "Notice how the Apostle says that **the law of Moses brings wrath,**" and "**Where that law will not be found, neither will there be violation.**" . . . How will they deal with those who committed violations prior to

---

1. That is, that they would have a child in old age.

the law of Moses? If before the time of Moses no one was a transgressor, then no one would have been condemned or punished. How then will they explain the inhabitants of Sodom? What about those who were condemned in the flood? What about Cain? What about Adam himself? What will they say about Eve, of whom the Apostle said: *The woman was deceived and became a transgressor* (1 Tim 2:14)? If violations can occur only against the law of Moses, on what grounds does the Apostle call Adam and Eve transgressors?

As we have often said in our previous comments, in this letter the Apostle refers to different laws. Sometimes he speaks about the law of Moses; other times he refers to the law of faith, as when he says: *Where is your boasting? It is excluded, not through the law of works, but through the law of faith* (Rom 3:27). He refers to still other laws, for example: *I delight in the law of God in my inmost self, but I see in my members another law resisting the law of my mind, making me captive to the law of sin* (Rom 7:22-23). He moves from one law to another so easily that even a careful and diligent reader can barely follow and grasp his intention. Therefore, we must see whether that law which the Apostle says brings wrath might be the one in our members making us captive to the law of sin. It certainly brings down wrath upon the person made captive to the law of sin. No violations can occur in the absence of some law, and those subject to that law will definitely not become **heirs.**

Now if someone wants to propose the law of Moses as the one that brings wrath, this could be supported by its prescription that a sinner be immediately stoned or burned to death, or its enumeration of other penalties for sinners. In these instances, the wrath to which the Apostle refers seems to be the punishment itself, which is inflicted on the sinner according to the law. The same holds for the term **violation.** In this passage the Apostle refers not to every violation in general, but only to an offense by someone subject to the law. Thus the sin of a person who actually lived under the prohibitions of the law is shown to be more serious than that of a person who was not warned by the law.

Note as well that the Apostle did not say: "Where there was law, there was violation." He said: **Where there is no law, neither is there violation.** Here he shows that violation is impossible in the absence of law, not that the very presence of law produces all sorts of transgressions. For a law can exist without violations, but violations cannot occur where no law is in force. Apply this to the law of Moses: it does not follow that everyone who lived under the Mosaic law thereby became its violator, since that would implicate the prophets and all the righteous. A response might be that all the righteous and prophets lived not under the law but under faith, while sinners and the unrighteous were bound by the chains of the law.... Whether the law in question is that of Moses or the one in our members which brings wrath, it remains that those who are subject to that law cannot be **heirs.** The inheritance belongs only to those who are under the law of faith, the faith by which Abraham was justified.

(3) Origen on verses 16-17

Previously Paul posited a distinction between a wage and a grace: a wage is something owed; a grace is something not owed but bestowed gratuitously. In the present passage he intends to show that God gives the promised inheritance as a grace rather than as something owed. Therefore, he says that the inheritance is bestowed by God on those who believe and as a gift for faith, not because of a debt owing as a wage. For example, our very existence cannot be understood as a reward for something that we have done; our being is a gift from God and a grace of the creator who willed us to exist. Similarly, if we receive the inheritance of the promises of God, this will be by divine grace, not as reward for any deed or as payment of some debt.

Perhaps something coming from faith would not seem to be freely given, since a person might first have to offer faith and thereby merit grace from God. To answer this question, one should attend to the other places where the Apostle addresses the matter. In the passage where he lists the gifts of the Spirit, which he says are given to believers according to the measure of their faith, he also states that the gift of faith is itself bestowed by the Holy Spirit. After listing several other gifts, he says, *to another is given faith in the same Spirit* (1 Cor 12:9), thus showing that faith itself is given through grace. Elsewhere the Apostle teaches the same thing, *for God has given you not only the grace to believe in Christ, but also to suffer for him* (Phil 1:29). The same point is made in the Gospels when the apostles realize that the faith which humans offer must be completed by the addition of that faith which is given by God. They say to the Savior, *Increase our faith* (Luke 17:5). All this clearly confirms what the Apostle says in this passage: **For this reason it depends on faith, in order that the promise may rest firmly on grace.** Even that faith by which we appear to believe in God is itself confirmed in us by a gift of grace. . . .

In the next verse he adds: **Who gives life to the dead and calls to things that do not exist in the same way as to those that do.** Here we understand **the dead** as referring to the sin of the soul, since, as is said, *the soul that sins shall die* (Ezek 18:4). When the body dies, the senses perish and the body no longer sees, hears, smells, tastes, or touches. In the same way, those who have lost the spiritual senses in the soul can no longer see God, or hear the words of God, or smell the sweet odor of Christ (2 Cor 2:15), or taste the true goodness of God (Heb 6:5), or touch the word of life (1 John 1:1). Such people are rightly called "dead." At his coming, Christ found us in this condition, but he has brought us to life through his grace. . . .

Let us investigate what he means by **and calls to things that do not exist in the same way as to those that do.** We have often observed in other places that God alone says, *I am who I am* (Exod 3:14). God is that one reality which always exists. Anyone who adheres to that which truly is becomes one spirit with God (1 Cor 6:17), and thus can be said to exist through the one who always exists. But the person who is far from God can neither participate in God nor even be considered existing, just as we Gentiles did not exist before we came *to a knowledge of the divine truth* (1 Tim 2:4). This is why it is said of God that he **calls to things that do not exist in the same way as to those that do.** Among those who exist, that is, who participate in the one who is, we include Abraham, Isaac, Jacob, and the other saints. And so because the Gentiles enter into the faith of Abraham by believing, the Apostle rightly proclaims that God has **and calls to things that do not exist in the same way as to those that do.**

Romans 4:18-25

18In hope he believed against hope, that he should become the father of many nations; as he had been told, *So shall your descendants be* (Gen 15:5). 19He did not weaken in faith when he considered his own body, which was as good as dead because he was about a hundred years old, or when he considered the barrenness of Sarah's womb. 20No distrust made him waver concerning the promise of God, but he grew strong in his faith as he gave glory to God, 21fully convinced that God was able to do what he had promised. 22That is why his faith *was reckoned to him as righteousness* (Gen 15:6). 23But the words, *it was reckoned to him*, were written not for his sake alone, 24but for ours also. It will be reckoned to us who believe in him that raised from the dead Jesus our Lord, 25who was put to death for our trespasses and raised for our justification.

(1) Ambrosiaster on verses 18-25

Hoping against hope. The matter is clear. Although Abraham had no hope of begetting a child, he believed in God; he had faith against hope that he would beget, knowing that God can do everything. **He believed that he would become the father of many nations, according to what was said, *So shall your descendants be.*** This is from Genesis (15:5). Showing him the stars of heaven, God said, *So shall your descendants be.* He believed and was made righteous, for he believed what everyone considers impossible. Nature cannot make old people become parents and assure them that their progeny will multiply until they cannot be counted. Faith is precious because, contrary to what it sees and expects, it believes that the improbable will actually happen. Faith takes comfort in hope because God makes the promise and can be trusted to accomplish more than human weakness can comprehend.

He did not weaken in faith, he did not consider his own body, which was as good as dead, because he was about a hundred years old, and Sarah's dead womb. No distrust made him waver concerning the promise of God, but he grew strong in his faith as he gave glory to God, fully convinced that God was able to do what he had promised. Therefore, his faith *was reckoned to him as righteousness.* Paul asserts that Abraham deserved praise; though he knew his own weakness, he strengthened it by faith that through God's power he could accomplish what was impossible according to the laws of the bodily world. He deserved more from God because he believed in God despite his own knowledge. He did not doubt that God, as God, could do what he knew everyone considered impossible. For he firmly judged that God is beyond human understanding and that the creation cannot set limits on its creator. The believer, therefore, deserves a reward from God for recognizing that the creator can accomplish more than a creature can comprehend. Such belief would not be particularly praiseworthy if it were just common sense; the widespread lack of faith, however, makes the faith of believers precious in God's sight. Paul, therefore, exhorts the Gentiles to this firmness of faith: that by trusting in the precedent of Abraham, they would embrace the promise and grace of God without wavering. Affirming what the world considers incredible and foolish wins greater praise for the believer. Indeed, the more ridiculous a belief is generally considered, the more honor does it bring to the believer. Yet, to believe something so improbable would indeed be foolish were it assumed to happen without God's intervention. Abraham's faith outshines the faith of others and is more praiseworthy than that of others because it was not in response to miraculous signs.

The universe is governed by an unchanging power and system of laws; God rules it in a precisely determined way. Human beings, however, because of their affection for corporeal reality, see only its rational structure and neglect God, its creator. To destroy error and to demonstrate divine dominion over all things, God willed that it be proclaimed that God could do and actually had done what the natural world could not. Those who believed this preaching would be set apart and saved as subjects of God's reign; those who ignored God and were puffed up with worldly reasoning would be damned.

But the words *it was counted for him,* **were written not for his sake alone, but for ours also. It will be counted for us who believe in him who raised from the dead Jesus our Lord, who was handed over because of our trespasses and rose for our justification.** Paul says that in Abraham a model was given to Jews and Gentiles, so that following his example we might believe in God and Christ and the Holy Spirit, and that righteousness might be reckoned to us. Even though what we believe now is different, nonetheless faith receives the same gift as Abraham. We receive what we believe: believing that Christ is the Son of God, we are adopted as God's children. Being acknowledged as the children of God is the greatest gift God could give to believers; unbelievers are disinherited. For we are called the children of God, but they do not deserve even to be called servants. In keeping with the infinite divine generosity, the gift which God has given to those who love God is measured not by what these humans themselves deserve to receive but by what is befitting for the divine majesty to grant. In gift-giving, the status of the giver takes precedence over that of the recipient. Thus, great praise is due to God for the wondrous gifts bestowed through Christ upon the lowly. He allowed himself to be put to death for our sake, so that by granting us forgiveness, he might rescue us from the second death, the punishment of hell. He rose from the dead so that, in the celebration of his triumph in conquering death, he might grant us the grace of justification and make us worthy to be called children of God.

Those who were baptized before Christ's passion received only the forgiveness of sins. Out of envy, Satan then killed the Savior. But after the resurrection, those baptized both before and after were all justified through that confession of faith made when they were baptized, faith in the Trinity. They received the Holy Spirit, who is the sign for believers that they are children of God. To bring our righteousness to its fullness, the risen Christ gave his precepts the power to increase the merits of those who zealously obey them. Through the faith which makes us righteous, we can escape the power of death, attain glory, and shine brilliantly in the kingdom of God. Though death had earlier ruled because of sin, it was conquered by the passion of the Savior and now does not dare lay hold of those he has justified.

(2) Origen on verse 18

Consider: if **Abraham trusted in hope beyond all hope**, do not the children of the faith of Abraham also **trust in hope beyond all hope** concerning everything they believe, either in the resurrection of the dead or the inheritance of the kingdom of the heavens or the kingdom of God. For human nature, these things are indeed against hope, but because of the divine power and God's faithful promises, such things are within the hope of those who have hope because they believe. To believe is to trust in hope, and on this account *faith, hope, love abide* (1 Cor 13:13). I think faith indicates the beginning, hope the progress, and love the fulfillment.

(3) Augustine on verses 20-21

God promised to Abraham the faith of the nations in his seed, saying, *I have made you the father of a multitude of nations* (Gen 17:5). Thus the Apostle says, **For this reason it depends on faith, in order that the promise may rest firmly on grace for all his descendants.** God promised that this would be accomplished by divine predestination, not by the power of our willing. God promised what God was going to accomplish, not what humans would achieve. Even when humans perform the good works required for the service of God, God causes them to fulfill the divine commands; humans do not move God to accomplish what God has promised. Otherwise, the fulfillment of God's promises would depend on human rather than divine power, and humans would actually deliver what God had promised to Abraham. That, however, is not what Abraham believed: **he grew strong in faith as he gave glory to God, being fully convinced that God was able to do what God had promised.** Paul did not say that God was able to predict or able to foresee. God could, of course, predict or foreknow someone else's achievements. Instead, Paul said **that God was able actually to do** and thus affirmed that the accomplishment would be God's rather than another's.

(4) John Chrysostom on verse 20

God did not offer a proof or work a sign. Rather, these were bare words, promising what nature could not deliver. Nevertheless, Paul says, **he did not waver.** Not, "he did not disbelieve," but **he did not waver**, that is, he did not doubt even though great obstacles lay in the way of the promise. So we learn that even if God were to make ten thousand impossible promises, when someone who hears them rejects them, that arises not from the weakness of physical nature but from the folly of the person who does not believe them. **He grew strong in faith.** Notice Paul's wisdom. Since he is comparing those who do works and those who believe, he shows that the believer actually performs more works and needs greater power and strength. The believer undertakes no ordinary labor. Because his opponents were disparaging faith as not requiring much effort, Paul disputes this very point. He acknowledges that the person who succeeds in temperance or some other such virtue does need strength, but the one who exercises faith needs even greater strength. The person who works at temperance needs strength to get rid of the mental temptations to intemperance; the person who shows faith also needs a strong soul to expel thoughts of disbelief. How did Abraham become so strong? Paul says that unless he had relied on faith rather than reason, he would have fallen. So how did he succeed at faith? Paul says, **He gave glory to God.**

(5) Origen on verses 23-24

Let us examine why Abraham's faith has been described as belief in the resurrection of the Lord. Did Abraham believe in God as raising the Lord Jesus from the dead, even though Jesus had not yet been raised from the dead? I want to consider what Paul meant when he promised that just as faith was reckoned as righteousness to Abraham as a believer, so too will it be reckoned to us who believe in the God who raised our Lord Jesus from the dead. In my own limited intelligence, I suggest that for God to have raised our Lord Jesus from the dead was a much more praiseworthy and magnificent act than to have made the heaven and the earth, to have created the angels and established the heavenly powers. Creation involved making something that did not yet exist, which had not been ruined; resurrection meant reconstructing what had perished, restoring what had been destroyed. The one was accomplished by a decree, the other by suffering. Yet the figure and image of this great and magnificent mystery had already been realized in the faith of Abraham. He was commanded to sacrifice his only son, but he believed that God was able to raise him from the dead. He even believed not only that this would happen for Isaac, but that the full reality of this mystery would be accomplished in his promised offspring, Christ. This is the reason he even rejoiced in offering his only son; he realized that this action was not the destruction of his entire progeny but the restoration of the world and even the revival of the whole creation, which was renewed through the resurrection of the Lord. This was what the Lord meant in saying of him: *Your father Abraham rejoiced to see my day, and he saw it and was glad* (John 8:56). The faith of Abraham, therefore, can be reasonably compared to the faith of those who believe that God has raised the Lord Jesus: he believed that it would be, we believe that it has been accomplished.

(6) Augustine on verse 25

Our Lord Jesus Christ, as the Apostle says, **died for our offenses and rose for our justification.** As we are sown through his death, so do we begin to grow through his resurrection. The end of our life is symbolized by his death. Listen to what the Apostle says: *We were buried with him by Baptism into death, so that as Christ rose from the dead, so we might walk in newness of life* (Rom 6:4). Christ went up on the cross without any sin; he had nothing of his own to set right on the cross. We are the ones set right on his cross; there we put all the evil we have amassed, so that we may be justified by his resurrection. Thus we distinguish: **he was handed over for our offenses, and rose for our justification.** He did not say, handed over for our justification and rose for our offenses. His being handed over indicates the offense; his resurrection expresses the justice. He died to sin and rose to righteousness.

Romans 5

In the first part of chapter 5, Paul encouraged his readers to stand fast and even rejoice in adversity, with the assurance that God was bringing them to salvation in Christ. The divine goodness is evident in Christ's dying to make sinners righteous. Augustine pointed out that God was already loving humans when they were still sinful and acted to reconcile them.

This section includes the statement which Augustine made central to this theology: that the love by which the Christian loves God was itself the gift of divine love, the operation of the Holy Spirit within the human heart. Origen had noticed this interpretation but had not exploited it.

Beginning at verse 12, Paul turned to a complex comparison of Adam and Christ. The commentators had to explain not only Adam's negative influence on his progeny but also Christ's greater effect in bringing them to salvation. All affirmed that Adam's sin had brought mortality, which weakened humanity and resulted in many, if not all, following him into sin and guilt. On the basis of the Latin translation of Rom 5:12 — "through one man sin entered into the world and through sin death, and thus it spread to all people because all sinned" — Augustine alone argued that all humans were present in and sinned together in Adam. All the commentators worked to explain how the personal sins of his descendants were like or unlike those of Adam — a task complicated by different ancient versions of the key text of Rom 5:14 — and how Christ's saving action was more influential than Adam's failure. In Origen's interpretation, Adam and Christ had parallel influences: through generation and regeneration, and through opposite forms of education. Ambrosiaster explained that not everyone imitated Adam's particular kind of sin but that Christ forgave other sins and opened the door to heaven, shut because of Adam's sin. Augustine recognized that Christ had a greater effect than Adam only on the saved; he conceded that most sins are not forgiven and that the majority of humans are condemned. Chrysostom explained that Paul was primarily interested in Christ's power to bring life to others and that he had not really explained the deadly effects of Adam's sin in this part of his letter.

Romans 5:1-5

1Therefore, since we are justified by faith, we have peace with God through our Lord Jesus Christ. 2Through him we have obtained access by faith to this grace in which we stand; and we rejoice in our hope of sharing in the glory of God. 3More than that, we

rejoice in our sufferings, knowing that suffering produces endurance, and ₄endurance produces character, and character produces hope, ₅and hope does not disappoint us, because God's love has been poured into our hearts through the Holy Spirit which has been given to us.

(1) Ambrosiaster on verses 1-5

Therefore, since we are justified by faith, we have peace with God through our Lord Jesus Christ. Faith, not the law, brings a person to peace with God. Faith reconciles us to God by removing the sins which made us enemies of God. We have peace with God through the Lord Jesus, since he bestows the grace of faith. Now faith is greater than law because the law is about our actions while faith is about God's. While the law is responsible for discipline in the present time, faith is concerned with everlasting salvation.

Through whom we have obtained access by faith to this grace in which we now stand; and we boast of our hope in the glory of God. Through Christ we have access to the grace of God. The mediator between God and man lifted us up by his teaching, made us hope in God's grace, and enabled us to stand in faith. Formerly we were laid low, but now we are upright; once we believe, we rise up and exult in hope of the glory which he promised us.

And not only that, but we also boast in our sufferings. Paul teaches that we should exult even in our sufferings because through them we gain entrance to the kingdom of God. When suffering is added to hope, our reward grows. Suffering proves that hope is steadfast and thus shows that we deserve to be crowned. Hence the Lord says, *Blessed are you when people persecute you and utter all kinds of evil against you for the sake of God's righteousness. Rejoice and be glad, for your reward is great in heaven* (Matt 5:11-12). To despise present goods and enticements, and not to yield to adversity in hope of future realities win great merit before God. The more one believes in the good to be attained, the more steadfast will one prove in suffering. Thus should we boast in suffering.

Knowing that suffering produces endurance. Suffering produces endurance when it repulses weakness or doubt. **And endurance wins approval.** Clearly, if endurance is as strong as we have said, it will appear as a firm approval. **And approval gives hope.** The person who has been tried has hope and is acknowledged as worthy of reward in the kingdom of God.

And hope does not disappoint us, because God's love has been poured into our hearts through the Holy Spirit that has been given to us. Hope does not disappoint us when unbelievers consider us foolish and stupid for believing things which the culture considers impossible. We have within ourselves the pledge of the love of God through the Holy Spirit who is given to us. The Holy Spirit, who is given to the apostles and to us, proves that God's promise is trustworthy. The Spirit supplied the variety of languages by which uneducated people could speak in such a way to confirm the hope placed in God (Acts 2:3-11), and thus assure us of God's love for us. Since people cannot deceive those they love, we were made secure in the promise, both because of God who made the promise and because God made it to those whom God loves.

(2) Origen on verse 1

May we who have been **justified by faith have peace with God through our Lord Jesus Christ.** Let us enjoy that peace in which the flesh does not oppose the spirit, and the law in our members does not resist the law of God. May conflict cease within us. Let us all speak as internally unified and so be prudent; may no strife be found within our selves or among us. Then we shall enjoy peace with God through our Lord Jesus Christ. This must be clearly understood: one who is malicious can never be at peace. A person constantly planning to harm a neighbor and always on the lookout for opportunities to hurt others never rests in peace.

If you asked me how the just person can have peace while attacked by the devil and assaulted by temptations, I would reply that such a person really is at peace, more than all others. Notice how precisely the Apostle expresses himself. He does not say: "After we have been justified by faith, may we have peace." He seems to pause after speaking of our justification and then he adds: **we have peace with God**, knowing that war against the devil assures peace with God. We enter more fully into the peace of God when we struggle persistently against the devil and contend against the failings of the flesh.

(3) Augustine on verses 1-2

Therefore, since we are justified by faith, we have peace with God through our Lord Jesus Christ, through whom we have obtained access to this grace in which we now stand; and we boast of our hope of the glory of God. To add a few words of the Apostle to those of the psalm which we are considering together,[1] dear friends, is indeed delightful. Let us see how they fit together. **Since we are justified by faith, we have peace with God.** *Righteousness and peace will kiss each other* (Ps 85:10). **Through our Lord Jesus Christ.** *Truth has sprung up from the ground* (Ps 85:11). **Through whom we have obtained access to this grace in which we now stand; and we boast of our hope of the glory of God.** He did not say, "in our own glory," but **of the glory of God**. He can say this because righteousness has not come forth from us, *but looked down from the sky* (Ps 84:11). Therefore *let whoever boasts, boast* not in self *but in the Lord* (1 Cor 1:31).

(4) John Chrysostom on verses 2-5

If when we were far away God brought us close, how much more likely is God to protect us now that we are near. Notice that Paul always makes these two points: some things come from God and some from us. A great variety of things come from God: God died for our sake, reconciled us, brought us near, and gave us grace beyond description. We, however, have brought only faith. For this reason he says, **by faith ... to this grace in which we now stand.** Tell me, what grace? To become worthy of the knowledge of God,

---

1. Augustine is preaching on Psalm 85.

to be delivered from error, to recognize the truth, to attain all the good things which come through Baptism. God has brought us near to receive these gifts. We not only receive remission of sins and deliverance but enjoy thousands of honors as well. God did not stop even there but promised much more as well, the ineffable goods which surpass both mind and reason. . . .

Since we think that the present pains are great, let us consider how great the future reward will be. The gift of God is so great that it includes only pleasant things. Though the quest for external goods entails toil, pain, and suffering, the rewards for such labor are enjoyable. The gift of God is different: the struggles bring no less pleasure than the rewards. In the past, temptations were many, the kingdom was still an object of hope, and fearful things were close at hand while good things were expected in the distant future. This situation unnerved the weak. By saying that we must boast even in suffering, however, Paul bestows the honors even before the rewards. He does not say, "You should boast," but, **we boast**, presenting his own case as encouragement. What he said seems strange and implausible: to exalt while still struggling, hungry, in chains and tortured, maltreated and disrespected. Yet he insists on this by saying that we must brag not only because of the future reward but also because of these present sufferings themselves. These sufferings must be taken as good in and of themselves. Why? Because they encourage patience. Thus Paul says, **let us boast in our sufferings**, and adds a reason, **knowing that suffering produces endurance**. Notice again how Paul loves to construct his arguments, how he turns an objection around into its opposite. Sufferings had made them give up and lose hope in the future. Paul says that precisely because of these sufferings, they must take courage and not despair about what lies ahead.

What then? Does our good lie in hope? Yes, but not hope in humans, which fails and usually embarrasses those who hope, as, for example, when we count on someone who dies or changes his mind about helping us. Such is not the case with us: our hope is sure and unchanging. For the one who promised to help us lives forever, and even though we who enjoy God's help will die, we shall rise again. Indeed, nothing at all can confound us, as it would if we had put our trust rashly in an unsound hope and in vain.

Now that Paul has fully addressed all their doubts, he does not conclude his discourse with considerations of the present life. He knew that the weak seek what is to be had in the present life, even though they will be dissatisfied with it, so he turns to future things. He grounds hope for the future things on the basis of the blessings which they had already received. For someone might say, "What if God does not want to give us these blessings? We all know that God has the necessary power and that God lives forever. But how do we know that God will want to give them?" This we know from the blessings God has already given. To which blessings is he referring? The love which God has shown to us. "What did God do?" someone asks. Gave the Holy Spirit. For this reason, Paul said, **hope does not disappoint us**; he proved this **because God's love has been poured into our hearts**. He did not say, "It has been given," but, **it has been poured into our hearts**, thereby indicating the abundance of the blessings. For God gave the greatest gift: not just earth, sea, and sky but a more noble gift. This gift transformed humans into angels, into children of God, into brothers and sisters of Christ. What is this gift? The Holy Spirit. If

God did not intend to give us great rewards after our labors, God would not have bestowed such great benefits upon us even before we had toiled. God shows us the warmth of divine love by giving not a slight or middling honor but by pouring out the fountain of divine blessings all at once. God did this even before our struggles had begun. So even if you are not really worthy, do not despair; the love of the judge will serve as a mighty advocate for you. So by saying, **hope does not disappoint us,** Paul ascribed everything not to our achievements but to God's love.

(5) Origen on verse 5

I must also consider whether he is saying love is that virtue by which we love God or the one by which God loves us, **poured into our hearts by the Holy Spirit.** The interpretation that understands love as the virtue by which we love God does not need to be proven. Because he said that the love of God has been implanted in our hearts, however, the statement should also be understood as indicating the love by which God loves us. Moreover, he would consider love the supreme and greatest gift of the Holy Spirit, an endowment first received from God which then empowers us to love God, because we are cherished by God. For Paul himself names the Spirit of love (2 Tim 1:7). God is called love (1 John 4:8), and Christ is called the Son of love (Col 1:13). But if the Spirit of charity and the Son of charity and God are all identified as love, then certainly both the Son and the Holy Spirit must be recognized as coming from a single source, the paternal Deity. From this overflowing fullness the profusion of love flows out into the hearts of the saints so that they may share in the divine nature, as the Apostle Peter taught (2 Pet 1:4). Thus through this gift of the Holy Spirit the words of the Lord are fulfilled: *Just as you, Father, are in me, and I am in you, so may these be in us* (John 17:21). Indeed, they have become partakers of the divine nature through the abundance of love given by the Holy Spirit.

(6) Augustine on verse 5

The wicked are hardened to endure evils only to the extent that they desire the present world; the righteous are strengthened for enduring them to the degree that they are filled with the love of God. The desire for the present world originates in the choice of the human will, grows through the enjoyment of pleasure, and is firmly established by the chains of habit. The **love of God,** however, **has been poured into our hearts,** not indeed from ourselves, **but through the Holy Spirit that has been given to us.** The patience of the righteous, therefore, comes from the one who **pours out their love.** When the Apostle was praising this love and exhorting us to it, among its good qualities he named its *bearing all things* (1 Cor 13:7). *Love is generous,* he said (1 Cor 13:4). Then, later, *it endures all things* (1 Cor 13:7). The greater the love of God in the saints, the greater their tolerance of all things, for the sake of what they love. Similarly, the greater the lust for this world in sinners, the more they tolerate for the sake of what they desire. Thus the true patience of the righteous springs from the same source as that love of God which is in them. The false patience of the wicked comes from the same source as their desire for this world.... The human will alone, by this false patience and without any help from God, makes them just as tolerant as they are lustful; the more wicked, the readier to withstand adversity. For those who have true patience, however, the human will is not strong enough unless it is enkindled and assisted from above. The Holy Spirit is the fire which enflames them with that love of unchangeable good, without which they could not bear up under the evils they suffer.

Then when he had said, **God's love has been poured into our hearts**, in order to prevent anyone from thinking that they loved God by their own power, he immediately added, **through the Holy Spirit that has been given to us**. In order for you to love God, then, God dwells in you, and God loves himself from within you; God moves you to loving God, enkindles you, illumines you, arouses you.

(7) Augustine on verse 5

With all our resources and energy, we must oppose teachers who think that we can fulfill the demands of justice, or make any progress toward that goal, without the help of God but by the power of the human will alone. When they are pressed to explain their claim that righteousness can be accomplished without the divine assistance, they must be made to understand that this view is irreligious and unbearable. They must be taught to restrain themselves and never be so rash as to express this thought. They offer two reasons for asserting that human beings can be righteous without divine aid: God created humans with free choice of the will and then gave commandments to teach humans the right way to live. They concede that God provides help by the teaching which removes human ignorance, so that people will know what they ought to seek and to avoid in their actions. Using the free choice with which they are naturally endowed, people should then follow the path God has pointed out. By living chastely, justly, and devoutly, they can make themselves deserving of eternal life.

In contrast, we say that God helps people to do what is right not only by creating humans with free choice and then teaching them how they ought to live but by giving the Holy Spirit. The presence of the Spirit brings into the human soul a love for and delight in the highest, unfailing good, who is God. Thus even now, while they *walk by faith and not yet by sight* (2 Cor 5:7), they are inflamed by this first installment of the gracious gift promised them. They cling to the creator and they burn for a share in God's true light, so that the one who first gave them being might make their existence good. Granted: if the way of truth is hidden, free will is good for nothing but sinning. Still, even when God has revealed what we ought to attempt and accomplish, unless we love and take delight in those actions, we will not undertake and perform them, and we will not live well. That right actions might attract and delight us, however, **God's love has been poured into our hearts** not through the free choices which we make but **through the Holy Spirit who has been given to us**.

Romans 5:6-11

₆While we were still weak, at the right time Christ died for the ungodly. ₇Why, one will hardly die for a righteous man — though perhaps for a good man one will dare even to die. ₈But God shows his love for us in that while we were yet sinners Christ died for us. ₉Since, therefore, we are now justified by his blood, much more shall we be saved by him from the wrath of God. ₁₀For if while we were enemies we were reconciled to God by the death of his Son, much more, now that we are reconciled, shall we be saved by his life. ₁₁Not only so, but we also rejoice in God through our Lord Jesus Christ, through whom we have now received our reconciliation.

(1) Ambrosiaster on verses 6-11

To what purpose, then, when we were still sinners, did Christ die for a time for the ungodly? Indeed, rarely will anyone die for a righteous person — though perhaps for a good person someone might actually dare to die. If for the sake of unbelievers and enemies of God, Christ gave himself over to death **for a time** — he died for only a time because he rose again on the third day[2] — how much more, now that we have believed in him, will he strengthen us with his aid! He died to acquire life and glory for us. From his dying for those still enemies, we ought to understand how much he will do for his friends. From the perspective of humans, that is, **for a time**, he appeared to die, but actually he was still alive in the underworld, breaking down the gates of hell by his mighty power.

Paul wants to call our attention to the Savior's love for us when he says, **rarely will anyone die for a righteous person**. If one is hardly ever willing to die for a righteous person, how could someone be ready to die for ungodly people? One might be willing — or unwilling — to die for a single good person, but either would be difficult to choose freely. How could someone ever decide, however, to die for the sins of a whole multitude? Suppose that someone might choose to die for a righteous or good person, motivated by sympathy or appreciation of the person's goodness. But for one who is evil, by contrast, there is no good reason, and the idea is repulsive. Most people would be hesitant to advance their own credit in order to rescue a self-centered debtor. Christ died for the impious actions of a people which was not yet his own.

Paul distinguishes between two different types of people: the **righteous** and the **good**. Although a righteous person should be called good, Paul nevertheless distinguished the two categories: **righteous** refers to a person's practice; **good** refers to a state into which one is born, a kind of innocence based on simplicity. Now in the context of this discussion, the righteous are more deserving than the good. Still Paul says, **perhaps for a good person someone might actually dare to die**. Innocence attracts greater sym-

---

2. The Latin version which Ambrosiaster was using — *secundum tempus* — could be read as he did, "according to time," rather than carrying the more precise meaning of the Greek — *kata kairon* — "at the right time."

pathy and thus might be able to move a person. In this way, parents are willing to die for their good children, though I would not presume to say that wives are willing to die for husbands because they are good. If we compare the good and the righteous, sometimes we find the righteous better but other times the good seem preferable. If we judge according to the law of God, however, a righteous person is better than a good one, than one who has not made efforts to progress in goodness. The righteous person has improved the goodness originally given by nature. If that righteousness is measured by the world's standards, however, the innocence of the good is preferable, because worldly justice always entails harshness and is thereby never completely free of malice. All nature is good, then, but righteousness is the fruit of God's law which is in accord with nature. Consequently, this kind of righteousness is goodness. Thus these righteous are always called good as well as righteous. Good people are not always called righteous, however, since that goodness depends on their innocence rather than what they have done. Righteousness is goodness perfected by doing what is given in nature.

But God proves his love for us. God favors us with the divine love by being gracious to those who are still enemies, by sending the one who will save them, although they certainly do not deserve this. **Since, if while we still were sinners Christ died for us, how much more surely then, now that we have been justified in his blood, will we be saved through him from the wrath of God.** Paul argues that if God has allowed the Son to be killed for the sake of sinners, then God will do even more for the justified, by saving them from wrath, that is, by preserving them from the deceits of the devil. Thus they will be confident on the Day of Judgment, even when divine vengeance begins to destroy the infidels. Because divine goodness prefers that no one perish, God bestowed mercy on those deserving death. Thus any who recognize God's graciousness toward them can attain honor and glory as well. People who refuse God's call are guilty of ingratitude; by rejecting the divine grace, they persist in their error and ill-will.

For if while we were enemies we were reconciled to God through the death of his Son, much more surely, having been reconciled, will we be saved in his life. Clearly if God surrendered the Son to death in order to reconcile us, how much more will God make those now reconciled safe through the life of the Son. Someone generous for the good of enemies cannot be stingy in the love of friends. If the death of the Savior came to our aid while we were still ungodly, how much more will the Son's life, once he rose from the dead, help us now that we have been made righteous? Just as his death rescued us from the devil, so shall his life free us on the day of God's judgment.

But more than that, we even boast in God through our Lord Jesus Christ, through whom we have now received reconciliation. Paul teaches not only that we should give thanks to God for the salvation and security that we have received, but that we should exult in God through Jesus Christ. Through the Son's mediation, God saw fit to call us friends, although we had been impious and hostile. Thus we should rejoice in all the benefits which we have received through Christ. Because we have come to know God through him, we boast of him and honor him as equal to God the Father — as Christ, in fitting witness to himself, preached, *so that they may honor the Son just as they honor the Father* (John 5:23).

(2) Origen on verses 6-7

This is clearly a sign of Christ's divine goodness. For unless he was of the divine substance and the Son of that Father of whom he said: *no one is good except God the Father* (Mark 10:18), he surely would not have been able to manifest his goodness toward us.

On the evidence of such benevolence, he himself is recognized as good: **for this good man perhaps someone might even dare to die**. Since everyone has recognized the great generosity of Christ toward us and love for him is inspired in every heart, each of us will be ready not only **to die on behalf of this good man** but even to die courageously. We often see this happening when those to whom the love of Christ has been abundantly given freely and with great courage present themselves to their persecutors and confess the name of Christ openly before angels and humans (Matt 10:32). They proclaim themselves ready not only to suffer injury for the sake of his name but even to submit to death because of his goodness, an act hardly anyone chooses on behalf of a righteous person. Yet the love of this earthly life is so great that even when a just cause for death does present itself, hardly anyone willingly submits to that death. The laws of nature bring death upon us justly. Though we may recognize death as just because of our mortal condition, still the soul yields to the laws of nature only with difficulty. **So scarcely anyone is prepared to die for a righteous man.** But **on behalf of this good man someone might be ready to die** and to confront death with confidence, especially if this person understands **that while we were still faithless and weak, Christ had already suffered death for us.**

(3) Augustine on verse 8

The love by which God loves is neither changeable nor comprehensible. God did not first begin to love us when we were reconciled to God through the blood of God's Son. God loved us before the establishment of the world, before we even existed, so that we too might then become God's children, along with God's Only-Begotten. When we hear that we were reconciled to God through the death of God's Son, we should not understand this as meaning that while God hated us, the Son reconciled us to the Father, and only then did God begin to love us. This is the way enemies are reconciled to one another, so that they become friends and begin to love instead of hate one another. No, we were reconciled to God who was already loving us, even while we were still holding enmity against God through our sin. The Apostle makes clear that I am telling the truth: **God shows love for us in that while we were still sinners Christ died for us.** God was extending love toward us even while we were still building our animosity against God by the evil deeds we performed. Yet the Scripture truly says to God, *You hated, O Lord, all those who do evil* (Ps 6:8). Thus in some wondrous and divine way, God loved us even while God hated us. God hated us for being other than what God had made us. But since our wickedness had not yet completely consumed God's good work in us, God was able, simultaneously in each of us, to hate what we had made of ourselves and to love what God had made in us. This is a general truth about God, understood in all God does: *you hate nothing that you have made* (Wis 11:25). What God hated would not be allowed to exist; nor could anything exist without the Omnipotent's tolerance. In anything God hates, therefore, must be something God loves.

(4) John Chrysostom on verses 9-11

The only one who is going to save us is that one who so loved sinners that he gave himself up for them. Do you fail to appreciate how much hope this gives us for the future? Before this time, two obstacles blocked our salvation: first, that we were sinners; second, that we could be saved only through the death of the Lord. Before the death of the Lord actually took place, no one could have believed such a thing possible, so great was the love necessary for it. Now that it has been accomplished, the remaining requirement is easier. For we have been made friends and death is no longer necessary. Moreover, in order to spare us while we were still enemies, God did not spare the Son; now that we are friends and God need no longer deliver up the Son for us, will God not protect us?

Someone may say, "How could one who loves us threaten us with hell, punishment, and vengeance?" God does this *because* of love for us. The whole divine purpose is to cut away the evil in you. God uses fear like a bridle to hold back your tendency toward evil. Through blessings and sufferings, God stops you from rushing downward. God draws and leads you away from evil, which is itself worse than hell.

These objectors consider the punishment worse than the sin. It is, in fact, just the other way round. If punishment were really an evil for the sinner, God would not have piled new evils on top of existing ones, nor would God have willed to make sinners worse by punishing them. God does everything to remove evil and would do nothing to increase it. Punishment, then, is not imposed as an evil in retaliation for our transgression. Indeed, not to punish sinners would itself be evil, like not nursing the sick. Nothing is so evil as unbridled passion. When I say unbridled, I refer to lust for luxury, vainglory, domination, in short, the passion for anything which violates the limits of what is necessary. Someone living a soft and loose life may seem happier than others but is actually more wretched than all, because this way of life subjects the soul to demanding mistresses and tyrants. For this reason, God has made the present life toilsome for us, intending to set us free from slavery to it and thereby lead us to perfect freedom. For this reason, God threatens punishment and imposes labors on our lives, binding our vaunting spirits.

Someone may object, "What would you say about those who are often made worse by tribulation?" I would say that becoming worse results not from the tribulation itself but from their own weakness. If a person was unable to tolerate a bitter medicine which hurts a sick stomach even though it could cure it, we would blame the sickness of the bodily organ rather than the medicine. Likewise in this case of the objection, we should accuse the weakness of the person's resolve rather than the tribulation itself. Moreover, anyone who becomes worse through suffering would be even more likely to fail through an easy life. For anyone who falls even when propped up by tribulation would be more prone to failure without it. If a person becomes worse when braced, how much more probable is a fall without any support.

Someone may object again, "How can I not become worse under tribulation?" Well, remember that you must endure what afflicts you, whether you are willing or not. If you bear suffering graciously, you will derive great profit. But if you become disgruntled, if you are upset and complain, you will make things worse and even more burdensome. Let us remember this and thereby turn what we cannot prevent into something of our own choosing.

Romans 5:12-14

12Therefore as sin came into the world through one man, and death through sin, and so death spread to all men because all men sinned — 13sin indeed was in the world before the law was given, but sin is not counted where there is no law. 14Yet death reigned from Adam to Moses, even over those whose sins were not like the transgression of Adam, who was a type of the one who was to come.[3]

(1) Ambrosiaster on verses 12-14

Therefore, just as sin came into the world through one man, and death came through sin, and so it spread to all men, in which man all have sinned. Since Paul showed above that the grace of God was given through Christ in accordance with the order of truth, he now explains the plan of God the Father through the one Christ, the Son. Because the one Adam — the reference is actually to Eve, because the woman is also Adam — sinned in everyone, so the one Christ, Son of God, conquered death in everyone. Paul explains the plan of the grace of God for the human race; in order to clarify the origin of sin, he started from the first sinner, Adam. He teaches that, through the agency of a single individual, the providence of God has restored what had failed and been consigned to death through the agency of another individual. Christ is the one through whom we have been saved, to whom — by the will of the Father — we owe the same reverence as we do to God the Father. For Paul says in another place, *One who serves Christ in these things is acceptable to God* (Rom 14:18), since it is written, *You shall worship the Lord your God, and serve only the Lord* (Matt 4:10; cf. Deut 6:13). If, therefore, Scripture says that God alone must be served, and Paul commanded them to serve Christ, then Christ must be within the divine unity, neither dissimilar from God nor a second God. The law warns that God alone must be served, and Scripture says that serving Christ pleases God. Therefore, **just as sin came into the world through one, and death came through sin**, so through the one Christ, eternal life comes through the condemnation and death of sin.

In which man, that is, in Adam, **all have sinned**. The reason why Paul said, **in which man**, although he was actually referring to the woman, was that his reference was generic rather than specific. In Adam, all have sinned as a single lump. Once Adam was corrupted through sinning, all those whom Adam generated were born under sin. All coming out of Adam are sinners because we are all from Adam. Death entered when

---

3. The commentators note and address the different versions of the text.

through transgression Adam lost the favor of God and became unworthy to eat from the tree of life. This first death is the separation of soul from body. We suffer another death, which is called the second death in hell, not through the sin of Adam but through our own sins, as a result of the opening Adam allowed to sin. Good people were not subject to this second death. They were indeed in hell, but in its upper, free part.[4] As still bound by the sentence which had been handed down in Adam, however, they could not yet ascend into heaven. The condemnation written in these decrees was removed by the death of Christ. The sentence in these decrees was that the body of each human should be dissolved into the earth and the soul should be bound by the chains of hell and suffer death.

Sin was indeed in the world before the law, but sin is not counted when there is no law. Paul says that all sinned in Adam, as I have explained above, and that until the giving of the law sin was not called to account. People thought their sinning would go unpunished by God, though not by their fellow humans. The natural law had not entirely faded from human consciousness: people retained the belief that they ought not do to others what they did not want to have done to themselves. Thus sin was far from being unrecognized in human society. For example, when Jacob's father-in-law, Laban, was searching Jacob's camp for his idols, Jacob declared that the person found guilty of the theft deserved to die (Gen 31:32). Joseph too was imprisoned as guilty, though admittedly as a result of false accusation. Pharaoh's baker and butler were consigned to chains for some offense (Genesis 40), and Moses fled in terror from the law after having killed an Egyptian (Exod 2:11). How, then, was **sin not counted when there was no law**? If law was unknown, why do these texts tell of punishment being inflicted? Well, the natural law always exists; there was no time when it was not known. People believed, however, that its authority was limited to the human world, that it did not make one guilty before God. They did not realize that God would judge the human race, and thus they claimed that God was unconcerned with and paid no attention to sin. Once the law was given through Moses, it became clear that God does care what humans do and thus that evildoers who manage to evade punishment in the present life will not escape it in the future.

The natural law has three parts. First, that the creator be honored, that divine glory and majesty be attributed to no one else — except the Son. The second part is concerned with behavior, namely, that one should live well, with discretion as the governing principle. Awareness of the creator should not be sterile; it should produce a life restrained by law. The third part involves teaching others. Knowledge of God the creator and the example of a good life should be shared with others, so that they may learn how to earn merit in the judgment of the creator. This is true Christian prudence.

Yet death reigned from Adam to Moses. Since sin was not thought to be judged by God before the law was given through Moses, as I have explained, death usurped control and ruled unhindered, realizing that humans had been handed over to it. So death exercised an unchallenged dominion over both those who were still temporarily evading it and those who were already paying the penalty for their wicked actions. Death knew that everyone was subject to it, because *everyone who commits sin is a slave to sin* (John 8:34).

---

4. The reference is not, as will be clear, to the state of eternal punishment but to the condition of awaiting liberation by Christ.

Believing that they were escaping unpunished, people sinned more freely. They were particularly given to those sins which their culture promoted as lawful acts. This made Satan happy and confident in possession of the human race, which God had abandoned because of Adam's sin. In this sense, death reigned.

Even over those whose sins were like the transgression of Adam, who is a type of the one to come. We will show that **Adam is the type of the one to come.** Clearly, then, death did not rule over everyone, because not everyone **sinned like the transgression of Adam**, that is, in contempt of God. Who, then, sinned with contempt for God if not those who had become slaves to the creation by ignoring the creator, those who set up gods for themselves and worshiped them in contempt of God? The devil rejoiced over those people, recognizing them as imitators. Abraham's father Terah, Nahor, and Laban, for example, all had their own gods (cf. Josh 24:2; Gen 31:30). Adam's sin was itself a type of idolatry: he transgressed by believing that a human could thereby become a god. He judged the devil's proposal more advantageous than God's command; he put the devil in God's place and was, as a result, subjected to the devil. People who transgress against God by serving creatures sin in a similar but not fully identical way — similarity means being both the same and yet different. They cannot be charged with having received a command not to eat from the tree, as Adam did. Thus they sin not by despising God but by violating the natural law. Consider, for example, someone who has recognized and revered God, either by tradition or natural instinct, who confers the honor of God's name and majesty upon no other. Now if such a person sins — and it is impossible not to sin — then that sin would still be committed in subjection to God, whose authority to judge it is acknowledged, rather than against God. Death did not reign in such a person; as I have said, it reigned in those who served the devil under the guise of idols.

Because the law had not been authoritatively promulgated, people failed to foresee that God would judge. The majority did not realize that God would judge, and thus very few escaped the rule of death. After what is called the first death, those over whom death reigned were held by the second death for future punishment and destruction. Those, however, over whom death did not reign, because they did not **sin like the transgression of Adam**, were reserved in hope of freedom, in anticipation of the coming of the Savior. Thus we read that Abraham was in the underworld but set far apart (Luke 16:23). An immense chasm divided the righteous from sinners, and the godless were separated even further. Even before the judgment, what each one deserved was no longer hidden: the just were in cool repose, sinners in feverish anxiety, and the ungodly in burning agitation. Thus death reigned over them; the craftiness of its operation led them, like enemies, to punishment. It was no secret that this first human had been created in the world to proclaim the ruling authority of the one God, against which Satan had rebelled.

The Apostle's saying that sinners were not called to account because the law was not yet given does not help us understand why death reigned from Adam to Moses. At that time almost everyone served idols and thus worshiped the devil; through this practice death reigned. But if death ruled even over those who did not **sin like the transgression of Adam** (as some Greek manuscripts read), then death ruled because they died, and death would continue to reign because even holy people still die. If death ruled at that time only because of idolatry, then it would still rule now. But death does not rule now.

Even in the earlier time, then, death ruled not because of idolatry alone but also because of depraved living. Every day now, however, people who had been children of the devil become children of God. Thus death does not rule now. The law was given so that the guilty would become answerable to the judgment of God; they would then become subject to God and no longer to the devil. In this way, the giving of the law brought an end to the reign of death. By the law, everyone began to recognize that God the creator would judge the human race; gradually, they began to draw back from death's domination.

Now, Adam was the **type of the one to come**, because even at that time God had secretly decided to correct the sin committed by the one Adam through the one Christ, as it says in the Apocalypse of the Apostle John, *The Lamb who has been slain from the foundation of the world* (Rev 13:8).

(2) Origen on verses 12-14

First let us see how **through one man sin entered into this world and then through sin, death.** . . . If Levi, who was born in the fourth generation after Abraham, is said to have been in the loins of Abraham, so much more were all the human beings who have been born and lived in this world in the loins of Adam (Heb 7:9-10). While he was still in paradise, all humans were with him or in him; when he was expelled, they too were exiled from paradise. As a result, that death which came upon him because of his transgression also passed through him into them who were held in his loins. Thus the Apostle rightly states: *If all die in Adam, so also will they all be brought to life again in Christ* (1 Cor 15:22). Therefore sin entered in and through sin death entered into all humans, neither from the serpent who had sinned before the woman nor from the woman who transgressed before the man but through Adam, from whom all mortals draw their origin. . . .

When that death of sin, which passed into everyone, came to Jesus and tried to pierce him with its sting — *the sting of death is sin* (1 Cor 15:56) — it was repulsed and broken. He was life; life could not fail to destroy death. Then was it said: *O death, where is your sting? O death, where is your victory?* (1 Cor 15:55). Indeed, because death had earlier defeated everyone, Paul addresses it: *O death, where is your victory?*

He said that sin entered **into the world**, not into every man, and that death had come not into the world but **into every man**, and that it had not **come into** but **passed through**. I do not believe that Paul made these distinctions without reason. For I judge that by **the world** he means those who are earthly and completely taken up with earthly affairs; by **men**, however, he means those who have already begun to understand themselves and recognize that they have been created in the image of God. He says that sin **came into** those whom he calls **the world** or the earthly, and never leaves them. But he says that sin **passed through** those whom he wants to understand as **men**; it was in them, but it was driven out through that turning that is performed in repentance; it passed through but does not remain in them. . . .

Thus a more indirect approach is demanded by us and a digression from Paul at that line in which he says: **sin was indeed in the world before the law, but sin is not counted when there is no law.** We find him speaking again in this way later in this epistle:

Apart from the law, sin lies dead. I was once alive apart from the law (Rom 7:8-9). The same meaning seems to me expressed in both sections. For what was lacking in one passage, he supplied in the other by a single word. **Sin was in the world before the law**: the word *dead* was lacking, which he later expressed more clearly. If we may add that word here, then, we might express his idea: **sin was *dead* in the world before the law, but sin is not counted when there is no law.** This interpretation makes the passage read clearly.

We have often stated that in this epistle Paul discusses many laws, though more frequently he speaks about the natural law, which is especially discussed in this passage. **Before the** (natural) **law** — which starts at the age when a person begins to be capable of reasoning and of distinguishing between just and unjust, right and wrong — sin was dead or without power over a person, but then it comes to life. At that time the interior law which forbids and the faculty of reason which commands begin to operate.

To make our point clearer, let us use a simple example. It has been written: *Whoever strikes father or mother shall be put to death; whoever curses father or mother shall be put to death* (Exod 21:15, 17). If a young child of four or five years becomes angry, as often happens, and strikes its father or mother with a rod, the child would be subject to death under the principle of this mandate. Because the natural law is not yet operative in the child and does not instruct the child not to injure its father or mother, the child does not realize that its action involves the crime of disrespect. It commits a kind of sin by striking or insulting its mother; but sin itself is dead in the child. Because the natural law is not yet operative, the sin cannot be imputed. The reasoning capacity within the child is not yet adequate to judge that it ought not do this. Thus, even its parents treat the child with grace and humor rather than as guilty. In this way, I think, we can comprehend what the Apostle states: **Sin was indeed *dead* in the world before the law. Sin is not counted when there is no law.** . . .

Death therefore ruled from Adam to Moses, according to the explanation which we proposed above, not over all but only **over those who have sinned in a manner similar to the transgression of Adam.** Death indeed entered into the world; it passed through everyone but did not exercise dominion over all. To pass through is quite different than to rule. Sin passed through the just and gave them a slight fever. The reign of sin captures and with all its power dominates the transgressors, those who subject themselves to sin with full intention and action. Death thus ruled from Adam, who first opened the way for sin into this world by his transgression, down to the time of Moses, to the establishment of the law. Through the law purification from sins began to be possible; the tyranny of sin began to be challenged through sacrifices, various atonements, offerings, and precepts. Because sin's dominion was greater than the powers of the law, the prophets were then sent to strengthen the law. They came to realize that the power of this tyrant was beyond their strength as well, so they prayed fervently for the coming and presence of the king himself, calling out to God: *Send forth your light and your truth* (Ps 43:3); and again, *Bow your heavens, O Lord, and come down* (Ps 144:5); and again, *Arise, O Lord, and come to our help* (Ps 44:26). Then came Jesus Christ, the Son of God. Because the flesh had weakened the law, God sent the Son in the likeness of sinful flesh. Through sin *he condemned sin in the flesh* and *reconciled the world to God* (Rom 8:3; 2 Cor 5:19). Moreover, he *stripped away the rule and power of the tyrant, triumphing over them through himself* (Col

2:15). We seem to have been carried away by this discussion, so let us now return to the proposition itself.

As a result, **the death of sin reigned from Adam to Moses**, that is, until the coming of Christ. The law is named for Moses; that law, as it is written, held sway up to the time of John the Baptist, when Jesus began to proclaim the kingdom of God (Luke 16:16). Paul seems to assign a special status to certain people over whom death had ruled — those who sinned in **likeness to the transgression of Adam**. He seems to imply some hidden mystery by this expression. Might there have been some humans, even down to the time when humans were placed under the law as their instructor, who acted somewhat as Adam did in paradise, were smitten by the tree of the knowledge of good and evil, were ashamed of their nakedness, and gave up their home in paradise?

Perhaps. But, in fact, this can be explained more simply. The meaning of **likeness to the transgression of Adam** must be read as referring to all who are born from Adam the transgressor. They have in themselves a likeness to his transgression not only by being born from him but through their upbringing. All born into this world are not only nurtured but also trained by their parents; thus they are both the children and the students of sinners. Once they have grown up and attained the freedom to do as they see fit, children either follow the way of their parents — as is written of not a few kings (1 Kgs 15:26), or they walk in the way of the Lord their God. . . .

Some manuscripts read, **even over those who have *not* sinned in the likeness of the transgression of Adam.** If death can be described as having ruled over them, then the death in question is the one which holds souls in the underworld. We recognize that even virtuous persons fell under that death, by the general law of mortality even if not as a punishment for sin. Thus Christ descended into the underworld, not only so that he would then break free from the power of death but so that he could free those who were being held there by their mortal condition rather than on the charge of transgression. Thus it is written: *many bodies of the saints who had fallen asleep were raised. After his resurrection they came out of the tombs and entered the holy city* (Matt 27:52-53). The prophet's statement about Christ is here fulfilled: *Ascending on high, he led captivity captive* (Ps 67:19; Eph 4:8). Through his resurrection, he destroyed the reign of death and is thus said to have liberated captivity itself. . . .

He then added: **who is a type of the one to come**. To me this appears ambiguous. Adam was called the type (prefiguring) of the one who was still going to come. Was this based on the time when the Apostle was actually writing these words, so that the reference would be to a future age? Or is the time that of Adam himself, so that **the one to come** would refer to Christ himself, whose coming was already past rather than future when the Apostle wrote this? Referring to Adam and Eve in another place, the same apostle said: *This is a great mystery; I am applying it to Christ and the Church* (Eph 5:32). Using this as a model, he would seem to have intended that we understand **the type of the one to come** to designate Adam as a type of Christ, who would come and join the Church to himself.

In the present passage, however, I am not sure that anyone could understand Adam as a figure of Christ, since the question is about his transgression, his sin, and the death passing through him into all humans. This might be explained, however, through the principle of opposites, in the way the Apostle does in another passage when he says: *For as death came through one man, the resurrection of the dead has also come through one man* (1 Cor 15:21); and again: *For just as by the one man's disobedience the many were made sinners, so by the one man's obedience the many will be made righteous* (Rom 5:19).

We might understand that the Apostle was referring to the time at which he was writing, when he said that Adam is the **type of the one to come**. Then all will be clearer: just as in this age death ruled because of the one man Adam and all humanity was made subject to death, so in the future age life will reign through Christ and all humanity will be endowed with immortality.

(3) Augustine on verse 12

Julian wrote:[5] The Apostle said that death, not sin, had spread. Pay attention to the order of the words: **As through one man sin came into the world, and through sin death, and thus it spread to all people, in which all have sinned.** The great teacher of the Church weighed carefully what he should say: **through one man sin entered, and through sin death, and thus it spread to all.** He had just named both death and sin. What need had he, in specifying what had spread, to separate death from its relationship to sin so that he could clearly indicate that sin had entered into this world through one man and then death through that sin? What had spread to all humans was not sin but that death which was imposed by the severity of the sentence, as an avenger of the transgression, to pursue not the bodily seed but the moral vices. So what then? His point was only to forewarn and forearm us carefully, so that we would never think he had provided any support for your interpretation.

Augustine: The passage that says, **though one man sin entered into the world, and through sin death, and thus it spread to all people**, is ambiguous: it might mean either that sin, or death, or even both spread to all people. But the reality itself clearly shows which of these Paul intended. If sin itself had not spread, then every human being would not be born with *the law of sin which is in the members* (Rom 7:23). If death had not spread, then all humans, who are caught in this mortal state, would not be going to die. When the Apostle says, **in which all sinned**, that **in which** can only be understood as referring to Adam, **in which man** Paul says that they all die. It would not be not just and fair for the punishment to spread but not the crime itself.

(4) Theodoret on verses 12-14

When the Lord God created Adam and endowed him with reason, God gave him one command regarding its exercise. A person who was in possession of reason and had the capacity to discriminate between the good and its opposite could not escape every form of law in performing any action. Adam was utterly seduced and violated this one direc-

---

5. Julian was bishop of Eclanum in Italy; he was the ablest and most persistent of Pelagius's defenders.

tive. At the outset, the lawgiver had imposed a threat of punishment along with the law. Then, while under this penalty of death, Adam begot Cain and Seth and the others; all of them, by being born under such a mortal condition, became subject to death. The mortal condition requires many supports — food, drink, clothing, housing, and a variety of skills — and the need for such supplies often incites the passions to excess and thus involves sin. Therefore, the holy Apostle states that because Adam had sinned and had been made subject to death because of that sin, both of these defects passed into the human race. The condition of death prevails over all humanity, then, because all have sinned. So each person stands under sentence of death, not on account of the sin of the first parent but through each one's own transgression.

Sin was indeed in the world until the law, but sin is not reckoned when there is no law. Paul does not, as some suppose, arraign only those who have violated the (Mosaic) law; instead he indicts all alike. For the phrase **until the law** does not mean, up to the beginning of the law, but until its termination. So while the law is in force, sin retains its effect. For in the absence of law, transgression cannot occur.

Yet death exercised dominion from Adam to Moses, even over those whose sins were not like the transgression of Adam, who is a type of the one who was to come. He calls it the Mosaic law, and we find this term in the Gospels, as in, *They have Moses and the prophets* (Luke 16:29). So also when the holy Apostle in the Second Epistle to the Corinthians states, *Indeed, to this very day whenever Moses is read, a veil lies over their minds* (2 Cor 3:15), he had in mind the law. Therefore he means that death held power from Adam until the appearance of the Savior, which brought the law to its end. *The law and the prophets were in effect until John came; since then the good news of the kingdom of God is proclaimed, and everyone tries to enter it by force* (Luke 16:16).

Death also ruled over those who had not sinned in ways similar to the transgression of Adam. Even if they had not violated that particular commandment, they had engaged in other transgressions. The Apostle called Adam a type of Christ, and for this reason he calls Christ the future Adam. That first human being, Adam, was the first to sin, and thus came under the penalty of death; the whole human race followed its progenitor into this condition. When the Lord Christ fulfilled the supreme demands of justice, he broke the power of death, and in being the first to arise from the dead he restored human nature to the fullness of life. Thus in calling Adam a type of Christ, the Apostle shows the preeminence of the Lord.

(5) Cyril of Alexandria on verse 12

For as I said, the death derived from sin came upon the first human and the source of the race. Then the entire race was affected. And the serpent, the originator of sin, strengthened by the wickedness of Adam, gained access to the human mind for evil purposes. *They have all gone astray, they are all alike perverse* (Ps 14:3). Then humanity turned from the face of the most holy God, since from its earliest days consciousness eagerly inclined toward evil (Gen 8:21), and our lives were all opposed to reason. Then death gained strength and consumed us, as the prophet says: *Then death extended its power and opened its mouth without restraint* (Isa 5:14). For since we have repeated the transgression of Adam, we have all sinned and have incurred the same penalties. Yet earth under heaven did not remain without help. For sin was purged, Satan fell down, and death was abolished.

(6) John Chrysostom on verses 13-14

By saying **until the law sin was in the world**, I think Paul means that after the (Mosaic) law was given, the sin which arose from transgression prevailed as long as the law existed. **For sin cannot continue**, he says, **if no law exists.** If he means that the sin which arose from the transgressions of the law gave birth to death, then why would everyone have died before the law? If death had its root in sin and no one is guilty of sin in the absence of the law, how could death have prevailed before the time of the law? This argument makes clear that he is not speaking of the sin which arises from the transgression of the law, but rather of that sin which comes from the disobedience of Adam; that was the sin which ruined everything. What is the proof of this? That everyone died even before the law. **Yet death exercised dominion**, he says, **from Adam to Moses, even over those who did not sin.** How did it reign? **In the likeness of the transgression of Adam, who is a type of the one who was to come.** In this way Adam is also a type of Jesus Christ. How is he a type? Adam, by eating from the tree, was the cause of death to all those who derived from him, even though they did not eat from the tree. Similarly, Christ became the ambassador of righteousness — which he granted to us through the cross — for all those who came from him, even if they did not perform acts of righteousness.

(7) Augustine on verse 13

When he had said, **in whom all sinned**, he then added, **sin was indeed in the world until the law**, that is, because the law could not take away sin. The statement, *The law came in to increase sin* (Rom 5:20), refers both to the natural law, by which anyone who has the use of reason begins to add their own sins to the original sin, and to the written law, which was given to the people through Moses. *If a law had been given which could make alive, then righteousness would indeed be by the law. But the scripture consigned all things to sin, that what was promised to faith in Jesus Christ might be given to those who believe* (Gal 3:21-22). **But sin was not assigned when there was no law.** What does **was not assigned** mean except that it was overlooked and not recognized as sin? That does not mean that God also treated it as non-existent, since it is written, *All who have sinned without the law will also perish without the law* (Rom 2:12).

Yet death reigned from Adam until Moses, that is, from the first human to the divinely promulgated law, because even that law could not abolish the **reign of death**. By the **reign of death** he means the situation in which the guilt of sin so dominates humans that it prevents them from attaining eternal life, which is true life, and draws them down into the second death, which is an eternal punishment. Only the Savior's grace destroys this **reign of death** in anyone. That grace worked even in the ancient saints, all those who, before Christ had come in the flesh, lived by his helping grace rather than by the letter of the law, which can command but cannot help. Through a most just arrangement of the times, this was hidden in the Old Testament and is now revealed in the New. **Therefore death reigned from Adam until Moses** in everyone whom the grace of Christ did not assist by destroying the **reign of death** in them. **These did not sin in the likeness of the transgression of Adam**, that is, they did not sin by their own personal choice as he did. Instead they drew the original sin from him. He **was a type of the one to come**, because in him was established the pattern of condemnation for all who would follow after, who would come into being by generation from him. Thus from that one, everyone would be born into that condemnation from which only the grace of the Savior would set anyone free. I realize that many Latin copies have the reading: **death reigned from Adam until Moses in those who sinned in likeness of the transgression of Adam.** Yet, even those who read the text this way grasp the same meaning. They understand that the ones who **sinned in the likeness of the transgression of Adam** are those who sinned in him, so that they were then created like him. As they were humans from a human, so also they were sinners from a sinner, bound to death from one bound to death, condemned from one condemned. The Greek copies, from which the Latin versions were made, either all or almost all read as I first stated the text.

Romans 5:15-19

15But the free gift is not like the trespass. For if many died through the one man's trespass, much more have the grace of God and the free gift in the grace of that one man, Jesus Christ, abounded for the many. 16And the free gift is not like the effect of that one man's sin. For the judgment following one trespass brought condemnation, but the free gift following many trespasses brings justification. 17If, because of one man's trespass, death reigned through that one man, much more will those who receive the abundance of grace and the free gift of righteousness reign in life through the one man, Jesus Christ. 18Then, as one man's trespass led to condemnation for all men, so one man's act of righteousness leads to acquittal and life for all men. 19For as by the one man's disobedience many were made sinners, so by the one man's obedience many will be made righteous.

(1) Ambrosiaster on verses 15-19

But the free gift is not like the trespass. Because he said that the one Adam is the **type** of the one Christ, he adds, **but the free gift is not like the trespass.** He does not want to give the impression that the work of Christ is like that of Adam. Adam is the type of Christ only in this respect: that as a single individual sinned, a single individual reversed the failure.

For if many have died through the one man's trespass, how much more surely have the grace of God and the gift in the grace of the one man, Jesus Christ, abounded

for the many. Many have died by imitating the transgression of one man and repeating his sin, but God's grace and gift have been more abundant toward the greater number of people who take refuge in God. More people receive grace than died by the sin of Adam. From this, it is clear that Paul was not thinking about that bodily death which is common to all, since absolutely everyone dies but not everyone receives grace. Nor has death ruled over everyone but only over those who are called dead because of the sin of Adam, the ones whom he says sinned *like the transgression of Adam* (Rom 5:14). These are the dead he has in mind when he says that many died through the sin of that one. The grace of God is abundant toward a greater number, however, because in the descent of the Savior the grace of God has abounded both to those who sinned like Adam and thus died through Adam's sin, and also to those who did not sin by a transgression like Adam's but still had been sent into the underworld by the divine judgment because of that sin of their forefather. Christ bestowed a blessing on all of them when he led them up to heaven in triumph.

And the free gift is not like the effect of the one man's sin. For the judgment following one trespass brought condemnation, but the free gift following many trespasses brings justification. The difference is evident: by the one sin of Adam, those who sinned in the likeness of his transgression were condemned; by remitting their sins, the grace of God through Christ justified people not only from that one offense but from many others. Paul shows the magnificent compassion of God and Christ. The second death held many in the lower part of hell through the sin like Adam's. Though they would have been justly punished, God's gift of grace not only forgave but justified them.

If, because of the one man's trespass, death reigned through that one man, much more surely will those who receive the abundance of grace and of righteousness reign in life through the one man, Jesus Christ. Notice that Paul is developing a single idea here and does not contradict himself. He says that death had reigned, not that it continues to reign now; those who understood through the law that God was going to judge have escaped from death's empire. Death ruled for a time because, without an open proclamation of the law, the fear of God was nowhere to be found on earth. This then is the idea he expressed: because *death ruled from Adam up until Moses over those who sinned in the likeness of the transgression of Adam* (Rom 5:14), so much the more will grace reign for life by the abundance of the gift of God through the one, Jesus Christ. For if death reigned, why will grace not reign even more, since grace justifies many more than death ruled? How much more must we trust the rule of that grace which grants life through Christ.

Therefore, just as one man's trespass led to condemnation for all, so one man's act of righteousness leads to justification and life for all. As the sin of one human individual brought condemnation to all who sinned in the same way, so too, all who believe in the righteousness of another single human individual shall be justified. Moreover, those who believe that the condemnation is universal should recognize a similarly general justification. That is not right, however, because not everyone believes.

For just as by the one man's disobedience numerous people were made sinners, so by the one man's obedience the many will be made righteous. Paul here uses **numerous** and **many** for the **all** of which he spoke before. For a number — but not all — imitated the offense of Adam by transgressing. So, too, many will be made righteous through faith in Christ — but not all. So death did not rule over those who did not sin *in the likeness of the transgression of Adam* (Rom 5:14).

(2) John Chrysostom on verses 15-16

Thus the free gift is not like the trespass. For if many have died through the one man's trespass, how much more surely have the grace of God and the free gift of the one man, Jesus Christ, abounded for the many. He says, "If sin — even the sin of one man — had such great power, will not grace exceed that power, that is, the grace of God, not just of the Father but also of the Son?" This is much more reasonable. For to punish a person on account of someone else does not seem fitting or fair, while one person being saved through another is more appropriate and credible. Since the former did happen when all died through the sin of one person, the latter appears more likely to occur through the gift of grace through Jesus Christ. By these arguments, Paul has demonstrated that this is plausible and reasonable. If the first argument is proven, then the rest should be readily admitted. He proves that the first event has actually happened by the following considerations. How does he prove it? **The free gift is not like the effect of the one man's sin. For the judgment following one trespass brought condemnation, but the free gift following many trespasses brings justification.** What is he saying? One sin had the power to introduce death and condemnation. Grace took away not that sin alone but other sins as well which came after that one. The **like** and the **thus** in the text might suggest equal measures of good and evil, so that, when you hear "Adam," you could think that only the sin which he introduced was taken away. To avert this misunderstanding, Paul says that many offenses were taken away. How do we know that? Because after the many sins which followed on that one sin committed in Paradise, there was righteousness. Life and innumerable goods assuredly and necessarily follow upon that righteousness, just as death assuredly follows from sin. For righteousness is greater than life, since it is the source of life. Therefore, Paul demonstrated that greater goods have been given and that all sins, not just that one sin, were taken away, since **the free gift following many trespasses brings justification.**

Further, from this statement he concludes that death has been totally eradicated. He still has to construct the rest of the argument, since he said that the second effect is greater than the first. For earlier he said, **if the sin of one person killed all people, much more will the grace of one person be able to save all people.** Then he demonstrated that not only was this sin taken away through grace, but all the rest of the sins as well. Not only were sins taken away, but righteousness was also given. Christ's benefit to us not only matched but surpassed Adam's harm.

(3) Augustine on verse 15

What he then added about Adam — *who was a type of the one to come* (Rom 5:14) — cannot be understood in only one way. It could refer to Adam as a contrary type of Christ, so that as all die in Adam so all are made alive in Christ, and **as by one man's disobedience many were made sinners, so by Christ's obedience many will be made righteous** (Rom 5:19). It could also mean that he was a type of what was to come because he instituted the pattern of death which would be replicated in his descendants. The better understanding is to take it as the first, a contrasting pattern, which the Apostle advances in many other passages. Then, to prevent our thinking that the two patterns are equivalent, he adds: **But the gift is not like the trespass. For if many died through one man's trespass, much more have the grace of God and the gift in the grace of that one man, Jesus Christ, abounded for many.** This should be understood not as referring to a greater number, since the wicked who are condemned are more numerous. Rather, it abounded more because the type of death coming from Adam prevails only temporarily in those redeemed by Christ, but the type of life coming through Christ continues forever. Therefore, he says, even though Adam may set a contrary pattern for the future, still Christ does more good to those he regenerates than Adam does harm to those he generated. **And the gift is not like that one man's sin. For the judgment following one trespass brought condemnation, but the grace following many trespasses brings justification.** The inequality of the contrasting patterns, he says, is not only in Adam harming temporarily those whom Christ redeems eternally. They are also unbalanced because Adam's descendants are dragged into condemnation for his one trespass unless Christ redeems them but Christ's redemption takes away the many offenses which the abundance of wickedness has added to that first transgression.

(4) Augustine on verse 16

What is indicated by, **from one trespass brought condemnation**, if not that one trespass by which Adam sinned? And what is **from many trespasses brings justification** except a reference to the grace of Christ which not only forgives the one trespass by which the infants generated from that one man are bound but also the many trespasses which they add by their own evil behavior once they grow up? He says, however, that the one trespass which originated in that first human and binds all by carnal generation is sufficient to lead to condemnation. Therefore, the Baptism of infants is not superfluous, because by regenerating them it releases from the condemnation to which they were bound by their generation. As no human can be carnally generated apart from Adam, so no one can be spiritually regenerated apart from Christ. Carnal generation is subject to that one trespass and its condemnation; spiritual regeneration abolishes not only that one trespass for which infants are baptized but the many trespasses which individual wicked lives have added to that one in which people were generated.

(5) Origen on verses 17-18

He asserted that the gift of grace extends to many more than the fault of that one man has made sinners. I think a mystery is hidden in this statement. Elsewhere he says that *death exercised dominion from Adam to Moses* (Rom 5:14), not over everyone but only over those who sinned in a way *similar to the transgression of Adam.* Yet a simple explanation can be given for his statement that more received grace. Although those made sinners from Adam are many, yet those brought to life through the grace of Christ are called more because even that one individual, from whom the death caused by sin passed into others, was himself added to the number brought back to life by Christ. Along with all those he involved in the fault, he too will be saved. Thus the Scripture says about wisdom: *Wisdom protected the first-formed father of the world when he alone had been created; she delivered him from his transgression* (Wis 10:1). What wisdom was this that freed the first human from his sin? What wisdom but Christ who is *the power of God and the wisdom of God* (1 Cor 1:24)? Thus Christ led more back to life than Adam had led to death, because Christ restored Adam himself to life, who was the cause of death for others. Thus what the Apostle wrote a little further on is also true: **through the grace of one man leads to justification and life in all.** Since Adam is certainly to be counted among all humans, the justification of life reached him as well.

But perhaps you will say that if death passed to everyone by one sinner and then the justification of life came to everyone by the righteousness of one person, it would appear that we ourselves do nothing for which we deserve to live or die: Adam is the cause of death, and Christ the cause of life. We have already stated above that parents not only give life to their children but educate them; those born to them become not only their sons and daughters but their pupils. As a result, they are guided to the death of sin by their training rather than their nature. For instance, if people turn away from God to worship idols, will they not then teach any children they raise to worship idols and offer sacrifice to evil spirits? Adam's example had this kind of effect; death rules in his children starting from Adam, that is, from birth, until the time of the law, through which they gained some ability to distinguish good from evil for themselves and were thereby empowered to receive the grace of Christ. At that point a person leaves behind Adam, the parent or teacher of death, and follows Christ, who both teaches and regenerates to life.

Do you want to make sure that death ruled from Adam not only because of generation but also because of instruction? Consider the following sets of contraries. The Lord Jesus Christ came to correct actions which were wrong because that first birth from Adam was producing death. So he initiated a second birth, which he called not generation but regeneration; through it he removed the defect of the first birth. Just as he replaced birth with rebirth, he also substituted a new type of instruction for that earlier training. When he sent his disciples out to do his work, he said not only: *Go, baptize all nations,* but *Go and teach all nations, baptizing them in the name of the Father and of the Son and of the Holy Spirit* (Matt 28:19). Knowing that both were defective, he provided a remedy for both: mortal generation would be transformed by the regeneration of Baptism; instruction in piety would supplant training in moral laxity. Thus death did not rule over us without our actually committing any sins; nor will life rule in us if we are negligent and make no effort. Christ gives the beginning of life not to the unwilling but to those who believe. The fullness of life is then attained by perfecting the virtues, just as death came earlier through the likeness of transgression and the full range of vices.

(6) Augustine on verse 17

If, because of one's trespass, death reigned through that one, from which trespass children are purified through Baptism, **much more will those who receive the abundance of grace and righteousness then reign in life through the one man, Jesus Christ.** They will reign more fully in life because that kingdom will be of eternal life while death will pass through them temporarily and will not reign forever.

(7) Cyril of Alexandria on verses 18-19

The holy Paul brings his previous thoughts to a kind of conclusion, **Therefore, just as one man's trespass**, and so on. For we have been condemned in Adam, as I stated earlier, and from that initial root came a curse, whence death has passed into everyone. We have also been absolved and reborn into life through the righteousness of Christ. The ancestor by his neglect of the commandment given to him broke his relationship with God and then experienced the effects of divine wrath — he sank into a corrupt condition. Then sin entered into human nature, and so many sinners rose up, over all the earth. But someone might say: "Yes, Adam fell. After he disregarded the divine commandment, he was condemned to corruption and death. Yet how did so many then become sinners on account of him? Why did his failures come down upon us? How, in sum, were persons not yet born condemned along with him? God says, *Parents shall not be put to death for their children, nor the children for their parents, only for their own crimes may persons be put to death* (Deut 24:13; 2 Chr 25:4)."

What argument might we give in response to this objection? Surely the soul caught up in sin shall die. We have become sinners in just this sense through the disobedience of Adam. For he had been created free of corruption and endowed with life; his existence was correspondingly simple in the comfort of Paradise. His mind was completely and continuously occupied with divine visions; his body flourished in undisturbed wonder; all shameful pleasures were under control, for the clamor of indecent excitements was not in him. When he fell under sin and sank into corruption, however, pleasures and impurities entered the nature of the flesh and their provocative movements began in our members. In this way, the disobedience of one person, Adam, infected our nature with the disease of sin. Then many became sinners, not because they had transgressed with Adam — they were not yet alive — but because they shared his nature and thus became subject to the law of sin in it. For just as in Adam human nature was ruined by corruption through disobedience and was invaded by the passions, so this same nature was afterward restored and liberated in Christ. For he was obedient to God the Father; he did not commit sin.

(8) Augustine on verse 19

When it is said, *through one man sin spread to all* (Rom 5:12), and later, **for as by one man's disobedience many were made sinners,** the meaning is that they are **many** because they are **all**. Similarly, when it is said, **so by one man's justification to all people for** the justification of life; and again it is said, **through one man's obedience many will be made righteous**, these **many** should be understood as meaning **all** without exception. Not that everyone is justified in Christ but that all who are actually justified can be justified only in Christ. In the same way we could say that everyone enters a house through one door; not because everyone enters that house but because no one enters except through that door. All come to death through Adam, then, and all to life through Christ. *For as in Adam all die, so also in Christ shall all be made alive* (1 Cor 15:22). From the first beginnings of the human race, no one came to death except through Adam, and through Adam everyone came to death; and no one came to life except through Christ, and through Christ no one came to anything but life.

(9) John Chrysostom on verse 19

For just as by the one man's disobedience the many were made sinners, so by the one man's obedience the many will be made righteous. What Paul says seems to present no small problem. That problem is easily solved, however, by close attention. What is the problem? He says that through the disobedience of one many became sinners. It is not implausible that because Adam sinned and became mortal, all those who came from him also became mortal. But how does it follow that because of the disobedience of one man other persons should become sinners? No one would be judged deserving of punishment who did not sin through personal choice. What then does the word **sinner** mean here? I think it means someone liable to punishment and condemned to death. Through many arguments, Paul clearly shows that we have all become mortal because Adam died. The question is, why did this happen? Paul has not yet addressed this question because it is not relevant to the present discussion: he is contending here against a Jew who questions and mocks the idea that righteousness can come through one person. He responds by showing that punishment for everyone originated from one person, but he does not explain why this happened. He focuses on what is necessary for the argument, not what is irrelevant to it. The rules of disputation did not oblige him to say anything more, just as it did not oblige the Jew to say anything more. So he left the question unsolved.

If anyone wants to learn the answer to this question, then I would say that [because of Christ] we are none the worse for this death and condemnation, as long as we are vigilant. We can even benefit from having become mortal. First, we do not sin in an immortal body. Second, we have innumerable reasons for living virtuously; death, whether present or anticipated, persuades us to be moderate, temperate, restrained, and free of all evil. Beyond these things, or rather even before them, death has brought us even greater goods: through this death have come the crowns of the martyrs and the trophies of the apostles.

Romans 5:20-21

20Law came in, to increase the trespass; but where sin increased, grace abounded all the more, 21so that, as sin reigned in death, grace also might reign through righteousness to eternal life through Jesus Christ our Lord.

(1) Ambrosiaster on verses 20-21

But law stole in, with the result that the trespass multiplied. The law was given in writing to make it public. This law, which was willingly received when the Jews said to Moses, *Whatever the Lord has said we will do* (Exod 24:7), had been sown in nature itself. It **stole in** because, once willingly received, it showed the guilt of those who had already sinned. For they recognized that God would demand the fruit of the seed of righteousness, which had been sown in nature. To **steal in**, therefore, is to enter without attracting notice and then to dominate. Once the law entered, sin flourished, because the law exposed both the older sinners from the time before the law and those sinning after the law. Indeed, sin became greater after the law because the adversary was inflamed with envy at God's concern for humans and used the law to make them culpable and thereby unworthy of God's attention. . . .

Someone might object: "To prevent the growth of sin, the law should have been withheld. If there was less sinning before the law, then nobody needed it." The law was clearly necessary to show that God was taking account of sins, which people thought would go unpunished, as well as to help them recognize what they should avoid. Thus the prophet Isaiah says, *The law was given as a helper* (Isa 8:20 LXX). The seeds of righteousness had been implanted in nature; the law was then added, so that by its authority and teaching, this natural capacity would grow up and produce the fruit of justice. For just as birth is in vain unless nutrition is then supplied to foster development, so the natural instinct for justice does not easily thrive without being given something to observe and respect; instead it weakens and falls into sins, which then overwhelm it. It is beaten down by the custom of sinning, prevented from producing fruit, and thus snuffed out. As the prophet attests, the law was meant to provide assistance; by holding to their customary practices, however, the people multiplied its sins. After accepting the law, therefore, the people began to sin more than they had before. Once the law was given, sins multiplied rather than diminished. Thus the Apostle shows not what the law itself did but what happened as a consequence of the giving of the law. . . .

But where sin increased, grace abounded all the more. When sin flourished, as I have said, grace became even fuller: the gift of God found in the promise covered everyone's sins and frustrated the devil's envy. This must be spelled out. Although the law had been given for humanity's good, the devil subverted that purpose by persuading humans to do what was forbidden. When its commandments were despised, the law which had been given to help had the opposite effect. What resulted from the law, then, was not the gift of God's grace but a sentence of punishment. To prevent the devil from winning glory by a triumph over human beings, the just and merciful God decided that the Son should come to forgive all sins. The joy produced by this gift of grace would then be greater than the grief resulting from sin. For the happiness occasioned by God's gift lifted up even those whom Satan had failed to conquer. Thus grace surpassed the sin instigated by Satan. . . .

So that, just as sin reigned in death, so grace might also exercise dominion through justification leading to eternal life through Jesus Christ our Lord. Sin dominated when it succeeded in bringing death to sinners; so it won glory. In the same way, grace too reigns **through justification leading to eternal life through Jesus Christ our Lord.** As the sin begun through Adam reigned, so too has the grace brought by Christ. If we follow the paths of justice once our sins are forgiven, then grace reigns in us through justice. Grace produces fruit in those good people whom it has redeemed; it reigns unto eternal life, since we shall endure forever. Grace also excels because it reigns eternally while sin reigned only temporarily. For the dominion of grace is the kingdom of God, just as the rule of sin is the kingdom of the devil. Paul refers everything to Christ, so that all God's grace may be learned from Christ.

(2) Origen on verses 20-21

I do not understand what period of time they may be able to identify as prior to the law when there was no sin. . . . [Origen then reviews the biblical record of the period from Cain and Abel to Moses, finding sin in every generation.][6] In this passage, therefore, the law should be understood as the law of nature, which has been *written not with ink but with the Spirit of the living God, not on tablets of stone but on tablets of human hearts* (2 Cor 3:3). This law was inscribed on the ruling part of the heart when God created human beings in the beginning. It was written down so that at the proper time, when the pages of the mind itself had grown, or rather, as the Scripture describes it, when *the tablets of the human heart* began to be opened by the advance in age, its message might start to spread through the recesses of the conscience and fill the senses with rational power. Then in opposition to the precepts which naturally spring from this law, the will of the flesh rises up and produces contrary desires. The Apostle himself called this *the law in the members, at war with the law of the mind* (Rom 7:23). Thus in this passage, the Apostle seems to have intended this *law in the members,* which, he says, **stole in, with the result that sin multiplied.** For the very word which he used seems to me to indicate this interpretation. It is one thing to **enter**, but another to **steal in**, just as to lead is different than to mislead, or to draw than to withdraw. **To steal in** indicates that someone enters with another and gains access by hiding behind another. The argument we have presented shows that under the pretext of natural law, which the Apostle called *the law of the mind* and which conforms to the law of God, the *law in the members* arose, which stimulates the desires of the flesh and makes a person captive to pleasures and desires, thereby causing sin to multiply. In this way, **the law stole in so that trespass multiplied.**

But where sin increased, grace abounded all the more. The grace of Christ abounded all the more because it not only absolved people from their prior sins but protected them from future ones. This then indicates the two kingdoms in humanity, the one whereby sin reigned unto death and the other whereby grace will rule through justice for life. Grace therefore overthrows and expels sin from its realm, that is, from our members. Death was forced out along with sin, so that in the end grace establishes its reign in us through justice, so that eternal life can now abide where death had once been.

---

6. See the parallels at Rom 3:9; 4:15.

(3) Theodoret on verses 20-21

The law entered so that sin might increase. The holy Apostle made this statement not to start an argument, but as part of his exposition of the matter at hand. He wishes to make clear that in earlier times God had not left humans without care. God gave the Jews the law, and through their observance God revealed the light of devout obedience to the other nations as well. Paul used the term **entered**, since Christ was the fulfillment of the promise given to the patriarch. *For through your seed*, God says, *all the nations of the earth will be blessed* (Gen 22:18; 26:4). Between the time of Abraham and that of Christ, the law was interposed. It taught more clearly about the evil of sin. Though all sins did not then display their power in the same way, all increased greatly. Because of the greater number of transgressions, more commandments were then set down. The holy Apostle offered a fitting resolution: **where sin increased, grace abounded all the more.** Sin, he says, did not impede the loving attention of God.

Now that Paul has come to the end of the discussion, he teaches that, just as sin brought forth death and exercised dominion over mortal bodies by arousing the passions to excess, so grace bestowed righteousness through faith on those who believe; grace rules a kingdom which is for the ages and is unending, far greater than the temporary rule of sin. Sin ruled over our bodies, but at their death its dominion ended. According to the holy Apostle, *whoever has died is freed from sin* (Rom 6:7). But after the resurrection, when our bodies have become incorruptible and immortal, grace will rule over them. Sin will have no kingdom left to it. After the passions have ceased, sin will have no domain.

(4) Augustine on verse 20

Law stole in, to increase the trespass, either when people pay no attention to what God commands, or when they rely on their own resources, do not beg for the help of grace, and thus add pride to their weakness. When, however, by means of the divine vocation, they understand that they should cry out and call upon the one in whom they have rightly believed, saying: *Have mercy on me, O God, according to your great mercy* (Ps 51:1); and *I said, Lord, have mercy on me; heal my soul, because I have sinned against you* (Ps 41:4); and *In your righteousness give me life* (Ps 119:40); and *Put false ways far from me, and have mercy on me by your law* (Ps 119:29); and *Let not the foot of arrogance come near me, nor the hands of sinners move me* (Ps 36:11); and *Guide my way according to your word, and let not iniquity rule over me* (Ps 119:133); and *A person's steps are guided by the Lord, and his path speeds along* (Ps 37:23). These and many other such prayers were written to remind us that to fulfill what we are commanded, we must seek help from the one who commands us. When, therefore, people exert themselves and implore God, what follows in the text then happens: **where sin increased, grace abounded all the more**; and *many sins are forgiven her, because she loved much* (Luke 7:47); and *the love of God is poured into the heart, whence the fulfilling of the law*, not through the power of choice in us, *but through the Holy Spirit who is given to us* (Rom 5:5; 13:10).

(5) Augustine on verses 20-21

When the Apostle had said, **Law stole in, to increase trespass; but where sin increased, grace abounded all the more**, he immediately added: **so that, as sin reigned in death, grace also might reign through righteousness unto eternal life through Jesus Christ our Lord.** When he had just said, **so that, as sin had reigned in death**, he did not add, "through one man" or "through the first man" or "through Adam," because he had just said, **Law stole in, to increase trespass.** This increase of sin results not from generation by the first man but from the perversity of human behavior. One trespass alone held infants bound, but sin increases through the wickedness of those who are older. All the sins that have accumulated — even what does not derive from the source of that one sin — is forgiven by the grace of the Savior. So when he had said, **so that grace might reign through righteousness unto eternal life**, he added, **through Jesus Christ our Lord.**

Romans 6

In the sixth chapter, the commentators focused on Paul's discussion of the Christian's dying with Christ in Baptism and thereby escaping sin and death. Origen's interpretative lens was individual responsibility for sin, both in Christ and the Christians: a person is called to separate from the collective body of sinners and be joined into the collective body of Christ. Ambrosiaster added the understanding of personified sin as the devil but otherwise tends to follow Origen's explanation. Augustine and Cyril used the second section of the chapter, 6:5-11, to explain the way in which Christ's death destroys the power of sin in his own flesh and thereby liberates the Christian from both sin and death. The two interpretations wonderfully illustrate the techniques of Alexandrian and African theology in explaining the efficacy of the redemptive work of Christ: the one using the identity of nature shared by Christ and humans that was achieved through the Incarnation and the other extending a sacramental model from the church to Christ.

In the final sections, the interpreters followed Paul in a moral or voluntary understanding of servitude to good or evil. Augustine, characteristically, insisted upon the primacy of divine grace over human self-determination.

Romans 6:1-4

₁**What shall we say then? Are we to continue in sin that grace may abound?** ₂**By no means! How can we who died to sin still live in it?** ₃**Do you not know that all of us who have been baptized into Christ Jesus were baptized into his death?** ₄**We were buried therefore with him by baptism into death, so that as Christ was raised from the dead by the glory of the Father, we too might walk in newness of life.**

(1) Ambrosiaster on verses 1-3

What then are we to say? Should we continue in sin in order that grace may abound? By no means! Should we always be sinning so that the gift of God might then increase to cover our sins? Should we put the grace of Christ on display by continually hoping for the remission of new sins from a faithful God? Certainly not. For God has taken pity on us through Christ so that we might stop sinning, that our good merits and God's grace might guide our lives. By returning to the old self and past ways of living, a people take their lives away from the governance of God's grace and hand them over to sin. We have received mercy for two purposes: to deprive the devil of dominion and to preach the reign of God to those who do not know it. This is the way to attain the honor we seek.

How can we who died to sin go on living in it? When we lived for sin, we were dead in God's sight. To commit sin is to live for sin, just as to avoid sin is to live for God. When, therefore, the grace of God comes to us through Christ and spiritual washing regenerates us through faith, we begin to live for God and to die to sin, that is, to the devil. To be dead to sin is to be set free from sin and become a servant of God. Thus, once we are dead to sin, we must not return to our former evil ways, lest we once more live for sin and, by dying to God, lose our exalted status and incur once again the punishment we had escaped.

Do you not know that all of us who have been baptized into Christ Jesus were baptized in his death? Once baptized, we must sin no more because when we are baptized we die with Christ, we are **baptized in his death**. In that Baptism all our sins die, so that we are renewed, casting off death and rising to new life. Just as Christ himself died to sin and rose, we too have the hope of resurrection through Baptism.

(2) Origen on verse 1

What then are we to say? Should we continue in sin in order that grace may abound? By no means! How can we who died to sin go on living in it? He said earlier that *where sin had increased, grace abounded all the more* (Rom 5:20). He now faces a question occasioned by this assertion: if an abundance of sin provokes a superabundance of grace, then sin ought to be committed so that grace may abound the more. Paul gives an immediate response — **By no means!** — and follows with an explanation. He observes that those in whom grace abounds are dead to sin: since a dead person cannot sin, one who is really dead to sin cannot continue to sin.

To clarify the issue let us consider the meaning of living and dying to sin. Just as the person who lives according to the will of God lives to God, so the one who lives according to the will of sin lives to sin. The Apostle expresses the same idea in saying, *Do not let sin exercise dominion in your mortal bodies, to make you obey their passions* (Rom 6:12). Thus he shows that obeying the desires of sin is living to sin. If to satisfy the desires of sin is to live to sin, then if we do not satisfy the passions of sin or obey its dictates, we die to sin.

(3) Augustine on verses 2-3

Paul says: **How can we who died to sin still live in it?** Then, to show that we are dead to sin, he writes: **Do you not know that any of us who have been baptized into Christ Jesus were baptized in his death?** If, then, we are told here that we died to sin because we were baptized into the death of Christ, it clearly follows that even children who are baptized into Christ must die to sin, since they are **baptized in his death**. No exception is noted:

any of us who have been baptized into Christ Jesus were baptized in his death. And this was said to prove that we were dead to sin. To what sin could children die by being reborn, if not that one they contracted by birth?

(4) Origen on verses 3-4

Wishing then to show the meaning of being dead to sin, Paul asks: **Do you not know that whoever of us have been baptized in Christ Jesus were baptized in his death? Therefore we have been buried with him by baptism into death.** In this statement, he taught that a person who has previously died to sin is then buried with Christ in baptism; but someone not already dead to sin cannot be buried with Christ. No one is ever buried alive. Yet a person is not properly baptized unless buried with Christ. . . .

We have all been baptized according to that form passed down in the churches — with visible water and oil. Yet only a person truly baptized in the Holy Spirit and invisible water from above is dead to sin, truly baptized in the death of Christ, and buried with him through Baptism into death.

Notice more carefully the sequence of this mystical order. You must first die to sin, and only then can you be buried with Christ, since only the dead should be buried. Indeed, if you are still alive to sin, you can neither be buried with Christ nor be interred in his new tomb. For in that case, your old self is still alive and you cannot walk in newness of life. The reason the Holy Spirit carefully specified in the Scriptures that Jesus was buried in a new sepulcher and that he was wrapped in a clean, fresh cloth, was to ensure that all who want to be buried with Christ through baptism would realize that nothing old should be brought into this new tomb and nothing unclean wrapped in this pure, fine cloth. The Apostle refers to this blessed dying when he says: *always carrying in the body the death of Jesus* (2 Cor 4:10), and again, *I die every day* (1 Cor 15:31). Also, when he says: *All things are yours, whether Paul or Apollo or Cephas or the world or life or death* (1 Cor 3:21-22), he intends the death by which we die to sin and are buried with Christ. . . .

So a deeper understanding of the Apostle's words yields this insight: just as no one still alive can be buried with the dead, so no one still living to sin can be buried with Christ, who is himself dead to sin. Therefore, those who approach Baptism must first take care that they have already died to sin, so they can be buried with Christ through Baptism and can say: *always carrying in the body the death of Jesus, so that the life of Jesus may also be made visible in our bodies* (2 Cor 4:10). Paul himself explains how the life of Jesus Christ may be displayed in the body when he says: *it is no longer I who live, but it is Christ who lives in me* (Gal 2:20). The Apostle John writes the same thing in his epistle, *every spirit that confesses that Jesus Christ has come in the flesh is from God* (1 John 4:2). The Spirit of God surely does not move the ones who only say the words or go along with the community's profession; no, the Spirit moves those who have ordered their lives, brought forth the fruit of their labors, and manifested by the devotion of their thoughts and deeds that Christ has come in the flesh, is dead to sin, and alive to God. . . .

For you must not imagine that a life can be renewed once and for all. On the contrary, this newness must, so to speak, itself be renewed again and again, even daily. Thus the Apostle says, *Even though our outer nature is wasting away, our inner nature is being renewed day by day* (2 Cor 4:16). For just as that old life is ever aging and is getting older day by day, so this new reality is always being renewed and its stature should be constantly and continuously growing. Just consider those who are making progress in the faith and whose virtues sparkle daily. See how they are always adding even better actions to their existing good works and eagerly seeking ever more noble achievements to add to their already great accomplishments, how they advance in understanding, knowledge, and wisdom. The things which earlier were poorly understood, they later grasp as plain and evident. Would you not agree that this sort of person is really being renewed just as the person who began to grow old and then continues to get worse is daily getting more elderly and feeble? So then we should walk in newness of life, showing ourselves to God, who *raised us with Christ* (Eph. 2:6) as renewed daily and every more beautiful persons. Let us compare our faces with Christ, and *seeing the glory of the Lord as though reflected in a mirror, we are being transformed into the same image* (2 Cor 3:18), because Christ, by rising from the dead, ascended from earthly lowliness to the glory of the Father's majesty.

(5) John Chrysostom on verses 3-4

Paul says, **Do you not know, brothers and sisters, that all of us who have been baptized into Christ have been baptized into his death? Therefore we have been buried with him through Baptism into his death.** What does he mean by **we have been baptized into his death**? He means that we die in the same way that Jesus died: Baptism is the cross. Baptism has become for us what the cross and the tomb were for Christ, although not in the same way. Christ died and was buried in the flesh, while we experience death and burial to sin. For this reason Paul did not say "planted together" in death, but *united with him in a death like his* (Rom 6:5). What Christ experienced and what we experience is death, but not the same kind of death. The death of Christ was death of the flesh; the death we experience is death to sin.

(6) Ambrosiaster on verse 4

In Baptism, we have been buried together with Christ, so that henceforth we may lead that life in which Christ rose. Thus Baptism is a pledge and an image of the resurrection, so that thereafter we remain steadfast in the commands of Christ, and do not turn back to the concerns of our past life. A person who has died sins no more: death puts an end to sinning. Baptism is celebrated with water because water washes dirt from the body. So we believe that through Baptism our incorporeal selves are invisibly washed, that we are spiritually cleansed from all sin and renewed.

(7) Augustine on verse 4

Beloved, consider Christ's resurrection. As his passion signified our old life, so his resurrection is a symbol of our new life. Thus the Apostle says: **We were buried with Christ through Baptism into death, so that as Christ has risen from the dead, so we too might walk in newness of life.** You believed and were baptized. The old life died; it was killed on the cross and buried in Baptism. The old, in which you lived wickedly, is buried. Let the new arise. Live well; live so that you may live. So live that when you have died, you may not die.

Romans 6:5-11

5 **For if we have been united with him in a death like his, we shall certainly be united with him in a resurrection like his.** 6 **We know that our old self was crucified with him, so that the sinful body might be destroyed, and we might no longer be enslaved to sin.** 7 **For he who has died is freed from sin.** 8 **But if we have died with Christ, we believe that we shall also live with him.** 9 **For we know that Christ, being raised from the dead, will never die again; death no longer has dominion over him.** 10 **The death he died he died to sin, once for all, but the life he lives he lives to God.** 11 **So you also must consider yourselves dead to sin and alive to God in Christ Jesus.**

(1) Origen on verses 5-7

The Apostle, well aware that in the present passage he was dealing not with natural death but with the death of sin, said not, **if we have been united in his death**, but **in a likeness of his death.** Christ died once to sin because *he committed no sin, nor was guile found on his lips* (1 Pet 2:22). That freedom from sin cannot be found in anyone else. *No one is pure from sin, even if his life on earth lasts one day* (Job 14:4-5 LXX). We cannot avoid all taint of sin, and so we cannot die the same death that Jesus died to sin, for he did not commit any sin. Yet we can achieve its likeness by imitating him; by following in his path, we can refrain from sin. Human nature can develop into the likeness of his death by imitating him and not sinning. Christ alone, however, has absolutely no experience of sin. . . .

What the Apostle says about **the body of sin** requires careful examination. Two ideas can be distinguished here: either our own body is a body of sin, or sin has its own proper body which must be destroyed by those who want to be enslaved to sin no longer. Either meaning might fit the sense, so we will explain both. Sin might have its own body in the sense of what is said about those who are reborn and renewed: *you are the body of Christ and individually members of it* (1 Cor 12:27). By contrast, those who have not crucified the old self might be called the body of sin and its members. The head of this body of sin would be the devil, just as Christ is the head of the body of the Church, which is *without stain or wrinkle* (Eph 5:27). The members forming this body of sin would be those vices which the Apostle counted earlier as belonging to this world: fornication, impurity, immodesty, avarice, contention, anger, deceit, strife, dissension, heresies, jealousy, rioting, and similar actions (Rom 1:29). These sins are appropriately characterized as members composing **the body of sin**, which is called **the old self**. Anyone who destroys that body through Christ's cross and is transformed into a new person created according to God will be enslaved to sin no longer. In contrast, anyone who serves the vices which are the members of **the body of sin** is a slave to sin.

If, however, the Apostle is understood to mean that our own body is **a body of sin**, he could be interpreted according to what David said of himself: *I was born guilty, a sinner when my mother conceived me* (Ps 51:5). The Apostle himself says elsewhere: *Who will rescue me from this body of death?* (Rom 7:24). He also calls our body a *body of humiliation* (Phil 3:21). He says of the Savior: *by sending his own Son in the likeness of sinful flesh, and to deal with sin, he condemned sin in the flesh* (Rom 8:3), indicating that while our flesh is the flesh of sin, the flesh of Christ is *like the flesh of sin*. Christ's flesh was not conceived from human seed, but *the Holy Spirit came over Mary, and the power of the Most High overshadowed her, so that the one born of her might be called the son of Most High* (Luke 1:35). By the unspeakable divine wisdom granted to him, therefore, Paul discerned a hidden and concealed meaning in our body being called a body of sin, death, and humiliation....

Thus our body is a **body of sin** because it is written that Adam sexually knew his wife Eve and begat Cain only after sinning (Gen 4:1). Note as well that the law requires a sacrifice of two turtledoves or two young pigeons for a newborn infant: one as a sin offering and the other as a burnt offering (Lev 12:8). For what sin are the birds offered? Can a newborn infant sin? Yet the offering of the sacrifice is commanded because of some sin, which makes the infant unclean even if it has lived for only a single day. David must have been referring to this sin when he said, as noted above, *my mother conceived me in sin* (Ps 51:5). Yet the Scripture contains no reference to his mother's sin. For this reason, the church received from the apostles the practice of baptizing infants.[1] Because the secrets of the divine mysteries were committed to the apostles, they knew that everyone is born with the stain of sin, which must be cleansed through water and the Spirit. Because of these inborn stains, the body itself is called **a body of sin**. Those who believe in the transmigration of souls think that this cleansing is for sins the soul committed in a prior body. They are wrong: the washing is necessary because the soul has been made in a body of sin, death, and debasement, as is written, *You have debased our soul in the dust* (Ps 44:25). These are the different ways in which we understand the expression **the body of sin**. Let the reader decide which, if either, of these two interpretations fits the Apostle's meaning.

In another passage, the Apostle states that we have already been *raised up with Christ and seated with him in heavenly places* (Eph 2:6). In this passage, however, he says: **if we have been united with him in a death like his, we will certainly be united with him in a resurrection like his.** There he said that it had already been accomplished; here that it will be and is still in hope. This is the basis for positing a double resurrection: now we rise with Christ in mind, intention, and faith, passing from earthly to heavenly con-

---

1. This explanation may be an adaptation added by Rufinus, who made the Latin translation of Origen's Greek text in which it survives. This statement, then, may reflect the practice of the late-fourth-century Latin church rather than the mid-third-century Greek one.

cerns and seeking what is yet to come; later will come the general resurrection of all in the flesh. Therefore the resurrection of faith in the mind begins to be realized now only in those who *seek the things that are above, where Christ is, seated at the right hand of God* (Col 3:1). That general resurrection of the flesh which affects everyone is still in the future. The fullness of each resurrection, however, will be accomplished only at the coming of the Lord.

(2) Ambrosiaster on verses 5-6

For if we have been united with him in a death like his, we will certainly be united with him in a resurrection like his. If we have been united with him **in the likeness of his death**, then we can rise in blessedness. Once brought into new life in Baptism, if we then set aside all our vices and sin no more, eventually we will be united with him in the likeness of his resurrection. Likeness in death brings likeness in resurrection, as the Apostle John says, *What we do know is this: when he is revealed, we will be like him* (1 John 3:2). We will rise immortal and glorious. This likeness will not eliminate all difference, of course, since our resurrection will be like his not in the divine nature but in bodily glory....

By the **old man** Paul means past actions. Just as the new self has a pure life through faith and Christ, so the prior self was old because of its unbelief and evil deeds. These actions have been crucified — he means killed — so that **the body of sin**, which is the accumulation of all crimes, **might be destroyed**. All sins taken together form a **body**, which is destroyed by good living and catholic faith.

(3) John Chrysostom on verse 5

Therefore Paul distinguishes two types of mortality and death. Christ suffered death of the first type; we must undergo the second type by earnestly seeking it. Christ granted us the gift of burying our former sins. Now, even if we acknowledge that God gives us much help, we must ourselves work hard to remain dead to sin after Baptism. Baptism has the power not only to forgive past transgressions but also to protect us against future ones. Just as you exercised faith to gain remission of the former sins, you should also show that your desires have changed by resisting sin in the future: do not defile yourself again.

(4) Augustine on verses 6-8

We know that our old self was crucified at the same time so that the sinful body might be destroyed. This refers to what Moses said, *Cursed is everyone who hangs from a tree* (Deut 21:23). The cross of the Lord symbolized crucifixion of the old self, just as his resurrection symbolized the renewal of our new self. According to Paul, we bear the old self, which is cursed. Because of that old self, the Lord himself was called sin and carried our sins and even sinned for us. By this sin, he condemned sin. What does it mean to condemn sin? Paul explains: **that we might no longer serve sin, if we have died with Christ**, that is, if we are crucified with Christ. He says in another place, *those who belong to Christ Jesus have crucified the flesh with its passions and desires* (Gal 5:24). Moses, therefore, did not curse Christ but prophesied what his crucifixion would signify.

(5) Augustine on verses 6-11

What does it mean to be *baptized in the death of Christ* (Rom 6:3) if not to die to sin? For this reason he says, **he died to sin; he died once for all.** This points to *the likeness of the flesh of sin* (Rom 8:3) and the great mystery of his cross, where **our old self was crucified so that our body of sin might be destroyed.** If infants are baptized into Christ, they are baptized into his death. If they are baptized into his death, then they are *united with him in the likeness of his death* (Rom 6:5) and they **die to sin. The death he died to sin was once for all; the life he lives he lives to God.** What follows tells what he means by *united with him in the likeness of his death.* **So you all must consider yourselves dead to sin and alive to God in Christ Jesus.** Could he be saying that Jesus himself **died to sin**, even though he committed no sin? No! And yet **the death he died to sin, he died once for all.** His death signified our sin, which is how death itself came about. To say that he **died to sin** means that he died to death (which comes from sin), so that he would no longer be mortal. What, therefore, he himself first signified in *the likeness of the flesh of sin*, through his grace we then accomplish in *the flesh of sin* itself. As Paul proclaimed that Christ **died to sin** by dying in *the likeness of sin*, so whoever is baptized into him actually dies to the very reality of sin, of which Christ's flesh was a likeness. He died a real death in true flesh; therefore, real sins are actually forgiven in Baptism.

(6) Cyril of Alexandria on verse 6

We must inquire who this **old self** of ours is, and what kind of body is rendered barren by sin, and how it has been crucified with Christ. Some might think that our body is called flesh of the earth because of sin, and that it was assigned to a human soul as a sentence for having sinned before coming into this body. Some believe that this is the right way to think and to speak about it. We reject this opinion of the pagan Greeks as false. Paul calls this **body marked by sin** and our **old self** an earthly body because since the ancient times of Adam when we were condemned, the body has been bound to corruption. Because of this weakness, we also love pleasure; by nature the flesh has these inbred passions. How then can one be crucified with Christ? The Only-Begotten Son became human and took on flesh derived from the earth, as I said, which has been afflicted with death since the ancient times of Adam, and because of its inbred passions has a burning desire for sin.

    The law of sin was suppressed in the holy and chaste flesh of Christ. We assert that the excesses of human passion were never aroused in him, leaving in him only those not rooted in sin, such as hunger, thirst, fatigue, and whatever the law of nature itself does in us without any guilt. If then the law of sin was not active in Christ because it was restrained by the power and the action of the indwelling Word, then we can conclude that the nature of the flesh itself was no different in Christ than it is in us. His body included in itself the whole of human nature; so when he was crucified, we too were crucified with him.

The curse called down for Adam's guilt afflicted the whole of human nature. In a similar way, we will be raised up with Christ and gathered together in the heavens. For even if Emmanuel exceeds us in power by his divinity, yet he came among us as one of us; as one of us, he rose from the dead and sits in council with the Father. As a result, our **old self** was crucified in him and the power of that old curse was abolished through his resurrection. The **body of sin** was destroyed in him — though in our own flesh this is not yet completely accomplished. The inborn wildness of passion in our flesh constantly draws our minds toward shameful deeds and incites us to earthy pleasures, as though our minds were mired in mud and filth. How could anyone doubt that in Christ this flaw of human nature has been corrected? For Paul states clearly: *God has done what the law, weakened by the flesh, could not do: by sending God's own Son in the likeness of sinful flesh, and to deal with sin, God condemned sin in the flesh* (Rom 8:3). Do you understand how **the body of sin was destroyed**? The urge for sin was condemned in the flesh; sin died first in Christ, then from him and through him grace has passed into us.

(7) Augustine on verses 8-11

If we have died with Christ, we believe that we shall also live with Christ, knowing that Christ, being raised from the dead, will never die again; death no longer has dominion over him. The death he died he died to sin, once for all, but the life he lives he lives to God. So you also must consider yourselves dead to sin and alive to God in Christ Jesus. Julian of Eclanum[2] explains this passage as follows: "Just as Christ **died to sin once for all** — that is, he **died once for all** because of our sins — and **will never die again** but lives in the glory of God; **so you also must consider yourselves dead to sin**, you must live to serve the virtues alone."

What an astonishing explanation! The Apostle says, **Christ died to sin**, and Julian says this means, "Christ died <u>because of our sins</u>." So when Paul says, **so you also must consider yourselves dead to sin**, should we think he means: "consider yourselves dead <u>because of your sins</u>?" Paul did not mean that, and Julian does not understand the statement that way. He recognizes that it means: "you are dead to sin, so do not live to sin." So he should explain **Christ died to sin** in such a way that the Apostle's next phrase, **so you also**, would reasonably follow from it. Clearly, Christ must have died in order to take away our sins. But Paul actually says, **he died to sin**. How could he have **died to sin** when he had no sin at all, either original or individual, to which he could die? How indeed but *in a likeness* (Rom 8:3)? By bearing a likeness, he assumed the name of the corresponding thing. We know that Christ came in *the likeness of sinful flesh* (Rom 8:3) because he came in true flesh but not in sinful flesh, like other human beings. He then died to that *likeness* of sin which he bore in his mortal flesh and so fulfilled the mystery of our salvation. As a

---

2. On Julian, see above, Augustine, p. 118, n. 5.

result, we can die to that sin whose *likeness* he had borne. We are baptized into his death: just as true death occurred in him, so true forgiveness occurs in us.

(8) Origen on verses 8-10

It seems to me that we must distinguish several deaths which Paul says *are at work in us* (2 Cor 4:12). The first occasion for the death of Christ is where it is written: *Then Jesus cried again with a loud voice and breathed his last* (Matt 27:50). Another time of death was when he lay behind the sealed entry in the tomb. Yet a third, when he was sought but not found in the tomb because he had already arisen — no one saw the beginning of the resurrection. So also we who believe in Christ should consider three times of death. First, the death of Christ must be manifest in us by confession in words: *For one believes with the heart and so is justified, and one confesses with the mouth and so is saved* (Rom 10:10). Second, we always carry the death of Christ in our body by mortifying our earthly members, as Paul says: *so death is at work in us* (2 Cor 4:12). Third, even now we rise from the dead and *walk in newness of life* (Rom 6:4). To summarize and clarify: the first time of death is the renunciation of the world; the second is the rejection of the faults of the flesh; and the third is the fullness of perfection in the light of wisdom on the day of resurrection. Yet only one to whom the secrets of hearts are revealed can discern these differences and stages of progress in each of the believers.

(9) Ambrosiaster on verse 8

But if we have died with Christ, we believe that we will also live with him. Obviously, those who have crucified the flesh — the world — with its vices and cravings, die to the world and die with Christ. Thus they bear the image of eternal life and salvation, and they deserve to become like Christ in glory. The flesh — the body — is crucified when its desires are beaten down; those desires began in the transgression of the first humans and are continued by the sin remaining in the flesh. The devil is also crucified in the flesh, since the devil deceives us through the flesh. Flesh, then, can mean different things: the world and the powers ruling it, the human body, or even the soul itself when it pursues bodily vices.

(10) John Chrysostom on verse 10

He died to sin. What does the expression **to sin** mean? That Christ was not liable to sin but became subject to death only because of our sin. Christ died for this reason — to destroy sin and cut out its sinews. Did you see how he terrified the powers of sin? If Christ dies only once, then there is no second cleansing from sin. Since there is no second cleansing, you must not slide back into sin. Paul says these things to oppose those who say, *Let us do evil so that good may come of it* (Rom 3:8), and also, *Let us continue in sin that grace may* *abound* (Rom 6:1). He wrote this to put away such notions. **But the life he lives he lives to God.** He means that he is incorruptible, no longer controlled by death. For if Christ died the first time on account of the sins of others, even though he was not himself subject to sin, he will certainly not die a second time because he has already destroyed sin.

Romans 6:12-14

12Let not sin therefore reign in your mortal bodies, to make you obey their passions. 13Do not yield your members to sin as instruments of wickedness, but yield yourselves to God as men who have been brought from death to life, and your members to God as instruments of righteousness. 14For sin will have no dominion over you, since you are not under law but under grace.

(1) Origen on verses 12-14

How is it possible for sin not to rule in our flesh? We must do what the Apostle directs: *Put to death whatever in you is earthly* (Col 3:5), and be *always carrying in the body the death of Christ* (2 Cor 4:10). Sin simply cannot rule when we bear the death of Christ. Indeed, the cross of Christ has such great power that if it were always before our eyes and faithfully kept in mind and the mind's eye was ever intent on the death of Christ, then no pressing desire, no lust, no wrath, no sinful spite would be able to prevail over us. That entire army of sin and the flesh would immediately be put to flight by the appearance of the cross. Sin itself does not stand fast in the fight; it has no substantive reality of its own but is operative only in our works and deeds.

Within us are both the concupiscence of sin which holds power in the flesh and the concupiscence of the spirit which finds its strength in the mind, as we have stated above: *What the flesh desires is opposed to the spirit, and what the spirit desires is opposed to the flesh* (Gal 5:17). The concupiscence of the flesh means desiring what is neither permitted nor fitting nor expedient. The concupiscence of the spirit, in contrast, means desiring and longing to see the salvation of God. A mediating soul seems to be placed between the flesh and the spirit. If that soul indulges the desires of sin, it joins the flesh and is united to the body. If it joins itself to the Lord, it becomes one spirit with the Lord. This follows what is said: *Whoever is united to a prostitute becomes one body with her. Anyone united to the Lord becomes one spirit with the Lord* (1 Cor 6:16, 17). Do not be surprised, then, if Paul calls the flesh a harlot, which suggests that all the faults and sins previously listed were its shameful lovers.

(2) Ambrosiaster on verses 12-14

Paul called the body mortal not because of its corruption but because of the punishment of hell: thus a person who deserves hell is called mortal. Those who obey sin do not escape that second death from which the Savior has freed those who believe in him. By the **mortal body**, then, Paul meant the whole human person; all who obey sin are called mortal. *For*, it says, *the one who sins shall die* (Ezek 18:4), that is, the whole self. No one will be judged without the body.

No longer present your members to sin as instruments of wickedness. Paul shows that the devil attacks us with our own weapons. Our sins provide the opportunity. When God deserts us, the devil gets the power to mock and destroy us. We ought to restrain our members from all evil deeds, therefore, so that we can catch our enemy unarmed and gain the victory. . . .

But present yourselves to God as those living from among the dead. By **death** he means ignorance and unbelief, along with an evil life. **Life** is to know God through Christ. . . . Ignorance and shameful behavior are death, for these vices lead to death — not to the common death of all but to the death of hell, as I indicated above. Similarly, knowledge of God as our parent and holy conduct lead to life — again not the present life which is subject to destruction, but the life of the age to come which is called eternal. For this reason, **present yourselves**, he says, **to God**; by knowing God, you advance toward salvation; by turning away from shameful behavior, you become **as alive from among the dead**.

And present your members to God as instruments of righteousness. He wants us to conduct our lives with such discretion that our actions advance us in divine righteousness rather than the righteousness of this world, and thus equip Christ with means to defend us. The righteousness of this world places no faith in Christ; it is more death than life. When we furnish armaments to God by our good deeds, we become worthy of being helped, but divine justice pays no heed to the unworthy. The Holy Spirit dwells where the righteousness of God is found and assists our weakness. We supply weapons to sin when we act wrongly, but we arm righteousness when we behave well and restrain our members from all indecency.

For sin will have no dominion over you, since you are not under law but under grace. If we walk according to the instructions he gives, Paul says that sin cannot rule over us in the way it masters those who sin. When we do not walk in the way he teaches, we are under the law. If we do not sin, however, we are subject not to the law but to grace. Thus if we sin, we will return to the realm of the law, and sin will once again rule our lives. Every sinner is a servant of sin.

(3) Theodoret on verses 12-14

A kingdom differs from a tyranny in that a tyranny has unwilling subjects, while a kingdom is governed by their agreement. Paul urges us not to consent to the ruling power of sin, since the Lord incarnate overthrew that kingdom. As lawgiver for us mortals who are still subject to suffering, he establishes laws adapted to our failings. He does not say, "Do not let sin tyrannize you," but rather, **Do not let it rule you.** Ruling by tyranny is characteristic of sin, but subjecting oneself to its governance requires our intentions. The excitement and annoyance of the passions exist in our nature, but the mind must make a choice about what is forbidden. By calling the body mortal, Paul reminds us that this conflict will be not last long. For when the flesh reaches its end in death, the assault of the passions ceases. Thus he gives us orders, not that we should end the tyranny of sin, but rather that we not yield to it, even though it incessantly stirs up the desires of the flesh.

And present your members to God as instruments of righteousness. He has demonstrated that the body is not evil, that it is the workmanship of the good God. If the soul guides it well and honestly, the body can render service to God. An inclination toward evil offers the bodily members as tools for sin, but a delight in knowledge of the good disposes the members to observe the divine laws. In self-controlled harmony, the tongue offers fitting music to the God of the universe; if drunk and careless, it madly brays out in harsh blasphemy. It is honored by truth-telling but disgraced by lying. So too the eye sees what is chaste and licentious, cruel and humane. The hand can either kill or offer mercy. Generally speaking, a person's will can make all parts of the body tools of justice — or submit to sin's dominion.

Since you are not under the law but under grace. He maintains that before the coming of grace, the law taught only what ought to be done but offered no help to those on whom it was imposed. Grace provides assistance to supplement the law's commands. Since its help removes difficulties, grace provides a more perfect legislation.

(4) John Chrysostom on verses 12-13

Let not sin therefore reign in your mortal bodies, to make you obey their passions. Paul did not say, "Do not let the flesh live or act," but, **Let not sin reign.** Christ came to set right, not to destroy, the freedom that is ours by nature. So Paul shows that iniquity holds us fast not by coercion or compulsion but by our own free choice. He did not say, "Do not let it tyrannize you," which would have meant compulsion, but he says, **Let not sin reign.** How absurd that those led into the kingdom of heaven should let sin be their sovereign and that those called to reign with Christ would choose to be slaves of sin. This would be like knocking the crown off Christ's head and enslaving oneself to some frantic beggar-woman clothed in rags. Because overcoming sin can be difficult, Paul showed how to make it easy. He lightens the effort needed to prevail over sin by saying, **in your mortal bodies**, to remind us that the struggles are temporary and quickly brought to an end. At the same time he recalls our prior wrongdoing and the root of death, since the body became mortal through sin, contrary to the way it was created. Even in a mortal body, however, a person can still avoid sin. Notice the abundance of Christ's grace. Although he did not yet have a mortal body, Adam fell. You can be crowned, although you received a body subject to death.

Someone might ask, "How can sin exercise dominion?" It reigns because of your negligence rather than by its own power. Thus Paul says, **Let it not reign**, and then shows how it would reign by adding, **to obey sin in the passions of the body.** Granting the body everything it demands brings no one respect; such is rather the lowest form of slavery and height of dishonor. By doing what it desires, the body is actually deprived of all freedom. By being restrained, however, the body's own value is especially maintained.

No longer present your members to sin as instruments of wickedness, but as in-

struments of righteousness. Like an instrument, the body is capable of evil and virtue. The person using it determines which it will serve. Both the soldier who fights for his country and the thief who arms himself against the inhabitants of that country defend themselves with their weapons. We do not fault the armaments themselves but the person who uses them for evil purposes. The same can be said of the flesh, which acts in different ways, not by its own nature but at the soul's direction. If the flesh is curious about the beauty of another, the eye becomes the weapon of unrighteousness, not through its own action — the function of the eye itself is just seeing, not seeing wickedly — but because an evil mind commands it. If a person controls the eyes, they can become the armor of righteousness. The same can be said about the tongue, the hands, and all the other members of the body.

(5) Augustine on verses 12-13

But if in the flesh you must serve the law of sin, at least do what the Apostle himself says: **Let not sin therefore reign in your mortal bodies, to make you obey their passions. Do not yield your members to sin as instruments of wickedness.** He did not say, "Let not sin be," but **Let sin not reign.** As long as sin has to be in your members, at least deprive it of dominion: what it commands must not be allowed to take place. Does anger boil up? Do not let anger take over your tongue for cursing; do not lend anger your hand or foot for striking. That irrational anger would not arise unless sin were in our members; but take away control from it and deny it the arms by which it could assault you. It will learn not to rebel when it begins to find no armaments available. **Do not yield your members to sin as instruments of wickedness** or your whole self will all be held captive and you will not be able to say, *I serve the law of God with my mind* (Rom 7:25). If the mind holds onto its weapons, then the members will not act in the service of violent sin. Let the interior ruler hold the citadel; in taking this stand it will be supported by a higher power. Let it bridle anger and imprison lust. What is within needs to be bridled; what is within needs to be restrained; what is within needs to be controlled. Would not the righteous person who *serves the law of God with the mind* prefer that what must be bridled be driven out? This everyone who strives for perfection must attempt. If one is making progress, unbridled desire should daily grow weaker as the members refuse to obey it.

(6) Augustine on verse 14

When, then, you hear: **Sin will have no dominion over you**, do not rely on yourself to keep sin from dominating you but rely instead on the one to whom the holy man prayed, *Guide my way according to your word, and let no iniquity get dominion over me* (Ps 119:133). We must be careful that when we hear, **Sin will have no dominion over you**, we do not praise ourselves and claim that we accomplish this by our own strength. The Apostle saw this danger and immediately added, **since you are not under law but under grace.** Grace prevents sin from having dominion over you.

Romans 6:15-19

₁₅**What, then? Are we to sin because we are not under law but under grace? By no means!** ₁₆**Do you not know that if you yield yourselves to anyone as obedient slaves, you are slaves of the one whom you obey, either of sin, which leads to death, or of obedience, which leads to righteousness.** ₁₇**But thanks be to God, that you who were once slaves of sin have become obedient from the heart to the standard of teaching to which you were committed,** ₁₈**and, having been set free from sin, have become slaves of righteousness.** ₁₉**I am speaking in human terms because of your natural limitations. For just as you once yielded your members to impurity and to greater and greater iniquity, so now yield your members to righteousness for sanctification.**

(1) Ambrosiaster on verses 15-17

What, then? Have we sinned because we are not under law but under grace? By no means! Since the law is from God, Paul acts to forestall a possible objection: "If the law is from God, why should we not be subject to the law?" Then he explains that Christ fulfilled the will of God, who had given the law, by releasing us from subjection to it. The law was given for two reasons: to show that people who had sinned before it was given were actually culpable in God's judgment, and to deter them from sinning in the future. Yet, because the human race was weak and unstable, people could not restrain themselves from sinning and thus were condemned to death in hell. Moved by the goodness of that divine clemency by which God always aids the human race, God opened a way through Christ for those who had given up hope of a cure. By receiving the forgiveness of sins, they were rescued from the law which held them guilty. Once raised up and restored by God's help, they struggled against the vices which had previously dominated them. Thus we did not sin as though disregarding God's law, but through Christ we are under God's wise governance.

Do you not know that if you present yourselves to anyone as servants ready to obey, you are servants of the one whom you obey, either of sin or of obedience to righteousness. We are not to profess one thing and do another, not to call ourselves servants of God and have our deeds show us actually slaves of the devil. Paul thus warns and threatens that we are the servants of whoever's will we carry out in our actions. To profess God as our Lord and still serve the devil in our deeds is destructive. . . .

But thanks be to God, that you who were once servants of sin have become obedient from the heart to the form of teaching to which you were entrusted. Because, by believing in Christ, we have been made servants of righteousness. We are called servants of the one whom we obey. Because it is right to obey Christ — for he is righteousness itself and his teachings are just — Paul says that we have been made servants of righteousness **from our hearts** and not from the law, in freedom and not in fear, so that our profession of faith should be manifest in our decisions. For we have been brought to faith not by the law but by nature. God formed this teaching in us by the same command that created nature itself. From nature we have the means of recognizing from whom and through whom and in whom we have been created. These are the truths which the creator has naturally shaped in us. Paul said above, *They are a law to themselves* (Rom 2:14), because they understand that what they believe is built into their own nature. As a result, the Gentiles believe from their hearts the things that the Law and the Prophets foretold to the Jews about Christ. Thus Paul gives thanks to God that, though we were slaves of sin, we obeyed from within our hearts, believing in Christ, so that we might serve God through the natural law rather than the law of Moses.

(2) Origen on verse 15

What, then? Should we sin because we are not under law but under grace? By no means! This seems similar to that statement which we explained previously: *What then are we to say? Should we continue in sin in order that grace may abound? By no means!* (Rom 6:1-2). The same exposition may suffice for both instances. The only difference between the two statements seems to be in the first, *Shall we continue in sin?* Those words appear to be directed to people who have not yet stopped sinning, urging them not to remain in that condition. Here the question may be posed by those who have already stopped sinning. There the question is about the abundance of grace which is not yet given, while here the grace is already present. Thus Paul adds here: **we are not under law but under grace.**

(3) Origen on verse 16

The words of Paul are consistent: **if you present yourselves to anyone as obedient servants, you are servants of the one whom you obey, either of sin or righteousness.** By our own will, through our own consent and not coercion, we show ourselves servants of either sin or justice. We should always remember this and not make excuses for our sin, blaming the devil, the demands of nature, fate, or the position of the stars.

(4) John Chrysostom on verse 18

You, having been set free from sin, have become slaves of righteousness. Here Paul points out two gifts from God: being freed from sin and serving righteousness, which is a gift even greater than freedom. A parallel might be someone's taking an orphan who had been carried off by barbarians into their land, delivering the child from captivity, placing it in the care of a guardian, and then bestowing the highest honor on the child. This is exactly what God did for us. Having freed us from the ancient evil and led us to the angelic life, God has paved the way to the highest form of life by placing us under the protection of righteousness, exterminating the old evils, executing the old self, and leading us by the hand toward immortal life. Let us continue living such a life — for many of those who appear to breathe and walk about are in a worse condition than the dead. There are different forms of dying. One death is of the body, by which Abraham is dead, and yet not dead. *For God*, Christ said, *is the God not of the dead, but of the living* (Matt 22:32). A second is death of the soul, to which Christ referred when he said, *Let the dead bury their own dead* (Matt 8:22). A third, praiseworthy dying is accomplished by religious practice. Paul spoke about this death when he said, *Put to death whatever in you is earthly* (Col 3:5). Baptism also produces this type of death, as Paul says, *our old self was crucified*, put to death (Rom 6:6). Understanding these distinctions, we should flee that death of the soul in which we die while still alive and should not fear the bodily death common to all. Let us choose and strive for both ways leading to the third death: since Baptism is blessed because God has given it, and self-restraint is praiseworthy because God helps us do it. David pronounces the baptized blessed when he says, *Happy are those whose transgression is forgiven* (Ps 32:1). Paul praises the self-controlled when he writes to the Galatians, *Those who belong to Christ have crucified the flesh* (Gal 5:24). Of the other two types of death, Christ says that the one is easy to despise and the other should be feared, *Do not fear those who kill the body but cannot kill the soul; rather, fear the one who can destroy both soul and body in hell* (Matt 10:28). For this reason, let us flee the first two types of death and choose instead both forms of the third, which are blessed and praised. We may flee bodily death and fear spiritual death. If we do not live a life of good works, seeing the sun or eating and drinking does us no good. Tell me, what would a king accomplish by dressing in the purple robe and piling up armaments if he had not a single subject and no army to protect him from whoever wanted to attack and insult him? In the same way, a Christian gains no benefit by having faith and the gift of Baptism but remaining subject to all the passions. Indeed, the outrage is even greater. Just as the person who wears the diadem and the purple robe gains no honor from the garment itself but would even degrade that dignity by shameful behavior, so also a believer who leads a corrupt life will become an object of scorn, not a model of respect.

(5) Ambrosiaster on verse 19

For just as you once presented your members to serve impurity and to greater and greater iniquity, so now present your members to serve righteousness for sanctification. To prevent our accepting faith in fear, which would make it harsh and burdensome, Paul urges us to serve God in the same way that we previously served the devil. We ought to serve God even more willingly than we did the devil, to be more eager for salvation than damnation. This spiritual physician demands nothing more from us, lest we find these commands too heavy for our weakness, take to flight, and remain in death as a result. As the Lord says, *Take my yoke upon you, because my yoke is easy and my burden is light* (Matt 11:29-30).

(6) Augustine on verse 19

Prefer the delights of the mind to those of the senses. Illicit pleasures delight your flesh; the righteousness which delights the mind is invisible, beautiful, chaste, holy, melodious, and sweet; it does not coerce by fear. If I am forced by fear, I am not yet delighted. You must shun sin not for fear of punishment but by love of justice. This is what the Apostle says: **I am speaking in human terms because of the weakness of your flesh. For just as you once yielded your members to serve impurity and to iniquity for iniquity, so now yield your members to serve justice unto sanctification.** What did I say? **I speak in human terms,** I told you what you can manage. When you yielded your members to iniquity in perpetrating outrages, were you pushed by fear or drawn by delight? What do you say? Answer yourselves. Those of you who live virtuously now might have lived wrongly in the past. When you used to sin, did you enjoy your sins? Did fear or attraction draw you to sinning? Would you answer, attraction? So, did attractiveness once lead you to sin and now fear drives you to righteousness? Test yourselves, examine yourselves. Let the one who threatens you take away your gold. Righteousness is still more attractive, and justice more shining. The one who promises it will not really deliver the gold, but righteousness is preferable to gold and gives greater joy. It is more sparkling, brilliant, attractive, delightful. If, therefore, people have tested themselves and won this battle, then they have listened to the Apostle, **I speak in human terms because of the weakness of your flesh.** Doubtless, he has mercy on weakness. I do not know what he could have said that would be more gracious to those who were less worthy.

Romans 6:20-23

20When you were slaves of sin, you were free in regard to righteousness. 21But then what return did you get from the things of which you are now ashamed? The end of those things is death. 22But now that you have been set free from sin and have become slaves of God, the return you get is sanctification and its end, eternal life. 23For the wages of sin is death, but the free gift of God is eternal life in Christ Jesus our Lord.

(1) Origen on verses 20-21

What benefit did you get from the things of which you are now ashamed? The end of those things is death. Divine Scripture teaches that both good and evil deeds produce a crop, as the Savior himself states in the Gospel: *Either make the tree good, and its fruit good; or make the tree bad, and its fruit bad; for the tree is known by its fruit* (Matt 12:33). *A good tree cannot bear bad fruit, nor can a bad tree bear good fruit* (Matt 7:18). In these sayings the tree, whether good or bad, seems to represent the intention and will; its fruits signify deeds. Someone who converted to righteousness in will and intention would undoubtedly become ashamed of earlier actions and recognize that **the end of those things**, that is, the deeds done under the rule of sin, **is death.**

I want to determine which death this is. Certainly it is not the common form of death because no one converts to justice or becomes ashamed for past evil actions after that death. Which death then? Does he mean the death brought on by sin, since *the soul which sins will die* (Exod 18:4)? Or should we understand it as our dying to sin with Christ and putting an end to our vices and iniquities, so that we hear, **The end of those things is death. But now that you have been freed from sin and have become servants of God, the benefit you get is sanctification. The end is eternal life?** Paul compares the results to one another. The fruits of sin shame us once we have been freed from sin and become servants of God, but death puts an end to them. The fruits of justice bring sanctification and result in eternal life.

(2) Augustine on verses 20-22

Free choice has not perished in the sinner because all who sin with delight actually exercise free choice to its full potential by loving the sin and doing what pleases them. The Apostle says this: **When you were servants of sin, you were not ruled by righteousness.** Sinners, then, can serve sin only by using a different kind of liberty. They escape the rule of righteousness only by the choice of their will; they are freed from the rule of sin, however, only through the grace of the Savior. For this reason, that admirable teacher distinguishes the terms themselves: **when you were servants of sin,** he says, **you were not ruled by righteousness. But then what benefit did you get from the things of which you are now ashamed? The end of those things is death. But now that you have been set free from sin, you have become servants of God, and the benefit you have is sanctification and its end of eternal life.** He said that they were **not ruled by righteousness**, not that they were "set free." He did not say they were free of sin but that they were "not ruled" by sin, choosing his words carefully, lest they claim this had been accomplished by their own efforts, He was referring to the Lord's statement: *If the Son sets you free, then you will be free indeed* (John 8:36). Since human beings do not live well unless they have been made children of God, why do the Pelagians insist on attributing the power of living well to our own free choice? This power is bestowed only by the grace of God through Jesus Christ our Lord, as the gospel says: *But to all who received him, he gave the power to become children of God* (John 1:12).

(3) John Chrysostom on verses 22-23

But now that you have been freed from sin and enslaved to God, the advantage you get is sanctification. The end is eternal life. The fruit of the former actions was shame — even after deliverance — but the fruit of the later actions is holiness. Where there is holiness, there is also great boldness. The result of the former actions was death, but the outcome of these later actions is eternal life.

Do you see how Paul shows both the gifts already given and the gifts for which we still hope? From the gifts already given, he also displays the gifts for which we hope; moving from holiness to eternal life. To prevent anyone from asserting that all the gifts are still yours only in hope, he shows that you have already gathered some fruit for yourself: first, you have been freed from iniquity and from those evils you are ashamed even to recall; second, you have become a servant of righteousness; third, you enjoy holiness;

fourth, you have obtained life unending, not just for the present. However, this is also the situation. Paul directs you to continue serving as you did before. Even if the master is far preferable, if the benefit and reward of the service is much greater, I demand nothing more. Then, he continues with the metaphor of a king and armaments: **For the wages of sin is death, but the free gift of God is eternal life in Christ Jesus our Lord.** After referring to **the wages of sin**, Paul did not use these same terms to talk about goodness: he did not say, "the wages of your good works," but **the free gift of God.** He indicates that they had not freed themselves by their own power, nor had they received what was owed them, nor payment of goods in exchange for deeds. Rather, all was accomplished through grace. So this part was better too, not just because God changed them and made them better people, but because God accomplished it and they did not have to labor or struggle for it. And God not only changed them but bestowed on them something much better, through the Son. Paul inserted all these points because he had been discussing grace and would next overthrow the law. Between these discussions, he inserted a section on living a virtuous life, so that those other two considerations would not wear them down. He took every opportunity to exhort his listeners to practice virtue. When Paul calls **the wages of sin death**, he again strikes fear in them and he arms them to face the future. He reminds them of their former way of life but at the same time inspires gratitude and makes them more secure against anything that may yet happen to them.

(4) Origen on verse 23

For the wages of sin is death, but the free gift of God is eternal life in Christ Jesus. His words, **the wages of sin is death**, are like what he had just stated, **the end of these things is death.** What things? Doubtlessly, those that shame us and whose results he deems unworthy of further mention. **But the free gift of God is eternal life in Christ Jesus** is itself similar to his statement: **the advantage you get is sanctification. The end is eternal life.** He continues to use the earlier metaphor or image of campaigning or serving sin as one's king, even submitting to that tyranny. He even says that death is the stipend due to be paid. God, however, does not give wages like those due to soldiers, but offers a gift, the grace of **life eternal in Christ Jesus our Lord.**

Sin therefore offers death as a fitting stipend for the legions it commands. This does not mean bodily death but that death of which it is written: *the soul which sins will itself die* (Ezek 18:4). Because the present passage requires that I briefly recap what was said elsewhere about the different kinds of death, I hope this exercise will not be too much trouble to me or a burden to my readers. Death is a single term in the Scriptures, but it conveys many meanings. It names the separation of the body from the soul. This kind of death is neither bad nor good; it is neutral or indifferent. In another sense, the separation of the soul from God is termed death occurring through sin. This condition is plainly evil, and it is also called **the wages of sin**. God did not create this death, nor does God find any satisfaction in the loss of the living; but *through the devil's envy, this death has entered into the world* (Wis 2:24). As the cause of this death, the devil is also called death and named *the last enemy of Christ to be destroyed* (1 Cor 15:26). That hell in which souls are imprisoned by death is also given the name of death (1 Pet 3:19). But there is also a praiseworthy death in which a person dies to sin and is buried with Christ, a death which sets the soul right and brings it eternal life (Rom 6:2-4).

(5) Ambrosiaster on verse 23

For the wages of sin is death. He says that the wages of sin is death, because death comes through sin, and thus, those who abstain from further sin will receive the payment of eternal life. Whoever avoids sin is free from the second death.

But the grace of God is eternal life in Christ Jesus our Lord. As those who give themselves over to sin earn death, similarly those who give themselves over to the grace of God and the faith of Christ which forgives sins will have eternal life. For this reason, they rejoice in being discharged at the proper time, knowing that they will attain a life which is free of all burdens and does not give way to yet another life. In his desire for that life, holy Simeon prayed to be discharged from this life, *to be dismissed in peace* (Luke 2:29), into that life which suffers no distress. Paul testifies that this gift is given to us by God through Christ our Lord, so that we may give thanks to God the Father through no one but the Son.

(6) Augustine on verse 23

Since grace alone causes all our good merit, what merit could a person have before receiving grace, for which grace would then be given as a reward? God rewards God's own gifts in rewarding our merits. From the outset of our faith, we received mercy not because we had been, but so that we might become faithful. And so to the very end, to eternal life, *God crowns us,* as it is written, *with compassion and mercy* (Ps 103:4). Nor do we sing to God in vain, *God's mercy will go before me* (Ps 59:10), and *God's mercy will follow me* (Ps 23:6). For this reason, therefore, that eternal life which we will possess in the end without end itself remains a gift of grace, even though it is given as a reward for preceding merits. The very merits which it rewards were accomplished in us through grace; we did not earn them through our own power. That grace itself is called "grace" precisely because it is given gratuitously. Because grace is given without merits, it follows that the merits for which eternal life is then given are themselves gifts. We even find eternal life being termed a grace in the writings of the same great defender of grace, the Apostle Paul: **the wages of sin is death**, he says, **but the free gift of God is eternal life in Christ Jesus our Lord.**

Notice, I beg you, how precisely and carefully he chose his words. Attending to them diligently can illumine somewhat the obscurities of this question. When he had said, **the wages of sin is death**, who would not have expected that he would continue on — properly and consistently — by saying, "the wages of righteousness is eternal life"? And this could be true in a way: as death is paid as a kind of wage for the merit of sin, so would eternal life be paid as a kind of wage for the merit of righteousness. Or, if he preferred to avoid saying righteousness, he could have said faith, *since the just lives by faith* (Rom 1:17; Gal 3:11; Heb 10:38; Hab 2:4). In just this way, eternal life is called a payment in many places in the Holy Scriptures. Righteousness and faith, however, are never called a payment; rather, a payment is given to righteousness or faith. Payment is to a worker, in the terms being used here, as wages are to a soldier.

The blessed Apostle is working against self-aggrandizement, which constantly tries to get control of the great. He speaks about this because of *the messenger of Satan sent to harass him* (2 Cor 12:7), lest he be exalted by presumption. Vigilantly campaigning against elation as a plague, he says: **the wages of sin is death.** Death is truly a wage because it is owed, because it is duly handed out, because it is paid for merit. Then, he prevented righteousness from applying the same standard, that evil merit among human beings is certainly sin; he did not say that righteousness is based on human merit. He did not say, "the wages of righteousness is eternal life," but instead: **the grace of God is eternal life.** And lest this grace be sought from some source other than the mediator, he added: **in Christ Jesus our Lord.** Thus he is saying: "Hearing that **the wages of sin is death**, you are all set to brag about yourself, you proud one, not for true righteousness but instead for that pride that claims the title of righteousness. Are you ready to praise yourself? Are you burning with a desire to claim eternal life — the opposite of death — as a wage owing to you? To what is eternal life owed, except only to true righteousness? If, however, that righteousness is true, then it did not arise from you; it is *from above, descending from the Father of lights* (Jas 1:17). To have it, if indeed you do have it, you must have received it: *What good have you that you have not received?* (1 Cor 4:7). Therefore, if you are going to receive eternal life, in itself it will indeed be the wages of righteousness, but for you it will be a grace, because your very righteousness is itself a grace. It would be paid to you as owed, but only if your righteousness was itself your own, something belonging properly to you. Now, in truth, we receive from the fullness of God not only that grace by which we live righteously in our labors until the end, but we even receive *grace for this grace* (John 1:16) so that afterward we may live in rest without end. Faith believes nothing more salutary than this, because our understanding discovers nothing more true. We should listen to what the prophet says: *Unless you have believed, you will not understand* (Isa 7:9 LXX).

Romans 7

Most but not all commentators note that Paul's analogy for the Christian's relationship to the law — a marriage being dissolved through death of one of the partners — was not developed consistently. Their explanations, however, differ as to how Paul understood being freed from sin by Christ.

Paul discussed the conflict between the law and sin. Origen identifies the law in question as that which resides naturally in the human mind and becomes operative in guiding choices as a child matures. The other commentators argue that Paul intended the law revealed through Moses, which unmasks human sinfulness. They explain the power of sin to resist the law in different ways: as the devil defending a dominion over humans, as human desires arising from mortality, or as self-love that only divine grace can overcome.

A major question in the second half of the chapter, in which Paul discussed the conflict within the person, was the status of the speaker. Origen judges that Paul spoke not for himself but for recently converted Christians who were still struggling against their vices. Ambrosiaster and Augustine — in his later works — explain that this power of sin was not removed by Baptism but remained in the Christian until the body was freed in the resurrection from that mortality brought on by sin. In some of his statements, then, Paul could have spoken for himself not only before but even after he had become a Christian. Augustine argues that the delight in the law of God which Paul claimed actually arose not from natural instinct but was the work of divine grace. In that part of the chapter, therefore, Paul had to be speaking as a Christian, as someone strengthened by grace.

Romans 7:1-6

1Do you not know, brethren — for I am speaking to those who know the law — that the law is binding on a person only during his life? 2Thus a married woman is bound by the law to her husband as long as he lives; but if her husband dies she is discharged from the law concerning the husband. 3Accordingly, she will be called an adulteress if she lives with another man while her husband is still alive. But if her husband dies she is free from that law, and if she marries another man she is not an adulteress.

4Likewise, my brethren, you have died to the law through the body of Christ, so that you may belong to another, to him who has been raised from the dead in order that we may bear fruit for God. 5While we were living in the flesh, our sinful passions, aroused by the law, were at work in our members to bear fruit for death. 6But now we are discharged from the law, dead to that which held us captive, so that we serve not under the old written code but in the new life of the Spirit.

(1) Origen on verses 1-6

Brothers — for I am speaking to those who know the law — I want you to know that you left the law like a deceased husband. Its death was brought about when Christ came and assumed a body. Now you belong to another and are joined to a new husband, to one who rose from the dead and is no longer subject to death, the death which your previous husband, the law, has died. . . .

The law is binding on a man only as long as it is alive. Alive refers not to the person but to the law itself. This Paul makes clear when he says, **a married woman is bound to the law as long as her husband lives.** His example makes the point clearer: he gives the law the role of the husband and says of the woman, that **if her husband dies she is free from that law of the husband.** . . .

And so, **she will be called an adulteress if she lives with another while her husband is still alive.** If a person comes to Christ and is joined in marriage to Christ as her second husband, she must not allow her first husband, **the oldness of the letter**, to remain alive for her. If she keeps the law alive within herself, she will be an adulteress by taking a second husband while her first is still living. Paul made the same point earlier by another illustration, saying that the Christian should die and be buried with Christ.

And so, my brothers, you have died to the law through the body of Christ, so that you may belong to another, to him who has been raised from the dead in order that we may bear fruit for God. Notice that while Paul uses a variety of images, he focuses on a single point. He says the law is dead for us, and he wants us to understand that we are dead to the law through the body of Christ, in which *he bore our iniquities and carried our sins* (Isa 53:4, 11) and in which *he disarmed the ruler and authorities, triumphing over them in his body* (Col 2:15). Let us hasten, then, to this second marriage, which is far happier than the first. . . .

This argument can be made not only about the law of Moses interpreted according to the letter but about any such spouse. Those whose lives are guided by social institutions and cultural customs are under a kind of law that regulates their behavior. They must die to this law or the law to them, lest they come to Christ still joined to another spouse, that is, to those prior laws with which they have been living, and so enter not into marriage with Christ but into an adulterous union. . . .

While we were living in the flesh, the vices of sin, which came from the law, were at work in our members to bear fruit for death. But now we are discharged from the law and dead to what held us, so that we serve in the newness of the Spirit and not in the oldness of the letter. In using these images, Paul seems to be moving between unmarked rooms through hidden passages. The preceding statements seem to focus on the letter of the law and thus appear addressed to those who place their trust in circumcision. Now he has moved to discussing the law in terms of the flesh and the vices; he seems to be addressing a wider audience, not only those who identify themselves by circumcision. So he says, **while we were living in the flesh.** He is not speaking literally: he was still living in the flesh when he said this. **While we were living in the flesh** means living according to the flesh. **The vices of sin, which came from the law, were at work in our members.** What law was this which set the sinful passions to work? Certainly the law of Moses, even if followed literally, does not rouse sinful passions. Obviously, he means the law in the members which resists the law of the mind, which we discussed above in treating the text, *Law came in, with the result that the trespasses multiplied* (Rom 5:20). This law makes trespasses multiply in those who live according to the flesh and **bear fruit for death.** This law is in our members; it resists the law of the mind, makes us captive to sin, and offers these fruits to death.

But now we are discharged from the law and dead to what held us. We are now free of the law that held us captive. What is the meaning of this **now**? Surely, it means the time when we died with Christ, were crucified with him, and were buried with him in Baptism. Thus Paul says, **we are discharged from the law, dead.** A person can be set free from that law only by dying with Christ. I know that some copies of the text read, **from the law of death, in which we were held**, but the reading, **dead**, is more accurate and true.

(2) Cyril of Alexandria on verse 1

Throughout his writings Paul shows the danger of voluntarily subjecting oneself to the law. In place of this, he urges his readers to focus their thoughts fully on thirsting after grace through faith, which is righteousness in Christ. He assured those who had been baptized that they were buried together with Christ and that, once having died to sin, they could live to God in righteousness. For this reason, he also said, *Therefore do not let sin reign in your mortal body to obey its passions, nor present your members as weapons of unrighteousness for sin, but present yourselves to God as those who have returned to life, and your members as weapons of righteousness for God; for sin will no longer rule over you; for you will not be under the law but under grace* (Rom 6:12-14). Notice how he commands them to abandon the rule of the law and seek the grace found in Christ.

Filled as he was with the Spirit, Paul certainly anticipated that in reply someone might say or rather argue: this means that our ancestors strayed from the straight path of life; the law did not benefit them at all, and the glory of their way of life has already vanished. For if it is unreasonable to seek to follow the law — which was the ancients' goal in life — can we not say that they strayed from what was appropriate? So Paul, with Christ in him, countered and argued with them. Cleverly, he first pretends to agree with those who preferred to live under the law. Then he subtly turns things around to show that they must not cling stubbornly to the ancient customs once the opportunity arises to answer the call to faith. For this reason Paul says, **Or do you not know, brothers (for I speak to those who know the law), that the law rules over a person for as long as he**

lives? This is a general rule applying to those subject to any law. For example, the laws determine what a person subject to civil authority can and cannot do. But it applies only to those who are still living. When someone subject to the civil law is set free from bodily life, he is thereby freed from the power of that law. In the same way, the law loses power over anyone who dies to sin. So it is true that the law rules over a person only as long as he lives in sin.

We must also explain the purpose of this argument. Paul introduces two important points simultaneously. We were buried together with Christ through Baptism and have died to sin; because we have been transformed into another type of life, we are beyond the power of the law. But those who lived before Christ's coming — and therefore had not undergone spiritual death in Christ — still lived in sin and were therefore subject to the law while they were living. Paul illustrates this point by alluding to a husband's rule over his wife. If a married woman's legitimate husband is still living, she cannot have sexual intercourse with another man without thereby incurring guilt. But if her husband dies, Paul says, she is beyond the scope of that law, even if she should voluntarily choose to continue following its rule. In the same vein, I think, anyone who has not yet experienced death to sin in Christ is living in sin and therefore under the law, since it rules over a person as long as he so lives. But those who are already living in Christ under grace, through which they died to sin and to the flesh (i.e., to the passions of the flesh), live a blameless life independently of the law, so long as they do not behave as if they were living in the world. They have died, as Paul says, *through the body of Christ* (Rom 7:4). By being made righteous through faith, they died to the law.

(3) Ambrosiaster on verses 2-6

Just as a wife, on the death of her husband, is freed from the law of marriage but not from the law of nature, so by the grace of God these people have been freed from the law which held them guilty. For them the law is dead and they are not made adulterers by becoming Christians. If the law continues to live among them, however, they will be adulterers; they will gain no advantage from being called Christians but instead will be liable to punishment. If after the death of the law a person was joined to the gospel but then reverted to the law, that person would be an adulterer — against the gospel rather than the law. The law is pronounced dead when its authority ceases.

But if her husband dies she is freed from that law, and would not be an adulteress if she marries another husband. People who have been taken out from under the law by receiving the forgiveness of sins and being joined to the gospel are not adulterers against the law because the law is dead for them. But if they try to come to the gospel while continuing to observe the law, they will be guilty of adultery; by joining themselves to the faith while the law remains alive, they would commit adultery against both.

Therefore, my brothers, you too have been made dead to the law through the body of Christ. Paul says that we were saved through the body of Christ because the Savior allowed the devil to crucify his body, knowing that this would work against him and for us. To die to the law is to live for God, because the law governs sinners. By having one's sins forgiven, a person dies to the law and is thereby liberated from the law. This benefit comes to us through the body of Christ. By surrendering his body, the Savior conquered death and condemned sin. When the devil killed Christ even though he was innocent and utterly untouched by sin, he sinned against Christ. The devil was himself found guilty of the very crime with which he charged humans in order to claim them. Once sin itself — which is the devil — had been condemned, then, all believers in Christ were rescued from the law. Sin was defeated through the body of Christ, and the devil had no further authority over those belonging to its conqueror.

Though Christ did not sin and he was killed as though he were guilty, he overcame sin by sin. He allowed the devil to commit a sin against him and then convicted the devil of that sin. Christ thus annulled the sentence which had been pronounced on the sin of Adam. Then, when he rose from hell, Christ set a pattern for those who believe in him: they too cannot be held by the second death. In this way, we died to the law through the body of Christ. Anyone who has not died to the law remains guilty, however, and those who are guilty cannot escape the second death. . . .

The vices of sins, which are made plain through the law, were at work in our members to bear fruit for death. Clearly the one who does not believe acts under sin and like a captive is forced to submit to the vices, and thus to bear fruit for the second death. When sin is committed, death gains an advantage. To avoid any suggestion that he denigrates the body, Paul says that the vices are at work **in the members**, not in the body. The tongue is charged with speaking evil; the hand is blamed for theft; the ears are rebuked for inattentiveness; and so with the other members. All these vices are acted out in the members but arise from the heart. . . .

But now we have been freed from the law of death in which we used to be held. Receiving the forgiveness of sins freed us from the law. The law has no further power over us, since it dominates only unbelievers and sinners. In punishing the guilty, it inflicts death on sinners and is thus called **the law of death.** In so doing, it acts justly and is not evil. The law does cause harm to those who suffer the punishment it inflicts, but the law itself is not evil because its wrath is just. In sum, toward sinners the law is just, not evil. . . .

So that we serve in the newness of the Spirit and not in the oldness of the written code. Though the law to which he refers is judged inferior, it is not opposed to the law of faith. He says that we were rescued from the law of death so that we might obey the law of faith, which itself provides that saving help which the old law could not. Let us not make grace void by continuing to obey the old law.

(4) John Chrysostom on verses 1-3

Do you not know, brothers and sisters — I am speaking to those who know the law? Since Paul said that we have died to sin, he shows here that neither sin nor the law has power over them. If the law has no power, sin must have even less. Paul makes his argument more intelligible by using an example from human experience. He makes a single point but offers two related arguments. The first argument: when a man dies, the wife is no longer subjected to the law of her marriage. Her dead husband cannot stop her from becoming another man's wife. The second argument would be this case in which the husband died, but the wife has also died. This would suggest that a person can enjoy two types of freedom. If the husband dies, the wife is freed from his authority, but a woman is even freer when she herself has died.[1] If the first event frees her from her husband's authority, both events together make her freer still.

Since Paul wants to prove both of these arguments, he begins by praising his audience, **Do you not know, my brothers and sisters — for I speak to those who know the law?** In other words, I am saying something which everyone with a good knowledge of the law agrees upon and recognizes as certain: **that the law is binding on a person only during that person's lifetime.** He did not specify male or female but man (anthrōpos), a term commonly used to refer to both. *For whoever has died*, Paul says, *is freed from sin* (Rom 6:7). Therefore the law is laid down for the living; it is not intended for the dead. Do you see how he clarifies this double freedom?

Next he deals with the argument about the woman. **A married woman is bound by law to her husband as long as he lives; but if her husband dies she is discharged from the law concerning the husband. Accordingly, she will be called an adulteress if she lives with another while her husband is still alive. But if her husband dies she is free from that law, and if she marries another man she is not an adulteress.** He makes this point over and again, confidently and with great precision. He then replaces the husband with the law, and the wife with all believers. But he does not draw his conclusion directly from these premises. The conclusion that should follow would be, "And so, my brothers and sisters, the law has no power over you, for it is dead." But Paul does not say this. He hints at this as he argues but avoids offending when he introduces a wife who has died; he says: **likewise, my friends, you have died to the law.**

Since the same freedom is achieved in both these cases, why could he not show favor to the law, since his case would hardly suffer from that? **Thus a married woman is bound by the law to her husband as long as he lives.** Where now are those who denigrate the law? Let them hear how Paul, even when apparently forced to it, avoids stripping the law of its dignity. He speaks highly of its authority: if indeed the law is living, the Jews are bound by it, and those who transgress or abandon the law while it is still living commit adultery. But we should not be surprised if they abandon the law after it has died, since no one is blamed for doing this in a human relationship. **But if her husband dies, she is discharged from the law concerning the husband.** Notice how he argues that the law itself has died in the example he gives but not in the conclusion? **She will be called an adulteress if she lives with another while her husband is still alive.** Paul dwells upon the charges against those who violate the law while it is still alive. Since he has put an end to the law, however, he can respect it without endangering or harming the faith. He says, **she will be called an adulteress if she lives with another while her husband is still alive. In the same way, my friends**, the natural conclusion should have been: "since the law is dead, you are not guilty of adultery by being with another husband." Yet he does not say this; instead, he says, **You have died to the law.** If you are dead, you are not under the law.

---

1. The death in question would have to be spiritual, such as the baptismal death to sin.

For if the wife is no longer subject to her husband once he has died, how much more is she free from her husband when she herself is dead.

(5) Augustine on verse 2

He says, **a married woman is bound to her husband by the law as long as he lives; but if her husband dies she is discharged from the law concerning the husband**, and so on. We should note, however, that the example is different from the situation which it is used to illustrate: it shows that when her husband dies, a woman is freed from the law concerning him and is therefore free to marry anyone she chooses. The soul is compared to the wife, the husband to the sinful passions which are **at work in the members of the body to bring forth the fruit for death**, so that the children appropriate to such a union are born. The law is given not to take away or to liberate from sin but to point it out before grace is given. Those subject to the law are then carried away by a more urgent desire to sin, and their sin is even greater because it is a transgression of the law. Three things are here involved: the soul as the wife, the sinful passions as her husband, and the law as the rule concerning her husband. The soul is said to be set free, however, not because the sins represented by the husband die but because the soul itself dies to sin and is freed from the law. Thus the soul becomes the wife of another husband, Christ, when it has died to sin even though the sin itself goes on living. This happens when desires for and attraction to sin remain alive in us but we neither obey nor approve them. With our minds, we follow the law of God because we have died to sin. The sin itself will die only in the resurrection, when the restoration of the body has been accomplished. He refers to this in saying, *he will give life to your mortal bodies also through his Spirit which dwells in you* (Rom 8:11).

(6) Augustine on verses 4-6

Some might think that the Apostle considered the law evil. He said: *Law came in, to increase the trespass* (Rom 5:20); *the dispensation of death, carved in letters on stone* (2 Cor 3:7); and *the power of sin is the law* (1 Cor 15:56); **you have died to the law through the body of Christ, so that you may belong to another, to him who rose from the dead; and sinful passions, which come from the law, were at work in our members to bear fruit for death. But now we are discharged from the law, dead to that which held us captive, so that we serve in the newness of the Spirit, not the oldness of the letter.** When we realize that the Apostle has said these and similar things, we should understand them as meaning that the law's prohibition provokes lust and then binds with guilt by making sin a transgression. It commands what humans, because of their weakness, cannot accomplish, unless they devoutly turn to the grace of God. Thus Paul says that they are subject to the law which reigns over them; that it reigns over those it punishes; that it punishes all transgressors. Moreover, all who receive the law transgress it unless, through grace, they also acquire the power to do what the law commands. Thus the law reigns over those who had been condemned in fear of it, but only until they are under grace and fulfill it through charity.

(7) Cyril of Alexandria on verse 5

By "flesh," Paul means a carnal attitude, as he says elsewhere, *Those who are in the flesh are not able to please God* (Rom 8:8). Is this not true? Paul judged this point relevant to those he was teaching. What he intends to communicate, however, is not always clear. **When we were living in a fleshly manner and an earthly attitude had power over us,** he says, **then the passions of the flesh were also actively operating in us through the law so that we would be fruitful for death.** Someone might then wonder whether the law incited the passions of the flesh. If so, would not the law itself then be guilty of a crime? What can we say in response to this question? The law did not stir up the passions of the flesh; rather, they arise from an inborn desire for pleasure, which then attacks the weak spiritual faculty. Paul clearly explains this to us when he says, *The flesh desires against the spirit, and the spirit against the flesh, and they oppose each other* (Gal 5:17). In this instance, he says that the flesh wars against the spirit, omitting any reference to the law and thus placing nothing between these two. It follows, then, that the passions of the body are stirred up in us naturally rather than through the agency of the law. The puzzle is that the passions of the body actually oppose the command of the law, as Paul himself says somewhere, *the mind set on the flesh is hostile to God; for it does not obey the law of God, for it is not able* (Rom 8:7). If the attitude of the flesh wars against the law, would it not seem to follow that the law itself provokes opposition to itself and thus brings the passions into operation? What then is Paul saying? He is addressing those who have been buried together with Christ in Baptism, who have died to sin, who have already benefited from the death of the passions. Because such people have been freed from the passions which had been condemned by the law, they are no longer bound by the limits of the law. When, however, our attitude was still fleshly, **then the passions of the flesh were also actively operating in us through the law.** At that time, we were answerable to the law, because sin was still alive in us.

Romans 7:7-13

7What then shall we say? That the law is sin? By no means! Yet, if it had not been for the law, I should not have known sin. I should not have known what it is to covet if the law had not said, *You shall not covet* **(Exod 20:17; Deut 5:21). 8But sin, finding opportunity in the commandment, wrought in me all kinds of covetousness. Apart from the law sin lies dead. 9I was once alive apart from the law, but when the commandment came, sin revived and I died; 10the very commandment that promised life proved to be death to me. 11For sin, finding opportunity in the commandment, deceived me and through it killed me. 12So the law is holy, and the commandment is holy and just and good.**

13Did that which is good, then, bring death to me? By no means! It was sin, work-

ing death in me through what is good, in order that sin might be shown to be sin, and through the commandment might become sinful beyond measure.

(1) Origen on verses 7-13

So he says: **What then should we say? That the law is sin?** Did you think, he said, that I would say that the law of Moses is sin? **By no means!** Let the **by no means** do double duty: I am not talking about the law of Moses and I am not calling it sin.

Yet, I did not know sin except through the law. I would not have known what it is to covet if the law had not said, *You shall not covet.* Understand, he says, which law I am talking about, which law is necessary for a person to recognize sin. Was it the Mosaic law by which Adam recognized his sin and hid himself from God's sight? Was it the Mosaic law by which Cain acknowledged his sin and said, *My sin is greater than I can bear* (Gen 4:13)? Or was it the law by which Pharaoh understood his sin and said, *the Lord is in the right, and I and my people are in the wrong* (Exod 9:27)? If each of these three, and innumerable others, recognized his sin before the Mosaic law was given, then clearly the Apostle is not referring to the Mosaic law when he says, **I did not know sin except through the law**, or when he said, **I would not have known what it is to covet if the law had not said,** *You shall not covet.* This law, as we have frequently explained, is *written not with ink but with the Spirit of the living God* (2 Cor 3:3) on human hearts, and teaches each person what should be done and what avoided. Through this natural law, every person recognizes sin. Clearly, then, he means that we are ignorant of this law until we come to the age at which we recognize the distinction between good and evil. This law speaks within our conscience and says to us, **You shall not covet.**

Because this law is not always present in human beings, and is not recognized at the time of each one's birth, however, each person lives without this law for a considerable period of time, until, as one matures, the law can no longer be ignored. Paul himself acknowledges, **I was once alive apart from law.** During the time we lived without the law, we did not recognize covetousness. Paul did not say, "I did not have," but, **I did not know.** These covetous desires existed but were not recognized as such. When reason begins to operate and the natural law takes its place within us by our advance in age, it begins to teach us what is good and to forbid evil. Thus when it says, **You shall not covet**, we learn from it what we did not know before: that concupiscence is evil.

But sin, seizing the opportunity in the commandment, produced in me all kinds of covetousness. What he calls **the commandment** here is that law about which he says: **I would not have known what it is to covet if the law had not said,** *You shall not covet.* Then he says that by forbidding us to covet, this commandment gave sin an opportunity to flare up within us and to work every form of covetousness in us. Because *what the flesh desires is opposed to the Spirit* (Gal 5:17), it is opposed to the law which commands, **You shall not covet.** Sin opposes this law and wages war against it, so to speak, not only for the satisfaction of its desire but in order to conquer the enemy standing against it. . . .

Apart from the law sin lies dead in us, and this occurs before our minds mature. Earlier, we explained this with the example of a little child who strikes or curses its father or mother. Because the law forbids striking or cursing one's father or mother, then, according to the law, this child would commit a sin. The child's sin is called dead, however, because the law is not yet present in the child to teach that this action is wrong. During the years of childhood, Paul and everyone else live without this law. At that age, everyone is alike incapable of knowing this natural law. . . .

Paul said that sin was dead during this time, not that it did not exist in the child. Afterward, when the natural law became operative and began forbidding concupiscence, sin revived. This law raised sin from the dead. This follows from the very definition of sin: doing what the law forbids. **When sin revived, I died.** Whom does he intend? Clearly, the soul that did what the law forbade; as the prophet says, *the soul that sins shall die* (Ezek 18:4). **The very commandment that promised life** to the soul by teaching it which works would lead to life itself **proved to be death**, since instead of fleeing from forbidden things, the soul pursued them more eagerly. . . .

When the commandment comes, even though it **is holy and just and good**, sin revives in us and kills us: **sin, seizing an opportunity in the commandment, deceived me and through it killed me.** By saying that the commandment provided the opportunity for sin to kill me, Paul is not accusing the commandment itself. On the contrary, his conclusion is only a logical inference from the preceding statements. A law or commandment teaches what should be done and what avoided. To do this effectively, it must inform us of the characteristics of things, so that we can more easily guard against the ones we should avoid; no one can steer clear of an unidentified danger. If, however, a person acts on the law's instruction about the nature of things by doing rather than avoiding what the law calls evil, the law itself did not instruct the person to do it and to die. It only provided the opportunity to learn what should not be done. In this way, then, **sin, seizing an opportunity in the commandment, deceived me and through it killed me.** . . .

But someone will surely raise the objection: **Did what was good, then, bring death to me? By no means!** To which Paul would then respond, "The goodness of the law and the commandment did not inflict death on me," **it was sin, working death in me through what is good**, that brought death, **in order that sin's true evil might be apparent.** The commandment is good when it is observed; when it is not obeyed, the commandment necessarily becomes an evil for the one who loses a good by violating it.

(2) Ambrosiaster on verses 7-13

I would not have known what it is to covet if the law had not said, *You shall not covet.* Paul did not distinguish this covetousness from what he had earlier called sin. He is amazed because he had no prior suspicion that covetousness was not permitted by God. So he says: "I realized that it was a sin." In his own person, he addresses the situation of humanity as a whole. So the law prohibits covetousness, which had not been thought sinful because it was enjoyable. Desiring one's neighbor's property appeared to be harmless; then the law proclaimed it sinful. For people given to the values of this culture, however, nothing seems so harmless and gratifying as pleasure.

But sin, seizing the opportunity in the commandment, produced in me all kinds

of covetousness. By **all kinds of covetousness**, Paul means the whole range of sins. Earlier, he specified that covetousness which the law forbids; now he includes all the other vices in saying that **all kinds of covetousness** were activated in humanity at the instigation of the devil — whom Paul signifies by the term **sin**. In this way, that law which had been given as a help for humanity became harmful. The devil had been well satisfied with the collaboration established through his own sin and that of Adam. Then he recognized that the law attacked that alliance, for it gave help to humanity. By being subjected to the law, and learning how to avoid the punishment of hell, humans could escape from demonic domination. The devil boiled over with anger against humans and devised a way to turn the law against them: if they did what it forbade, they would offend God once again and thus fall back into the devil's power. When God's jurisdiction over humans was asserted by the giving of the law, the devil had lost the right to rule them. Rather than giving a contrary set of commandments, the devil set to work by deceit.

Apart from the law sin lies dead. This can be understood in two ways: the term "sin" can be taken as referring either to the devil or to a particular sinful action. In the first sense, the devil was "**dead**" because before the law it was enjoying secure and untroubled dominion over humans; it was not viciously attacking and deceiving them. In the second sense, sin was **dead** because people thought that God was paying no attention to it. The sinful action itself was not hidden, but people thought that God would not pass judgment on it. . . .

For sin, seizing an opportunity in the commandment, deceived me and through it killed me. In this instance, sin should be understood as the devil, the author of sin. Through the law, the devil found an opportunity to indulge its cruelty by ruining humans. The law threatened sinners. At the urging of the devil, humans regularly accepted what was forbidden; they offended God and incurred the punishment given in the law. Thus the very law which had been given to help humans resulted in their condemnation. The law was given in defiance of the devil and inflamed its envy of humanity; the devil worked even harder to pollute humans with sinful pleasures and thus prevent their escape. . . .

But sin, in order that it might be shown to be sin, brought about death for me through something good. The devil seized the opportunity provided by the good law to work evil in human beings by leading them away into death. The law revealed in the Scriptures was given to expose the sinfulness of the evil deeds which had been committed through beguiling desire before the time of the law, and so put an end to them. What was undeniably good made Satan furious; realizing that humans would be helped by the law, he persuaded them to do what was forbidden, so that death rather than life would result. This outcome can also be charged to human negligence: they so enjoyed sinning that they enfeebled their natural power to resist the devil's wiles. The enemy — here signified by sin — used the opportunity which the law had provided to bring about humanity's death and thus exposed it as an enemy. . . .

So that sin, by sinning through the commandment, might become sinful beyond measure. . . . The measure to which the Apostle refers was the level of sin before the law, which was greater after the law. The fear inspired by the law should have stopped human sinning completely. The envy and cunning of the devil turned the divine governance to humanity's disadvantage. In order to thwart the envy of the devil and to establish divine governance over humanity, God then instituted a new plan: Christ was sent as Savior to overcome the devil and liberate humanity.

(3) Apollinaris of Laodicea on verse 7

Let no one hearing these statements mock the Apostle and say that if the law proscribes what brings death to make known what is good and evil (since the Lord himself identified evil and good in his own sayings), then the level road would be undone by sin, at least in the view of unbelievers. For the difference between the law and Christ is very great. The law consists of words alone and bestows no power for righteousness; it leaves everything to be accomplished by the hearer. Our Lord Jesus Christ, in contrast, fully accomplished the salvation of his own and created anew those of us who believe; he transformed and shaped us by bestowing the divine in-breathing upon us and shaping us by it. He did indeed exhort us with words to prepare us to be formed by the working of the Spirit; he did not leave to us to our own devices. For if he had done that, we would be condemned again because we are weak in faith and the knowledge of sin would be imposed on us from the outside rather than arising from within. But he is preparing us to become vessels for the Spirit; we abandon, day by day, affection for this world, we loose the carnal bonds and become ever more receptive of the Spirit.

The law is swift to punish, but the Spirit is patient. The law has its own method of directing humanity toward righteousness, but the Spirit itself guides our healing. For the law inflicts vengeance on the person whose life has not been changed, making him an example of its power. The Spirit has the power to correct those who believe, even if they are initially too weak to be reformed by it. The Spirit neither dismisses the sin nor swiftly punishes it; instead it guards the person who is being disciplined by its saving work. Thus Paul said, *hand him over to Satan for the destruction of his flesh, so that the spirit may be saved* (1 Cor 5:5). For the Spirit of the Lord is sent forth until the return of Christ, until that time when creation will be perfected. Its work continues until that judgment has been completed in which it rejects those who have not been corrected and are then found unprepared for the eternal life which is to follow.

Thus the Apostle adds elsewhere: *It is God who works in you both to will and to do for his good pleasure* (Phil 2:13), not by destroying our self-determination but by guiding us by the power of virtue given by God. When he rose, the Savior breathed the Holy Spirit upon the disciples. In this same way, he dwells with us and he tells us not to worry about what we should say: *It will not be you who are speaking, but the spirit of your Father who is speaking within you* (Matt 10:19-20). Even before this, that prophetic word which identified the new covenant as the giving of the Spirit spoke in God's name to Israel: *And this is my covenant for them; my Spirit is upon you, and the words which I have put into your mouth will not ever depart from your mouth and your descendants, says the* Lðrd, *from now until eternity* (Isa 59:21). These words were spoken through Isaiah. God promises a new covenant through Jeremiah: *This is the covenant which I shall set forth for them in those days, putting my laws in their hearts, and I shall inscribe the laws on their consciousness, and no one will teach his neighbors, saying, "Know the* Lord*" because all* *will know me, from the small to the great, because I will be merciful to their sin* (Jer 31:33-34). He promises the power of the Spirit working in their hearts. God will accomplish propitiation; God will forgive the sins of which the law reckoned them guilty, and God will give that perseverance of spirit that brings salvation. Again, through Ezekiel God promises the *gift of a new heart and a new spirit* (Ezek 36:26), for the fulfillment of his own will in us.

In this passage, then, the Apostle defines life in Christ. He says that we are liberated from the power of sin not by the letter, since the Spirit's gift consists not in the knowledge of sin and its judgment by the law but in the remission of sins and the working of righteousness by divine rather than human power. This Paul announced at the beginning of this epistle, *The righteousness of God is revealed* through the gospel (Rom 1:17).

(4) John Chrysostom on verse 8

Sin took the opportunity through the command and produced every type of desire in me. Do you see how Paul defended the law against accusations? He says that **sin**, not the law, **took the opportunity**, increased desire, and brought about the opposite of what the law intended. This happened through weakness, not malice. For when we are prevented from obtaining what we desire, the flame of longing blazes up. Paul's burning desire did not come from the law, however, because the law itself laid down prohibitions to lead us away from sin. But sin, that is, your laziness and evil disposition, used this good for the opposite purpose. The doctor is not at fault if a patient misuses a drug. For the law was given not to enflame desire, but to extinguish it. Yet the opposite happened. The responsibility, however, falls on us and not on the law. If by forbidding a feverish person to have a desirable cold drink, a physician thereby increases the patient's desire for this deadly pleasure, then to accuse the doctor of causing that increased desire would be unjust. The doctor can only set up an obstacle; the patient must say no. What difference does it make that sin took the opportunity provided by the law? Many bad people do greater evil in the way they respond to good commandments: this is how the devil destroyed Judas, by plunging him into avarice and getting him to steal money from the poor. The theft happened not because Christ entrusted him with the purse but because his dispositions were evil.

(5) John Chrysostom on verse 12

So the law is holy, and the commandment is holy and just and good. Allow me to introduce into this discussion the argument of those who misunderstand this passage. This will make our own reasoning clearer. Some explain that Paul is not speaking here about the law of Moses; others say he is speaking about natural law; still others say that he is speaking about the commandment which was given in Paradise. Indeed, Paul always intends to put an end to the Mosaic law, but he has no problem with those other laws. His concern with the law is quite reasonable because the Jews were so fearful and trembling before the law that they fought against grace. Neither Paul nor any other writers seem to have applied the name "law" to the commandment given in Paradise.

To clarify his argument, let us go through the earlier reasoning using Paul's own words. After he had discussed the conduct of life with them in detail, he went on to say, *Do you not know, brothers and sisters, that the law is binding on a person only during that person's lifetime? You have died to the law* (Rom 7:1, 4). Therefore, if Paul were talking about the natural law, we would have to conclude that we no longer possess the natural law. But that would make us more foolish than the irrational animals. So he cannot be talking about the natural law. We will not discuss the law which was given in Paradise, lest we undertake an unnecessary argument, stripping for a battle over points which are conceded by everyone. How can Paul say, **if it had not been for the law, I would never have known sin**? He is describing not what had been a total ignorance of sin but the process of acquiring a more certain knowledge of it. If he were considering the natural law, how could he make the following statement, **I was once alive apart from the law**? Neither Adam nor anyone else ever lived without natural law. God created Adam and placed that law in him at the same time, establishing it as a sure companion for all those who share his nature. Besides, as noted, Paul nowhere called the natural law a commandment. Yet he calls that law with which he is concerned here both a just and holy commandment, and a spiritual law. Further, the natural law was not given to us by the Spirit, since both Greeks and barbarians have this law. From these considerations, it becomes clear that in every instance Paul is discussing the law of Moses.

(6) Augustine on verses 7-13

Why, then, should the law have been given, if not to implant or to root out sin but only to make it apparent? By exposing sin it makes the human soul recognize its guilt instead of allowing it to continue in a secure but false sense of its own innocence. Anxiety over guilt could lead the soul to seek the grace of God, for without grace sin cannot be overcome. For this reason, he did not say: "except for the law, I would not have committed sin," but: **except for the law, I would not have known sin.** Nor, again, does he say: "I would not have coveted, unless the law had said, 'You shall not covet,'" but instead: **I would not have know what it is to covet if the law had not said,** *You shall not covet.* Thus he shows that the law did not cause covetousness but only uncovered it. The result, however, was that covetousness was amplified because it could not be resisted until grace was received. Covetousness became worse, moreover, when the actual transgression was added to the sinful desire; this happens when a person violates a law rather than acting in the absence of any prohibition. For this reason, he adds: **But sin, finding opportunity in the commandment, wrought in me all kinds of covetousness.** The covetousness was present even before the law, but it was not full and complete until the act of transgression of a law was added. For this reason, he says in another place: *but where there is no law there is no transgression* (Rom 4:15). When he continues, **Apart from the law sin lies dead**, the meaning is the same as saying it is hidden and considered dead. Then he says the same thing: **I was once alive apart from the law**, that is, I was not afraid of death arising from sin, because before the law came, it was not revealed. **But when the commandment came, sin revived**, that is, it became evident, **and I died.** I died in the sense that I recognized that I was dead, or because the act of transgression led to the penalty of death.

Paul's saying, **when the commandment came, sin revived**, implies that sin had been alive — that it had been recognized — at some time in the past. I think that this refers to the transgression of the first humans, since they had received a commandment. For Paul says in another place, *the woman was deceived and became a transgressor* (1 Tim 2:14), or again, *in the likeness of the transgression of Adam, who is a type of the one to come* (Rom 5:14). Only something that had been alive at an earlier time can revive. Sin had been dead, that is, hidden. Born mortal and without any commandment of a law, humans lived by following the desires of the flesh; they acted without understanding because they had no prohibition. **I once lived apart from the law**, he says, and thus shows that he speaks not as an individual but for humans in general. **But when the commandment came, sin revived and I died; the very commandment that promised life proved to be death to me.** If the commandment is obeyed, it gives life. The commandment proved to be the source of death when people violated it. Sin had been committed even before the commandment, but the sin became greater and more harmful because people sinned knowingly and in defiance of the commandment.

For sin, finding opportunity in the commandment, deceived me and by it killed me. Sin did not use the law legally. The prohibition actually increased the evil desire; sin became sweeter, and thus it deceived. Sweetness is deceptive when it results in greater and more bitter punishments. People who have not yet received spiritual grace find something forbidden even more pleasant. This false sweetness of sin deceives. And because the sin is accompanied by the guilt of transgression, it kills.

So the law is holy, and the commandment is holy and just and good. It commands what ought to be commanded and forbids what should be forbidden. **Did that which is good, then, bring death to me? By no means!** The failure arises from the evil use of the law, not from the commandment itself, which is good, *since the law is good, if anyone uses it lawfully* (1 Tim 1:8). The law is put to evil use by those who do not humbly subject themselves to God, so that they can fulfill the law through grace. Unless the law is used properly, its reception results in the sin, which had been hidden before its prohibition, becoming manifest through transgression of the law, and by the addition of a violation of the commandment to the sin itself. Thus he continues and adds: **Sin, that it might be shown to be sin, worked death in me through what is good, so that through the commandment the sinner or the sin might go beyond all measure.** What he had intended in saying earlier, **Apart from the law sin lies dead**, now becomes clearer. Not that something should come into being that had not existed before the law, but that it should become apparent. Similarly, **sin revived.** Not that it might then become what it already was even before the law but that it might be made manifest by being committed in violation of the law. When he says here: **Sin, that it might be shown to be sin, worked death in me through what is good**, he did not say, "that it might be sin," but **that it might be shown to be sin.**

(7) Augustine on verses 12-13

Now respond to those who blame the law by appealing to the authority of the Apostle. Listen to the Apostle when he says: **the law is holy, and the commandment is holy and just and good. Did that which is good, then, bring death to me? By no means! It was sin, working death in me through what is good, in order that sin might be shown to be sin.** Why did this happen if not because you feared rather than loving the commandment you received? You feared the punishment; you did not love the justice. Anyone who is afraid of the punishment would actually prefer, were it possible, to do whatever they like and not to suffer the fearful punishment. God forbids adultery; you lust for another's wife. Yet you do not pursue her; you do not do it. You have the opportunity; you have the time; a place is available; no one will know. Yet you do not do it. Why? Because you are afraid of the consequences. But no one will know about it. Not even God? That's the point: you hold back because God knows what you want to do. You tremble when God threatens, but you do not love when God commands. Why do you hold back? Because if you did it, you would be sent to hell. You are afraid of the fire. O, if you loved chastity, you would not do it, even if you could escape the punishment completely. If God were to say to you: alright, go ahead and do it; I will not condemn you; I will not damn you to hell; I'll will only deny you seeing my face. If this threat held you back, then you would be acting out of love of God, not fear of judgment. But perhaps you would still do it; in that case you might commit the adultery. I am not in a position to judge. Let grace help you, that grace which makes saints. If you do not do it, then, it is because you are horrified by the pollution of adultery, because you love the one commanding, because you seek the one promising, not because you fear the one condemning. That, indeed, would be the work of grace; do not take it as your own achievement; do not attribute it to your own strength. You act from delight, good. You act from charity. Good. I approve, I agree. Charity is at work in you when you act willingly. If you trust in the Lord, you can already taste the sweetness.

Romans 7:14-25

14**We know that the law is spiritual; but I am carnal, sold under sin.** 15**I do not understand my own actions. For I do not do what I want, but I do the very thing I hate.** 16**Now if I do what I do not want, I agree that the law is good.** 17**So then it is no longer I that do it, but sin which dwells within me.** 18**For I know that nothing good dwells within me, that is, in my flesh. I can will what is right, but I cannot do it.** 19**For I do not do the good I want, but the evil I do not want is what I do.** 20**Now if I do what I do not want, it is no longer I that do it, but sin which dwells within me.**

21**So I find it to be a law that when I want to do what is good, evil lies close at hand.** 22**For I delight in the law of God, in my inmost self,** 23**but I see in my members another law at war with the law of my mind and making me captive to the law of sin which dwells in my members.** 24**Wretched man that I am! Who will deliver me from** this body of death? 25Thanks be to God through Jesus Christ our Lord! So then, I of myself serve the law of God with my mind, but with my flesh I serve the law of sin.

(1) Origen on verses 14-25

The Holy Scripture often and without warning changes the persons, the subject, and the issues about which it seems to be speaking, and even their names. In other instances, Scripture uses the same names for entirely different things. For example, in the present passage the Apostle says: **for we know that the law is spiritual.** His judgment, that **the law is spiritual**, is pronounced with apostolic authority. Only someone who has the indwelling Spirit of God knows **that the law is spiritual**; those who are carnal and sold in slavery to sin do not know **that the law is spiritual.** This statement can be applied to the law of Moses, since that law is a spiritual law and a life-giving Spirit for those who understand it spiritually. It is a law of the letter and a letter which kills, however, for those who understand it according to the flesh. Thus when Paul says: **but I am of the flesh, sold into slavery under sin**, he is speaking as a teacher of the Church and has assumed the voice of the weak, in the same way he does elsewhere, for example: *To the weak I became weak, so that I might win the weak* (1 Cor 9:22). Here, too, Paul becomes as it were **of the flesh, sold into slavery under sin** to whoever is weak **of the flesh, and sold into slavery under sin.** He repeats the things such people usually say to cover themselves by an excuse or an accusation. Speaking in their voice, he says of himself, **I am of the flesh, sold into slavery under sin**, that is, living according to the flesh and sold into the power of sin for the price of lust and concupiscence.

I do not understand my own actions. For I do not do what I want, but I do the very thing I hate. In saying, **I do not understand my own actions**, he does not mean that the actor does not know what was actually done in living according to the flesh, but rather that the person does not understand the reason for doing it. The statement, **For I do not do what I want, but I do the very thing I hate**, shows that although the speaker might be **of the flesh and sold into slavery under sin**, still through the instinct of natural law such a person can still offer some resistance to the passions, even though the person's will is assaulted and overpowered by those vices. This happens often and in many different ways. A person may resolve to endure a provocation patiently but in the end be overcome by anger and suffer this passion unwillingly. Anger breaks out despite the resolve not to become angry. Fear can terrify with dread and apprehension, against a person's will. Elation from a sudden and unexpected honor can make a person arrogant and uncharacteristically puffed up. People who are not yet spiritual but do not want to be carnal fail in each case because their desire is not yet strong and determined enough to sustain the struggle for virtue even unto death. These are not the kind of people whose *yes means yes and whose no means no* (Jas 5:12); these kinds of people cannot do what they should but do what they would prefer not to do.

In not willing the evil that is actually done, a person **agrees that the law is good**, that it is right in forbidding evil. The natural law is approved as supporting the law of God in that the two approve and disapprove the same things. If with our will we consent to God's law, then it is no longer we who do the evil but sin working within us, that law and will of the flesh which makes us captive to the law of sin.

Surely, Paul is speaking as a carnal person in saying, **it is no longer I that do it, but sin that dwells within me.** Speaking elsewhere as a spiritual person, Paul says, *I worked harder than any of them — though it was not I, but the grace of God that is with me* (1 Cor 15:10). In that instance, he attributed his labors to the grace of God working in him rather than to himself; in this case, the carnal Paul ascribes the evil works not to himself but to **sin which dwells in me** and performs them. On this basis, he says, **it is no longer I that do it, but sin that dwells within me. For I know that nothing good dwells within me, that is, in my flesh.** Christ is not yet dwelling in him, nor is his body a temple of God.

Nevertheless the person portrayed here is not a complete stranger to the good; this person has begun to seek the good by will and intention but is not yet able to realize it in deed and action. Those just beginning their conversion suffer from this weakness: they want to accomplish every good deed all at once, but performance does not follow immediately upon the willing. So he reflects to himself, discerns that anger should be avoided, for example, and willingly resolves to guard against it. The vice of anger has become dominant, however, by regular practice and long-standing habit; it impedes the reforming will and intention; the person breaks out in a rage, following an accustomed pattern. The vice of lust works the same way. By the same chronic disease, lying sneaks in and fear terrifies. In each case the person who has already begun the process of conversion can rightly say: **I can will what is right, but I cannot do it. For I do not do the good I want, but the evil I do not want is what I do.**

If I can judge what is good but my will is opposed and subverted by the habitual carnal vices — what are called the law of the flesh and the law of the members — then I make a choice for the good, even though I actually do the evil. Because I act against my preference, I still **agree that the law of God is good.** I hate the evil, and I desire to do the good that the law commands. But if I do evil against my will, overcome by vicious habits and by the regular practice of sinning, then **it is no longer I** — the inner person who wills the good — **that do it, but sin that dwells within me.** The term **sin** is used here to designate the habit of sinning.

So I find it to be a law that when I want to do what is good, evil lies close at hand. For I delight in the law of God in my inmost self. In these statements, as we have often remarked, the expressions seem not to be fully developed and the connections are obscured by excessive or inappropriate language. To get the meaning clear, we must read the text in a certain order. **Evil lies close at hand when I want to do good**; still I judge the **law of God** good, and **I delight in it according to the inner self.** In this he shows that the inner self, that is, the will and intention by which he took the first steps in converting to the Lord, agrees with the **law of God** and **delights in it.** As we said above, a person cannot succeed in the practice of good works just by deciding to turn toward the good. The will is quick, and it converts without being blocked by any impediment; performance is slower, however, because it requires practice, skill, and effort in actual working. An illustration will make this clearer. A person decides, let us say, to seek wisdom but does not thereby become wise as soon as that decision is made. The willing has to come first; no one can become wise without willing it. Once the willing is in place, the person must engage in labor and study, solicitude and vigilance, teaching and instruction. Yet even with long practice and continuous reflection, a person scarcely ever becomes wise. From the very beginning, our aspirant had the will to become wise, but the achievement of wisdom did not follow immediately. Indeed, in the very effort to become wise, one does many things which are foolish and opposed to wisdom. Being devoted to wisdom, the student could understand that past actions had been foolish, but was not yet wise enough to avoid doing anything further that was unwise. The same sequence can be applied to chastity: a person does not become fully chaste in practice and root out all the promptings of lust just by deciding to make a commitment to chastity. That can be said for gentleness, patience, and each of the other virtues. In each case, a person can say, **I delight in the law of God**, in the virtues, **in my inmost self.**

I see in my members another law at war with the law of my mind, making me captive to the law of sin that dwells in my members. When he said earlier, **I can will what is right**, he called this will for good the law of the mind; it agrees with the **law of God** and affirms it. The impulses of the body and the desires of the flesh he named the **law of the members**, which leads the soul captive and subjects it to the **law of sin.** The desires of the flesh certainly pull the soul toward sin and subject it to those laws. The **law of the mind**, which agrees with **the law of God**, will lead the soul to **the law of God** if it can gain control of it. Similarly, the **law in the members** and the concupiscence of the flesh will subject the soul to the law of sin if they can seduce it.

By assuming the voice of this weaker character, Paul taught that struggles do occur within a person and showed that through the desires of the flesh and the practice of sinning, the soul is violently dragged off against its will into the dominion of sin. In that assumed role he exclaimed, **Wretched man that I am! Who will rescue me from this body of death?** With so many different laws fighting against each other within him and so many battles going on, he clearly saw his own wretchedness. The flesh fights against the spirit, and the spirit against the flesh; the **law in the members** opposes the **law of the mind** and takes the soul captive to the law of sin; it remains under that yoke even though the interior person **delights in the law of God.** In the midst of such great and multiple evils, what person would not admit to being wretched and living in a **body of death**? A body in which sin, the cause of death, is dwelling is rightly called a **body of death**.

This exclamation is in the voice of a person who has begun the process of conversion, whom the Apostle describes as able to will the good but not to bring it into effect. This person lacks the power to carry out the good, not yet having learned to practice and exercise the virtues. This sort of person cries out, **Who will rescue me from this body of death?** Paul then responds not in the voice of the person he assumed but in that of apostolic authority: **Thanks be to God through Jesus Christ our Lord!** And so it becomes clear that the Apostle's purpose in describing this entire situation and laying bare the evils which were at work within us was, in the end, to show and teach us the many evils and the various forms of death from which Christ has rescued us. . . .

So then with my mind I myself serve the law of God, but with my flesh the law of sin. Perhaps someone will claim that the Apostle, who up until now had been speaking not with his own voice but with that of the weaker character he had assumed, here indicates a change in the speaker by the words, **I myself**, to show that what follows should be attributed to the person of the Apostle himself. The statement, **with my mind I serve the law of God, but with my flesh the law of sin**, moreover, seems to indicate a force of sinning so strong and a tyranny of the flesh so powerful that not even the Apostle could escape them. Moreover, he had said elsewhere, *I punish my body and enslave it, so that after proclaiming to others I myself should not be disqualified* (1 Cor 9:27). To assign this statement to the Apostle himself, however, would seem to bring down despair upon every soul: no one would be able to escape sinning in the flesh, which is what **serving the law of sin with the flesh** means. I think more likely, therefore, that Paul is still speaking for that person whom he described above as having turned toward the better by will and intention, already serving the law of God with mind and soul, but not yet having arrived at bringing the flesh into obedience to the mind's purpose.

(2) Ambrosiaster on verses 14-24

To be **sold into slavery under sin** is to originate from Adam, who sinned first, and then by one's own transgression to become subject to sin. As the prophet Isaiah says, *For your sins you have been sold* (Isa 50:1). Adam sold himself first, and consequently all his seed has been subjected to sin. For this reason, humans are too weak to observe the precepts of the law unless they are strengthened by divine assistance. Hence he says: **the law is spiritual; but I am of the flesh, sold under sin**, that is, the law is strong, just, and blameless, but humans are fragile and in bondage to ancestral or personal transgression, so that they cannot exercise their own power to obey the law. They must take refuge in God's mercy to escape the severity of the law and, once freed from their sins, to resist the enemy with God's help. For what is subjection to sin, if not to have a body corrupted by the vices of the soul, a body in which sin implants itself and drives a person to follow its orders, like a captive to crime? Thus the Lord says, among other things: *the devil comes and takes away the word from their hearts, so that they may not believe and be saved* (Luke 8:12). In another letter, the Apostle Paul says: *Our struggle is not against enemies of blood and flesh, but against the rulers, against the authorities, against the cosmic powers of this present darkness, against the spiritual forces of evil in the heavenly places* (Eph 6:12), forces which are recognized as allies of Satan. Prior to humanity's sin, before humans beings delivered themselves over to death, the enemy had no power to enter the inner self and plant opposing thoughts there. The enemy had to use its cunning to trick humans through conversation, using a serpent. After he overcame and subjugated humans, however, the enemy received power over them. He could assault the inner self and so insinuate himself into the mind that as a result one could distinguish one's own thoughts from those of the enemy only by recourse to the Law. . . .

But in fact it is no longer I that do it, but sin that dwells within me. Since Paul sees that his actions are forbidden by the law and agrees that they should not be done, he concludes that something else — **sin** — drives him to these actions. He always says **sin** when he means the devil because none of this would be happening now unless the first humans had sinned. Thus it is that sin does all this. **For I know that nothing good dwells within me, that is, in my flesh.** He does not say, as some people think he does, that the flesh is bad but that the sin dwelling in the flesh is not good. How can sin dwell in the flesh? It is not some substantial reality but a violation of the good. The body of the first man was corrupted by sin and thereby became capable of dissolution, and this corruption of sin remains stamped on the body as a result of the offense, as the force of that divine sentence pronounced upon Adam. It is the mark of the devil, at whose instigation Adam sinned. Because the cause itself remains, sin is said to **dwell in the flesh**, and the devil approaches it as something under its own jurisdiction. It is now the flesh of sin, and sin — the devil — abides in that sin. The devil can deceive a person by evil suggestions and impede doing what the law teaches. . . .

Now if I do what I do not want, it is no longer I that do it, but sin that dwells within me. As he stated earlier, this refers to the devil. The will of the devil is accomplished; the person's own will is oppressed and subjugated to sin. Is the person then innocent of any crime because the sinning is coerced, as Paul says, because some power forces the person to act contrary to intention? Certainly not. This condition is the consequence of the person's own vice and negligence. Sin rules by right over a person who has surrendered by assenting to sin. The devil first persuades and then dominates the one he has defeated. . . .

I delight in the law of God, in my inmost self. Paul says that his soul is delighted by what the law teaches. He speaks of the inner self because sin dwells not in the soul but in the flesh. This flesh belongs to sin because of its origin and because generation has made all human flesh the flesh of sin. Sin is not allowed to dwell in the soul, however, because of the free choice of the will. Therefore, sin dwells in the flesh, at the gates of the soul, thereby preventing the soul from going where it wishes. . . .

I see in my members another law resisting the law of my mind, making me captive to the law of sin that dwells in my members. . . . Paul names four laws. The first is the spiritual law, which is also the natural law, which was reformed and established in its authority by Moses. This is the law of God. He names as second the law of the mind which assents to the law of God. The third is the law of sin which he says dwells in the bodily members as a consequence of the sin of the first humans. The fourth law is discerned in the members when it makes an evil suggestion and then draws back. But these laws have been doubled; what are presented as four are in fact only two, the laws of good and of evil. The law of the mind is identical with the spiritual or Mosaic law, which is also called the law of God. The law of sin is the same as the one seen in the members, which contradicts the law of our mind. . . .

Wretched man that I am! Who will rescue me from this body of death? . . . **This body of death** consists in the whole body of sins: though many, the sins form one body, like individual members of a single agent. A person rescued from these sins by God's grace through Baptism has escaped the second death in hell. Paul would not claim to have been rescued from the fleshly body while he was still living in it. Instead, Paul is talking about that body which is destroyed through Baptism and the observance of the law. When he says, **from this body of death**, he shows that some other body does not belong to death. . . .

Freed, then, **from the body of death** by the grace of God through Christ, **with my mind**, or rational soul, **I serve the law of God, but with my flesh the law of sin.** The law control and have actually begun to practice it but are then overcome by the attractions of foul pleasure. Once they have sunk to a low spiritual state and have committed sin, they are truly filled with remorse. Those who have become sick in this way, even almost unwillingly, can rightly say again: **Now I no longer do this, but sin which dwells in me.**

(4) Gennadius of Constantinople on verse 15

Paul says, **sold under sin**, presenting sin as the mistress and himself as her slave. Then he adds: **For I do not understand what I am doing.** This is what we expect of the slaves in a household, since they are subject to their master's orders and do not decide for themselves. In the same way, he says again, **I myself do something although I do not choose to do it.** For **I do not understand** does not mean that he is ignorant. When a person does something, how could he possibly be ignorant of his own action? Or how could it even be accounted as his sin? The meaning of **I do not understand** here is like that of the Savior's statement in the Gospels: *I do not know you, depart from me* (Matt 7:23). It means that he is doing something not right for him, not willingly or with pleasure, not enjoying the accomplishment. He is not following his own preference but that of someone else. This is clearly what he means in saying: **For I do not do what I want, but I do the very thing I hate.** By the things he hates, he means what he could never prefer for himself. In doing such things, he acknowledges that he violates the natural and comprehensive law of the Savior: Through such things, he says that he transgresses that law of the Savior which is natural and containing all things. *Whatever you want people to do to you, you do so to them, for this is the law and the prophets* (Matt 7:12).

(5) John Chrysostom on verses 17-20

But in fact it is no longer I that do it, but sin that dwells within me. For I know that nothing good dwells within me, that is, in my flesh. Those who hate the flesh and the enemies of God's creation use this text to attack us. What, then, should we say? Paul says the same thing here as he said in the earlier passage, that these problems have their origin in sin. He did not say, "The flesh accomplishes this"; rather, he says the opposite, **it is no longer I that do it, but sin that dwells within me.** When Paul says that **good does not dwell in his flesh**, he is not making any accusation against the flesh. For the flesh is not evil simply because good does not dwell in it. We admit that the flesh is lesser than the soul and inferior to it, but it does not oppose the soul, nor does it wage war against the soul, nor is it evil. Just as the cithara is inferior to the cithara player, and as the ship is inferior to the pilot, so the flesh is inferior to the soul. Such things are not in opposition to the people who guide and use them. In truth, they are partners, though they are not as valuable as the skilled person. Just as someone who observes that the skill resides in the pilot and cithara player rather than in the cithara or the ship, does not find fault with the instrument, but notes the great difference between them. In the same way, when Paul said, **nothing good dwells within me, that is, in my flesh**, he was not finding fault with the body but pointing out the superiority of the soul.

The soul has been endowed with the skill of piloting or playing what has been entrusted to it, something Paul shows by assigning governing power to the soul. By dividing the human being into soul and body, he says that the flesh is less rational and devoid of intelligence, classed among the things which are led rather than among those that lead. The soul has more wisdom; it is able to discern what should be done and what must not be done. Yet the soul is not always powerful enough to govern its instrument in the way it wishes. When this happens, it is the fault not of the flesh alone but also of the soul, which knows what it needs to do and yet does not accomplish the things that are good for it. **I can will what is right**, Paul says, **but I cannot do it.** When he says in this passage, **but I cannot do it**, he is speaking not about ignorance or difficulty, but about sin's abuse and hostile assault which he clearly indicated when he added what follows.

For I do not do the good I want, but the evil I do not want is what I do. Now if I do what I do not want, it is no longer I that do it, but sin that dwells within me. Do you see how he has defended the essence both of the soul and the body against blame, and has shifted all the accusations to the evil deed itself? If he does not desire to do evil, then the soul has been acquitted; if he himself does not do it, then the body too has been declared innocent. He has assigned the sin to evil choice alone. The natures of soul, body, and choice are not the same: the first two are works of God; the third is a movement which arises from ourselves and inclines wherever we decide to direct it. For the will itself is something natural and from God, but willing in any particular way originates from us and from our own mind.

(6) Augustine on verses 14-17

The Apostle has just said: *So the law is holy, and the commandment is holy and just and good. Did that which is good, then, bring death to me? By no means! Sin, that it might be shown to be sin, worked death in me through what is good, so that the sin might go beyond all measure by sinning against the commandment* (Rom 7:12-13). There he is properly understood as speaking about his own past, when he was living under the law and not yet under grace. For he uses words in the past tense, saying; *I did not know sin, except through the law* (Rom 7:7); and *I did not know what it is to covet* (Rom 7:7); and *it wrought in me all kinds of covetousness* (Rom 7:8); and *I once lived apart from the law* (Rom 7:9), which would have been when he did not yet have the use of reason; and *when the commandment came, sin revived and I died* (Rom 7:9); and *sin, finding opportunity in the commandment, deceived me and by it killed me* (Rom 7:11); and *through that which is good, it brought death to me* (Rom 7:13). All these statements refer to the earlier time when he lived under the law and was overcome by carnal desires because he was not yet helped by grace.

When, however, he says: **the law is spiritual but I am carnal**, he shows that he is actually experiencing the conflict. He did not say, "I was carnal," or "I used to be carnal," but **I am carnal**. He distinguishes the different times more clearly when he says: **Now it is no longer I that do it, but sin which dwells within me.** He is no longer himself the cause of these movements of evil desire, to which he does not consent and thus commit sins. By the phrase, **the sin which dwells within me**, he names the lust itself which arose from sin and itself conceives and gives birth to sin when it succeeds in enticing and drawing a person's consent. The statements that follow are all the words of a person already established under grace, right down to the point where he says, **So then, I of myself serve the law of God with my mind, but with my flesh the law of sin.** He is still struggling against his lust but is not sinning by consenting to it. He is suffering the desires of sin but resisting them.

(7) Augustine on verses 14-25

What follows does, though not obviously, apply to Paul himself. **We know,** he says, **that the law is spiritual but that I am carnal.** He does not say, "I was," but **I am.** How could the Apostle have been carnal when he wrote this? Did he speak about his body? He was still in the body of this death, not yet having attained that body which he speaks about elsewhere: *It is sown a physical body; it is raised a spiritual body* (1 Cor 15:44). When that has been accomplished, even the body will be spiritual and he will be a spiritual person, in his whole self, in both the parts of which he is constituted. Nor is it ridiculous to think that in that future life even the flesh can be spiritual, since the spirit itself can be carnal in this present life, at least among those who have a taste for the carnal. This, then, is the reason the Apostle said, **I am carnal**; he did not yet have a spiritual body. He might have said, "I am mortal," which could have been understood only about his body, since it had not yet been endowed with immortality. What he then added, **sold under sin**, has to be understood in the same way. No one should think that he had not yet been redeemed by the blood of Christ. The statement is rather to be understood by what he says elsewhere: *We ourselves, who have the first fruits of the Spirit, groan inwardly as we wait for adoption as sons, the redemption of our bodies* (Rom 8:23). If then he spoke of himself as **sold under sin** because he was not yet redeemed from the corruption of his body, or **sold** in the original transgression of the command so that he had a corruptible body which burdens the soul, what prevents us from understanding that the Apostle is speaking of himself here? He could have meant it about himself, but not himself alone, intending that it apply to all who recognize themselves as using their spiritual desires to contend against and not consent to the tendencies of the flesh.

Should we be afraid of what follows: **I do not understand my own actions. For I do not do what I want, but I do the very thing I hate**? Might someone think, on the basis of this statement, that the holy Apostle was consenting to the desires of the flesh in performing evil actions? Notice what he adds: **Now if I do what I do not want, I agree that the law is good.** He says that he agrees with the law more than with the desires of the flesh, to which he applies the term "sin." He says, therefore, that what he does and performs comes not from his disposition of preferring and carrying out his own choice but by the stirring of cupidity. In this, he says, **I agree that the law is good**: I agree with the law because I do not want what the law forbids. Then he says: **Now then it is no longer I that do it, but sin which dwells within me.** To what time does this **now** refer, if not to living under grace, which had liberated the affections of the will from consent to cupidity? The best way to understand **I do not do it** is that he does not consent to his members being used by sin as tools for iniquity. For if he had desired and consented to the desire and acted on it, how could he say **it is no longer I that do it,** even if he regretted his action and grieved deeply for having been overcome?

Does not what follows clearly show the position for which he is speaking? **For I know that nothing good dwells within me, that is, in my flesh.** If he had not made the statement precise by adding, **that is, in my flesh,** then we might have understood his saying **within me** differently. He keeps pondering the same point, repeating it, and driving it home: **I can will what is right, but I cannot accomplish it.** To do the good would be to have no evil desires. Good remains incomplete as long as one lusts, even though one does not consent to the evil desire. **For I do not do the good I want,** he says, **but the evil I do not want is what I do. Now if I do what I do not want, it is no longer I that do it, but sin that dwells within me.** He repeats it, driving home the point, as though he were trying to rouse someone from sleep. **So I find a law,** he says, **that when I want to do good, evil lies close at hand.** When he is willing to do the good, the evil of lust lies right to hand, to which he says that he does not consent: **it is no longer I that do it.**

What follows makes both points clearer: **For I delight in the law of God, in my inmost self, but I see in my members another law at war with the law of my mind and making me captive to the law of sin which dwells in my members.** His words, **making me captive,** could raise a question if no consent were involved. These three statements, the two earlier ones we have already discussed — **but I am carnal** — and then — **sold under sin** — and now this third — **making me captive by the law of sin which is in my members** — could make it appear that the Apostle is describing a person still living under the law and not yet under grace. However, we have already explained the first two by reference to the flesh which is still corruptible, and this third can also be understood in the same way. He means **making me captive** by the flesh rather than the mind, by tendency rather than consent. He says, **myself being made captive,** because the flesh belongs to our own nature, not to some alien one. This is the way he himself explains what he said: **For I know that nothing good dwells within me, that is, in my flesh.** We should follow his own explanation and understand this passage as saying, **making me captive** — that is, my flesh — **by the law of sin which dwells in my members.**

Then he comes to the point of the whole discussion: **Wretched man that I am! Who will deliver me from this body of death? The grace of God through Jesus Christ our Lord.** From this he concludes: **So then, I of myself serve the law of God with my mind, but with my flesh I serve the law of sin.** I serve the law of sin with my flesh when I have evil desires; I serve the law of God with my mind by not consenting to those evil desires. He continues, *There is therefore now no condemnation for those who are in Christ Jesus* (Rom 8:1). Only those who consent to the desire for evil in the flesh are condemned. *The law of the Spirit of life in Christ Jesus has set you free from the law of sin and death* (Rom 8:2), lest the evil desires of the flesh win over your consent. . . .

At one time, I thought that in this passage the Apostle was describing a person who was under the law (rather than in grace), but afterward these words forced themselves on me: **Now it is not I that do it.** What he says next is also related to this: *There is now no condemnation for those who are in Christ Jesus* (Rom 8:1). Nor do I see how this statement could be true about a person under the law: **I delight in the law of God, in my inmost self.** This very delight in good, by which he does not consent to evil out of a love of justice rather than from fear of punishment — this is what it means to delight — must be attributed to the grace of God alone.

He says: **Who will deliver me from the body of this death?** Who will deny that the Apostle was still in **the body of this death**? The impious are never delivered from it; they are given back those same bodies to suffer eternal torments. Therefore, **to be delivered from the body of this death** is to have all the weakness arising from the lust of the flesh healed and to receive back the body for glory, not punishment. A later statement also fits with this one: *we ourselves, who have the first fruits of the Spirit, groan inwardly as we wait for adoption as children, the redemption of our bodies* (Rom 8:23). We do groan with that moaning, **Wretched man that I am! Who will deliver me from the body of this death?** When he says, **I do not know what I do**, what else could he mean but, "I do not will it; I do not approve it; I do not consent to it; I do not do it"? Otherwise, the statement would be incompatible with the things he said earlier: *through the law comes knowledge of sin* (Rom 3:20); and *if it had not been for the law, I should not have known sin* (Rom 7:7); and *It was sin, working death in me through what is good, in order that sin might be shown to be sin* (Rom 7:13). How could he not know the sin which he had come to know through the law? How could sin be shown and still not be known? Thus in this instance, **I do not know** means "I do not do"; it means, I myself commit it but without consenting to it. In the same way, the Lord will say to the impious: *I never knew you* (Matt 7:23), even though nothing can be hidden from him. Similarly, *he who did not know sin* (2 Cor 5:21) has to mean he did not commit it; he could not have been ignorant of what he condemned.

(8) Augustine on verses 24-25

O you Christian, plead as much as you can; cry out and say: **Wretched man that I am! Who will deliver me from the body of this death?** You will receive an answer: "You will reach safety not by yourself but by your Lord; you will be saved by the pledge you have received. Hope to reign with Christ in his kingdom, since you already hold the blood of Christ as a pledge." Say and say again, **Who will deliver me from the body of this death?** Then you will hear in response, **the grace of God through Jesus Christ our Lord.** To be **delivered from the body of this death** does not mean that you will not have this body. You will have this body, but it will no longer be **the body of this death.** It will be itself and not itself. It will be itself because it will be flesh; it will be not itself because it will not be mortal. Just so will you **be liberated from the body of this death** *because the mortal will put on immortality and the corruptible will be clothed in incorruption* (1 Cor 15:53). By whom? Through whom? **By the grace of God through Jesus Christ our Lord.** *For as by one man came death, so by one man has come the resurrection of the dead. As in Adam all die* — thence what you bewail — *in Adam all die*, and from this comes what you bemoan, from this your conflict with death, from this **the body of this death.** *But as in Adam all die, so in Christ all shall be made alive* (1 Cor 15:21-22). Once you are made alive by receiving an immortal body, then you will say, *O death, where is your claim?* (1 Cor 15:55). You will be **delivered from the body of this death** — not, however, by your own power but **by the grace of God through Jesus Christ our Lord.**

Romans 8

The chapter deals with many different topics that are not unified into a single argument. In the initial sections, the commentators are concerned to rule out any interpretation that would make the human body itself the source of evil. Later, some depict the liberation of creation from futility as the restoration of the whole of creation to that incorruption and immortality which was lost through the sin of human beings.

Paul's assertion that Christ overcame sin by sin required specifying which sin was used to destroy the power of sin. Ambrosiaster and Chrysostom offered the most common explanation: the devil sinned by killing the innocent Christ and thus lost dominion over other sinners. Origen and Augustine identify the sin as a term used for the sacrifice offered for sin.

In the last sections, Paul introduces the topic of election, which will play a major role in the following chapter. Augustine stakes out his characteristic position on the gratuity and efficacy of divine operation; in general, other commentators think it important to defend divine fairness, that is, the integrity of God's justice, by insisting on the (foreknown) human intention to which God responds.

Romans 8:1-4

₁**There is therefore now no condemnation for those who are in Christ Jesus.** ₂**For the law of the Spirit of life in Christ Jesus has set me free from the law of sin and of death.** ₃**For God has done what the law, weakened by the flesh, could not do: by sending his own Son in the likeness of sinful flesh, and for sin, he condemned sin in the flesh,** ₄**in order that the just requirement of the law might be fulfilled in us, who walk not according to the flesh but according to the Spirit.**

(1) Origen on verse 1

Now then, there is no condemnation for those who are in Christ Jesus. For in Christ Jesus the law of the Spirit of life has set you free from the law of sin and death. In the preceding section, Paul has pointed out that different forces were locked in battle within those who follow the law of God with their minds but are driven by the desires of the flesh and the law of sin. Now he is addressing those who are no longer caught between the flesh and the Spirit, but are fully in Christ. Nothing deserving condemnation is found in them, he declares, because **the law of the Spirit of life in Christ Jesus has set them free from the law of sin and of death. The law of the Spirit of life** is the same as the law of God, just as the law of sin and the law of death are one. There will be no condemnation for those fully liberated from the law of sin, that is, the law of death, and who serve the law of God, which is the law of the Spirit.

(2) Cyril of Alexandria on verses 2-3

Just as Paul identifies the law of sin and death as the carnal spirit which leads us into every form of evil, so also he calls the law of the spirit of life the will of the spirit, that inclination of the rational faculty toward the good. So one who sows in the flesh will reap the corruption of the flesh, but one who plants in the spirit will harvest the eternal life of the spirit. Therefore, the law of the spirit of life, that is, the will of the mind which leads toward life, was in us long ago when we were serving the law of God in the mind. But it was powerless to resist. Humanity was overcome by the desires of the flesh and condemned by the law. When this disease passed, we were strengthened through Christ. For through him we have been marked with the seal of the Holy Spirit,[1] and we have been clothed in power from above. In this way we have been ransomed and are no longer under the yoke of evil; we have been restored to dignity in freedom. Therefore, he says that the law of the spirit of life, that is, the will of our reason which inclines us toward good works and a good life, is freed from its old weaknesses, once it has received grace through Christ. Then the law of the spirit despises the evils of sin and liberates us, because it has become stronger than the habits of the flesh. Still this law itself has not granted us full freedom; it is rather a guardian of the freedom we have through the merits of Christ. For just as those under the law of sin must be bound by the snares of death, so those freed through Christ are not under that law. They are beyond the reach of death, not subject to corruption, and strive to lead a life of sanctity.

(3) Origen on verse 3

Paul's words, **in the likeness of sinful flesh**, show that we have **sinful flesh** but that the Son of God did not have **sinful flesh** itself but **the likeness of sinful flesh.** For all human beings who have been conceived from the male seed through intercourse with a woman must join in the confession of David: *For I was conceived in iniquity, and my mother conceived me in sin* (Ps 51:5). But when one came without contact with a man but only, *by the Spirit coming upon a virgin, and the power of the Most High overshadowing her* (Luke 1:36), then that one has our body's nature in its unblemished state and does not share the pol-

---

1. A reference to Baptism.

lution of sin which is passed down to those conceived through the operation of concupiscence. So he says that the Son of God came **in the likeness of sinful flesh.**

For sin, he condemned sin in the flesh. . . . **For sin,** that is to say, through the sacrifice of his flesh which he offered for sin, **he condemned sin in the flesh, so that the just requirement of the law might be fulfilled in us who walk not according to the flesh but according to the Spirit.** After this sacrifice of Christ's flesh, which was offered for sin and condemned sin, put sin to flight and took it away, the righteousness of the law is fulfilled in us who obey the law according to the Spirit rather than the flesh.

(4) Cyril of Alexandria on verse 3

I greatly admire Paul, who initiates us into the mysteries of the faith and carefully guides us toward knowledge of God, though he himself says that he is *unskilled in speaking* (2 Cor 11:6). Since he admits this of himself, we are free to recognize that in his written presentations, such as this one, he leaves out what is necessary for full understanding. When he said, **What the law, weakened by the flesh, was unable to do,** he should have added, "this weakness was destroyed or has ceased." Then he could have shown how what comes next follows from that: **For God, sending his own Son in the likeness of sinful flesh, and for sin, . . . condemned sin in the flesh,** and what comes after that. Since this was what he meant in writing these words, let us examine how we are healed through Christ, how the weakness of the law has ended, what that weakness is, and which law is being considered.

Paul, who speaks for God, discusses such matters with great subtlety. He concedes that it is useful for his readers to know both the written law of God and the law of the spirit, through which we have the capacity to will what is good, even if we are not able to complete the good actions. When he said, *I can will what is right, but I cannot do it* (Rom 7:18), he was referring to the situation in which sin has control and the law of the flesh turns our spiritual powers to its own use even when we are unwilling. I think that what Paul himself says about the weakness of the law could be reasonably understood in this way. His words would refer both to the weakness of the written law given through Moses, as I just noted, as well as to that inborn law, according to which *the Gentiles, who have not the law, do by nature what the law requires, [and] are a law to themselves, even though they do not have the law. They show that what the law requires is written on their hearts,* as Paul has written (Rom 2:14-15). Next we should investigate how both types of law are weak.

The written law was the teacher of good behavior and guide to the best way of life, but it did not make anyone righteous. The other law is inborn in us, the one Paul calls the law of the spirit; it does incline us toward good, yet it is weaker than the written law, which enumerates shameful things. The weakness and lack of strength of both the written law and the inborn law came to an end through Christ. The flesh has died at least to some extent, and the power of pleasure within us has been nearly rooted out. As a result, the law of the spirit or, rather, of the spiritual faculty, is now strong.

Let me explain how the power of sin within us has died, at least to some extent. By the good pleasure of the Father, the Word of God was made **in the likeness of sinful flesh** in order to **condemn sin in the flesh.** He became a human being, *emptying himself* (Phil 2:6). Could anyone doubt that his body had the same appearance and nature as our bodies? The difference was that everyone else's body could be called **sinful flesh**, made sick by the desire for disordered pleasure. Now no one would say that Christ's body is sinful flesh (may it not be so!), but is instead **in the likeness of sinful flesh**; it resembled our bodies, but it was not sickened by the impurities of the flesh. That divine temple was holy from his mother's womb. Everyone recognizes that because he was flesh, he had the natural movements by which he thought and reasoned as a human being. Since the Logos who sanctifies all creation took up his dwelling in that flesh, however, the power of sin was condemned in it, so that this restored nature could be transmitted to us as well. As a result, we have been transformed here and now both spiritually and physically. For when Christ abides in us through the Holy Spirit and through a mystical blessing, the law of sin is also certainly condemned in us. Therefore, we can truly say that the weakness of the law, its being sickened through the flesh, was brought to an end through Christ, who condemned and abolished sin in the flesh so that the righteousness of the law might be fulfilled in us. For the righteousness of the law, that is, the precepts of the law that guide the will toward virtue, has been fulfilled. The law inborn in us is no longer weakened by being held captive to our natural inclination toward pleasures. Therefore, the righteousness of the law has been fulfilled in those who do not walk according to the flesh but instead desire to live spiritually.

(5) Ambrosiaster on verses 3-4

The womb of a virgin was chosen for the birth of the Lord so that the flesh of the Lord could be distinguished from our flesh by its sanctity. His flesh is similar in condition but different because it is not afflicted by the substance of sin. Paul called it **like** because, although it comes from the same substance of flesh, it did not have the same type of birth, and because the body of the Lord was not subject to sin. The flesh of the Lord was purified by the Holy Spirit, so that he was born in the kind of body Adam had before sinning, though the sentence passed on Adam remained. By sending Christ, **God condemned sin from sin**, that is, God condemned sin by its own sin. When Christ was crucified by sin, that is, by Satan, sin itself sinned against the body of the Savior. By this means, God then **condemned sin in the flesh**, specifically in the very place where it had sinned, as Paul says in another letter, *triumphing over them in him* (Col 2:15), that is, in Christ. Thus whenever a person is convicted, one asks for what crime the condemned was found guilty, for example, for murder. Thus **sin was condemned in the flesh**, that is, for the sin which it committed in the flesh. By this sin, therefore, Satan incurred guilt and lost his dominion over the souls which had been held. Now Satan does not dare to hold in the second death those who are signed with the cross on which he was defeated. . . .

    So that the just requirement of the law might be fulfilled in us, who walk not according to the flesh but according to the Spirit. . . . **The just requirement of the law is fulfilled in us** by the forgiveness of all sins, so that, with all sins removed, a person may be justified by serving the law of God in the mind. Thus **to walk not according to the**

flesh but according to the Spirit is accomplished when the devotion of the mind or spirit does not consent to the desire for sin, which sows the lusts of the soul in the flesh, where sin dwells.

If sin has been condemned, how does it continue to dwell there? Sin has been condemned by the Savior in three different ways. In the first place, he condemned sin by refusing to sin. Secondly, sin was condemned on the cross, because the devil sinned. By that sin, the devil has lost the authority to hold humans in hell because of the transgression of Adam; he no longer dares to hold those signed with the cross. Third, the Savior condemned sin by granting the forgiveness of sins and thus loosening the bindings of offenses. Since the sinner was condemned for having committed sin, the Savior condemned the sin itself by granting forgiveness. Then, by following the example of the Savior in not sinning, we too condemn sin.

(6) Augustine on verses 2-4

The Apostle continues by saying, **There is therefore now no condemnation for those who are in Christ Jesus.** Even if they have carnal desires, they do not consent to them; even if the law in their members continues to fight against the law of their minds and tries to take it captive, they are not condemned. Through the grace of Baptism and the washing of new birth, that guilt with which they were born has been loosed; the [baptismal] font also removes any consent they gave to evil desires or shameful action, to any crime, any evil thought or word. You entered it a slave and came out free. Because of your Baptism, **There is therefore now no condemnation for those who are in Christ Jesus.** What once was, is now no more. *From one came condemnation to all* (Rom 5:18). Being born brought evil upon you, but being reborn has brought about good. **For the law of the Spirit of life in Christ Jesus has set you free from the law of sin and death.** Although the law of sin and death remains in your members, it does not make you guilty. You have been set free from it. So fight against it as a free person, being careful not to let it overcome and enslave you once again. You struggle in the fight, but you will rejoice in victory.

I have already spoken to you about this conflict, and you must never forget what you have learned. Even a person who lives well cannot escape this conflict; indeed, the conflict occurs precisely in those who live well; others put up no resistance and are just dragged along. This conflict must not lead you to believe in two different types of being which derive from opposed sources struggling against each other, like the foolish Manichees who believe that the flesh did not derive from God. That is wrong: both flesh and spirit come from God. By sinning, humanity brought this conflict on itself. This is a weakness; it is now being healed and someday will be no more. The present discord between spirit and flesh is actually a struggle to achieve concord; the spirit strives to bring the flesh into accord with itself. In the same way, husband and wife might be at odds with one another within a family; they should strive to come to agreement in what is right, so that the household will be at peace.

Having said, **the law of the Spirit of life in Christ Jesus has set you free from the law of sin and death**, Paul explains the different laws for us. Pay careful attention and distinguish them from one another: these distinctions are important for you to know. **The law of the Spirit of life** — this is one law — **has set you free from the law of sin and death** — this is the other law. Then he continued, **what the law, weakened by the flesh, could not do** — here is a third law. Or is this third law actually the same as one of the other two? Let us consider this question and see what we can figure out with the Lord's help.

What did Paul say about that good law? **The law of the Spirit of life has set you free from the law of sin and death.** He did not say that this law was too weak to accomplish the liberation. **The law of the Spirit of life has set you free**, he said, **from the law of sin and death.** This good law has set you free from that bad law. What, then, is the evil law? *I see in my members another law at war with the law of my mind and making me captive to the law of sin which dwells in my members* (Rom 7:23). Why is this called a law? It is appropriately named: humans refused to obey their Lord and were then legitimately deprived of the obedience of their own flesh. Your Lord is above you and your flesh below. Serve the greater so that the lesser may obey you. As it is, you disdained the higher and as a result are tormented by the lower. This, then, is **the law of sin**, and **of death** as well. *Death came through sin* (Rom 5:12). *For in the day that you eat of it you shall die* (Gen 2:17). That law of sin drags the spirit down and tries to dominate it. *I delight in the law of God in my inmost self* (Rom 7:22). This then is how the conflict arises; in the midst of this struggle he says, *I serve the law of God with my mind, but with my flesh I serve the law of sin* (Rom 7:25).

The law of the Spirit of life has set you free from the law of sin and death. How has this law of the Spirit of life set you free? First it granted the forgiveness of all sins. For this is the law about which we say to God in the psalm: *Have mercy on me by your law* (Ps 119:29). This is the law of mercy, the law of faith and not of works. What then is the law of works? You have already heard about the good law of faith: **the law of the Spirit of life has set you free from the law of sin and death.** Then you heard about the other **law of sin and death. What the law, weakened by the flesh, could not do.** I am still uncertain what this third law is unable to accomplish. The **law of the Spirit of life** did succeed: it **has set you free from the law of sin and death.** The law named third, however, is the law which was given to the people through Moses on Mount Sinai; it is the one referred to as the law of works. It has the power to threaten but not to empower; it can command but cannot help. This is the law which says, *"You shall not covet."* It is the reason why the Apostle says, *I should not have known what it is to covet if the law had not said, "You shall not covet"* (Rom 7:7). Of what advantage to me was it for the law to say, *"You shall not covet?" But sin, finding opportunity in the commandment, deceived me and by it killed me* (Rom 7:7, 11). I was forbidden to covet. I did not fulfill the command; I was overcome. Before the law, I was a sinner; once I received the law, I became a transgressor as well. *But sin, finding opportunity in the commandment, deceived me and by it killed me* (Rom 7:11). . . .

The law of the Spirit of life in Christ Jesus has set you free from the law of sin and death, from which the law of the letter could not. **The law, weakened by the flesh, could not do this.** Your flesh rebelled; your flesh conquered you. Your flesh heard the law, and your lust was incited all the more. Because the law of the letter was weakened by the flesh, it was unable to liberate from **the law of sin and death.**

God sent his Son in the likeness of sinful flesh, not in the flesh of sin. The flesh of all other humans was the flesh of sin; Christ alone was not in the flesh of sin, because his mother conceived him by grace rather than lust. Since Christ had **the likeness of sinful flesh**, he could hunger and thirst, could eat and drink, could grow tired and sleep, could die. **God sent his Son in the likeness of sinful flesh. And from sin, he condemned sin in the flesh.** From which sin? Condemned what sin? **From sin, he condemned sin in the flesh, in order that the just requirements of the law might be fulfilled in us.** The righteousness of the law is now fulfilled in us; that justice which is commanded is now accomplished in us through the Spirit who helps us. This means that through the Spirit of life, the law of the letter is fulfilled in us, **who walk not according to the flesh but according to the Spirit.** Which sin did the Lord condemn, and from which sin?

Indeed, I can see it: *Behold, the Lamb of God, who takes away the sin of the world!* (John 1:29). What sin does he take away? Every sin; he condemned all our sin. But from which sin? He did not have any sin of his own. Of him was it said, *He committed no sin; no guile was found in his mouth* (1 Pet 2:22). None at all: he derived none from Adam; he added none of his own. He had no sin, either from his origin or from his own wickedness. His origin is evident in that he was born of a virgin; his holy manner of life proved that he had done nothing deserving of death. Thus he said: *Behold, the ruler of this world is coming* — referring to the devil — *and he will find nothing in me* (John 14:30). The prince of death will not find any reason to justify killing me. Why then will you die? *So that all may know that I do the will of my Father, let us go hence* (John 14:31). He went forth to the suffering of his death, to a death not forced upon him but a voluntary death, of his own choice. *I have power to lay down my soul, and power to take it up again. No one takes it from me; I lay it down, and I take it up again* (John 10:17-18). If you are in awe at this power, reflect on his majesty. Christ speaks as God speaks.

From which sin, therefore, did he condemn sin? Some have considered this question and arrived at an answer that is not necessarily wrong. Though their explanation is not bad in itself, I judge that they have not really discerned what the Apostle intended. Let me first tell you what they think and then what seems right to me. In any case, what the divine Scripture itself says is most true.

The puzzling question is to identify that sin from which he condemned sin. He did not himself have any sin from which to condemn sin, did he? They agree that in, **from sin he condemned sin**, Paul is not referring to Christ's own sin. Still, **from sin he condemned sin.** If not from his own sin, then from whose? From the sin of Judas, the sin of the Jews? **From** which action did he shed his blood for the forgiveness of sins? Crucifixion by the Jews? Betrayal by Judas? When the Jews killed him, when Judas betrayed him, did they act well or did they sin? Clearly, they sinned. There, they say, is the sin in question, **from sin he condemned sin.** This is true because from the sin of the Jews, Christ condemned every sin: by their persecuting him, he shed the blood which washed away all sin.

Consider, however, what the Apostle says in another of his letters. *So we are ambassadors for Christ, God making his appeal through us. We beseech you on behalf of Christ,* as though Christ himself were beseeching, for him we beseech you, *be reconciled to God.* He continues, *him who did not know sin,* God *(to whom we beg you to be reconciled) made him who did not know sin* and is himself God, *made him who* is Christ and *did not know sin, to be sin for us, so that in him we might become the righteousness of God* (2 Cor 5:20-21). Now in this passage, could we really understand *sin* as a reference — as those others suggest — to the sin of Judas, the sin of the Jews, or the sin of any other person? How do you understand, *him who did not know sin, he made sin for us*? Who made whom? God made Christ. God made Christ *to be sin for us*. He did not say, "God made him a sinner for us," but *God made him sin*. If saying that Christ committed sin would be outrageous, will anyone tolerate our saying, *Christ was sin*? Yet, we cannot contradict the Apostle. We cannot say to Paul: what you are saying? To say that to the Apostle would be saying it to Christ himself. As the Apostle says in another place, *Do you want proof that Christ is speaking in me?* (2 Cor 13:3).

What then? Please, dear friends, attend carefully to this great, deep mystery. You will be blessed if you love what you understand and attain what you love. Yes, indeed, Christ our Lord, Jesus our Savior, our Redeemer *was made to be sin for us so that we might be the righteousness of God in him* (2 Cor 5:21). How? Listen to what the law says. Those of you who know it will recognize what I say; those who do not should read it or listen to it being read. In the law sacrifices which were offered for sins were themselves called sins. For instance, when a victim for sin was led forward, the law says: *the priests shall lay their hands on the sin* (Lev 4:3-4),[2] referring to the victim for sin. What, however, is Christ if not a sacrifice for sin? *As Christ loved us and gave himself up for us as an offering and a sacrifice to God in an odor of sweetness* (Eph 5:2).

This, then, is the sin from which **he condemned sin**: from the sacrifice which he made for sins, **he condemned sin**. This, then, is **the law of the Spirit of life, which has set you free from the law of sin and death.** That third law, the law of the letter, the law which commands, is good indeed: *the commandment is holy and just and good* (Rom 7:12), but it **was weakened by the flesh**. What it commanded, it could not accomplish in us. One law, as I began to explain, pointed out sin to you and another took it away: the law of the letter manifested sin; the law of grace removed it.

(7) John Chrysostom on verse 3

Although Paul seems to disparage the law, a closer look reveals that he actually praises it highly. He shows that it agrees with Christ and highlights the same things. Paul does not say, "the evil of the law," but "its lack of power," and again, **it was weakened**, not "in that it did evil" or "that it plotted evil." Paul attributes this weakness not to the law but to the flesh: **the law, weakened by the flesh**. Again, when Paul refers to the flesh in this passage he means not human nature itself, but a carnal mentality. In this way he defends the body and acquits it. . . .

For in Christ the flesh remained invincible by not sinning. Indeed, the flesh conquered and condemned sin by dying; the flesh, which had been despised, now became

---

2. Augustine seems to have conflated Lev 4:3 and 4:4. In the LXX, the Vetus Latina, and the Vulgate 4:4 reads: the high priest shall "lay his hand on the head of the bull calf," not on the "sin," as Augustine has it. But in 4:3 it is said that "he shall offer a young bull for his sin." Reading the passage from Leviticus in light of Rom 8:3, "from sin he condemned sin in the flesh," Augustine cited Lev 4:4 as "laid hands on the sin" rather than "on the head of the bull," the victim that was the sin offering.

threatening to sin. In this way, flesh destroyed the power of sin and abolished death, which was introduced through sin. For as long as sin held sinners bound, it justly pressed on to its fullness in death. When sin came upon a sinless body, however, and still brought it to death, sin itself was condemned as unjust. Do you perceive the rewards of victory? The flesh is not enslaved by sin; flesh conquered and condemned sin. The flesh did not simply condemn sin: it convicted sin as itself sinful. For Christ first convicted sin of being unjust, then he condemned sin not only by his might and power but also by the rule of justice. Paul made this clear when he said of sin: **he condemned sin in the flesh**, as though to say, "he convicted it of having sinned greatly, and then he condemned it." Do you see how Paul constantly condemns sin, but not the flesh? In fact, he even crowns the flesh with honor and pronounces judgment against sin.

Romans 8:5-13

5For those who live according to the flesh set their minds on the things of the flesh, but those who live according to the Spirit set their minds on the things of the Spirit. 6To set the mind on the flesh is death, but to set the mind on the Spirit is life and peace. 7For the mind that is set on the flesh is hostile to God; it does not submit to God's law; indeed, it cannot; 8and those who are in the flesh cannot please God.

9But you are not in the flesh; you are in the Spirit, if in fact the Spirit of God dwells in you. Anyone who does not have the Spirit of Christ does not belong to him. 10But if Christ is in you, although your bodies are dead because of sin, your spirits are alive because of righteousness. 11If the Spirit of him who raised Jesus from the dead dwells in you, he who raised Christ from the dead will give life to your mortal bodies also through his Spirit which dwells in you.

12So then, brethren, we are debtors, not to the flesh, to live according to the flesh — 13for if you live according to the flesh, you will die; but if by the Spirit you put to death the deeds of the body, you will live.

(1) Ambrosiaster on verses 5-7

For those who live according to the flesh think about the things of the flesh. Paul says this because a person who obeys a suggestion made by the flesh sets the mind on fleshly things. For the mind follows what it is set upon, seeking the enjoyment of what opposes the good and straying after carnal things. All forms of worldly straying are symbolized by the flesh.

But those who live according to the Spirit sense the things of the Spirit. These people have overcome the tendency to stray from the good and suppressed the desires of the flesh; they put the world behind them and do not serve the flesh even while living in the flesh; they seek praise from God and not from other human beings. They are steadfast in spiritual labors, and they **think about the things of the Spirit** of God, by whose precepts they live.

The prudence of the flesh is death. The cunning[3] of the flesh is death because it is seriously sinful, the kind of sin which leads to death. It is called **prudence**, although it is foolish, because the guiding principles which worldly people derive from what they can see, in thought or deed, seem wise to them. Yet these people oppose the law of God, particularly because all their effort and cunning are dedicated to sinning. They consider themselves wise when they devote themselves to sinning, although nothing is more foolish. There is another type of **prudence of the flesh**; puffed up by worldly modes of thought, it denies that anything can happen contrary to the principles of this world. Thus it ridicules the virginal conception and resurrection of the flesh.

The prudence of the Spirit is life and peace. True wisdom brings life and peace. Anyone who seeks spiritual things and despises the enticements of the present life will have life with peace, without anxiety. Where there is disquiet, however, there is also punishment.

The wisdom of the flesh is hostile to God; it does not submit to God's law — indeed, it cannot. Paul assigns this enmity not to the flesh itself but to **the wisdom of the flesh**, which is not itself substantial but rather acting or thinking badly or holding opinions based on error. **The wisdom of the flesh** is, in the first place, astrological calculation presumptuously undertaken by humans and, secondly, delight in visible things. These activities are hostile to God because they assert that events can occur only according to the principles of this world and thus equate the lord of the elements and the creator of the universe with the things that were made. They deny that God caused a virgin to bear a child and the bodies of the dead to rise again. It is foolish, they claim, to say that God would do things that transcend human understanding, and for this reason they insist that God did not do them. O prudent people, belonging to this world, who think that God cannot do anything other than what the creation made by God can do and who think that God is like creatures. They are so blind that they do not even see how they are insulting God. These people ridicule as incredible and foolish the very works by which God chose to manifest the divine glory. So this **prudence of the flesh cannot submit to the law of God**. It is firmly set on resisting the acts of God.

(2) Augustine on verses 5-8

The wisdom of the flesh is death, but the wisdom of the spirit is life and peace. For the wisdom of the flesh is hostile to God. It does not submit to the law of God; indeed, it cannot. What does he mean, **indeed, it cannot**? Not that a human being cannot, nor that the soul cannot, nor finally that the flesh — itself a creature of God — cannot. The wisdom of the flesh cannot; that is, vice, not what is by nature, cannot. Similarly, you might say, "Limping does not submit to the rule of proper walking; indeed, it cannot." The foot can, but the lameness cannot. Take away the limp and you will see proper walking. But as long as the lameness persists, the person cannot walk aright. Similarly, as long as the wisdom of the flesh continues, it cannot be subject to God. Eliminate the wisdom of the

---

3. The Latin term prudentia used here is not restricted to wisdom but refers to a mind-set, worldview, or a kind of proficiency.

flesh and the person can be subject to God. **The wisdom of the Spirit is life and peace.** Now, when he says that **the wisdom of the flesh is hostile to God**, we should not understand it as an enemy which could harm God. Its hostility is in resisting, not in eliminating God. Instead, the wisdom of the flesh harms the person in whom it exists: just as the defect in a nature harms that nature in which it is found. Medicines were discovered for the sake of getting rid of such defects and thus curing the nature. The Savior came to the human race and found no one healthy: he came as the great physician.

The Apostle made this statement because the Manichees wanted to introduce another kind of nature, an evil nature that would be opposed to God. They thought that some parts of the testimony of the Apostle could support their false teaching. Thus they figured that because he said things like, **it cannot; it is hostile to God; it does not submit to the law of God; indeed, it cannot**, he must have been talking about the nature itself. They did not notice that **it cannot** was said not about the flesh nor about human beings nor about the soul; instead, **it cannot** was said about the **wisdom of the flesh**. That wisdom is a defect, a fault. Do you want to know the meaning of being wise according to the flesh? **It is death.** The same human person, living in the same nature created by the true and good Lord God, yesterday was wise according to the flesh but today is wise according to the Spirit. The fault was driven out; the nature was healed. As long as that wisdom of the flesh persisted in it, the nature could not be subject to the law of God. As long as lameness is present as a defect, a person cannot walk properly. When the defect is cured, the nature is restored. *Once you were darkness, but now you are light in the Lord* (Eph 5:8).

Notice, then, what follows. **Those who are in the flesh**, that is, who trust in the flesh, who follow and live according to its desires, who delight in these pleasures, who identify the blessed and happy life with these joys, these are **in the flesh and cannot please God.** To say that **those who are in the flesh cannot please God** is not to say that human beings cannot please God so long as they are in this earthly life. Did not the holy patriarchs please God? Did not the holy prophets please God? Did not the holy apostles please God? Did not the holy martyrs please God — who even before they had laid aside the body by confessing Christ and suffering not only despised pleasure but endured pain with great patience? They all pleased God, but they were not **in the flesh**. They bore flesh but did not rely on the strength of the flesh. They were like the paralytic who was told, *Take up your pallet* (Mark 2:11). **Those, therefore, who are in the flesh**, as I have already said and explained, **cannot please God**, not because they live in this age but because they give themselves over to the desires of the flesh.

(3) John Chrysostom on verse 8

Those who are in the flesh cannot please God. Someone might respond: "What, then? Should we cut the body into pieces in order to please God? Should we depart from the flesh? Are you commanding us to murder ourselves in order to lead us to virtue?" You see how absurd it would be for us to take this text without careful consideration? When he uses the word **flesh** in this passage, Paul does not mean "the body" or the nature of body. Instead, he refers to a carnal and worldly lifestyle, full of wantonness and wastefulness, which transforms the whole person into flesh. For just as those who take flight in the spirit make the body spiritual, so those who reject the spiritual to enslave themselves to their stomach and to pleasure, turn their soul into flesh; they do not change the nature of the soul but destroy its dignity.

(4) Origen on verse 9

We could understand his saying, **Anyone who does not have the Spirit of Christ does not belong to him**, in another way. It is introduced abruptly into the discourse and could be taken to mean that a person who has not met a certain standard and thereby deserved to have the Spirit of Christ should be considered completely cut off from him. But the psalm says, *The wild animals of the forests and the beasts on the mountains and the cattle are mine* (Ps 50:10). If the wild animals and the cattle are his, how could all human beings not be his as well?

The Apostle's statement might be understood in the same way as the saying in the Gospel, *Whoever does not carry his cross and follow me is not worthy of me* (Matt 10:38). In this sense, **Anyone who does not have the Spirit of Christ** in himself is not being led by the same Spirit, is not ready to serve righteousness and truth, to proclaim the word of God and preach the kingdom of heaven, to reject the letter and reveal the spirit of the law, to struggle against sin. Someone unprepared to do all these even until death is not Christ's disciple. Whoever is not like this, whoever does not have this kind of internal disposition, certainly remains Christ's creature, along with *the wild animals of the forests and the beasts on the mountains and the cattle* (Ps 50:10), but is not his disciple. So then, **Anyone who does not have the Spirit of Christ does not belong to him**. . . .

I wish to investigate the meaning of Paul's saying that **the Spirit of Christ**, or **the Spirit of God**, or even **Christ himself, dwells in us.** Does it mean that the Spirit is given to everyone in the beginning and subsequently flees if their evil actions separate them from God, as it is written: *My Spirit shall not abide in mortals forever, for they are flesh* (Gen 6:3)? Or is the Spirit given later because of the merits of life and the gift of faith, as is taught in the Acts of the Apostles, where it says that the Holy Spirit came upon each one like tongues of fire (Acts 2:3); or as we are taught in the Gospel, that after he rose from the dead, the Savior said to the disciples, *Receive the Holy Spirit* (John 20:22), and breathed on each of them? I would conclude from these texts that this gift is acquired by merits, retained by an innocent life, and increased in each person by progress in faith, and by God's gift. The more the soul regains its purity, the more generously the Spirit is poured into it.

The text, *My Spirit shall not abide in mortals forever, for they are flesh* (Gen 6:3), refers to the way these particular souls refused to serve the Spirit and gave themselves over completely to the vices of the flesh. They received the name of that flesh to which they had given themselves in marriage and to which they had joined themselves. **The Spirit of God**, or **the Spirit of Christ**, can then be obtained in various ways. It may be received by divine inspiration, as I just mentioned above, as it says: *he breathed on them, and said to them, "Receive the Holy Spirit"* (John 20:22), or as was done in the Acts of the Apostles when the apostles spoke different languages, or as recorded in the

Books of Kingdoms,[4] *the spirit of God possessed Saul, and he fell into a prophetic frenzy* (1 Sam 10:10). The Spirit can be given in yet another way. After the resurrection the Savior traveled along with Cleopas and another disciple, opened the Scriptures to them, and set them afire by the Spirit of his mouth, as they later said, *Were not our hearts burning within us while he was opening the scriptures to us?* (Luke 24:32).

(5) Ambrosiaster on verses 10-13

Those who live according to the flesh will be abandoned by the Holy Spirit and die in their iniquity. By saying, **the body is dead because of sin**, Paul means that the whole person dies on account of sin, just as the prophet has in mind the whole person when he uses the word *soul*, naming a part for the whole, *The soul which sins shall die* (Ezek 18:4). Will the soul die without the body? Paul here uses **body** to mean the whole person, just as the prophet used *soul*. Another prophet used flesh for the whole person, *All flesh shall see God's salvation* (Isa 40:5 in Luke 3:6). Further, the Holy Spirit given to someone purified by Baptism is called the spirit of that person. Paul compares the rest of the person to its body. So when the soul sins, it is called flesh, bearing the name of the part of the person it follows. In a similar way, to show that his divinity had no fear of his passion but that the sorrow belonged to the humanity, the Lord said, *the spirit is indeed willing, but the flesh is weak* (Matt 26:41), indicating the divine by *spirit* and the human by *flesh*.

But if the Spirit of God who raised Jesus from the dead dwells in you, he who raised Jesus from the dead will give life to your mortal bodies also through his Spirit that dwells in you. Paul expresses the same idea here: he says **bodies** to indicate whole human beings. He said earlier that because of sin, the body dies the second death; here he promises that through good living, mortal bodies will be returned to life. In both, he intends the whole person.

So then, brothers, we are debtors, not to the flesh, to live according to the flesh. Clearly and evidently, we ought not follow the initiative of Adam, who acted according to the flesh; he was the first to sin and bequeathed to us an inheritance of death. Instead, we should serve the law of Christ, who redeemed us from this death by acting according to the spirit. We are his debtors. We had polluted ourselves with carnal vices, but he cleansed us by the bath of the Spirit; he justified us and made us children of God. First we lived in the flesh by the example of Adam and were subject to sins; now we are liberated and owe our service to the redeemer.

(6) Augustine on verse 10

The Apostle did not say, "the body is mortal because of sin," but **the body is dead because of sin.** Before sin, the body might have been called mortal in one sense and immortal in another: mortal because it could die; immortal because it was capable of not dying. God

---

4. In the Septuagint, the books of Samuel and Kings are called Kingdoms. So the first book of Kingdoms is 1 Samuel.

created certain immortal natures incapable of dying; to be capable of not dying is different. In this second sense, the first humans were created immortal not by the constitution of their nature but by being given access to the tree of life. Unless they had sinned, the first humans could have avoided death; once they sinned and were separated from the tree of life, however, they would die. They were mortal by the nature of their animated body but immortal by the gift of their creator. If the body was animated, then it was capable of dying and thus mortal; it was also immortal because it was capable of not dying. It will be immortal in the sense of being incapable of dying only when it becomes spiritual, as we are promised in the resurrection. So the human body was originally animated and thus mortal; it will finally become spiritual through righteousness and thus fully immortal; through sin, it did not become mortal — which it was already — but rather something dead. It could have escaped becoming dead had the first human avoided sinning.

(7) Origen on verses 12-13

I have already explained on many occasions that living according to the flesh means indulging the desires of the flesh. In this statement, Paul denies that we are debtors to the flesh, just as he says elsewhere, *make no provision for the flesh, to gratify its desires* (Rom 13:14). He forbids satisfying the flesh's lusts, but allows caring for its needs. Here he says something similar: **If you live according to the flesh, you will die.**

He adds, **but if by the Spirit you put to death the deeds of the flesh, you will live.** I have already spoken about how **the body** should **be dead because of sin, but the spirit has life because of righteousness.** Whoever acts according to the Spirit and puts to death the deeds of the flesh shall live by the indwelling Spirit of life. The deeds of the flesh are put to death by the Spirit in the following way. *Love is the fruit of the Spirit* (Gal 5:22) but hatred the work of the flesh; charity puts hatred to death and snuffs it out. *Joy is the fruit of the Spirit* (Gal 5:22), but *worldly grief which produces death* (2 Cor 7:10) is the deed of the flesh; grief is quenched when the joy of the Spirit is within us. *Peace is the fruit of the Spirit* (Gal 5:22), but dissension and conflict arise from the flesh; peace can certainly put discord to death. The *patience of the Spirit* (Gal 5:22) puts an end to the impatience of the flesh; goodness extinguishes malice; gentleness overcomes fierceness; continence, intemperance; chastity kills immodesty. In this way, those who **by the Spirit put to death the deeds of the flesh will live**.

Paul says, **if you live indeed according to the flesh, you will die**, referring to the death of sin, not to that death common to all. In the same way, he intends not this common life but that eternal life as the destination of those who put to death the deeds of the flesh through the fruits of the Spirit. We should recognize that the deeds of the flesh are put to death through penance and that this is accomplished gradually rather than all at once. The evil deeds must first be weakened in beginners. As they start to advance more eagerly and are more generously filled with the Spirit, the deeds of the flesh not only become weaker but begin to disappear. When they come to that perfection in which no signs of sin arise in thought, word, or deed, then may we believe that they have fully destroyed the deeds of the flesh and completely handed them over to death.

(8) Augustine on verse 13

The Apostle says, **If you live according to the flesh, you will die; but if by the Spirit you put to death the deeds of the flesh, you will live.** Using these words, humans have glorified themselves, thinking that they could **put to death the deeds of the flesh** through the power of their own spirits. **If you live according to the flesh, you will die; but if by the Spirit you put to death the deeds of the flesh, you will live.** Clarify for us, O Apostle, which spirit you are considering here. Human beings have a spirit which is proper to their own nature; it makes them human. Humans are made up of body and spirit. So, *No one knows a man's thoughts except the spirit of the man which is in him* (1 Cor 2:11). Thus I understand that each of us has a spirit of our own proper to human nature. But then, O Apostle, I hear you saying, **but if by the spirit you put to death the deeds of the flesh, you will live.** So I ask, which spirit, my own or God's?

Listen to what follows and understand. The question is resolved by the words that follow. Once the Apostle had said, **but if by the spirit you put to death the deeds of the flesh, you will live**, he immediately added: *all who are led by the Spirit of God are children of God* (Rom 8:14). You move if you are led; you move well if you are led by what is good. Thus the Apostle said to you, **but if by the spirit you put to death the deeds of the flesh, you will live.** You had been uncertain which spirit he was talking about. In the words which followed, understand your teacher and acknowledge your redeemer. For this redeemer gave you the spirit by which you put to death the deeds of the flesh, for **all who are led by the Spirit of God are children of God** (Rom 8:14). They are not children of God, however, if they are not led by the Spirit of God. If, however, they are led by the Spirit of God, they strive; for they have a mighty helper. God does not watch these fighters in the same way that the crowd watches hunters fight wild beasts in the arena. That crowd can encourage a hunter, but it cannot help him when he is in danger.

Romans 8:14-17

14**For all who are led by the Spirit of God are sons of God.** 15**For you did not receive a spirit of slavery to fall back into fear, but you have received the spirit of sonship. When we cry, *Abba! Father!* (Mark 14:36),** 16**it is that Spirit himself bearing witness with our spirit that we are children of God,** 17**and if children, then heirs, heirs of God and fellow heirs with Christ, provided we suffer with him in order that we may also be glorified with him.**

(1) John Chrysostom on verse 14

For all who are led by the Spirit of God are sons of God. This honor is far greater than the former one. For this reason Paul did not simply say, "all who live by the Spirit of God," but **all who are led by the Spirit of God.** He thus shows that he wants the Spirit to be ruler of our lives, as the pilot is master of a ship and the charioteer is master of a team of horses. Paul subjects not only the body but the soul to such guidance. He does not want the soul to be autonomous, but has placed its authority under the power of the Holy Spirit. To prevent you from neglecting the proper way of life by relying on the gift of Baptism, Paul says that, if you do not intend to be led by the Spirit after receiving Baptism, you destroy the dignity and the privilege of adoption bestowed upon you. For this reason he did not say, "all who received the Spirit," but, **all who are led by the Spirit**, that is, those who live in this way for their whole lives **are sons of God**.

(2) Origen on verses 15-17

Let us consider the meaning of the statement, **You did not receive a spirit of slavery to fall back into fear.** It is written in the prophet Malachi, *A son honors his father, and servants their master. If then I am a father, where is the honor due me? And if I am a master, where is the respect due me? says the Lord of hosts* (Mal 1:6). Clearly, a person becomes a child of God by the Spirit of adoption and a servant of God by the Spirit of fear. Because *To fear the Lord is the beginning of wisdom* (Sir 1:14), the first step in serving God is being filled with the Spirit of bondage while one is still called a child. Fear is the child's guardian. For this reason, the Apostle says of this child, *heirs, as long as they are minors, are no better than slaves, though they are the owners of all the property; but they remain under guardians and trustees until the date set by the father. So with us; while we were minors, we were enslaved to the elemental spirits of this world* (Gal 4:1-3). You see that Paul, acting on the wisdom granted him by God, identifies the spirits of servitude which are given in fear as the guardians and tutors of children. They guard each one of us in fear as long as we are children in our inner selves, until we come to the age at which we become worthy to receive the Spirit of adoption as sons, and so become the heir and ruler of all. . . .

After this, the Apostle weaves an argument which can be laid out in a kind of syllogism: "If we have received the Spirit of adoption, we are thereby children. If we are children, then we are certainly heirs. Now a servant awaits a reward, but a child hopes for an inheritance." Then his conclusion follows: **If children, then heirs, heirs of God and joint heirs with Christ.** A person becomes an heir of God by meriting divine attributes: incorruption and the glory of immortality, the hidden treasures of wisdom and knowledge. This person becomes a joint heir with Christ when *he will transform the body of our humiliation that it may be conformed to the body of his glory* (Phil 3:21), and they become worthy to attain what the Savior sought for them, *Father, I desire that they may be with me where I am* (John 17:24). These joint heirs with Christ will share a further honor: as *the Father has given all judgment to the Son* (John 5:22), so the Son says to his joint heirs, *you will sit on twelve thrones, judging the twelve tribes of Israel* (Matt 19:28). Thus Christ incorporates his joint heirs into a sharing not only of his inheritance but of his dominion as well. . . .

Christ *humbled himself and become obedient to the point of death — even death on a cross. Therefore, God also highly exalted him and gave him the name that is above every name* (Phil 2:8-9). All those who suffer with Christ and imitate the example of his sufferings will be exalted in glory with him. This is the way Christ opened up for his joint heirs, that they might be exalted not through strength or wisdom but through humility, and that by patience in afflictions they might attain to the glory of an everlasting inheritance.

(3) Ambrosiaster on verses 15-16

You have received a spirit of adoption of sons, in which we cry, *Abba! Father!* Freed from fear by the grace of God, we have received the **Spirit of the adoption of sons**, so that reflecting on what we were and what we have attained by the grace of God, we may guide our lives with great care, so that the name of God the Father may not be demeaned in us and that we may not revert ungratefully to everything we have escaped. For we have received a grace by which we dare to say to God: ***Abba!*** that is, ***Father.*** Thus Paul warns that the trust placed in us should not make us reckless. If we openly follow a different way of life, we offend God by using the title ***Father.*** The divine goodness has indulged us with a gift higher than our nature: what we are unworthy to receive as we are, we merit by our works.

It is that very Spirit bearing witness with our spirit that we are sons of God. When we behave well and thereby retain the indwelling of the Spirit of God, this Spirit bears witness to our utterance and to our soul so that when we pray, ***Abba***, that is, ***Father***, we do not say ***Abba***, that is, ***Father***, rashly. Because the Spirit dwells in us, we are presenting a life worthy of this utterance. The proof of being children is that the character of the Father is manifest in us through the Spirit.

(4) Augustine on verses 15-17

But you have received the spirit of sonship, in which we cry, *Abba, Father.* The heart cries, *Our Father, who art in heaven* (Matt 6:9). Therefore why not say only ***Father***, why cry, ***Abba, Father***? If you asked what ***Abba*** means, the answer would be, "Father." ***Abba*** means "Father" in Hebrew. Why, then, did the Apostle put down both terms? Because he was thinking about the cornerstone, the one *the builders rejected, which became the head of the corner* (Matt 21:42; Ps 117:22). It is called a corner because it embraces two walls coming from different directions. Here those of the circumcision, there those of the foreskin; far apart among themselves and from each other; so far from the corner. But as they approach the corner, they draw close to each other and are finally joined together at the corner. *For he is our peace, who has made us both one* (Eph 2:14). Those of the circumcision, those of the foreskin, the concord of the walls, the glory of the corner. **You have received the spirit of sonship, in which we cry, *Abba, Father.***

What must the reality be like that has such a pledge? Actually, it should be called a deposit rather than a pledge. A pledge is returned when the promised reality itself is delivered. A deposit is part of that reality whose delivery is being promised; thus when the reality is handed over, what was originally given as a deposit is completed rather than exchanged. Let everyone pay attention to their own hearts: do you say ***Father*** from the innermost depths of your hearts, with sincere charity? The question now is not how great that love is: large, small, or medium. I am asking only whether it is present at all. If it has been born, it will grow in secret, will mature by growing, and once perfect will endure. Upon attaining maturity, it does not then decline into old age and thence arrive at death. It matures and continues forever. Notice what follows. **We cry, *Abba, Father.* The Spirit itself bears witness to our spirit that we are children of God.** The Spirit bearing witness to our spirit that we are children of God is not our own but the Spirit of God. The deposit bears witness to the reality which has been promised to us. **The Spirit itself bears witness to our spirit that we are children of God.**

And if children, then heirs. We are not children in vain. Here is the reward, **then heirs.** He talked about this a little earlier: our physician not only restores our health but grants us a reward as well. What is that reward? The inheritance. Not, however, in the way a human father leaves an inheritance. He leaves it to his children but does not enjoy it with them. Still he considers himself generous and expects to be thanked because he decides to give them what he cannot take along with him. What if he could take it with him when he dies? If he could, I suspect his children would see none of it. As heirs of God, however, we have God as our inheritance, as the psalm says to us, *The Lord is the portion of my inheritance* (Ps 16:5). **Heirs of God.** If that seems insufficient for you, listen to the rest, **heirs of God and fellow heirs of Christ.**

Romans 8:18-23

18I consider that the sufferings of this present time are not worth comparing with the glory about to be revealed to us. 19For the creation waits with eager longing for the revealing of the children of God; 20for the creation was subjected to futility, not of its own will but by the will of him who subjected it in hope; 21because the creation itself will be set free from its bondage to decay and obtain the glorious liberty of the children of God. 22We know that the whole creation has been groaning in travail together until now; 23and not only the creation, but we ourselves, who have the first fruits of the Spirit, groan inwardly while we wait for adoption as sons, the redemption of our bodies.

(1) Origen on verse 18

If the seeds of future glory can be gathered up during the present life, he says, these seeds will be harvested from afflictions and sufferings. As the same Apostle says elsewhere, *this slight momentary affliction is preparing us for an eternal weight of glory beyond all measure, because we look not at what can be seen but at what cannot be seen* (2 Cor 4:17-18). He shows that those who look for the eternal realities that cannot be seen consider any affliction that they endure, however harsh and persistent, as momentary and light. Even while the body is being afflicted with torture by rack and claw, if a person concentrates on the future glory to be revealed, and considers that through these very torments this body of humiliation is being transformed into conformity to the glorious body of the Son of

God, then the present afflictions will be regarded as momentary and light, and the weight of future glory recognized as great and eternal. The more pains and afflictions are multiplied, the more will the one who suffers grasp the weight and magnitude of glory being piled up.

(2) Ambrosiaster on verses 19-22

For the creation waits with eager longing for the revealing of the sons of God. Since Paul just said that **the sufferings of this present time are not worth comparing with the glory** of the future, he adds that creation awaits the time when the number of children of God destined for life will be completed, so that finally creation itself may be relieved of its duty of service and rest in peace.

For the creation was subjected to futility, not of its own will. Because creation is in the power of God its creator, it was not subjected to futility of its own accord; this subjection is for our benefit, not that of the creation itself. It has been **subjected to futility** because its offspring are destined to die. Though it goes about its work, its fruit is subject to corruption. It is corruption, then, that is the **futility.** For all things born in the world are impermanent, destined to perish, corruptible, and in this sense futile. They are futile because they cannot maintain their status. For the whole creation is distorted by a process of flux and its nature reverts toward chaos. Solomon says something similar about these things, *All is vanity* (Eccl 1:2).[5] David does not disagree when he says, *Truly the life of every person is futile* (Ps 38:6 Vg). Is it not futility to eat and drink, to worry about the things of this world? And yet this futility has its advantages. People born in this world are benefited by learning the mysteries of the creator through the bodily troubles they suffer. In comparison to eternal realities, things of this world are indeed futile, but they are good and even necessary in their own realm.

The creation itself will be set free from its bondage to decay into the freedom of the glory of the sons of God. Since creation cannot gainsay its creator, it was subjected for God's purpose but not without hope. In the midst of its struggle, it is consoled by knowing that it will have rest, once all whom God knows are going to believe have actually come to believe, since it was subjected for their sake.

We know that the whole creation has been groaning and giving birth until now. To be **in labor** is to be in pain. The meaning is that all creation, through its daily toil, is groaning and in pain up until this time. **Until now** means as long as this text is read. The elements themselves perform their works with care: the sun and moon labor in completing their appointed circuits, and the spirit in animals is constrained to accomplish its service with great groaning. We see them complaining when they are forced to work. All are waiting for the rest that will release them from this servile labor.

Now if this were a service by which God's favor could be won, the creation would be rejoicing, not suffering. But it suffers because it is subjected to this service of corruption for our sake. Every day it sees its accomplishments perishing. Every day its work rises

---

5. The Greek and Hebrew terms translated as *futility* and *vanity* are closely related.

and falls. A creature is right to grieve when its work serves corruption and does not endure. As far as we are given to understand, the creation is fully occupied with our salvation, knowing that the sooner we earn the good graces of our maker, the sooner will it be released from its servitude. Realizing this, let us with all care and diligence show ourselves worthy to serve as an example for others. Let us be moved not only by compassion for ourselves but by sympathy for the creation which groans as it suffers day and night. We are usually concerned more for others than for ourselves.

(3) Augustine on verse 20

The creation was subjected to futility. This refers to, *Vanity of vanities! All is vanity. What does one gain by toil, by laboring under the sun?* (Eccl 1:2-3). Who was told: *In toil will you eat bread* (Gen 3:19)? **The creation was subjected to futility, not of its own will.** It was good that he added, **Not of its own will.** Humans sinned by their own will but were condemned against their will. The sin against the command to speak truly was indeed voluntary, but the punishment for that sin was that one became subject to deceit, so **the creation was subjected to futility not of its own will but because of him who subjected it in hope.** God's justice and mercy left neither the sin unpunished nor the sinner beyond healing.

(4) Theodoret on verse 20

He describes vanity as moral corruption. After a few other observations, he points out that creation itself will be liberated from slavery to corruption. He explains that all the visible creation shares in mortal nature, since the creator of all things foresaw the transgression of Adam and the sentence of death that would be imposed upon him. It was neither reasonable nor just that the rest of creation should remain uncorrupt while the very one on whose account these things had been made should become mortal and subject to suffering because of his actions. By virtue of the resurrection, Adam will receive immortality; and the rest of creation will also participate in this freedom from corruption. He concludes that the visible creation now awaits this transformation. For it has become subject to change, not for its own sake but by embracing the decision of the creator. By seeing God's care for us, the whole universe holds a hope of transformation, so that creation may be freed from the bondage to corruption. Holy David gives witness to this transformation, for in referring to the heaven and the earth he says, *They will perish, but you endure* (Ps 102:26).

(5) John Chrysostom on verses 20-21

For the creation was subjected to futility, not of its own will but by the will of him who subjected it. What is the meaning of **creation was subjected to futility**? It means that the creation became perishable. What caused it to become perishable? Because of you, human being. For when your body became mortal and subject to suffering, the earth was also cursed and brings forth thorns and thistles. After the heaven has become old along with the earth, it will then be transformed into something far better. Listen to what the prophet says, *Long ago you laid the foundation of the earth, and the heavens are the work of your hands. They will perish, but you will endure; they will all wear out like a garment. You change them like clothing, and they pass away* (Ps 102:26). Isaiah demonstrates these things when he says, *Lift up your eyes to the heavens, and look at the earth beneath; for the heavens will vanish like smoke, the earth wear out like a garment, and those who live on it will die like gnats* (Isa 51:6). Do you see how creation is enslaved to futility and how it is freed from corruption? For the prophet says, *You change them like clothing, and they pass away.* And Isaiah says, *those who live on it will die like gnats.* He does not mean complete destruction, since the inhabitants, that is, the human race, will not undergo such a total extermination, but rather a temporary destruction. Through this destruction humanity will be transformed into incorruptibility, and creation along with it. Paul calls this futility, showing why such a thing comes about and assigning its cause to us human beings. . . .

The creation itself will be set free from its bondage. What does he mean by **the creation itself**? Not only you, but also whatever is inferior to you, whatever does not share in reasoning or sensation, this too will share blessings with you. **It will be set free**, Paul says, **from bondage to decay**, that is, it will no longer be corruptible but will imitate the beauty of your body. For just as when your body became corruptible, this creation also became corruptible; so when it becomes incorruptible, this creation also will follow it again.

(6) Origen on verses 20-22

Let us examine more carefully **the futility to which the creation** is said to be **subjected**, and **the decay from whose bondage** the creation hopes to be set free. I think these expressions refer to the substance of our corruptible, material bodies. For decay exercises dominion only over bodies. The inner self has been created like God and was made in the image of God to be incorruptible and invisible; it can even be called incorporeal in its own way. The outer person, however, is both corporeal and corruptible. Thus Paul said: *Even though our outer nature is wasting away, our inner nature is being renewed* (2 Cor 4:16). Because the inner self is a rational mind, its renovation consists in the acknowledgment of God and the capacity for the Holy Spirit.

In order to commit to paper a brief and summary consideration of these deep matters, let us form a sketch from the inner man, the substance of the soul and mind, of how **the creation was subjected to futility, not by its own will but because of him who subjected it in hope.** Let us focus our attention on Paul, whose soul and mind, his inner self, surpasses and transcends everything corporal, visible, or subject to sense and scrutiny, who became capable of understanding the divine nature itself. Still the substance of such a great soul as his, which could understand and grasp the principles of heavenly and divine realities (God alone knows how), was subjected to the servitude of a corruptible body and overcome by futility. Consider the needs of the body: the appetite for food, the embarrassment of digestion, the shame involved in generating offspring, as children are sown, brought forth, and raised. Notice the futility in all of these exercises, the great corruption to which that noble and reasonable creature, the soul, is unwillingly subjected; subjected in hope, however, looking forward to the time when it will be set free, when the hour of the **freedom of the sons of God** arrives. This is what the Apostle has already said even more clearly of himself: *while we are still in this tent, we groan* (2 Cor 5:4). Speaking through Solomon, wisdom says the same: *a perishable body weighs down the soul, and this earthly tent burdens the thoughtful mind* (Wis 9:15). The same Apostle says, *while we are at home in the body, we are away from the Lord* (2 Cor 5:6), though he would prefer to be away from the body and at home with the Lord. He indicates the same more clearly when he says, *I am hard pressed between the two: my desire is to depart and be with Christ, for that is far better; but to remain in the flesh is more necessary for you* (Phil 1:23-24). In this he clearly shows that he was not willing to serve this decay and futility for what he considered the interests of his own soul but did it because God willed it and for the sake of our salvation. He remained in the flesh for our sake. When we have been revealed as children of God and gathered into one through the Church which he promised *to one husband, to present you as a chaste virgin to Christ* (2 Cor 11:2), then he too will be freed from bondage to decay, as he says, *I am already being poured out as a libation, and the time of my departure has come. I have fought the good fight, I have finished the race, I have kept the faith. From now on there is reserved for me the crown of righteousness* (2 Tim 4:6-8). This is what it means to be freed from servitude to corruption in the **freedom of the glory of the sons of God**.

From these examples, let us ascend together to higher considerations. Notice how the services of the sun itself, of the moon and stars of the heavens, and indeed of the whole world are subjected to futility and decay. For the benefit of humans, they nourish the crops and bring forth the fruit of the trees and the plants of the fields. They rotate in the same cycles each year. They renew what passes away, and they allow what has been reborn to pass away again. If you attend to the meaning of Paul's statement, *Are not all ministering spirits in the divine service, sent to serve for the sake of those who are to inherit salvation?* (Heb 1:14), you will understand that the angels perform these things and are subject to this regimen. I believe that they also do so **not by their own will but because of him who subjected them in hope**. *Who can resist God's will?* (Rom 9:19). The sayings of the prophets draw me to a similar understanding of the archangels. What could you find more futile and corrupting than waging wars in this world, inciting kings and peoples to fight one another? Yet you should notice that this is the primary work of the archangels, as the prophet Daniel testifies in saying that an archangel told him that he had fought against the Persian ruler, and said, *Michael, one of the chief princes, came to help me* (Dan 10:13). In each of these instances, you can understand that the rational creation **was subjected to futility, not by its own will but because of him who subjected it in hope**. That hope is to be released eventually from these corruptible, bodily things. The rational creation looks forward to the revelation of the children of God, for whose sake the angels were placed in these offices, so that, along with those they have served, they might receive the inheritance of salvation and that there might be one flock including both earthly and heavenly beings, and one shepherd, and that God might be all in all.

To confirm the points which he had made, Paul added more clearly, **We know that the whole creation has been groaning and suffering until now.** He had said earlier, **I consider that the sufferings of this present time are not worthy comparing with the future glory.** There he said that he **considered** it, but here that he **knows** that **the whole creation has been groaning and suffering**, thereby removing all doubt. Although the creation is subjected unwillingly, by acceding to the will of God who subjects it, it demonstrates a certain affection and love for those in whose interest it was subjected; it suffers for their sufferings and groans for their groaning. But if we read the text as it appears in some copies, **it suffers and gives birth**, we would take this reference to a birth like those the Apostle describes in saying that he had begotten through the gospel those whom he brought forth into the light by faith in Christ (1 Cor 4:14), or as he says elsewhere of a different group, *My little children, for whom I am again in the pain of childbirth until Christ is formed in you* (Gal 4:19). In this way, the creation **gives birth** to those whom it brings forth into salvation.

Some reader might inquire why Paul named the creation three times in this passage without once saying, "all creation," until he says in the final phrase, **we realize that all creation has been groaning and suffering.** That could be explained as follows. The whole creation does not groan and suffer from being subjected to the needs of a corruptible body; the whole creation, however, grieves with those who grieve and groans with those that groan. The whole higher creation attends to our contests and conflicts; it grieves when we are defeated, and rejoices when we are victorious. Indeed, those higher beings watching us are more likely than we to rejoice with the rejoicing and grieve with the grieving.

(7) Augustine on verses 22-23

Let us ask the Apostle Paul how humanity came into captivity. Longing for the eternal Jerusalem, Paul is in the forefront of those who groan in that captivity, and he teaches us to groan in the same Spirit with which he was filled in his groaning. This is what he says: **The whole creation groans together and sorrows until now.** And again, **The creation was subjected to futility, not of its own will but because of him who subjected it in hope.** He says that **the whole creation groans together in travail**, even in those people who do not believe yet but who will believe. Would this not imply that it groans only in those who do not yet believe? Does the creation neither groan nor give birth in those who do believe? **Not only the creation**, he says, **but we ourselves who have the first fruits of the Spirit**, meaning we who already serve God by the Spirit, who already believe in God with our minds and in this faith have produced some first fruits, so that we ourselves may then follow after our first fruits. **Therefore, we ourselves groan inwardly as we wait for adoption as sons, the redemption of our bodies.** So, Paul groaned and all the faithful groan, **waiting for adoption as sons, the redemption of our bodies.** Where do they groan? In this mortal condition. What redemption do they await? **Of their bodies**, which has already been accomplished in the Lord, who rose from the dead and ascended into heaven. Before this is accomplished in us, we must groan, even though we are faithful and hopeful.

Romans 8:24-25

24For in this hope we were saved. Now hope that is seen is not hope. For who hopes for what he sees? 25But if we hope for what we do not see, we wait for it with patience.

(1) Ambrosiaster on verses 24-25

For in hope we were saved. Paul says that, by hoping for what God promised in Christ, we are rewarded by being set free. We are set free in hope because what we believe will indeed happen.

Now hope that is seen is not hope. Obviously hope is not for what is seen but for what is yet unseen. Believers deserve a reward because they hope for what they do not see.

For who hopes for what is seen? But if we hope for what we do not see, we wait for it with patience. Clearly, unseen things are hoped for and expected to happen. Waiting is the patience which earns a great reward from God. The believer eagerly awaits the coming of the kingdom of God day-in and day-out and does not doubt because it is delayed.

(2) John Chrysostom on verse 24

We must not expect to receive everything in this life; we must also have hope. For believing in God's promise of the things to come is the only gift we have to offer to God, and the only way we were saved. If we lose this hope, we have lost everything we have to offer. For I ask you, Paul says, were you not guilty of countless sins? Were you not in despair? Were you not under sentence? Were you not worn out worrying about your salvation? What brought you salvation? Only hoping in God and trusting God for the things God promised and gave — you had nothing else to offer. If this hope saved you, then hold onto it even now. Hope has brought you such great blessings; clearly it will not disappoint you in what is still to come.

(3) Augustine on verse 24

Once the Apostle had said, **we ourselves groan inwardly**, he then added, **as we wait for adoption, the redemption of our bodies.** He seemed to be responding to an objection, "What use is Christ to you if you are still groaning; how has the Savior saved you?" Anyone groaning is still sick. So he added: **For in this hope we are saved. Now hope that is seen is not hope. What a person sees is not hoped for. But if we hope for what we do not see, we wait for it with patience.** This then is why and how we groan: what we hope for, we still await and do not yet hold. Until we possess it, we will sigh for it, because we desire what we do not yet possess. Why? **Because we are saved in hope.** Our kind of flesh, taken from ourselves, has already been saved in the Lord, saved not in hope but in reality. In our head, our saved flesh has resurrected and ascended; in his members, it still remains to be saved. Because the members have not been abandoned by their head, they rejoice in security.

Romans 8:26-27

26Likewise the Spirit helps us in our weakness; for we do not know how to pray as we ought, but the Spirit himself intercedes for us with sighs too deep for words. 27And he who searches the hearts of men knows what is the mind of the Spirit, because the Spirit intercedes for the saints according to the will of God.

(1) Origen on verse 26

The Spirit is like a teacher who takes on an untrained student, one who does not yet know even the alphabet. To be able to teach and instruct, the teacher has to stoop down to the initial steps of the pupil, has to sound out the names of the letters so that the student can learn by repeating them. Like a beginning student, the teacher sounds out and practices the things the beginner should say and do. In the same way, when the Holy Spirit sees our spirit being harassed by the attacks of the flesh and not knowing what it ought to ask in prayer, the Spirit acts like a teacher, first saying the prayer which our spirit should then follow if it wishes to become a student of the Holy Spirit. The Spirit utters the groans by which our spirit learns to groan and to win God over for itself.

(2) Augustine on verse 26

We might argue that the merit of praying comes first as a means of acquiring the gift of grace. Still the prayer itself, by its very begging, would show that anything it seeks is itself a gift of God, lest people think they can provide it for themselves. If it were in their own power, they would not be asking God for it. This must be taken a step further: people should not think that the merits of prayer precede, so that grace is repaid for those merits and is not given gratuitously. For in that case, grace would no longer be a gift but a wage paid out as owed. Thus praying must itself be counted among the gifts of grace. **For we do not know how to pray as we ought**, says the teacher of grace, **but the Spirit pleads for us with sighs too deep for words.** What does **plead** mean here if not "make us plead"? To plead with sighs is a very clear sign of neediness. No one could possibly believe, however, that the Holy Spirit is in need of anything. So **plead** must be used here to indicate that the Spirit moves us to plead and inspires in us the urge to plead and groan, as the gospel says: *It is not you who speak, but the Spirit of your Father speaking through you* (Matt 10:20). Nor is this accomplished in us without our doing anything. The Holy Spirit's way of helping is expressed by saying that the Spirit does what the Spirit causes us to do ourselves.

The Spirit which **pleads with sighs too deep for words** must be understood not as our own spirit but as the Holy Spirit, who helps our weakness, as the Apostle clearly shows. He introduces the consideration by saying, **the Spirit helps our weakness**. Then he continues, **for we do not know what we should pray for**, and so forth. A little earlier, he clearly said about this Spirit: *you did not receive the spirit of slavery to fall back into fear, but you have received the spirit of adoption as children, in which we cry out, "Abba, Father"* (Rom 8:15). Notice that here he did not say, "That Spirit cries out by praying," but instead, *in whom we cry out, "Abba, Father."* In another place he states: *Because you are children, God has sent the Spirit of the Son into your hearts, crying, "Abba, Father"* (Gal 4:6). That time he did not say, *in whom we cry out*, but preferred to attribute the crying out directly to the Spirit, who moves us to cry out. Similarly, in those other passages: **the Spirit pleads for us with sighs too deep for words** and *the Spirit of your Father speaks through you* (Matt 10:20).

(3) Cyril of Alexandria on verse 26

With loud groans the spirit — clearly our own spirit — makes a plea on our behalf. For when we moan we are making supplications to God. We also learn to do this through the Holy Spirit, for the Spirit is wise, like the Son. Paul says: **We do not know how to pray as we ought.** We must consider what he says, since we learned how we ought to pray from Christ, who plainly told us: *Pray then in this way, Our Father in heaven, hallowed be your name. Your kingdom come, your will be done on earth as it is in heaven* (Matt 6:9-10), and so on with the other matters in their order. Since we have already learned how we should properly express our prayers, what could be the meaning of this apostolic letter or what does Paul intend to explain? We pray by making petitions for what is good: we seek first the glory of God and then the means to live virtuously and conduct our lives with integrity. Having thus begun in the spirit, we groan within ourselves as we await our adoption as heirs, the liberation of our bodies. This happens in particular when **we do not know how to pray as we ought.** For if God has promised *what no eye has seen, nor ear heard, nor the human heart conceived, what God has prepared for those who love God* (1 Cor 2:9), what will we seek when we come to prayer? How can we recognize and specify things that are beyond our mental perception and unknown to the human heart? God alone, the skilled artisan of such things, knows what the redemption or transformation of the body would be, and how it would be changed into an imperishable and glorious state. The Savior's disciple admonished the ignorant about their prayer: *You ask and do not receive, because you ask wrongly, in order to spend what you get on your pleasures* (Jas 4:3). It would be appropriate and reasonable for people like these to admit: **we do not know how to pray as we ought.**

Thus with loud groans we will seek in the Spirit what we believe will come, though we are completely ignorant of how it will be done. Our nature, he says, is weak; were we to rely on our own resources, we would refuse to believe that we shall rise. The promises made to us are great and holy; we cannot comprehend them, nor can our hearts conceive them. Yet we have the great help of the Spirit as an aid to our faith in these great things. For such realities are beyond our prayer; we do not even know how to ask for them.

(4) John Chrysostom on verse 26

The Spirit intercedes with sighs too deep for words. Paul's meaning here is hidden from us because the wonders which used to occur frequently in his time have now ceased. For this reason, let me teach you something about events at that time, so that the matter will be more intelligible. What, then, was happening at that time? God gave different gifts of grace to everyone who was baptized. These gifts were called spirits, as Paul says, *And the spirits of the prophets are subject to the prophets* (1 Cor 14:32). The gift of prophecy enabled a person to foretell the future. The gift of wisdom instructed many people. The gift of healing healed the sick. The one who received the gift of power raised the dead. The one with the gift of tongues spoke in different languages. Among these was also the gift of prayer, also called a spirit; the one who had this spirit prayed for all the people. Since we are ignorant of many things that would be profitable for us, and we ask for things that are unprofitable, one particular person received the gift of prayer. That person was responsible for the common good of the whole church and for all the prayers, and also instructed others. By "**the spirit**," Paul means both this particular gift and the soul which receives the gift and intercedes with groans to God. The person judged worthy of such a gift stands with much compunction, falls down before God with a mind full of groaning, and begs for what is helpful for all. Today, the deacon offering up the prayers of the people symbolizes this gift. Paul clarifies this point when he says, **the Spirit intercedes with sighs too deep for words.**

(5) Ambrosiaster on verse 27

And he who searches the heart knows what the Spirit desires, because the Spirit intercedes for the saints according to the will of God. Obviously the prayer of every spirit is known to God, to whom nothing is silent or hidden. How much more so the prayer of the Holy Spirit, who is divine in substance and speaks not by moving the air, nor even as the angels or other creatures speak, but speaks in a way proper to divinity. The Spirit speaks to God beyond our hearing; the Spirit sees but is not seen; the Spirit asks for things which the Spirit knows are pleasing to God and beneficial for us. When the Spirit knows that we are asking for harmful things out of ignorance rather than arrogance, the Spirit intervenes on our behalf.

Romans 8:28-30

28 We know that in everything God works for good with those who love God, who are called according to his purpose. 29 For those whom he foreknew he also predestined to be conformed to the image of his Son, in order that he might be the first-born among many brethren. 30 And those whom he predestined he also called; and those whom he called he also justified; and those whom he justified he also glorified.

(1) Cyril of Alexandria on verse 28

All things work together for good for those who love God, who are called according to purpose. But according to whose purpose? What does the phrase **according to purpose** mean? Surely the meaning would follow the prior phrase *according to the will* (Rom 8:27). The subjects of this statement have been called according to someone's will. But is this the will of the one calling or of those being called? Every impulse which attracts us toward righteousness comes to us from God the Father. For Christ has said: *No one can come to me unless drawn by the Father who sent me* (John 6:44). Still, even in this case, a person would not be mistaken in explaining that some have been called for a purpose which includes the will of both the caller and those called.

(2) Origen on verses 29-30

He says, **those whom he foreknew and predestined to be conformed to the image of God's Son.** Let us not pass over his statements: **he foreknew and predestined.** He has said neither that everyone is predestined, nor that everyone is foreknown. We have to attend to the scriptural use of language rather than to the popular opinion which thinks that God foreknows both good and evil. The reader who is learned in the Scriptures should try to think of a passage saying that God foreknows the wicked — as the present passage clearly says of the good, **those whom he foreknew and predestined to be conformed to the image of his Son.** If those whom God foreknew, **he predestined to be conformed to the image of God's Son**, and if no evil person can be **conformed to the image of his Son**, then the statement must be restricted to the good: **those whom he foreknew and predestined to be conformed to the image of his Son.** God does not foreknow the others; God does not know them at all. *The Lord knows those who belong to the Lord* (2 Tim 2:19). The Savior said to those unworthy to be known by God, *I never knew you; go away from me, you evildoers* (Matt 7:23). This is precisely the meaning of the present passage: **those whom God foreknew and predestined to be conformed to the image of his Son.** Scripture does not say that God foreknows the others. Although nothing can be hidden from that nature which is present everywhere and absent nowhere, all wickedness is unworthy of divine knowledge or foreknowledge. . . .

Attentive readers might also ask why he says **conformed to the image of his Son**, rather than "conformed to God's Son." They should notice that the Son, who is called *the image of the invisible God* (Col 1:15), is not the same person as God, whose image the Son is. In the same way, what is called the image of God's Son should be distinguished from the Son whose image it bears. Hard and difficult as this is to understand, we might be able to say something about it. Although all those who develop themselves into that form we have just discussed are the image of God, that is, the image of God's Son, still the soul of Jesus himself is the special and proper image of God's Son because it received the Son fully and completely, and it formed that image in itself. That soul so adapted itself to the Word and Wisdom of God that no deviation from God's likeness can be found in it. Thus whoever aspires to attain the highest perfection and happiness must aim toward that image and likeness which is, primarily and above all others, itself the image of the Son of God, so that this soul of Jesus might become **the first-born among many brethren.** That soul holds the first place among these who are **conformed to the image of God's Son.** . . .

I think that we need to reconsider the preceding exposition of the way God knows or foreknows, so that we take into account the language which Scripture uses when describing how persons know. When Scripture says, *the man knew his wife Eve* (Gen 4:1), it means that he had intercourse with her. Similarly, it calls Rebecca *a virgin, whom no man had known* (Gen 24:16). It says that the sons of Levi will punish transgressors because none of them *had known his father and his mother* (Deut 33:9). The clear meaning here is that they had not joined themselves to their fathers and mothers in affection and love. You will find many instances in which Scripture speaks of knowing in this way. The Apostle is employing this customary scriptural mode of speaking in the present case: he shows that God foreknows those upon whom God bestows divine love and affection, knowing what their character will be. Thus is it written, *The Lord knows those who belong to him* (2 Tim 2:19), even though in the general meaning of knowing, God is no more ignorant of those who wander from God than of those who belong to God. God is said to know God's own, however, in the sense of loving them and uniting with them.

Those whom he foreknew he also predestined; and those he predestined he also called; and those whom he called he also justified. We will have to solve this question: How did God justify whoever was called? Our earlier explanations followed the statement, *many are called but few are chosen* (Matt 22:14). I think that God has different ways of calling, as we have discussed in an earlier chapter, since all are called but not all are **called according to purpose.** Those **called according to purpose** are the ones called according to that good intention and purpose which they exercise in worshiping God. These are the ones who are both called and justified. Their good intention lacked only a divine call. Those who have no good and definite intention toward either the worship of God or good works are indeed called. Otherwise, they might find occasion to make an excuse and a plea at the judgment: "if we had been called we could certainly have been justified and not only justified but glorified." These too are called, therefore, but like seed sown on rocky soil which springs up quickly. Under the blazing sun of afflictions, however, they immediately burn up and die because they did not have the deep roots of good intention. The Apostle says of them, *certain persons have suffered shipwreck in the faith* (1 Tim 1:19).

Therefore, those whom God has called according to their own good intention, God has also justified. Our interpretation would still fit, however, even if the **according to purpose** were referred to God's purpose, so that they are called according to the purpose of God precisely because God knows who are religiously disposed and have a desire for salvation. In this scenario, the foreknowledge of God would not be the cause of our salvation or ruin; nor would justification depend on the vocation alone; nor would being glorified be taken completely out of our discretion.

God's foreknowledge could even be taken in its popular meaning. An event will not happen because God knows that it will; God knows it in advance because it is actually going to happen.

(3) Ambrosiaster on verses 29-30

Those he foreknew and predestined. God chooses the ones whose devotion God foreknows, and they receive the promised rewards. Others begin and seem to believe but do not remain steadfast in the faith; they are judged not to have been chosen by God. Those God chooses actually persevere. Some, like Saul and Judas, are chosen for a particular time because of the righteousness they have at that time, but not because of God's foreknowledge. . . .

Those he predestined he has also called. To call means to assist someone who is thinking about the faith or to move someone known to be attentive.

Those he called he also justified; and those he justified he also glorified. This repeats what was said above: those whom God foreknows are the ones attached to God, and they are the ones who persevere in faith, because events develop according to God's foreknowledge. God justified them and thereby glorified them so that they would become like the Son of God. The others, whom God does not foreknow, do not receive this grace, because God foreknows that they will not be worthy of it. Even though they might be chosen as believers for a time — because they seem to be good, and righteousness should not be treated with contempt — still they do not persevere and thus are not glorified. These are like Judas Iscariot and those other seventy-two who had been chosen but drew back after the Savior scandalized them (Luke 10:1-20; John 6:60-71).

(4) Theodoret on verse 29

God predestined on the basis of foreknowledge, not arbitrarily. In stating all this with precision, Paul did not say "conformed to God's Son," but **to the image of his Son.** He made this point more clearly in the Epistle to the Philippians. There he stated: *Our citizenship is in heaven, and it is from there that we are expecting a Savior, the Lord Jesus Christ.* He then added, *He will transform the body of our humiliation that it may be conformed to the body of his glory* (Phil 3:20-21). Our body will be conformed not to his divinity, but *to the body of his glory.* Thus God called those judged worthy to be **conformed to the image of the Son**, that is, to the body of the Son. Though the divine nature is invisible, the body can be seen; so the divinity is adored through the body as in an image.

(5) Augustine on verses 29-30

Whoever, therefore, is freed from that original condemnation by the generosity of divine grace is assured not only a hearing of the gospel but that they believe what they have heard, and then persevere in that *faith which works through love* (Gal 5:6). If they ever lose it, they are rebuked and corrected; even if some are not rebuked by another human being, still they do return to that path from which they had strayed. Death removes some of them from the dangers of this life shortly after they have received grace, at whatever age that happens. God accomplishes all these things in those who are made vessels of mercy. God chooses them by grace in the Son, before the constitution of the world. *If it is by grace, then it is no longer from works; otherwise grace would no longer be grace* (Rom 11:5-6). They are not only called but also chosen, unlike those others described by the saying: *Many are called, but few are chosen* (Matt 22:14). Instead, because they are **called according to purpose**, they are most certainly *chosen by grace,* as has been said, rather than because of their own prior merits. In them, grace has the function of merit.

The Apostle speaks of these people: **For we know that everything works for good in those who love God, in those who are called according to purpose. For those whom he foreknew he also predestined to be conformed to the image of his Son, so that he might be the first-born among many brethren. And those whom he predestined he also called; those whom he called he also justified; those whom he justified he also glorified.** None of them perishes because they are all chosen, and chosen because they are **called according to purpose.** This is God's purpose, not their own. Paul speaks of it elsewhere: *in order that God's purpose of election might continue, not because of works but because of his calling, she [Rebecca] was told, "The elder will serve the younger"* (Rom 9:11-12). And again: *not in virtue of our works but in virtue of his own purpose and grace* (2 Tim 1:9). Thus, when we hear, **those whom he predestined he also called**, we should acknowledge that they are called according to purpose. Keep clearly in mind the course of the discussion. It began, **we know that everything works for good for those who are called according to purpose.** It continued, **For those whom he foreknew he also predestined to be conformed to the image of his Son, so that he might be the first-born among many brethren.** Then the Apostle said, **those whom he predestined he also called.** Paul wants us to understand that these people are called according to God's purpose; thus no one may entertain the notion that some among them are called but not chosen. As the Lord says elsewhere, *Many are called, but few are chosen* (Matt 22:14). Granted that all the elect must be called, that being called does not of itself place a person among the elect. The elect, as has often been said, are those **called according to purpose**, the ones not only called but also predestined and foreknown. If any of these were to perish, then God would have failed; but because God cannot fail, none of them perish. If any of them were to perish, then God would have been overcome by a human failure. Because nothing can impede God, none of them perish.

Romans 8:31-39

31**What then are we to say to this? If God is for us, who is against us?** 32**He who did not spare his own Son, but gave him up for us all, will he not also give us all things with him?** 33**Who shall bring any charge against God's elect? It is God who justifies;** 34**who is to condemn? Is it Christ Jesus, who died, yes, who was raised from the dead, who is at the right hand of God, who indeed intercedes for us?** 35**Who shall separate us from the love of Christ? Shall tribulation, or distress, or persecution, or famine, or nakedness, or peril, or sword?** 36**As it is written,**

> *For your sake we are being killed all day long;*
> *we are regarded as sheep to be slaughtered.* (Ps 44:22)

37No, in all these things we are more than conquerors through him who loved us. 38For I am sure that neither death, nor life, nor angels, nor principalities, nor things present, nor things to come, nor powers, 39nor height, nor depth, nor anything else in all creation, will be able to separate us from the love of God in Christ Jesus our Lord.

(1) Ambrosiaster on verse 31

What then shall we to say to these things? If God is for us, who is against us? The meaning is plain: seeing that God provides us with a testimony, who will dare to accuse us? For the judge has foreknown us and judged us worthy.

(2) Origen on verses 32-34

But handed him over for all of us refers not to the kind of **handing over** about which Scripture says, *Brother will hand over brother to death, and a father his child* (Matt 10:21). God handed him over in the sense that although in the form of God, the Son was allowed to be emptied and take the form of a slave, and come to death on a cross, so that he might display an example of obedience and open the way for the resurrection of the dead. . . .

Attend carefully to the way the Apostle never abandons his innate caution in his statements. He did not say, "Who will bring any charge against those who are called?" but **against the elect**. Unless you have been chosen, unless you have shown yourself acceptable to God in everything, you will have an accuser. If your cause is evil, if your crime binds you tightly, what good will it do you to have Jesus himself acting as your defender? Jesus is truth; truth cannot lie for your sake. An advocate can prevent your being overwhelmed by the false testimony of your accuser, so that your past sins removed through Baptism will not be held against you. If you sin again after Baptism and have not washed those sins away by the tears of penance, however, you will provide grounds for your accuser to bring charges against you. Although Jesus will intercede for us, still Jesus cannot argue that darkness is light or bitter is sweet. If you want to emerge victorious in the judgment, then do what is written about the just: *Guide your speech with a view to the judgment; prepare your works for the end; in all you do, remember the end of your life and then you will never sin* (Ps 111:5 LXX; Sir 7:36). Do this lest what is written about someone else happens to you, to wit, *when he is tried, let him be found guilty* (Ps 109:7). Take care how you understand Jesus' intercession for us. It is written elsewhere of him, *The Father judges no one, but has given all judgment to the Son* (John 5:22). As he is both the victim and the priest, as he is both in the form of a slave and in the form of God, so will he be both the advocate and the judge.

(3) Augustine on verse 32

The Lord himself said, *Greater love has no one than this, that a person lay down life for friends* (John 15:13). The love of Christ for us was shown in just this way: he died for us. How is the Father's love for us shown? Because God sent the only Son to die for us, as the Apostle Paul says, **He who did not spare his own Son, but handed him over for us all, will he not also give us all things with him?** The Father handed over Christ; Judas also handed him over. These were not both the same sort of action, were they? Judas was a betrayer; was God the Father also a betrayer? By no means! But not just because I say it. The Apostle says: **Who did not spare his own Son, but handed him over for us all.** God the Father gave him up; Christ gave himself up. The same Apostle says, *he loved me and handed himself over for me* (Gal 2:20). If the Father gave up the Son, and the Son gave himself up, what did Judas do? The Father handed over; the Son handed over; Judas handed over; the same thing was done by all three. What makes the difference between the Father's handing over the Son, the Son's handing over himself, and the disciple Judas's handing over his teacher? The Father and Son acted in love; Judas acted in treachery. You understand that we have to take into consideration not just what a person does but the disposition and intention in which the person acts. We find God the Father doing the same thing that Judas does; we bless the Father but we detest Judas. Why do we bless the Father but detest Judas? We bless the charity but detest the malice. What a great thing for the human race that Christ was handed over. Was Judas intending that benefit in handing him over? God's objective was the saving action by which we were redeemed; Judas's objective was the price for which he sold the Lord. The Son himself considered the price he paid for us; Judas considered the price he received in the sale. A different intention makes for a different action. If we evaluate this same reality on the basis of these different intentions, we realize that one should be loved but the other condemned; one praised but the other vilified. This is the great value of charity. Notice that it alone distinguishes; by itself it separates one person's action from another's.

(4) Augustine on verse 34

The Apostle says that even after the resurrection, our Lord Jesus Christ **sits at the right hand of God, who intercedes for us.** Why does he intercede for us? Because he agreed to be a mediator. What is a mediator between God and human beings? Not between the Father and human beings, but between God and human beings. Who is God? The Father, the Son, and the Holy Spirit. Who are human beings? Sinners, wicked and mortal. This man was made a mediator between the Trinity and those weak, wicked human beings. He was weak but not wicked. Because he was not wicked, he could join you to God. Because he was weak, he could draw near to you. For a mediator to function between God and human beings, *the Word was made flesh* (John 1:14). This means that the Word became human, because human beings are called by the name "flesh."

(5) Ambrosiaster on verses 35-39

Who shall separate us from the love of Christ? Who shall be able to turn us away from loving Christ, who has bestowed on us such great and innumerable acts of kindness? **Tribulation?** It cannot, because no torments overcome the love of a true Christian. Being forbidden to love the one whose generosity has been experienced would stir up the charity of the lover all the more. For when a person thinks of throwing away these undeserved benefits, the blessings themselves rise up to restore the love. **Shall distress? Shall persecution? Shall famine? Shall nakedness? Shall peril? Shall the sword? As it is written:** *For your sake we are slain all day long; we are regarded as sheep to be slaughtered.* No, in all these things we are more than conquerors through him who loved us. This is written in Psalm 43/44 (Ps 44:22). The meaning is plain, then: all the disasters that Paul enumerates — tribulations, afflictions, and death — cannot be compared or equated with **the love of Christ** he has planted in us. For we hold Christ's acts of kindness as greater than all these other things that seem to be adversities. If we die for him — the worst of all the threats — you see that he has died for us. He died for our benefit, but our death brings him no advantage. For we pay with our temporal life, so that eternal life may be delivered to us. And what wonder if servants die for a good master, since the master has died for the servants, even for bad ones? So the acts of kindness gain the victory; they encourage the soul to persevere for him who has loved us.

For I am confident that neither death. . . . That confidence rests on the pledge of Christ, whereby he promised that in time of tribulation he would assist the faith that is pledged to him.

Nor life, nor angels, nor rulers, nor height, nor depth, nor things present, nor things to come, . . . nor any other creature, will be able to separate us from the love of God in Christ Jesus our Lord. All these are threats deployed by the devil to lead us away. Paul's purpose in recalling them is to strengthen us so that, if they come out against us, we may fight them off, armed with faith and confident in the hope and help of Christ.

(6) Augustine on verses 35-39

The festivals of the holy martyrs are exhortations to martyrdom; they make us desire to imitate what we delight in celebrating. The reading from Holy Scripture which we have just heard exhorts and even inspires us, as the Apostle says: **Who shall separate us from the love of Christ? Shall tribulation, or distress, or persecution, or famine, or nakedness, or peril, or the sword? As the Scripture says,** *For your sake we are being killed all day long; we are considered as sheep to be sacrificed.* Then follows a list of things that seem capable of separating us, but Christ gives us victory over them all, lest we be separated from him who is himself not separated from us. Because of these afflictions and threatening forces, the faithful guarantor and gracious benefactor promised us that he would be with us, *to the close of the age* (Matt 28:20). **For I am sure,** the Apostle says, **that neither death, nor life, nor angels, nor principalities, nor things present, nor things to come, nor powers, nor height, nor depth, nor any other creature** — he could not name every one of them — **will be able to separate us from the love of God in Christ Jesus our Lord.** We need to be fortified by hope and faith against all the temptations of this age, lest we be separated from Christ. Our own strength will certainly prove inadequate if we are abandoned by the divine assistance. So Paul said above, **If God is for us, who is against us?** After having summarized the things which savagely attack Christian faith, the Apostle armed us to bear all these things for Christ, lest they **separate us from the love of Christ.**

(7) John Chrysostom on verse 37

For the apostles did not simply conquer; they amazed their opponents to show that the conflict was not against these human adversaries but against an invincible power. Notice how the Jews had the apostles in their control and still did not know what to do with them, and said, *What shall we do with them?* (Acts 4:16). They held them as prisoners, responsible for their actions. They chained and beat them. Still, they were helpless; they could not decide what to do with them. The very means by which they expected to conquer brought defeat upon them. Neither the tyrant nor the people nor the battle array of demons nor the devil could prevail over the apostles. All of their enemies were defeated with great losses; they saw everything they plotted against the apostles actually turn back on themselves. For this reason Paul said, **we are more than conquerors.** This was a new law of victory: to prevail through their adversaries' own stratagems; never to be defeated; to enter into conflict as masters secure of the outcome.

Romans 9

In this chapter, Paul considered God's fidelity to the promise made to Abraham about his descendants; he argued that the promise of divine blessing had been made not to all of Abraham's descendants but to those who shared a spiritual relation to him, primarily his faith in the promise itself. Most commentators explained that God chose those intended in the promise through foreknowledge of their own faith, thus defending God's limiting of the gifts of grace as just. Augustine broke from this established tradition to insist that God's gift caused the faith of the elect rather than granted favor in response to it. He appealed to the universality of human sinfulness to argue that God was just in granting salvation to some while not giving it to others. A literal reading of Paul's text, he insisted, yielded the judgment that the efficacy of divine mercy could not depend upon human cooperation or be frustrated by human resistance.

Romans 9:1-5

1I am speaking the truth in Christ; I am not lying; my conscience bears me witness in the Holy Spirit, 2that I have great sorrow and unceasing anguish in my heart. 3For I could wish that I myself were accursed and cut off from Christ for the sake of my brethren, my kinsmen by race. 4They are Israelites, and to them belong the sonship, the glory, the covenants, the giving of the law, the worship, and the promises; 5to them belong the patriarchs, and of their race, according to the flesh, is the Christ. God who is over all be blessed forever. Amen.

(1) Ambrosiaster on verses 1-2

Since he earlier seemed to criticize the Jews, who think they are justified by the law, Paul now clearly shows what his prayer is for them and how deep is his affection for them. With his conscience as his witness, and speaking in Christ Jesus and the Holy Spirit, he has no desire to be considered an enemy of their faith. For this reason he gives as his witnesses Christ and the Holy Spirit, from whom nothing is hidden and whose testimony cannot be rejected. They support and bear witness to the Apostle by the power of the signs which they perform through him.

(2) Origen on verses 3-5

Paul realized that he had just asserted that no opposing power on heaven or on earth, present or future, could separate him from the love of Christ. He might, then, appear to be contradicting himself and so not trustworthy when he now professed his willingness to be cursed and cut off from the same Christ — to whom he had earlier claimed to be inseparably bound in love. To avoid being branded a liar, then, he immediately offered assurances that his statement was true: **I am speaking the truth in Christ; I am not lying; my conscience bears me witness in the Holy Spirit.**

Why did he say, **I am speaking the truth in Christ**? Did he imply another kind of truth that was not **in Christ**? Can we find a way to distinguish **the truth in Christ** from some other truth that is not **in Christ**? Elsewhere Paul says, *the truth of Christ is in me; I am not lying* (2 Cor 11:10). There he implies that *the truth of Christ* can be found wherever those other virtues which are personified in Christ can also be found. Wherever righteousness, peace, or the Word of God is found, there as well is *the truth of Christ*. A certain type of truth, however, can be found in unrighteousness. Consider, for example, the account in the Acts of the Apostles of the demon of Pythia[1] which was dwelling in the slave girl. She followed the apostles, calling out, *These men are servants of the Most High God, who proclaim the way of God* (Acts 16:17). Truth was in those words: what was said was true. But because that truth was not **in Christ**, Paul turned back to face her and said, *Shut up and get out of her* (Acts 16:18). Similarly, Caiaphas spoke the truth: *It is expedient for you that one man should die for the people, and that the whole nation should not perish* (John 11:50). But that truth was not **in Christ**. To distinguish his own statement from that kind of truth which is not in Christ, therefore, the Apostle said, **I am speaking the truth in Christ**.

I think that his statement, **my conscience bears me witness in the Holy Spirit**, will allow the same interpretation. Conscience also bears witness to the Gentiles, as the same Apostle says earlier, *their conscience also bears witness and their conflicting thoughts accuse or perhaps excuse them* (Rom 2:15). When their thoughts accuse them and their conscience comes to their defense, this cannot mean that their conscience bears witness in the Holy Spirit by excusing their evil deeds. In the Apostle, whose thoughts no longer have any accusations to make, conscience bears witness in the Holy Spirit. Notice how magnanimous the Apostle is. He cannot be separated from the love of God; whatever he says is said in Christ; whatever is in his conscience is held by the Holy Spirit. What minds, I ask, in the heavens or among those thrones endowed with the heavenly powers, have such capacity to encompass the whole Trinity?

I have great sorrow and unceasing anguish in my heart. Suppose you are sorrowful; suppose you are filled with anguish at the loss of your blood relatives; would you prefer to be accursed by Christ? What good would their salvation do you if it resulted in losing your own salvation? What salvation can you bring to others if you yourself perish? That is not what I mean, he says; I have learned from my teacher and Lord that *whoever would save his life will lose it, and whoever will lose his live will save it* (Mark 8:35).

---

1. Associated with the oracle at Delphi.

What is so astonishing, then, if the Apostle should be prepared to be an outcast for the sake of his fellow Jews? He knows that the one who *was in the form of God emptied himself, taking the form of a slave* (Phil 2:6-7) and *became a curse for us* (Gal 3:13). Is it so astonishing, then, that the servant wants to become an outcast for the sake of his fellows, when the Lord himself became a curse for the sake of slaves? I believe that Moses said the same thing to the Lord when the people sinned: *But now, if you will only forgive their sin — but if not, blot me out of the book that you have written* (Exod 32:32). What then? Do you consider Paul inferior to Moses? Moses asked to be blotted out of the book of life for the sake of his people; should Paul not be ready to be an outcast for his fellow Jews? . . .

You see, then, that Paul was heard: by offering to be cast out himself, he won salvation for his fellows. I think that Paul earlier made the claim that *no force could separate him from the love of God* (Rom 8:35), so that when he later offered to become an outcast for the sake of others, you would not presume that he could actually suffer rejection. The one who is by nature immortal and inseparable from the Father entered into death and descended into hell. Paul then imitated his teacher: though he could not be separated from the love of Christ, he would become an outcast for the sake of his fellows by devotion rather than transgression.

That the Israelites are Paul's **kindred according to the flesh** requires no explanation.

To them belong the adoption of sons. The children of Israel were adopted by God at the time *when the Most High apportioned the nations, when he divided humankind, he fixed the boundaries of the peoples according to the number of the angels; the Lord's own portion was God's people, Jacob God's allotted share* (Deut 32:8-9). This is their adoption as children.

The glory, the covenants, the giving of the law. The glory of that law which was given has been discussed many times already. As the Apostle himself says: *For if what was set aside* — the Old Testament — *came through glory, much more has the permanent* — the proclamation of the gospel — *come in glory* (2 Cor 3:11). In saying, **the covenants, the giving of the law**, he might be referring to a single reality, since the law which was imposed is itself also called the covenant. Or, a distinction could be made: the giving of the law was a single event, accomplished through Moses, but covenants were established over and over again. When the people sinned and were abandoned, they were disinherited. When God was propitiated, they were called back and restored to the possession of their inheritance. God renewed the covenants and again recognized them as heirs.

The worship, and the promises. By **worship**, he means the priestly duties. **Promises** were made to their ancestors, which they hoped would be fulfilled for those called children of Abraham through faith. Certainly, even according to the flesh, not only the ancestors but Christ himself came from that Israelite race. Christ is from them according to the flesh.

(3) Theodoret on verse 3

And he did not say "I willed" but **I could wish that I myself were cut off from Christ for the sake of my own kindred according to the flesh**, that they might be joined to him and attain the fruit of salvation. His inserting the words, **I myself**, was quite fitting since it recalled what he had said about the love of Christ. He would be saying: "I, *whom neither death, nor life, nor things present, nor things to come, nor anything else in all creation, will be able to separate us from the love of God in Christ Jesus our Lord* (Rom 8:38-39), would gladly be separated from him for the salvation of the Jews." In saying this he is certainly not preferring them to the Savior but is declaring his love and desire for them, wanting to see all of them submit and freely receive the message of salvation.

(4) Ambrosiaster on verse 5

In this context he says of the Savior: **who is over all, God blessed for evermore. Amen.** Since the Father's name is not mentioned here and the statement itself is about Christ, the conclusion cannot be avoided that Christ is being called **God**. Because of belief in one God, Scripture frequently adds a reference to the Son when it speaks of God the Father; it calls the Father "God" and the Son "Lord." Anyone who thinks that the phrase **who is God** does not refer to Christ must be prepared to name the person to whom it does apply, since this section of the text contains no mention of God the Father. Why the surprise at Paul's plainly naming Christ as **God over all** in this text? In another epistle he confirms this idea with a similar statement: *so that at the name of Jesus every knee should bend, in heaven and on earth and under the earth* (Phil 2:10). These are the **all** over whom Christ is God. There are no others than these, as though Christ is not **God over all**. Nor can all creation bend the knee to anyone but God.

Romans 9:6-13

₆But it is not as though the word of God had failed. For not all who are descended from Israel belong to Israel, ₇and not all are children of Abraham because they are his descendants; but *Through Isaac shall your descendants be named* (Gen 21:12). ₈This means that it is not the children of the flesh who are the children of God, but the children of the promise are reckoned as descendants. ₉For this is what the promise said, *About this time I will return and Sarah shall have a son* (Gen 18:10). ₁₀Not only so, but also when Rebecca had conceived children by one man, our forefather Isaac, ₁₁though they were not yet born and had done nothing either good or bad, in order that God's purpose of election might continue, not by works but because of his call, ₁₂she was told, *The elder will serve the younger* (Gen 25:23). ₁₃As it is written, *Jacob I loved, but Esau I hated* (Mal 1:2-3).

(1) John Chrysostom on verses 6-7

It is not as though the word of God had failed. Paul shows that he had the courage to endure all these sufferings through the word of God, the promise that had been made to

Abraham. Moses seemed to act as spokesman for the Jews, but actually he did everything for the glory of God. *Lest they say,* Moses says, *"because God was not able to save them, God led them out to be destroyed in the desert,"* put an end to your wrath (Deut 9:28). So Paul too says, *I could wish that I myself were accursed* (Rom 9:3), so that they do not say that the promise of God failed, that God lied in making the promise, and that the word did not produce results. He is not speaking about the Gentiles: this promise was not made to them, nor did they worship God, so no one blasphemed God because of them. Paul wished this for the sake of the Jews who received the promise and who were singled out from the others to become God's own people. And so, you see that if he had expressed this wish for the sake of the Gentiles, he would have been seen as acting for the glory of Christ. Since he was willing to be accursed for the sake of the Jews, however, it was clear that he desired this only because of Christ. . . .

Paul recognizes that on the basis of these statements, yet another difficulty might arise. Why did God even make the promises to the Jews if God did not intend to fulfill them? Human beings cannot see the future and thus are often mistaken; they promise gifts to those who turn out to be unworthy. But God foresees both the present and the future; God clearly knows that they will make themselves unworthy of the promises and, as a result, that they will actually receive nothing God promised. Why, then, does God even make the promise? How does Paul solve this problem? By identifying the real Israel to whom God actually made this promise. When this becomes clear, he is able to show that all the promises have been fulfilled.

(2) Origen on verses 6-8

Many belong to the race of Israel, but not all are called Israel. Israel's name was given for seeing God, as Jacob himself says: *I have seen God face to face, and yet my life is preserved* (Gen 32:30). Therefore, the one who saw God was called Israel. Anyone who has not seen the one who said, *Whoever has seen me has seen the Father* (John 14:9), cannot be called Israel.

Nor are all the seed of Abraham also his children. This point was made already about Abraham when his posterity was assigned to Isaac alone, who was born because of the promise of a future inheritance. Abraham had many children, whom the Apostle calls children of the flesh. And now, therefore, among the descendants of Abraham are included only children of the promise made about Isaac, the children of that faith through which Abraham became worthy to receive the promise of a future inheritance. The line of inheritance is realized in them.

(3) Ambrosiaster on verses 6-7

But the word of God did not fail. The word of God which says, **Through Isaac your descendants shall be named,** has not failed. What God said would occur has been accomplished: the descendants of Abraham would not be those according to the flesh but those who received that faith by which Isaac was born. That faith was revived in the time of Christ; then it became universal rather than remaining particular. Thus, what Abraham believed about Isaac, these descendants believe about God and Christ: that the Son of God was born to restore the salvation of the human race.

For not all who are descended from Israel belong to Israel, nor is the whole seed of Abraham his sons. But *Through Isaac your descendants shall be named.* Paul wants them to understand that simply being children of Abraham does not make them all worthy. Instead, only the children of the promise are worthy — those whom God foreknew would accept the promise, whether they come from among the Jews or the nations. The people worthy of being called Israelites are those who, seeing God, believed.

(4) Origen on verses 9-13

In all these statements, the Apostle is attempting to prove that if either Isaac or Jacob had been chosen by God on the basis of merits which they acquired while in the flesh or if they had earned justification through works of the flesh, then the grace attained by these merits might have affected their flesh and blood descendants. Since, however, they were chosen not on the basis of their works but because of God's purpose and the decision of the one calling them, then the grace of the promises is fulfilled not in the children they generated by the flesh but in those who, like them, were chosen according to God's purpose and adopted as children. What was explained earlier is realized in them: *For those whom he foreknew he also predestined; those whom he predestined he also called; and those whom he called he also justified; and those whom he justified he also glorified* (Rom 8:29-30).

(5) Ambrosiaster on verses 9-13

For this is what the promise said, *About this time I will return and Sarah shall have a son.* This is how Genesis reads (Gen 18:10). Christ fulfilled what is here prefigured. The promise was that the coming Christ would be a son of Abraham and that all the nations of the earth would be blessed in the Christ who fulfilled the promise. This promise was made to Abraham when he heard, *by your offspring shall all the nations of the earth gain blessing for themselves* (Gen 22:18). He was promised that Christ would come from the line of Isaac. We now see this promise fulfilled in him.

Not only her, that is, Sarah, but also Rebecca, who **conceived children by our forefather Isaac**. Paul says that both Sarah's bearing of Isaac and the childbearing of Isaac's wife Rebecca must be understood as prefigurings. They were different, however, because Isaac was born as a foreshadowing of the Savior himself, while Jacob and Esau were symbolic of two peoples, believers and non-believers. Though they were sons of the same father, they were different. Each of them signified a nation, a people united in either faith or infidelity. The many individuals symbolized in their persons are joined not by fleshly descent but by a shared commitment. In this way, some who are actually born from Esau must be recognized as children of Jacob, and some born from Jacob must be classified as children of Esau. . . .

Though they had not yet been born or done anything either good or bad, in order that God's purpose of election might continue, not by works but because of his call, she was told, *The elder will serve the younger.* **As it is written,** *Jacob I loved, but Esau I hated.* This is to be found in Malachi (Mal 1:2-3). Paul is insisting on God's foreknowledge: things cannot turn out differently from what God knows they will be. Knowing what each of them was going to be, God said, "The younger is worthy and the elder unworthy." By foreknowledge God chose one and spurned the other. **God's purpose continues** in the one chosen, because nothing can happen differently from what God knows and intends for him: that he be worthy of salvation. **God's purpose continues** in the one rejected as well; what God intended for him, because he will be unworthy. God intends these things by foreknowing, but not as favoring particular individuals. God neither condemns a person before he sins nor crowns someone who has yet to win a victory.

(6) Theodoret on verses 9-13

But Ishmael was also a son of Abraham, and indeed the firstborn. Why then are you presumptuous, Judea, claiming to be the only descendant of Abraham? You would be wrong in assuming that the child was cast out of the family because he was half-slave. Sacred Scripture usually traces descent from the father rather than the mother. And the holy Apostle could also have introduced those children born of Keturah and shown that, although these had been born of a free woman, they were not called the descendants of Abraham. He could easily have pointed to the twelve sons of Jacob, born of different mothers — four of them also half-slaves — and all still bearing the name Israel. There the servile status of the mothers did not affect their sons. Limiting his inquiry, Paul omitted these, and successfully won the argument using the abundant evidence that remained. For when the words spoken by God to Abraham had been set down, *It is through Isaac that descendants shall be named for you,* they showed that not all of his offspring shared in this blessing. Indeed, one of his sons received the blessing which was denied to the other.

If you think, he says, that Isaac was given preference over Ishmael and the children of Abraham born of Keturah on account of Sarah (Gen 25:1-6), what would you say about Rebecca and her children? In this case there is one mother, one father, and one conception, and the sons are twins. This then is what he said: **she had conceived children by one husband**; she conceived both children at the same time from this one father. But the one child was loved by God, and the other proved undeserving of God's care. God did not wait for the actual experience of these events; even while they were in the womb God foretold the difference between them. God made the prediction by foreknowledge of their intentions. For the election was not unjust; it corresponded to their individual intentions. Paul then added a prophetic testimony, as it was written: *I have loved Jacob, but I have hated Esau.* God does not attend to nature but looks for virtue.

(7) John Chrysostom on verses 9-10

The promise and the Word of God formed and begot Isaac. What matter if a woman's womb and belly are involved? For the power of the promise, not the strength of the belly, gave birth to the child. We are begotten in the same way through the words of God. For in the water of the baptismal font the words of God are the instruments by which we are begotten and formed. We were begotten when we were baptized in the name of the Father and of the Son and of the Holy Spirit. Such a birth comes from the promise of God, not from nature. For God prophesied the birth of Isaac and then fulfilled it. In the same way God announced our birth many years ahead of time through all the prophets, and has accomplished it afterward. What a great thing God has set forth; when God had promised something great, it was very easily accomplished.

(8) Augustine on verses 9-12

No one could claim that Jacob's actions had won God's favor before he was born, so that God would say: *The elder will serve the younger.* So not only was Isaac himself promised when it was said, *At this time I will return and Sarah will have son,* but Isaac had not done any good works to win God's favor so that his own birth should be promised and that **in Isaac Abraham's descendants would be named**. God promised that they would share the lot of the saints in Christ, that they would recognize themselves as children of the promise, that they would not boast of their own accomplishments but would consider themselves fellow heirs of Christ by the gift of being called. When this was promised for them, they did not yet exist and so had done nothing to deserve it. **But when Rebecca, by a single sexual union with Isaac our father** — Paul spoke with utmost care — **by a single sexual union**. They were conceived as twins, so that the merits of their father would have no effect on the outcome. Otherwise, someone might claim that this son was born as he was because of the dispositions of either his father when he sowed him in his mother's womb or of his mother when she conceived him. He sowed both of them together at the same time, and she conceived them at the same time. . . .

He recalled these events in order to break up and throw down that pride of people ungrateful for the grace of God, of those people daring to boast of their own achievements. **Though they had not yet been born nor had they done anything either good or bad, not because of works but because of the one calling, she was told,** *The elder would serve the younger.* The grace, therefore, is from the one who calls; the good works that follow the grace belong to the one who receives it. The grace brings forth the works; the works do not themselves produce the grace. Fire heats because it is hot, not to become hot; a wheel rolls smoothly because it is round, not to get rounded. In the same way, a person acts well because grace has already been received, not in order to acquire grace. How can someone who has not been already justified live justly? Just as a person who has not yet been sanctified cannot live a holy life, neither can someone who has not already been justified. Grace justifies so that the person who has been justified can then live justly. Grace, therefore, comes first, then good works follow, as Paul says elsewhere, *Now* *to one who works, wages are reckoned not as a gift but as due* (Rom 4:4). After good works, therefore, immortality might even be demanded as one's due, as Paul says: *I have fought the good fight, I have finished the race, I have kept the faith. Henceforth there is laid up for me the crown of righteousness, which the Lord, the righteous judge, will award to me on that day* (2 Tim 4:7-8). Because he said, *award,* it might appear that the crown was owed. But *when he ascended on high he led captivity captive,* and he did not award but *gave gifts to humans* (Eph 4:8). How then could the Apostle have presumed that the crown would be awarded to him as owed unless he had earlier received — but not as owed — the grace by which he was justified and empowered *to fight the good fight* (2 Tim 4:7)? He had been a blasphemer, persecuting and attacking, but he received mercy — as he testified — and believed in the one who justifies not the faithful but the unfaithful, and makes them faithful by justifying them.

(9) Augustine on verses 11-13

The teacher of the nations in faith and truth (1 Tim 2:7) witnesses that those twins had not yet been born and had done nothing of good or evil, so that the grace of God might be praised. Thus, **The elder will serve the younger** might be understood as said **not because of works but because of the one calling**, so that **God's purpose according to election might stand** and would not be preceded by human merits. Paul was not referring to a divine election of human will or human nature, since both of these were subject to death and condemnation. He referred to an election which was clearly of grace, an election that does not seek out those who deserve to be chosen but chooses them. Later in the same letter, he speaks of this election: *So too at the present time there is a remnant, chosen by grace. But if it is by grace, it is no longer on the basis of works; otherwise grace would no longer be grace* (Rom 11:5-6). This statement agrees fully with the present one, where he recalls, **not because of works but because of the one calling, was it said, The elder will serve the younger.** Why then does this man [Pelagius] foolishly oppose this most excellent promoter of grace by appealing to the free choice of infants and the works of those who are not yet born? Why do his supporters insist that merits precede grace when grace would not be gracious if it was given according to merit? Why do they assault that salvation which was sent to the lost and came to the unworthy, with such sharp, extensive and elaborate — barely Christian — arguments?

How, he says, would God escape the charge of malice, if divine loving itself distinguishes between people who are not separated by any merits of good works? He demands this of us, as though the Apostle himself had not noticed the question, considered it, and responded to it. Paul saw what humans, in their weakness and ignorance, would think when they heard this; so he posed the same question to himself: *What shall we say then? Is there injustice on God's part?* He responded immediately, *By no means!* (Rom 9:14). In justifying that response, *By no means!* he did not refute the charge of *injustice on God's part,* by claiming, "God judges the merits or works of infants, even if they are still living in their mother's womb." He could not have made that argument because he had already said, **not because of works but because of the one calling, was it said, The elder will** *serve the younger,* about brothers who were still unborn and had as yet done nothing good or bad. When he came to show that God could not be charged with injustice in this matter, he said instead, *For he says to Moses, "I will have mercy on whom I will have mercy, and I will have compassion on whom I have compassion"* (Exod 33:19; Rom 9:15). What was he teaching us here if not that anyone being rescued from that lump coming from the first human, to which death was rightly due, owes this salvation not to human merits but to the mercy of God? No injustice may be charged against God, who is unjust neither in forgiving nor in exacting the debt. Where punishment would be just, leniency is gratuitous. The greatness of the favor bestowed on those who are liberated from a due punishment and freely justified is more clearly manifest when other equally guilty persons are actually punished, without any injustice on the part of the judge. . . .

How, they ask, was Esau not undeserving of his condemnation, if **not because of works but because of the one calling it was said,** *The elder will serve the younger*? If no good works had preceded by which he might have brought himself into God's favor, then likewise no bad deeds made him deserve God's punishment. Neither Jacob nor Esau had done any works of their own, either good or bad; both, however, were subject to that one *in whom all sinned* (Rom 5:12), so that all deserved to die in him. All were initially united in that one; they would later become so many individually. That sin would have been of one alone, therefore, had no one been born from him. Since, however, the shared nature was in that one, no one is protected from his fault. If, therefore, both of them — who had not yet done anything good or evil of their own — were born guilty because of their origin, let the one set free give thanks for the mercy and the one punished not blame the judgment.

Romans 9:14-18

14 **What shall we say then? Is there injustice on God's part? By no means!** 15 **For he says to Moses,** *I will have mercy on whom I have mercy, and I will have compassion on whom I have compassion* **(Exod 33:19).** 16 **So it depends not on man's will or exertion, but upon God's mercy.** 17 **For the scripture says to Pharaoh,** *I have raised you up for the very purpose of showing my power in you, so that my name may be proclaimed in all the earth* **(Exod 9:16).** 18 **So then he has mercy on whomever he wills, and he hardens the heart of whomever he wills.**

(1) Ambrosiaster on verses 14-16

What then are we to say? Is there injustice on God's part? By no means! Because God loves one person and hates another, Paul is saying, "Does that mean God is unjust?" This is not the case, for God is just. For God knows what God is doing, and God's judgment never needs review. As has been noted above, here is what the prophet Malachi says: *I have loved Jacob, but I have hated Esau* (Mal 1:2-3). Here God is speaking in judgment; earlier God spoke out of foreknowledge, *The elder shall serve the younger* (Gen 25:23). On the basis of foreknowledge that Pharaoh was not going to respond to correction, God determined that he should be condemned. God chose the Apostle Paul when he was still a persecutor in the foreknowledge that he would become a believer. God anticipated events by taking the initiative with Paul, because he was needed; God condemned Pharaoh before the future judgment to come, in order to bring people to believe that God would pass judgment.

For God says to Moses, *I will have mercy on whom I will have been merciful, and I will have compassion on whom I will have had compassion.* **Well then, God says,** *I will have mercy on whom I will have been merciful.* That is, "I will have mercy on the one of whom I knew in advance that I will have mercy, knowing that the person will be converted and remain faithful." *And I will have compassion on whom I will have had compassion.* That is, "I will have compassion on the person whom I knew in advance will turn back with an upright heart after straying." In reality, this is only giving to the person who ought to receive and not giving to the person who ought not receive; God calls those God knows will obey and does not call those God knows will be completely disobedient. Calling, in this context, means goading the conscience to make it receptive to faith.

So it depends not on the one willing or striving, but on God who shows mercy. Exactly! Fulfilling a request should depend not on the will of the petitioner but on the discretion of the giver. The giver ought to consider and decide whether it should be given. Saul sinned and sought pardon but did not receive it; yet David, when he sinned and asked to be forgiven, received pardon. Thus the judgment of God, in giving and not giving, must be accepted; God wishes all to be saved but maintains justice. Thus God does not judge unjustly. God examines the heart of the petitioner and knows whether its dispositions deserve that the request be fulfilled.

(2) Cyril of Alexandria on verses 14-18

Since it was likely that people who love finding fault would think that even before Jacob and Esau were able to choose right or wrong God was disposed to love Jacob by a special grace and to hate Esau, the Apostle rightly demolishes this harmful opinion, and defends the divine judgment by his own arguments. The difficulty, however, is that this defense itself seems to set up a contrary opinion. For if, as he says, even before the infants did anything, and before they even tried to do anything, the one was worthy of love but the other deserved hatred and being enslaved to the younger, this still suggests that God was unjust. That would be astonishing! Suppose that Jacob had not turned out to be a good man or Esau an evil one, the allegation could be made that either God's foreknowledge was erroneous or, worse, that what God ordained for each of them was based on a whim or a fickle will. Since Esau was in fact very wicked and Jacob wise, however, God's foreknowledge would not have resulted in an unjust decision. In anticipation, God granted to the good man the love of which he would prove worthy but to the bad man the condemnation he would deserve. For God is long-suffering and awaits the proper time for things to be done when what one is becomes evident in what one does.

The grace of election and the gift given on the basis of foreknowledge foreshadow the mystery that God accomplishes what is best when the time is right. Through the birth of the children God gave assurance that Isaac, although he was Abraham's only son, would be the father of the countless nations who were called by faith on the basis of the promise. Even if God is merciful to those whom he chooses according to his knowledge, or rather to those who deserved to be shown mercy (**for he said somewhere to Moses:** *I will be gracious to whom I will be gracious, and I will show mercy on whom I will show mercy*) accusations will still be leveled against him. The Apostle seems to have anticipated that some people would think that the divine will causes some people to be good and others to be disobedient. For this reason, he responds to their ignorance and says: **Therefore, it is not by some human will or human exertion, but from God who shows mercy.** For if Esau was hated even before doing anything evil, and if Jacob was honored before he began to do good, and if God has mercy on whomever he wants to have mercy, would we not be correct to conclude that whoever exerts himself or wills something (i.e., whoever chooses to do something good) gains nothing, but that everything we do depends on God's will?

Paul then gathers arguments that would support their opinion about this and says, **For the Scripture says to Pharaoh:** *I have raised you up for this very purpose of showing my power in you.* He then adds the obvious conclusion and says: **Therefore, he has mercy on whomever he chooses, but he hardens whomever he chooses.** *You will say to me then, "Why does he still find fault? For who can resist his will?"* How, then, can we defend God? Paul is not clear here, and even seems to be accepting their arguments. However, here is our defense: nothing can exist in God which is not reasonable and fitting. Since God confers upon each person what is appropriate to him, he has compassion and mercy on those for whom it is fitting but he punishes the guilty even if his vengeance does not immediately follow their crimes. Because he is long-suffering, some people might think that God is not concerned with what happens on earth.

(3) John Chrysostom on verse 15

For God says to Moses, *I will have mercy on whom I have mercy, and I will have compassion on whom I have compassion.* Here was the one sin which all the Jews committed, making the golden calf. Some of the Jews were punished for making it, others were not (Exod 32:25-29). For this reason, God said, *I will have mercy on whom I have mercy, and I will have compassion on whom I have compassion.* For it is not yours to know, Moses, which individuals are worthy of my love for humanity; this is my business. If this is not for Moses to know, then even less is it our business. For this reason, Paul did not simply quote the passage; he also reminded us to whom it was addressed: **God says to Moses.** Thus he cut off any objection by calling attention to the status of the person being addressed.

(4) Origen on verses 16-18

Paul's statement, **so it depends not on human will or exertion, but on God showing mercy**, should be taken in the same sense as what David says in a psalm: *Unless the* LORD *builds the house, those who build it labor in vain. Unless the* Lord *guards the city, the guard keeps watch in vain* (Ps 127:1). In that text, David's objective was not to teach the one who intends to build a house to do nothing and remain passive, so that the Lord could build it. On the contrary, the builder must give the matter as much thought and attention as one can; God brings that work to completion by removing all the obstacles. So this text teaches that humans must exercise their labor and care, but that God bestows the success and completion of the operation. With God and the human agent each doing their proper parts, therefore, we should piously and religiously attribute the whole of the work to God rather than to human effort. In the same way, he said: *Paul planted, Apollos watered, but God gave the growth* (1 Cor 3:6). Then he added, *so neither the one who plants nor the one who waters is anything, but only God who gives the growth* (1 Cor 3:7). This is the way to interpret the present passage: **So it depends not on one willing or running, but on God showing mercy.** For "the one who wills and the one who strives" clearly corresponds to *the one who plants* and *the one who waters*. The Apostle says that *the one who plants* and *the one who waters* are nothing, not because they actually do nothing, but because they may be counted as nothing in comparison with God, *who gives the growth* or brings the work to successful completion.

Let us now consider what God says to Pharaoh: ***I have raised you up for the very purpose of showing my strength in you.*** God not only knows each person's will and intention, but knows them in advance. Knowing and even foreknowing them, God then uses the intentions and efforts of each person, like a good and just manager, to bring about those works which the soul and will of each one chooses. Take, for example, a wise and good father of a household with a large group of servants. Will not such a wise manager discern, as best he can, which of them are well disposed for cultivating the soil and assign those to the fields, which one has a head for business, which for taking care of animals, which for household service, and which the talent to look after his own personal affairs? Will he not test their characters and wisely assign each to duties fitting their dispositions?

Moreover, as head of a household or even a ruler of a people, such a person would realize that subjects regularly rebel or undermine standards of discipline, and that correction and punishment could be necessary. So the ruler will have to choose those who are apt and disposed for this office, so that when the occasion does arise these servants will be aroused to violence and moved by their own emotions to administer the correction necessary for the offenders. Let us then suppose that this householder or ruler saw that the time was right to correct some subjects who had engaged in many actions violating both morality and discipline. He then selected a particularly cruel person, one much more savage than those who need correction — he was himself a criminal who deserved execution rather than rehabilitation. Since he wants to use the destruction of this one to correct the others, the ruler then sends that condemned person to those whom he intends to correct by the execution. He says to that one: ***I have raised you up for the very purpose of showing my strength in you, so that my name may be proclaimed in all the earth.*** That scripture did not say, "I have made you for this purpose"; which would have made the creator responsible for the crimes of the condemned person. Instead it reads, ***I have raised you up for the very purpose,*** that through the malice of your own heart, which you have brought on yourself by acting without restraint or fear of God, an effective and helpful warning might be driven home to others, that your spectacular destruction may serve as an example for posterity.

Paul seems to be citing Exodus in saying, **so then he has mercy on whom he wills, and he hardens whom he wills**. Scripture says there, *I will harden Pharaoh's heart, so that he will not let the people go* (Exod 4:21). This is how Pharaoh's heart was hardened. God was unwilling to inflict sudden and total vengeance upon him. Although Pharaoh was a person of consummate malice, God is patient and did not want to deprive even him of an opportunity for repentance. So God struck him lightly in the beginning and gradually increased the weight of the blows. God's patient approach, however, actually resulted in Pharaoh's hardening into contempt, storing up wrath for himself. Thus the saying of the Apostle could be applied to him, *Do you despise the riches of his kindness and forbearance and patience? Do you not realize that God's kindness is meant to lead you to repentance? But by your hard and impenitent heart you are storing up wrath for yourself on the day of wrath* (Rom 2:4-6). God does not intend to harden; the one who refused to bend to God's patience was hardened.

(5) Augustine on verse 16

If you attend carefully to the meaning of the words, **So it depends not upon a person willing or striving, but upon God being merciful**, you will notice that the Apostle not only says that we cannot accomplish what we choose without God's assistance but also that he intends something like what he says elsewhere: *Work out your own salvation with fear and trembling; for God is at work in you both to will and to do for God's good pleasure* (Phil 2:12-13). In that place, he states clearly that God himself brings about a good will in us. If he had said, **it depends not upon a person willing but upon God being merciful**, only because a person's willing is inadequate for just and righteous living unless we are assisted by the divine mercy, then the statement could also have been reversed, "So it depends not on God's being merciful but upon the person's own willing," because the mercy of God alone would be inadequate unless the consent of our willing were added. That we would will in vain unless God were merciful is plainly evident. I do not know how it could be said, however, that God's mercy is in vain unless we willingly assent. If God is merciful, then we actually will, for our being willing must itself be attributed to the same divine mercy, since *God is working in you both to will and to work in good willing* (Phil 2:12-13).

Now if we were to ask whether a good will is the gift of God, I would be surprised if anyone dared deny it. Because a call precedes a good will, but good will does not precede a call, we are right to credit God for our willing well but we cannot claim being called as something we earned. Thus, we should not think that Paul said, **it depends not upon a person willing but upon God being merciful**, because we need God's help to accomplish what we choose. Instead, he means that without God's calling, we do not even will.

Now, if God's calling produces good willing so effectively that everyone who is called responds positively, how will *many are called, but few are chosen* (Matt 22:14) still be true? If it is true, however, both that not everyone called always obeys the call, and that rejecting God's call is within the power of the person's own will, then it could rightly be said, "So it depends not on God being merciful but upon the person's own willing and exertion." In this case, God's mercy in calling would not be effective unless the person being called decided to obey.

Might it be, however, that those who do not respond when they are called in some particular way might willingly consent to faith if they were called in some other way? This might explain how the statement, *many are called, but few are chosen* (Matt 22:14), can be true: although many are called in one way, yet because everyone is not moved in the same way, only those whom it finds disposed to accept the call actually accept it. In this way, that other statement might also be true: **So it depends not upon a person's willing but upon God's being merciful**, because God called in some particular way that was suited to those who accepted the call. The call did indeed go to others; because their own dispositions made them unfit to receive and respond to the call, however, it did not move them; thus they could be said to have been called but not chosen. In that situation, the reversal of Paul's statement, "So it depends not on the God's being merciful but upon the person's own willing and exertion," would not be true. The effect of God's mercy cannot be subject to human willing, so that God's mercy is in vain because a person refuses it. In this explanation, if God had willed to be merciful even to those others, God could have called them in some way that would have been suited to them; then they would have been moved, would have understood, and would have accepted the call. Thus is it true that *many are called, but few are chosen* (Matt 22:14).

The elect, then, are those called in a way suited to them; those who are not apt and disposed toward that kind of vocation are not chosen; although they are called, they do not respond. In the same way, **it depends not upon a person willing and striving, but upon God's being merciful**. Although God calls many, God is merciful only to those whom God calls in such a way that they are disposed to follow. It would be false, however, to say, "So it depends not on God's being merciful, but upon the person's own willing and exertion," because God is never merciful in vain. When God is merciful to a person, God calls that person in the particular way that God knows is suited to the person, so that the person does not reject the call.

(6) Augustine on verse 18

The term "respecting of persons" is properly used to describe a situation in which a judge disregards the merits of the case under review and decides in favor of one person over another because that person is for some reason considered deserving of respect or mercy. If, however, a creditor has two debtors and chooses to forgive the debt of one and exact payment from the other, the creditor makes a gift to one but does not defraud the other. The proper term for this would be "acceptance of persons," and it involves no injustice. Nevertheless, people who understand little or nothing might think that "respecting of persons" was operative when the owner of the vineyard gave the same amount of pay to those workers who had done an hour's work as he gave to those who had borne the weight of the day and the heat. He made their rewards equal even though their labors were so different. What did this householder reply to those who were complaining of what they considered his respecting of persons? *Friend, he said, I am doing you no wrong; did you not agree with me for a denarius? Take what belongs to you and go; I choose to give to this last as I give to you. Am I not allowed to do what I choose with what belongs to me? Or do you begrudge my generosity?* (Matt 20:13-15). I choose to do this, and it is completely just. I paid you; I made a gift to this other worker. In making that gift to him, I did not deprive you of what I owed you, or lessen it, or refuse it. *Am I not permitted to do what I choose? Is your eye evil because I am generous?* (Matt 20:15). So no respecting of persons occurs when one person is gratuitously honored without depriving another of what is owed.

In the same way, one person is called according to God's purpose while another is not called in that way. The call according to God's purpose is given as an undeserved good, and the calling is itself the instrument of that good. Evil is repaid to the one not called, because all are guilty through the sin that entered into the world through one man. In the story of the workers, when those who worked one hour received one denarius, according to human considerations — which are useless — those who worked twelve hours should have received twelve denarii for the amount of work they had done. In that case, however, all were made equal in good; some were not exonerated and others condemned. Those who worked more, who were called so that they responded, who were fed so that they did not wear out, received all of this from the householder himself. Here it is said, **He has mercy on whom he wills, and he hardens whom he wills.** *He makes one vessel for honor and another for contempt* (Rom 9:21). The good given is undeserved and gratuitous, because the one to whom it is given comes from the same lump. The bad is repaid deservedly and as owed, because in the lump of perdition evil is paid to evil people but not in an evil way. Being made a vessel for menial use is an evil for the one to whom it is repaid because it is a punishment. To the one who repays it, however, it is good because the action of repaying is right. Nor is there any respecting of persons in dealing with two debtors who are equally guilty if the debt equally owed by both is forgiven for one and exacted from the other.

Romans 9:19-23

19**You will say to me then, "Why then does he still find fault? For who can resist his will?"** 20**But who indeed are you, a man, to answer back to God? Will what is molded say to its molder,** *Why have you made me thus?* (Isa 45:9). 21**Has the potter no right over the clay, to make out of the same lump one vessel for beauty and another for menial use?** 22**What if God, desiring to show his wrath and to make known his power, has endured with much patience the objects of wrath made for destruction;** 23**in order to make known the riches of his glory for the vessels of mercy, which he has prepared beforehand for glory —**

(1) Ambrosiaster on verses 19-20

Why then does [God] still find fault? For who can resist God's will? First Paul teaches that God cannot be resisted; he is more powerful than anyone else. Then he says that God is the parent of all and wishes evil on no one; he wants what has been made to continue safe and sound. Nor can God be thought unjust. His benevolence is manifest not only in bringing into being things that did not exist but in giving them eternal life and glory, so that these works would share a majesty like God's own. The justice of the God who is so good and caring should not be questioned.

But who indeed are you, a man, to answer back to God? Great indeed is the presumption and shame of the argument of humans against God: the wicked against the just, the evil against the good, the ignorant against the perfect, the weak against the strongest, the corruptible against the incorrupt, the mortal against immortal, the servant against the lord, the creature against the creator.

(2) Theodoret on verses 19-20

Since you have asked, Paul says, "**Who can resists God's will?**" **But who indeed are you, a man, to argue with God?** If you did not enjoy autonomy, you would not choose a course of action according to your own judgment; instead you would follow the directives of the divine will. Like an inanimate creature, moreover, you would do so without protest, acquiescing in your condition. But since you have been endowed with reason, you both say and do what seems good to you; you do not simply accept events as they happen but investigate the reasons for the divine dispensations.

Will what is molded say to the one who molds it, *Why have you made me like this?* **Has the potter no right over the clay, to make out of the same lump one object for special use and another for ordinary use?** Consider the clay of the potter: lacking reasoned judgment, it does not challenge the craftsman who shapes it. Even if it is intended to be used as a cheap vessel, it accepts its role in silence. But you resist and oppose, for you are not bound by natural necessity, nor are your transgressions opposed to your own will. Rather, you freely embrace evil or by your own choice you undertake the labor of virtue. Therefore, the judgment of the God of the universe is right and just. By right, it punishes sinners for daring to do evil by their own decision. But God justly extends clemency as well: when we provide the opportunity, God offers us mercy.

(3) Origen on verses 20-21

The person who longs to understand the governance of divine wisdom should attend to what Paul, who was privy to the hidden things of God, says in another place, where he is discussing the workings of divine wisdom: *In a large house there are vessels not only of gold and silver but also of wood and clay, some for special use, some for ordinary. If a man cleanses himself of the things I have mentioned, he will become a special vessel, dedicated and useful to the owner of the house, ready for every good work* (2 Tim 2:20-21). Notice how Paul explained the diversity of vessels when he was not facing an impudent objector. In that passage he talked about golden, silver, wooden, and clay vessels; in the present text when the hearer was an objector who did not deserve his attention, however, he mentioned only vessels of clay; in both he refers to special and ordinary uses. The reason why some are put to special and others to ordinary use is not mentioned in the present passage, but it is mentioned in the other one: *If a man cleanses himself of these things* — clearly referring to the filth of sin — *he will become a special vessel, dedicated and useful to the owner of the house, ready for every good work.* Thus it follows that those who do not cleanse themselves and wash away the stains of sin by penance will be vessels for ordinary use. If their malice increases and they turn away, if they are contemptuous with a closed mind and an impenitent heart, then they will become not only vessels for ordinary use but vessels of wrath.

(4) Cyril of Alexandria on verses 17-24

Paul opposes those who say that human willing and effort accomplish nothing, that all is determined by the decision of God. He directs the force of his argument at their examples — Esau and Pharaoh. He addresses both cases by saying: **Who are you, a man, to answer back to God? Will the creation say its creator:** *Why did you make me this way?* His point shows clearly that opposing the divine judgment entails great difficulties. If a person follows this argument to its conclusion, he will recognize that the all-knowing God has the ability to judge each thing because he sees it, and he will not doubt that everything God chooses to do is holy, since by his power he created each thing with its unique character. Therefore Paul vehemently censures those who scrutinize the divine judgments and question their goodness. Instead, they ought to imitate the potter's products and accept without complaining whatever comes from God. **For the creation will not say to its creator:** *Why did you make me in this way?*

Someone may, however, respond: If God makes things as he pleases, like a potter, and **he makes one a vessel for honor but another for dishonor**, then each person will have a character exactly corresponding to the way God made him. Thus, one person was allotted a nature suited **for dishonor**; another person was made, or rather raised up, hard-hearted **in order** (as is said) **to proclaim his name in all the earth**. What accusation can then be made against those who actually fall after they were created to fall?

Here is how one might respond specifically to those who claim that the argument indicates that God makes different kinds of natures. Scripture did not say that some people are made cruel and hard, that is, **a vessel of dishonor**; nor did it in any way assign such a nature to them. Rather, it leads us to think that people are created like clay vessels, **some for beauty and others for menial use**. We see an example of this type in the words of the prophets. If one reads the actual words of Jeremiah, it is clear that people are shaped like clay, some for beauty and others for menial use, and there is a reason for this. Here is what he says: *Arise, and go down to the potter's house, and there you will hear my words. And I went down to the potter's house, and there he was working at his wheel. And the vessel in his hand fell, and he reworked it into another vessel, as seemed good to him to do. "Do I not have the power to do with you, O house of Israel, just as this potter did? Behold, you are in my hands like the clay of the potter. At some time, I shall warn a nation or a kingdom that I intend to destroy it, and if that nation turns back from its evil ways, I shall not do* *the evil things which I contemplated for them. And at some other time, I shall proclaim to a nation and to a kingdom my intention to build and plant it, and if they then commit evil deeds in my sight, not listening to my voice, I shall not do the good things which I said I would do for them"* (Jer 18:2-10). Do you grasp how some people are created for honor and some for dishonor, not because they arbitrarily received a nature created for this purpose, but because they received a fair and appropriate repayment for what they did? Therefore if the creator of all punishes anyone who changes from good to bad and honors whoever changes from bad to good, we can truly acknowledge that at least some people have become evil because they were shaped this way through their own fault. They became *vessels of menial use* because they turned away from pleasing God and willingly became weak and prone to evil.

But, someone observes, God himself hardened Pharaoh's heart. God said: **I have raised you up for this very purpose of showing my power in you.** If God himself hardens some people and raises them up **as vessels of wrath, which are designated for destruction**, why does God still blame them? **For who has withstood his will**? How could someone hardened by God become good?

How should one respond to this argument? In order to know the truth, it is enough to hold firmly that God could never create evil, for whatever God created is very good. If they maintain that the Egyptian (Pharaoh) was not a human being and they demonstrate that he did not share the same nature as we do, then we will be silent. But if he was one of us, then they must either openly attack the divine decree for not distinguishing what is good from what is not good, or — if they are horrified at that — let them confess that everything which God has brought into existence is good and thereby abandon this reckless opinion. The phrase directed to Pharaoh, **For this very purpose I have raised you up,** means not "I have established" or "I have created," but rather "I have called you that you might set your will against me — not from the time you were born, but when Moses was sent to save Israel." In his wisdom, Paul states clearly for us why and for what purpose Pharaoh was called: **For God desires that his wrath be made known**, and what follows.

The whole world wandered in error in times past: some people worshiped creation itself; others worshiped whatever seemed good to them. But Abraham alone was called to know God, and thus brought forth from himself a nation devoted to the worship of God. But when the Israelites went down to and remained in Egypt for a long time, they fell into error and worshiped the gods of that land. But God remembered his promises to their fathers and sent Moses as a messenger to free Israel from slavery. His purpose was to persuade not only those already called to worship God but everyone else on earth that the God of the Hebrews was revealed after a long period of time. By marvelous deeds, he also strengthened faith in himself and his glory by showing that God is not mute and impotent like other gods, but that he governs the universe and his wrath falls upon those who resist his commandments. He also wished to show that when God decides to work wonders, he does so for a good reason. So Pharaoh was raised up according to the divine plan, and was hardened against the divine will. His punishment was not unjust since he was an evil man, an idolater, and was afflicting the Israelites by forcing them to make bricks out of mud and then rewarding them with even more hard work. By these actions, Pharaoh had become a vessel of wrath and had prepared himself for destruction; that is, he drove himself to such monstrous evils that in the end he was a vessel of wrath and destruction. God then used this man to demonstrate his power, ***that God's name be proclaimed in all the world.*** Pharaoh showed that he deserved what he suffered. It was necessary that he suffer on account of his earlier sins, even though he may not have offended in what he did later.

Let God, therefore, be free from blame and ridiculous accusations. To manifest his wrath and make known his power, God patiently endured the vessels of wrath prepared for destruction, in order to benefit the vessels of mercy, **that is, those who have experienced mercy through faith,** since we were called **not only from the Jews but also from the Gentiles.**

(5) Origen on verses 22-23

Paul's style of composition is sometimes disjointed and unpolished, as I have remarked on many prior occasions and note again here. The phrase which begins the sentence, **That if God is willing,** is not clearly related to anything else. Later in this letter, he says, *That if the first fruits are holy, so is the whole batch* (Rom 11:16). But in the present passage, he does not make a similar connection and leaves the phrase ambiguous. If we disregard the initial words, the sentence will be clearer and we can understand it. Thus, for example, we could read this text as, "God, desiring to show his wrath and to make known his power, has endured with much patience the objects of wrath that deserve destruction, in order to make known the riches of God's glory in the objects of mercy." Read in this way, the statement means that when God endures and patiently bears with the unbelievers and the unfaithful, the divine patience and power are manifest to humans: patience is evident when God endures for a long time so that they might reconsider and convert; and power when God punishes occasionally and does not always allow their crimes to go unavenged. God manifests the riches of divine glory in the **vessels of mercy,** in those who cleanse themselves from all filth of sin, from which no one is pure, not even a day-old baby. God prepared these utensils for glory not by some unplanned or capricious gift, but because they had purified themselves from that defilement we just mentioned. . . .

Let us go back over this passage briefly and search out its inner meaning. How does God display anger? Through **vessels,** he says, **of wrath that are right for destruction.** I am amazed when I realize how carefully the Holy Spirit has planned the divine writings. The Scripture says that the wrath of God, which is extrinsic to the divine nature, is manifest to humans, as the Apostle indicates in this passage. It says that God's goodness and sweetness, which are intrinsic to the divine nature, are hidden and concealed, as David says, *How abundant is your goodness, which you have hidden for those who fear you!* (Ps 31:19). What reason can we discern for God's manifesting wrath to humans but concealing goodness? Clearly, God knows the weakness of the human race and its tendency to fail by negligence. Humans are helped more by being fearful of divine wrath than careless in their reliance on God's generosity and sweetness, as the Wisdom of God says, *Those who spare the rod hate their children. If you beat them with a rod, they will not die, but you will save their lives from Sheol* (Prov 13:24; 23:14-15). For this reason, God displays the divine power by correcting and attacking the wicked, so that as the Scripture says, *Strike a scoffer, and the simple will learn prudence* (Prov 19:25).

God makes known the riches of glory for the vessels of mercy, which he has prepared beforehand for glory. The riches of God are made known when divine mercy is bestowed upon people generally held of little importance, those who are humble and trust in the Lord rather than in their own riches and power. So at a time when it was considered hopeless by the nations and abandoned by God, the nation of the Hebrews obtained mercy. At the present time, another people has received mercy, a people taken from among the nations, one despised and regarded as hopeless by those who brag about their circumcision.

(6) Ambrosiaster on verses 22-23

That if God, desiring to show his wrath and to make known his power, has endured with much patience the vessels of wrath that are made for destruction. This means that unbelievers are being prepared for punishment by that will and long-suffering of God which is divine patience. Though God waited for a long time, they refused to be converted. They were awaited, therefore, so that they would be inexcusable when they perished; God knew they were not going to believe.

And in order to make known the riches of divine glory in the vessels of mercy, which he has prepared for glory. The patience and long-suffering of God prepare both the bad for destruction and the good for their reward. The good are those in whom the hope of faith is found. God sustains all, while knowing the final outcome of individuals. In this way, God's patience prepares for glory those who are reformed from evil and those who are steadfast in good. **The riches of glory** refers to that great variety of honors prepared for believers. God prepares for destruction, however, those who change from good to bad and then persist in that wickedness.

(7) Augustine on verses 19-23

People who refuse to live justly and faithfully will make excuses for themselves by saying: "What have we done? We behave badly when we are not given the grace by which we might act well." They cannot say that they do nothing wrong, since they admit to behaving badly; if they did no evil, they would be acting well. If they behave badly, however, this is because of their own evil — either what they inherited or what they have added to it. But if they are **vessels of wrath made for destruction**, which is being paid to them as their due, they should charge this to themselves. They were made from that lump which God has justly and deservedly condemned, because of the sin of that one in whom all sinned. If they are **vessels of mercy**, however, God has refused to pay their due punishment, though they were made from the same lump. They should not exalt themselves but glorify God, who has bestowed on them a mercy that they do not deserve. If they think differently, God will also reveal the truth to them.

Finally, then, how will these people make an excuse for themselves? By that appeal which the Apostle poses to himself in their own voice: **"Why does he find fault? For who can resist his will?"** Why blame us for offending God by behaving badly since no one can resist God's will and God has hardened us by not bestowing mercy? If they are so shameless as to contradict not us but the Apostle in offering this excuse, why should we be embarrassed to respond by repeating exactly what the Apostle said: **But who are you, a man, to answer back to God? Will what is molded say to its molder, Why have you made me thus? Has the potter no power over the clay, to make out of the same lump** — itself justly and deservedly condemned — **one vessel for honor** — undeserved but by the grace of mercy — **and another for contempt** — deserved and by the justice of wrath? **In order to make known the riches of God's glory in the vessels of mercy**, by showing what these are being given, while the vessels of wrath receive that punishment which all alike deserve? Let this response suffice for a Christian who is still living by faith during the present time and not yet seeing everything complete and finished — a Christian either knowing partially or believing that God saves only by gratuitous mercy through our Lord Jesus Christ. Why, however, God rescues one or does not rescue another, let anyone who is capable investigate the great depth of God's judgments — while being careful not to fall headlong into it. *Is there injustice on God's part? By no means!* (Rom 9:14). *But God's judgments are unsearchable, and God's ways inscrutable* (Rom 11:33). . . .

Therefore, God makes **vessels of wrath destined for destruction**, in order to show wrath and demonstrate the divine power which uses even evil things well, and to **make known the riches of God's glory in the vessels of mercy**, which God makes for an honor which the damnable lump does not deserve but rather receives by the liberality of grace. In these **vessels of wrath** made for dishonor, God is condemning, not causing an injustice which truth itself repudiates. God condemns them because of the merits of that lump which exists in human beings who were created for the good of their nature but who because of their crimes have been destined for wickedness as a punishment. As human nature, which no one should hesitate to praise, is attributed to the will of God, so sin, which no one refuses to condemn, belongs to the will of a man. The will of this man was either transmitted as a hereditary defect to the descendants whom he had within him when he sinned or was acquired through other vices as each individual behaves culpably. The sin was originally inherited, or piled up in individual lives by people not understanding or refusing to understand; it was made worse by the addition of transgressions after they were instructed in the law. No one is rescued from any of these evils and made righteous except by the grace of God through Jesus Christ our Lord. This grace bestows the remission of sins. Before this forgiveness, the same grace inspires faith and fear of God and imparts the salutary desire for, and practice of, prayer. Grace then heals all our weaknesses, redeems our life from corruption, and crowns us with compassion and mercy.

Romans 9:24-29

24[**which he has prepared beforehand for glory**] **even us whom he has called, not from the Jews only but also from the Gentiles?** 25**As indeed he says in Hosea,**

> *Those who were not my people*
> *I will call "my people,"*
> *and her who was not beloved*
> *I will call "my beloved."* (Hos 2:24)

26*And in the very place where it was said to them, "You are not my people,"*
they will be called "sons of the living God." (Hos 1:10)

27And Isaiah cries out concerning Israel, *Though the number of the sons of Israel were like the sand of the sea, only a remnant of them will be saved;* 28*for the Lord will execute his sentence on the earth with rigor and dispatch* (Isa 10:22-23). 29And as Isaiah predicted,

> *If the Lord of hosts had not left us children,*
> *we would have fared like Sodom*
> *and been made like Gomorrah.* (Isa 1:9)

(1) Ambrosiaster on verses 25-29

As indeed he says in Hosea, *Those who were not my people I will call "my people," and her who was not beloved I will call "beloved." And it will be in the very place where it was said to them, "You are not my people," that they shall be called "sons of the living God."* This is clearly a prediction about the nations, who previously were not the people of God. After obtaining mercy, they have been called the people of God, with the result that the Jews are shamed. Those who earlier were unloved have become beloved and adopted as children, while the Jews have given up that title. And so, that people which used not to be called the people of God is now called **"sons of the living God."** For people had been called children of God only in Judah, that is, in Jerusalem, where the house of God used to be. As Psalm 75/76 says: *In Judah God is known* (Ps 76:1). However, later on, in the prophet Zechariah, God says: *I will place Jerusalem in all the nations* (Zech 12:2 LXX), because the children of God would be everywhere and that house of God which is the Church would be in all places. Hence, the Lord says to the Jews: *the kingdom of God will be taken away from you and given to a people that produces the fruits of the kingdom* (Matt 21:43).

And Isaiah cries out for Israel. Paul says this because Isaiah cries out for those who believe in Christ, who are truly Israelites. As the Lord says about the most holy Nathanael: *Here is truly an Israelite in whom there is no deceit* (John 1:47).

Though the number of the sons of Israel were like the sand of the sea, only a remnant of them will be saved. When most of the Jews reject the promise and abandon the entitlement given to their ancestors, those few who persevere in believing in the trustworthiness of the promise are the remnant left behind. The Jews who do not believe that the one whom the law promised is adequate for salvation have abandoned the law itself; in rejecting Christ they are guilty of violating the law itself and must be regarded as apostates. Out of that great multitude, he says, only those who believe are saved, those whom God foreknew.

The sentence will be effective and quick in its justice, for the Lord will execute a short sentence on the earth. He promises that those called ***the remnant*** will be saved through a judgment which the Lord justly and decisively will execute quickly on the earth. Creation should, indeed, attain salvation only in the name of its lord and creator, that is, through faith. Now that all practices like new moons, the Sabbath, circumcision, the dietary law, and offerings of cattle have been abolished, faith alone is required for salvation. Faith is an abridgment of the law because what is believed is itself the principal element of the law, as the Savior says: *Moses wrote about me* (John 5:46). Therefore the remnant of the Jews is saved by this abridgment of the law; but the majority despise God's decision establishing salvation for the human race and thus cannot be saved.

And as Isaiah predicted, ***If the Lord of hosts had not left us seed, we would have fared like Sodom and been made like Gomorrah.*** This **seed** which he says remained alone of all things and was preserved for the renewal of the human race is Christ and his teaching (Gal 3:16), as he himself says: *The seed is the Word of God* (Luke 8:11). God promised long ago to remove the burdens of the law and leave us a way to redemption; by receiving the forgiveness of sins, we would not be punished under the law, as Sodom was destroyed. Paul is therefore saying that the Savior was preserved for us as a support for life, which the law could not supply. From the beginning God planned that the birth of this one, who alone was free of all sin, would defeat the enemy of humanity and take away the sins of all. There is also this text in the Apocalypse of John: *No one in heaven or on earth or under the earth was able to open the scroll or to look into it* (Rev 5:3), except the Savior who conquered death. This, therefore, is the seed promised of old which God kept in reserve, to bear fruit once the sins of both Jews and Gentiles had reached their full strength. For if Christ, whom he calls the **seed** because the human race was restored through him, had not been kept in reserve, then the progeny of Abraham would have died out: they had been overwhelmed by sins, and the law could not help them. Paul teaches, therefore, that they should follow Christ, who brought protection for life.

(2) John Chrysostom on verses 26-27

There they shall be called "children of the living God." Even if they say that this passage referred to the Jews who believed, Paul's argument is still effective. For then after receiving so many benefits, a people so hard-hearted and alienated that it had even destroyed its own identity as a people could be so fully transformed, then what of those who were strangers from the beginning, instead of being estranged after having been made God's own people? What could hinder them from being called and — provided they obey — being judged worthy of the same blessings? Paul was not satisfied by introducing only the prophet Hosea; he also produced the prophet Isaiah, who agrees with Hosea: **And Isaiah cries out concerning Israel,** ***Though the number of the children of Israel were like the sand of the sea, only a remnant of them will be saved.*** Notice that this prophet also says that not everyone but only the worthy will be saved. For God means, "I do not respect the multitude, nor does the race being spread out everywhere distress me; I only save those who make themselves worthy." Isaiah did not mention ***the sand of the sea*** without a purpose; he was actually reminding them of that ancient promise of which they had become unworthy. Why are you upset, then, thinking that the promise itself had failed when all the prophets affirm that not everyone is saved?

(3) Origen on verse 29

And as Isaiah foretold, *If the Lord of hosts had not left a seed to us, we would have fared like Sodom and been made like Gomorrah.* Which offspring did Isaiah say was left by the Lord? It was that seed indicated by the Apostle when he recounted what had been said to Abraham, *I will give this land to you and your offspring* (Gen 12:7); *It does not say, "And to offsprings," as of many; but it says, "And to your offspring," that is, to one person, who is Christ* (Gal 3:16). Isaiah is referring to the same one, *If the Lord had not left us a seed*; that is, unless the Lord had given Christ to be born of us, our impiety would have been as great as Sodom's — although something even worse was done by the Israelites. The residents of Sodom were indecent and impure toward visitors; the people of Israel violated the holiness of the one who desired to become and to be accepted as their brother, though he was the majestic Lord. Unless God had left that one offspring through whom the remnant and the vessels of mercy would be saved, the people would have been exterminated like the residents of Sodom. Isaiah intentionally called this remnant a **seed,** since seed is sown in the earth and bears abundant fruit. Thus he taught that Christ would be sown, buried in the earth, and rise from it, in order to bring forth much fruit among the multitudes which make up the whole Church. As the Lord himself says, *unless a grain of wheat falls into the earth and dies, it remains just a single grain; but if it dies, it bears much fruit* (John 12:24).

(4) Augustine on verses 24-29

Those of us whom he has called, not from the Jews only but also from the Gentiles, that is, the vessels of mercy which he has prepared for glory, include neither all the Jews nor all the Gentiles but some from the Jews and some from the Gentiles. The one lump of sinners and wicked deriving from Adam is a mixture that includes both the Jews and the Gentiles who have lost the grace of God. If then the molder of the clay takes portions of this same mixture to make one vessel for honor and another for contempt, then both kinds of vessels are made from both the Jews and the Gentiles. They all belong to the same mixture.

Then he begins to cite prophetic witnesses for each type but in the opposite order. He had spoken first of the Jews and then of the Gentiles, but here he offers testimonies first for the Gentiles and then for the Jews. **For, as Hosea says,** *Those who were not my people I will call "my people," and the one who was not beloved I will call "beloved"; and in that place where it was said: "you are not my people," they will be called "children of the living God."* This should be understood as referring to the Gentiles because they did not have a single place set aside for sacrifices, as the Jews did in Jerusalem. The apostles were sent to the Gentiles so that they might believe in their own places. Then all to whom God gave the power to become children of God would offer a sacrifice of praise in whatever place they had believed.

And Isaiah cries out concerning Israel. Lest we believe again that all the Israelites have been destroyed, Paul teaches that some of them were made vessels of honor and others of contempt. ***Though the number of the children of Israel be as the sand of the sea, a remnant will be saved.*** The other multitude are vessels destined for destruction. ***For the Lord will execute his sentence upon the earth completely and quickly.*** God will save the believers through grace by a simple profession of faith rather than through the many elaborate observances that burdened and enslaved that multitude. Through grace, God made a pronouncement on earth which was short but effective: *My yoke is easy, and my burden is light* (Matt 11:30). A little later Paul said this: *The word is near you, in your mouth and in your heart, that is, the word of faith which we preach. Because, if you confess with your mouth that Jesus is Lord and believe in your heart that God raised him from the dead, you will be saved. A person believes with the heart for righteousness, and confesses with the mouth for salvation* (Rom 10:8-10; Deut 30:14). This is the short but effective word that the Lord spoke on earth. By its power and brevity, that robber was justified, even though all his limbs were affixed to the cross and he had only these two free; he *believed with his heart for righteousness, and confessed with his mouth for salvation* (Rom 10:8-10). Thus he merited to hear at once: *Today you will be with me in Paradise* (Luke 23:43). His good works would have followed had he lived longer among us after receiving this grace. His good works had not preceded, however, to earn that grace by which he was taken to the cross as a robber and from the cross carried to Paradise.

Paul points out that Isaiah had foretold: ***Unless the Lord of hosts had left us a seed, we would have fared like Sodom and been made like Gomorrah.*** Here he says, ***Unless God had left us a seed;*** and there, ***a remnant will be saved.*** Everyone else will perish, as vessels destined for destruction by due punishment. That the entire people did not perish as did Sodom and Gomorrah, was not due to its merits but to the grace of God preserving a remnant, from which another harvest might grow up, all over the world. This he says a little later: *So too at the present time there is a remnant, chosen by grace. But if it is by grace, it is no longer on the basis of works; otherwise grace would no longer be grace. What then? Israel failed to obtain what it sought. The elect obtained it, but the rest were blinded* (Rom 11:5-7). The vessels of mercy received mercy, while the vessels of wrath — taken from that same mixture — were blinded. The same division is found in the fullness of the Gentiles.

Romans 9:30-33

30What shall we say, then? That Gentiles who did not pursue righteousness have attained it, that is, righteousness through faith; 31but that Israel who pursued the righteousness that is based on the law did not succeed in fulfilling that law. 32Why? Because they did not pursue it through faith, but as if it were based on works. They have stumbled over the stumbling stone, 33as it is written,

Behold, I am laying in Zion a stone that will make men stumble,
a rock that will make them fall,
and he who believes in him will not be put to shame. (Isa 28:16)

(1) Ambrosiaster on verses 30-31

What then are we to say? That Gentiles who did not strive for righteousness have attained it, that is, righteousness that is from faith. Since righteousness is from that law entrusted to the world which forbids the committing of sin, Paul says that what the nations have grasped is not the righteousness which can be recognized by nature's teaching, but the righteousness which comes from faith in Christ. Professing faith in Christ is true and lasting righteousness in the sight of God. For who is so righteous as the one who knows God the Father, from whom all things exist, and God's Son Christ, through whom all things exist? Righteousness is first to recognize the creator, and then to obey God's teaching. Previously, the nations did not seek after righteousness, that is, the law which bore witness to the creator. When they did attain it at the coming of Christ, they discovered a superabundant righteousness beyond that of the scribes and Pharisees. Those who earlier had not sought even the lesser, later grasped the greater. The Jews were under the law and ought to have advanced beyond the others, but they became worse.

But Israel, striving for the law of righteousness, did not succeed in fulfilling that law. The fulfillment of the law is through faith. When the nations grasp this, they are proven to have fulfilled the whole law. Through their bad will, the Jews did not believe in the Savior. They claimed the righteousness that was commanded in the law, that is, the Sabbath, circumcision, and the rest, but they did not thereby attain the law, that is, they did not fulfill it. Not having fulfilled the law, they then became guilty by the standards of the law. The person who moves from the law of Moses to faith in Christ actually fulfills that law.

(2) Origen on verses 31-33

But Israel, pursuing the law of righteousness, did not succeed in fulfilling that law. In this passage, Paul uses the term "law" in different senses within the same verse, as we have noted about other texts as well. Certainly, **Israel, pursuing the law of righteousness**, according to the letter, **did not succeed in fulfilling that law**. Which law did it fail to fulfill? That of the Spirit. Otherwise the Apostle would not have said that they had not fulfilled that very law which they sought, held, and possessed. Then he gives the reason why Israel could not fulfill the law: **Because they did not pursue it on the basis of faith, but as if it were based on works.** We have already discussed faith in Christ and the works of the law in great detail in the beginning of this letter. To avoid going over all that again, we will explain the present passage by using a few words from the Apostle himself: *Being ignorant of the righteousness that comes from God, and seeking to establish their own, they have not submitted to God's righteousness. For Christ is the end of the law, so that there may be righ-*

teousness for everyone who believes (Rom 10:3-4). They sought the law not according to the works of God's justice but according to the works of their own justice. **They have stumbled over the stumbling stone, as it is written, *See, I am laying in Zion a stone of stumbling, a rock for falling down, and whoever believes in him will not be ashamed.***

(3) Ambrosiaster on verses 32-33

They have stumbled over the stumbling stone, as it is written, *See, I am laying in Zion a stone that will make people stumble, a rock that will make them fall, and whoever believes in him will not be put to shame.* This is found in Isaiah (Isa 28:16). By parallels in many other texts, it can be shown that *rock* or *stone* refers to Christ. For the prophet Daniel gave the name of stone to the one who was cut out of the mountain without human hands and who struck and threatened all kingdoms and filled the whole earth (Dan 2:34-35). Clearly, he was referring to Christ. In the law, too, Christ is called the rock from which water flowed, as the Apostle himself attests: *They drank from the spiritual rock that followed them, and the rock,* he says, *was Christ* (1 Cor 4:10). The Apostle Peter, too, says to the Jews: *This is the stone that was rejected by you, the builders* (Acts 4:10). **The stumbling block placed in Zion,** therefore, is Christ. Zion, of course, is the mountain or the city of Jerusalem itself, which is deservedly called exalted because there God was known. In Jerusalem, the Savior was set by his Father as a preacher; he became a stumbling block to the Jews when he preached that he was the Son of God, born of a woman by the Holy Spirit.

(4) Augustine on verses 30-33

Those mentioned here anticipate rewards as owed for their merits and attribute the merits to themselves, to the strength of their own wills, not to the grace of God. They are doing what was said about Israel according to the flesh: **they pursued the law of righteousness but did not succeed in fulfilling that law. Why? Because they did not seek it from faith but from works.** This righteousness based on faith is what the Gentiles have attained, about whom it was said: **What shall we say, then? That Gentiles who had not known righteousness have attained it, that is, righteousness through faith. Israel, however, pursuing the law of righteousness, did not succeed in fulfilling that law. Why? Because they did not seek it from faith but from works. They have stumbled against the stumbling stone, as it is written, *Behold, I am laying in Sion a stumbling stone and a rock for failure, and whoever believes in him will not be ashamed.*** This is the righteousness which comes from faith by which we believe that we are justified, that is, that we are made righteous by the grace of God through Jesus Christ our Lord, *so that we may be found in him, not having a righteousness of our own, which comes from the law, but that righteousness which is through the faith of Christ, the righteousness in faith which comes from God* (Phil 3:9). This is indeed the faith by which we believe that righteousness has been divinely given to us, not that we perfect it in ourselves by our own power.

Romans 10

In this chapter, Paul continues his discussion of the relation between Israel and the nations. The commentators, drawing on texts from the Old Testament cited by Paul, take him to mean that the preaching of the gospel has gone to everyone, and in particular to the Jews. God has brought the nations into the promises fulfilled in Christ in order to move the Jews to accept the gospel. Only Augustine dissents: he insists that the preaching of the gospel has not been universal in either time or place. He wishes to highlight the grace of divine election and the operation of God's predestination. No one deserves to be called to faith in Christ, he argues; even when the gospel is preached, only those whose hearts God prepares to accept it actually believe and are saved.

In keeping with his insistence on the necessity of actually hearing and responding to the gospel, Augustine argued that faith in Christ had to be publicly professed and lived in the Church. He noted that Peter and many others sinned by failing through fear to confess what they actually held in their hearts.

Romans 10:1-4

1Brethren, my heart's desire and prayer to God for them is that they may be saved. 2I bear them witness that they have a zeal for God, but it is not enlightened. 3For, being ignorant of the righteousness that comes from God, and seeking to establish their own, they did not submit to God's righteousness. 4For Christ is the end of the law, that everyone who has faith may be justified.

(1) Ambrosiaster on verses 1-4

Brethren, my heart's desire and prayer to God for them is that they may be saved. I can testify that they have a zeal for God, but it is subject to misunderstanding. Paul is trying to convince them to abandon the law, which acts like a veil for the Jews (2 Cor 3:13-16). To prevent anyone from thinking that he hates the Jews, he displays his affection for them and affirms the value of the law. He teaches, however, that the time for observing the law has passed and explains that he desires to help them. When he praises their nobility and their ancestral tradition, he wants them to hear him and realize that he is not attacking them.

For, being ignorant of the righteousness of God, and seeking to establish their own, they have not submitted to God's righteousness. Paul says that they have not believed in Christ, but that they acted out of ignorance. **Having zeal for God** but not knowing God's will and purpose, they were acting against God even as they thought they were defending God. Paul is talking about those who did not accept Christ because of misunderstanding rather than malicious hatred. The Apostle Peter says the same: *And now, friends, I know that you acted in ignorance, as did also your rulers* (Acts 3:17). Failing to understand that this was indeed the Christ whom God had promised, they decided to await another and preferred their own justice based on the law to that of Christ, who is the righteousness of God in faith. Christ himself is righteousness, because in him God fulfilled what had been promised.

For Christ is the end of the law for the righteousness of everyone who believes. Whoever believes in Christ has fulfilled the law. No one was justified on the basis of the law, because only those who put their hope in the Christ who was promised could fulfill the law. That faith which believes in the fulfillment of the law has been established so that the legal observances could be set aside and this faith alone would suffice for the whole law and the prophets.

(2) Augustine on verse 1

Consider what is said in the gospel: *For this reason, they could not believe. For Isaiah again said, "He has blinded their eyes and hardened their heart, lest they should see with their eyes and perceive with their heart, and be converted, and I would heal them"* (John 12:39-40; Isa 6:10). I have recalled this passage so that you would understand, if you can, that people's hearts are blinded as a just punishment, and they do not believe; through mercy they are brought to believe by free will. Who does not realize that a person believes only through a free choice of the will? But *the will is prepared by the Lord* (Prov 8:35 VL); moreover, the will is rescued from the servitude which is due to its evil merits only when it is prepared by the Lord through gratuitous grace. If God did not transform a will from one that refuses to one that accepts, then we would not pray to God that those who reject faith would becoming willing. The Apostle showed that he did this for the Jews when he said: **Brethren, my heart's good will and my petition to God for them is that they may be saved.** They could attain salvation only by a believing will, which is what St. Paul prayed they would choose.

(3) Augustine on verses 2-3

Because the Jews thought that they could fulfill righteousness by their own power, they did not acknowledge the grace of Christ, and *they stumbled over the stumbling stone and the rock of ruin* (Rom 9:32). They received the law and became more guilty, rather than being liberated from guilt. What then did the Apostle say about them? **I bear them wit-**

ness that they have a zeal for God, but it is misguided. What did he mean in saying, the Jews have a zeal for God, but it is misguided? Listen to what misguided means: Being ignorant of God's righteousness, and seeking to establish their own, they did not submit to God's righteousness. They had a zeal for God which was misguided because they did not acknowledge God's righteousness; they wanted to establish their own, to make themselves righteous. They failed to acknowledge the grace of God because they refused to be saved gratuitously. Who, then, is saved gratuitously? The person in whom the Savior finds nothing deserving a reward but only condemnation. He finds not the merits of good works but those merits which deserve punishment. If the Savior were to judge according to the rule of the law, then the sinner should be condemned. If he acted according to this standard, whom would he save? He finds that all are sinners; he alone comes without sin (Heb 4:15) and finds us sinners.

(4) Origen on verse 2

The zeal of the Jews **was misguided. For, being ignorant of God's righteousness, and seeking to establish their own**, they sought what seems righteous to human beings. They should have obeyed the righteousness of God, which is Christ.

The statement, **they have a zeal for God, but it is misguided**, might not have been aimed at the Jews alone. The Apostle could say of others, "I can testify that they have fear of God, but it is misguided"; or of others still, "They have love of God, but it is misguided." People might have affection for God but not realize that *love should be patient, kind, not envious, not rude, not boastful, not self-seeking, not pursuing its own advantage* (1 Cor 13:4). Those lacking these dispositions of love and having only an affection for God might well be told, "They have love of God, but it is misguided." Others might be characterized as having a faith in God which is misguided. They might not understand that faith is dead without works (Jas 2:17, 26) and that faith consists not in reciting words composed and written by someone else but in an attitude of mind like that of the woman who said to herself, *If I only touch his garment, I will be made well* (Matt 9:21). If people believe but in their good works do not manifest the one in whom they place their faith, then they can be said to have faith in God, but it is misguided. Still others might be said to have the chastity of God, but it is misguided. A person who sought praise from others might care for the poor, but not in an informed way. A person who fasted in order to be noticed by others would be abstinent, but in an uninformed way. Thus in every good deed, unless we act with knowledge and understanding, we can be told that we are zealous for good works but in a misguided way. We must therefore be particularly attentive to the role of understanding, to prevent things turning out badly for ourselves, lest the faith we profess be in vain and we stray from goodness even in our efforts to do good works.

(5) Theodoret on verses 3-4

For since they are ignorant of the righteousness of God, and seek to establish their own righteousness, they have not submitted to the righteousness of God. Paul called observing the law after the proper time "their own righteousness," since they are zealous to observe it even though it is no longer operative. The righteousness which came about by grace through faith he called, "the righteousness of God." He added the following: **For the end of the law is Christ, for righteousness for each one who believes**. Faith in the Lord does not oppose but actually conforms to the law, since the law led us to Christ, the Lord. Paul expressed this well when he wrote, **for each one who believes**, and included the whole human race. It does not matter whether a person is a Greek or a barbarian. Everyone who believes will have a share in salvation.

(6) Augustine on verse 3

All those who are driven by their own pride and trust in their own power, relying on the assistance of the law alone and not the help of grace, are not children of God. These are people to whom the Apostle refers in saying, **Being ignorant of God's righteousness, and seeking to establish their own, they did not submit to God's righteousness**. He was referring to the Jews: they presumed upon themselves and rejected grace; for this reason, they did not believe in Christ. They tried to establish their own justice on the basis of the law, but not by establishing the law themselves. Rather, in believing that they could fulfill the requirements of God's law by their own power, they established their own righteousness. They were ignorant of the righteousness of God — not the righteousness which makes God just but that justice which humans receive from God.

(7) Augustine on verse 4

The report that *the children of Israel could not look at the face of Moses,* the agent of the Old Testament, *because of its brightness* (2 Cor 3:7), was a sign that they would not understand Christ in the law. *So a veil was placed between them and the face of Moses, so that the children of Israel, as it is written, might not behold it* (2 Cor 3:13). What is the end of the law? This is not my suggestion but the answer of the Apostle himself: **For Christ is the end of the law, that everyone who has faith may be justified**. This is the end which brings something to completion, not termination. An end, in this sense, is that for whose sake everything else is done, in whose service all else operates. Thus a goal is different from a duty: we are obliged to perform duties; a goal is the reason for which we act. All those things which the children of Israel experienced but did not understand actually happened for the sake of Christ. Their situation was symbolized by that veil which prevented their seeing the end itself, because the face of Moses was a symbol of Christ.

(8) John Chrysostom on verse 4

For Christ is the end of the law, so that there may be righteousness for everyone who believes. Notice Paul's wisdom. He is speaking about two different types of righteousness. Thus the Jews who believed were still newcomers to the faith; they might have thought that they had one type but were deprived of the other. They might have feared that they would be judged as outside the law. Nor should these Jews have expected to obtain this righteousness of Christ and then say, "Although we have not yet fulfilled the law, we will eventually fulfill it." Paul shows that there is only one righteousness, that the other righteousness is perfected in this one. Anyone who has laid hold of that righteousness which comes through faith in Christ has fulfilled that other one as well. But the person who despises this righteousness fails in both types. For if the end or goal of the law is Christ, then those who do not attain to Christ do not have that other righteousness either, even if they think they do. But those who have Christ receive all righteousness, even if they have not fulfilled the law.

For what did the law seek to accomplish? To make a person righteous. It could not do so, however, because no one actually fulfilled its provisions. The goal of the law was to justify people; all its prescriptions looked to this end and were established for this purpose: the feasts, the commandments, the sacrifices, and everything else. Christ actually accomplished this objective through faith. So do not fear, Paul says, that you may have violated the law when you came over to the faith. Actually, you transgress the law when you do not believe in Christ because of the law. So, if you believe in Christ, you have fulfilled that law and much more than it commanded; you have received a much greater righteousness.

Romans 10:5-13

5 Moses writes that the man who practices the righteousness which is based on the law shall live by it. 6 But the righteousness based on faith says, *Do not say in your heart, Who will ascend into heaven?* (Deut 30:12) (that is, to bring Christ down) 7 or *Who will descend into the abyss?* (that is, to bring Christ up from the dead). 8 But what does it say? *The word is near you, on your lips and in your heart* (Deut 30:14) (that is, the word of faith that we preach); 9 because, if you confess with your lips that Jesus is Lord and believe in your heart that God raised him from the dead, you will be saved. 10 For a man believes with his heart and so is justified, and he confesses with his lips and so is saved. 11 The scripture says, *No one who believes in him will be put to shame* (Isa 28:16). 12 For there is no distinction between Jew and Greek; the same Lord is Lord of all and bestows his riches upon all who call upon him. 13 For, *everyone who calls on the name of the Lord shall be saved* (Joel 2:32).

(1) Origen on verses 5-7

The differences in righteousness correspond to differences in life. Thus the righteousness of God is Christ, who became righteousness from God and peace for us; he says, *This is eternal life, that they may know you, the only true God, and Jesus Christ whom you have sent* (John 17:3). Thus righteousness offers not just life but eternal life. Paul recognizes that a person who achieves the righteousness of the law **will live**, but he does not say, "will live eternally." If *Christ is the end of the law* (Rom 10:4), then a person who does not accept Christ as *the end of the law* cannot fulfill the righteousness of the law without Christ. **But the righteousness that comes from faith**, which is a reality living and subsisting in Christ, says, *Do not say in your heart, "Who will ascend into heaven?"* **(that is, to bring Christ down) or "Who will descend into the abyss?" (that is, to bring Christ up from the dead)**. Do not be surprised that Christ, who is himself righteousness, seems to say these things about someone else when he means them of himself.

(2) Ambrosiaster on verses 6-8

But the righteousness that comes from faith says, *Do not say in your heart, "Who will ascend into heaven?"* This statement is in Deuteronomy (Deut 30:12), and Paul refers it to Christ, saying: **that is, to bring Christ down, or "Who will descend into the abyss?" that is, to bring Christ up from the dead.** This addition is the Apostle's own: the righteousness of faith entertains no doubt about the hope of God which is in Christ, so that a person might complain, **Who will ascend into heaven?** Christ endured his passion so that, after plundering the lower realm and conquering death by the Father's power, the souls he had rescued might accompany him as he ascended into heaven. Everyone who hoped for salvation from the Savior was set free when they saw him in the underworld. The Apostle Peter witnesses to this in saying, *the gospel was proclaimed even to the dead* (1 Pet 4:6). Those who have no doubt in their hearts about these things, therefore, are justified by that faith. The justice of the law, however, derives from fear. Seeing the law inflict punishment on sinners inspires fear of the law. Thus the law does not confer a significant righteousness and earns a reward only in the present world, not in the sight of God. Because unbelievers regard faith as foolishness, however, it wins a reward in the sight of God, in whom the believer hopes for things unseen (Heb 11:1).

But what does scripture say? *The word is near you, in your mouth and in your heart.* This is in Deuteronomy (Deut 30:14): what we are asked to believe is not far from our soul or nature. Although not seen with the eyes, what we believe is not discordant with the nature of souls or reasonable discourse. Seeds have been sown in nature itself which can then be cultivated by listening or willing so that they produce a testimony to the creator.

That is the word of faith that is preached. Paul says that in dealing with Christ, we must render faith alone and not the works of the law.

(3) Origen on verses 9-11

Notice what he says, **if you confess with your mouth that Jesus is Lord and believe in your heart that God raised him from the dead, you will be saved**. Some think this means that even if a person has no merits based on good works and has made no effort to acquire the virtues, still, by the very fact of having believed, that person will not perish but will be saved and enjoy salvation — though perhaps not qualifying for the glory of beatitude. Consider, however, whether the text should not be understood to mean that anyone who truly and without deceit confesses with his lips that Jesus is Lord and believes in his heart will with that same fidelity make a commitment to the rule of wisdom, justice, truth, and all the other things which are personified in Christ, and will not allow themselves to continue being governed by Mammon, that is, by avarice, injustice, impurity, or lying. Once he has confessed that Jesus Christ is Lord, he will offer no further service to any of these vices. **Believing in his heart that God raised him from the dead**, he will no doubt believe that he was raised up for their justification. Otherwise, what advantage do I gain by knowing and believing that God raised Jesus from the dead? If I do not have Christ raised up within myself, if I do not *walk in newness of life* (Rom 6:4) and flee from the old habits of sinning, then Christ has not yet risen from the dead for me. What follows should be taken in this same sense, **The scripture says,** *No one who believes in him will be put to shame,* which is written in Isaiah (Isa 28:16). So, if *no one who believes in him will be put to shame,* but all who sin will be put to shame, as Adam sinned, was ashamed, and hid himself (Gen 3:8), then anyone who blushes with sin would appear not to believe.

(4) Augustine on verse 9

When the text says, **If you believe, you will be saved**, some understand this to mean that one of these is required and the other offered. What is required would be within human power; what is offered is in the power of God. But why cannot both be in God's power, what is commanded and what is promised? God is asked to give what God commands: believers ask that their own faith be increased and that unbelievers be given faith. In its beginnings as well as in its stages of growth, faith is the gift of God. In this sense, then, is it written. **If you believe, you will be saved**. In the same way, it is written: *if by the Spirit you put to death the deeds of the flesh, you will live* (Rom 8:13). In both statements one thing is required and the other is offered: *if by the Spirit you put to death the deeds of the flesh, you will live* (Rom 8:13). It is required that by the Spirit we put to death the deeds of the flesh; that we will then live is offered in return. Would we be willing to say, however, that putting to death the deeds of the flesh is not the gift of God? Because we hear that we are required to accomplish this to gain the reward of life offered to us, do we therefore refuse to admit that it is the gift of God? Such a denial should not please those who share and defend grace. This is the damnable error of the Pelagians, those whose mouths the Apostle immediately shut by adding, *For all who are led by the Spirit of God are children of God* (Rom 8:14).

Thus we must not believe that we *put to death the deeds of the flesh* by our own spirit but by the divine Spirit. Paul spoke of this same Spirit of God when he said: *All these are accomplished by one and the same Spirit, who apportions to each one individually as the Spirit chooses* (1 Cor 12:11). Among these accomplishments, as you know, he named faith. Although *to put to death the deeds of the flesh* is a gift of God, it is still required of us to receive the life offered as a reward. In the same way, faith is also a gift of God, although it too is required from us for the reward of salvation, as it says, **If you believe, you will be saved**. Thus these things are demonstrated to be both required from us and gifts of God, so that we might understand both that we do them and that God causes us to do them, as the prophet Ezekiel says so clearly. What could be more explicit than his saying, *I will* *cause you to do it* (Ezek 36:27 VL)? Examine this scripture passage; you will see that God promises to cause them to do the very things which God commanded them to do. Their own merits are not ignored, but those merits are evil. For their evil, God repays good. God makes them obey the divine commands and causes them to have good works.

(5) Augustine on verse 10

Might one say something with the mouth that is not believed with the heart? A problem would arise from that passage to which I referred earlier: **For a person believes with the heart for righteousness and confesses with the mouth for salvation.** Was it not the case in time of persecution, however, that almost everyone actually did believe in Christ in their hearts, although they denied under trial that they believed? Still, they perished by not confessing orally for salvation, unless they were later restored by repentance. Who would be so empty-headed as to claim that the Apostle Peter had the same thing in his heart and his mouth when he denied Christ? In that denial, he held the truth within and pronounced a lie in his spoken words. Why did he then weep such tears for his spoken denial, if believing in his heart was sufficient for salvation? Why, while affirming the truth in his heart, did he punish by such bitter weeping the lie he had spoken? Why, indeed, unless because he realized what a disaster it was that he had **believed with the heart for righteousness but** had not **confessed with the mouth for salvation.**

(6) Cyril of Alexandria on verse 11

Everyone who believes in him will not be ashamed. Israel must not make salvation through faith exclusively its own. Everyone, Paul says, who would call upon the name of the Lord will be saved, whether Jew or Greek, whether slave or free. The God of all saves without distinction, for all things belong to God. Thus we say that all things are restored in Christ.

(7) Ambrosiaster on verses 11-13

The scripture says, *No one who believes in him will be put to shame.* When the general examination begins on the Day of Judgment, and all false inventions and erroneous teachings are reduced to confusion, those who believe in Christ will dance. The judgment will display for all to see that what Christians believed is true and what the unbelievers considered foolish is actually wise. The Christians will realize that they alone, whom everyone had disdained as contemptible and irrational, are glorious and wise. The real testing will come when rewards and punishments are handed out.

For there is no distinction between Jew and Greek. Paul is saying in these general terms that each person is either confounded for lack of faith or honored for belief. Without Christ, no one attains salvation in God's presence but only punishment or death. Nor will the privilege of their ancestors or the receiving of the law win any favors for those Jews who have not themselves accepted the reward and the promises made to their forebears. The nations, on the other hand, have nothing to recommend them — even in terms of the flesh — unless they believe in Christ.

One is Lord of all; he is generous to all who call on him. This obviously refers to everyone, both Jews and Greeks, since only those who call on the Lord Christ are alive in God's sight. He is Lord of all, as the Apostle Peter affirms, *he is Lord of all* (Acts 10:36). He is **generous**, however, only **to those who call upon him**, because they will receive a reward. To unbelievers, by contrast, he is not **generous**, because they do not share his goods; they will not receive what they did not believe he was going to give. Yet Paul says that God is **generous**, not "to all believers," but **to all who call upon him**. The soul, after coming to belief, must not cease to petition for what the Lord has taught it to ask always. In the Gospel of Luke, the Lord says that because of the subtle and cunning Enemy, we should *pray always* (Luke 18:1). Moreover, the forgiveness of sins is given only to believers. It follows, then, that a person dedicated to prayer will be saved from evil and is able to receive what God has promised to those who are watchful with their whole heart.

Everyone who calls on the name of the Lord shall be saved. This is a saying in Micah/Joel (Joel 2:32). For the God who appeared to Moses said, *My name is the Lord* (Exod 6:2-3). That was the Son of God, who was called both angel and God, so that he might be recognized not as the one from whom but as the one through whom all things are made (John 1:3). This one is called God because the Father and the Son are one, and is called angel because of being sent by the Father as the messenger of the promised salvation. Having been sent, this God is believed to be not the Father but the one generated from the Father. Thus, *everyone who calls upon the name of the Lord shall be saved.* Moses meant the same thing in saying: *everyone who does not listen to that prophet will be utterly rooted out of the people* (Acts 3:23).

Romans 10:14-17

14But how are men to call on him in whom they have not believed? And how are they to believe in him of whom they have never heard? And how are they to hear without a preacher? 15And how can men preach unless they are sent? As it is written, *How beautiful are the feet of those who bring good news!* **(Isa 52:7). 16But they have not all obeyed the gospel; for Isaiah says,** *Lord, who has believed what he has heard from us?* **(Isa 53:1). 17So faith comes from what is heard, and what is heard comes by the preaching of Christ.**

(1) Ambrosiaster on verses 14-17

But how are they to call on someone in whom they have not believed? Certainly the Jews themselves did not believe in Christ, whom Paul calls Lord. This follows from what I said earlier, that believing has to precede so that a person trusts enough to ask.

And how are they to believe in someone whom they have not heard? Clearly, they cannot believe in one whom they refused to **obey**.

And how are they to hear without someone preaching? Nor is this obscure: whoever rejects a messenger does not accept the sender.

And how are they to preach unless they are sent? Nor is there any question here: they will not be true apostles unless they are sent by Christ, nor can they proclaim without someone having sent them. No signs of power would bear them witness.

As it is written, *How beautiful are the feet of those who bring news of peace, who bring news of good things!* The prophet Nahum/Isaiah says this (Isa 52:7). By saying ***feet*** he has in mind the coming of the apostles as they go around the world and preach that the kingdom of God is at hand. For their arrival brought enlightenment to people, showing the way to go to God in peace, the way which John the Baptist had first come to prepare. Believers in Christ hurry toward this peace. Holy Simeon, rejoicing at the birth of the Savior, said, *Master, now you are dismissing your servant in peace* (Luke 2:29), because the world is full of conflict but the reign of God is peace. Discord will be brought to an end, and all will bend their knee to the one God. Thus the Jerusalem above, *who is our mother* (Gal 4:26), is understood as the city of peace.

But not all have obeyed the good news. This is true. Though the world may be illumined by the splendor of the Lord's teaching, some will reject it and call light darkness. The light of their minds is so dimmed that they do not perceive even the brightness of the true light. The gospel accuses them, *The light shines in the darkness, and the darkness did not comprehend it* (John 1:5).

Isaiah says, *Lord, who has believed our message?* That is: "Who has believed what we heard from you and spoke?" By this prophetic example, Paul asserts that the Jews opposed the truth of the gospel. The law itself accuses the Jews: as they were in former times, so now as well. Yet, this refers only to those Jews who did not accept faith.

So faith comes from hearing, and hearing comes through the word. This is clear: unless something has been said it can be neither heard nor believed.

(2) Origen on verses 14-15

And how are they to preach unless they are sent? This statement seems to give rise to certain problems: it seems to be saying that without a sending, no one preaches; without preaching, no one hears; without hearing, no one believes; without believing, no one calls; without calling, no one is saved. Thus the reason why they are not saved could be traced back to the initial agent who did not send preachers. Those of us who understand better should guide the discussion onto a more truthful path. We should read the text, **how are they to preach unless they are sent**, as the Apostle saying: "We who are heralds and preachers of Christ could not proclaim him, nor would we have any power to announce him unless the one who sent us was actually supporting us. If you choose not to hear what we proclaim to you, that is your fault. If you do hear it but do not believe, and by not believing do not call, then because you decide not to call, you cannot be saved."

(3) Augustine on verse 14

The question, however, is whether faith earns a person's justification or the mercy of God precedes the merits of faith, so that faith must itself be recognized as among the gifts of grace. Consider that in the passage where Paul said: *not because of works,* he did not then say, "but because of faith, *she was told, 'The elder will serve the younger.'*" Instead he said, *but because of the one calling* (Rom 9:12). For no one can believe without being called. The merciful God calls, however, and gives the call without any prior merits, even those of faith; the merits of faith follow the call rather than preceding it. **How are they to believe someone they have not heard? And how are they to hear without a preacher?** Unless, therefore, the mercy of God precedes by calling, no one can believe and thereby begin to be justified and to receive the capacity to do good works. Grace, therefore, goes before all merits: Christ died for those who were wicked. Because of God giving the call, and not because of any merits of his works, the younger received the service of the elder. As it is written, *Jacob I have loved* (Rom 9:13), was based on God calling rather than on Jacob working.

(4) Origen on verse 17

So faith comes from hearing, and hearing comes through the word of Christ. Here **the word of Christ** means the preaching about Christ. Those who heard Christ the Lord himself speaking were not the only ones to believe; those who hear others preaching about him are far more numerous. The Lord himself foretold this in saying to Thomas, *Have you believed because you have seen me? Blessed are those who have not seen and yet have come to believe* (John 20:29). **The word of Christ** refers to every word which the apostles and those others who receive that gift from Christ preach about him. Even in the church, if anyone speaks the wisdom which comes from God and the truth of God, if anyone teaches Christ as the way to God or explains his righteousness, then what is spoken is undoubtedly **the word of Christ**.

(5) Augustine on verses 17-18

If the nature of the human race generated from the flesh of a single transgressor had the power in itself to fulfill the law and achieve righteousness, it should have been confident of receiving the reward of eternal life, even though in a certain nation or in some earlier time, faith in the blood of Christ was unknown. God is not unjust and would not defraud the righteous of the wages of justice, even if they had received no announcement of the mystery of the divinity and humanity of Christ revealed in the flesh. **How could they believe what they have not heard? And how could they hear without a preacher? Faith comes from hearing,** as it is written, **Hearing, though, through the word of Christ. But I ask, have they not heard?** *Their voice has gone out to all the earth, and their words to the ends of the earth.*

But what about the time before this preaching had started or before it reaches the ends of the whole earth — since there are still some nations, even though we are told that they are only a few, to whom this has not yet been preached? What does human nature accomplish, or what did it accomplish, before people had heard what was going to happen or even now still do not know what has happened? Without having been enlightened by faith in the passion and resurrection of Christ, does human nature have the capacity to believe in the God who made heaven and earth, and to recognize that it was itself made, and then to fulfill the divine will by behaving well? Even if human nature could have or can accomplish all this, I would still have to face the assertion which the Apostle made about the efficacy of the law: *therefore Christ died for no purpose* (Gal 2:21). If Paul made this point about that law which the one nation of the Jews received, how much more could it be made about the law of nature, which the whole human race received? If righteousness comes through the power of nature, *then Christ died for no purpose*. If, however, Christ did not *die for no purpose*, then only through faith and the mystery of the blood of Christ can the whole of humanity be justified and redeemed from punishment by the most just wrath of God.

Romans 10:18-21

18 But I ask, have they not heard? Indeed they have; for

> *Their voice has gone out to all the earth,*
> *and their words to the ends of the world.* (Ps 19:4)

19 Again I ask, did Israel not understand? First Moses says,

> *I will make you jealous of those who are not a nation;*
> *with a foolish nation I will make you angry.* (Deut 32:21)

20 Then Isaiah is so bold as to say,

> *I have been found by those who did not seek me;*
> *I have shown myself to those who did not ask for me.* (Isa 65:1)

21 But of Israel he says, *All day long I have held out my hands to a disobedient and contrary people* (Isa 65:2).

(1) Ambrosiaster on verses 18-19

But I ask: Have they not heard? They have heard and have refused to believe. Although faith comes from hearing, some hear but do not believe. They hear and do not understand (Matt 13:13), since their hearts are blinded by their ill will.

Their voice has gone out to all the earth, and their words to the ends of the world (Ps 19:4). Paul is testifying that God's preaching has been so widely heard by the Jews that he can even declare that the whole world is filled with the divine proclamation. For just as, according to the words of the prophet David, the craftsmanship of the world proclaims the creator (Ps 19:1), similarly the gospel preaching reaches every place; for in places where no one has actually spoken, the **voice** or even a rumor has arrived, in the same way as a report of the mighty acts performed in Egypt had reached all nations, as Rahab the harlot testified (Josh 2:10). If the apostolic preaching reached every place, then the Jews could not fail to hear it, so that none of them is excused from the charge of unbelief.

Again I ask, did Israel not know? Israel knew. Through the testimonies given above, Paul has charged the people of Israel with failure to believe. But to avoid complaining and being upset about all Israelites, Paul affirms that Israel has understood and accepted what was promised to it in the law — thus intending the spiritual rather than the carnal Israel, the Israel which God knew in advance was going to believe. For all Jews heard but not all believed.

(2) John Chrysostom on verses 18-19

But I ask, have they not heard? What does it matter, Paul asks, since these people did not listen when preachers were sent out and preached what they were directed to preach? Then he goes beyond the whole solution to this objection: ***Their voice has gone out to all the earth, and their words to the ends of the world.*** What do you mean, Paul asks, they did not hear? The whole world and the ends of the earth heard, and you, among whom the preachers spent so much time and from whom they set out, you did not hear? Does this make sense? If the ends of the world heard, how did you not hear? Then another objection comes: ***Again I ask, did Israel not understand?*** What does it matter that they heard, if they still did not understand what was said and thus did not grasp that these were preachers who had been sent? Does this ignorance not make them deserving of forgiveness? Not at all! Isaiah described their character when he said, *How beautiful are the feet of those who proclaim the good news of peace!* (Rom 10:15; Isa 52:7). Above all, Paul cites the lawgiver himself, adding, **First Moses says, *I will make you jealous of those who are not a nation; with a foolish nation I will make you angry.*** So then, they ought to have recognized the preachers from the prophecy: not only did they not believe, not only did those preachers preach peace, not only did they proclaim those blessings, not only was the word sown everywhere throughout the world, but even more they saw that people from nations inferior to their own were surpassing them in honor. Those other people suddenly loved the wisdom which their ancestors had not heeded. This mark of high honor for the nations galled the Jews, made them jealous, and reminded them of the prophecy of Moses, ***I will make you jealous of those who are not a nation.*** The great honor alone was not sufficient to make them jealous; Moses added that the nation which enjoyed that honor had been despised and considered unworthy even to be called a nation. ***I will make you jealous of those who are not a nation,*** Moses said, ***with a foolish nation I will make you angry.*** For who had less understanding than the Greeks? What was more worthless? God has used all these means to give the Jews clear signs and warnings about these times, in order to pierce their blindness.

(3) Origen on verses 18-19

But I ask, have they not heard? Indeed they have; for *Their sound has gone out to all the earth, and their words to the ends of the world.* This is from Psalm 18/19, where it says, *There is no speech, nor are there words; their voice is not heard; yet their sound goes out through all the earth, and their words to the end of the world* (Ps 19:3-4). The nations are represented in these verses by the reference to the variety of tongues and speech. It says that the *sound* of the apostles of Christ *has gone out to all the earth,* while *their words* rather than their *sound* reached *to the ends of the world.* This can be understood by referring *earth* to persons who are crude and unteachable, to whom not the *words,* which contain the meaning of faith and the exposition of wisdom, but the *sound went out,* as a general and simple proclamation. He calls those who are better educated and more prudent *the ends of the world,* since the *end* indicates a thing's perfection. So he says that not *the sound of the voice* but *the word* and reason came to those who, when they heard the preaching of the faith, could examine and inquire into the divine Scriptures, so that they could recognize the truth of the words which were communicated to them through the apostles. . . .

Again I ask, did Israel not know? First Moses says, *I will make you jealous of those who are not a nation; with a foolish nation I will make you angry.* In what he just said, Paul seems to have been speaking about the nations. As is his practice, he then adds something about Israel and intends to present proper evidence that Israel has no excuse. Speaking in the person of God, Moses says, *I will make you jealous of those who are not a nation,* referring no doubt to the Christians whom God raised up in order to anger the unbelieving and contemptuous Jewish people. Moses might appear in this to have insulted that nation which was chosen by God for the merits of its faith and devotion; he referred to it as *not a nation,* treating it as unworthy to be called a nation or at most *a foolish nation.* Moses, the friend of God, however, does not insult those whom God has chosen, nor will his expression appear disparaging once its meaning is properly discerned. Each nation, such as the Egyptians or Syrians or Moabites, is called a nation because it has its own proper borders, language, dress, customs, and practices; thus the Syrians are never called Egyptians, nor the Moabites Idumeans, nor the Arabs Scythians. The Christians are not a nation like these others but a people taken from all the nations. For this reason, Moses paid them the highest compliment in calling them *not a nation,* because they are not one nation but, if the term be allowed, the nation of all nations. In what follows, however, this interpretation does not seem to work out. When he says, *with a foolish nation I will make you angry,* he seems to call this nation of all nations foolish. Even in this, however, God's servant Moses did not insult the people of God. In the power of the Spirit, he foresaw that anyone who wanted to be wise should become a fool in this world, in order to be wise before God. Because *the world did not know God through wisdom, God decided, through the foolishness of the proclamation, to save those who believe* (1 Cor 1:21). Also through the preaching of the cross of Christ, which is foolishness to the nations, a people would be gathered together which would appear foolish in this world, so that it might be wise in God's sight.

(4) Origen on verses 20-21

The nations were clearly the ones who neither knew to seek nor learned to inquire about Christ. Yet they found the one for whom they had not searched because he sought them. He is the good shepherd and looks for the lost sheep; he is the wisdom which searched for the lost coin and found it by seeking (Luke 15:4, 8). The Jews are still looking for Christ and questioning the scriptures about him; because his cross is an obstacle to them, they have not found him. Thus he says to them, **I held out my hands all day long to a rebellious people** when he was hanging on the cross. Not only did they not find him but they challenged him, *If you are the Son of God, come down from the cross and we will believe in you* (Matt 27:40, 42). Notice as well what the Wisdom of Solomon said, *he is found by those who do not put him to the test, and manifests himself to those who do not distrust him* (Wis 1:2).[1]

(5) John Chrysostom on verse 21

Paul then shows that what happened came about not only through the grace of God but also through the choice of those who responded, just as the falling away of the others was provoked by the contentiousness of the disobedient. Notice what he adds: **But of Israel he says,** *All day long I have held out my hands to a disobedient and contrary people.* By *day* here Paul means the whole period before his own time. By **holding out my hands,** he means the calling, the attractions, the summons. Then Paul asserts that the entire fault was their own by saying, **to a disobedient and contrary people.** Do you understand the significance of such an accusation? They did not obey when God summoned them. Instead, they contradicted God, not just once, twice, or three times, but continuously, even though they could see what God was doing.

God was needling them and provoking them to jealousy. You know the tyranny of this passion and what great power jealousy naturally has even for bringing conflicts to an end and rousing those who have lost heart. Is it necessary to prove this about adults when the power of jealousy is so evident in irrational animals and in children before they reach maturity? For very often a child will not obey and remains obstinate when its father calls it. When the father pays attention to another child, however, the first child runs up to the father's lap even without being called. Jealousy effected what an invitation could not accomplish. God did the same thing with the Jews. Not only did God summon and reach out, but God also roused up in them the passion of jealousy, and brought in much inferior people — which especially provokes jealousy. God introduces these others not to the blessings of the Jews but into blessings which were much better and more necessary than theirs, blessings of which they had never even dreamed.

---

1. The text of Isa 65:2 is written in Hebrew and Greek on the front of a church facing the synagogue in the Jewish ghetto in Rome. Apparently in the Middle Ages sermons were preached to the Jews at that spot.

Romans 11

In this chapter, Paul reflects on the fidelity of God toward Israel, even in its infidelity, and the complexity of the divine plan for the salvation of both Israel and the nations. Origen, Ambrosiaster, and Chrysostom attempt to broaden Paul's exposition of the divine plan by extending the pattern back to the election of Israel. All follow Paul in recognizing that only a part of Israel is made righteous in the present time; Ambrosiaster, Augustine, and Cyril explicitly assert that only a remnant will eventually be saved. The complexity of the divine plan is manifest in God's using free human actions — both good and evil — to achieve the divine plan of salvation. All hold humans responsible for their failures, and each explains how the grace of God guides and assists sinners to come to righteousness. Most of the commentators insist upon some type of independent human response to and cooperation with God's help. Origen, for example, identifies ritual observances as the "works" which do not merit divine grace. Others are less specific, but Augustine insists that no morally good works precede and earn the initial gift of conversion. He alone recognized a gratuitous and effective divine grace at work in the salvation of the elect, a grace preceded by no meritorious works and through which God produced those righteous works which brought salvation.

Using the Old Latin version of Ps 59:11 in his commentary on verse 11, Augustine introduced his theory that Israel was preserved as an independent witness to the text of the Old Testament which prophesied the work of Christ. This assigned contemporary Jews an integral role in the salvation of Christians.

Romans 11:1-6

1I ask, then, has God rejected his people? By no means! I myself am an Israelite, a descendant of Abraham, a member of the tribe of Benjamin. 2God has not rejected his people whom he foreknew. Do you not know what the scripture says of Elijah, how he pleads with God against Israel? *3Lord, they have killed your prophets, they have demolished your altars, and I alone am left, and they seek my life* **(1 Kgs 19:10). 4But what is God's reply to him?** *I have kept for myself seven thousand men who have not bowed the knee to Baal* **(1 Kgs 19:18). 5So too at the present time there is a remnant, chosen by grace. 6But if it is by grace, it is no longer on the basis of works; otherwise grace would no longer be grace.**

(1) Ambrosiaster on verses 1-6

I say, then, has God rejected his people? By no means! Because Paul has just shown that the people of Israel were unbelieving, to prevent anyone thinking that he meant that the whole of Israel was unfaithful, he shows that God had not withdrawn the divine inheritance which had been promised to the children of Abraham. If God had known that none of them would be faithful, he would not have promised them a kingdom. The Lord's inheritance, according to the law, is the children of Abraham, but only the faithful among them.

I myself am an Israelite, a descendant of Abraham, of the tribe of Benjamin. By using himself as an example, he shows that part of Israel is saved, the part which God foreknew should be saved, or still could be saved, and that the other part of Israel was consigned to destruction because of its burden of infidelity.

God has not rejected his people whom he foreknew. Here is what the Savior meant, *Father, I protected those you have given me, and not one of them was lost except the one destined to be lost* (John 17:12). Thus none of those whom God foreknows will believe has been deprived of the promise, because things happen as God foreknows they will.

Do you not know what the scripture says of Elijah, how he pleads with God against Israel? *Lord, they have killed your prophets, they have demolished your altars; I alone am left, and they seek my life.* **But what is the divine reply to him?** *I have kept for myself seven thousand who have not bowed the knee before Baal.* The meaning here is clear. He shows that Elijah had remained dedicated to God and had not adored idols, but that many others had persevered in fidelity to God. In the same way a good number of Jews later believed in Christ. This statement reflects what happened according to the historical record. Many had hidden in caves because of Ahab, the king of Samaria, and his wife Jezebel, who believed the false prophets, persecuted the prophets of God, and urged the people to practice idolatry.

So too at the present time a remnant, chosen by grace, has been made safe. So, he says, these remain within the promise of the law, while many others, whom God had foreknown, withdrew. Those who accepted Christ as the one promised in the law stood firm in the law, but those who did not receive him abandoned it. So the believers who remained in the law are called the remnant.

But if it is by grace, it is not on the basis of works. This is clear because grace is the gift of God, not a reward owing to works; it is bestowed gratuitously by the intervention of mercy.

Otherwise grace would no longer be grace. A reward is not given by grace. Because it is not a reward, it is doubtless a grace. To forgive sinners is nothing but grace, especially to those who do not seek it, to whom it is offered so that they might believe. The grace is double, therefore, because God, who abounds in mercy, seeks them out and then heals them by grace.

(2) Augustine on verses 1-7

The gifts of God are given to the elect, who are called according to God's purpose. The foundational gift is to believe and then to persevere in faith until the end of this life.

These gifts of God would not be foreknown by God unless the kind of predestination we are defending were actually operative. But they are foreknown, and, for us, this is the meaning of predestination. Sometimes, indeed, predestination is referred to as foreknowledge, as in the statement of the Apostle, **God has not rejected his people whom he foreknew.** In this case, foreknowing can be understood properly only as predestining, as the context of the passage itself makes clear. Paul is talking about that remnant of the Jews which was saved while the others perished. He had noted earlier that the prophet had said to Israel, *"All day long I have held out my hands to an unbelieving and contrary people"* (Rom 10:21). Then, as though he were responding to the question, "What has happened to the promises which God made to Israel?" he goes on to say: **I ask, then, has God rejected his people? By no means! I myself am an Israelite, a descendant of Abraham, a member of the tribe of Benjamin.** He says, "I am part of the people." Then he added the sentence which concerns us here: **God has not rejected his people that he foreknew.** He next shows that this remnant had been preserved by the grace of God rather than through the merits of their good works. **Do you not know what the scripture says of Elijah, how he pleads with God against Israel? What is God's reply to him?** *I have kept for myself seven thousand who have not bowed the knee before Baʿal.* God replied neither, "There remain for me," nor "They have kept themselves for me," but *I have kept for myself.* Paul continued, **So too at the present time a remnant, chosen by grace, has been made. But if it is by grace, it is no longer on the basis of works; otherwise grace would no longer be grace.** He then drew the conclusion from his argument: What then? (Rom 11:7). And in response to his own question: *Israel failed to obtain what it sought. The elect obtained it, but the rest were blinded* (Rom 11:7). In this election and in this remnant established through the election of grace, he was referring to that people whom God foreknew and therefore did not reject. This is the election by which God chose the elect in Christ before the establishment of the world, that they might be holy and pure in God's sight. God predestined them in charity for adoption as children. Anyone who understands what is being said here could not possibly deny or doubt that when the Apostle says, **God has not rejected his people whom he foreknew**, he meant predestination. God foreknew that remnant which God was going to establish according to the election of grace. This means that God predestined. If God predestined, then clearly God foreknew. For God to predestine is for God to foreknow what he himself is going to do.

(3) Origen on verses 1-2

On the basis of what has already been said, it would appear that the Jewish people have been rejected by God and no longer have any hope. God *made that people jealous of those who are not a nation, and made them angry with a foolish nation;* and *God was made manifest to those who did not seek him, and has been found by those who did not search for him* (Rom 10:19-20). For this reason, the Apostle wants to help them and to make clear that a way to salvation remains for the people of Israel, if they believe. To show that they were disowned because they refused to believe and not because they are the race of Israel, he says: **God has not rejected his people whom he foreknew.** To provide contemporary proof, he then adds: **I myself am an Israelite, a descendant of Abraham, a member of the tribe of Benjamin**, and yet I am teaching faith in Jesus and proclaiming that he is the Christ. My being **an Israelite from the seed of Abraham** did not prevent my becoming a believer in Christ and being justified by faith in him. So then, **God has not rejected his people whom he foreknew**.

(4) John Chrysostom on verses 2-5

Paul is saying something like this: God did not cast off his people. If God had cast them off, God would not accept any of them. But God accepted some, so he did not cast them off. "And yet," someone might say, "if God did not cast them off, he would accept all of them." This inference is wrong. Even in the time of Elijah the number of the saved was reduced to seven thousand persons. At the present time, there are probably many more believers. Do not be surprised if you do not know who they are, since the prophet himself, such a great and important man, did not know. God arranged his own affairs, even though the prophet did not know it.

(5) Origen on verses 5-6

So too at the present time a remnant, chosen by grace, has been made. But if it is by grace, it is not now on the basis of works; otherwise grace would no longer be grace. I must try my best to show the parallel between what happened at the time of Elijah, when the prophet judged that the whole people had been rejected but seven thousand men were shown to have remained faithful to God's covenant, and what happened at the coming of Christ, and at the time when Paul was preaching. Perhaps we can put John the Baptist, who went before the coming of the Savior, in the place of Elijah. The gospel itself assigns him this role by testifying that he would come *with the spirit and power of Elijah* (Luke 1:17), and the Lord said of him, *if you are willing to accept it, he is Elijah who is to come. Let anyone with ears listen* (Matt 11:14-15). He then, who had come *with the spirit and power of Elijah,* so despaired of this people that he called them not the children of Abraham but a *brood of vipers* (Matt 3:7), and then continued, *Do not presume to say to yourselves, "We have Abraham as our ancestor"; for I tell you, God is able from these stones to raise up children to Abraham* (Matt 3:9). Our Lord and Savior could respond to John's complaints about the people, *I know whom I have chosen* (John 13:18), and *My sheep hear my voice. I know them, and they follow me* (John 10:27), and again, *I have other sheep that do not belong to this fold. I must bring them also* (John 10:16). . . .

He continued, **But if it is by grace, it is no longer on the basis of works**. We must realize that the works which Paul repudiates and frequently criticizes are not those of justice which are commanded in the law. People who observe the law according to the flesh take pride in other works, like circumcision of the flesh, the rituals of sacrifices, and the commemoration of Sabbaths and new moons. These and like things are the works that Paul criticized, because no one can be saved through them; as he says in the present passage, **no longer on the basis of works; otherwise grace would no longer be grace.** Because anyone made righteous by such observances would not be justified gratuitously, they are in no way required of those justified by grace. Still, one should take care that once grace has been received it is not wasted, as Paul says, *God's grace toward me has not been in vain; on the contrary, I worked harder than any of them* (1 Cor 15:10). He then continues, remembering that it was a gift, *though it was not I, but the grace of God that is with me* (1 Cor 15:10). By adding to the grace of God works worthy of that gift, a person does not waste the grace and thus show ingratitude toward God. A person who sins after receiving grace is ungrateful to the giver. If you do not let it lie idle, then God's grace will be increased in you and you will receive a multitude of gifts as a sort of reward for good works. This Paul says, and Peter writes in his letter, *May grace and peace be yours in abundance in the knowledge of God* (2 Pet 1:2), and elsewhere, *Like good stewards of the manifold grace of God* (1 Pet 4:10).

(6) John Chrysostom on verse 6

But if it is by grace, it is no longer on the basis of works; otherwise grace would no longer be grace. For when Paul says that even in the present time a remnant has been selected by grace, he shows that these are saved by grace. He not only states this himself but also cites the text: *I have kept for myself.* He quotes this statement to prove that God has made the greater contribution. Someone might object, "If we are saved by grace, why are we not all saved?" Because not all want to be saved. Grace, if it is to be truly gracious, saves those who want to be saved — not those who are unwilling, who turn away from it, who continually fight against it, and who oppose it.

(7) Augustine on verse 6

And again, **But if it is by grace,** he says, **it is no longer on the basis of works; otherwise grace is no longer grace.** How, I ask, could this be true if good works precede and earn for us the merit for acquiring grace, so that it would not be gratuitously given to us but paid as owed? Does one run to God without the help of God, in order to attain the help of God? Do we cling to God without any divine assistance, so that we may then be helped by God? If a person has already been able, by the use of free choice alone, to become one in spirit with God, could the grace then given in response to this provide anything of greater value?

(8) Cyril of Alexandria on verse 6

Paul says, **if by grace, then not from works, since that grace would no longer be grace.** When someone might think becoming well-pleasing to God resulted from works, the name and strength of grace have been made altogether purposeless and superfluous.

Wages for the worker, he says, *are not reckoned according to grace but according to what is owed* (Rom 4:4). Therefore if grace comes from works, it would no longer be grace.

Romans 11:7-10

7What then? Israel failed to obtain what it sought. The elect obtained it, but the rest were hardened, 8as it is written,

> *God gave them a spirit of stupor,*
> *eyes that could not see and ears that could not hear,*
> *down to this very day.* (Isa 29:10)

9And David says,

> *Let their table become a snare and a trap,*
> *a pitfall and a retribution for them;*
> 10*let their eyes be darkened so that they cannot see,*
> *and bend their backs forever.* (Ps 69:22-23)

(1) Ambrosiaster on verses 7-10

What then? Israel failed to obtain what it was seeking. The elect obtained it. The carnal Israelites think they can justify themselves by the works of the law and thus have not attained that righteousness before God which comes through faith. Moreover, all are guilty through the law, because *cursed be anyone who does not uphold the words of this law by observing them* (Deut 27:26). Even if they did uphold all the words of the law, which is scarcely possible, that would not make them righteous in the sight of God, because *the righteous live by their faith* (Hab 2:4; Rom 1:17). A person is righteous in the present age by the law, but one is righteous before God by faith.

But the rest were blinded, as it is written. Isaiah reads, *God gave them a spirit of regret, eyes that could not see and ears that could not hear, down to this very day.* **And David says,** *Let their table become a snare and a trap, a pitfall and a retribution for them; let their eyes be darkened so that they cannot see, and keep their backs forever bent.* These two prophetic quotations have a double meaning; they were spoken and written in two different ways, and two different types of people were intended. Some are forever blinded because of the malice of their wills, so that they will not be saved. Their wills are so evil that they insist they do not know what they have heard, even when they actually understand it. They said about the Savior: *What does he mean? We do not know what he is talking about. Why listen to him? He has a demon and is out of his mind* (John 16:18; 10:20). The others are the true Israel, which opposed them, *These are not the words of one who has a demon. Can a demon open the eyes of the blind?* (John 10:21).

Because the first group hated the Savior, they wanted to appear not to understand what they heard. Thus, when the lawyers and Pharisees pretended not to understand, people would think that what Christ said was absurd and contrary to the law. That could then turn others away from faith. The Savior said to these people, *you have taken away the key of knowledge; you did not enter yourselves, and you hindered those who were entering* (Luke 11:52). Who would not follow the advice and counsel of these lawyers and Pharisees, who were not silly but serious people and defenders of the law? Thus they said to the true Israelites, *Has any one of the authorities believed in him?* (John 7:48). In this way, those filled with hatred could appear justified in not believing in Christ by gathering many others into their party. What only a few people uphold seems to be implausible. As a result, they were blinded, so that they could no longer believe and be saved. The whole process became easier as it developed: because they called false what they knew was true, they could no longer understand what was true and they became convinced that those false things they preferred were actually true.

The other type to which the prophets refer sought the righteousness of the law and thus did not accept the righteousness of Christ. Jealousy for the tradition of their ancestors led them astray; they did not act through spite or malice. These were blinded for a time. The miracles of Christ should have brought them to understand that a person whose magnificent power was displayed in such deeds could not deceive them. They should have compared his preaching to the promise of a new covenant given through the prophets; thus they should have been able to confess that Christ was the one who had been promised. Instead, they ignored God and trusted in human beings. They were then blinded temporarily. When the Gentiles were admitted to the promise, they would be moved to envy. In their jealousy, they would then return to faith in God. Some of the Jews, then, resisted the Savior out of jealousy for their law. These acted in ignorance rather than malice, and for this reason they were not blinded forever.

(2) Augustine on verses 7-8

What then shall we say in response to the other prophetic witness which Paul cites: **Israel failed to obtain what it sought. The elect obtained it, but the rest were blinded, as it is written, *God gave them a spirit of regret, eyes that could not see and ears that could not hear, down to the present day.*** You hear the question which is posed here, brothers, and you certainly perceive how profound it is. We will address it as best we can. *They could not believe* (John 12:39) because the prophet Isaiah foretold it. The prophet foretold it because God foreknew that it would happen. If I were asked why they were not able to believe, I would immediately answer that they refused. God foresaw their evil will; God, from whom the future cannot be hidden, announced it in advance through the prophet. But the prophet, you object, did not attribute the failure to their will. What cause did the prophet assign? ***God gave them a spirit of regret, eyes that could not see and ears that could not hear;*** *God blinded their eyes and hardened their hearts* (John 12:40). I reply that their wills had deserved this. God blinds and hardens people by deserting and not helping them — something God can do by a judgment that is hidden but not wicked. Religious devotion must guard this principle firm and inviolate. The Apostle affirms it in addressing the same difficult question: *What shall we say* *then? Is there injustice on God's part? By no means!* (Rom 9:14). No injustice can be attributed to God's decision, either when God acts mercifully and helps, or when God acts justly and does not help. God does all things by deliberation, not arbitrarily. If the judgments of the saints are just, how much more those of the sanctifying and justifying God? These judgments are just but hidden. So these kinds of questions arise: one person is treated one way and another person differently; one is deserted by God and thereby blinded, while another is helped and thereby enlightened. Yet, we must not presume to review the judgments of such a judge; we must rather tremble and cry out with the Apostle: *O the depth of the riches and wisdom and knowledge of God! How unsearchable are God's judgments and how inscrutable God's ways!* (Rom 11:33). Thus is it said in the psalm: *Your judgments are like the great deep!* (Ps 36:6).

(3) Origen on verses 8-10

People can use their bodily eyes to see either good or evil. They have the power to raise their eyes up to heaven, and through what they see to acknowledge their maker and praise their creator. Or they can give their eyes over to the spectacles in the circus or the theater, or the amusements of other filthy sights which stoke the fires of lust or greed or the other vices. I think we can apply this to the eyes of the soul. Some use them to learn the word of God and the doctrine of truth, to advance daily in its wisdom; others use these eyes for opposite purposes: they train every day and search for ways to destroy the true teachings and to attack what they understand of the faith of Christ. Let us suppose, then, that someone prayed for these people who are cunning and well versed in false knowledge, saying, "May God give them eyes that will not see the shrewdness of perverted opinions and ears that will not hear the teachers of lies, and may their eyes be darkened so that they do not see." Would you not approve someone wishing for them the kind of things that would mitigate their sins? Far better not to understand at all than to understand wrongly. . . .

In this sense, then, is it said of Israel, **Let their eyes be darkened lest they see,** and **May God give them eyes with which they will not see.** Things like this seem to be said in reference to that blindness of the eyes which God gave to unbelieving Israel as a sort of remedy, which prevented its seeing clearly. . . .

As best I can understand, **their table** is the whole of the Scripture, what we call the Old Testament, which Israel possessed before the coming of Christ: *In the first place, they were entrusted with the oracles of God* (Rom 3:2). If people wanted to eat God's word at this table, the laws and the prophets were set out before them. . . .

All Scripture, then, is the table of wisdom. Let us then investigate the sense in which David prays that, **this table become a snare and a trap, a pitfall and a retribution for them** — the unbelieving Israelites. Scripture becomes **a snare** for them when they read what has been prophesied about Christ, *He will build my city and set my exiles free* (Isa 45:13), and they claim that Jesus has not fulfilled it. He neither built the city of God, they say, nor did he restore the people from captivity. They say this because they do not follow the advice of Solomon for eating at the table of the powerful, *to understand intellectually* *the things set before them* (Prov 23:1). It was prophesied that Christ would do these things not visibly but intellectually, that is, spiritually. Christ did indeed build the city of God, but out of the living stones from which he raised up children of Abraham, from whom he built the Church of God. He restored from captivity that people which the devil held captive in sin. For those, therefore, who do not understand in this way, the table of the Holy Scriptures has become **a snare and a trap**. This table can also be seen as a **trap** when the Lord snared those to whom he posed the question, *"What do you think of the Messiah? Whose son is he?" They said to him, "The son of David." He said to them, "How is it then that David calls him Lord, saying, 'The Lord said to my Lord?'" No one was able to give him an answer* (Matt 22:42-46). The table becomes **a retribution** for them, briefly, according to the saying of the Lord, *Do not think that I will accuse you before the Father; your accuser is Moses* (John 5:45), and according to what the Apostle says, *All who have sinned under the law will be judged by the law* (Rom 2:12). The table will become **a pitfall** for them in another way. The Jews learned from the Scripture that *the Messiah remains forever* (John 12:34).[1] Seeing Jesus in the flesh — not only in the flesh but in death and the death of the cross — they stumbled on him. They did not understand that even though he suffered in the weakness of the flesh, *he lives by the power of God* (2 Cor 13:4). Because they did not understand spiritually each of the things *set before them at the table of the powerful* (Prov 23:1), they were scandalized and the very table of the Holy Scriptures became **a stumbling block** for them and **their eyes were darkened**, as we have explained earlier, **and their backs forever bent**. For those who sinned against the creator of heaven and the Lord of Glory should be allowed to look no longer upon the heavens.

Romans 11:11-12

11So I ask, have they stumbled so as to fall? By no means! But through their trespass salvation has come to the Gentiles, so as to make Israel jealous. 12Now if their trespass means riches for the world, and if their failure means riches for the Gentiles, how much more will their full inclusion mean!

(1) Origen on verses 11-12

Now if their trespass means riches for the world, and if their reduction means riches for the nations, how much more will their fullness mean! Consider the wisdom of God in all of this: even offenses and failings result in profit. As people transgress according to the intentions of their own freedom, the divine wisdom governs the world so that the negligence which leads to loss and impoverishment for some results in the enrichment of others. *When God apportioned the nations, when God divided humankind, God fixed the*

---

1. Origen means that the Jews learned from their Scripture, that is, the law, that the Christ, that is, the Messiah, remains forever. His source for this would have been the full passage in John 12:34, which reads: "We [the Jews] have heard from the law that the Christ [i.e., the Messiah] remains forever."

boundaries of the peoples according to the number of the angels of God; the Lord's *own portion was his people, Jacob his allotted share* (Deut 32:8-9). The angels to whom the portion of the nations was allotted seduced people away from the portion of the Lord, perverted them, and made them sin. Thus the Lord said through the prophet, *they have made my pleasant portion a desolate wilderness* (Jer 12:10). Once that portion had been rejected and repudiated, the Lord had to take a different portion on the face of the earth which would receive the glory, the covenants, the laws, and the proper rites for worshiping God — all the riches which had belonged to the Lord's portion. This would then be called the Lord's portion as the replacement of that portion which had sinned. Thus the offense of that first portion brought riches to the world. Now then, not only the one nation of the Hebrews but the whole world has been made the portion of the Lord. This is what the Savior said, *for I come not to judge the world but to save the world* (John 12:47).

The term **world** can be ambiguous: sometimes it is used to designate the heaven and the earth, other times only the earth, or even all humanity. For this reason, the Apostle repeats the phrase and makes his meaning clear, **their reduction means riches for the Gentiles**. What was taken away and removed from those who offended was then bestowed as wealth on the nations that through faith had become the portion and heredity of the Lord. Paul is balancing **loss** and **fullness**. His use of the term **fullness** for the people of Israel conveys a deeper meaning. I will explain this as far as I am able. Now, as all the nations are coming to salvation, the riches of God are being gathered from the multitude of believers; as long as Israel persists in unbelief, however, the full portion of the Lord remains incomplete. The people of Israel is missing from its perfection. When the fullness of the nations has entered and when Israel finally comes in through faith during the last days, then that people who had been first will arrive last; it will complete the fullness of the portion and heredity of God. Thus Israel is called the **fullness** because it will bring to completion what was missing from the portion of God. In this way the governance of the good and omnipotent God makes the offenses of some bring profit to others, just as now Israel's **offense means riches for the world, and their loss means riches for the nations**.

(2) John Chrysostom on verse 11

But through their stumbling, salvation has come to the Gentiles, so as to make Israel jealous. This statement is not just Paul's assertion; parables in the Gospels also communicate this truth. The man who made a wedding feast for his son ended up inviting those on the thoroughfares, since those first invited had refused to come (Matt 22:9). The man who planted the vineyard rented it to others, since the original tenants murdered the heir (Matt 22:38-41). Without using a parable Christ said, *I was sent only to the lost sheep of the house of Israel* (Matt 15:24). To the Canaanite woman who persisted, he said again, *It is not right to take the children's food and throw it to the dogs* (Matt 15:26). Paul also says to those Jews who were disputing with him, *It was necessary that the word of God should be spoken first to you. Since you reject it and judge yourselves to be unworthy of eternal life, we are now turning to the Gentiles* (Acts 13:46).

Through all these examples, it is clear that the original intention was that the Jews should enter first and then the Gentiles. But when the Jews refused to believe, the order was reversed; the disbelief and offense of the Jews resulted in the Gentiles entering first. For this reason, Paul says, **through their stumbling salvation has come to the Gentiles, so as to make Israel jealous**. Do not be surprised if he treats the final result as something which happened in advance. Do not be amazed: he wants to comfort their stricken souls. This is what Paul intends. Jesus came on behalf of the Jews. They did not receive him, although he performed thousands of miracles; instead they crucified him. Then he drew the Gentiles near so that their being honored would sting the insensibility of the Jews; even though this provoked the Jews to envy against the Gentiles, it would persuade the Jews to approach. They ought to have been received first, and only then would we be received. For this reason, Paul says, *the power of God for salvation to everyone who has faith, to the Jew first and also to the Greek* (Rom 1:16).

Since the Jews wandered off, those who were second became the first to enter. Thus you see what great honor Paul bestows upon the Jews even in this: first, he says that we were called when the Jews refused to respond; second, he says that we were called not only for our own salvation but so that it would make the Jews jealous and provoke them to improve. "What do you mean?" someone may object, "Would we not be called and saved if it were not for the Jews?" We would not be called and saved before them, but in the order which had been foretold. For this reason when Jesus spoke to the disciples, he did not simply say, "Go to the lost sheep of the house of Israel," but *Go rather* (Matt 10:6), showing that they should go out to the lost sheep of the Gentiles only after the lost sheep of the Jews. Also, Paul did not say, "It is necessary that the word of God should be spoken to you," but, *spoken first to you* (Acts 13:46), showing that he had to speak to us in second place. These things were said and done so that the Jews would not be able to excuse themselves shamelessly by claiming that they had been neglected and as a consequence had not believed. Indeed, God came to them first for this very reason, although God also knew everything beforehand.

(3) Augustine on verse 11

The Jews, however, who killed him and refused to believe in him — because he had to die and rise — suffered the misfortune of being destroyed by the Romans and completely losing their state, in which they were already under foreign rule. They were uprooted and dispersed throughout the earth, so that no place is now without their presence. Through their Scriptures they serve as witness for us that we did not concoct the prophecies about Christ. Indeed, many of the Jews studied these prophecies and came to believe in Christ both before his passion and even more after his resurrection. Of these was it foretold: *Though the number of the children of Israel may be like the sand of the sea, only a remnant of them will be saved* (Isa 10:22). The rest of them were blinded, as is foretold of them: *Let their own table before them become a snare, a punishment and an obstacle. Let their eyes be darkened so that they do not see; let their backs be bent forever* (Ps 69:22-23, quoted in Rom 11:9-10). When they do not believe, moreover, our Scriptures (their own, which they read blindly) are being fulfilled in them. The charge might have been made that the Christians had invented the prophecies about Christ, like those which are brought forward under the name of the Sibyl or some other seers, if there are any, who are unrelated to the Jewish people. We have adequate evidence, however, which can be cited from the books of our enemies, whom we acknowledge because of the testimony which they unwillingly bear for us by possessing and preserving these books among all the nations, where they have been dispersed and to which the Church of Christ has spread. This very fact is foretold in a prophecy in the Psalms, which they also read, where it says: *My God will go before me in mercy; my God will praise me in the presence of my enemies. You shall not kill them, lest my law should be forgotten. Scatter them in your power* (Ps 59:10-11 VL).[2] God has shown the grace of divine mercy to the Church in its enemies, the Jews, just as the Apostle says, **through their trespass salvation has come to the Gentiles**. God did not kill them, that is, they did not stop being Jews, although they had been defeated and trampled by the Romans. God preserved them lest they forget the law of God and then the witness they provide for us lose its validity. It was not enough, therefore, for Scripture to say, *You shall not kill them, lest my law should be forgotten;* the addition was necessary, *Scatter them* (Ps 59:11 VL). If they had been preserved only in their own land with the witness of their Scriptures and were not found everywhere, then certainly the Church, which is everywhere, would not have had them as witness to all the Gentiles of the prophecies which had been made about Christ.

Romans 11:13-16

13Now I am speaking to you Gentiles. Inasmuch then as I am an apostle to the Gentiles, I magnify my ministry 14in order to make my fellow Jews jealous, and thus save some of them. 15For if their rejection means the reconciliation of the world, what will their acceptance mean but life from the dead? 16If the dough offered as first fruits is holy, so is the whole lump; and if the root is holy, so are the branches.

(1) Ambrosiaster on verse 13

Now I am speaking to you Gentiles. Since I am an apostle to the Gentiles, I glorify my ministry in order to make my own people jealous, and thus save some of them. Here Paul displays to the Gentiles the affection he has for the Jews and glorifies his own ministry as apostle to the Gentiles. By his efforts, he hopes to win the Jews to the faith as well, because of his love for them. If he won over to life even those to whom he was not sent, he would deserve greater honor. He would win greater praise from their forebears, moreover, if he rescued his relatives who were perishing.

---

2. This version of the text is found only in the Old Latin version made from the Greek Septuagint, which Augustine read before Jerome made the Latin Vulgate translation directly from the Hebrew.

(2) John Chrysostom on verse 14

Paul does not say, "my brothers and sisters," or "my relatives," but **the flesh**. Then, when he points out the contentious spirit of the Jews, he does not say, "If somehow I persuade," but **I make them jealous and thus save**, and here he does not mean the whole people, but **some of them**. How hard-hearted they were! In this criticism, he revealed the luster of the Gentiles: even if the Jews became a cause of salvation for them, yet this was not in the same way as the Gentiles did for the Jews. For the Jews passed along blessings to the Gentiles through their disbelief, but the Gentiles conveyed blessings on the Jews through their faith. For this reason, the status of the Gentiles seems to equal and even surpass that of the Jews.

What would you say, then, O Jew? "If we had not been cast out, you would not have been called so soon?" A Gentile could reply: "If I were not saved, you would not have been moved to jealousy. Notice how we have the advantage over you: I am saving you through believing; you stumbled and let us go in before you."

(3) Origen on verse 15

If then, he says, the rejection of the Israelite people provided reconciliation for the world; and if the grace given to that nation was so great that when taken away it was adequate to reconcile the whole world to God; how much more do you think the world will deserve once that nation too is worthy to be reconciled to God? Paul shows in summary form what the world will attain from the reconciliation of Israel: **life from the dead**. The reception of Israel will happen when the dead receive life, when the corruptible world becomes incorruptible, and when mortals will be endowed with immortality. Since Israel's offense had given reconciliation to the world, it would be absurd for their reception not to bestow something even greater and more excellent on the world.

Romans 11:17-21

17But if some of the branches were broken off, and you, a wild olive shoot, were grafted in their place to share the richness of the olive tree, 18do not boast over the branches. If you do boast, remember it is not you that support the root, but the root that supports you. 19You will say, "Branches were broken off so that I might be grafted in." 20That is true. They were broken off because of their unbelief, but you stand fast only through faith. So do not become proud, but stand in awe. 21For if God did not spare the natural branches, neither will he spare you.

(1) Origen on verses 17-20

We hold that all humans, indeed all rational creatures, share a common nature, which makes all of them equally capable of salvation, or of damnation if they are negligent.

Thus an objection could be raised: Why does Paul use the example of the olive and the wild olive? If he knows that all have the same nature, it would seem that he should not have used different species of trees. Our response is to point out that all bodily matter is of the same nature; it is differentiated through what is found in the various species of bodies, trees, or plants. In a similar way, one nature endows all rational beings with individual freedom of choice so that by its own exercise of this power each soul becomes subject to virtue or to lust and is shaped into a particular species of good or evil tree. It is called a good or a bad tree, depending on whether it has loved good or evil things. In this way each person, in accord with the exercise of his or her intention, is named a good olive by following the path of virtue or a wild olive by traveling the opposite path. Thus the Lord said in the Gospel, *Either make the tree good, and its fruit good; or make the tree bad, and its fruit bad* (Matt 12:33), to show that good and bad trees are made rather than born. This solution is not subverted by the ineffable divine governance through which the free will is affected by things or events outside itself that provoke to evil or exhort to good. This rational nature has within itself a power to choose freely in such matters: it can choose to obey the provocation; it can refuse and reject the exhortation. . . .

Because, as I have said, the freedom of choice exists always in nature itself, someone belonging to the people of Israel and a branch on the good olive tree can fall into unbelief and be broken off. Again, someone from the nations who had chosen to be a guilty sinner, and thus to be called a branch of the wild olive, could later convert to the faith — freedom of choice empowers everyone to convert to the good — and be grafted into the good olive through faith and thus share in the richness of the root of the olive. Some take this root to be Abraham, others Seth, and still others one of the worthy ancestors. I, however, acknowledge only my Lord Jesus Christ as the holy root and holy firstfruits. He is the firstfruits, the first portion of all, as the present text of the Apostle puts it, and, as he says elsewhere of Christ, *he is the firstborn of all creation* (Col 1:15). Into this root are grafted all who are being saved, and by this holy portion the whole lump of the human race is sanctified. Like a holy root, he supplies the richness of sanctity to all the branches which remain in him. Through the Holy Spirit, he gives life to those who adhere to him, nourishes them with the word, makes them blossom in wisdom, and makes them bear rich fruit in the fullness of all the virtues. Thus he says of them, *I am like a green olive tree in the house of God* (Ps 52:8). If some branches are broken off because of infidelity and if those remaining hold fast by faith, then in whom do they stand but Jesus Christ? Could unbelief break them away from someone other than the one in whom they did not believe? Whenever, therefore, foreigners were joined to the faith and practices of Israel, they were grafted into Christ, who is the true Israel. Especially from the time of his coming many wild olives were grafted into this stock and into its branches, the apostles and prophets of God, so that those who are inserted share the richness of the root of Christ.

Then, the Apostle warns us not to taunt or mock the Israelite branches which were broken off because **it is not we that support the root, but the root that supports us.** *We have nothing that we have not received. And if we have received it, why do we boast as though it were not a gift?* (1 Cor 4:7). Paul then turns to those who are arrogantly jeering at them and saying, "**Branches were broken off,** and rightly so because of their unbelief, **so that I,** a believer, **might be grafted in.**" The Apostle rebukes them: "**They were broken off**

because of their unbelief, but you stand only through faith. *Remember, all who exalt themselves will be humbled* (Luke 18:14); do not think too highly of yourselves; do not hold forth in such a high and mighty way...."

It should not go unremarked that in this passage the Apostle did not present the example of the olive and the wild olive according to the actual practice of farmers. They usually graft a cultivated olive branch into a wild olive tree, not the other way around. Using his apostolic authority, Paul changed the natural order and adapted the example to his argument rather than his argument to the example.

(2) Ambrosiaster on verses 17-21

But if some of the branches were broken off. That is, if any of them have not believed, they were cut off from the promise.

And you, a wild olive, were grafted into them, to share the root of the olive tree. Paul means that, because many Jews did not believe, the Gentiles have been grafted into the hope of the promise through faith, and have become a source of pain for the Jews. This example does not fit the normal agricultural practice: a good shoot is grafted into a root which is not as good. The Gentiles, however, were from a bad root and were grafted into a good tree. Paul says that a wild olive was grafted in so that the shoot would share in and bear the fruit of the root.

Do not praise yourself at the expense of the branches. Do not rejoice in their unbelief. God is displeased when someone enjoys another's loss, as Solomon says (Prov 24:17). Further, they were not rejected for the sake of the Gentiles; rather, by not believing, they provided an opportunity for the mission to the Gentiles.

If you do boast, you do not support the root, but the root supports you. If you boast about yourself and despise the people into whose stock you have been grafted, you are insulting the race which has adopted you and changed you from bad to good. You will not remain standing long if you destroy your support.

You will say, "Branches were broken off so that I might be grafted in." Paul speaks in the person of Gentile believers, who think that they should rejoice over the fall of the unbelieving Jews, and are saying, "Their rejection made space for the Gentiles." The Jews have not, however, been rejected by God in order that the Gentiles might enter; rather, they brought condemnation on themselves by despising the gift of God, and as a consequence they gave the Gentiles an opportunity for salvation. Paul intends to suppress this Gentile arrogance so that they may rejoice together over salvation rather than mock the weakness. For someone who mocks a sinner is easily misled.

You say well and rightly that branches were broken off and you were grafted it. **They were broken off because of their unbelief.** Not for your sake but because of their offense. They were unfaithful and you were called to salvation to make them jealous. You should give thanks for the gift of God through Christ, not mock them. Instead, you should pray that they might return to their roots, since their loss brought you salvation. Then you will please God, who had mercy on you. God called you so they might be led back to grace by envy of you.

But you stand through faith. Since the Jews fell by unbelief, he tells them to stand by faith. Since the first group fell by infidelity, the second began to stand by faith.

So do not think too highly of yourself, but be afraid. Do not be proud, but be careful lest you too give offense.

For if God did not spare the natural branches, God might not spare you either. This is the truth. Because of their unbelief, God blinded those who had been dignified by the privilege of the ancestors and had been promised adoption as children of God. What will God do to these other people, who were raised up with nothing to commend them and had no prior distinction, if they doubt or conceive too high an opinion of themselves?

(3) Augustine on verses 17-21

The Gentiles who were already believers in Christ wanted to raise their own status at the expense of the Jews who had crucified Christ. One wall came from this people, meeting at the angle, which is Christ himself, the other wall coming from the uncircumcised, that is, the Gentiles. Since the Gentiles raised themselves up higher, this is the way Paul subdued them: **If you**, he says, **cut from a wild olive, were grafted in among them, do not boast against the branches. If you do boast, it is not you that support the root, but the root that supports you.** So, he says that certain branches were broken off the root of the patriarchs because of their infidelity. A wild olive — that is, the Church coming from the Gentiles — was grafted there, to share in the richness of the olive. Why graft the wild olive into the cultivated olive? The normal procedure is to graft the cultivated olive into the wild olive; we never see a wild olive grafted onto a cultivated olive tree. For whoever did such a thing would find nothing but wild olives. What is grafted in is what grows and produces fruit of its own kind. The fruit is determined not by the root but by the cutting.

In this way, the Apostle shows that God accomplished by divine omnipotence that the wild olive was grafted into the cultivated olive and bore good olives rather than wild olives. Directing their attention to this divine omnipotence, the Apostle says: **If you were cut from the wild olive and contrary to the natural process were grafted into a good olive tree, then do not boast**, he says, **against the branches. But you will say, "Branches were broken off so that I might be grafted in." That is true. They were broken off because of their unbelief; but you must stand fast by faith. So do not think too well of yourself, but fear.** What does, **do not think too well of yourself**, mean? Do not become proud because you were grafted in, but fear lest you be broken off because of unbelief, just as those others were broken off. **They were broken off because of their unbelief; but you must stand fast by faith. So do not think too well of yourself, but fear. For if God did not spare the natural branches, neither will God spare you.**

(4) Theodoret on verses 17-18

He calls the **first fruits** the Lord Christ according to his human nature, and calls **the root** the patriarch Abraham, and **the branches of the olive tree** the Jewish people, that they may bear fruit, and **the richness of the olive** the lesson of piety. Thus he exhorts those Gentiles who have faith not to be arrogant toward the Jews who do not believe, whom he calls **the broken branches**. Consider, he says, that you came from other stock, have been grafted into this one, and are receiving the richness of this faithful, receptive root. But if you indulge in boasting: you do not hold up the root, but rather the root bears you. And consider this, **that it is not you that support the root, but the root that supports you**; you are in need of it, and not it of you.

Romans 11:22-24

22Note then the kindness and the severity of God: severity toward those who have fallen, but God's kindness to you, provided you continue in his kindness; otherwise you too will be cut off. 23And even the others, if they do not persist in their unbelief, will be grafted in, for God has the power to graft them in again. 24For if you have been cut from what is by nature a wild olive tree and grafted, contrary to nature, into a cultivated olive tree, how much more will these natural branches be grafted back into their own olive tree.

(1) Ambrosiaster on verses 22-24

Note then the kindness and the severity of God: severity toward those who have fallen, but God's kindness toward you, provided you continue in God's kindness; otherwise you too will be cut off. Paul testifies that God has been kind to the Gentiles because even though they worshiped idols and deserved death, God patiently waited for them; though they did not seek God, God called them and forgave their sins. God was severe toward the Jews, blinding them because they spurned the divine gifts. The Jews to whom he refers here are those who are blinded forever because of their ill will; for this reason he says that **they have fallen**. The others, whom he mentioned earlier, have *stumbled* but not *so as to fall* (Rom 11:11), because he shows that they were blinded only temporarily. Thus God's severity was toward those who were blinded forever and are apostates.

And even those, if they do not persist in unbelief, will be grafted in, for God has the power to graft them in again. He makes clear that divine justice is not unendingly severe toward those whom it blinded temporarily, nor indeed toward those who were refusing to believe, if they change and do believe. God has not so cut off the Jews that they cannot be grafted in again, if they convert. This is the God who said through the prophet: *I will replant those who return to me* (Jer 24:6). Knowing this, the Christian Gentiles should not mock the Jews, but should be certain that the mercy of God is being held ready for those who stumbled.

For if you have been cut from what is by nature a wild olive tree and grafted, contrary to nature, into a cultivated olive tree, how much more will these natural branches be grafted back into their olive tree. Let us interpret the olive tree as the faith through which Abraham was justified; the wild olive signifies infidelity because it is uncultivated and unfruitful. According to this interpretation, if these people, who had always been enemies of God, have been converted to the faith of Abraham and grafted into his root, from which they did not originate, how much more should the Jews, if they turn from infidelity to belief, be returned to their ancestral nature and be grafted once more into their own promise?

(2) John Chrysostom on verse 23

If they do not persist in unbelief, they will be grafted in. God did not cast off the Jews; they broke themselves off and fell. Paul uses the appropriate phrase **they broke themselves off**, because God never cast them out, even though they regularly committed many sins. Notice the authority of free choice and the power of the mind. None of these things continues without change, neither your good nor another's evil. Do you realize how God raised the Gentiles up from their hopeless despair and humbled the Jews in their arrogance? Do not give up when you hear talk of being cut off; do not become arrogant when you hear about divine goodness. God cut you off with such severity to make you want to return. God displayed kindness, so that you would remain. Paul did not say, "in faith," but **by kindness**, that is, if your behavior conforms to God's love toward humanity. For faith alone is not sufficient. God allowed neither the Gentiles to be humbled nor the Jews to be arrogant; God provoked the Jews to jealousy and through the Gentiles granted the Jews the ability to stand in the Gentiles' place, just as the Gentiles had earlier entered the Jews' place. Paul instills fear into the Gentiles by the example of what happened to the Jews, so that the Gentiles would not be puffed up on account of the Jews' failure. He tried to encourage the Jews by what had been granted to the Greeks. For, Paul says, since the Jews were cut off, you also might be cut off by your negligence. Since you were grafted in, the Jews who make the effort will be grafted in. In his great wisdom, Paul turns the whole argument toward the Gentiles, since his usual practice is to correct the weak by rebuking the strong.

(3) Augustine on verse 23

Notice that some branches were broken off and you were grafted in. Do not consider yourself greater than those broken branches but instead say to God: *How fearful are your works!* (Ps 66:3). Brothers and sisters, if we should not make ourselves greater than the Jews who were once cut away from the root of the patriarchs but rather should fear and say to God, *How fearful are your works!* how much less should we make ourselves greater than those more recently cut off? The Jews were cut off and the Gentiles grafted in; then, from this grafting, the heretics were cut out. We should not, however, make ourselves better than them, lest we ourselves merit being cut out because we enjoy insulting those cut out. Brothers and sisters, when you hear the voice of any kind of bishop, we ask you to be cautious. Those of you inside the church must not insult those who are outside; instead pray that they too may be inside. **For God has the power to graft them in again**, just as the

Apostle said about those Jews. This did happen to them. The Lord rose and many believed; they had not understood when they crucified him; but afterward they believed in him and were forgiven for that great sin. The blood of the Lord poured out was given to homicides. I will not call them deicides because, *If they had known, they would never have crucified the Lord of glory* (1 Cor 2:8). The spilled blood of the innocent one was given to those who were only homicides. Through grace they then drank the very blood which they had shed in their frenzy. Say then to God: *How fearful are your works!* (Ps 66:3). Why fearful? Because **Israel was blinded so that the fullness of the Gentiles might enter in.** O fullness of the Gentiles, say to God: *How fearful are your works!* Rejoice so that you tremble in fear. Do not mock the branches cut off. Say to God: *How fearful are your works!*

Romans 11:25-32

25**Lest you be wise in your own conceits, I want you to understand this mystery, brethren: a hardening has come upon part of Israel, until the full number of the Gentiles come in,** 26**and so all Israel will be saved; as it is written,**

> *The Deliverer will come from Zion,*
> *he will banish ungodliness from Jacob;*
> 27 *and this will be my covenant with them*
> *when I take away their sins.* (Isa 59:20-21; 27:9)

28**As regards the gospel they are enemies of God, for your sake; but as regards election they are beloved for the sake of their forefathers.** 29**For the gifts and the call of God are irrevocable.** 30**Just as you were once disobedient to God but now have received mercy because of their disobedience,** 31**so they have now been disobedient in order that by the mercy shown to you they also may receive mercy.** 32**For God has consigned all men to disobedience so that he may have mercy on all.**

(1) Augustine on verses 25-29

Paul said: **God does not regret and reverse his gifts and call.** Consider for a moment what was under consideration in this section. He had said, **Lest you be wise in your own conceits, I want you to understand this mystery, brothers: a hardening has come upon part of Israel, until the full number of the Gentiles has come in, and so all Israel will be saved; as it is written,** *The one who liberates will come from Zion, he will banish ungodliness from Jacob; and this will be my covenant with them when I take away their sins.* He then added something which requires careful attention: **As regards the gospel they are enemies, for your sake; but as regards election they are beloved for the sake of the fathers.** What could be the meaning of, **As regards the gospel they are enemies, for your sake,** except that the enmity by which they killed Christ was, as we have seen, an advantage for the gospel? This shows as well that it happened according to the divine economy, since God knows how to use even evil deeds well. This does not mean that the vessels of wrath are themselves a benefit to the gospel, but that because God used them well, they bring good to the vessels of mercy. What could be clearer than the statement: **as regards the gospel they are enemies, for your sake**? For the evil have it in their power to sin, but that their malice should bring about one result rather than another is not in their power but in the power of God, who divides the darkness and imposes order. So, even when they act against the will of God, only God's will is actually accomplished. We read in the Acts of the Apostles, *When the apostles were released by the Jews, they went to their friends and reported what the chief priests and the elders had said to them. They lifted their voices together to the Lord and said: "Lord, who are the one who made heaven and earth, and the sea, and all that is in them, who said through the mouth of our father David, your holy servant, 'Why did the Gentiles rage, and the peoples imagine vain things? The kings of the earth took their stand, and the rulers gathered together, against the Lord and against the Lord's Christ?'* (Ps 2:1-2) *For truly in this city there were gathered together against your holy servant Jesus, whom you anointed, both Herod and Pilate and the people of Israel, to do whatever your hand and plan had predestined to happen"* (Acts 4:24-28). Notice what was said, **As regards the gospel they are enemies, for your sake.** The hand and the plan of God predestined that the Jewish enemies would do those things necessary to the gospel, for our sake.

But what is the meaning of what follows: **As regards election they are beloved for the sake of the fathers**? Are the enemies elect and beloved, those who perished in their enmity, who oppose Christ, who are even now perishing from the people? By no means! Only a fool would say this. But the two characteristics, enemy and friend, although they are opposed to one another and cannot be found in the same individual, can be found in the one Jewish people, among the fleshly descendants of Israel, for some as lameness and for others as blessing, but both belonging to Israel himself. Paul made this point more clearly above when he said, *Israel failed to obtain what it sought. The elect obtained it, but the rest were blinded* (Rom 11:7). Both groups, however, are in the same Israel. When we hear, then, *Israel failed to obtain,* or, *the rest were blinded,* we must understand these as references to those **enemies for our sake**. When we hear, *the elect obtained it,* we should recognize those **beloved for the sake of the fathers**, those ancestors to whom these things were promised. *The promises were made to Abraham and his offspring* (Gal 3:16). Into this olive tree was grafted the wild olive of the Gentiles. Further, that election, which he calls according to grace rather than merit, had to be carried out, since *a remnant was made through the election of grace* (Rom 11:5). *These elect obtained it; the rest were blinded* (Rom 11:7). The Israelites **beloved for the sake of the fathers** are these elect. They were called by the vocation given to the elect, not by that of which it is said, *many are called* (Matt 22:14). For this reason, once Paul had said, **As regards election they are beloved for the sake of the fathers**, he continued, **God does not regret and withdraw his gifts and call**, that is, they are firmly established and do not change.

(2) Origen on verses 25-26

A person wise in the ways of God's graciousness does not mock those who have been rejected but gives thanks with fear for the divine mercy. This mystery is not understood by those who mock others. In the dispersion of the children of Adam, the other nations were apportioned according to the number of angels but Israel became God's own portion. I have discussed elsewhere, as well as a little earlier in this exposition (Rom 11:11-12), how the promises, the covenants, and the law were given to them. As long as the Lord's portion retained its status, we who belonged to the other nations could not enter into God's heritage and gain access to the rights of God's reign. For this reason, then, God allowed a part, that is, some but not all of the Israelites, to be blinded by a veil of envy and jealousy inflicted, no doubt, by those angels who had been allotted governance of the other nations. God allowed this to happen and decided not to block what could have been prevented. In place of those who were misled by blindness and fell into hardness of heart, God would then take the portions of the angels who had deceived them and turn them into God's own portion, thus catching the angels in their own trap. By using the attractions of sin to turn God's people toward themselves, the angels opened a place for the nations to enter into God's own heredity. God acts toward the angels with a recognized and most strict justice. During the time they held God's original people in captivity by blindness, some people taken from the nations replaced those whom the angels had led away from that nation which had originally been God's portion and separate inheritance. When the fullness from the nations has been completed and Israel has been seized by envy of their salvation, the Jews will shake off their blindness of heart and raise their eyes to gaze upon Christ, the true light. Thus, according to the earlier prophets, a provoked Israel will seek the salvation which a blinded Israel had lost, repeating the prophecy to itself, *I will return to my first husband, for it was better with me then than now* (Hos 2:7).

(3) Ambrosiaster on verses 25-28

So that you may not claim to be wiser than you are, brethren, I want you to understand this mystery: a hardening has come upon part of Israel, until the full number of the Gentiles has come in. And thus all of Israel will be saved. This passage is not obscure: those Jews who were jealous for the law were afflicted with the stupor of a temporary blindness, so that they did not see that the gift which had been promised by God had actually arrived and was being preached by Christ. In their zeal, they were blinded; they thought that the law of ritual observances should never come to an end, and thus were jealous of Sabbath observance. Because of this offense, the minds of some were dulled, so that they would be tormented for their unbelief when they saw the Gentiles joyously declare that they had received the gifts promised to Abraham. Once the mass of the Gentiles had been admitted, the mist was wiped away from the eyes of their minds, so that they could believe. God drove from their hearts the *sluggish spirit* (Rom 11:8) which had caused their blindness and restored the free choice of their wills. Because their unbelief was motivated by misunderstanding rather than malice, they could be corrected and then saved.

As it is written. He brings forward an appropriate citation from the prophet Isaiah to prove that God has held this gift in reserve for them. He teaches that the grace which freed the Israelites who already believe could free them as well. Grace is not exhausted but always overflows.

Out of Zion will come the one who will tear out and banish ungodliness from Jacob. And this is my covenant with them when I take away their sins. The meaning of this citation is always relevant, as long as some believe. It refers to the Lord Jesus, who was promised to come from heaven for the liberation of the human race. Daily, Christ forgives the sins of those who turn to God. Nor does it condemn unbelievers at once but is patient, knowing that they can make progress in knowing God.

As regards the gospel they are enemies, because of you. Because of their unbelief, they are enemies of the gospel. Their error and offense, however, opens a way through which the Gentiles enter into faith before the time of the Jews, as I have explained already. First, then, the preaching went to all the Jews; then the Gentiles were to believe the word of God. But because the Jews did not believe, the kingdom was taken from them and given to the Gentiles. Because their offense helped the Gentiles, he warns that the Jews are not to be mocked — although a sinner whose failure harmed others might be reviled. No one should deride their infidelity; rather, all should mourn their delay in converting. Thus, as the Gentiles rejoiced because the sin of the Jews brought them to salvation, they will also celebrate the Jews' conversion. The Gentiles received the grace of God earlier through the opportunity provided by the Jews.

But as regards election they are beloved because of their fathers. The Jews have sinned gravely and deserve death for rejecting the gift of God. Still, they are the descendants of good people, through whose privilege and merits they too have received many benefits from God. Thus, they will be received with gladness when they return to faith, because God's love is awakened in them by the memory of their ancestors.

(4) Cyril of Alexandria on verse 25

Look at this again and observe closely. For Paul says that the fullness of the Gentiles will enter in, and all Israel will be saved. Someone might choose to respond to this statement: "And yet, many of the Gentiles died without believing. How then has the fullness of the Gentiles entered in?" But neither will all Israel ever be saved — if it is true that the Jews will receive the man of lawlessness (2 Thess 2:8) because they had contempt for the love for Christ. For Christ himself said this: *I came in the name of my Father, and you do not receive me. If someone should come in his own name, you will receive him* (John 5:43). Paul, a truly wise man, said, *Because they did not receive the love of the truth in order to save them, on account of this, God sends them the delusion of error in order that they believe the lie* (2 Thess 2:10-11). What shall we say to this? We say that since God offers grace through faith ungrudgingly to all, and does not exclude anyone at all. How can it be said that the fullness of the Gentiles will not enter in, since indeed it reached the intention and goal of the one who had chosen them? We should not judge the word of Scripture false because some people voluntarily slipped and fell and failed to attain the gift. For although they could have had a share in the things which were given, they made for themselves a voluntary decision to the contrary. Therefore, to the extent that they reached the kindness and love for humanity of the one who called them, not only has the fullness of the Gentiles entered in, but all Israel has been saved. Some might remain unconverted and, Paul says, this part will become hard-hearted.

(5) Theodoret on verse 25

A mystery is something not known to everyone but only to those who are confident in their belief. He says therefore: **So that you may not claim to be wiser than you are, brothers, I want you to understand this mystery.** What then is the mystery? That **a hardening has come upon part of Israel, until the full number of the Gentiles has come in, and so all Israel will be saved**. He included reference to that **part**, thus showing that not all of Israel lacked faith. Many of them did believe; he urges them not to lose hope for the salvation of those others. After the Gentiles have received this proclamation, those others will have belief, when the great Elijah shall have come and brought to them the teaching of the faith. For the Lord also says in the holy Gospels: *Elijah is indeed coming and will restore all things* (Matt 17:11).

(6) Origen on verses 28-29

As regards the gospel they are enemies of God, for your sake; but as regards election they are beloved for the sake of their fathers; for the gifts are irrevocable, as the calling of God. . . . The Apostle is still considering the question of Israel and the Gentiles, particularly the wild olive branches which were mocking those branches broken off the olive tree. He makes a further point: **As regards the gospel** Israel has become an enemy of God, because it has not believed in Christ; but as regards the honoring of its ancestors, Israel is elect and beloved of God. Once the election is made and love bestowed upon the children of the ancestors, God will preserve the gifts and calling for the descendants of those whose merits originally received the gift. God does not suffer regret and become inconstant; even the benefits promised to their ancestors are actually conferred upon offspring who seem less deserving of them. The distinction frequently made has to be applied in the present passage as well. The Israel which is the enemy of God are those who cried out for Christ, *Away with him! Away with him! Crucify him!* (John 19:15). How can someone who said that then or says it now be considered anything but an enemy of God? The words, **for your sake**, refer to those whose salvation they begrudge: they forbid the apostles to speak to the nations (1 Thess 2:16) and persecute those who proclaim the Christ. The remnant are those who will be saved, whom the election of believers has chosen out of Israel. **They are beloved for the sake of their fathers**, in whose faith they follow, believing *in God, who raised Christ Jesus from the dead* (Rom 4:24). In regard to this type of offspring, **the gifts and the calling of God are irrevocable**.

(7) Augustine on verses 30-32

The statement of the Apostle, **God has consigned all to unbelief in order to have mercy on all**, was not intended to indicate that no one would be condemned. The preceding context makes Paul's meaning clear. The Apostle wrote his letters to Gentiles who had already believed; here he was speaking to them about the Jews who would come to believe only later. **Just as you once did not believe in God but now have received the mercy of their unbelief, so they too now have not believed in the mercy you have received, so that they too may obtain mercy.** Then he added, **Thus they delude themselves by going astray**, and then, **God has consigned all to unbelief in order to have mercy on all.** The "all" here refers to the groups he has been discussing, "you and them." God, therefore, has consigned to unbelief both the Gentiles and the Jews whom he has foreknown and predestined to be conformed to the image of the Son. By being joined together in repenting the bitterness of their infidelity and converted to the sweetness of God's mercy by believing, they could cry out the message of the psalm: *O how abundant is your sweetness, Lord, which you have set aside for those who fear you and wrought for those who trust,* not in themselves but, *in you!* (Ps 31:19). God, therefore, has mercy on all the vessels of mercy. What does "all" mean here? It includes those from among both the Gentiles and the Jews whom God has predestined, called, justified, glorified (Rom 8:30). God will condemn no one included among these, but he will not spare absolutely everyone.

(8) Cyril of Alexandria on verse 30

Paul shows that both faults are equal; the faults of the Greeks and Israel were healed by one grace. For Israel was called at a certain time through Moses and was freed from suffering in Egypt. But the servants of the demons, that is to say, the Gentiles represented by the Egyptians, at that time did not believe in the mercy bestowed upon Israel, for they did not believe the signs which God worked through Moses. They did not want to know the God of the Hebrews. But the Jewish people had hardly set out to offer sacrifice in the desert when they were taken captive by the ancient error. Because Israel fell away, now the Gentiles have received mercy in turn. Israel also responded by refusing to believe in the mercy bestowed upon the Gentiles. Thus Israel will again receive mercy at the proper time. So, as I said, the faults of both are equal, since they were equally in need of help from someone who would take pity on them. Paul says that God shut them all up together in unbelief, in order to have mercy on them all. Surely we do not attribute some people's lack of faith to the working of the divine will, so that they would be shown mercy only after they had fallen into disbelief. Rather, God shut them up together in unbelief in order to show both that all were guilty of the sin of unbelief, and that they could receive mercy for these very sins. So, then, they needed only to be pitied and to receive mercy; thus they all arrived at so much happiness.

(9) Ambrosiaster on verses 30-32

Just as you once disbelieved God but have now received mercy because of their distrust, so they have now been unbelievers in order that by the mercy shown to you they too may now receive mercy. Paul reminds the Gentiles of their own unbelief to make them blush and prevent their glorifying themselves. They should not mock the Jews who had not believed but rather entice them to acknowledge God's promise. "When the pronouncements of God were entrusted to the Jews," he says, "you among the Gentiles refused to accept them. Now you have been granted mercy, not because of your merits but for the purpose of dishonoring them. Why would they not be granted greater mercy when they do convert, since the promises were made to them and they had lived earlier according to the law of God?"

For God has imprisoned all in unbelief, so that he may be merciful to all. From ancient times, the Gentiles lived in impiety and ignorance, deprived of God. The law was then made manifest in writing, so that those plunging headlong into ruin could be restrained. Through the cunning of the adversary, however, sins began to mount up; the prohibition made people even more guilty. By the clemency proper to divine goodness, God always takes care of humanity. So God decided on a plan to remove all the sins committed both apart from and under the law. Since the law offered humanity no hope, God specified that all sins would be abolished through faith alone and that all might be saved through the mercy of God. This is the meaning of **having imprisoned all in unbelief**. The gift decreed by God would come when everyone was troubled and lacking confidence; the graciousness of the gift would then be all the more welcome. Let no one be arrogant, for one who has been pardoned and then turns proud is truly wretched.

(10) John Chrysostom on verses 30-32

Just as you were once disobedient to God but have now received mercy because of their disobedience, so they have now been disobedient in order that by the mercy shown to you they too may now receive mercy. For God has imprisoned all in disobedience so that he may be merciful to all. In this passage Paul shows that the Gentiles were called first. Then when they refused, the Jews were chosen; afterward, the same thing happened again. Since the Jews refused to believe, the Gentiles were brought back in again. But it did not stop there; God did not end the process with the rejection of the Jews. Rather, God extends it to include showing mercy to the Jews as well. See how much God gives to the Gentiles: just as much as had been given to the Jews in the past. For when the Gentiles disobeyed in the past, Paul says, the Jews came in. When the Jews disobeyed in their turn, the Gentiles came in. They will certainly not perish forever. **For God has imprisoned all in disobedience**, that is to say, God has convicted them. God has demonstrated that they disobeyed, not to make them remain disobedient, but to save one group through the contentiousness of the other: the Jews through the Gentiles, and the Gentiles through the Jews. Reflect on this: the Gentiles were disobedient and the Jews were saved. Then the Jews were disobedient and the Gentiles were saved. The Gentiles were not saved so that they would then go out again, like the Jews had, but so that by remaining inside, they would draw the Jews back in through jealousy.

(11) Theodoret on verse 32

He said God **imprisoned all** rather than "God reproached all." God reproached the Gentiles who had accepted a natural interpretation of things and believed that created

Romans 11

matter is the principal source for knowledge of God, so that they profited from neither God nor creation. And God reproached the Jews, who had received the fullness of doctrine. For in addition to nature and creation, they also received the Law and the Prophets to instruct them in what was necessary. Thus, they were subjected to greater punishments. Though both Gentiles and Jews deserved to be completely destroyed, God would judge them worthy of salvation if only they chose to have faith.

Romans 11:33-36

33 O the depth of the riches and wisdom and knowledge of God! How unsearchable are his judgments and how inscrutable his ways!

> 34 *For who has known the mind of the* LORD,
> *or who has been his counselor?* (Isa 40:13)

> 35 *Or who has given a gift to him*
> *That he might be repaid?* (Job 35:7; 41:11)

36 For from him and through him and to him are all things. To him be the glory for ever. Amen.

(1) Ambrosiaster on verses 33-36

O the depth of the riches and wisdom and knowledge of God! How unsearchable are God's judgments and how inscrutable God's ways! With all praise and thanksgiving, Paul confesses God's eminence and immensity in the riches of divine wisdom and knowledge; God's plan and judgment are beyond comprehension. From the beginning, God has known the habits and deeds of humans and has understood that the human race can neither be saved by the severity of justice alone nor attain full dignity by mercy alone. After first allowing each person to follow individual judgment and come to know righteousness under the guidance of nature itself, God has decided what ought to be preached in each particular age. Because the habit of sinning had paralyzed the natural capacity for righteousness, the law was given so that its presence would frighten and restrain the human race. Because people did not control themselves and were held guilty by the law, a mercy was proclaimed which would save those who took refuge in it and temporarily blind those who rejected it. This divine mercy would also invite the Gentiles, who had earlier refused to follow God's righteousness as set forth through Moses, to enter into the promises of those who did. When that people living under Mosaic law begrudged salvation for the Gentiles, they too would be moved by their jealousy to restore themselves to their origin in the root of the Savior. This is **the depth of the riches of the wisdom and the knowledge of God**, whose different ways of governing have brought so many to life, both Jews and Gentiles.

For who has known the mind of the LORD, *or who has been the* LORD'S *counselor?*

Or who has first given a gift to him to receive a gift in return? This is found written in Isaiah (Isa 40:13). Obviously, God alone possesses all counsel and alone needs nothing, because all things come from God. For this reason, God's plan can be neither comprehended nor judged by anyone else, since the lower mind cannot contain the higher. Consequently, Jewish believers thought it impossible that God's plan and will was for the redemption of the Gentiles. Likewise, the Gentiles judged it improbable and incredible that Jews who had not believed could be converted or, if they did believe, would be accepted for salvation. This, among other things, is the plan of God which was hidden and could not be understood.

For from him and through him and in him are all things. To him be the glory forever. Amen. Paul made clear why the mind and counsel of God cannot be investigated. He says, **For from him and through him and in him are all things. To him be the glory.** By saying this, he revealed a meaning hidden to the world. Since God is the creator of all things, **all things are from God.** Since all come from God, they came into being through God's Son, who is of the same substance and whose work is the same as the Father's works. Because God acts through the Son, **all things are through God.** Then, since the things which are **from God** and **through God** are in the Holy Spirit once they are reborn, **all things are in God.** Because the Holy Spirit is from God the Father, the Spirit knows the things which are in God. Therefore the Father is also in the Holy Spirit. What is from God the Father cannot be different from what God the Father is. Thus, **to him be glory** because **all things are from him and through him and in him.** Therefore, the things which came into being and have their being **from him and through him and in him** cannot know his mind and counsel. He knows all things, because **all things are in him**. Paul has revealed the mystery of God which, as he said above, he *wanted them to understand* (Rom 11:25).

(2) Augustine on verses 33-36

How unsearchable are God's judgments! You have heard it, let that be enough for you. **How inscrutable God's ways!** *For who has known the mind of the Lord, or who has been his counselor? Or who has given a gift to God and is owed a repayment?* Who first gave to God, since everything has been received freely? **Or who has first given a gift to God and is owed a repayment?** If the Lord wanted to repay anyone, what could that be other than the punishment due? They did not give anything, that a gift should be given to them in return. *You save them without cost* (Ps 55:8 Vg). **Who has first given to God,** as though from the gift of their own merits? **Who has first given to God**; who has anticipated that grace which is given freely? If any merits precede grace, then grace is repaid as due, not freely given. If it is not freely given, however, why is it called grace? **Who has first given to God and then been repaid? For from him and through him and in him are all things.** What things, if not all the good things that we receive from God, including our being good? *Every good endowment and every perfect gift is from above, coming down from the Father of lights who is free from all change* (Jas 1:17). You have changed for the worse; yet the one *who is free of all change* supports you. God is free from even a moment of darkness, but you lie in the darkness of your own night. All things come from God. No one has given God anything first; no one collects a debt from God. *By grace you have been saved through faith; and this is not your own doing, it is the gift of God* (Eph 2:8).

(3) Augustine on verse 33

We are not surprised that you[3] are unable to investigate God's unsearchable ways. Let us pass over in silence the innumerable things which are given to some people and not to others by the Lord God, *who never respects persons* (Rom 2:11), things which cannot be attributed to the merits of their wills: such as quickness, strength, good health, bodily beauty, wonderful dispositions, and the natural talents of minds for a multitude of arts, or even the things which are external to a person, such as riches, social status, honors, and other things like this. Certainly that a person may have any of these lies only within God's power. . . .

Consider the Baptism of infants, who surely do not already belong to the kingdom of God — as the Pelagians would have it. Why is Baptism provided to one infant and not to another? To receive and not to receive it are both in God's discretion; yet no one will enter into the kingdom of God without that sacrament. But to leave these matters aside, let us focus on the things which are under consideration here. We are concerned with those people who do not persevere in good, who die after falling from good into evil by the failure of their good will. Let our opponents explain, if they can, why during that time when they were still living faithfully and piously, God did not snatch them away from the dangers of this life, *lest evil change their understanding or guile deceive their souls* (Wis 4:11). Did God not have power to do this? Did God not know the evils ahead? Only the most perverse or stupid people would assert either of these. Why, then, did God not do it? Let them answer, those people who laugh at us when we are faced with such questions and can reply only by exclaiming: **How unsearchable are his judgments and how inscrutable his ways!** Nor is it the case that God does not grant such a gift to those God chooses, unless the scripture is lying when it describes the early death of a righteous person: *He was caught up lest evil change his understanding or guile deceive his soul* (Wis 4:11). God acts neither with malice nor with partiality, and God has the power to determine how long any person remains in this life, which is a trial upon earth. Why does God grant such a great favor to some people and not to others? Our opponents are thus forced to acknowledge that for a person to end this life before turning from good to evil is actually a gift of God. Yet they do not know why God gives this gift to some and not to others. So they should confess with us that according to the Scriptures, which I have already cited extensively, perseverance in good is a gift of God. Why this gift is given to some and not to others, they should join us in admitting that they do not understand but without complaining against God.

---

3. Augustine wrote this letter to the monks at Hadrumetum, a city about seventy miles south of Carthage, on the eastern coast of modern Tunisia.

(4) Origen on verses 35-36

Next he uncovers the deep and hidden reasons for their own unbelief and explains it to them. You among the nations once did not believe in God, and yet God did not completely abandon you. In this final age you have obtained mercy because the unbelief of the people of Israel provided an occasion for mercy to be extended to you. In the same way, those of the people of Israel who do not now believe and have been left in their unbelief so that the mercy of God could be directed to you, will not be abandoned to their unbelief forever. Once the divine governance has completed the fullness of the nations, even the Israelites will obtain mercy. The Apostle wanted to display the mercy of God at work in the process by which the unbelief of some brought salvation to others. **For God has imprisoned all in disobedience**, he said, **so that God may be merciful to all**. God did not force them into unbelief; but through their own decision not to believe, God provide an opportunity for others who had themselves been unbelievers. . . .

The holy Apostle reflects on the great richness of the divine goodness and the great workings of the divine wisdom with rational natures, and how rich in mercy God is, and how generous to all who call upon God, and how wonderful are the riches of the divine goodness, patience, and forbearance. He suddenly sees them with the inner eyes of his heart and perceives their immense grandeur; then, struck by fear and wonder, he cries out, **O the depth of the riches and wisdom and knowledge of God! How unsearchable are God's judgments and how inscrutable God's ways!** How could the human mind conceive such a plan? Everyone's free choice is preserved, yet the evil deed of one promotes the salvation of another; the same malice brings destruction to those who succumb to it and the palm of victory to those who overcome it.

Once the Apostle has grasped this general pattern, he cries out and exclaims that the depth of God's riches and the depth of God's wisdom and the depth of God's knowledge — depth refers to all of these attributes — is so great that no one can search the judgments by which God governs each soul and the whole rational creation. Nor can anyone examine the ways by which God's providence proceeds.

Romans 12

In this chapter, Paul turns from the meditation on the status of Israel to life within the Christian community: making an offering of self to God, the distribution of spiritual gifts, and resolving conflicts within the local church. Origen and Ambrosiaster note differences between the Greek and Latin texts at 12:11 and 12:13, but each finds an interpretation for either version. The commentators differ in considering the distribution of spiritual gifts: Origen, Ambrosiaster, and Theodoret explain that the faith of each person is a basis for the gift each receives; Chrysostom and Augustine refuse to recognize personal merits as determinative of God's choices. Each of the commentators was concerned about Paul's exhortation to treat enemies generously in order to "bring down coals of fire" on their heads; they insisted that one should not do good in order to increase another's punishment. Similarly, Augustine worked to resolve an apparent discrepancy between Paul's exhortation to bless but not curse and the behavior of both Christ and the prophets, who seemed to have called down evil on others.

Romans 12:1-2

1 I appeal to you therefore, brethren, by the mercies of God, to present your bodies as a living sacrifice, holy and acceptable to God, which is your spiritual worship. 2 Do not be conformed to this world but be transformed by the renewal of your mind, that you may prove what is the will of God, what is good and acceptable and perfect.

(1) Origen on verses 1-2

What, then, are you urged to do? **To present your bodies as a living sacrifice, holy and acceptable to God, so that it might be your reasonable service.** He calls this service the worship of God. Earlier, divine worship had consisted in offering the bodies of irrational animals, but he says that worship is now offered in the bodies of reasonable humans: your bodies, rather than those of cattle, become the sacrifice to God and are placed on the holy altars. Those, then, who eradicate the tendencies to lust and rage from their bodily members and who make their bodily actions pleasing to God spiritually **present a**

living sacrifice, holy and acceptable to God. According to a spiritual understanding, they fulfill the sacrificial law which was laid down in Leviticus. Thus, for example, following that law they might have offered first a calf or second a ram or third a goat or fourth turtledoves or even young doves, so that through each of these their souls might have been purified from a different kind of action. Now, by purifying their bodies and understanding these things according to their spiritual meaning, they offered **a living sacrifice to God by a reasonable service**. . . .

Paul appeals to those who believe in Christ **to present their bodies as a living sacrifice, holy and acceptable to God**. He calls **a living sacrifice** one that carries in itself life, that is, Christ. Thus he says: *carrying in our body the death of Jesus, so that the life of Jesus may also be manifest in our body* (2 Cor 4:10). That body in which the Holy Spirit dwells is called holy, as he says elsewhere: *Do you not know that you are God's temple and that God's Spirit dwells in you?* (1 Cor 3:16). The sacrifice pleases God because it has been purified of sins and vices. All this is the reasonable worship of God; a person could provide a reason for such worship and show that offering such victims is worthy of God. No right and true understanding would offer rams, goats, and calves to the immortal and incorporeal God. . . .

A living sacrifice, holy and acceptable to God, would appear then to mean a body free of impurity. Since, however, we observe that a good number of saints and even some of the apostles had wives, we cannot define this purity simply in terms of virginity, although virgins might hold the first rank in this type of sacrifice. In the law, some sacrifices were specified for the priests, others for the rulers, others for the assembly of the people, and others for individual souls (Leviticus 4). Now in the Church, the sacrifice of the martyrs follows immediately after that of the apostles, then the virgins, and after them all those who have renounced sexual practice. My opinion, however, is that even those who live in the married state and by mutual consent abstain for a time for the sake of prayer, fulfilling their vows like the Nazarites, cannot be denied **to present their bodies as a living sacrifice, holy and acceptable to God**, as long as they otherwise behave in a just and holy way. Nor, in contrast, can the bodies of the virgins and the continent be considered **a sacrifice holy and acceptable to God** solely because of their bodily virginity, if they are polluted by the blemishes of pride, the dirt of avarice, or the uncleanness of lying and cursing. According to the law, the victim to be offered in sacrifice had to be examined carefully by the priest not only to determine that it was among the clean animals but to be sure that it had no defect in its eyes or ears or feet. No lame, blind, or blemished animal could be brought to the divine altar. . . .

Notice that the Apostle adds renewing of the mind to what he had already said: **that you may prove what is the will of God, what is good and acceptable and perfect**. Certainly, unless the mind is renewed in all knowledge and illumined by the full wisdom of God, it cannot discern the will of God. In many instances, what is thought to be the will of God in truth is not. The person whose mind is not renewed will then be mistaken and err in this. To determine what is the will of God in each individual thing we do, say, or think belongs not just to any mind but to one completely renewed, so that it has been reformed according to the image of God. Such a mind does, says, or thinks only what it judges is according to the will of God.

(2) Ambrosiaster on verses 1-2

This passage is a reminder to them, that they not forget they have received mercy, and that they be diligent in obedience to the one who bestowed that mercy, through which they were gratuitously purified from impiety. They should know that the living sacrifice, holy and acceptable to God, is to preserve our bodies in purity, unlike the unbelievers who cultivate pleasure. *This is the will of God, our sanctification* (1 Thess 4:3). Bodies subject to sin are considered not living but dead and without hope for the promised life. Sins are cleansed by the gift of God so that by living a pure life afterward we may win God's love for ourselves, and the work of grace does not remain fruitless in us. In earlier times, animals offered in sacrifice were killed to signify that humans were subject to death because of sin. Now, however, because humans have been purified by the gift of God and set free from the second death, they should offer a living sacrifice, one that may be a sign of eternal life. Then, bodies were immolated in place of other bodies; now, however, not the bodies themselves but their vices should be killed.

(3) Augustine on verses 1-2

A true sacrifice is any action by which we attempt to cling to God in a holy bond; its objective is that fullness of goodness by which we are truly blessed. Thus even the mercy by which we help another person is a sacrifice only if we do it for the sake of God. Though a sacrifice is performed or offered by a human being, it belongs to the divine realm — indeed, the old Latins called it a "divine reality." For this reason those people who are consecrated to the divine name and dedicated to God are themselves sacrifices, because they die to the world in order to live to God. This dedication is an act of mercy which they bestow on themselves. For this reason, it is written, *Have mercy on your soul and be pleasing to God* (Sir 30:24 Vg). It is a sacrifice when we correct our bodies by temperance and do this for God's sake, as we should, so that we do not *yield our members to sin as instruments of wickedness but to God as instruments of righteousness* (Rom 6:13). In urging us to this, the Apostle said: **I appeal to you therefore, brothers, through the mercies of God, to present your bodies as a living sacrifice, holy and acceptable to God, which is your rational worship**. If the body, which the soul uses as a servant or tool, is a sacrifice when it is used properly and well by being directed toward God, then how much more does the soul itself become a sacrifice when it directs itself toward God, when it is inflamed by the fire of love for God, casts off the appearances dictated by the values of the present age, is reformed by an unchanging disposition of submission to God, and pleases God by sharing the divine beauty. The Apostle says just this: **Do not be conformed to this age but be reformed by the renewal of your mind, that you may show in yourselves what is the will of God, what is good and well pleasing and perfect**. True sacrifices are works of mercy, either for ourselves or our neighbors, which are directed toward God. The whole purpose of works of mercy is to free ourselves from suffering and gain happiness, which can be attained only by that good of which it is said, *for me it is good to cling to God* (Ps 73:28). This whole redeemed city, which is the assembly and association of the saints, is offered to God as a universal sacrifice by that great priest who also offered himself for us in his passion, so that we might be the body of such a head, in his servant form. He offered this servant form and was offered in it, because in this form he is the mediator, the priest, and the sacrifice.

(4) John Chrysostom on verses 1-2

Someone may say, "How should the body be a sacrifice?" Prevent your eye from looking at something evil; it has become a sacrifice. Do not let the tongue say something shameful; it has become an offering. Do not let the hand perform a lawless action; it has become a whole burnt offering. Yet these things are not enough; we must also perform good works: let the hand give alms, let the mouth bless those who abuse, let the hearing devote itself continuously to listening to divine speech. For sacrifice has nothing impure about it; sacrifice is the firstfruits of all other actions. Let us then make a sacrifice to God of the firstfruits of our hands, feet, mouth, and all the other members of our body.

Since your body is going to be presented to the King of all as a sacrifice, cleanse it of every stain; if it had a spot, it would no longer be a sacrifice. For an eye cannot be sacrificed if it looks at lewd things; a grasping and greedy hand cannot be offered, nor a foot which limps and goes to the theater, nor a stomach enslaved to food which kindles the desire for pleasure, nor a heart filled with anger and lascivious lust, nor a tongue which speaks shameful things. We have to search out the stains all over our body.

Those who offered sacrifice in ancient times were commanded to examine everything very carefully. They were not permitted to offer any animal that had its ears cut off, or a maimed tail, or scabs, or sores. So much the more must we, who do not offer irrational animals but our very selves, exercise great care and be pure in every respect. Thus we too might say, as Paul did, *For I am already poured out as a libation, and the time of my release is at hand* (2 Tim 4:6). He called himself a libation because he was purer than any sacrifice. We will be the same if we strip off the old self, if we kill our members on earth, if we crucify the world to ourselves. Thus we will have no further need of a knife, an altar, or fire. We will need all these things, but not the ones made by hands; the ones we need will come to us from above. The fire will come from above; the fire and the altar will be the breath of heaven. When Elijah offered his visible sacrifice, the flame came down from above and consumed everything it contained — the water, the wood, and the stone. This will happen even more fully to you. If you have anything fleeting and worldly about yourself, when you bring it as a sacrifice with a proper intention, the fire of the Holy Spirit will come down upon and consume that worldly thing; it will perfect the whole offering.

Paul means either, "Be renewed in order to learn what things are profitable and what the will of God is," or "You can be renewed, if you learn what things are profitable and what God wills." For if you understand this and distinguish the natures of things, you have attained the whole meaning of virtue. "Who does not know the things that are profitable," someone may say, "and what the will of God is?" The answer is: those who covet the things of this present life, those who think that riches ought to be desired and poverty disdained, those who pursue power, those who seek praise from others, those who consider themselves great because they build magnificent houses and buy expensive tombs, have a herd of slaves, and go around with a great swarm of eunuchs. For such people are ignorant about what is profitable for them and about the will of God — which are one and the same. For God wills what is profitable for us, and whatever God wills is profitable for us.

For this reason we must above all have right judgment about things. We should praise virtue, even if we do not seek it. Even if we do not flee from evil, we should still reproach evil, so that for the present we at least have an uncorrupted judgment. This way we advance on the road and will eventually be able also to accomplish the good works themselves. Finally, for this reason also Paul commands that you be renewed, "so that you test what is the will of God."

(5) Theodoret on verse 2

And do not conform yourselves to this age. Paul uses the term *appearance* to designate the affairs of the present age, such as wealth, authority, and other forms of fame. He calls **reality** the things that are future, that are stable and lasting. Thus he says elsewhere: *For the appearance of this world is passing away* (Rom 6:13). Many people fall from the heights of abundance into abject poverty. Some born in poverty are entrusted with the highest offices. Others arch their eyebrows, puff out their cheeks, and assume that they are better than everyone else; then they are suddenly snatched away and turned into odorous dust. The divine Apostle wishes, therefore, that we should not be awed by these things, that we should not love the appearances of this life, but that we should pursue things which secure eternal life.

But be transformed by the renewal of your mind, in order for you to test what is the good, well-pleasing, and perfect will of God. Paul exhorts those who incline toward bad things to ascend instead to better things. This is what he means by **be transformed**. He was also teaching how attachment to present things differs from virtue. For he called those things *appearance* and virtue *form*. The form of true things is meaningful, but false appearances are easily destroyed.

Romans 12:3-8

3**For by the grace given to me I bid every one among you not to think of himself more highly than he ought to think, but to think with sober judgment, each according to the measure of faith that God has assigned him.** 4**For as in one body we have many members, and all the members do not have the same function,** 5**so we, though many, are one body in Christ, and individually members one of another.** 6**Having gifts that differ according to the grace given to us, let us use them: if prophecy, in proportion to our faith;** 7**if service, in our serving; he who teaches, in his teaching;** 8**he who exhorts, in his exhortation; he who contributes, in liberality; he who gives aid, with zeal; he who does acts of mercy, with cheerfulness.**

(1) **Origen on verses 3-8**

One should note that here Paul, as elsewhere, is speaking through the gift bestowed upon him rather than in the persuasive words of carnal wisdom. A great difference separates speaking through grace from drawing on human wisdom. Experience frequently confirms that eloquent and learned men who excel in both understanding and rhetoric make presentations in the church that are received with ringing applause; yet the hearts of none of their hearers are struck by the things they say; they are not moved to progress in either faith or fear of God by recalling what had been said. They take away only a sweetness and delight in their ears. In contrast, people of little or no eloquence, who do not labor over their presentations, still convert many unbelievers to faith; by their simple and unadorned speech, they attract the proud to humility and goad sinners to conversion. This is certainly a sign that the preacher is speaking **by the grace which was given to him**, as the Apostle says in this passage. I think, moreover, that this grace is operative in all aspects of life, not just in those who instruct the Church in the word of God — if their speech moves rather than only delights the hearer and so leads to progress in virtue. Some people have a grace in what they say and do; others speak with greater care or act with greater diligence and labor but then find grace in neither the things said nor those done. . . .

To make these points stand out more clearly, the Apostle offers an example: **For as in one body we have many members, and not all the members have the same activity, so we, who are many, are one body in Christ, and individually we are members one of another**. Through this observation, he joins together in an ordered way the whole body of the Church. Each member of the body has a proper role and each devotes himself to his function, and they cannot fail to cooperate with one another in mutual accord. So he says that in the Church which is the body of Christ, we individually have different roles. For example: one person is zealous for God's wisdom, attends to the teaching of the Word, and continues night and day in meditation on the divine law; such a person is an eye of this great body. Another is devoted to caring for the members of the community and the poor; a hand of this holy body. Another is a diligent hearer of the Word of God; an ear of the body. Another is active in tending to the sick, searching for the afflicted, and rescuing those in danger; that person would be called a foot of the Church's body. Thus you will find that each one is occupied in one office or another; each performs some one task in particular while others have different roles.

We are not implying that a particular duty is the sole concern of one person but are elaborating on the point of the example. So, the eye has the special role of seeing, but it is one among many members; it collaborates with the other members, and they in turn act with it. So whoever has gained a special gift through the grace of faith is principally concerned with it but shares in all the activities of the body; each one is associated and participates with all the others. We have already explained many times how this body is in Christ, that it has the truth, wisdom, justice, and holiness which are proper to Christ. Now, someone might be an eye, for example, which is the most noble organ in the whole body, or a hand, which holds the next place, or an ear or tongue or some other of the honored members; or someone might be one of the bodily parts considered less honorable. I believe that we cannot understand whether these members individually did something which has resulted in their having one or another role in the body or whether God assigned the tasks without any prior cause. . . .

We have gifts that differ according to the grace given to us; prophecy, in proportion to faith; ministry, in ministering; the one who teaches, in teaching; the one who exhorts, in exhortation; the giver, in simplicity; the leader, in solicitude; the compassionate, in cheerfulness. Having said that each of the believers is a member of the one body of Christ, Paul now enumerates the diverse roles of the various members. As, for example, he attributed seeing to the eye, he assigns the role of prophecy to the mind, which is the interior eye; he ascribes ministry to another, like a hand; he grants teaching to another, like a tongue; and so with each of the others. He clarifies here that point which was unclear to us earlier: whether persons were assigned a more or less honorable station in the body because of some cause they had given or whether they were given these honorable or less than honorable tasks by the will of God alone, and not for any prior cause. . . .

He asserts that the diversities of graces are assigned according to the measure of each one's faith. Thus a person becomes this or that member of the body of Christ by receiving a grace, and he sets down the measure of faith as the reason for obtaining particular graces. Writing to the Corinthians, he says: *To each is given the manifestation of the Spirit as is useful* (1 Cor 12:7), and a little later he adds, *All these are activated by one and the same Spirit, who allots to each one individually just as the Spirit chooses* (1 Cor 12:11). Thus in writing to both the Romans and the Corinthians, he appears to teach three ways of receiving grace, showing that we do earn something for ourselves but that the office comes primarily through the largess of God. He specifies that a person receives grace through the measure of faith, that gifts are given that will be useful, and that the Spirit allots offices as the Spirit chooses. . . .

At this point, the question arises whether any type of prophecy can be obtained to some extent by human effort and does not come completely from God. Some consider this completely impossible, but Paul exhorts: *Strive for the greater gifts* (1 Cor 12:31), *and especially that you may prophesy* (1 Cor 14:1). In this passage, as one strives for the gifts of ministry, teaching, and exhortation, and the others by expending effort and working for them, so the Apostle shows that they should also work for prophecy. Thus the prophecy to which Paul refers here should not be understood as that by which a person says, *Thus says the Lord* (e.g., Jer 26:2). This type of prophecy continued only up until John, as it is written in the Gospel, *The law and the prophets were in effect until John came* (Luke 16:16). The form of prophecy which can now be attained is rather that to which the Apostle refers in saying, *those who prophesy speak to other people for their upbuilding and encouragement and consolation* (1 Cor 14:3). Thus to seek this kind of prophecy is possible for us. We can labor with such a standard or measure of faith that even the other form of prophecy — which is from God — might also be given to us. According to the Apostle, there is yet another kind of prophecy: *If you prophesy, an unbeliever or outsider who enters is reproved by all and called to account by all. After the secrets of the unbeliever's heart are disclosed, that person will bow down and declare that God is truly among you* (1 Cor 14:24-25).

As the Spirit of God examines all things, so also the Word of God scrutinizes all that is hidden, especially *since the Word is living and active, sharper than any two-edged sword, piercing until it divides soul from spirit, joints from marrow* (Heb 4:12). When a moral exhortation is given in the church, all are prodded by their consciences by what is being said; they are moved to recognize their own sins and remember any committed in secret. Sometimes the shrewdness of the wise, which makes inferences from expressions, gestures, and actions, is like a form of prophecy. This is what we have to say about the gift of prophecy. . . .

The one who exhorts, in exhortation. Exhortation is a type of teaching by which afflicted souls are comforted by discourses in which texts from the divine Scriptures are prudently selected and gathered together for them. A kind of despair often comes upon the soul because of the immensity of its troubles; it cannot be renewed and restored by just any words, no matter how polished and appealing. A sermon filled with the power of God's grace will penetrate the heart and bring consolation and hope; it will draw the soul back from the despair which overcame it, as the Lord said through the prophet: *Priests, speak to the heart of Jerusalem* (Isa 40:2).

The one who gives, in simplicity. He says that those who provide for the needy should act in simplicity of heart. In their hearts they should not be seeking human praise when they appear to be assisting the poor. Simplicity is not found where the hands seem to be doing one thing while the heart seeks another. The one who is in charge of the brethren or is the head of the church should be concerned not with human issues or worldly matters — this kind of solicitude should be alien to those who are leaders of the church. Instead, they should undertake that concern which the Apostle describes, *Solicitude for all the churches rushes upon me every day. Who is weak, and I am not weak? Who is hindered, and I am not outraged?* (2 Cor 11:28-29).

The one who is merciful, in cheerfulness. The giver, in simplicity, might seem to mean the same as **the compassionate, in cheerfulness**. I think that the work itself might be the same but not the disposition involved. To give to the needy is not the same as sharing the affection of mercy with the one in need: Paul wants sadness to have no place in that work. A non-believer who distributes money has no hope of receiving a return and as a result grieves the loss. But the person who gives with faith and hope acts in cheerfulness and joy, certain that what little was paid out here on earth to fulfill God's command will return great wealth in heavenly riches and eternal life besides.

(2) Ambrosiaster on verse 3

For by the grace given to me I bid every one among you not to think of yourself more highly than you ought to think, but to think with sober judgment, each according to the measure of faith that God has assigned. Paul is clearly teaching that we should exercise a wisdom that does not transgress the bounds of justice, so that it will both profit us and not harm others. For prudence consists in helping rather than hindering others and in being satisfied with our role, which God has measured out according to each one's merit and faith, and in not claiming for oneself what has not been granted. This is **not to think of yourself more highly**, because everything cannot be assigned to any one person.

A person who lives a good life does not thereby have the right to claim the wisdom which belongs to teaching, nor should one versed in the law expect to be accorded the deference proper to the clergy. Paul exhorts and teaches, therefore, **by the grace given to him**. This grace is understood as skill in the divine discipline, through which he asserts that each must strive for humility and justice.

For as in one body we have many members, and all the members do not have the same role, so we, though many, are one body in Christ, and individually members one of another. By using the example of the body, he shows that we cannot each have everything; because we are members of one another, we must depend on one another. For this reason we should exercise care for one another and not hinder each other, because we each benefit from the functions which others perform. Loving Christ, then, will mean that the members exhort one another to fulfill the roles by which the body of Christ is made perfect.

We have gifts that differ according to the grace given to us. Now he begins to enumerate the roles which are assigned to the members according to the merit of faith. Each member must discern the function assigned to it and not compete with another member, to whom a different office is given, but rejoice with it. Thus will the body of the church be perfected.

If prophecy, in proportion to our faith. He begins with prophecy, which is the first proof that we have good reason to believe, since believers used to prophesy when they received the Holy Spirit. This is given in the way appropriate to the receiver, adapted to the purpose for which it is bestowed.

If ministry, in ministering. This is given to strengthen the minister, to provide that service to the church which each believes should be offered. No one should work at an office which is beyond the power of that individual's faith; this would result in the person's wearing out and then failing. A person succeeds by working from the heart.

The one who teaches, in teaching. Likewise, he says that the teacher is aided in teaching, so that as that person's faith is dedicated to teaching, the teacher will pass along the heavenly discipline.

The one who exhorts, in exhortation. In the same way, the exhorter makes the effort and is prepared by the help of the Spirit to act with grace in making appeals, so that the believers are urged to good and the unbelievers to faith.

The one who gives, in simplicity. Here Paul says that one who gives with a good heart will always be supported by the care of the Spirit and that one who gives generously will never be in want, as Solomon says, *Whoever gives to the poor will lack nothing* (Prov 28:27). One who gives generously does so not as a pretense for winning human praise but to gain merit from God for the action.

The one in charge, in solicitude. The one who accepts the responsibility of leading the community receives vigilance and authority, in the measure of faith, to be successful in the undertaking and produce fruit in those who are governed.

The one who is merciful, in cheerfulness. According to Paul's understanding, the one who shows mercy from a joyful heart — not having it wrung out of an unwilling heart — is supported and strengthened by God, and suffers no weakness in this work, remembering what Solomon said, *When you have the opportunity, do good* (Prov

3:27). But this statement can be understood in different ways. Since he had already said above, **the giver, in simplicity**, why did he repeat it, unless he intended to indicate different good works by the one term, **mercy**. Acts of mercy take many forms: to forgive sinners, to supply someone caught in need or oppressed, to clothe the naked, to break bread for the hungry, to take in exposed infants, to bury a body, and other such works. Thus a person who does these things energetically and tirelessly has this work in the present and a reward in the future. All acts of mercy should be performed in both generosity and joy: generosity prevents hypocrisy; joy trusts in future hope and bears witness to the judgment.

(3) John Chrysostom on verse 3

Since the distribution of divine gifts upset many people among both the Romans and the Corinthians, Paul clarifies the cause of this sickness and removes every trace of it. After he said that we must think soberly, he added, **To each person as God has distributed the measure of faith**, to indicate that faith is itself among the divine gifts of good things. By saying, "distributed," he consoled the person who received less and humbled the person who enjoyed more. For if God distributed the gifts and they are not your accomplishment, why are you proud?

If someone should argue that the faith mentioned in this passage is not called a divine gift, that would show even more clearly that Paul was humbling proud boasters. If the cause of the divine gift is faith, through which miracles occur, and these wonders are from God, then what is the basis for your pride? For if God had not come and taken on flesh, then faith would not have amounted to much. All blessings have their origin in this mystery. If God gives good things, then God knows how to distribute them. And if God created all people, then God likewise cares for all people. Just as God's giving flows from divine love for humanity, so too the amount that God gives to each comes from that same love. Having demonstrated generosity by bestowing divine gifts, God would not then cheat you in determining the measure of that gift. If the objective was to dishonor you, God would not have given you anything in the first place.

(4) Augustine on verses 3-5

This passage makes clear that none are righteous by their own justice, as though they made themselves righteous, but, as the Apostle says, **according to the measure of faith which God has granted to each**. He then continues: **For as in one body we have many members, and all the members do not have the same activity, so we, though many, are one body in Christ**. Because of this, no one can be righteous in separation from the unity of this body. If a member is severed from the body of a living person, it cannot retain the spirit of life. So persons cut off from the righteous body of Christ simply cannot retain the Spirit of righteousness, even if they keep that appearance of a member which they had acquired in the body.

(5) Theodoret on verse 3

Paul says, **for I say through the grace which was given to me, not to know more than I ought to know, but to know for self-control**. He does not say these things simply to lay down a law, but that through them he might share the grace of the Spirit. For, he says, I am an instrument of that grace. He called the mind's health **self-control**, thereby teaching that pride is a sickness of mind. Indeed, he emulated his own Master. For the Lord in the sacred Gospels declared those who have acquired humility first among the blessed. *For blessed,* Christ says, *are the poor in spirit, because theirs is the kingdom of heaven* (Matt 5:3). He lays these things down as a law for everyone, both for the sick and for the poor, for slaves and for masters, for men and for women. This is what he means by **for each among you**. He also sets a limit to proud thoughts.

For each person as God has appointed a measure of faith. Paul called grace "faith," because the gifts of grace comes from faith, and are supplied according to the measure of faith. He directs us to measure the self-regard of the soul by the grace given.

(6) John Chrysostom on verses 4-5

Paul made two statements designed to suppress their madness: that we are all one body and members of one another; not just that the humble person is a member of the great person, but that the greatest person is a member of the least. Actually he makes three statements, because he also displayed that one divine gift which was given. **Do not think great thoughts**, then, "for the gift was given to you by God. You did not take it, nor did you find it." For this reason, when he discusses the divine gifts, he did not say, "One received more, another less." What did he say? **Different**, he said, **having the divine gifts**; not more or less, but different. What does it matter if you do not exercise the same office, as long as the body remains the same? He begins from a divine gift and ends with good deeds. He talks about prophecy, service, and such things; he concludes with mercy, hope, and help. Since some were probably virtuous but did not have prophecy, Paul values that divine gift as much greater than the others, just as he insisted in his letter to the Corinthians (1 Cor 13:1-3). He also shows that it is greater because love has a reward, while the others have no recompense. For the whole is a gift and grace.

(7) Theodoret on verse 7

Whether prophecy according to the proportion of faith, or ministry in ministry, or the one who teaches in teaching, or the one who exhorts in exhortation. The one who supplies good things measures grace according to the faith of each person. Paul calls **prophecy** not only the foreknowledge of things to come, but the knowledge of hidden things. He calls the service of preaching **ministry**. He calls the learning of divine doctrines **teaching**. He calls the persuasion to virtue **exhortation**.

The one who is handing over in simplicity. Not the one pursuing praise from others, but the one who supplies those in need; not the one who indulges in calculating whether his possessions are sufficient for him or not, but the one who has confidence in God; this is the one who eagerly provides for others.

(8) John Chrysostom on verse 8

It is not enough to be merciful; we must be merciful with liberality and free of anxiety. Indeed, we must do it not only without pain, but even with a cheerful and joyful attitude. For to rejoice is not the same as not to suffer. Paul wrote this same thing to the Corinthians, and he insisted on it very earnestly. In order to inspire them to generosity, he said, *Whoever sows sparingly will also reap sparingly. Whoever sows bountifully will reap bountifully* (2 Cor 9:6). He amended this opinion and added, *Not with sorrow or from necessity* (2 Cor 9:7), for someone who is merciful must be free from envy and pleasure. Why do you cry when you give alms? Why are you distressed when you are merciful and thereby abandon the fruit of your good work? If you are distressed, you are not merciful, but cruel and inhuman. If you are distressed, how will you be able to lift up a person who is in sorrow? The poor are barely able to trust your intention even when you give with joy. Nothing seems to be so shameful for humans as to receive from another person. So, unless you take away that shame by great cheerfulness and show that you are the recipient rather than the donor in the exchange, you will cast down rather than lift up the one to whom you give. For this reason Paul says, **The one who shows mercy with cheerfulness**.

Who is gloomy if he receives a kingdom? Who remains dejected when he receives forgiveness of sins? Do not be focused on the expenditure of money but on the return from that investment. If the sower rejoices, even though he sows without knowing the profit from his work, how much more does a heavenly farmer rejoice! In this way, even if you give little, you will give much. On the contrary, if you give much sullenly, you will have transformed that great amount into very little.

Romans 12:9-13

9Let love be genuine; hate what is evil, hold fast to what is good; 10love one another with brotherly affection; outdo one another in showing honor. 11Never flag in zeal, be aglow with the Spirit, serve the Lord. 12Rejoice in your hope, be patient in tribulation, be constant in prayer. 13Contribute to the needs of the saints, practice hospitality.

(1) Origen on verses 9-13

Let love be genuine. I think that all love which is not guided by God is false and a pretense. God, the creator of the soul, has implanted the affection of love in it along with the other virtues so that it might delight in God and the things which God wills. Since God gave this role to the soul for its love, any love which delights in something other than God and the things which please God should be recognized as a sham and a pretense. Loving the neighbor but failing to warn and correct a friend who goes astray is likewise only pretending to love. Love, therefore, must have nothing of flattery or deception about it, as the Apostle says elsewhere, *love that comes from a pure heart, a good conscience, and sincere faith* (1 Tim 1:5).

Hate what is evil, hold fast to what is good. You might be surprised that the Apostle, in talking about the other benefits of the virtues, includes hatred as something necessary. Clearly, then, the affection of hatred is in the soul; it is praiseworthy to hate vices and sins. A person who does not hate the vices cannot love and preserve the virtues. For example, a person intending to guard purity can protect it only by harboring a kind of hatred and detestation of impurity. It would be difficult, very difficult indeed, for continence to prevail when what it rejects is desired, and for the lust of the soul to be held in check only by fear of the future judgment. The virtues are in danger, great danger, unless we follow the advice of the Apostle to **hate what is evil and hold fast to what is good** by waging unrelenting war against the things we hate. Notice that, just as he says elsewhere, *anyone united to the Lord becomes one spirit with him* (1 Cor 6:17), so he says here, **hold fast to what is good**, doubtlessly so that we might be identified with the good.

Love one another with brotherly affection. This commandment, that we love one another just as God has loved us, follows immediately on the primary command. The chief commandment is to love God, but in human relations the first is to love one another. I do not understand how we can disregard it as the lowest and least important in dealing with our fellows, how we can reverse the proper order and direct against the good that hatred which was implanted in us to be used against evil, how we can hate our fellows but love sins and the vices of the flesh. We hate the wrong things only because we already love the wrong things. We are commanded to love our fellows, not to judge them. If you think someone is evil and therefore decide to withhold your love, just remember that Christ died for the unjust. Or if you think your neighbor is a sinner and thus ought not be loved, then recall that Christ Jesus came into this world to save sinners. A just neighbor is even more deserving of your love than a sinful one, since God loves the just....

Serve the Lord. The person who truly serves the Lord can say, *for us there is one Lord, Jesus Christ, through whom are all things and through whom we exist* (1 Cor 8:6). That person is not ruled by lust or avarice or vainglory. I know that some of the Latin manuscripts[1] read, **serving the time**. I think this is an improper reading, unless it is taken in the way the Apostle speaks elsewhere: *The appointed time has grown short; from now on, let even those who have wives be as though they had none* (1 Cor 7:29), or *making the most of the time, because the days are evil* (Eph 5:16)....

Contribute to the needs of the saints. I recall that in the Latin manuscripts the text reads: **contribute to the remembrances of the saints**. We neither dispute that practice nor judge the accuracy of the text, especially since both readings are edifying. For to contribute to the needs of the saints properly and appropriately, we do not give a handout to

---

1. Rufinus, the translator of the Latin version in which alone Origen's Commentary survives, notes that his readers will find this version of the text of Romans different from the Latin version to which they are accustomed.

the poor but share the wealth which we hold in common with them. So too, it seems right and fitting to remember the saints, whether in the solemn assembly or in order to make progress by recalling their deeds.

Extend hospitality. He has expressed the magnificence of hospitality in a single word. In saying that hospitality must be extended, he shows that it consists not only in receiving the guest who comes to us but in looking for, pursuing, and searching out guests everywhere, so that no one is left sitting in the street or sleeping with no roof over them. Remember Lot, and you will recall that he sought out his guests; they did not seek him out. It was Lot who extended hospitality.

(2) Ambrosiaster on verses 9-11

Let love be genuine. A devout mind is intent on loving the neighbor, knowing that this is pleasing to God, its creator, and does not seek praise in the present life. The Spirit assists it to complete this service. They hear what the Lord said: *I give you a new commandment, that you love one another* (John 13:34).

Hate what is evil, hold fast to what is good; be affectionate toward one another with brotherly love; outdo one another in honor. Paul says that avoiding evil is not a great achievement unless a person holds fast to good — the one comes from fear and the other from love. Nor is affection or love of neighbor great unless they outdo each other in service. . . .

Serve the time. The Greek is reported to have here, **Serve the Lord**, which does not fit the context. Paul is going through the individual elements of service and obedience to God, so why would he need to include on the list this summation of all devotion? The service of God is demonstrated in every one of the actions he enumerates. He explains elsewhere what it means to **serve the time** when he says: *making the most of the time, because the days are evil, so that you may know how you ought to answer everyone* (Eph 5:16; Col 4:6). Because he had just said, **be ardent in spirit**, he wanted to prevent their speaking about religion at an inappropriate time, without discrimination and prudence, and thus create an impediment to others. So he immediately added, **serve the time**, so that they would speak about religious faith simply and modestly, at the right place and time, and to the right people. Some people, even in this time of peace, are so terrified of God's word that they angrily curse the teaching of Christ whenever they hear it. Paul himself **served the time** when he did what he did not want to do. To placate the madness of the Jews, he reluctantly had Timothy circumcised, then shaved his own head, purified himself according to the law, and went into the temple (Acts 16:3; 21:24).

(3) John Chrysostom on verses 10-11

Do you see how Paul seeks to stretch further every time? He did not just say, *Give*, but *with liberality;* he did not just say, *Rule*, but *with zeal;* not just, *Have mercy*, but *with cheerfulness* (Rom 12:8); not just, **honor**, but **prefer**; not just, **love**, but **without dissimulation**; not just, **abstain from evils**, but **hate them**; not just, **be zealous**, but **without hesitancy**; not just,

have the Spirit, but **a fervent spirit**, that is, so that you are warm and roused up. If you have the things just mentioned, you will draw the Spirit to yourself; if the Spirit remains in you, it will make you zealous for these things. Everything will be easy because of the Spirit and of love, since you are fired up from both sides. Do you not notice that no one can withstand the bulls that carry fire on their backs?[2] In the same way, if you take both these flames, you will be unbearable to the devil. **Serving the Lord**. We serve God through all these things. For whatever you do to your brother or sister passes over to your master; he calculates your reward according to how well he has been served. Do you see the height to which he has lifted up the spirit of the person who has accomplished these things?

(4) Theodoret on verse 11

Paul called grace "spirit." He ordered that zeal offer substance to it, like wood to fire. He also says this elsewhere: *Do not extinguish the Spirit* (1 Thess 5:19). The Spirit is extinguished by those unworthy of grace. Since the eye of their mind is not pure, they do not perceive that splendor. They are like those who suffer bodily blindness; even the light is darkness, and they labor in gloom even at midday. For this reason, Paul commands us to be fervent in spirit and ardently to desire divine things.

(5) Augustine on verse 12

In the hope of attaining the reward of the devout, we lead this temporary and mortal life with more tolerance than joy. We now bravely bear its evils with good guidance and divine assistance. We rejoice in the faithful promises of God and our faithful anticipation of eternal goods. The Apostle exhorted us to do this: **Rejoicing in hope, patient in sufferings**. By speaking first of **rejoicing in hope**, he showed why we are **patient in sufferings**. We are urged to this hope through our Lord Jesus Christ. The divine teacher — with the majesty of his divinity hidden and the weakness of his flesh evident — gave this instruction not only through the oracle of his speaking but by the example of his passion and resurrection. He showed in the one what we should bear and in the other what we should hope to attain. We will become worthy of God's grace unless we are puffed up and bloated with pride, unless we vainly try to construct for ourselves that blessed life which God alone has truly promised to provide for the devout after this life.

(6) John Chrysostom on verse 13

Paul did not say, "Provide for their necessities," but, **share in their necessities**. He shows that they receive more than they give, and that the whole business is mutual trade, a sharing in fellowship. So you supply money to them? They contribute boldness before God to

---

2. The reference may to a deceptive tactic of Hannibal, described by Livy in Ab urbe condita libri 22.16.

you. **Pursuing hospitality**. Paul did not say, "providing," but **pursuing**; he teaches us not to wait for someone to come to us and ask for hospitality, but to run after them and pursue them. Lot acted in this way; Abraham acted in this way. For he spent the day in this pursuit, waiting for this good prey; when he saw it, he jumped up and ran to meet them and fell down on the earth in worship and said, *Lord, if I have found favor in your sight, do not pass by your servant* (Gen 18:3). That is not how we act. Whenever we see a stranger or a poor person, we knit our brows, we do not consider them worth talking to. If we relent after thousands of entreaties and order our servants to give them a little silver coin, we think that we have accomplished everything required of us. But Abraham did not act that way. Rather, he assumed the role of a suppliant and a slave, even though he did not know whom he would be receiving into his house.

But we clearly know that we receive Christ, and still we do not become gracious. Abraham invited and begged and worshiped; we, in contrast, treat those who come to us outrageously. Abraham practiced this hospitality himself and with his wife, but we do not even practice it through our servants. If you considered the table which he spread, you would find great bounty there. He did not do this because he was a wealthy man, but because he had the wealth of a willing spirit. Indeed, how many wealthy people were there at that time? But not one of them did anything like this. How many widows were there in Israel? But not a single one cared for Elijah. Again, how many wealthy people were there at the time of Elisha? But the Shunammite woman alone gathered the fruit of hospitality. In his time, Abraham acted with the same generosity and eagerness. We are right to be greatly astonished by this: even though he did these things, he did not know the identity of the men who arrived. Do not then be curious whom you are receiving, because it is on account of Christ that you care for a needy person.

Romans 12:14-18

14Bless those who persecute you; bless and do not curse them. 15Rejoice with those who rejoice, weep with those who weep. 16Live in harmony with one another; do not be haughty, but associate with the lowly; never be conceited. 17Repay no one evil for evil, but take thought for what is noble in the sight of all. 18If possible, so far as it depends upon you, live peaceably with all.

(1) Origen on verses 14-16

Bless and do not curse. The word "blessing" is used in different ways in the Scriptures. God is said to bless humans or the other created things, while humans and other creatures are commanded to bless God. God's blessing always bestows some gift on those whom God blesses. When humans are said to bless God, it means to give God praise and thanksgiving. When the Apostle says here, **bless and do not curse**, he is warning that when we are provoked by enemies or upset by insults, we should not return curses for curses but do what he writes about himself, *when reviled, we bless* (1 Cor 4:12).

Rejoice with those who rejoice, weep with those who weep. We must make a right and proper distinction here. The rejoicing of Christians is not to be seen as just any kind of celebration, nor are their tears just any kind of weeping. When I see people celebrating a financial gain or great possessions or high worldly honors, I should not congratulate them; I know that wailing and tears follow on this kind of rejoicing. How could we rejoice over such things when the Lord did not allow his disciples to rejoice even when they saw the demons subject to them; he said to them, *do not rejoice at this, that the spirits submit to you; but rejoice that your names are written in the book of life* (Luke 10:20). We should rejoice with people when we see them doing works which are worthy of being written in heaven — a work of justice or charity or peace or mercy — and the works are performed in a way that merits their being included in the book of life. And we should rejoice with people when we see them turn from error and leave the darkness of ignorance to come to the light of truth, to merit the forgiveness of sins and the grace of Holy Spirit. Likewise, to weep with the weeping. We are not ordered to join those who weep for their dead or wail over worldly losses, since we know that *worldly grief produces death* (2 Cor 7:10). We should not join such persons with our tears but should weep with those the Lord identified: *Blessed are those who mourn, for they will be comforted* (Matt 5:4). But if they weep over their sins, if they turn to penance after offending and wash away their error with tears, if they groan while living in this habitation and long to return to Christ and assuage their holy desire by pouring out tears, then we should join our tears to theirs and share their groaning. *Godly grief produces a repentance that leads to salvation* (2 Cor 7:10).

Wishing the same for one another. This statement is not unclear in itself but requires interpretation. He means that we should be as careful for our fellows as for ourselves and that we should wish for them what we wish for ourselves. Thus the Lord says in the Gospel, *Do to others as you would have them do to you* (Matt 7:12).

Do not be haughty, but associate with the lowly. Pride — the meaning of being haughty — is to be avoided in everything. One ought to flee from pride, because the Scripture says, *The beginning of forsaking the Lord is pride* (Sir 10:12). He explains the practice of humility at the same time. To associate with the humble and love the humble and be gracious to them is to accustom oneself to imitate him *who, though he was in the form of God, took the form of a slave, and humbled himself to the point of death* (Phil 2:6-8).

Do not be cunning in dealing with one another. People who are too much concerned with themselves are stupidly arrogant. Those who cultivate their own foolishness as though it were wisdom cannot recognize the true wisdom of God. In the earlier parts of the letter, Paul explained that this caused the unbelief of the Jews: *being ignorant of the righteousness of God, and seeking to establish their own, they have not submitted to God's righteousness* (Rom 10:3). By relying on their own wisdom, people cannot share God's.

(2) Augustine on verse 14

A question arises here which must not be ignored. The Lord commanded us to love our enemies, to do good to those who hate us, and to pray for those who persecute us. This seems to be opposed by many other scriptural passages, at least when these are not carefully and prudently interpreted. In the prophets, for example, we find many appeals to God against enemies which look like curses, such as: *Let their own table become a snare* (Ps 69:22), and the other things said in that passage. Or *May his children be fatherless and his wife a widow* (Ps 109:9) and the rest that is said through the prophet both before and afterward in the same psalm, which is directed against the person of Judas. Many other passages are to be found elsewhere in the Scriptures which would seem to violate both this precept of the Lord and that of the Apostle where he says: **Bless and refuse to curse**. Similarly, the Lord is described as cursing the cities which did not receive his word, and the Apostle himself said about someone: *the Lord will requite him for his deeds* (2 Tim 4:14).

But these conflicts are easily resolved: because through these curses the prophets proclaimed by imprecation what was going to happen, not praying for something they hoped for, but foreseeing it by the spirit. The same can be said about both the Lord and the Apostle; in their words we find not what they hoped for but what they foretold. Thus when the Lord said, *Woe to you, Capernaum* (Matt 11:21, 23), he did nothing more than describe the evil which, because of its infidelity, was going to befall it. By divine power, the Lord discerned what was going to happen; he did not maliciously pray for it. Similarly, the Apostle did not say, "May God requite," but *the Lord will requite him for his deeds* (2 Tim 4:14). This kind of speech is a foretelling, not an appeal for divine action. In the same way, he addressed the hypocrisy of the Jews, whose overthrow he saw about to happen: *The Lord will strike you, you whitewashed wall!* (Acts 23:3). Actually the prophets do most of their predicting in the form of a threat, just as they often foretold what was going to happen as though it was already accomplished. For example: *Why did the nations conspire and have the peoples plotted in vain?* (Ps 2:1 Vg). He did not say, "Why do the nations conspire and the people plot in vain?" In this instance, however, the prophet was not recalling things that had happened but looking forward to what was going to happen. In the same way, in the passage: *They divided my garments among them, and cast lots for my clothing* (Ps 21:19 Vg), he did not say, "They divide my garments and cast lots for my clothing." So the only people who would complain about these "cursing" passages are those who fail to appreciate the way in which figures of speech do not detract from the truth of the matter but add a great deal to its impact on the mind.

(3) Ambrosiaster on verses 15-18

Rejoice with those who rejoice, weep with those who weep. Paul says the same in another place: *If one member suffers, all suffer together with it; if one member is honored, all rejoice together with it* (1 Cor 12:26). By bringing consolation to a fellow in difficulty, a Christian lifts up the troubled spirit and wins merit in God's sight, by showing love to a member of the body of Christ. If consolation is offered to a non-believer, that person will be well disposed toward the discipline of the Lord.

Wishing the same for one another. This is the same as what preceded: that they should suffer the troubles of their fellows. Paul says in another epistle, *Take care that you are not tempted. Bear one another's burdens* (Gal 6:1-2).

Do not be haughty. Haughtiness is pride — the devil fell away by being haughty. A haughty attitude leads people to presume that their own situations are secure and so not to feel for their fellows in trouble but to condemn them as sinners. This is pride, in which people sin by thinking more highly of themselves than of others. The Lord denounces it: *first take the log out of your own eye, and then you will see clearly to take the speck out of your neighbor's eye* (Matt 7:5). Haughtiness is a sin; even a person not already a sinner — which is impossible — would become one if filled with pride. Thus Solomon says, *Toward the scorners God is scornful* (Prov 3:34).

But associate with the lowly. Put aside your pride and make the other's cause your own, and your own the other's. Thus you may find favor with God, since *all who exalt themselves will be humbled* (Luke 14:11).

Do not be cunning in dealing with one another. This is written in the prophet Isaiah (Isa 5:21), and Paul makes the saying his own. Justice should be common; a person should not claim justice for self and be unjust toward others.

Do not repay anyone evil for evil. This is what the Lord says, *Unless your righteousness exceeds that of the scribes and Pharisees, you will never enter the kingdom of heaven* (Matt 5:20). The command in the law was: *You shall love your neighbor and hate your enemy* (Matt 5:43; Lev 19:18). This, apparently, was justice. But to make the justice of Christians greater, they were taught not to repay evil, that they might be perfect and a reward might be paid to them in the judgment of God. The imitator of heavenly justice surpasses justice itself by not doing what is allowed and is thus better. The justice which God allows for this world makes a person innocent in time, but heavenly justice makes a person perfect and earns merit in God's sight.

Take thought for what is noble not only before God but also before humans. To take thought is to have future goods in mind, so that a person does things whose accomplishment will deserve praise rather than blame from both God and humans. Do not think that even if something is permitted it cannot displease God and that God does not care whether it scandalizes another person. Thus Paul warns that one's actions should neither displease God nor harm a fellow human being. Something might be permitted, but God is not pleased when it scandalizes another. God warns us to care for the salvation of others. Take thought, therefore, **for what is noble before God and humans**; even though something is permitted, it must be performed in a way that does not cause scandal.

If it is possible, so far as it depends upon you, live peaceably with all. He wants all who observe divine justice to be peaceable. Some people may reject this peace, so that one is not at peace with others, either because they reject correction or because they covet another's possessions. Those whom Paul addresses, however, are to be at peace with all who do good. Not to be peaceable is to reject the spirit of the law and follow one's own sense of right, even though David said: *I was peaceable with those who hate peace* (Ps 120:6). But this was unavoidable because of the power of the persons involved. By humility, one might win over a person haughty and proud who despises the commands of the law. By fearing God and not retaliating for offenses, a peaceable person can maintain peace with someone who hates peace. This would be overcoming evil with good, overcoming by gentleness a person who does not submit to the commands of the law. **If it is**

possible, so far as it depends upon you, he says, so that by acting well they may display a love of peace.

You must try to be peaceable, as best you can, even if others do not love peace. If another person remains disrespectful and blasphemous, and so makes peace impossible, at least the failure will not be attributed to you — since the Apostle John forbade even greeting those who denied that Christ had come in the flesh. We are therefore prepared to be at peace with everyone, if it can be done. However, it can be impossible not through our fault but because others resist and refuse to abandon a conflict with us. So a peaceable person is one who does not harm others.

(4) John Chrysostom on verse 15

"Yes," someone may say, "it is reasonable for him to command us to join the sorrow of those who mourn, but why in the world did he order that other thing, **rejoicing with those who are rejoicing**, since it is not very important?" Yet **to rejoice with those who are rejoicing** requires a soul with a deeper grasp of the faith than **to weep with those who are weeping**. For nature itself moves us to weep, and no one can remain unmoved and dry-eyed when another is in trouble. But rejoicing requires a really noble soul not only in order to avoid jealousy when another enjoys success but even to find pleasure in the good fortune of the other. For this reason, Paul puts the rejoicing first. Nothing so binds love together as sharing another's joy and sorrow. Do not then be slow to sympathize, even if the terrible situation is not a threat to you. For you ought to take upon yourself your neighbor's tribulations. So, join in with another's tears to raise their low spirits; join in with another's joy to make their good cheer strike deep roots. You will firmly establish love and serve yourself as well as your neighbor: you make yourself merciful through weeping, and you purify yourself of jealousy and envy through sharing the pleasure.

(5) John Chrysostom on verse 16

What does Paul mean by, **Having the same mind toward one another**? Have poor people come to your house? Adapt your dispositions to theirs. Do not take pride in your wealth. There are no rich or poor in Christ. Do not then be ashamed of them on account of their outward appearance, but receive them because of their inward faith. If you see them suffering, do not consider them unworthy of your help. And if you see them cheerful, do not be embarrassed to share in their pleasure and rejoice with them. Have the same regard for them that you have for yourself. Paul says, **Having the same mind toward one another**. For example, do you think you are great? Then think that they are great. Do you consider them lowly and little? Then hold the same opinion about yourself and banish all inequality. How should we do this? By getting rid of madness. For this reason Paul adds, **Do not think high thoughts, but accommodate yourselves to the lowly**, that is, bring yourself down to their lowly condition, identify with them, walk together with them. Do not be humble only in your mind but take action to help them; stretch out your hand to them, personally rather than through another, just as parents care for their children, just as the head takes care of its body.

(6) Origen on verses 17-18

Do not repay anyone evil for evil. If to inflict evil is to sin, then to repay evil is not itself just, as some think, but equally sinful, or even more grave, as I think. For the person who inflicts the injury first does not realize that it is evil. The person who is moved to take revenge and repays the evil, by that very fact realizes that the response is evil. Therefore we must always defer to God, who says, *Vengeance is mine, I will repay, says the Lord* (Rom 12:19).

But take thought of what is good in the sight of all. A person **take[s] thought for what is good in the sight of all** not in order to please all who indulge in vices or bad conduct. That would contradict the statement of this very Apostle, *If I were still pleasing people, I would not be a servant of Christ* (Gal 1:10). Those who **take thought of what is good in the sight of all** balance their life, practices, and actions so that no one can reproach them. Notice that the Apostle does not say here that we should please everyone but that we should **take thought of what is good in the sight of all**. He means that we should do what is good whether it pleases them or not.

If it is possible, so far as it depends on you, live peaceably with all. Perhaps someone will say, "How is it possible to be at peace with everyone? How will we understand the scripture which says, *You make friends with a thief when you see one, and you keep company with adulterers*" (Ps 50:18)? This is the reason why the Apostle adds so wisely: **so far as it depends on you**. This is appropriate for your intention and faith. To have peace and friendship with evil-doers is not proper for our faith and intention, although another distinction could be made. To love persons is not to love their crimes. To love a human is to love a creature of God; to love crimes is to pursue the inventions of the devil. For the perfect, the very hating of crimes is the loving of human beings; to hate their crimes is not to stop loving what God created.

(7) John Chrysostom on verse 18

If it is possible, as far as you can, live at peace with all humanity. That is, *Let your light shine before humanity* (Matt 5:16), not that we live for good appearances but that we provide no occasion for those who seek to attack us. For this reason Paul says in another place, *Do not give offense to the Jews and to the Greeks and to the Church of God* (1 Cor 10:32). In what follows he clarifies his meaning well by saying, **If it is possible, as far as you can**. Sometimes this is impossible, as when religion is at issue or the injury is done to another. Why are you surprised that peace with others is not always possible? Paul expected that it could fail between a husband and wife when he said, *If the unbelieving spouse separates, let him be separated* (1 Cor 7:15). Paul means this: take care of your own affairs and give no one occasion for conflict and strife, either Jew or Greek. But if you ever find religion being attacked, do not prefer harmony to the truth; stand nobly even unto death. Do not let this battle enter your soul and do not turn back in your belief, but give way only in conflict over possessions.

(8) Theodoret on verse 18

If it is possible, so far as it depends on you, be at peace with all men. Paul added **if it is possible** and the **on you** with precision. He says, let nothing happen from your side, but offer every option for peace. This follows from what has already been said. What ill will those bring upon themselves who bless the one who persecutes them and do not take revenge on the one who has done them an injustice?

Romans 12:19-21

19**Beloved, never avenge yourselves, but leave it to the wrath of God; for it is written,** *Vengeance is mine, I will repay, says the Lord* (Deut 32:35). 20No, *if your enemy is hungry, feed him; if he is thirsty, give him drink; for by doing so you will heap burning coals upon his head* (Prov 25:21-22). 21**Do not be overcome by evil, but overcome evil with good.**

(1) Origen on verses 19-21

Beloved, never avenge yourselves, but leave room for wrath. For it is written, *Vengeance is mine, I will repay, says the Lord.* Two ways occur to me of understanding how those who do not avenge themselves **leave room for wrath**. By the very fact of not returning blow for blow or abuse for abuse, they leave a space for the wrath of the person who caused the injury to pass over and die down. People are not so violent that if they injured someone and suffered no injury in return, they would continue to rage. Their fury, spent and dissipated, would die down. Great profit is achieved by holding down the number of the offender's sins, and patience in tolerating an injury is praiseworthy in God's sight. Another way to understand **leave room for wrath** is that those who sin by inflicting injury store up wrath for themselves, according to Paul's opinion, on the day of wrath when God will repay all according to their works (Rom 2:5-6). If we take revenge for ourselves, it is a small thing that we pay back for the injury we suffered: a slap for a slap, a stone for a stone, or a verbal insult for what was only a verbal insult. But if we hold these back for God to take revenge on the person who injured us, we make room for that wrath which our attacker's evil actions are certainly storing up, and in which God will exact much harsher punishments than we could inflict.

   If your enemy is hungry, feed him; if he is thirsty, give him something to drink, for by doing this you will heap burning coals on their heads. The Lord commands this in the

Gospels as well. The meaning is perfectly clear, following what was said above: to the extent that we not only do not retaliate against an enemy or attacker but provide them with benefits, we thereby heap up their punishments at God's judgment. The charge will be made before the Lord that they inflicted evils on the very persons from whom they received good treatment; just condemnation will follow. Let us inquire, however, whether this command might contain some more worthy meaning. The prophet Jeremiah said to the sinful daughter of Babylon: *You have coals of fire; sit on them; they will be a help to you* (Isa 47:14-15). Perhaps these coals of fire which are heaped up on the heads of the enemies are there for their own good. Perhaps the wild and barbarous souls of the enemies will be moved to compunction of heart by experiencing our help, by being treated with humanity, affection, and piety. Perhaps the enemies will regret what they have done and thus a fire will be kindled in them which will torture and sear their conscience for their evil deeds. These coals of fire would have been heaped on their heads by our works of mercy and piety. The head is the name given to the ruler of the heart; it is appropriately called the head because its understanding and wisdom guide all the members.

Do not be overcome by evil, but overcome evil in good. A person who returns evil when provoked by evil is actually overcome by evil. The one who returns goods for the evils suffered overcomes evil by good. The nature of evil is to grow and increase by feeding on what is like it, like adding fire to fire, or clouds to the darkness of night. By returning good, however, you will wipe out evil. Contraries are destroyed by their contraries, as fire is extinguished by water and darkness is put to flight by light.

(2) Ambrosiaster on verses 19-21

Beloved, never defend yourselves, but leave room for wrath. Paul warns that anger must be avoided so that opportunities for peace can be maintained. Anger leads to sin because people agitated by anger tend to exact more than the offense requires; they cause problems for themselves by demanding a disproportionate revenge even for more grievous sins; they maim a person whom they could have corrected and cured. Thus Solomon says: *Do not be too righteous; why should you destroy yourself?* (Eccl 7:16). A person who tries to respond to every sin can cause death by seeking vengeance, either one's own or that of the person being beaten. People usually sin in punishing. He forbids exacting even a proportionate vengeance not only from one's inferiors but also from one's equals and betters. We should not seek revenge from someone who has sinned against us but should forgive and leave the matter to God's judgment. Otherwise, we might leave an opening for the enemy to tempt and persuade us to do what brings us no advantage.

For it is written. To be more persuasive, he confirms this with an example, citing what is written in Proverbs: **Vengeance is mine, I will repay, says the Lord.** He shows that by failing to follow his direction, we would hold God in contempt. A double benefit is gained by leaving vengeance to God: a person is perfected by leaving wrath to God and will be vindicated in God's judgment.

If your enemy is hungry, feed him; if he is thirsty, give him something to drink; for by doing this you will heap burning coals upon his head. We should not just leave vengeance to God but should confer benefits on our enemies. We will thereby demonstrate that we do not deserve to have enemies, since we even try to turn them away from doing evil by overcoming them with kindness. If they persevere in enmity and hold to the impiety of their minds, our good service will either increase their punishment or will strike them and bring them back to life, like dead coals. Paul wants to make us so perfect that we win life not only for ourselves but for others, just as the Lord not only forbids us to repay our enemies in return but through Solomon urges us to move them to friendship by our humanity.

Do not be overcome by evil, but overcome evil in good. This is the point of the Apostle's exhorting us not to repay our enemies. Yielding to their malice will greatly benefit us. The person who seems to be overcome by evil at the time actually achieves a victory over evil. When he did not resist, the Savior won such a victory over evil. Malice acted against its own interests and thought that it was winning, even as it was being defeated. By attacking us, the enemy tries to draw us away from our good purpose and seeks an opportunity to make us sin. So if we do not repay in kind when provoked by the enemy, we overcome the enemy by good. We do not resist so that we may preserve the good, setting aside the justice of retribution which drives us to seek revenge.

(3) Theodoret on verses 19-20

Do not defend yourselves, my beloved, but give place to anger. For it is written: *Revenge is mine, I will repay,* **says the Lord. Therefore, if your enemy is hungry, give him bread. If he is thirsty, give him something to drink. By doing this, you heap coals of fire on his head.** By referring to the judge and by recalling God's just decrees (this is what he means by ***Revenge is mine, I will repay,* says the Lord**), Paul orders us to bear bravely the injustices which befall us, to repay those who do us injustice with the opposite, and to give the necessities of life to those who are hostile toward us. These actions weave crowns for those who love the wisdom of the faith, and they increase the punishment of those who commit injustice. Nevertheless, we must recognize that we should not serve those who are hostile to us for the purpose of increasing the punishment they suffer. For the divine Apostle added these things because he wanted to extinguish the anger of the person suffering the injustice, not because he was trying to use good to increase evil.

(4) Augustine on verse 20

The text which says, *If your enemy is hungry, feed him; if he is thirsty, give him drink; for by so doing, you will heap coals of fire upon his head,* appears to many people as being at odds with the Lord's command to love our enemies and pray for those who persecute us, or even with what the Apostle himself said a little earlier, *Bless those who persecute you; bless and do not curse* (Rom 12:14). Or again, *Repay no one evil for evil* (Rom 12:17). How is a person loving someone by giving food and drink in order to **heap coals of fire on his head,** provided that **coals of fire** are here understood as indicating some grave punishment? For this reason, this passage has to be understood as urging a means of moving the people who have harmed us to repent of their evil deeds because we responded by doing something good for them. Such coals of fire have the effect of burning and pressing the spirit, which is like the head of the soul; all wickedness is burned up in the spirit when a person is changed for the better through repentance. These coals of fire are like the ones of which the psalm says: *What shall be given to you or what appointed to you for a deceitful tongue? The sharp arrows of the powerful, with ravaging coals!* (Ps 120:3-4).

(5) Augustine on verse 21

They say: many evil people means many evils. So what do you want? Do you want to get good from evil people? Do not look for grapes on a bramble bush. You are forbidden to do this. *Out of the abundance of the heart the mouth speaks* (Luke 6:45). If you can do anything, if you are now no longer evil yourself, then desire that the evil person become good. Why do you rage against the evil? "Because they are evil," you say. But you join them when you rage against them. Let me give you some advice: Is an evil person displeasing to you? Do not double the number of evil persons. You reproach that person and yet you add yourself: you increase the number of those you subject to condemnation. Do you want to overcome evil with evil? To conquer malice with malice? There will be two wicked people, both of whom have to be overcome. Do you not hear the counsel of your Lord given through the Apostle: **Do not be overcome by evil, but overcome evil in good.** Perhaps the other person is worse, but if you become evil, then there are two evil people. I would prefer that at least one of them be good. Finally, suppose the evil person rages all the way up to the point of dying. What happens after death, where no further punishment can reach the one evil person, and only the malice of that other, living evil person is left? It is madness, not to be vindicated.

Romans 13

In the opening section of this chapter, Paul addressed the topic of the relation between Christians and the state. Because each of the commentators knew that Christians had suffered persecution at the hands of Roman authorities, they had to nuance Paul's optimistic presentation of the state. All agreed that God has established rulers to govern human life on earth, that rulers provide important services, and that they acted as ministers of God by enforcing the moral standards of the natural law. Although governing authority is derived from God, individual rulers are not chosen by God, particularly those who abuse their power. Such rulers should be resisted when they persecute those who follow God's law in spiritual matters. Augustine argued that the rulers had a role in religious matters because they should punish crimes against God. Origen alone asserted that Christians could exempt themselves from submission to earthly rulers by withdrawing from engagement in worldly affairs.

The remainder of the chapter is occupied with moral exhortation. In commenting on the love of neighbor, Origen included the reinterpretation of the parable of the Samaritan which identifies Christ as the rescuer of a wounded humanity. Augustine identified the final section of the chapter as the call by which God worked his own conversion.

Romans 13:1-7

1Let every person be subject to the governing authorities. For there is no authority except from God, and those that exist have been instituted by God. 2Therefore whoever resists authority resists what God has appointed, and those who resist will incur judgment. 3For rulers are not a terror to good conduct, but to bad. Would you have no fear of him who is in authority? Then do what is good, and you will receive its approval; 4for he is God's servant for your good. But if you do wrong, be afraid, for he does not bear the sword in vain; he is the servant of God to execute his wrath on the wrongdoer. 5Therefore one must be subject, not only to avoid God's wrath but also for the sake of conscience. 6For the same reason you also pay taxes, for the authorities are ministers of God, attending to this very thing. 7Pay all of them their dues, taxes to whom taxes are due, revenue to whom revenue is due, respect to whom respect is due, honor to whom honor is due.

(1) Origen on verses 1-7

Let every soul be subject to the more exalted powers. I think that Paul is to be commended for saying that it is the **soul** that is to be subject to the more sublime powers. He would never have said, "Let every spirit be subject to the authorities"; rather, he says, **every soul.** We have often explained the difference between these two, soul and spirit: sometimes he names the human being by its soul, sometimes by its flesh, and sometimes by its spirit. He uses the term "spirit" when the human is being named by its better part, which is spiritual; when by the lesser part, it is called soul; and when it is called by its lowest part, flesh. This is something we have noted often. Here the Apostle is laying down directives for believers; in this life, he wants us to live as quietly as we can and to maintain peace. If we are already united with the Lord and are one spirit with him, then we are recognized as subject to the Lord. If we are not yet so joined to the Lord but still have in us that common soul which participates in this world and is bound to its concerns, then the Apostle addresses us in laying down these precepts and says that we are subject to the authorities of this world. The Lord said that those who bear the inscription of Caesar must repay to Caesar what belongs to Caesar (Matt 22:21). Peter and John had nothing to repay to Caesar. Thus Peter said, *I have no silver or gold* (Acts 3:6). People who have no part in these have nothing to give back to Caesar, nor are they subject to the higher authorities. Those who have either money or possessions or business in this world must attend: **Let every soul be subject to the more exalted powers.**

For there is no power except from God. Some will perhaps reply: "What is this? Is that power from God which persecutes the servants of God, attacks faith, and subverts religion?" To this we will respond briefly. Everyone recognizes that sight, hearing, and understanding are all given to us by God. Once we have these things from God, it is in our power to use vision for good or for ill; and so with hearing, the movement of the hands, and the thinking of the mind. The judgment of God is just when by evil and iniquitous operations we abuse the powers given us for good use. In this way, then, all authority is given by God for the punishment of the evil and praise of the good, as the Apostle himself says in what follows. Thus the judgment of God will be just upon those who use the power they receive for their own wickedness and do not restrain themselves by the divine laws.

Thus he says, **Therefore whoever resists power resists God's organization.** He is not referring here to those authorities who persecute the faithful. The proper response to these is, *We must obey God rather than any humans* (Acts 5:29). Instead, he applies this to the common authorities, who **are not a terror to good conduct, but to bad.** Those who resist such authority will earn damnation for themselves because of the nature of their own behavior.

Do you wish to have no fear of the power? Then do what is good, and you will receive its approval; for he is God's servant for your good. But if you do what is wrong, you should be afraid, for he does not bear the sword in vain. He is the servant of God to execute wrath on the wrongdoer. I am disturbed by Paul's saying that the authority of this age and the judgment of the world are the ministers of God. He says it, moreover, not once but a second and even a third time. I need to investigate how a judge of this world could be the minister of God. We find written in the Acts of the Apostles that the apostles gathered together and made decisions which we among the nations who have believed in Christ ought to obey. The following is included in these: *The apostles and elders send greetings to all our fellows from among the nations who have believed, in Antioch, Syria and Cilicia. Since we have heard that certain persons who have gone out from us, though with no instruction from us, and have said things to disturb you* (Acts 15:24); and then a little further on, *For it has seemed good to the Holy Spirit and to us to impose on you no further burden than these essentials: that you abstain from what has been sacrificed to idols and from blood and from what is strangled and from fornication. If you keep yourselves from these, you will do well. Farewell* (Acts 5:28-29). Now in these precepts, they say that no further burden is to be imposed on those coming from among the nations who have believed, except *to abstain from what has been sacrificed to idols and from blood and from what is strangled and from fornication.* Many things are not forbidden: neither homicide nor adultery nor theft nor sleeping with persons of the same sex nor any of the other crimes which are punished by both divine and human law. So if the decree says that only those specific points must be observed by Christians, then it would seem that they left all the other matters to personal decision. But notice the operation of the Holy Spirit: all these other crimes are punished by the laws of this age. Hence, it would appear unnecessary for divine law to forbid things sufficiently punished by human law. Thus, the apostles legislated only for those crimes on which human law was silent and which were proper to religion. So it is clear that the judge in this world fulfills the major part of God's law. All these crimes God wants to be punished by the judge of this world, not by the bishops and leaders of the church. On this understanding, Paul correctly called that judge the minister of God and the one who punishes evil-doers.

What he says about this authority, **do what is good, and you will receive its approval**, requires further investigation. The secular powers are not accustomed to praise those who do not break the laws. They punish those who sin, but usually do not praise those who do not sin. Let us see whether Paul might have inserted some mystery here, even when he seems to be giving only moral instruction. He knows that all who sin against the law will be judged according to the law, and in that judgment the law will accuse each on the basis of behavior. Moreover, we have just seen that the Holy Spirit provides a role for human law in judging many crimes. Thus on the day of judgment, a person who has not violated these laws will be praised when God says, *Well done, good and trustworthy servant; you have been trustworthy in a few things, I will put you in charge of many things* (Matt 25:21). It must be remembered, however, *that the law is laid down not for the innocent but for the lawless and disobedient, for criminals, murderers, the vile, for perjurers and others of this sort* (1 Tim 1:9-10). These are the ones who fear the law. Those who do good, who act not for fear of the law but for love of the good, all live not under the law of the letter but the law of the spirit.

Therefore one must be subject, not only because of wrath but also because of conscience. For the same reason you also pay taxes, for they are God's servants, attending to this very thing. Paul governs the church of God so that it will do nothing in opposition to the rulers and authorities of this age; through peace and tranquility of life, it should perform the work of justice and piety. If we were to say, for example, that those who believe in Christ are not subject to the rulers of this age, do not pay taxes or revenues, owe no one fear or honor, would Christians not thereby invite the governors and rulers to take action against them, would they not excuse their persecutors and make themselves culpable? Obstinacy rather than faith would be under attack; it would be a capital case deserving an unworthy death. . . .

Pay to all what is due them — taxes to whom taxes are due, revenue to whom revenue is due, fear to whom fear is due, respect to whom respect is due, honor to whom honor is due. . . . Those who still belong to the world, who care for the things of the world, and who seek what pertains to the flesh, must submit to the officials of the world. That person is subject, however, because of the wrath which is being stored up from sins. This, I think, is the reason why he says: **Therefore one must be subject, not only because of wrath but also because of conscience.** People are subject to conscience when conscience finds something in them to accuse. Because of sins, we also pay taxes as long as we live according to the flesh and think about what is proper to the flesh. If we cultivate the vineyard of the Lord and the true vine which is Christ, we will occupy ourselves with that vine; we will not pay taxes to the officials of this age but will deliver fruit to the Lord at the proper time. This is what the Savior himself said in the Gospels: *He will take the vineyard from those evil tenants and give it to other tenants, who will give him the produce at the right time* (Matt 25:42). What he says first, **Pay to all what is due them — taxes to whom taxes are due, revenue to whom revenue is due,** seems to be different from what he then adds, **fear to whom fear is due, respect to whom respect is due, honor to whom honor is due.** Taxes and revenue are due to those whom we have just called officials: they collect from us taxes on our land and revenue from our business. Why am I saying, "from us"? Even our Lord Jesus Christ paid taxes when he was in the flesh; he said that he paid them not because he owed but to avoid giving scandal. He had nothing belonging to Caesar in him, and in him the prince of this world found nothing of his own when he came (John 14:30) because he was free — he even went down into death so that he might be free among the dead — and yet he paid the tax (Matt 17:27; 22:21). How much more must we pay those taxes of the flesh and of our business? If, however, we trade in the pearls of the kingdom of heaven, we must pay those revenues which the spirits exact from us through the various temptations. We should refer fear and honor to the one who says through the prophet: *Do you not call me father and master? If then I am a father, where is the honor due me? And if I am a master, where is the respect due me?* (Mal 1:6),

(2) Ambrosiaster on verses 1-7

Let every person be subject to the more exalted powers. For there is no power except from God. Paul had commanded that the law of heavenly justice must be followed but did not want to appear to be neglecting the law of the present time. He praised it by saying that it must be observed in order that the heavenly law be kept. The earthly law is like a tutor, giving initial instruction to children, so that they might enter on the path to a greater righteousness. A person failing in justice cannot be recognized as merciful. In order to confirm the justice and fear of natural law, he bears witness that God is its author and that those who administer it are established by God. Thus he adds: **those that exist**

have been instituted by God. Thus no one should despise this law as a human invention; let them acknowledge that divine authority has been delegated to human rulers. To submit to those powers means to avoid out of fear of God what they prohibit.

Therefore, whoever resists the power resists what God has arranged. This is directed against those who mock the law because they trust in their own power or think they cannot be caught. He argues that this is God's law and that they will not evade the judgment of God, even though they escape temporarily. **Those who resist will bring condemnation on themselves.** Clearly, every person will be justified or condemned by their works. Those who sin with knowledge of the law are inexcusable.

For rulers are not a terror to good conduct, but to bad. By rulers he means those kings who were established to correct conduct and prohibit transgressions. They bear the image of God, so that all may be under this one rule. **Do you wish to have no fear of the power? Then do what is good, and you will receive its approval.** The ruler praises a person who is innocent.

For he is God's servant for your good. Clearly, governors are given to prevent evil. **But if you do what is wrong, you should be afraid, for he does not bear the sword in vain.** The warning is given that if the authority is disregarded, it will punish. **He is the servant of God to execute wrath on the wrongdoer.** God set the future judgment and yet wants no one to perish, so governors were placed in this age to act as guides by the fear they instill in humans. They teach them what they ought to do to avoid incurring punishment in the future judgment.

Therefore you must be subject, not only because of wrath but also because of conscience. Paul says that they should be subject, **not only because of wrath** — the present punishment where anger begets vengeance — but because of the future judgment. If they evade this earthly judgment, punishment will be waiting for them in that one, where they will be punished by their accusing conscience.

For the same reason you also pay taxes, for they are God's ministers, serving in this very thing. He says that taxes, or what is called the imperial revenues, are handed over as part of their submission, and through these they know that they are not free but act under a power which is from God. They are subject to their ruler, acting as the agent of God, as the prophet Daniel said: *Dominion belongs to God, and is given to whom God wills* (Dan 4:14 Vg). Thus the Lord says: *Give to Caesar the things which are Caesar's* (Matt 22:21). They must then submit to these rulers as to God. The proof of their subjection is their paying the taxes.

Pay to all what is due them. He wants them to pay what they owe to each other, because even the powerful are debtors of their subjects, required to fulfill what their merits deserve. **Taxes to whom taxes are due, revenue to whom revenue is due.** Paul orders that those debts which are due to the royal authority should be paid first, because the cause or need is greater there. **Fear to whom fear is due.** Fear is to be shown toward authority because fear prevents sin, and also toward a parent or an earthly lord, so that they may be favorably disposed toward their Christian child or servant. **Honor to whom honor is due.** Honor can be shown to those who seem to be highly placed in the world, so that by observing the humility of the servants of Christ they might praise rather than vilify the evangelical discipline.

(3) Augustine on verses 1-5

When Paul says, **Let every soul be subject to the more exalted powers. For there is no power except from God**, he is right to warn people not to be puffed up in pride because they have been called to freedom in becoming Christian, and then decide that during the journey of earthly life they are not required to maintain their place in society, and think that they need not submit to the higher authorities, who have been assigned responsibility for governing earthly affairs for the present time. We are made up of body and soul. Since as long as we are in this temporal life we depend on its goods to support our living, we ought therefore to be subject in our bodies to the authorities responsible for what makes up this life, to the people who are generally recognized as managing human affairs. With that part of ourselves with which we believe in God and are called to the kingdom of God, however, we should not submit to any human being who tries to deprive us of the goods which God has chosen to bestow on us for attaining eternal life. A serious error has overtaken those who think that because they are Christians they are not required to pay taxes, or provide services, or show the respect due those who exercise authority in these matters. A great error has also befallen those who judge that they ought to submit in matters of faith to persons who have attained a certain eminence by managing temporal affairs. The proper way to act is according to the instruction of the Lord himself: *Render to Caesar the things that are Caesar's, and to God the things that are God's* (Matt 22:24). Although we are called to a kingdom in which the authorities of this world will have no role, as long as we are on this journey and until we arrive at that age *where every rule and authority will be destroyed* (1 Cor 15:25), let us be patient with our assigned status in the order of human society. We should not act by pretense; in these matters, we should obey God rather than humans, as God commands us.

Do you wish to have no fear of the power? Then do what is good, and you will have praise from it. Some people might be disturbed by this, remembering that Christians have often suffered persecution at the hands of the authorities. Were these Christians behaving improperly? For the authorities not only did not praise them; they punished and even killed them. The words of the Apostle require careful attention. He did not say, "Do what is good and the authorities will praise you," but **Do what is good, and you will have praise from it**. Whether they approve your good deeds or persecute you, **you will have praise from it**; by serving God either you profit from their praise or you earn a crown as a result of their persecution. This is made clear in the following statement, when he says, **For they are God's servants for your good**, even if it means their loss.

He says, **be subject because of necessity**, and means that we should understand that it is necessary for the sake of this life that we be subject and not resist, even when they want to confiscate goods over which they have been allowed authority. These things are temporal and passing; thus our submission is not in lasting goods but only in those necessary for this time. Still he said, **be subject because of necessity**, and then to prevent anyone being subject to these sorts of authorities with anything less than their whole mind and pure love, he added: **not only because of wrath but for the sake of conscience.** He intended not only that you escape wrath, which could be accomplished even by pretense, but that in your conscience you should be careful to act for love of the authority to which you have been subjected by the command of your Lord, *who wills all to be saved and to come to the acknowledgment of truth* (1 Tim 2:4). When the Apostle wrote this, he was talking about these earthly authorities. He urged servants to do the same in another place: *not serving for their eyes, as though you were trying to please humans* (Eph 6:6), so that in being subject to their masters they would not hate them or try to gain their favor by deceit.

(4) Augustine on verses 1-4

[Gaudentius[1]], erase these statements of the Apostle if you can; if you cannot delete them, then go ahead and continue to despise them. Make your negative judgment about what he is saying. Do not give up your free choice, or at least state your position clearly if you dare, because you are human and ashamed to say this before your fellow humans. Murder should be punished; adultery should be punished; all sorts of other crimes or outrages of lust and disgrace should be punished. We want sacrilege to be the only offense which the rulers do not punish by their laws. Are you saying something different when you proclaim: "To be protected by humans is a great insult to God. A person who chooses to use violence for God's sake must think that God has no power to avenge those injuries"?

When you say this, what else could you mean but that no human power must oppose or impede our free choice when we attack God? What an outrage! Ancient times were deprived of such advice, since you had not yet been born. Back then, Moses gently bore injuries done to himself but he punished most severely those committed against God. Now you, the more learned, proclaim with all the hatefulness of your heretical presumption: *God created humans and left them to make their own choices* (Sir 15:14). Will some human emperor try to deprive me of that freedom which God has given? This, then, is what you are asserting: human beings must respect your free decision to assault God, who created humanity with free choice. Other people might have joined you in saying this, particularly those who were forbidden by the decree of King Nebuchadnezzar from speaking against the God of Shadrach, Meshach, and Abednego under the threat of terrible punishments — their own execution and the dispersal of their households — and would have been harshly treated if they disregarded that decree (Dan 3:29). They could have argued exactly as you do: "To be protected by humans is a great insult to God. What must those who want to use violence to defend God think about God? That God does not have the power to avenge those injuries?" They could have said exactly what you are saying, and perhaps they did — with the same folly if not the same freedom.

---

1. Donatist bishop of Timgad who was defying an imperial official sent to confiscate his church building.

(5) Theodoret on verses 1-2

Let every soul be subjected to the powers over them. Whether it is a priest or a bishop, or one who professes the monastic life, let them yield to those who have been entrusted with authority. This is clear, as long as the authority is exercised with piety, since we are not permitted to obey rulers if they oppose the commandments of God. **There is no power except from God. The powers that exist are ordered by God.** Such things depend on the providence of God, who cares for the good order we enjoy together. He regulates both those who rule and those who are ruled, restraining those who do injustice with the fear of the rulers like a bridle. We should know, however, that although the divine Apostle teaches that either to rule or to be ruled depends on the providence of God, he does not say that any one particular person has that authority. For if it happens that an unjust person should exercise the power, the choice is not of God but the result of the natural patterns of leadership. Yet, since God is gracious, God gives authority to rulers who honor justice: *For I shall give them,* God says, *shepherds according to my heart, and they will shepherd them with knowledge* (Jer 3:15); and again, *I will restore your judges, as before, and your counselors, as from the beginning* (Isa 1:26). Since God wills to punish those who commit sin, God allows them to be ruled even by evil rulers. *I shall establish,* God says, *young men as their rulers, and deceivers will dominate them* (Isa 3:4)....

So that whoever opposes authority has opposed the ordinance of God. Paul has frightened them enough. **Those who have opposed authority will receive judgment for themselves.** That is, they will become liable to punishment.

(6) Theodoret on verses 3-4

For those who rule are not afraid of good works, but of evil. For they punish those who pass their lives in evil.

You do not want to fear authority, do you? Accomplish the good, and you will have praise for it. For he is a servant of God for you for the good. God shows that the ruler is worthy of respect as a servant of God. He also exhorted people to perform good works by saying that rulers praise good works.

But be afraid if you commit evil. For he does not bear a sword in vain. For he is the servant of God, an avenger of anger for someone who commits evil. If you love good works, honor the authority, as the one who laid down these laws. But if you pursue the opposite, fear its decision, for it has been established by God for the punishment of evil-doers.

(7) Theodoret on verses 5-7

For this reason it is necessary to be subordinate, not only on account of the wrath but also because of conscience. Paul calls punishment **wrath**. He orders us to be submissive, both for fear of punishment and a desire to accomplish what is appropriate. Paul named the latter **conscience**.

For on account of this you also pay taxes. For they are ministers of God and serve for this very purpose. You sleep, and the ruler cares for the common good. You stay at home, but the ruler goes out to war for the sake of peace.

Therefore give what is due to everyone. To the one to whom tribute is due, give the tribute; to the one to whom tax is due, give the tax; to the one to whom fear is due, give fear; to the one to whom honor is due, give honor. He calls the property tax for land **tribute**; but he calls payment for trade **tax**. He calls **debts** not only these things but also fear and honor. For subjects owe these things to their rulers.

(8) John Chrysostom on verses 1–7

For there is no power, Paul says, **unless it is from God.** What are you saying? Has every ruler been elected by God? Paul says, "I am not saying this, and I am not talking about individual rulers, but about power itself. I am saying that the operation of the wisdom of God has established ruling powers, that some people rule and others are ruled. Human affairs do not proceed in confusion, with people tossed around this way and that, like the waves." For this reason, Paul did not say, "There is no ruler except from God." He is talking about the power itself, and says, **For there is no power unless it is from God. God has ordered any power that exists.** In the same way, when the wise teacher said, *The woman is joined together with the man by the Lord* (Prov 14:14 LXX), he was observing that God created marriage, not that God joins each individual man to the particular woman who is united with him.

Therefore after Paul explained the source of power, he went on to say, **So that whoever opposes the power opposes the ordinance of God.** Notice how he has addressed the issue and made it something fearsome, as a matter of obligation. He intends to prevent the faithful saying, "You are really disrespecting us and making us contemptible by subjecting to earthly rulers people who are destined to enjoy the kingdom of God." So he shows that he is subjecting them not to earthly rulers but to God, since whoever is subject to these earthly rulers obeys God. But Paul is not saying directly that we obey God when we obey earthly rulers. Instead he approaches the question from the opposite perspective. He instills fear and crafts a more accurate argument by saying that we are not doing rulers a favor by our obedience: we owe them that obedience. In this way, he entices the unbelieving rulers to piety and the faithful to obedience.

For he does not bear the sword in vain. Notice how Paul has presented the ruler, arming him like some soldier, displaying him up as terrifying to sinners. **For he is God's servant for wrath, an avenger to the person who commits evil.** To prevent your pulling back when you hear about punishment, vengeance, and the sword again, Paul says that the ruler fulfills the law of God. What happens if the ruler does not know this? God formed him in this way. So, if the ruler is the servant of God by punishing, by honoring, by avenging virtue, by driving away evil, by doing whatever God wills, why do you oppose the government, since the ruler accomplishes so much good and brings you so many advantages? Many people initially seek virtue because of their rulers, and later achieve it through the fear of God. Some people are rather dull and are not as interested in what will happen in the future as they are in what is happening in the present. Therefore, the title "Servant of God" is reasonably applied to a person who uses fear and honor to prepare the souls of many people and make them ready for the word of instruction.

For this reason it is necessary to be subject, not only because of wrath but also because of conscience. What does Paul mean by **not only because of wrath**? He means not only that when you refuse submission to the ruler, you are resisting God, you are earning great evils for yourself from God and from the people, but also that the ruler is your benefactor in matters of great importance, since he secures the peace and manages the state. Cities enjoy a multitude of benefits through these authorities. If you were to destroy them, everything would be ruined; no city, no countryside, no house, no marketplace, nothing at all would remain in place. Everything would be overturned; the strong would devour the weak. So, even if no wrath were to result from a person's disobedience, you should still be subject to your rulers. Otherwise, you would show that you lack both conscience and gratitude toward your benefactor.

For this reason pay tribute, Paul says, **for they are ministers of God, being faithful in this very thing.** Paul did not speak in detail of the benefits which rulers provide for cities, such as good order, peace, and the other services of soldiers and officials who perform public works. Instead, he illustrates the point by one example. Paul says that by paying him a salary, you admit that the ruler provides benefits to you. Oh, the wisdom and intelligence of the blessed Paul! The system of requisitions by rulers seems to be burdensome and grievous, but Paul makes this system an example of the care rulers exercise for their people. Why, Paul asks, do we pay tribute to the king? Are we not paying a salary to the person who is providing for us and who is responsible for caring for us? We would not have paid the tribute unless we knew from the beginning that we would profit from their governance. For this reason, from the very beginning, common opinion has held that we should maintain rulers. They neglected their own affairs, they took care of the common business and spent all their leisure on these affairs, and through their work our personal possessions are kept safe. After Paul mentioned these external goods, he turned his argument back to the prior consideration, which was more likely to persuade the believer. He summarizes his former argument by this one phrase: **They are servants of God.**

Therefore give to everyone what is due: to the one owed taxes, give taxes; to the one owed custom duties, custom duties; to the one owed fear, give fear; to the one owed honor, give honor. Do not think that by standing up or uncovering your head when a ruler is present you are really abandoning your own dignity and lowering the value of your own way of life. If God laid down these laws at the time when the rulers were Gentiles, such things are even more necessary now that the rulers are believers. Even if you claim that you have been entrusted with something greater than the rulers have, you must recognize that the present age is not your proper time, for here you are a stranger and sojourner. The time will come when you will shine more brightly than all the rest; but now your life is hidden with Christ in God. *When Christ appears, then you too will ap-*

Romans 13:8-10

₈Owe no one anything, except to love one another; for he who loves his neighbor has fulfilled the law. ₉The commandments, *You shall not commit adultery, You shall not kill, You shall not steal, You shall not covet* (Exod 20:3-17), and any other commandment, are summed up in this sentence, *Love your neighbor as yourself* (Lev 19:18). ₁₀Love does no wrong to a neighbor; therefore love is the fulfilling of the law.

(1) Origen on verses 8-10

What he then adds, that no one should owe another, must refer to the rulers to whom one incurs a debt by sinning. We have shown often and in many places that sin is a debt. Paul therefore wants us to pay off every debt of sin and not to continue to owe a debt of sin. The debt of charity, however, should be with us always and never cease. We must pay this daily and always owe it. . . .

Then in what follows he lays out the great power of love: **The one who loves his neighbor has fulfilled the law. The commandments,** *You shall not commit adultery, You shall not murder, You shall not steal, You shall not covet,* **and any other commandment, are summed up in this word,** *Love your neighbor as yourself.* Finally, summarizing the reason behind this great good, he says: **Love does no wrong to a neighbor; therefore love is the fulfilling of the law.** He had just said, **The one who loves his neighbor has fulfilled the law.** Because understanding how the whole law could be included in a single statement was difficult, he then added a fuller reason: **Love does no wrong to a neighbor; therefore love is the fullness of the law.** Include love in each of the commandments of the law and see how easily they are all fulfilled. Can a person kill a beloved neighbor? Clearly, one who loves does not murder. Therefore, through love the commandment, *you shall not kill* (Exod 20:13), is fulfilled. Will a person commit adultery against the spouse of a beloved neighbor? Certainly not. If, then, you love your neighbor, you will not commit adultery. Similarly, a person will not steal what belongs to a beloved neighbor. A person will not give false testimony against a beloved neighbor. And so with all the other commandments of the law: if one loves the neighbor, these will be observed without any difficulty. But I think that the Apostle intended to teach us something more in this. Now if you were to inquire more deeply into who your neighbor is, you will learn from the Gospels (Luke 10:29-37) that our neighbor is the one who came and found us prostrate, wounded by robbers, and stripped by demons. He loaded us on the beast of his body and took us to the inn of the Church and gave the innkeeper — Paul himself or whoever leads the Church — for our care and needs, two coins — the New and the Old Testament — for the cost of our care. If we love this neighbor, we will fulfill every law and all the commandments for love of him.

(2) Ambrosiaster on verses 8-10

For the one who loves his neighbor has fulfilled the law. To love one's neighbor fulfills the law of Moses. The command of the new law is to love even one's enemies.

For *you shall not commit adultery, you shall not murder, you shall not steal, you shall not covet.* Moses received this from God in writing, for the renewal of the natural law. **And any other commandment is summed up in this word:** *Love your neighbor as yourself.* This is written in Leviticus (Lev 19:18). While the commandments cited above remain in force, therefore, he says that this law is fulfilled in love. Even if there are other commandments which he does not mention here, love will still satisfy for all the commandments. For if the human race had loved from the beginning, iniquity would have no place on earth. Discord is the manifestation of injustice. To iniquity, then, love is an evil; what is good to the good is evil to the evil.

Love of neighbor does no wrong; therefore love is the fulfilling of the law. Love does not do wrong because it is good and one cannot sin by that virtue which fulfills the law perfectly. Paul wants to make the transition from the words of the law to the meaning of the gospel. Thus he recalls the highest point of the law, then links it to the gospel, in order to show that the two agree and come from a single author. That Christ should supplement the law was entirely proper; he directed that enemies as well as neighbors should be loved. Thus Paul inserts, **love is the fulfilling of the law**: justice is to love one's neighbor, but full and perfect justice is to love one's enemy as well. What does loving an enemy mean if not being willing to put a stop to the hatred and seek nothing harmful to that other? To love the enemy is to wish for whatever would make God merciful to the other. This is heavenly justice. God the Father does this in bestowing seasonal blessings on those who do not worship God. The Lord, hanging on the cross, prayed for his enemies and demonstrated that fullness of justice which he had taught.

(3) Augustine on verses 8-10

When the Apostle was dealing with the question of love of neighbor in the letter to the Romans, he said, **Those who love their neighbor have fulfilled the law. For the commandments,** *You shall not commit adultery, You shall not kill, You shall not steal, You shall not covet,* **and any other commandment there might be, are summed up in this sentence,** *You shall love your neighbor as yourself.* **Love of neighbor does no wrong. The fullness of the law is love.** Since, therefore, love is fulfilled in the two commandments of love of God and of neighbor, why does the Apostle address only the love of neighbor in that letter? Isn't the reason that people can lie about the love of God that the temptations which test it are relatively infrequent, while people are more frequently shown to fail in love of neighbor when they treat others badly? It follows, however, that those who love God with their whole heart and whole soul and whole mind will also love their neighbor as themselves, because this is the command of the one who loves with his whole heart and soul and mind. Indeed, who could love their neighbor — every human being — as themselves unless they loved God, through whose command and gift they can accomplish the love of neighbor? Neither of these precepts can be fulfilled without the other; to address one of them is usually sufficient for a discussion of the works of righteousness. Still, to focus on the one which a person can more easily be shown to violate is more appropriate. This is why John says: *How could those who do not love their fellows, whom they see, love God whom they do not see?* (1 John 4:20). Daily experience of people hating their fellows belies their claims to love God. He says elsewhere, *If you bite and devour one another, beware lest you be eaten up by one another* (Gal 5:15). They nourished these conflicts among themselves through the vices of rivalry and pernicious envy, speaking evil of one another, seeking their own advantage and empty victories, actions by which a community is eaten up as people divide into factions. This sort of thing can be prevented only by their walking in the Spirit and not following the lusts of the flesh. The first and greatest gift of the Spirit is humility and gentleness. For this reason, the Lord proclaimed, *Learn from me, because I am gentle and humble of heart* (Matt 11:29). And the prophet says, *Upon whom shall my spirit rest except on the humble and quiet, who trembles at my word?* (Isa 66:2).

(4) John Chrysostom on verses 8-10

For whoever loves the other has fulfilled the law. I beg you, do not think that you love the other as a gift. Even this is a debt, since you owe love to your brother and sister because of your spiritual relationship. You owe love not only because of this relationship, but because we are also members of one another. If we fail in this love, the whole body will be torn in pieces. And so, love your fellows. If by loving them you achieve the great benefit of fulfilling the whole law, then you owe them love, since you are helped by them.

Paul is not seeking simple love, but an intense love. He does not say only, **Love your neighbor**, but adds **like yourself**. For the same reason, Christ also said that the Law and the Prophets depend on this love. See how Christ has praised this love by positing two types of love. After he said, *This is the first commandment, "You will love the Lord your God,"* he added the second, and he did not stop there, but added, *like this one, "And your neighbor like yourself"* (Matt 22:37-39). What could equal this love for humanity? What could equal this gentleness? Although we are infinitely distant from God, Christ compares this love we have toward one another to the love we have for God; he says that our love for one another is like our love for God. For this reason, Christ makes the measure of each of these types of love nearly the same; about love of God, he says: *with all your heart, and all your soul* (Matt 22:37); about love of our neighbor, he says, *like yourself* (Matt 22:39).

Let us love one another, so that in this same way we will love God, who loves us. When you are dealing with humans, if you love a person who is loved by someone else, that lover resents your love. But when you are dealing with God, you are considered worthy to share divine love. God does not hate the person who shares in divine love. Humans are full of envy and malice, but God is free from all passion. For this reason, God seeks out those who would share in divine love. God says, "Love another together with me, and then I will love you all the more." Do you recognize here the words of a vehement lover? If you love the one whom I love, then I consider that you love me greatly.

Romans 13:11-14

11Besides this, you know what hour it is, how it is full time for you to wake from sleep. For salvation is nearer to us now than when we first believed; 12the night is far gone, the day is at hand. Let us then cast off the works of darkness and put on the armor of light; 13let us conduct ourselves becomingly as in the day, not in reveling and drunkenness, not in debauchery and licentiousness, not in quarreling and jealousy. 14But put on the Lord Jesus Christ, and make no provision for the flesh, to gratify its desires.

(1) Origen on verses 11-13

Besides this, we know the time, how it is now the hour for us to wake from sleep. For salvation is nearer to us now than when we began to believe; the night has gone, the day draws near. Let us throw away the works of darkness and put on the armor of light; let us walk honorably as in the daytime. Now that he has spoken extensively about the Gentiles and the Jews, the Apostle introduces moral considerations, so that he might increasingly incite his hearers to renewal. He introduces the question of the time, which is pressing toward the culmination of all things. The brightness of a new day awakens everyone, no matter how sleepy and drowsy; the sun shining in their eyes opens them up. The soul also has a kind of sleep. The soul has its own eyes and ears, hands and feet, as we have often said, which are not like the bodily members but are understood as virtues by which it is moved and motivated. So sleep can come upon the eyes of the soul when it does not respond to God at the proper time but becomes lazy and idle. Therefore Paul, the herald of Christ, goes about in a world which is stuck in the idleness of sleep and announces that the light has come, that it is time to rise from sleep, that humanity's night of ignorance is far spent, that the rising sun of justice is drawing near, that the darkness is dissipating, that the day of knowledge is dawning. Therefore he sounds the wake-up call, lest through laziness the night should continue during the light. He calls his hearers to throw off the works of darkness and put on the arms of light.

The works of darkness are the actions opposed to God; the arms of light are the virtues. As we said, to stay asleep as the day advances is shameful, and even more shameful to perform the works of darkness in the daylight. The coming of this light and day can be understood in two ways: a general one which applies to everyone and a special one which applies to each individual. Light and day will come to everyone in common when the future age arrives; in comparison with that brightness, the present world is called a place of darkness. That time is coming quickly, as each day slips away; as the duration of the past increases, the length of the future decreases. Thus he says, **our salvation is nearer to us now than when we began to believe**, and it draws closer each day. Thus the Lord pointed to the signs of the consummation of the age: *When these things begin to take place, raise your heads, because your redemption is near* (Luke 21:28). This day also arrives for individuals. If Christ is in our hearts, if he brings the daylight, if reason and understanding chase away our ignorance, if we turn away from unworthy behavior and pursue what is holy and honorable, then we will be established in the light and walk honorably in the day.

(2) Ambrosiaster on verses 11-14

Besides this, you know what time it is, how it is now the hour for you to wake from sleep. It is time for us to advance toward our reward. **To wake from sleep** is to do good in the daylight and in the open; forbidden things are done at night and in hiding. Since we are set in the open, in the sight of God, we should recognize how we ought to behave and make an effort to live purely so that we may attain the promised reward. We should shake off sleep, which is ignorance or negligence. **For salvation is nearer to us now than when we became believers.** By living well and making an effort to love after Baptism, we are not far from the reward of the promised resurrection. The good life of a Christian is a sign of salvation to come. In Baptism, we each receive forgiveness but not the crown; afterward we draw near to eternal life by walking in newness of life.

The night has passed, the day is near. Night signifies the old self, which was renewed in Baptism. It has faded away like night, and the day has dawned, the sun of justice, by whose light truth will appear to us, so that we can know what we ought to do. We were in darkness when we did not know Christ, but when we learned of him, light dawned on us; we came over from falsehood to truth. **Let us then cast away the works of darkness and put on the armor of light.** Darkness names the vices of the flesh, which are engaged with worldly attractions. These deserve the darkness, as the Lord says: *Take him and bind him hand and foot, and throw him into the outer darkness* (Matt 22:13). To put on the armor of light means to do good deeds. Evil actions are assigned to the darkness, because people who do evil act in secret; so those who do good act in the open, because they are joyous rather than fearful. Good actions are then the armor of light; they fight against the darkness, which represents the vices of the flesh.

Let us live honorably, in the light of day. Let us act as one acts in public, because no one sins in public. Nothing is so public as truth. **Not in reveling and drunkenness.** Revels are luxurious banquets, which are either celebrated by gathering everyone together or arranged from time to time by clubs. No one is ashamed to say or do anything at one of them; they all consider the party their own, and shame restrains them only at someone else's table. They gather to drink frightful quantities of wine and are incited to various lustful pleasures. Thus Paul commands that such banquets be avoided. **Not in debauchery and licentiousness.** He adds what usually follows these luxurious banquets: impure sexual intercourse, which is the fruit of this lust. **Not in quarreling and jealousy.** Because all quarreling and jealousy gives rise to enmity, he warns us to avoid them. All these things he calls darkness, because they cannot lead to the reward of light.

Instead, put on the Lord Jesus Christ, and make no provision for the flesh, to gratify its desires. He forbids caring for the flesh, that is, for pleasure, so that the desire for everything the law forbids will be prevented or, if it arises, at least it will be overcome. These are the works of the flesh, which they should put off in order to be clothed with the Lord Jesus Christ. Once renewed through Christ, they should restrain themselves from all these evils. Those who put on Christ separate themselves from all error and wickedness, lest they be discovered without a new garment at the wedding banquet, and be cast out into the darkness in disgrace. If they do not separate themselves, they have put on their old rags over those new garments with which they were clothed in Christ. Having stripped off the old self, they should continue in newness of life.

(3) John Chrysostom on verses 11-14

Their passion would probably have been greatest at the very beginning of their journey, but in time this zeal would die away. Paul instructs them that just the opposite should be true: they should not relax as time goes by; their zeal should continue to grow into full bloom. The closer the King comes, the more prepared they must be. The closer the prize comes, the more focused they should be on the contest, as even runners do. As they approach the end of the course and the prize is close at hand, they make even greater efforts. This is why Paul says, **Now our salvation is closer than when we believed.**

Let us walk decently as in the day. The day is already present. He uses decency, which influences most people, to bring them along. The applause of the crowd is a powerful incentive for them. Paul does not say, "Walk," but, **Let us walk**, in order to make the exhortation inoffensive and the rebuke light.

Not in revelries and drunkenness. Paul does not forbid drinking, but drinking immoderately; he does not forbid enjoying wine, but enjoying it to drunkenness. He lays down the same moderation in the next verse: **Not in wantonness and lasciviousness.** He does not forbid all heterosexual intercourse here, but fornication. **Not with strife and envy.** Paul is preventing opportunities arising for the passions, particularly lust and anger. For this reason he excludes not only the passions but whatever feeds them. Nothing so ignites desire and kindles anger as strong drink, and too much of it. For this reason, Paul first says, **not in revelries and drunkenness**, and then adds, **not in wantonness and lasciviousness, not in strife and jealousy.**

Paul did not stop there but went on to a stronger, more striking argument. He gave us the Master and King himself as our clothing; for whoever puts on Christ has every possible virtue. When Paul says, **Put on**, he orders us to place Christ all over ourselves, just as he says elsewhere, *If Christ is in you* (Rom 8:10), and again, *Christ lives in the inner person* (Eph 3:16-17). He wants our soul to be a dwelling place for Christ, and Christ to surround us like a garment, so that Christ is all things for us, both inside and outside ourselves. He is our fullness, for *the fullness of the one filling all things in all things* (Eph 1:23). He is our way, our husband and bridegroom: *I have betrothed you as a pure virgin to one husband* (2 Cor 11:2). He is our root, drink, food, and life: *For I live, yet no longer I, but Christ who lives in me* (Gal 2:20). He is our apostle, high priest, teacher, father, brother, fellow heir, and sharer of tomb and cross: *For we were buried together with him, and we have been planted together with him in the likeness of his death* (Rom 6:4, 5). He is our intercessor — *We have become ambassadors in place of Christ* (2 Cor 5:20) — and our advocate with the Father, for *He makes intercession for us* (Rom 8:34). He is our house and our inhabitant: *Whoever dwells in me, I also dwell in him* (John 15:5). He is our friend: *For you are my friends* (John 15:14). He is our foundation and cornerstone. And we are his members, his field, his dwelling, his branch, and his fellow workers. Why would he not want to be part of us, since he cements and joins us together with himself in every way? This is characteristic of someone who loves vehemently. So be convinced; and, after you have risen up from sleep, put him on; and when you have put him on, submit your flesh to him as obedient to his guidance.

Do not make provision for the flesh to gratify its desire. Just as he forbids neither drinking nor marrying but getting drunk and acting in licentiousness but not marrying, so too he forbids not making provision for the flesh but acting from desire, by exceeding what is necessary. As proof that he even gives instruction to make provision for the flesh, listen to what he says to Timothy, *Use a little wine on account of your stomach and your frequent infirmities* (1 Tim 5:23). So here too he takes care of the flesh, but for the sake of health, not to satisfy licentiousness. You would not be making provision when you kindle the flame and stoke the furnace. To understand better what it means to make provision for the flesh to gratify its desire, and then to avoid making such provision, consider the drunkards, the gluttons, those who adorn themselves with clothing, those who are effeminate, those who are living a soft and wasteful life. Then you will understand what Paul means. For they do all this not to be healthy, but to divert themselves and kindle desire. You who have put on Christ and have rejected all these things should seek only to have a healthy body. Make provision for the flesh up to this point and no farther; spend all your energy caring for spiritual things. In this way you will be able to arise from your sleep, since you will not be weighed down by a multitude of desires.

Let us then shake off this evil sleep. If we are still asleep when the day overtakes us, we will die forever. Before that day, we will be subject to attack by all enemies here, both humans and demons. If they want to destroy us, there is no one to prevent them. If many had been keeping watch, we would be in no such danger. But only one or perhaps two have lighted their lamps and are watching, while others are sleeping in the deepest night. We need to be watchful and on guard constantly so that we do not suffer these deadly evils. Does the day not seem bright now? Do we not think that everyone is watchful and sober? Perhaps you will laugh at what I have to say, but I will say it anyway. We all seem like people who are sleeping and snoring away in the depths of the night. If it were possible to make a bodiless being visible, I could show you how most people are snoring and how the devil is breaking through the walls and killing the people lying sound asleep in their houses, how he is emptying the houses of all their possessions. He does all these things without any fear, just as though he were acting in deep darkness.

I am giving this advice not only to the rich but also to the poor, and especially to those who enjoy drinking parties with friends. For this is not enjoyment or relaxation, but punishment and vengeance. Enjoyment is not saying shameful things, but talking about holy things; it is to be full, but not to burst from overeating. If you think this is pleasurable, show me that it can last till the end of the day. You would not want it to go on that long! I am not yet speaking about the resulting harm; I have been discussing with you that pleasure which immediately fades away. No sooner does the drinking party break up than whatever produced the enjoyment vanishes. What would you say were I to bring up the vomiting and the headaches, the thousands of illnesses, and the captivity of the soul? Are only the poor freed from an obligation to behave shamefully? I am not trying to forbid you to gather or to have dinners together, but to behave shamefully. I want enjoyment to be enjoyment, not licentiousness or wantonness or drunkenness or riotousness. Let the Gentiles see that the Christians know best how to enjoy themselves, and that in a dignified manner. The psalmist says, *Rejoice in the Lord in fear* (Ps 2:11). How should you rejoice? By singing hymns, by praying, by introducing psalms instead of those slave songs. Christ will also be present at your table and bless your entire feast: when you pray, when you sing spiritual songs, when you invite the poor to share what is served, when you maintain good order and temperance in the party. In this way you transform the hall into a church, singing hymns to the Lord of all instead of shouting and singing. Do not tell me that this is not customary; instead, correct your bad behavior. Paul says, *Whether you eat, whether you drink, whether you do anything, do everything to the glory of God* (1 Cor 10:31).

(4) Theodoret on verses 11-14

And this, since you know the proper time, that it is already time for us to arise from sleep. In other words: it is most certainly the proper time for waking, not for sleeping.

For now our salvation is closer than when we believed. For day by day we draw nearer to the coming of the Master.

The night has progressed, the day draws near. He calls the time of ignorance **night**, but he calls the time after the coming of the Master, **day**. For the sun of righteousness has risen and has illumined the universe with the rays of divine knowledge.

Therefore, let us put aside the works of darkness, and let us put on the weapons of light. He calls ignorance **darkness**, and he calls deeds contrary to the law **the works of darkness.** He gives knowledge the name **light**, and the doing of good works **the weapons of light.**

Let us walk nobly as in the day. Paul illustrates spiritual truths from bodily experience. Those who embrace a life opposed to the law do those things in the night; during the day, they dress themselves in the costume of decency. And so he wishes to be liberated from evils, when the night has passed and when ignorance has ceased. This he teaches in what follows.

Not in carousing and drunkenness, not in sleeping around and lasciviousness, not in strife and jealousy. Some were accustomed to carouse in banquets and to pollute their tongues with shameful songs. Drunkenness causes these things; indeed, it is the very mother of lasciviousness, the teacher of strife and quarreling.

But clothe yourself with the Lord Jesus Christ. Not that they should receive another Baptism but that they should recognize the clothing which they had already put on.

And make no provision for the desires of the flesh. Here Paul shuts the mouths of the heretics who accuse the flesh; he did not forbid caring for the body, but he ruled out wantonness and failure in self-control. He did not say, "Do not make for yourselves a care for the body," but **make no provision for the desires of the flesh.** In other words, do not make it grow proud through wantonness. After dealing with active virtue, he returned again to discuss teaching. First, he had to address the goal of the apostolic teaching, to make the meaning of what he said clearly understood. The Gentiles who believed had embraced the evangelical way of life, but many of the Jews who responded to the preaching of the gospel were observing the prescriptions of the Mosaic law, following the observance of particular days and eating those foods which that law commanded. Great strife and quarreling resulted, since the Jews looked down on the Gentiles, who ate foods indiscriminately; they observed the law to an extreme degree and spat on the Gentile Christians from this pinnacle of righteousness. Therefore the divine Apostle healed these divisions and offered each side appropriate advice. But first he urged the Gentiles to love their brothers and sisters.

(5) Augustine on verse 12

God divided the light from the darkness; God first called the light day and then the darkness night, counting a single day from the appearance of light to the following morning. Thus, those days began with the light, continued through the night, ending with the following dawn. After humans had been created and had turned away from the light of righteousness to the darkness of sin from which the grace of Christ later freed them, we began to count days beginning at dusk. Our journey now is not from light to darkness; we are trying, with the help of the Lord, to travel from this darkness and arrive at the light. This is what the Apostle says: **The night has passed; the day is at hand. Let us then cast off the works of darkness and put on the armor of light.**

(6) Augustine on verse 13

Dearly beloved, we too shall see one another's hearts, but only later. For the present time, we still carry about with us the darkness of this mortality and we walk by the lamp of Scripture, as the Apostle Peter says: *We have the prophetic word made more sure. You will do well to pay attention to this as to a lamp shining in a dark place, until the day dawns and the morning star rises in your hearts* (2 Pet 1:19). Moreover, dearly beloved, we are ourselves the day — at least in comparison to the unfaithful — because of the faith we place in God. We were once with them in the night of infidelity but now we are light, as the Apostle says: *Once you were darkness, but now you are light in the Lord* (Eph 5:8). Left to yourselves, you are darkness, but in the Lord you are light. He says the same in another place: *For you are all children of light and children of the day; we are neither darkness nor night* (1 Thess 5:5). **Let us walk properly as in the day.** In comparison to those who do not believe, we are day. We are still night, however, in comparison to that day on which the dead will rise, and *the corruptible with be clothed with incorruptibility, and this mortal will put on immortality* (1 Cor 15:53). The Apostle John speaks of us as already living in the day: *Beloved, we are God's children* (1 John 3:2). But because it is still night, what follows? *It has not yet appeared what we shall be. We know that when he appears, we will be like him, for we shall see him as he is* (1 John 3:2). That is our reward, not our achievement. *We shall see him as he is,* is the reward itself. Then will be the day, brighter than any could be. Now, therefore, let us walk properly in the present day; in what remains of the night let us not judge one another. Notice that the Apostle Paul, in saying: **Let us walk properly as in the**

day, did not oppose or disagree with his fellow apostle Peter, who said, *We have the prophetic word made more sure. You will do well to pay attention to this as to a lamp shining in a dark place, until the day dawns and the morning star rises in your hearts* (2 Pet 1:19).

(7) Augustine on verses 13-14

I said these things, and I wept in the bitter regret of my heart. Then, behold, I heard a voice coming from the neighboring house of someone speaking in singsong, repeating over and over, like a child: "Take and read, take and read." My disposition changed suddenly, and I began to think whether children usually sang out something like this in some game of theirs. But I could not remember ever having heard anything like it anywhere else. Holding back the rush of my tears, I rose up with the clear realization that I was being directed by God to open the book and read whatever I found there first. I had once heard a story that Antony had been prompted by a reading from the Gospel which he happened to hear, as though it were addressed to him in particular: *Go; sell all you have; give it to the poor, and you will have treasure in heaven; then come, follow me* (Matt 19:21). By this revelation Antony was immediately converted to you. I rushed back to the place where Alypius[2] was sitting, where I had left the book of the Apostle when I got up. I grabbed and opened it. I read in silence the first paragraph that my eyes fell upon: **Not in reveling and drunkenness, not in debauchery and licentiousness, not in quarreling and jealousy. But put on the Lord Jesus Christ, and make no provision for gratifying the desires of the flesh.** I read no further, nor had I any need to do so. Immediately, at the end of this sentence, the light of freedom poured into my heart and all the shadows of doubt were scattered.

(8) Augustine on verse 14

When he says, **do not devote yourselves to caring for the desires of the flesh**, he shows that it is not blameworthy to care for the flesh by providing what is necessary for bodily health. If, however, we care for superfluous pleasures and luxuries, for enjoying what the flesh desires, then it is appropriately denounced as **devoting yourselves to caring for the desires of the flesh.** *For they who sow to the flesh*, that is, those who enjoy carnal delights, *will from the flesh reap corruption* (Gal 6:8).

---

2. Alypius was Augustine's close friend and subsequently his collaborator as bishop of Thagaste, where Augustine had grown up.

Romans 14

This section of the letter deals with conflicts within the community at Rome over matters of eating and drinking. Each of the commentators attempts to discern the nature of the conflict. Origen and Augustine propose figurative interpretations of the text, but all the commentators finally deal with the conflict as focused on food. All agree that Paul is holding two values in tension: all foods are edible by Christians; Christians must adapt in love to the weakness of their fellows. They explain that a Christian must not act if uncertain about the rightness or wrongness of the proposed action; so the weak would sin by eating what they considered unclean. Those of stronger faith should abstain and gradually try to bring their fellows to a better understanding.

Origen explained that the original function of the laws on food was to segregate the chosen people from others. Because all humans are called to faith in Christ, that separation is no longer appropriate and the food rules should not be followed.

Origen and Augustine extend the requirement that good action must proceed from a clear conscience to those who are not Christians: the apparently virtuous actions of heretics and pagans are not truly good.

Romans 14:1-4

₁As for the man who is weak in faith, welcome him, but not for disputes over opinions. ₂One believes he may eat anything, while the weak man eats only vegetables. ₃Let not him who eats despise him who abstains, and let not him who abstains pass judgment on him who eats; for God has welcomed him. ₄Who are you to pass judgment on the servant of another? It is before his own master that he stands or falls. And he will be upheld, for the Master is able to make him stand.

(1) Origen on verses 1-4

Welcome the man who is weak in faith, but not for the purpose of quarreling over opinions. One believes he may eat anything, while the weak man eats only vegetables. Now he speaks about weakness in faith, focusing on someone who believes that not everything should be eaten; that faith is so weak that the person believes only vegetables are permitted as food. Paul's advice could be addressed to Gentile believers who are so taken with the freedom of a faith that considers nothing profane or unclean and attack believers who came from Judaism and are still observing the distinction of foods according to the practice of the law. Paul is rebuking and admonishing these Gentiles not to insult those whose long habit of following the classification of foods makes them somewhat hesitant. He commands that any person who is so weak in faith must be welcomed rather than turned away as an unbeliever. To be weak in faith is not the same as not believing: the unbeliever has no faith, while the weak hesitates over some elements of the faith.

In an effort to order the body of the Church in peace, the Apostle says: **Let not him who eats despise him who abstains, and let not him who abstains pass judgment on him who eats; for God has welcomed him. Who are you to pass judgment on the servant of another? It is before his own master that he stands or falls. And he will stand, however, for the Master is able to make him stand.** Conflict over food should not arise among believers. Paul's statement seems to have a more profound meaning. The law did not include any command about eating only vegetables; the statement, **the weak man eats only vegetables**, would not seem to apply to converts coming from Judaism. It would appear, then, that Paul is speaking symbolically about the food of the Word; he is saying that the weak in faith are not mature enough for their minds to eat all the food of the Word of God. The same Apostle says something similar in another place: *But solid food is for the mature, for those whose faculties have been trained by practice to distinguish good from evil* (Heb 5:14). Again, he says to others: *I fed you with milk, not solid food; for you were not yet ready* (1 Cor 3:2). Are we so silly as to think that the Apostle, who was sent to preach the Word of God, carried with him milk to give the Corinthians to drink? Clearly, he refers here to the way he presented the Word. Thus he is saying, "Those weak in understanding and so immature in faith that they are incapable of comprehending a discourse about the more secret mysteries ought not be drawn into arguments over ideas which they cannot understand."

Some believe in eating anything. Paul is not urging his disciples to eat everything — he is not a trainer of palate and gullet — he is talking about those whose faith is mature and unimpeded by any differences in the Word of God. The Apostle elsewhere calls them *spiritual*, when he says: *Those who are spiritual discern all things* (1 Cor 2:15). These are the ones of whom he says: **Some believe in eating anything.** Consider that the Lord said to the apostles, before they received the Holy Spirit: *I still have many things to say to you, but you cannot hear them now. The Paraclete, the Spirit of truth, will come and teach you all things* (John 16:12-13). These, then, are the *all things* which people believe they can eat, once the maturity of their faith through the grace of the Holy Spirit has made them capable of understanding the more secret teaching. The weak believers have something to eat from the Word of God, a kind of teaching which the Apostle here called vegetables. This food does sustain and keep the understanding hearers from starving, but it does not make them strong and robust. . . .

Those whose faith is so great that it can eat everything and digest every form of the Word are instructed not to grow proud and despise those who are lesser. Those who are not capable of the more perfect teaching are ordered not to judge those whose minds are more open and whose understanding is higher. In a perverse way, the inexperienced judge the experts and the lazy condemn those who are eager to learn. Occasionally, those who have grasped the rudiments of knowledge become puffed up and place themselves above those who seem less capable. For this reason, Paul uses his apostolic authority to reprimand the insolence of both parties when he says: **Who are you to judge the servant of another? It is before his own lord that he stands or falls.** Here he adapts **stands and falls** to those he rebukes. For the less capable, when they see someone expressing something more profound than they can grasp, judge that the wiser person has fallen away from the faith. Similarly, the person puffed up with knowledge rather than love, as Paul warns, expresses a similar opinion about those who are less learned. Paul refuses to grant one Christian the power to judge another. He quite rightly calls them *the servants of another*, because the Lord says: *You are all students* (Matt 23:8). *All* means the whole creation, as there is only one Lord Christ Jesus, who is *Lord of all and generous to all* (Rom 10:12). At the same time, he shows the ineffable goodness of God when he says of the one who seems to have fallen or has actually fallen: **the Lord is able to make him stand.** For *the Lord upholds all who are falling* (Ps 145:14).

(2) Augustine on verses 1-4

He says, **Welcome the man who is weak in faith, but not in quarreling over opinions.** Paul says that we should welcome those who are weak in faith, support their weakness with our strength, and avoid quarrels over their opinions — that we should not dare to make a judgment about another's heart, which we cannot see. He then continues, **One believes in eating anything, while the weak eats vegetables.** At that time many were already firm in faith and wise in knowledge of the Lord; they understood that what defiles a person is not what enters the mouth but what comes out of it (Matt 15:10-20). Thus they ate indiscriminately, without any scruples of conscience. Some of the weaker, however, abstained from meat and wine lest they unwittingly consume something which had been offered to an idol. At that time, meat which had been offered in sacrifice was sold in the market; the Gentiles poured out libations of the first fruits of the wine for their idols, and some of them even made the offerings right in the pressing rooms. So the Apostle commanded those who used such foods with an untroubled conscience not to despise the weakness of others who refused to eat meat and to drink wine because they were afraid of being polluted. This is the meaning of what he says next: **He who eats must not judge, that is, despise, him who abstains, and he who abstains must not pass judgment on him who eats.** The strong proudly condemned the weak, and the weak rashly judged the strong.

He says, **Who are you to pass judgment on the servant of another?** By this he means that in actions which can be performed with either a good or an evil intention, we should let God judge and not dare to make a judgment ourselves about the heart of another person, which we do not see. In other matters, however, which are so well understood that they cannot be done with a good and pure intention, we are not blamed for making a judgment. So when the question is about food, because we do not know the intention, he wants us not to act as judges but to leave that to God. But in the case of that shameful adultery, where the man had taken his father's wife, he ordered that the action should be judged (1 Cor 5:1-2). That man could not have claimed to be acting so foully and disgracefully with a good intention. So any deed which is so obvious that a person could not say, "I did it with a good intention," should be judged by us. When the behavior is such that the actor's intention remains unclear, we should not act as judge but leave the judgment to God, as it is written: *The secret things belong to God, but the manifest things to you and your children* (Deut 29:29).

(3) Ambrosiaster on verses 2-4

One believes in eating anything. This person, relying on a text, has no doubt that all things given for the purposes of humans are to be eaten. For Genesis says that all the things which God created are very good (Gen 1:31). Nothing, therefore, is to be rejected. None of the just are described as abstaining from them: neither Enoch, the first person to be pleasing to God, nor Noah, who alone was found pleasing at the time of the flood, nor God's friend Abraham, nor Isaac nor Jacob, likewise righteous and friends of God, among whom was Lot.

The weak eat only vegetables. Such people should eat vegetables because they think it right. They should not be persuaded to eat meat, lest they eat with uncertainty and sin by not following their judgment. . . .

Who are you to pass judgment on the servant of another? It is before his own lord that he stands or falls. Clearly, a servant ought not be judged by a fellow servant, who was given no authority in the matter. God, whose servants they are, is the judge of their intention in eating or abstaining. **He will stand, however, for God is able to make him stand. He will stand**, he says, in the sight of their Lord, because they are neither guilty if they eat nor blameworthy if they do not eat. They must act with devotion, however, and not avoid the food because they consider it evil.

(4) John Chrysostom on verses 1-2

Receive the weak person in faith and do not argue about distinctions. One person believes he should eat everything, another eats vegetables. I know that some find this statement difficult. For this reason, we must first discuss the whole passage, and determine what Paul is trying to correct. What is it, then, that he wants to correct? Many of the Jews who came to believe remained bound by conscience to the law; they preserved the practice of distinguishing types of food and did not dare to abandon the law completely. So, in order to avoid appearing to abstain only from pork, they refused to eat any meat and ate only vegetables. Thus they would seem to be fasting rather than observing the law. Others were more perfect and observed nothing of the kind; these became arrogant and reproached those who observed the law, becoming a burden to them. The blessed Paul therefore feared that in trying to set a small thing right, they would upset everything; in leading others to understand that foods are indifferent, they might occasion their falling away from the faith; by rushing to correct everything immediately, they could damage essential elements of their faith; by constantly censuring them and shaking their confession of Christ, they would leave the weak uncorrected about both Christ and the law. Notice his great wisdom and how he cares for both groups with his accustomed prudence. For he does not dare say to those who are censuring, "You are acting badly," since that would confirm the others in their observance of the law. Nor he does say, "You are acting well," since that would encourage them to more vehement accusations. Instead, he rebukes each appropriately. He seems to censure the stronger, but in addressing them he shows that he does not approve the practice of the weaker. . . .

Thus Paul immediately takes aim at the strong person by saying, **The person weak in faith.** Notice that the first blow is given to the strong person. But by saying **the weak person**, Paul showed that the other person is actually sick. Then he adds a second blow by saying, **Receive.** Again Paul shows that the other person needs attention. . . .

Then, by placing them side by side, Paul praises the one and accuses the other. He goes on to say, **This one believes he can eat everything**, commending that person's faith. In saying, **The other person who is weak eats vegetables**, he reproaches the weakness.

(5) John Chrysostom on verse 4

Who are you to judge the servant of another? From this verse it is clear that these people were judging and not just disrespecting the others. **For his own master he stands or falls.** Behold yet another blow! Paul's displeasure seems to be directed against the strong person, but he is actually attacking the weak person. When he says, **He will be held up**, he indicates that the weak are being tossed about and in need of much attention; they even need God as their physician. **For it is possible**, he says, **for God to hold them up.** Paul was deeply worried about them. But to prevent giving up on them, he called the weak person God's servant, saying, **Who are you to judge the servant of another?** Again, this is an indirect attack on the weak. Paul is saying, I do not forbid you to judge the weaker people because their actions are right but because they are the servant of another, that is, they answer not to you but to God.

Romans 14:5-6

5One man esteems one day as better than another, while another man esteems all days alike. Let everyone be fully convinced in his own mind. 6He who observes the day, observes it in honor of the Lord. He also who eats, eats in honor of the Lord, since he gives thanks to God; while he who abstains, abstains in honor of the Lord and gives thanks to God.

(1) Origen on verses 5-6

One judges different days; another considers all days alike. Each one is confident in his own judgment. According to the logic of the Apostle's writing, he seems to be dealing with self-control and freedom in using foods. The one who has been called to be in Christ recognizes no food as profane or unclean, but the ideal of self-control urges abstaining from even what is allowed. As he says elsewhere, not everything is appropriate or edifying simply because it is allowed (1 Cor 6:12; 10:23). Yet abstinence has a different meaning with vows and for the objectives of those who take them. Some make the judgment and decision in their souls to live out every day, and thus the whole of their lives, in abstinence. Others determine a particular time for abstinence, as is done in making a vow. Paul gives free choice to each: to take on self-control as a permanent yoke or for a period of time. He promises that both are acceptable to the Lord, and thus he continues.

He who observes a day, observes it in honor of the Lord. Also the one who eats, eats in honor of the Lord, and gives thanks to God; while the one who abstains, abstains in honor of the Lord and gives thanks to God. Both give thanks to God: one for the achievement of self-control, and the other for the freedom to eat. We showed earlier that the Apostle is dealing, in this spiritual interpretation, with something more profound than the idea of bodily food. Applying what we have just said above about some who judge every day and others who judge different days, we can understand that in the divine Scriptures, every chapter containing truth about piety and faith can be called a day. Like a day, it enlightens the mind, puts the shadows of ignorance to flight, and has within itself Christ, who is the son of justice. If some, then, labor and apply their effort to the divine writings, if they break open and search every day the meaning in the divine Scripture, if not one letter or one punctuation mark of the law escapes them, then these persons would seem to judge every day. Those who do not have such intelligence will grasp certain meanings, a few of the very many, but enough to suffice for complete faith, even if not for the fullness of knowledge. According to the counsel of the Apostle, both give thanks to God: one group because they judge every day alike and eat all things, because they recognize and understand everything; the other because, although they do not eat everything and do not comprehend the meaning of all points, still they are saved by the shorter confession of faith. Thus even though they do not eat everything and do not take in all knowledge, they still give thanks to God.

(2) Augustine on verses 5-6

He says, **One judges days as different; another judges all days to be alike.** Allowing that a better interpretation might be available, I think he is talking here not about two humans but about humans and God. Those who judge one day differently from another are humans. Humans can make one judgment today and a different one tomorrow. For example, today they condemn an evildoer who has confessed or been convicted; tomorrow they could judge the same person — now reformed — to be good. Or the opposite: today they could praise a person as just, but tomorrow condemn the same individual as depraved. The one who judges all days alike is God, because God knows not only what any person is like now but also every day in the future. **Let each be fully convinced in his own mind**, he says. Let a person judge according to the capacity of the human mind or an individual's ability. **The one who observes the day, observes it in honor of the Lord.** By judging well on a particular day, the person honors the Lord. To judge well according to the day means remembering that you must never despair of the future amendment of a person whose clear and manifest guilt you condemn in the present.

(3) Ambrosiaster on verse 5

One distinguishes between days. A person might like to eat at intervals. Some people have decided that meat should not be eaten on Tuesdays; others, on the Sabbath. Still others eat it from Easter to Pentecost. **Another judges all days to be alike.** These make all days the same and never eat meat. **Let each be fully convinced in his own mind.** Let each one make a choice of practice.

(4) John Chrysostom on verse 5

One person judges one day more important than another, another person judges all days equally. It seems to me that Paul is gently hinting at fasting. Some of those who were fasting might always have been judging those who were not fasting; or in the observances, they most likely abstained on fixed days and partook on fixed days. . . .

Let us be careful not to apply to all cases the verse, **Let each person be fully assured in his own mind.** For when the discussion is about doctrine, let them hear what Paul says, *If anyone preaches to you a gospel contrary to the one you received, even if it is an angel, let him be anathema* (Gal 1:9), and again, *I fear that, just as the serpent deceived Eve, so he will destroy your minds* (2 Cor 11:3). Writing his letter to the Philippians, he said, *Watch out for the dogs, watch out for evildoers, watch out for the cutting off* (Phil 3:2). But to the Romans, since he was discussing fasting and the time was not right to correct such things, he says, **Let each person be fully assured in his own mind.**

(5) Theodoret on verse 5

One person judges one day as different from another day, another person judges every day the same. Some people continuously abstained from foods forbidden by the law, but others only on certain days.

Let each person be fully convinced in his own mind. Paul did not make a universal statement on this subject, though he does not order them to think whatever they like about the divine doctrines. He anathematizes those who persist in teaching things opposite to the truth. *For if someone*, he says, *preaches to you another gospel than you received, let him be anathema* (Gal 1:9). Therefore, he assigned authority to individual conscience only in the matter of food. The Church has maintained this stance until the present time: one person practices self-control; another partakes of all foods freely. The former does not judge the latter, and the latter does not blame the former; but they follow the law of concord.

(6) John Chrysostom on verse 6

The one who regards the day, regards it for the Lord. And the one who does not regard the day, does not regard it for the Lord. The one who eats, eats for the Lord, for he gives thanks to God. And the one who does not eat, does not eat for the Lord, and he gives thanks to God. Paul continues on the same subject. What he means is that this passage is not dealing with fundamental matters. The question is whether the persons on both sides of this argument are working for God, whether in the end both are thankful and that each gives thanks to God. If both give thanks, no great difference separates them.

(7) Theodoret on verse 6

The one who pays attention to the day, pays attention for the Lord, and the one who does not pay attention to the day, does not pay attention for the Lord. And the one who eats, eats for the Lord, for he gives thanks to God. And the one who does not eat, does not eat for the Lord, and gives thanks to God. Paul says this with condescension; he is primarily concerned with the harmony of the Church. The God of all, he says, knows the purpose of those who eat and of those who do not eat. God pays attention not only to the deed, but also to the intention involved in doing it.

Romans 14:7-9

7None of us lives to himself, and none of us dies to himself. 8If we live, we live to the Lord, and if we die, we die to the Lord; so then, whether we live or whether we die, we are the Lord's. 9For to this end Christ died and lived again, so that he might be Lord of both the dead and the living.

(1) Origen on verses 7-9

No person sets himself up as a model for dying but follows the pattern of Christ, who alone died to sin. By imitating Christ, one may be separated from, and dead to sin. Nor do we set our own example for living, but we follow that of Christ's resurrection, as the Apostle says: *Just as Christ was raised from the dead by the glory of the Father, so we too might walk in newness of life* (Rom 6:4). The newness of life by which we live through faith in his resurrection is attributed to the Lord because it derives from him and not from us. Thus, **if we live, we live to the Lord, and if we die, we die to the Lord; so then, whether we live or whether we die, we are the Lord's.** The death to which Paul refers is that in which we were buried with Christ; in this baptismal death we died to sin. The life by which we were made strangers to this world and, as he says, *living from the dead* (Rom 6:13), we live not for ourselves, nor for the flesh, but for God, as he then adds: **For to this end Christ died and lived again, so that he might be Lord of both the dead and the living.** He says that Christ's death was part of the divine plan of his suffering; that he lived through the mystery of his resurrection. So, Christ left us an example first of suffering and dying, and then of resurrection and newness of life.

Some might be troubled that the Apostle says that **Christ died and lived again, so that he might be Lord of both the dead and the living.** Did he mean that unless Christ had died, he would not be Lord of the dead, and that unless he had returned to life after death, he would not have dominion over the living? I think the right response is to distinguish the two ways in which Christ has dominion over every creature. First, as the creator of all things and bearer of universal authority, he holds all things in subjection by the force of his majesty and his irresistible power. In this way, he rules over not only the good, holy minds and spirits but also over the bad and apostate and those whom the divine Scripture calls evil angels. Thus he is acknowledged as all-governing and almighty, as John specifies in the Apocalypse: *these things were said by the one who is, who was, and who is to come, the Almighty* (Rev 4:8). This is one of the ways in which Christ rules all things. The other way is as the good Son of the good Father, not willing violently to coerce the rational spirits into obedience to his law but waiting for them to come by their own initiative: so that they strive for good voluntarily and not under compulsion; so that he may persuade them by teaching rather than commanding, by invitation rather than threat. For this reason, he decided to go so far as to die in order to provide an example of obedience and a pattern of dying for those willing to die to sin and the vices. For this reason, the Apostle says here that **he died and lived again, so that he might be Lord of both the dead and the living.** The living are those who live a new and heavenly life on earth, according to the standard of his resurrection; the dead are those who carry around Christ's dying in their bodies and restrain their own earthly members.

(2) Augustine on verses 7-9

Do you fear that, though you belong to the Lord while living here, you might not be God's once you die? Listen to the Apostle promising you security: **If we live, we live to the Lord, and if we die, we die to the Lord; so then, whether we live or whether we die, we are the Lord's.** How will you belong to the Lord even when you are dead? He redeemed you, even when you were dead, by the price of his blood. How can he lose a servant who is dead, when his own death was the price he paid for you? So after he had said: **whether we live or whether we die, we are the Lord's,** he then showed the price he paid: **For to this end Christ died and rose, so that he might be Lord of both the dead and the living.**

(3) Ambrosiaster on verse 7

None of us lives for ourselves, and none of us dies for ourselves. Those who do not act according to the law live to themselves, but those who are guided by the law live not to themselves but to God, who gave the law; they live according to God's will. Those who die, die to God in the same way; they will be crowned or condemned by God's judgment.

(4) John Chrysostom on verse 7

What does this verse mean, **No one of us lives for self**? We are not free; we have a Master who wants us to live and wants us not to die, and both of these things matter more to him than they do to us. Paul shows that he cares for us more than we care for ourselves, so much more than we do; he considers our life as riches and our death as a penalty. If we should die, we do not die for ourselves alone but also for the Lord. The death he means here is the death of faith. That we live for the Lord and we die for the Lord convinces us that God cares for us.

(5) Ambrosiaster on verse 9

For to this end Christ died and rose, so that he might be Lord of both the living and the dead. The created order was made through Christ the Lord; through sin it then became alienated from its creator and was taken captive. To prevent the work from perishing, God the Father sent the Son from heaven to earth to teach what had to be done to escape from the hands of the captors. To achieve this purpose, he allowed himself to be put to death by the enemies and to descend into the lower world. Because he had been killed although he was innocent, he convicted sin and forced it to give up those whom it was holding in the lower world. He revealed the way of salvation to the living; he offered himself for the dead and liberated them from the lower world. Thus is he Lord of both the living and the dead. He took those lost and refashioned them into his servants.

(6) John Chrysostom on verse 9

For to this end, Paul says, **Christ died and rose and lived, in order to rule both the living and the dead.** So, let this persuade you, that God always cares for our salvation and correction. If God did not have such a great concern for us, why was the plan of salvation necessary? The Lord had such a great desire to make us his own that he took the form of a slave and died; will he despise us now that we have become his? Absolutely not! He would not have chosen to waste such a laborious task. Paul says, **For to this end he also died**, as though he were saying, "A person would not despise his slave, since he cares about his investment." Yet the Lord loves our salvation more than we love money. He put down his own blood, not money, for our sake; so he would not choose to lose those for whom he paid such a great price. Notice how Paul displays the unspeakable power of Christ: **For to this end, he died and lived, in order to rule both the living and the dead.** And he says earlier, **For if we live or if we die, we are his.**

Romans 14:10-13

10**Why do you pass judgment on your brother? Or you, why do you despise your brother? For we shall all stand before the judgment seat of God;** 11**for it is written,**

As I live, says the Lord, every knee shall bow to me,
and every tongue shall give praise to God. (Isa 45:23)

12**So each of us shall give account of himself to God.** 13**Then let us no more pass judgment on one another, but rather decide never to put a stumbling block or hindrance in the way of a brother.**

(1) Origen on verses 10-12

Why do you pass judgment on your brother? Or you, why do you despise your brother? Why indeed, if the flesh is put to death in you and the vices are not allowed to grow in you but are handed over to death in Christ; if, by the resurrection of Christ, you have attained newness of life and become a citizen of heaven? Paul captured the nature of this vice using the common terms, **why do you despise** and **why do you pass judgment**. Those who seem to have gained a bit of knowledge are accustomed to despise and look down on those who are unable to reach their level of understanding. The unlearned and unteachable also judge — they criticize and condemn — those who inquire into matters deeper and more profound than they can grasp or follow. To put a stop to these faults in each group, the Apostle forbade the less capable to reject and despise the others, and the more capable to judge themselves superior. He says that neither has the expertise for judging. Although he rebukes both those who despise their inferiors and those who judge their superiors, he overlooks the sin of contempt and emphasizes the presumption of the person who is judging. Thus he intends to show that passing judgment is a graver sin than disrespecting a fellow.

For we will all stand before the judgment seat of God. For it is written, *I live, says the Lord; every knee shall bow to me, and every tongue shall give praise to God.* **So then, each of us will be accountable to God. Let us therefore no longer pass judgment on one another, but resolve instead never to put a stumbling block or hindrance in the way of another.** Adding to the reasons why those who judge their fellows are not acting properly, he appeals to the model of God's judgment, which is right and just: **For we will all stand before the judgment seat of God.** Those who judge their fellows might then realize that by the arrogance of their actions they are usurping the judgment seat of God and preempting the judgment of the Only-Begotten. Let us examine the Apostle's appeal to the tribunal of God and see how it should be understood. He refers to the tribunal of God both here and in writing to the Corinthians: *So whether we are at home or away, we make it our aim to please him. For all of us must appear before the judgment seat of Christ* (2 Cor 5:9-10). In the prophet Daniel we find a description of the judgment: *As I watched, thrones were set in place and an Ancient One took his throne; his clothing was white as snow, and the hair of his head like pure wool; his throne was fiery flames, and its wheels were burning fire. A stream of fire issued and flowed out from his presence. A thousand thousands served him, and ten thousand times ten thousand stood attending him. The court sat in judgment, and the books were opened* (Dan 7:9-10). In the Book of the Twelve Prophets, the text says symbolically that in the Valley of Jehoshaphat the Lord will judge his people, and a little later it calls the Valley of Jehoshaphat the valley of judgment (Joel 3:2, 12, 14).

To explain singly each of the examples we have cited would take too long. By comparing what the Apostle wrote to the Corinthians with the present passage and the others we recalled from the prophets, however, we are certain that God will execute a judgment. In order to help humans understand the form this judgment will take, the Scripture has modeled its description on judicial proceedings in human societies. Thus we should know that an earthly judge ascends to a high place on what is called a tribunal, so that from it the judge might be higher and appear superior to those who being judged, and also that nothing may be hidden from the judge's gaze, either the supplications of the guilty or the intercessions of the innocent. We should infer that in a similar way Christ, the judge of all, excels all in nature and majesty, that he looks into the heart and conscience of each one, displays the hidden and reveals the concealed, so that he may bestow praise on good acts and exact the punishments which the evil deserve. This divine judgment is still in the future. In it, all will receive what their actions deserve; an explanation will also be required for every idle word, according to the statement of the Lord (Matt 12:36); the accusations of conscience will shame evil thoughts (Rom 2:15); each one of us will have to provide an explanation to God for everything about ourselves. **Let us therefore no longer pass judgment on one another**, as he says elsewhere: *Therefore do not pass judgment before the time, before the Lord comes, who will bring to light the things now hidden in darkness and will disclose the purposes of the heart. Then each one will receive commendation from God* (1 Cor 4:5). I think that our hearts will be stripped naked before every rational creature and that whatever is hidden will be revealed and displayed. There is a difference in these two actions. What will be revealed seems to apply to the evil, of whom he says: *it will be revealed with fire* (1 Cor 3:13). What will be displayed refers to the good, as he says, *everything that becomes visible is light* (Eph 5:13). Our hearts will be read by every rational creature like written books or inscribed tablets containing the accounts of our acts and thoughts. I believe that this is what is meant in Daniel, where it says, *and the books were opened* (Dan 7:10). These books are now veiled and concealed in the heart; they record whatever we do and are plowed like furrows in our conscience; they hold things known only to God. These books of our souls and the pages of our hearts will be opened in the sight of the throne of fiery flames, the wheels of burning fire, and the stream of fire issuing from the Ancient of Days. The angels and the million angels and the hundred million ministers will see and read. When even a single witness to our crimes makes us ashamed, we will suffer the witness of the innumerable band of celestial powers. Paul says, **we will all stand before the judgment seat of God**, and so includes himself among with those who appear before the tribunal of God. Who then could deceive and fool themselves by thinking that they will not appear before the judgment of Christ and his tribunal of inquiry, or suppose that all they have done rightly or less rightly will not be displayed? . . .

Let us return to the end and conclusion of the section we are discussing. Paul says that the truth of the judgment of God and Christ will be so great, so exact the examination in the future scrutiny, that we should no longer judge one another: **resolve instead never to put a stumbling block or hindrance in the way of another.** Resolve to do this, make this commitment: not to cause obstacles or impediments for your fellows through your food practices. We have already spoken about stumbling blocks and hindrances when we said that a hindrance is something encountered along the way which makes the feet of climbers or walkers stumble. These hurt those who have recently begun to travel the road of faith. The contentiousness, negligence, contempt, and pride of those going before them make them stumble. Shocked by these examples, they are turned away from the faith.

(2) Theodoret on verses 10-13

Why do you judge your brother? Paul says this to the Jews. **For we will all stand before the judgment seat of Christ.** Then he also confirms the argument by the witness of Scripture. **For it is written:** *For I live, says the Lord, because to me every knee bends, and every tongue will confess to God* (Isa 45:23). Christ is our judge; Christ is our jury; we have to stand before that judgment seat. Moreover, the testimony of the prophets teaches the height of the divinity of the Only-Begotten. For it was said by the prophet: *I am God from before the ages, and I am God first, and I am after these things, and I am in the future* (Isa 44:6), and *There was no other God before me, and there will be none after me, and there is none besides me* (Isa 43:10), and *There is no just person and savior besides me* (Isa 55:21); then he added, *I swore by myself, says the Lord, that every knee will bend to me, and every tongue will confess to God* (Isa 45:23). . . .

Then each of us will give an account of ourselves to God. Since Paul showed us the Lord's courtroom, he then exhorted us not to judge one another as we await Christ's decision. For again he added this: **Therefore let us no longer judge one another, but judge rather that you do not put an obstacle or stumbling block in the way of your brother or sister.** Here Paul addresses those Gentiles who did not tolerate the weakness of the Jewish believers but considered the partaking of foods without discrimination as the highest virtue and mark of fervent zeal. He teaches that none of these foods is cursed and unclean.

(3) Ambrosiaster on verses 11-13

I live, says the Lord, every knee shall bow to me, and every tongue shall give praise to God. This is written in Isaiah (45:23), that every tongue will acknowledge God in the faith of Christ. Since he rose again after being put to death, and will be the judge, he says truly,

I live, says the Lord. I not only live but I will also be the judge, and my enemies will acknowledge me and kneel before me, recognizing me as God from God. **So then, each of us will be accountable to God.** Since we will not be held accountable to one another, let us not condemn one another over the matters discussed above. **Let us therefore no longer pass judgment on one another.** Knowing this, let us stop our quarreling. **But resolve instead never to put a stumbling block or hindrance in the way of another.** He warns that judgments should be made only about what is beneficial and can be defended by the authority of the law. No impediment should be placed to a fellow either eating or not eating meat.

Romans 14:14-23

14I know and am persuaded in the Lord Jesus that nothing is unclean in itself; but it is unclean for anyone who thinks it is unclean. 15If your brother is being injured by what you eat, you are no longer walking in love. Do not let what you eat cause the ruin of one for whom Christ died. 16So do not let your good be spoken of as evil. 17For the kingdom of God is not food and drink but righteousness and peace and joy in the Holy Spirit; 18he who thus serves Christ is acceptable to God and approved by men. 19Let us then pursue what makes for peace and for mutual upbuilding. 20Do not, for the sake of food, destroy the work of God. Everything is indeed clean, but it is wrong for anyone to make others fall by what he eats; 21it is right not to eat meat or drink wine or do anything that makes your brother stumble. 22The faith that you have, keep between yourself and God; happy is he who has no reason to judge himself for what he approves. 23But he who has doubts is condemned if he eats, because he does not act from faith; for whatever does not proceed from faith is sin.

(1) Origen on verses 14-23

None of the creatures of God is naturally unclean — clearly everything the good God created is good and clean — **but it is unclean for anyone who thinks it is unclean.** This refers to those who in their minds consider something unclean but do not follow the practice of distinguishing foods, as he says in what follows: **But those who have doubts are condemned if they eat, because they do not act from faith; for whatever does not proceed from faith is sin.** In these statements, Paul has not excluded the distinctions of the law and pronounced absolutely that none of the things which the law specifies as unclean is actually profane or unclean. He set down first the reason why nothing is naturally profane: **I know and trust in the Lord Jesus.** In the Lord Jesus, therefore, nothing is profane by its nature and of itself. So he says: **it is unclean for anyone who judges and thinks it is unclean.** Do not be surprised that a person's opinion can pollute food which is neither profane nor unclean by its nature. In the opposite case, integrity of mind and the exclusion of all anxiety in judgment can cleanse food which is truly polluted, such as that which has been contaminated by being offered to idols. Again, even if the food is actually clean, but a person has an anxious conscience, then a suspicion that it was sacrificed to idols can make it polluted for that person.

If your brother is being injured by what you eat, you are no longer walking in love. Do not let what you eat cause the ruin of one for whom Christ died. By this apostolic teaching he first defined that through the Lord Jesus Christ nothing is to be judged naturally profane or unclean and thus gave absolute freedom in the use of food to every one of the faithful. Then, however, he set a limit to that liberty for the sake of mutual love. He says that even if nothing is profane and the use of all foods is properly allowed, still you may not take food which you think is allowed and thereby place an obstacle in the path of a fellow who is not yet capable of this knowledge. You would not be walking in love and demonstrating loving affection for your fellow. How are you harmed by abstaining from what is allowed in order to avoid bringing your fellow to grief? You commit no crime by abstaining from what is allowed; but the person who distinguishes between foods, and thinks a particular one is not allowed, would be defiled by eating it. **He who distinguishes is condemned if he eats.** Your eating will occasion the downfall of your fellow, for whom Christ died, and you will be responsible for the loss. . . .

The proper practice is to take food and do everything else in a way that prevents anyone saying, *their god is their belly* (Phil 3:19). All food should be avoided which is used for lust and concupiscence, sought out for pleasure, contrived for luxury. We must pay attention not only to what kind of food we eat but to when and how much or how little. This is the way that everything becomes clean for a clean mind; as the Apostle says, nothing is clean for the impure and unfaithful. Thus he shows that even those foods which the Jews categorized as clean cannot be clean for a person who is polluted and unfaithful. In Paul's teaching, clean foods become unclean for polluted people and those called unclean become clean for the saints and faithful. *It is sanctified by God's word and by prayer, for everything created by God is good, and nothing is to be rejected, provided it is received with thanksgiving* (1 Tim 4:4-5). These things are sanctified only through the prayer of those who lift up pure hands without anger or fraud. Do you want to learn a higher distinction between the clean and unclean, that they are determined not by bodies but by minds and souls? Listen to the statement of the Lord and Savior in the Gospel: *It is not what goes into the mouth that defiles a person, but it is what comes out of the mouth that defiles. For out of the heart come evil intentions, murder, adultery,* and the rest (Matt 15:11, 19).

It is the mind and thought that does not understand rightly that pollutes a person, not the kinds of food; no matter what the food is, it will pass through and be discharged in the same way. Do not be surprised that the saints sanctify the food they eat by the Word of God and prayer, since even the clothes they wear become holy. Paul's handkerchiefs and aprons were sanctified because of his purity to expel diseases and restore health when touched by sick bodies (Acts 19:12). What can I say about Peter, the very shadow of whose body bore such holiness that when he was moving about, anyone who was touched not by his body but even by its shadow was immediately freed from all illness (Acts 5:15). We have extended the discussion of clean and profane foods in order to consider the Apostle's meaning as fully as possible. . . .

So do not let your good be spoken of as evil. For the kingdom of God does not consist in food and drink but in righteousness and peace and joy in the Holy Spirit.

The one who serves Christ in these things is acceptable to God and has human approval. I ask how **our good** could **be spoken of as evil**? **Our good** is to understand the law spiritually and to avoid the impious and inept teachings of the heretics and the false philosophers like unclean and polluted foods. This is what the spiritual law approves. Now what if someone who was a Jew, for example, or from the group called Encratites[1] wished to believe in Christ but considered important the practice of abstinence either from the foods which are forbidden by the law or other foods considered harmful to chastity? Some of these judge that such foods should be rejected, even using the authority of Scripture. What would happen if you urged such people to eat all these unclean foods and told them that they could not be saved or attain faith and grace in Christ unless they ate all the foods they reject? The good of spiritual knowledge would be blasphemed, because the people you were pressuring would conclude that our faith and belief specified that one can be saved only by eating pork or some other profane and unapproved foods of this sort.

To this Paul adds, **For the kingdom of God does not consist in food and drink but in righteousness and peace and joy in the Holy Spirit.** Once again I am in awe of Paul's wisdom, who keeps the faults of the present time in check by appealing to the future mysteries and invokes the mystery of the kingdom of heaven to establish a standard for the Church. He asks why we should disturb mutual peace and love over an issue like the quality of foods and eating, since the kingdom of God, for which we work and run, does not consist in either food or drink; these are foreign to the kingdom of God and that future way of life. In that life, just as *they will neither marry nor be given in marriage, but will be like the angels of God* (Matt 22:30), so neither do they take food or drink but are like the angels of God in this as well. Therefore, the absolutely clear teaching and unambiguous judgment of the Apostle establish that bodily food and drink have no place in the kingdom of God, which consists in justice and peace in the Holy Spirit. So he urges us not to concern ourselves with this one good but to make every effort to acquire those other goods even here and now, to acquire those realities we can bring with us into the kingdom of heaven: peace and justice, and other such things which the Holy Spirit helps us seek and gather. These will be our food and substance in the kingdom of God. Therefore, he teaches that we should be anxious not about bodily food, which will have no place in the future, but about the virtues which will continue with us both in the present life and in the future kingdom of God.

And so he says, **The one who serves Christ in these things is acceptable to God and has human approval.** He says this about himself in another context: *Just as I try to please everyone in everything I do, not seeking my own advantage but that of many* (1 Cor 10:33). For this reason, as an apostle of Christ, he became a Jew to the Jews, doubtless to please and thereby save the Jews; and to those who were apart from the law, he too became apart from the law, to please and save them (1 Cor 9:20-21). He talks about pleasing people not by encouraging their vices but by patiently enduring their weaknesses. Let us not pass on without considering what he says: **The one who serves Christ in these things** — that is, in the Holy Spirit — **is acceptable to God and has human approval.** By serv-

---

1. Ascetics who avoided sexual activity and eating meat.

ing Christ in the Holy Spirit, he means what he says elsewhere: *No one can say, "Jesus is Lord," except in the Holy Spirit* (1 Cor 12:3). Paul himself served Christ in the Holy Spirit, since once he had received the grace of the Holy Spirit, he served the Word of God — served wisdom, justice, and all the other virtues which he identifies with Christ. Hence he says that God is pleased with those who fulfill God's will according to the witness God gave: *This is my Son, the Beloved, with whom I am well pleased; listen to him* (Matt 17:5). The one who listens to God and serves Christ, in whom God is pleased, both pleases God and wins human approval.

Let us then pursue what makes for peace and for mutual upbuilding. . . . Those pursue peace who preserve the things which nourish it, with their efforts, their losses, even their shame, and if need be even in peril of their lives and reputations. These things not only preserve peace but promote mutual development. Anyone who sees you striving for what benefits not you alone but others as well is encouraged. So the edifice of faith grows and the temple of God rises up as living stones are fitted together through love. Thus he says, **Do not, for the sake of food, destroy the work of God.** The person whose intemperance in using goods places a stumbling block to the community thereby destroys the work of God and tears down the edifice of love.

His statement, **Everything is indeed clean, but it is wrong for a person whose eating creates a stumbling block**, is like what he said above, **nothing is unclean in itself; but it is unclean for anyone who thinks it is unclean.** Therefore, all things are clean according to their nature and the principle of creation, by which all were made by God; nothing is unclean or what is called profane. He sets down two causes which can make clean things unclean or good things evil. In the present passage, he says, **but it is wrong for a person whose eating creates a stumbling block.** What is good by its own nature becomes evil by your behavior, by your eating those foods which harm and set up an obstacle to your fellows. The other cause by which something which is clean by its nature becomes unclean and profane is through someone's thinking and judging it profane. The thing then becomes profane or unclean only for that person who considers it so. In this way the Apostle clearly teaches that uncleanness and pollution consist not in the things themselves or in substances but in the actions and thoughts which fall short.

Although the law of Moses specified certain things as clean and others as unclean, its objective was to use these classifications to distinguish the people ruled by the law from the other nations. Now as long as that people had to be holy and separated from the other nations, the distinction between clean and unclean had a proper function, since it segregated and set apart the special people of God from the nations made unclean by ignorance of God and the cult of idols. When the gate of faith was later opened to the nations and all were invited to come to God, Peter was shown all the four-legged beasts and the serpents and the flying things in a sheet coming down from heaven; he was told: *Get up, Peter; kill and eat* (Acts 10:13). Since he remembered the legal norms, he replied to the Lord: *By no means, Lord, for I have never eaten anything that is profane or unclean* (Acts 10:14). A heavenly directive was then issued: *What God has made clean, you must not call profane* (Acts 10:15). When, therefore, the knowledge of faith cleanses all the nations from contamination, then food is also purified by the Word of God and prayer. For this reason, the Apostle says, **Everything is indeed clean**, as long as those actions are avoided which he specifies in what follows: that a person would transform the clean into the unclean by eating it in a way which injures a fellow. What he then adds, **it is good not to eat meat or drink wine**, would contradict what he just said unless he had continued, **or do anything that makes your brother stumble**. To eat or not eat flesh and to drink or not drink wine is neither bad nor good in itself, he teaches; it is neutral and indifferent. Those who are evil and strangers to the faith can reject eating meat and drinking wine, as some are known to do in the service of their idols. Occasionally, even practitioners of evil arts are reported to follow these rules. Many heretics customarily observe such things as well, and we do not immediately say, "Not to eat meat and not to drink wine is good for them." Obviously, however, that way of avoiding meat and wine which he set down in what followed, **or do anything that makes your brother stumble**, is no longer neutral or indifferent but truly good. To avoid posing a stumbling block or a hindrance to a fellow is itself good. For this reason, he says elsewhere, *Give no offense to Jews or to Greeks or to the church of God* (1 Cor 10:32).

Let them consider, therefore, whether those persons act properly who coerce others abstaining from meat and wine to taste them, in order to dispel a suspicion that they are practicing a superstitious distinction between foods. Let them notice what the Apostle did not say: "It is good to eat meat and to drink wine but not to eat meat and not to drink wine if it injures a fellow." He did not direct that those who would be injured by it should eat and drink, for the sake of those who judge that they should. Instead, he commanded that even those who judge they should eat must abstain for the sake of those who believe they should not eat. Caution must be exercised, lest by breaking down the wall of abstinence and insisting on freedom, a person might fall into a storm of gluttony and the depths of luxury, and then the shipwreck of chastity would follow. Everything must be done to prevent the destruction of God's work. Therefore, a person should eat if that will build up a fellow, or should not eat if that will advance the work of God. Similarly, drink if this will help a fellow's faith, and do not drink if that would result in either a fellow's losing faith or your suffering a loss of love.

The faith that you have, have as your very own before God. He is referring to that faith by which a person believes all things can be eaten, as he said above: **Some believe in eating anything.** This person believes that none of God's creatures is profane or unclean. Having this sort of conviction before God is sufficient; you do not have to coerce other people to eat when they do not have a faith which believes that everything can be eaten. His saying, **have as your own**, also eliminates the bragging which shows off belief rather than displaying virtue. . . .

Blessed is the person who does not judge himself for what he approves. But the one who distinguishes between foods is condemned if he eats, because he is not acting from faith; for whatever does not proceed from faith is sin. Blessed are those who remain constant and stable in what they have approved and determined, so that they do not question themselves or regret anything. He is saying that people should use foods according to the rule which he laid down earlier. Thus if through spiritual knowledge they approve eating all things and consider all things clean, they should not examine themselves again and fall into doubt about whether they should eat or not. Those who doubt whether what they eat is clean or unclean will be condemned when their conscience accuses them because of the uncertainty in their soul. The accusation is based on the doubt: they ate in doubt rather than faith. Then he makes a general pronouncement which applies to all situations: **whatever does not proceed from faith is sin.** By this statement, he tightly constricts those believers whose souls are negligent and lazy: they must do nothing apart from faith, say nothing apart from faith, think nothing apart from faith. You sin whenever you act or speak or even think apart from faith. This same warning is found in what he says elsewhere: *Whether you eat or drink, or whatever you do, do everything for the glory of God* (1 Cor 10:31).

Now someone will ask about the status of heretics: Should they be considered to act from faith when in their actions they follow the faith they have; or because they really have no faith and thus cannot act from faith, should everything they do be called sinful? In their case, I think that we are dealing with credulity rather than faith. As pseudo-prophets are sometimes falsely called prophets, and false knowledge is falsely called knowledge, and false wisdom is improperly called wisdom, so the credulity of heretics is falsely called by the name of faith. On this basis, we can determine that the good works which they seem to do are sinful because they do not proceed from faith, as it was once said, *let his prayer be counted as sin!* (Ps 109:7). Thus, chastity can sometimes be found apart from faith, specifically the practice of those *who pay attention to deceitful spirits and teachings of demons, through the hypocrisy of liars whose consciences are seared with a hot iron. They forbid marriage and demand abstinence from foods which God created* (1 Tim 4:1-3). This, therefore, is the false faith of those who have made shipwreck of the faith; it is false wisdom, belonging to this world and the rulers of this world, which will be destroyed.

(2) Ambrosiaster on verses 14-16

I know and I trust in the Lord Jesus that nothing is unclean in itself. Clearly, the beneficial work of the Savior made everything clean; he rescued humans from the yoke of the law and justified them, thereby restoring their original condition of freedom, so that they are worthy of enjoying the whole creation, as were the saints of old. Those who refused the pardon which has been given and remain under the law, however, are not allowed to use those things which the law forbids. These things are clean by their nature, but unclean because they are eaten in violation of the law. Thus the law reads: *these will be unclean for you* (Lev 11:4). **It is unclean for anyone who thinks it is unclean.** The one earlier called weak is a Christian, either a former Jew or a faithful Gentile, who thinks that things like this have to be avoided. Because of this uncertainty, the person is weak rather than strong. Such people consider things unclean and therefore not to be eaten. Because they act out of piety rather than superstition, their judgment must be respected. **If your brother is being injured by what you eat, you are no longer walking in love.** In another letter, he writes: *Food is meant for the stomach and the stomach for food, and God will destroy both the one and the other* (1 Cor 6:13). Because a person neither pleases nor displeases God in matters of food, Paul advises that we should give priority to love, through which God has deigned to set us free. Thus he said: *Because of his great love, God has had* *mercy on us* (Eph 2:4). Those who keep God's gift in mind cultivate love and prefer nothing to it; they do not contest even those great issues which they know do not gain the promise of God.

Do not let what you eat cause the ruin of one for whom Christ died. The value of the salvation of a fellow can be measured by the death of Christ. Thus those who know its worth should support their fellows, not set up obstacles which will make people uncertain about a matter of no consequence; they begin to doubt whether meat should be eaten or not, though earlier they might have eaten it with a secure conscience. Conflicts will disturb people, and they will begin to sin against God's creation and insult the creator, which will then lead to the doubters' downfall. **So do not let your good be spoken of as evil.** The teaching of the Lord, which is good and saving, should not be blasphemed over some insignificant matter. It is presented as evil, however, when doubt arises about God's creation. We could understand Paul's statement as meaning that our own good is being spoken of as evil. In that sense, a person does good works but is then reproached over some small matter, so that the good is overlooked and denigrated because of the evil accusation, as is written in Ezekiel: *The righteousness of the righteous shall not save them if they transgress* (Ezek 33:12). This is what happens when a person who is otherwise handsome has some facial blemish, which deforms the beauty. Therefore, Paul's advice is to seek the things which will not spoil the attraction of one's other goods.

(3) John Chrysostom on verses 14-15

Nothing is common of itself. By nature, Paul says, nothing is unclean; it becomes so by the choice of the person using it. Indeed, it becomes unclean for that person alone, and not for everyone. **For the person**, he says, **who considers something as common, for that person it is common.** Why then would he not correct the fellow, so that he does not consider it common? Why are you not leading him away from such a habit and assumption with all your authority, so that he does not make it common? I am afraid, Paul says, that I will disturb the person. . . .

Paul says, not only should you not lead them into distress; if it is necessary, you should condescend to them, and not hesitate to do so. For this reason he proceeds to say, **Do not destroy the person for whom Christ died on account of your food.** Or do you think that your fellows are not valuable enough for you to purchase their salvation by abstaining from foods? Even Christ did not refuse to become a slave nor to die for their sake, but you are unwilling even to despise food in order to save them? Even though Christ was not going to gain everyone, nevertheless he died for all, thus fulfilling his own duty. But do you know that because of your food you are upsetting them in greater matters, and are you still objecting? Do you consider people whom Christ desired so much to be so contemptible? Do you dishonor those whom Christ loved? He died not only for the weak person, but even for the enemy. Do you refuse even to abstain from food for the sake of weak persons? Christ performed the greatest act; can you not perform even the smallest act? And yet, he is the Master, but you are a fellow servant.

(4) Theodoret on verses 14-15

I know and I am persuaded in the Lord Jesus that nothing is common in itself.
He had added **in the Lord Jesus** out of necessity on account of the weakness of the Jews. So that they would not say, "Who are you, to oppose Moses," he taught that Jesus brought an end to the observation of the law and forbade them to think any food unclean. The phrase **in itself** means through Christ's giving of the law of the gospel. For Christ himself even said to the blessed Peter, *Whatever God has cleansed, do not consider common* (Acts 10:5).

Except for the one who thinks something is common, for him it is common. If someone thinks this food is unclean and partakes of it, he is unclean, not by the nature of the food but because of his judgment about the eating. After Paul settled the matter in this way, he again blamed the Gentiles who did not tolerate the weakness of the Jews.

If your brother is grieved over food, you are not yet walking in love. Paul added an appeal to the love of the intolerant person. Then he shows even more clearly the absurdity of what is happening. **Do not destroy someone for whom Christ died on account of food.** The Lord Christ underwent death for their sake, but you are unwilling to secure their life by abstaining from food. Instead your eating kills them.

(5) John Chrysostom on verses 17-21

So again Paul liberates the one from fear and the other from a love of quarreling by saying, **The kingdom of heaven is not food and drink.** We do not have to win approval through these things, do we? Just as he says elsewhere, *If we do not eat, we are not better, and if we do eat, we are not worse* (1 Cor 8:8). He does not need proof; the statement itself is sufficient. Paul is saying this: eating is not going to lead you into the kingdom, is it? He ridicules them because they have such a high opinion of themselves, and refers not to food alone but to drink as well. What are the things that bring us into the kingdom? Righteousness and peace and joy, a virtuous life, peace with our brothers and sisters to which this quarreling is opposed, the joy which arises from agreement, which this conflict destroys. Paul said these things not just to one of the parties but to both, considering this the right time to address both. Since he mentioned peace and joy, which are compatible with bad actions as well as good, he added, **in the Holy Spirit.** . . .

For the one who serves Christ in these things is pleasing to God and esteemed by men. For they will not admire you for perfection, but all will admire you for peace and harmony. For all will enjoy this good, but not even a single person will enjoy your supposed perfection. . . .

Indeed, then, let us pursue the affairs of peace and the affairs which build up one another. This statement is directed toward the one group to make them peaceful; it is directed toward the other group to prevent them from destroying their fellows. However, he has again joined both these groups into unity by saying, **of one another**, and by showing that without peace it is not easy to build up another person. . . .

All things are clean. But it is evil for the one who eats because of offense. That is, for those who eat with a bad conscience. If you would force them and they would eat, there would be no benefit. For eating is not what makes people unclean, but the attitude with which they eat. If you do not correct that attitude, then you have accomplished nothing, or you have actually harmed them. To think that something is unclean is not the same as to taste something while you still think that it is unclean. If you force them to eat, you are committing two sins: solidifying their wrong opinion by your contentiousness and making them taste something unclean. So, as long as you cannot persuade them, do not force them. . . .

What is Paul saying? **It is good not to eat meat.** Why does he say meat? Even if it were wine, or anything at all that causes scandal, avoid it. For nothing can be as valuable as the salvation of a fellow. Christ made this clear by coming from heaven and enduring everything which he suffered for us. Notice, I beg you, how he drives the point home by saying, **He stumbles or is scandalized, or is weak.** Do not protest, Paul says, that they fail for no reason; tell me that you can correct them. For the weak people have enough of a claim on your help for their weakness. And helping them does you no harm, for it requires not hypocrisy but edification and stewardship. For if you force them, they are destroyed and they will accuse you; not eating would have been better for them. But if you should condescend to their level, then they will love you and not be suspicious that you are correcting them. Then you will be given the opportunity to plant the right ideas in their minds.

But if they hate you once for all, you have impeded your own argument. Do not then force them; instead you should abstain for their sake, not pretending that you were abstaining from something actually unclean, but abstaining because they are disturbed by your eating. Then they will love you for doing it. For Paul also commanded, **It is good not to eat meat**, not because it is unclean, but because your fellow is harmed and weakened.

(6) Theodoret on verses 19-20

Therefore let us pursue the things of peace, and the things that build up one another. We should prefer useful harmony over all things, and do everything for the sake of helping one another. **Do not destroy the work of God on account of food.** The Lord names believing in him **the work of God**. *For,* he says, *this is the work of God, that you believe in the one whom God sent* (John 6:29). Paul was right to say, **Do not destroy the work of God on account of food**, because some of the Jewish Christians left the faith because they were unable to bear the criticism of the Gentile believers. But to prevent the Jewish believers from exploiting the toleration he urged as an excuse to continue observing the law, he also added: **Everything is ritually clean.** Paul says that none of these foods is unclean by nature. **But it is evil for the person who eats on account of scandal.** Nevertheless, partaking of this food brings you harm, because you are exercising no concern for your neighbor, and you despise the people whom you see yourself harming.

(7) Ambrosiaster on verse 20

Do not, for the sake of food, destroy the work of God. Human beings are the work of God in creation and then a second time when they are renewed by regeneration; food is also the work of God. But humans were not made for food; rather, food was made for humans. Thus they are of very different value. Paul is saying: do not destroy this work of God, which is splendid, for the sake of that other one which is quite ordinary. To avoid troubling one's fellows about food is a way of being concerned for their salvation. But raising a dispute about food provokes them to sin once again after having been set free from sin; it thereby makes the gift of God fruitless and in those people destroys the work Christ performed to free humans from sin. **Everything is indeed clean.** It is obviously true that all things are clean, especially since in Genesis one reads that all God made is *very good* (Gen 1:31). **But it is wrong for a person to eat because of scandal.** Although all things are by nature good and clean, they become unclean to those who are uncertain. If they eat while uncertain and not with a clear conscience, the food will be an obstacle to them because they are doing what they think is bad for them. Therefore, no one's practice of avoiding foods should be challenged.

(8) Ambrosiaster on verses 22-23

You have faith. Have confidence in it before God. Who are you, who eat without fear because God's creation is good? You have no need to judge another; it is more important for you to be at peace with your fellow, since this is pleasing in God's sight. Food is useful for the flesh; peace is useful for both the body and the soul. So these kinds of disputes must stop, and each one must act according to the disposition of his own heart. **Blessed is the one who does not judge himself because of what he approves.** Paul teaches that people should be condemned by their own judgment when they say they ought not do something and then do it. Those who perform the actions they consider good are indeed blessed. **Anyone who distinguishes between foods is condemned if he eats.** Those who judge that they should not eat and then eat are condemned. They make themselves guilty by doing what they think is not right for them. **Because they do not act from faith.** Those who judge that a food should not be eaten and then eat it are acting against their belief. **For whatever does not proceed from faith is sin.** What is done contrary to approval is rightly called sin. Because the Romans had been brought to faith under the law, as I remarked at the beginning of this letter, when those who had more correct beliefs arrived, questions arose about eating or not eating meat. The case made by those who said that meat should not be disapproved and could be eaten seemed stronger, because all things really are clean. For this reason, Paul characterizes as weak those who deny that it should be eaten, whether they were originally Jews or Gentiles, and he allows them to follow the course they have set in their hearts. Before God, abstaining brings no disadvantage nor does eating give an advantage. If they were not allowed freedom to do either, they might fail by eating in a state of uncertainty. When it comes to the conscience, he says that anything done against one's best judgment is a sin.

(9) John Chrysostom on verses 22-23

Do you have faith? Keep it to yourself. It seems to me that Paul is gently hinting at a danger of vainglory among the more perfect. This is what he is saying, "Do you want to show me that you are perfect and lacking nothing? Do not put yourself on display for me; let your conscience be sufficient." He is using the word "faith" here, not in regard to beliefs but to food practices. . . .

He who doubts is condemned if he eats. Again Paul says this to exhort them to spare the weak persons. How does it help him if the weak eat while they are still doubting and thus bring condemnation on themselves? I approve the one who eats without suffering any doubt. See how he expands the consideration beyond eating itself to eating with a clear conscience. Paul then adds the reason why such people are condemned, **because he does not eat from faith.** Not because they eat something unclean but because they do not eat it with faith. For they did not eat the food because they believed it was clean; they took it even though they continued to judge it unclean. Through this Paul shows them what great harm results when strong persons force those who remain unpersuaded to touch the things which they had considered unclean. He says this so that the strong would refrain from reproaching the weak. **Everyone who does not eat from faith commits sin.** How could people not sin, Paul asks, when they are confident, and they do not believe the food is clean?

(10) Theodoret on verses 22-23

Do you have faith? Have it concerning yourself before God. By exercising your faith, you will fulfill the law. Having faith is great and you deserve praise. But do not mistreat your neighbor. **Blessed is the one who does not judge himself in what he tries.** This statement hints that the Gentile believers forced the Jews to eat things they preferred not to eat. Paul teaches, therefore, that believers should suffer no harm from eating, but the one who eats with some degree of uncertainty eats food considered unclean. For this reason, he calls blessed those who do not bring judgment on themselves, that is, those who do not act with uncertainty. Interpreting this statement, he added: **The one who makes distinctions, if he eats, is condemned.** Then he explains the reason. **Because it does not come from faith. Anything that does not come from faith is a sin.** For whoever believes, eats without harm. The one who eats while uncertain about the food is subject to judgment.

(11) Augustine on verses 22 and 23

He says, **Blessed is the one who does not judge himself because of what he approves.** This should be understood in relation to what he said a bit earlier, **So do not let our good be spoken of as evil.** This is the same thing that he says in the prior sentence, **The faith that you have for yourself, maintain before God.** That faith is good by which we believe that all things are clean for the pure and we test ourselves by the standard of that faith; let us, then, use this good of ours well. If we abuse this good of ours by harming our weaker fellows, then we sin against them and we judge ourselves by that good. When we do harm to the weak, the faith which we love becomes the standard by which we are judged.

(12) Augustine on verse 23

What shall we say, then, about the conjugal chastity which is found among the impious? Should they be accused of sinning because they abuse this gift of God by not acknowledging and thanking God, from whom they received it? Or should we instead judge that when the unfaithful act well, this is not actually a gift of God, because of what the Apostle says, **Whatever does not proceed from faith is sin.** Who would dare to say that the gift of God is sinful? The soul and the body, and all the spiritual and bodily endowments, are gifts of God, even when they are in sinners. God, and not those sinners, made them. But **whatever does not proceed from faith is sin** refers to the deeds the unfaithful perform. When, therefore, people do these things, like practicing conjugal chastity, without faith, they are not holding themselves back from sin. Instead, they are overcoming one sin with another. They are trying to win human approval, either for themselves or others, or their depraved desires lead them to avoid the burdens of human life, or they are serving the demons. Fidelity to a spouse can truly be called chastity only when it is maintained for the love of God.

Romans 15

In the first half of the chapter, the commentators appreciate and amplify Paul's exhortation that the strong should support the weak and try to please them for the sake of the gospel. The strong recognize God as the source of their gifts and use them to give thanks for that grace. The Gentiles also recognize the mercy of God which extends salvation to them, to whom it had not been promised.

That Paul preached only in places where others had not already brought the gospel drew different explanations. Origen interpreted it as a means of achieving maximum spread of the gospel, but Ambrosiaster perceived a competition with the pseudo-apostles, whom Paul wished to forestall by preaching the true gospel before they arrived.

In his ministry to the saints in Jerusalem, only Theodoret recognized Paul's fear that the gift from the Gentiles would be rejected by Jewish Christians. Origen expanded the responsibility of the less perfect to appreciate and care for those more dedicated Christians upon whom they depended for spiritual understanding.

Romans 15:1-6

₁**We who are strong ought to bear with the failings of the weak, and not to please ourselves;** ₂**let each of us please his neighbor for his good, to edify him.** ₃**For Christ did not please himself; but, as it is written,** *The reproaches of those who reproached you fell on me* **(Ps 69:6).** ₄**For whatever was written in former days was written for our instruction, that by steadfastness and by the encouragement of the scriptures we might have hope.** ₅**May the God of steadfastness and encouragement grant you to live in such harmony with one another, in accord with Christ Jesus,** ₆**that together you may with one voice glorify the God and Father of our Lord Jesus Christ.**

(1) Origen on verses 1-4

We who are strong ought to bear with the failings of the weak, and not to please ourselves; let each of us please his neighbor for his good, to edify him. Paul seems to be placing himself among the strong in this passage, similar to what he did in his first letter to the Corinthians: *To the weak, I became weak, so that I might win the weak* (1 Cor 9:22). There, however, he did not say that he was weak but that he had become weak, which he could have done only if he were not already weak. You should not therefore think that he had forgotten the admonition: *Let another praise you, and not your own mouth* (Prov 27:2). He said that he was strong not to praise himself but because of what he had to say next. If, for the sake of humility, he had declined to place himself in the ranks of the strong, then who among those being asked to **bear with the failings of the weak** would have dared to shoulder that responsibility? Who would have presumed to be strong enough to try to bear the weakness of the others? Instead, Paul made this the responsibility of all, so that each one of us would **put up with the failings** of our fellows, at least in those cases where we appear stronger, even if we could not do it in every case. Thus he says elsewhere: *Bear one another's burdens* (Gal 6:2). The burdens to which he referred in that passage seem to be bodily needs; those who have greater resources should *bear the burdens* of the poorer and relieve their destitution from their own abundance.

In the text we are here discussing, when he says that the stronger should **bear with the failings of the weaker**, he must be referring to a situation in which some, in their weakness, offend the stronger. The stronger members then patiently bear the offense; they do not immediately despise, reject, and abhor those who are overcome by some vice; they do not expel them from the gathering of the community and the assembly of the church because of their impure life. Turning away from the weak would not be imitating the one of whom Isaiah said: *Surely he bears our infirmities and suffers for us; yet we accounted him stricken, wounded, and afflicted* (Isa 53:4). Since Christ bears our infirmities and God patiently tolerates our sins, how could we refuse to suffer the faults and negligence of those who seem to be slightly inferior to us? Surely, to do this would make Christ himself turn away from us and refuse to bear our infirmities. None are so perfect that God finds no weakness in them, and Christ bears no burden for them. In this statement, then, Paul is teaching us to be more sympathetic, to suffer and grieve with one another, as he wrote elsewhere: *forgiving one another, as God in Christ has forgiven you* (Eph 4:32). Paul is not commanding this to encourage greater laxity, which would facilitate failures and further debilitate the weak. Rather, he knows that if the weak are tolerated, either they will become ashamed of being carried and correct their vice or failure, or if they are not able to mend their ways, those bearing the weak will at least reap the benefit of not having made them worse and not watching them go from bad to worse. . . .

Someone might object that Paul contradicts himself when he commands us to please our neighbor because elsewhere he said, *If I were still pleasing humans, I would not be the servant of Christ* (Gal 1:10). This statement does indeed seem to oppose his precept that we each please our neighbor, as well as his other statement: *just as I try to please everybody in everything I do, not seeking my own advantage, but that of the many, so that they may be saved* (1 Cor 10:33). We can distinguish pleasing people by trying to win their praise from pleasing them by living blamelessly and thus being of advantage to all who see or hear of it. We should not try to please people by fulfilling their desires when these are contrary to faith, integrity, and religion, as he said: *If I were still pleasing humans* — the unbelieving and unfaithful Jews — *I would not be the servant of Christ* (Gal 1:10). . . .

So if someone asks us to do something which is opposed to justice, holiness, and the Christian rule of life, and threatens us with hatred and enmity unless we do, then we should remember Paul saying, *If I were still pleasing humans, I would not be the servant of Christ* (Gal 1:10). When he says, **let each of us please his neighbor**, he clearly specifies how we should be ready to please: **for his good, to build him up.** We please and build up our neighbor when we act and teach well. He urges not that we seek people's praise but that we encourage our neighbor by our acting and speaking, as the Savior says: *Let your light shine before others, so that they may see your good works and give glory to your Father in heaven* (Matt 5:16). Here Jesus is certainly not exhorting his disciples to seek glory from people but to live well and honestly in order to edify those who see them, so that God may be glorified for offering humans this way of progress and salvation. **For Christ did not please himself, but, as it is written, *The insults of those who insult you have fallen on me.*** He shows that Christ did not please himself, for *he did not consider equality with God as something to be exploited, but emptied himself* (Phil 2:6-7). Because he wished to please humans in order to save them, he bore the insults of those who despised him, as the Scripture says: ***The insults of those who insult you have fallen on me.*** This will become clearer if we recall what is written in the Gospels, how he ate and drank with sinners and publicans in order to help and save them, and how he bore the insults of the Jews for doing this: *Why does your master eat with tax collectors and sinners?* (Matt 9:11). Or again when he did not forbid the sinful woman to touch his feet and to wet them with her tears and dry them with her hair and anoint them with myrrh; for which the Jews insulted and reproached him: *If this man were a prophet, he would have known what kind of woman this is who is touching him — that she is a sinner* (Luke 7:39). . . .

For whatever was written was written for our instruction. This is like what he said elsewhere: *they were written down to instruct us, on whom the ends of the ages have come* (1 Cor 10:11). If you inquire in what sense these Scriptures were written, consider that they were written this way for us: *You shall not muzzle an ox when it is treading out the grain. Is it for oxen that God is concerned? Or does God not speak entirely for our sake?* (1 Cor 9:9-10; Deut 25:4). This was also written for our sake: *Abraham had two sons, one by a slave woman and the other by a free woman* (Gal 4:22); thus we would know that these statements are allegorical and that they represent the two covenants. For our sake, it was written that the people ate manna in the wilderness and drank water from the rock; thus we would understand that they ate spiritual food and drank spiritual drink from the rock following them, which rock was Christ. Both these and other such spiritual mysteries had been hidden from eternal times but are now manifest through the prophetic writings and the coming of our Lord and Savior Jesus Christ. To make even clearer how what was written down long ago about that earlier people was written for our sake, the prophet says to them: *You will listen with the ear but will not hear; looking, you will see but will not understand* (Isa 6:9). Of us, however, he said: *Those who have never been told of him shall see, and those who have never heard of him shall understand* (Isa 52:15). Consider, then, for whose sake these things have been written. What is written is certainly written for the sake of those who will understand and not for those who will neither see nor understand. Now those who do understand what was written will also experience what he then adds: **by steadfastness and encouragement of the scriptures we might have hope in God.** The person who believes and understands, rather than the one who does not, will receive consolation from the Scriptures.

(2) John Chrysostom on verses 1-3

We who are strong have the obligation. We have a duty, we are not doing a favor. What are we obliged to do? **To bear the weakness of those who are not strong.** You see how Paul praised them, not only by addressing them as strong, but by counting them alongside himself. This was not the only way he attracted them; he also emphasized how helpful they would be, and made it clear that what he was asking would not burden them. You are strong, Paul says, and compromising would not harm you; but, for other persons, the least issue presents a danger unless they are supported. Paul does not say "the weak," but **the weakness of those who are not strong**, enticing them and appealing to their mercy. He does the same in another place: *You who are spiritual correct such a one* (Gal 6:1). Are you strong? Repay God who made you strong. You will repay by correcting the weakness of the weak. For we were also weak, but by grace we have been made strong. We should not concentrate on just one issue, but should help those who have other weaknesses. For example, if someone is prone to anger, is insolent, or has some other such vices, we should bear it. How can we do this? Listen to the following: for when Paul says, **We ought to bear**, he added, **and not to please ourselves. Let each of you please your neighbor for good, for building them up.** Paul is saying this: Are you strong? Let the weak have evidence of your strength. Let them learn how strong you really are: please them. He did not simply say, **please**, but **for good**, and not simply **for good**, so that the strong person could not say, "Look, I am dragging him toward the good," but he added, **for building them up**. Even though you are rich, even though you are powerful, do not please yourself, but please the poor and needy person. In this way you will enjoy true glory and you will be of great help. The glory of the worldly person soon dissipates, but the glory of the spiritual person endures, if your purpose is to build up. For this reason, Paul requires it of everyone, not any one particular individual, but of **each of us**.

Because he was enjoining something important by commanding us to ignore our own perfection and correct the weakness of the other person, he followed his regular practice and reintroduced Christ into the argument by saying, **for Christ did not please himself.** For when encouraging them to give alms, he added, *Know the grace of the Lord, that for us he who is rich became poor* (2 Cor 8:9). When urging them to love, he exhorted them by this reflection, *just as also Christ loved us* (Eph 5:25). When giving advice about bearing shame and dangers, he fled to Christ, *who endured the cross for the joy placed before him, despising the shame* (Heb 12:2). Arguing here in the same manner, Paul shows that Christ also endured these things, and he appealed to the prophet who foretold it. Thus Paul added, **Just as it was written:** *The reproaches of those who reproached you fell on me.* What does he mean by, **He did not please himself**? He had the power to avoid the reproaches; he had the power to escape the things he suffered; he could have preferred his own advantage. However, he did not want this; he wanted instead to achieve our good. He set aside his own good. Why did Paul say, *He emptied himself* (Phil 2:7)? Not only to show that he had wanted to become human, but also that he was willing to be insulted and to be held in low repute by many people who considered him weak. *If you are the Son of God,* they said, *come down from the cross* (Matt 27:40), and *He saved others; he cannot save himself* (Matt 27:42). For this reason Paul recalled something useful in the present argument, and proves much more than he originally promised. He not only shows how Christ was reproached, but that the Father was also reproached. **For the reproaches of those who reproached you fell upon me,** he says. What he means is that nothing new or unusual happened; those who were intent on reproaching the Father in the Old Testament raged against the Son as well. These things were written to prevent our repeating them. Through this argument he strengthened them to endure temptation.

(3) Augustine on verse 1

Considering ourselves as members of the Church, let us distinguish what belongs to us and what to God. Then we will not stagger, then we will be grounded on the rock, we will be solid and stable against the winds, the storms, the floods, in short, against the temptations of the present age. Look at Peter, who was a symbol of ourselves at that time: one moment he was confident, the next he tottered; one moment he confessed the immortal one, the next he was afraid of dying. In the same way, then, the Church of Christ contains both the strong and the weak. It cannot lack either the strong or the weak. For this reason, the Apostle Paul says: **We who are strong ought to bear with the burdens of the weak.** When Peter said, *You are Christ, the Son of the living God* (Matt 16:16), he symbolized the strong. When he trembled and tottered, not wanting Christ to suffer, fearing death and not recognizing life, he symbolized the weak members of the Church. In that one apostle, Peter, first and foremost in the ranks of the apostles, in whom the Church itself was symbolized, both the strong and the weak had to be figuratively shown, because without both of them there is no Church.

(4) Ambrosiaster on verses 2-4

Each of us must please his neighbor for the good purpose of building him up. Now Paul speaks in his own name. He advises them to be attentive to charity and to please their neighbors in what is useful, in building up. As he says elsewhere, *I try to please everyone in everything* (1 Cor 10:33). **For Christ did not please himself, but, as it is written, The insults of those who insult you have fallen on me.** He says that in Psalm 68/69 (69:6) the Savior pleased not himself but God the Father, because he said, *For I have come down from heaven, not to do my own will, but the will of him who sent me* (John 6:38). Because he said this, the Jews who opposed him killed him as a sinner. Thus the psalmist speaks in Christ's person to the Father: **The insults of those who insult you have fallen on me.** This means: "When I did your will, they said that I sinned against you; in not receiving the one you had sent, they insulted you." The Jews sinned against God by not accepting the Christ whom God had sent and by killing him as a sinner against God; thus the sins of those sinning against God fell upon Christ. Though innocent, he was killed by sinners as a blasphemer, as is written in the Gospel.

For whatever was written was written to strengthen us, so that by steadfastness and by the encouragement of the scriptures we might have hope. The meaning is clear: everything has been written to instruct us, so that by this exhortation we may continue in hope and not distrust the promises, even if their fulfillment is delayed.

(5) Origen on verses 5-6

May the God of patience and consolation grant you to think alike, according to Jesus Christ, so that, being of one mind, you may with one voice honor the God and Father of our Lord Jesus Christ. Since patience is a virtue, and all virtue is from God, then patience comes from God. God's being called the God of patience would also seem to indicate that God is with those who have the virtue of patience in themselves, just as referring to the God of justice shows that God is in those who preserve justice, and so too with the God of truth and wisdom. In speaking of the God of consolation, he shows that God is with those who receive the consolation of the Spirit by a spiritual understanding of the divine Scriptures. **May the God of patience and consolation grant you to think alike, according to Jesus Christ.** In this, Paul called down blessings on the Romans in the way that the patriarchs and prophets did in the Scriptures. He prayed that God would grant them the same common sense. What a great blessing it is for all to share the same thought and judgment, that each would wish the same things for their neighbor and for themselves.

Do you want to understand the power of the gift of concord? The Savior said in the Gospels, *If two or three of you agree on any matter, whatsoever you ask from God will be done* (Matt 18:19). He said the same thing about himself, *Where two or three are gathered in my name,* that is, intending the same thing in the name of Christ, *there am I in the midst of them* (Matt 18:20). Do you want an example of Christ being in the midst of those agreeing? Look in the Acts of the Apostles, where it says that after the Lord's ascension, the eleven apostles with the others lifted up their voices and prayed together; the place in which they were standing was shaken, and they merited to receive the presence of the Holy Spirit (Acts 4:24, 30).

Romans 15:7-13

7 **Welcome one another, therefore, as Christ has welcomed you, for the glory of God. 8 For I tell you that Christ has become a servant to the circumcised to show God's truthfulness, in order to confirm the promises given to the patriarchs, 9 and in order that the Gentiles might glorify God for his mercy. As it is written,**

Therefore I will praise you among the Gentiles,
and sing praises to your name; **(Ps 18:49)**

10and again he says,

> *Rejoice, O Gentiles, with his people;* (Deut 32:43)

11and again,

> *Praise the Lord, all Gentiles,*
> *and let all the peoples praise him;* (Ps 117:1)

12and further Isaiah says,

> *The root of Jesse shall come,*
> *he who rises to rule the Gentiles;*
> *in him shall the Gentiles hope.* (Isa 11:10)

13May the God of hope fill you with all joy and peace in believing, so that by the power of the Holy Spirit you may abound in hope.

(1) Ambrosiaster on verses 7-12

Welcome one another, therefore, just as Christ has welcomed you, for the glory of God. As we were welcomed by Christ when he accepted our weaknesses and bore our infirmities, so should we support one another's weaknesses in patience, so that the honor of the name of God which has been conferred with us will not be in vain: we are called children of God through the favor of Christ. **For I tell you that Christ has become a servant of the circumcised on behalf of the truth of God, in order that he might confirm the promises to the patriarchs.** He praises the origins of the Jews, referring to the children of Abraham as the circumcised, on whom Christ bestowed the grace promised to the patriarchs. Thus the Savior said, *I am among you not to be served but to serve* (Matt 20:28), so that the truth of the promise made to the patriarchs might be established. Circumcision of the flesh was given to Abraham as a sign of circumcision of the heart, which the prophet later indicated in saying, *Circumcise the hardness of your heart* (Jer 4:4). Christ is the minister and the proclaimer of this promised circumcision, and then the apostles after him, to declare the circumcision of the heart to those circumcised in flesh. For Christ says, *As you have sent me into the world, so I have sent them into the world* (John 17:18). Circumcision of heart consists in cutting away the error which attaches itself to the heart like decay; once the truth is made clear, the heart can confess that God the creator is the Father of Jesus Christ, through whom all was created, so that the truth of God might be complete. God promised to have mercy and made this promise to the ancestors of the Jews. He had said to Abraham, *In your offspring, all nations will be blessed* (Gen 22:18), and to David, *One of the sons of your body, I will set upon your throne* (Ps 132:11), and, *a star shall come out of Jacob* (Num 24:17).

In order that the Gentiles might glorify God for his mercy. Because they were unworthy, no promise had been made to the Gentiles; they were brought to salvation by mercy alone, so that their confession might honor God, whom they had dishonored as unbelievers. **As it is written, *Therefore I will confess you among the Gentiles, and sing***

praises to your name. He proves this by a prophetic example: it is written in Psalm 17/18 (18:49) that the nations would be admitted to the favor of God, to attain salvation. This voice of Christ tells the future, that the preaching of him among the nations will bear fruit in their profession of the mystery of God. The Son, therefore, gives thanks to the Father for the obedience of the nations. Thence he says in the Gospel: *I thank you, Father, Lord of heaven and earth, because you have hidden these things from the wise and the intelligent and have revealed them to infants, for such was your gracious will* (Matt 11:25). This is the profession of one God in Trinity, which inspires joy; after confessing the truth, the joyful one sings of the mercy and gift of God.

And again he says, *Rejoice, O Gentiles, with his people.* This is in the canticle in Deuteronomy (32:43). **And again, *Praise the Lord, all you Gentiles, and all you peoples praise him.*** This verse in Psalm 106/117 (117:1) shows that God decided to make the Jews and the Gentiles of one heart by an intervention of mercy; that by receiving grace the Gentiles would become allies of the Jews, who had already been named God's people by that gift. The Jews were already honorable; the dishonorable Gentiles were made honorable through mercy, so that they might rejoice together in the recognition of truth. With the praises of the Gentiles, the whole people — the Twelve Tribes — would glorify the one God who added the Gentiles to increase the number of the people. Consequently, the Jews had complained about Peter's decision for Cornelius, but they were pacified by his explanation of the action and they praised God: *Then God has given even to the Gentiles the repentance that leads to life* (Acts 11:18).

And further Isaiah says, *The root of Jesse shall come, the one who rises to rule the Gentiles; in him the Gentiles shall hope* (Isa 11:10). To nurture the trust of the Gentiles and secure their hope, Paul establishes by these many witnesses that God had decreed that all the nations would be blessed in Christ. The reason was that the pride of the unbelieving Jews might not burden the souls of the believing Gentiles and make them worry that they had vainly held out hope that their faith had been accepted by the God of Abraham and that it would grow with joy and in security. Why, however, is Christ from **the root of Jesse** rather than the root of Boaz, a just person, or even Obed? He is called the son of David because of his kingship; as he was royally born from God, so he has his fleshly origin from King David. So the root is Jesse, the tree is David, which bore fruit through a branch, which is the Virgin Mary, who gave birth to Christ.

(2) Origen on verses 7-8

His saying, **Welcome one another,** should be referred back to what he first said when discussing their conflicting judgments on clean and unclean foods. He says, **Welcome one another, therefore, just as Christ has welcomed you,** because Christ was not put off by anyone's uncleanness, nor did he tally up anyone's transgressions. You must not make judgments about the uncleanness of animals, just as he did not consider the iniquities of believers. . . .

For I tell you that Christ was a servant of the circumcised on behalf of the truth of God, in order to confirm the promises of the patriarchs. . . . Christ's becoming a servant of the circumcised on behalf of the promises of the Father can be understood in two ways. First, that he received circumcision in his own flesh to manifest his origin from the seed of Abraham, to whom God promised that in his seed all nations would be blessed, and thus that the promises made to the patriarchs were being fulfilled in himself. This interpretation fits the objectives of the letter as a whole. Paul wants to restrain and repress those who were despising one another: the Jews who had believed and the Gentiles. He teaches, then, that those who continued the practices of the law should not be fully rejected, since even Christ had shown himself an observer of circumcision in his own flesh. A second way in which Christ could be called a servant of the circumcision is derived from what the Apostle says: *A person is not a Jew who is one outwardly, nor is true circumcision something in the flesh. Rather, a person is a Jew who is one inwardly, and real circumcision is a matter of the heart — it is spiritual and not literal. Such a person receives praise not from humans but from God* (Rom 2:28-29), and according to what the same Apostle says elsewhere: *In him also you were circumcised with a circumcision not done by hand in cutting off the flesh of the body, but in the circumcision of Christ, buried with him in Baptism* (Col 2:11-12). The promises to the patriarchs were clearly fulfilled in this circumcision.

(3) John Chrysostom on verse 7

Therefore receive one another, just as Christ also received you, to the glory of God.

Here again Paul mentions the example from the previous chapter, namely, Christ and his inestimable benefit. Christians joined in close unity give special glory to God. So even if you are troubled and at odds with your brother or sister, remember that you will glorify your Master by letting go of your anger; if not for the sake of your brother or sister, at least be reconciled for the sake of the ideal of unity. Indeed, let this be the primary reason for being reconciled. For Christ turned things upside down when he spoke to his Father, *In this all will know that you sent me, if they are one* (John 17:21).

Therefore let us be persuaded, and let us bind ourselves to one another. For here Paul raises up everyone, not just the weak. Even if someone prefers to be separated from you, do not respond by separating yourself. Do not be so cold-hearted as to say, "If the other loves me, I love in return; but if my right eye does not love me, I will pluck it out." Such statements are demonic and worthy only of tax collectors and small-minded Greeks. But since you are called to a better citizenship and have been enrolled in the heavens, you are subject to better laws. The point is not that you say these things, but whenever some refuse to love you, then show them an even greater love, in order to win them over, for they are also members [of the body]. Whenever some force cuts off a member from the rest of the body, we do everything we can in order to join it in once again, and we show even greater care afterward. The reward is even greater when someone who has refused to love is reconciled. For if Christ orders us to invite to dinner those who are unable to repay us, so that our reward might be greater, we ought to do this even more for love. For the one who is loved and loves in return has already given you your reward. Those who are loved and do not love in return have made God, rather than themselves, a debtor to you. Besides these considerations, when they love you, they do not give you cause for concern, but when they do not love you, then they need your help. Do not then let the cause for concern become the reason for negligence; do not say, "Since they are sick, I will not worry about them." For the chilling of love is a sickness. You must warm what is chilled. Someone may object, "What if they do not want to be warmed?" Keep doing what you have to do. "What if they become even colder?" Again, they will provide you a greater reward, and show that you imitate Christ carefully. For if to love one another is the sign of Christ's disciples — *For in this all will know that you are my disciples, if you love one another* (John 13:35) — think how much more is signified by loving someone who hates you. For your Master loved those who hated him and helped them; no matter how sick they were, he cared for them; and he proclaimed, *The strong have no need of a doctor, but those who are sick* (Matt 9:12).

He considered tax collectors and sinners worthy of his table. His concern for the Jewish people matched their disregard for him; actually his concern excelled their disdain. You must also strive to do the same. Success in this is no small matter, since without love not even the martyr can please God, as Paul says (1 Cor 13:3). So, do not say, "I do not love them because they hate me." This hatred imposes on you a greater obligation to love. Besides, someone who loves is not easy to hate. Even if people have the disposition of a wild beast, they at least love those who love them. Christ says that even the Gentiles and the tax collectors do this (Matt 5:46). If people love those who love them, who would not end up having to love some who still love them even while they hate those loving persons? So, show yourself to be that kind of person, and never stop saying, "No matter how much you hate me, I will not stop loving you." As a result you will overcome the strife, and mollify their whole souls. For this disease of hatred arises through either inflammation or coldness. The warming power of love is a customary cure for both these cases. . . .

So, are we not ashamed that the devil and his demons have such a powerful, passionate love (erōs) and we are unable to display an equally powerful spiritual love (philia) for God? Do you fail to understand that this passionate love is the devil's greatest weapon? Do you not recognize the evil demon standing ready, dragging off for himself that hate-filled member, and ready to claim it as his own? Do you run away and abandon the prize of this battle? Your brother or sister lies between you and the demon as a prize to be taken. If you prevail, you will win the prize, but if you are negligent, you will leave the contest empty-handed. So stop repeating that demonic phrase, "If my fellows hate me, I do not want to see them." Nothing is more shameful than this motto, and yet most people consider it evidence of a noble soul. Nothing, however, is more shameful or foolish or cruel than this attitude. I am especially grieved that the majority of people consider evil actions or attitudes virtuous, and that they believe that looking down on or despising others is somehow magnificent and holy. The devil's greatest snare is getting a good reputation for evil, which makes it very difficult to wipe out. I myself have heard many people bragging of shunning those who opposed them. Yet your Master takes pride in seeking out those who hate him. How many times have people spit at him? How many times have they opposed him? But he does not stop pursuing them! So do not say, "I am unable to approach those who hate me," but instead, "I am unable to spit at those who spit at me." This statement is appropriate for the disciple of Christ; the other one belongs to a disciple of the devil. This one makes a person radiant and glorious; that other makes a person shameful and ridiculous. This is why we admire Moses; when God said, *Allow me to wipe them out in my anger* (Exod 32:10), he was unable to spit on those who had so often rejected him; he said, *If you forgive them their sins, forgive. If not, destroy me too* (Exod 32:32). He acted this way because he was a friend and imitator of God.

(4) Cyril of Alexandria on verse 7

Therefore, receive one another, just as Christ received you, for the glory of God. We who are many constitute one body and are members of one another, according to the Scripture, since Christ binds us together in unity by the bonds of love. *For he . . . made both things one, and destroyed the middle wall of partition, and made the law of commandments void in dogmas* (Eph 2:14, 15). Therefore, we must indeed have the same mind toward one another; *If one member suffers, all members suffer together; and if one member is glorified, all the members rejoice* (1 Cor 12:26). **For this reason**, Paul says, **receive one another just as Christ received you, for the glory of God.** We shall receive one another when we choose to have the same mind, *bearing the burdens of one another* (Gal 6:2) and *preserving the unity of the spirit in the bond of peace* (Eph 4:3). In the same way, God received us in Christ. For he spoke truthfully when he said that *God the Father so loved the world that he gave his Son for our sake* (John 3:16). For he was given as an exchange for the life of us all; we have received the transformation of death; we have been saved from death and sin. Paul clarifies the purpose of God's eternal plan when he says, **Christ became the minister of circumcision for truth** and what follows. God promised to the ancestors of the Jews that God would bless the seed coming from them and make them as numerous as the stars of heaven. For this reason, Christ appeared in the flesh and became a human being, while existing as God, since he himself is the Word who both maintains all creation in existence and, as God, distributes its goodness to everything that exists. He came to the world with flesh, not to be served but rather, just as he himself says, *to serve, and to give his life as a ransom for many* (Mark 10:45). He proclaims that he came to fulfill the promise for Israel. For he said, *I was not sent except to the lost sheep of the house of Israel* (Matt 15:24). Therefore, Paul does not lie when he says that **Christ has become a minister of circumcision to confirm the promises to the ancestors**, and that God the Father made him the savior and redeemer for this purpose and to bring mercy for the Gentiles, so that they might glorify the creator and crafter of all things. The ineffable grace of God must not seem to be given in vain because of the great disbelief of the circumcised. They insulted him in an unholy way and refused to accept redemption from him, while only a few from Israel believed and were saved. Therefore, the Gentiles have received that peace from above which has been spread far and wide, intended for all; the mystery of wisdom in Christ has not failed to attain the kindness which is its goal. Because God is merciful, whatever lies under heaven has been saved to replace those who have fallen. By the testimonies of the prophets, Paul shows that this mystery had been announced beforehand through the voice of those holy ones who in the Spirit knew in advance the things that would later be done.

(5) Augustine on verses 8-9

The daughter of the ruler of the synagogue symbolized the Jewish people; that woman with the issue of blood, however, signified the church of the Gentiles. The Lord Christ, born from the Jews in the flesh, was revealed to the Jews in the flesh. He sent others to the nations; he did not go himself. His visible, bodily activity was performed in Judea. For this reason, the Apostle says: **For I tell you that Christ was a servant to the circumcised on behalf of the truth of God, in order that he might confirm the promises of the patriarchs** — Abraham was told, *In your seed, all the nations will be blessed* (Gen 22:18) — **and that the Gentiles might glorify God for his mercy.** So Christ was sent to the Jews. He went to raise up the daughter of the ruler of the synagogue. The woman intercepted him and was healed. She was first healed by faith, with the Savior apparently unaware of the cure. Why else did he say, *Who touched me?* (Luke 8:45)? Was God ignorant? This is a mystery of faith. Something else must be signified when someone who cannot be ignorant is presented as ignorant. So what does it signify? The healed church of the nations, which Christ did not see during the time of his bodily presence. His voice speaks in the psalm: *A people which I did not know has served me; in the hearing of the ear they obeyed me* (Ps 18:43-44). The whole earth heard and believed. The people in Judea saw; first they crucified but afterward they came to him. The Jews too will believe, but this will be at the end of the age.

(6) John Chrysostom on verse 9

That the Gentiles glorify God for God's mercy. This is what Paul means: The Jews had the promises, even though they were unworthy. You Gentiles did not enjoy this advantage; you were saved only because of God's love for humanity. Nevertheless, had Christ not come, the promise would have given no advantage to the Jews. In order to restrain the Jews and prevent their oppressing the weak, Paul recalls the promise. He then says that the Gentiles were saved by mercy alone and thus were truly bound to glorify God. Giving glory to God consists in being joined together, in being united, being of one accord in speaking well of others, in supporting those who are weaker, in not shunning someone who has broken fellowship with us. Then Paul also introduces testimonies, in which he shows that the Jews are to be joined together with the Gentiles, **Just as has been written:** *For this reason I shall praise you among the Gentiles, O Lord, and I shall chant to your Name,* and *Rejoice, Gentiles, with his people,* and *Praise the Lord, all you Gentiles, praise him, all you peoples,* and *There will be a root of Jesse, and the one who rises up to rule the Gentiles; on him will the Gentiles hope.* Paul introduced all these quotations to show that we must be united and glorify God. At the same time he restrains the Jews, so that they do not rise up against the Gentiles, since all the prophets called the Gentiles, and Paul persuades the Gentiles to be temperate by showing that they depend on a greater grace.

(7) Origen on verse 13

May the God of hope fill you with all joy and peace in believing, so that you may abound in hope in the power of the Holy Spirit. Paul quoted above what Isaiah said, *In him the Gentiles shall hope,* and here adds joyfully, **the God of hope.** If the Scripture had said, "The nations will believe in him," then Paul would certainly have added, "the God of faith." As it is, he calls down the God of hope on the nations because they hope in God. He prays that God's blessings on them will increase. That blessing is their being filled with all joy and peace. The prophet says something similar in one place: *In those days may righteousness flourish, and peace abound, until the moon is no more!* (Ps 72:7). But because this is spoken about Christ, we can refer the abundance of peace to him; by the blood of his cross, he brought peace not only on earth but in heaven as well. How the prayer of the Apostle might be fulfilled, that humans be **filled with all joy and peace**, is difficult for me to explain, particularly since the Apostle himself, in the gift he received through the Spirit, says that he *knows only in part and prophesies only in part* (1 Cor 13:9). I think, however, that believers can have the fullness of peace in being reconciled to God the Father, according to the saying of Paul: *We entreat you on behalf of Christ, be reconciled to God* (2 Cor 5:20); and in returning to peace with the Son of God through the blood of his cross; and in being united to the Holy Spirit by cleansing themselves from all impurities and being made holy vessels. So, a person would be filled with all peace by believing in the fullness of the Trinity. For this reason, the Apostle adds, **fill you with all joy and peace in believing, so that you may abound in hope in the power of the Holy Spirit.** If believers are strengthened with the power of the Holy Spirit, then they always have the fullness of joy and peace.

Romans 15:14-22

14 I myself am satisfied about you, my brethren, that you yourselves are full of goodness, filled with all knowledge, and able to instruct one another. 15 But on some points I have written to you very boldly by way of reminder, because of the grace given me by God 16 to be a minister of Christ Jesus to the Gentiles in the priestly service of the gospel of God, so that the offering of the Gentiles may be acceptable, sanctified by the Holy Spirit. 17 In Christ Jesus, then, I have reason to be proud of my work for God. 18 For I will not venture to speak of anything except what Christ has wrought through me to win obedience from the Gentiles, by word and deed, 19 by the power of signs and wonders, by the power of the Holy Spirit, so that from Jerusalem and as far round as Illyricum I have fully preached the gospel of Christ, 20 thus making it my ambition to preach the gospel, not where Christ has already been named, lest I build on another man's foundation; 21 but as it is written,

> *Those shall see who have never been told of him,*
> *and they shall understand who have never heard of him.* (Isa 52:15)

22 This is the reason that I have so often been hindered from coming to you.

(1) Origen on verses 14-15

Paul indicates the extent of their knowledge when he says, **you are able to instruct others.** He shows that they should all instruct others in what they have learned, and as fellow disciples meet together to admonish and edify one another. Mutual exchange, if it is done with charity, can produce a great deal of learning. One should look forward to the opinions of the more learned and perfect on profound and obscure matters, as Moses says: *Ask your parents, and they will inform you; your elders, and they will tell you* (Deut 32:7). . . .

I have written to you rather boldly in part, as one who is reminding you through the grace given me. Do you hear the Apostle saying, **I have written in part**? Then no one should be upset with us when we are unable to explain fully the meaning of the divine mysteries. You hear Paul, who passed these things on to us, saying that he did so partially. People should not be so confident in their knowledge that they claim to understand everything. Paul himself, by whom this knowledge has been transmitted to us, says that he understands and writes about it partially. Although Paul claims that he knows it in part, my opinion is that he knew much more than he wrote. He was a person who knew many things which he did not dare to say openly, since he described himself as acting boldly in committing some of them to writing.

(2) Origen on verse 16

When the priests were offering sacrifices, they had to make sure that the offering was free of blemish, fault, and defect, so that it would be acceptable and pleasing to God. So those who offer the gospel and announce the Word of God should take every precaution to prevent any blemish in their preaching, any defect in their teaching, and any fault in their instruction. Let them first sacrifice themselves if they can: exterminate their vices, kill the sin in their own members. Thus, not only by their teaching but also by the example of their lives, they will make the salvation of their disciples their own sacrifice acceptable to God.

(3) John Chrysostom on verses 16-17

To be the servant of Jesus Christ to the Gentiles, performing the sacred work of God. After giving abundant proof for the things he said, Paul takes the argument to a more exalted level, not simply talking about worship, as he did in the beginning, but about liturgy and sacred rites. For me, the priesthood means to preach and to proclaim; this is the sacrifice I offer. No one would find fault with a priest who zealously offers an immaculate victim. Paul was saying these things for multiple purposes: to elevate their thoughts, to show them that they are themselves the sacrifice, and to defend himself against accusations, because he had been appointed to this ministry. For my knife is the gospel, he says, the word of preaching. The goal is not to glorify myself or display my brilliance. It is rather **that the offering of the Gentiles become acceptable, sanctified in the Holy**

Spirit. That is, that the souls of those who are taught might be acceptable. For God led me to this ministry, not as an honor for me but for me to care for you. And how would they be acceptable? **In the Holy Spirit.** For we need not faith alone but a spiritual way of life as well, so that we possess the Spirit which was given once for all. For neither wood and fire, nor altar and knife mean anything to us; for us, the Spirit is everything. For this reason, I do everything not to extinguish that fire, as I am commanded. Why then do you speak to those who have no need of this? Not to teach you this, Paul says, but to remind you of it. Just as the priest stood by, tending the fire, so also I stood before you stirring up your zeal. Look, Paul does not say, "in order that it become an offering of yourselves," but, **the offering of the Gentiles.** By the Gentiles, he means the whole world, the earth and the sea together. He was anticipating their thoughts so that they did not despise having a teacher who was extending himself to the ends of the world. In the beginning he said, *As among the rest of the Gentiles, I am in debt to Greeks and barbarians, to the wise and to the unwise* (Rom 1:13-14). **Therefore I have a boast in Christ Jesus concerning the things pertaining to God.** Since he had so humbled himself, he again elevated the style of his speech. He did this for their sakes to prevent his appearing contemptible. In lifting himself up again, he recalls his own custom by saying, "Therefore I have reason to be proud."

(4) Origen on verses 17-22

There is no true boasting before God except in Christ Jesus. To boast before God without Christ is like thinking you could have glory in the sight of God without justice, wisdom, or truth. Christ is all of these, and therefore only in Christ can a person truly boast in God's sight. He says something similar elsewhere: *Let the one who boasts, boast in the Lord* (1 Cor 1:31). . . .

I will not venture to speak of anything except what Christ has accomplished through me to win obedience from the Gentiles, by word and deed, by the power of signs and wonders, in the power of the Spirit of God. What I describe, he says, are not works of someone else, nor have I become the herald of another's achievements; I write to you about what I know Christ has done through me, what he accomplished in me, in word and deed, for the obedience of the nations, by the word of preaching and the working of signs and wonders. The difference between signs and wonders has been more fully explained elsewhere and will be briefly summarized here. Something wonderful is called a sign when it points to a future event; but wonders have reference only to something marvelous. He speaks of signs and wonders when both are involved. Divine Scripture sometimes follows this usage, but occasionally it does not use the terms in their conventional sense and employs sign for wonders and wonder for signs. Paul, therefore, through the power of signs and wonders, by signs and wonders performed in the power of the Holy Spirit, spread the gospel of Christ from Jerusalem to Illyricum. God gave Moses and Aaron the power of signs and wonders, as it is written: *They performed God's signs among them, and miracles in the land of Ham* (Ps 105:27). By punishing Egypt they liberated the children of Israel, but they converted almost none of the Egyptians. With the power of signs and wonders which he received, Paul converted to the mystery of Christ not one nation, not two or three peoples, but all the nations and peoples in a circuit from Jerusalem as far as Illyricum, by the preaching of the Word and the power of works and miracles. He did not preach the gospel by adding his speech to the working and preaching of another. He did not want to steal the glory of another's work by imposing the building of his own preaching on the foundation of faith laid by another. This precedent should be noted by the leaders of the churches and followed with diligent effort: they should never appear to claim as their own anything that Christ has done but not through them; nor should they denigrate another's work and effort. They could indeed speak about something which Christ had not done through them, but only if they taught self-control without being continent, or preached sobriety and justice, giving away wealth, or despising power for sake of the kingdom of God when Christ had accomplished none of these in those teaching them. The Apostle offers himself as a model, therefore, saying that he presents and preaches to others what Christ has already accomplished in him.

But as it is written, he says, *Those who have never been told of him shall see, and those who have never heard of him shall understand.* The Apostle has carefully adhered to the prophetic utterance and preached Christ only to those to whom no one else had already preached, so that those who had not already been taught would thereby come to know him. In my opinion, this is the reason why he was repeatedly frustrated in his intention to go to Rome, as he says: **This is the reason that I have so often been hindered from coming to you.** Not, as he says in other cases, that he was *blocked by Satan* (1 Thess 2:18), but he was busy with his activities in founding churches, and starting them in places which had no prior foundation for the faith.

(5) Ambrosiaster on verses 17-20

In Christ Jesus, then, I have glory before God. For I will not venture to speak of anything except what Christ has accomplished through me to win obedience from the Gentiles, by word and deed, by the power of signs and wonders, in the power of the Holy Spirit. Paul has reason to boast before God through Christ Jesus. By believing in and serving Christ Jesus with a pure conscience, he earned merit with God the Father: he says nothing is lacking, nothing which Christ has failed to do through him for the encouragement of the Gentiles. Christ has worked signs and wonders through Paul, so that his preaching was confirmed by power. Because the divine power he has exercised was provided by God, he presents himself as having cause in Christ to brag before God. Because he was judged a good steward, he was empowered to bring about the conversion of the nations by working signs. He claims that he accomplished this because he was just as capable as the other apostles, who had been with the Lord, and because God exercised no less power among the nations. His purpose in these assertions was to build up the Gentiles by convincing them that they had received the same grace as the Jews, who could lay claim to the privilege of the patriarchs.

So that from Jerusalem and as far as Illyricum I have filled up the gospel of God and his Son, Jesus Christ. Thus I preached this gospel where Christ had not already been named, lest I build on someone else's foundation. He had a good reason for trying to preach **where Christ had not already been named**: he knew that the pseudo-apostles were presenting wrong teaching about Christ. They went about trying to convince people of a false teaching in the name of Christ; setting it right required enormous labor. So he wanted to arrive first and deliver pure preaching. He wanted his edifice to be strong, with straight lines, and on a firm foundation. As the teacher assigned to the nations, moreover, he should have been especially solicitous for teaching where Christ had not yet been proclaimed, both to establish his own authority and to achieve the full return of his labors in planting. As a result, the Church took up residence in every place. Afterward, however, the subtle malice of heresy tried to corrupt the meaning of faith and the law in the name of Christ.

(6) Ambrosiaster on verse 22

Paul returns to something he said at the beginning of the letter: *I have often intended to come to you,* he said, *but thus far have been prevented* (Rom 1:13). Now he explains why he was prevented. Though he wanted to come, he attended to a more pressing issue, to counter the false opinions of the pseudo-apostles. After preaching to everyone in his orbit, he says that he was finally free to come to Rome, as he had earlier hoped. By his letter, he was correcting the Romans, because they had been brought up under the law. Those who had not yet heard any preaching were more easily instructed by him in person; once they had been grounded on the right faith, they would not easily accept a different teaching. He promised to come when he was going to Spain, where Christ had not yet been preached nor even heard about. Because the journey was difficult for the pseudo-apostles, there was no danger in delaying his own trip a little.

Romans 15:23-29

23But now, since I no longer have any room for work in these regions, and since I have longed for many years to come to you, 24I hope to see you in passing as I go to Spain, and to be sped on my journey there by you, once I have enjoyed your company for a little. 25At present, however, I am going to Jerusalem with aid for the saints. 26For Macedonia and Achaia have been pleased to make some contribution for the poor among the saints at Jerusalem; 27they were pleased to do it, and indeed they are in debt to them, for if the Gentiles have come to share in their spiritual blessings, they ought also to be of service to them in material blessings. 28When therefore I have completed this, and have delivered to them what has been raised, I shall go on by way of you to Spain; 29and I know that when I come to you I shall come in the fullness of the blessing of Christ.

(1) Origen on verse 24

When I go to Spain, I do hope to see you on my journey does not mean that Paul cares so little about the Romans that he wants to see them only in passing and judged that he should visit them only on his way to another place. Notice what he says in what is added: **once I have enjoyed your company for a little while.** He seems to be leaving to their discretion how long he should stay with them before continuing his proposed journey. Thus, he elicits and fosters their love for him; if they develop a great affection for the Apostle, he wants them to know that he is prepared to stay with them and to go on to others only once he has fully enjoyed the gift of their love.

(2) John Chrysostom on verses 25-27

Notice how magnificently Paul uses words. He does not say, "I am going to carry alms," but **to serve.** Think how great it is for the teacher of the world to condescend to carry alms and, although he intended to travel to Rome and yearned so much to meet them, he prefers taking the offering to Jerusalem to coming to visit them.

For Macedonia and Achaea consented (i.e., they agree and wish to participate). **To some contribution.** Again Paul did not say, "alms," but **contribution.** He did not put in the **some** without reason, but to avoid giving the impression that he was reproaching them. He also did not say "to the poor," but **to the poor of the saints,** thereby giving them a double commendation, both for their virtue and their poverty. He would not be satisfied without adding, **they are debtors.** Then he illustrates this. **For if the Gentiles have fellowship with them in spiritual matters,** he says, **they also ought to serve them in bodily matters.** He means this: Christ came from the Jews and for the sake of the Jews; all the promises were made to them. For this reason Christ said, *Salvation is from the Jews* (John 4:22). From them are the apostles, from them the prophets, from them are all good things. The whole world shared in all these things. If, Paul says, you shared in better things, if you have entered in and become a partaker of the banquet prepared and laid out for the Jews according to the gospel parable, then you ought to share also in bodily goods and make a return gift to them. Paul also did not say, "to contribute," but **to perform a liturgy,** ranking them with those who serve as deacons, and with those who pay tribute to kings. He also did not say, "in your bodily matters," in direct parallel to, **in their spiritual matters.** For the spiritual goods belonged to the Jews, but bodily goods do not belong to the Gentile Christians alone; they are common to all people. He taught that money must belong to everyone, not only to those who possess it.

(3) Origen on verses 26-27

When he says, **for Macedonia and Achaia have been pleased to take up a collection for the poor among the saints at Jerusalem,** he is subtly and sensitively exhorting the Romans while praising the Corinthians. A devout mind is more easily moved to do good by example than by preaching. In adding, **they were pleased to do this, and indeed they owe it to them,** what did he intend the Romans to conclude, if not that since the Christians of Macedonia and Achaia were debtors of **the poor among the saints at Jerusalem,** so the Romans — who held the same faith in Christ — had also become debtors to them.

The Macedonians and Achaians were not alone in sharing the spiritual goods of the saints at Jerusalem and thereby obliged to minister to their carnal needs; so for the same reason, the Romans were also their debtors. He spoke only about the one, but the others understood his inference. This belongs to the literal interpretation; we have still to search out the accustomed magnificence of the writings of Paul. In my judgment, he did not think that all the poor among the saints — those whom he called the spiritual ones — were found in Jerusalem alone, which was only a single city in Palestine, thus excluding all the other Christians spread throughout the earth, whom he called the nations, or that all these others were obliged to provide bodily support to these inhabitants of Jerusalem, as though they were the only spiritual ones. Certainly there were spiritual people outside Jerusalem: it is not their location but holy living and the perfection of faith and knowledge that made them spiritual. This is what Paul wrote to the Corinthians: *Friends, if anyone is detected in a transgression, you who are spiritual should restore such a one in a spirit of gentleness* (Gal 6:1). What, then, should we think about this? That everyone who is spiritual, who serves God in the spirit and lives according to the spirit rather than the flesh, that everyone like this lives in Jerusalem, in the place of peace and established in the vision of peace? Such a person is **poor among the saints** and is among those blessed poor of whom is said: *Blessed are the poor in spirit, for theirs is the kingdom of heaven* (Matt 5:3). This is the blessed poverty which says: *I have no silver or gold, but what I have I give to you; in the name of Jesus Christ of Nazareth, stand up and walk* (Acts 3:6). This kind of pauper always lives in Jerusalem and is possessed of spiritual riches. For them, gold is wisdom and silver is the word of knowledge; clothing is Christ; banquets and riches are the table of wisdom and food abundant in the Word of God; they drink the wine of joy which Wisdom mixes in her bowl; they eat solid food from the sacrificial victims of understanding, and the Word made flesh. These are the spiritual riches in which those nations still living according to the flesh rush to share. It seems to me, then, that by "the nations" he refers the less perfect souls, who need the instruction of the perfect. If they are found worthy to share with them in understanding and spiritual knowledge, then they ought to support them in bodily goods; this means that when their spirits begin to be steeped in more lofty knowledge, then the flesh should also serve the spiritual precepts by submitting to the reins of self-control and chastity. If their flesh is still running heedlessly and unbridled in fleshly desires, then it might throw off its rider, the Word of God.

(4) Ambrosiaster on verse 27

Indeed they owe it to them; for if the Gentiles have come to share in their spiritual blessings, they ought also to be of service to them in material things. He says that they are debtors to the faithful Jews. As they have shared in their spiritual gifts, so the Gentile Christians should supply the bodily needs of the Jewish ones; through this service, the believers from among the Jews will rejoice and join in praising the providence of God for the salvation of the Gentiles. These Jews cared nothing for worldly things, had dedicated themselves totally to the service of God, and thus provided an example of good living to the other believers. The Apostle wants us to be humane and merciful, to consider ourselves debtors when we give alms and practice good works with a ready heart. Those who hope for the mercy of God should be merciful, showing that they are right to have this hope. If a human being can be merciful, how much more will God be. Moreover, a person who has received mercy makes a repayment in being merciful. Thus the Lord says: *Blessed are the merciful, for God will be merciful to them* (Matt 5:7).

Romans 15:30-33

30I appeal to you, brethren, by our Lord Jesus Christ and by the love of the Spirit, to strive together with me in your prayers to God on my behalf, 31that I may be delivered from the unbelievers in Judea, and that my service for Jerusalem may be acceptable to the saints, 32so that by God's will I may come to you with joy and be refreshed in your company. 33The God of peace be with you all. Amen.

(1) Origen on verse 30

Can anyone who reads that Paul appealed to the Christians in Rome to pray for him, then devalue or despise the prayers of the Church, even if those whose prayers are requested seem to be of little merit? Notice that Paul, although rich in apostolic merits, exhorted both the Romans and the Corinthians to pray for him. Consider the power of the religious obligations by which he binds them: **by our Lord Jesus Christ and by the love of the Spirit, help me in prayers to God.** Where our text reads, **help me in prayers**, the term in Greek means: **to help me in the struggle of prayers to God.** Thus he shows that he is in a contest of prayer, struggling against those opponents of whom he said, *For our struggle is not against enemies of blood and flesh, but against the cosmic powers of this present darkness, against the spiritual forces of evil in the heavenly places* (Eph 6:12). All of them attack faith and resist piety, just as they oppose justice, truth, and all that is good. Doubtlessly, then, they resist and fight against prayer. Thus when Paul thought it necessary to appeal for help from those living at Rome, he shows that prayer involves no small struggle. The demons and opposing powers are a hindrance in prayer, first by trying to prevent anyone from making the effort to lift up pure hands, free of anger, in the struggle of prayer. A person who can manage to get free of anger will often not escape contention, or be free of superfluous and vain thoughts. You will scarcely ever find a person who can be at prayer without any frivolous or foreign thoughts coming along which will drag down and break the intention which focuses the mind on God, tearing us away through irrelevancies. The struggle of prayer is then a mighty battle, for the assaults of the enemies distract the thoughts of the one praying, while the mind fights to keep its attention firmly focused on God, so that it might worthily proclaim: *I have fought the good fight, I have finished the race* (2 Tim 4:7).

(2) Ambrosiaster on verses 30-31

I appeal to you, brothers and sisters, by our Lord Jesus Christ and by the love of the Spirit, to join me in earnest prayer to God on my behalf, that I may be rescued from the unbelievers in Judea. He prays to be supported by their prayers and to escape the clutches of the unfaithful Jews, not that his own prayer was of less value, but to observe the rule that a church should pray for its leader. When many who are individually lowly gather together in harmony, they become mighty; the prayers of a multitude cannot be ignored. If, therefore, they really want to see the Apostle, they should pray earnestly that he will not be detained there and they will be able to welcome him in joyous love.

(3) John Chrysostom on verse 31

In order that I be delivered from those among the Jews who do not believe. A great contest then lay before Paul and is the occasion of his asking for their prayers. He did not say, "In order that I be engaged," but **that I be delivered**, as Christ directed, *Pray that you may not enter into trial* (Matt 20:41). By saying this, he showed that these evil people were wolves who would attack him, wild beasts rather than humans. From this statement Paul was leading to a second point, showing that he had good reason to take on the ministry to the saints; the unbelievers were so numerous that he prayed to be delivered from them. He knew that those living among so many enemies were going to perish from hunger. Therefore, he had to find support for these people from some other source.

And so that my ministry be acceptable in Jerusalem for the saints. In other words, so that my sacrifice may be received, so that they receive the offering with joy. See how Paul again praised the worthiness of those who were to receive it, even though he had to appeal to so many people for prayers that the gifts being sent would be received. From this, he derived another point, that giving alms does not guarantee that they will be acceptable. When someone is forced to offer alms or acts unjustly or from vainglory, the fruit of giving alms is destroyed.

(4) Theodoret on verses 31-33

Then, accurately perceiving the madness of the Jews, Paul asked for the Romans' prayers, not only for the sake of those who did not believe, but for those who believed as well. For the Jews considered him to be a transgressor of the law and thus were not well disposed toward him. For this reason he added: **So that my service for the saints is acceptable in Jerusalem.** He had struggled valiantly to collect these gifts, offering every kind of exhortation to the disciples, and then struggling with the recipients of the offering, lest their hatred overcome their need.

So that I may come to you in joy through the will of God, and rest with you. Paul desires to accomplish nothing apart from the divine will.

May the God of peace be with you all. Amen. Here Paul does not invoke **the God**

of peace as a simple title. He uses it as one who was not enjoying this peace, both because of those who were warring against him and because of those who regarded him with suspicion. He prayed for this peace for them because of their conflict over the observance of the law.

(5) Origen on verse 33

The God of peace be with all of you. He bestows a magnificent blessing on the Romans: that the God of peace be with them; that is, *that the peace of God, which surpasses all understanding, guard their hearts in Christ Jesus, who is our peace* (Phil 4:7; Eph 2:14).

Romans 16

The final chapter of the letter is largely dedicated to greetings, along with statements of praise and a final prayer or blessing. Origen and Ambrosiaster remark that the text calls Phoebe a minister of the church; Chrysostom explains that Paul prevented women from teaching but only in the assembly.

Origen finds a number of instances in which a figurative interpretation is necessary: Epaenetus as the firstfruits of Asia, the captivity Paul shared with Andronicus and Junias, that the name Satan can be applied not to an individual but to force contrary to the gospel, and how Paul is related to Lucius, Jason, and Sosipater.

Origen, Ambrosiaster, and Augustine discover dogmatic issues in the final blessing.

Romans 16:1-2

1I commend to you our sister Phoebe, a deaconess of the church at Cenchreae, 2that you may receive her in the Lord as befits the saints, and help her in whatever she may require from you, for she has been a helper of many and of myself as well.

(1) Origen on verses 1-2

I commend to you our sister Phoebe, a deacon of the church at Cenchreae, so that you may receive her in the Lord as is fitting for the saints, and help her in whatever she may require from you, for she has helped many and myself as well. This passage teaches us, with apostolic authority, that women were appointed to the ministry of the church. Paul describes Phoebe, who held office in the church of Cenchreae, with great praise and commendation. He lists her outstanding deeds and says, **she has helped many**, ready whenever they were in difficulty, **and myself as well**, in my troubles and my apostolic labors, with full devotion. I would compare her work to that of Lot; because he always offered hospitality, he merited to receive angels as guests. Similarly Abraham, who always went out to meet strangers, merited that the Lord and his angels would stop and rest in his tent. In the same way, Phoebe, since she offered and provided assistance to everyone, merited to become a benefactor of the Apostle. This passage provides two lessons:

women served as ministers in the church and those appointed to the ministry of the church should be benefactors to many and through their good services merit the praise of the apostles. The passage also encourages Christians to honor those who commit themselves to good works in the church; whether they serve spiritual or fleshly needs, they should be held in honor.

(2) Theodoret on verses 1-3

Cenchreae is a large village outside Corinth. Because of this, we can properly wonder at the power of preaching. In a short time Paul not only filled the cities with piety, but he even filled the villages. The congregation of the church of the Cenchreans was so great that they even had a woman deacon, who was highly regarded and famous. For she was so rich in accomplishments that she enjoyed praise from the mouth of the Apostle.

For she has been, Paul says, **a benefactor for many people and for myself.** I think he is calling hospitality and care a benefaction; he repays her with honor many times over. For she probably received him in her house for a short time, since he clearly spent time in Corinth. But he opened the universe to her, and this woman is now famous everywhere on earth. Not only do the Romans and the Greeks know her, but even all the barbarians.

(3) Ambrosiaster on verse 1

He recommended Phoebe, who was coming to them, as a sister they had in common, according to the law. In recommending her, he specified that she was a minister of the church at Cenchreae. She was worthy of their assistance on her journey, he says, because she had herself been of assistance to many. He urged that if she had already arrived, she be received without hesitation and helped with any need. He added that she had been part of his group, to show that they should be all the more prepared to fulfill in love the favor he was asking, relying on his own prominent status.

Romans 16:3-16

₃**Greet Prisca and Aquila, my fellow workers in Christ Jesus,** ₄**who risked their necks for my life, to whom not only I but also all the churches of the Gentiles give thanks;** ₅**greet also the church in their house. Greet my beloved Epaenetus, who was the first convert in Asia for Christ.** ₆**Greet Mary, who has worked hard among you.** ₇**Greet Andronicus and Junias, my kinsmen and my fellow prisoners; they are men of note among the apostles, and they were in Christ before me.** ₈**Greet Ampliatus, my beloved in the Lord.** ₉**Greet Urbanus, our fellow worker in Christ, and my beloved Stachys.** ₁₀**Greet Apelles, who is approved in Christ. Greet those who belong to the family of Aristobulus.** ₁₁**Greet my kinsman Herodion. Greet those in the Lord who belong to the family of Narcissus.** ₁₂**Greet those workers in the Lord, Tryphaena and Tryphosa.**

Greet the beloved Persis, who has worked hard in the Lord. 13**Greet Rufus, eminent in the Lord, also his mother and mine.** 14**Greet Asyncritus, Phlegon, Hermes, Patrobas, Hermas, and the brethren who are with them.** 15**Greet Philologus, Julia, Nereus and his sister, and Olympas, and all the saints who are with them.** 16**Greet one another with a holy kiss. All the churches of Christ greet you.**

(1) John Chrysostom on verses 3-5

Greet, Paul says, **Priscilla and Aquila, my fellow ministers in Christ Jesus.** Luke also witnesses to the virtue of these two when he says, *Paul stayed at their house, for they were tent-makers by trade* (Acts 18:3), and when he shows that the woman Priscilla received Apollos and instructed him in the way of the Lord (Acts 18:26). These deeds are great in themselves, but what Paul says about the people is much greater. What does he say? First, he calls them **fellow ministers**, showing that they shared in his unimaginable labors and dangers. Then he says, **Because they put out their own necks for my soul.** Do you recognize them as fulfilled martyrs? There were innumerable dangers under Nero, since he ordered all the Jews to be expelled from Rome (Acts 8:2).

I am not the only one who gives thanks to them, but also all the churches of the Gentiles. In this statement, he hints at their ministry of hospitality and monetary assistance, standing in wonder that they poured out their blood and handed over all their possessions to be shared property. You see here a noble woman whose feminine nature proved to be no obstacle on the road to virtue. This is to be expected, *For in Christ Jesus there is no male, no female* (Gal 3:28). Whatever Paul said about the man Aquila, he says about the woman Priscilla as well. **She has become the protector of many and of myself.** And again he referred specifically to the woman Priscilla, **I am not alone in giving thanks, but also all the churches of the Gentiles.** To prevent them from thinking he was engaging in flattery by saying these things, Paul adduces additional witnesses to Priscilla's merit.

And the church which meets in their house. Thus they were happy to make their house into a church, by making everyone in it a believer and by opening their home to strangers. For it was not Paul's custom simply to identify houses as churches, unless they were deeply rooted in piety and fear of God. For this reason, Paul said to the Corinthians: *Greet Aquila and Priscilla, with the church in their house* (1 Cor 16:19). Also, when he was writing about Onesimus he said, *Paul to Philemon and beloved Apphia and the church in your house* (Phlm 1-2). For even married Christians could be noble and admired.[1] See, then, that Aquila and Priscilla were married and had become honorable, and yet their livelihood was not noteworthy, since they were tentmakers. Their virtue, however, covered everything and showed them to be greater than the sun. Neither their trade nor their marriage hindered them, since they exhibited the love which Christ required. For *greater love than this no one has*, Christ says, *than to lay down one's life for one's friends* (John 15:13). They succeeded in displaying this characteristic sign of a disciple, for they took up

---

1. John Chrysostom lived at a time when the celibate life was considered the highest goal of Christians.

the cross and followed Christ. Although they did this for Paul's sake, they actually showed their courage for Christ's sake.

(2) Ambrosiaster on verses 3-4

Aquila and Priscilla were Jews who had believed and become collaborators of the Apostle. Because they truly believed, they had exhorted others to their faith. They had carefully instructed even Apollos in the way of the Lord, although he was himself well versed in the Scriptures (Acts 18:26). Thus Paul calls them his fellow workers **in Christ Jesus**; they were his collaborators in the gospel. Aquila is Priscilla's husband. Clearly, their coming to Rome had not been in vain; they were eager in their devotion to God. Everyone whom Paul addresses in this section should be understood as present in Rome for the purpose of strengthening the Christians there. Thus he says that not only he but **all the churches of the Gentiles give thanks to them**. He urges the Romans to care for these workers, whom they have heard are laboring for the benefit of the Gentiles by pleading with them to have faith in Christ.

(3) Origen on verses 4-7

He says, **to whom not only I give thanks but also all the churches of the Gentiles.** Thence it is clear that Prisca and Aquila had shown themselves dutiful and hospitable toward all their fellows among the faithful, not only those who had been Jews but also those Gentiles who had believed. Great grace is found in the practice of hospitality, not only in the sight of God but before humans as well. Because offering hospitality involves not only the will and decision of the masters but the gracious and faithful service of the household servants, Paul named everyone who was faithfully performing this service, with their masters, as their domestic church.

Greet my beloved Epaenetus, who was the first convert in Asia for Christ. I understand him as saying that this Epaenetus was the first of the Asians to believe; for this reason, Paul calls him the beginning of that church, or, as the Greek reads, **the firstfruits of Asia.** Perhaps these words signify something more profound, which we should understand: the angels of God who preside over the churches choose from among the believers certain individuals to offer to God as firstfruits. They would select these firstfruits not on the basis of temporal priority but because of their outstanding virtue and merit. Through the Spirit, Paul knew the election of Epaenetus and that he had been selected by the angels from the whole number of the faithful in Asia, and thus Paul called him **the firstfruits of Asia.** In another letter, he says of some: *they are the firstfruits of Achaia* (1 Cor 16:15). No doubt he perceives in them the same ideal of the mystery.

Greet Mary, who has worked very hard among you. In this passage as well, he teaches that women should work for the churches of God. They work by *teaching younger women to be modest, to love their husbands, to raise children, to be pure and chaste, to govern their homes well, to be kind, to submit to their husbands* (Titus 2:4-5), *to welcome guests,* *to wash the feet of the saints* (1 Tim 5:10), and to perform all the other roles which are listed in Scripture, things which are to be accomplished *in all chastity* (1 Tim 5:2).

Greet Andronicus and Junias, my relatives and fellow prisoners; they are prominent among the apostles, and they were in Christ before I was. These might have been Paul's blood relatives; they might have believed in Christ before he did and been distinguished among the apostles of Christ. He might have called them **prominent among the apostles** and among the apostles who preceded him because they were among the seventy-two who were also called apostles (Luke 10:1). But I am puzzled by his saying, **my fellow prisoners**. Where does Paul talk about a captivity which he shared with Andronicus and Junias? There might be a deeper mystery here: he could be referring to that captivity from which Christ came to set free, of which it is written that he came *to set captives free and give sight to the blind* (Luke 4:18; Isa 61:1). They might have been captives along with Paul in this sense.

(4) John Chrysostom on verse 6

Greet Mary, who did much labor for you. What is this? Again a woman is crowned and proclaimed victor; we men are once again put to shame, or, rather, we are both put to shame and honored. We are praised because the women among us have such outstanding characters; we are put to shame because we men are left so far behind them. If, however, we identify the source from which those women draw their adornment, we might swiftly leave them behind. So, what is the source of their ornaments? Let both men and women listen. Not bracelets or necklaces, not eunuchs and handmaidens, not gold-spangled clothes, but rather great labors for the sake of the truth. **For she**, Paul says, **did much labor for us.** She did this not for herself alone or for her own virtue — which many women do today when they fast or sleep on the floor — but to serve others, continuing the race run by the apostles and evangelists. How then does Paul say, *I do not permit women to teach* (1 Tim 2:12)? He prevents a woman from presiding in the midst of the assembly and from taking a seat in the altar area, but not from all teaching, since that would contradict what he says elsewhere to the woman who has an unbelieving husband, *For who knows, woman, if you might save your husband* (1 Cor 7:16)? How would he even allow a woman to admonish her children, when he says, *She will be saved through childbearing, if they remain in faith and love and holiness with self-control* (1 Tim 2:15)? How did Priscilla instruct Apollos in the faith (Acts 18:26)? So, Paul did not say this to forbid private discussions which would benefit others, but only those discourses in the midst of the congregation and in the public assembly which are appropriate for teachers. Or when the husband is a believer and fully endowed, and able to teach his wife. But when she is the wiser, Paul does not forbid her to teach and correct. Notice also that Paul did not say, "Who taught many things," but **Who performed many labors**, showing that, along with her teaching, she performed other ministries, such as risking dangers, dispersing money, and suffering exile.

The women of that time were more zealous than lions, sharing with the apostles in their labors of preaching. For this reason, they also traveled abroad with them and served them in every other way. In a similar way, women followed after Christ, ministered to the disciples from their possessions (Luke 8:3), and served the Teacher.

(5) Ambrosiaster on verse 13

Greet Rufus, chosen in the Lord, also his mother and mine. He named Rufus before his mother because he had been chosen to work for the grace of God, in which this woman has no place. He had been chosen and promoted by the Lord to care for his own work. His mother was so holy, however, that the Apostle here called her his own mother as well.

(6) Origen on verse 14

Greet Asyncritus, Phlegon, Hermes, Patrobas, Hermas, and the brothers who are with them. They are given a simple greeting, and no distinguishing praise is added. I think that this Hermas is the author of that book which is called *The Shepherd*, which I consider very useful and, in my judgment, divinely inspired. I suspect that Paul did not bestow any praise on him because, as that writing itself clearly indicates, he was moved to repentance after many sins — which would also explain why Paul did not reproach him. He had learned from the Scriptures not to blame a person who was repenting of sin. Nor did he attribute praise to him because he was still under the guidance of the angel of repentance, who would offer him to Christ again at the proper time. We understand that those who are associated with one another in the greeting must have been living together.

(7) Origen on verse 16

Greet one another with a holy kiss. From this passage and a number of similar ones, we can gather that the custom handed down to the churches was that Christians greet one another with a kiss after the prayers. The Apostle calls this **a holy kiss**. This name indicates, first, that the kiss given in the church was chaste; then that it was not a pretense, like the kiss of Judas who gave a kiss with his lips but a betrayal with his heart. The kiss of the faithful should be chaste, as we have said; it should also carry peace and sincerity in unfeigned love.

(8) John Chrysostom on verse 16

Greet one another with a holy kiss. Through this greeting of peace Paul expels every disturbing thought and every cause of resentment. An important person should not look down on an unimportant one, nor should a person of lower status speak ill of someone of higher status. This kiss mollifies and equalizes everyone, banishing grievances and jealousy. For this reason, Paul not only directs them to kiss one another in this way, but he also sends them the kiss of greeting from all the churches. For he says, **they greet you**, not of any one particular individual, but of everyone in common.

(9) Ambrosiaster on verse 16

All the churches of Christ greet you. From this we understand that some churches did not belong to Christ. Thus David calls a gathering of the wicked a church of the spiteful (Ps 26:5). He says that the churches of all places greet them, desiring that they grow in faith. This, therefore, refers to what he had said before: that salvation is in Christ; that the faithful people belong to Christ; that the whole creation lives by Christ's will. Some of them thought that they should trust in the law but, as the Apostle Peter said, Christ is the *Author of life* (Acts 3:15).

Romans 16:17-20

17I appeal to you, brethren, to take note of those who create dissensions and difficulties, in opposition to the doctrine which you have been taught; avoid them. 18For such people do not serve our Lord Christ, but their own appetites, and by fair and flattering words they deceive the hearts of the simple-minded. 19For while your obedience is known to all, so that I rejoice over you, I would have you wise as to what is good and guileless as to what is evil; 20then the God of peace will soon crush Satan under your feet. The grace of our Lord Jesus Christ be with you.

(1) Origen on verses 17-19

Inspired by the Spirit of God, Paul shows that quarrels and disputes are stirred up in the churches on account of the belly, that is, for the sake of profit and desire. This is the reason people go around to various houses, graciously speaking flattery and deceiving, not to build up souls in virtue by the Word of God but by sweet and ingratiating discourses to encourage them to continue or even advance in vice. They praise and approve things deserving of reproach, *putting darkness for light and light for darkness, bitter for sweet and sweet for bitter* (Isa 5:20). Thus they seduce the hearts of the innocent. The Romans should therefore carefully examine the objectives of the teachers, whether they are trying to win favor and honor from their hearers or striving to attain a reward from the Lord by the instruction and advancement of their students.

With great subtlety, Paul remarks on the indiscriminate and facile obedience of the Romans, saying that it is known, but not praised, everywhere. If he criticized them openly, he might drive them back into disobedience, so he adds: **so that I rejoice over you**. But, you ask, how can he be criticizing their obedience as undiscerning when he says, **I rejoice over you**? First, to disapprove their vice is not the same as stigmatizing the people themselves. He might be rejoicing over them because of the many other good qualities he observes in them; he would then criticize the fault which he disapproved, so that they would not think it had pleased him, along with their good qualities. A second reason for the Apostle's saying that he rejoiced over them was that disobedient people can be drawn neither to good nor to evil, while because of their inexperience, the obedient can be drawn to useless things. They do not realize that they are obeying what is not helpful; once they learn what is really useful, however, they will immediately ascend the road to virtue through the good practice of that obedience which they had already developed. Paul rejoices over them as obedient because he is certain that once they have learned not to obey indiscriminately as they have always carelessly done in the past, they will practice only proper obedience to God rather than humans. To know whose directives should be followed and whose rejected requires no little discretion, indeed a tested and experienced judgment. Finally, the Lord says in the Gospels: *Beware of those who come to you in sheep's clothing but inwardly are ravenous wolves* (Matt 7:15). An attentive mind and watchful eye are required, then, to distinguish the exposed simple-mindedness of the sheep from the hidden rapacity of the wolf. Consider the peril of those who neglect training themselves in the divine Scriptures, whence alone the discretion to examine such questions can be acquired. In this short statement, he shows the distinction he is proposing: since your obedience is facile and indiscriminate, you must learn what you ought to observe and what avoid.

I want you to be wise in what is good and guileless in what is evil. This is like what he wrote to the Corinthians: *be infants in evil, but adults in your thinking* (1 Cor 14:20). This supplements what the Lord said: *the children of this age are more shrewd in dealing with their own generation than are the children of light* (Luke 16:8). The children of this age are more shrewd in evil because they always find a more subtle and devious way to do greater harm and inflict grievous injury. These people are stupid in good, however; they can scarcely find any good to do. On the contrary, Paul wants us to be wise in good: always to be discovering more, searching out more, thinking more deeply about the good we might accomplish. So when some wickedness blocks our doing a particular good work, we can be shrewd enough to find a way forward: to speak a good word if we cannot perform a good deed; if even a good word is impeded, we can at least show good intention and spirit. Thus, we should be wise in good and simple in evil: if we are overcome by malice and injury, we should not become crafty and cunning, looking for stratagems and schemes by which we can repay evil with evil and wickedness for wickedness.

(2) John Chrysostom on verse 17

Those who make dissensions and offenses contrary to the teaching which you learned. Dividing the church is above all else overturning the church. This is a weapon of the devil; it turns everything upside down. As long as the body is united, the devil does not have the power to enter, but dissension opens an opportunity for offense. Whence does this dissension arise? From doctrines contrary to the teaching of the apostles. Whence do such dogmas come? From slavery to the stomach and to other passions.

For, Paul says, **such people do not serve the Lord, but their own bellies.** So if doctrines were not invented contrary to the apostles' teaching, then no dissension and consequently no offenses would result. Paul makes this clear from the phrase **contrary to teaching.** He did not say, "which we taught," but, **which you learned**, anticipating their response and showing that they had been persuaded, that they had been receptive and attentive to those teachers. What should we do to teachers who work such evils? Paul did not say, "Go forward together and attack," but, **turn away from them.** If they had done this in ignorance or by error, you should correct them; but since they sin knowingly, **turn away from them.** Elsewhere Paul says, *Withdraw from every brother who walks in a disorderly manner* (2 Thess 3:6). While speaking to Timothy about the coppersmith, he gives similar advice: *Watch him* (2 Tim 4:15).

(3) John Chrysostom on verse 19

For your obedience has reached to all people. Paul does this, not to allow them to behave impudently, but to win them over beforehand with praises, and to gain their commitment by a great number of witnesses. I do not bear witness alone, he says, but the whole world bears witness. He did not say, "your understanding," but, **your obedience**, meaning persuasion, which provided evidence of their great meekness. **Therefore I rejoice concerning you.** Even this phrase is not insignificant. After the praise comes an admonition. So that he does not make them worse by ignoring them after he delivered them from the earlier charges, he hints to them again, **I want you to be wise toward good but guileless toward evil.** Notice how he accuses them again, even though they do not suspect it. This statement seems to give a hint that some of them were led astray.

(4) Origen on verse 20

The God of peace will crush Satan under your feet quickly. Who is this Satan who is shortly going to be crushed? If Paul is referring to a single individual, it would seem to be the one designated in the Gospel: *I watched Satan fall from heaven like a flash of lightning* (Luke 10:16), the Satan who opposes the human race. Now if Paul is accurate in what he says, that this being will shortly be crushed beneath the feet of those to whom he is writing, then there would no longer be any Satan to stir up struggles, contests, and persecutions for believers. The facts do not allow this interpretation. It seems to me that in this passage, he used the name Satan for every spirit which opposes believers. In our language, *satan* means "adversary." Satan, then, is the name used for whatever resists and opposes a soul moving toward God, for whatever troubles its peace. This is why he begins the sentence with **the God of peace**, that is, the God who takes pleasure in peace, will crush the one who opposes peace and causes conflicts. This is what we read in the book of Kings, that God raised up Hadad the Edomite as a *satan*[2] to Solomon (1 Kgs

---

2. In the LXX version, the Hebrew is translated "adversary."

11:14); against Solomon, who was a peacemaker, an enemy was stirred up who opposed peace. The Apostle promises those he is teaching that if they act and conduct themselves according to his advice for the amendment of their lives, then God will swiftly crush Satan under their feet. But the God of peace will raise up a *satan,* an adversary, against those who do not guard peace with a pure heart and a clean conscience. Those who neglect the good of peace must bear the bitterness of assaults; in the midst of battle, they will recall the sweetness of the peace they violated. So let us be built up by both phrases of this passage from divine Scripture, that God raises up Satan to oppose the negligent and aids the earnest by crushing or subduing Satan. God incites one group to struggle and gives the palm of victory and the reward of virtue to the others who have overthrown their enemy....

The grace of our Lord Jesus Christ be with you. We should understand the grace of God and the grace of our Lord Jesus Christ as the same grace. Just as the Father gives life to those he chooses and the Son gives life to those he chooses, as the Father has life in himself and gave to the Son to have life in himself (John 5:21, 26), so too the grace which the Father gives is the same as that which the Son gives. We should know that everything humans have is a grace from God; nothing is owed to them. *Who first gave to God, so that God should repay?* (Rom 11:35). One who once was not and now is has nothing except through grace, a grace received from the one who always was, is, and will be.

(5) John Chrysostom on verse 20

The grace of our Lord Jesus Christ be with you. The greatest weapon, an unbroken wall, an unshaken tower. Paul reminded them about grace for the purpose of making them more zealous. If you have been saved from very serious things by grace alone, you will much prefer to be saved from less serious things; you have become friends and you have contributed your own part.

See how Paul does not propose either prayer without works or works without prayer. For after he testified to their obedience, he then prayed, thereby showing that we have need of both — what comes from our part, and what comes from God — if we intend to be saved by diligent effort. For not only in past times but even now, although we may be great and respected, we still need grace from God.

Romans 16:21-24

21Timothy, my fellow worker, greets you; so do Lucius and Jason and Sosipater, my kinsmen.

22I, Tertius, the writer of this letter, greet you in the Lord.

23Gaius, who is host to me and to the whole church, greets you. Erastus, the city treasurer, and our brother Quartus, greet you.

24The grace of our Lord Jesus Christ be with you all. Amen.

(1) Origen on verse 21

My helper Timothy and Lucius and Jason and Sosipater, all my relatives, greet you. Whoever examines Paul's writings carefully, because Christ is speaking in him, will certainly be troubled by this statement. Paul declared that he was a Hebrew of Hebrews, born in Tarsus of Cilicia. How, then, can he refer to either Timothy of Derbe, whose father was a Gentile, or Jason of Thessalonica or Sosipater of Berea as relatives, people related to him by blood? One explanation might be that all of them were part of the circumcised people; but this would not justify his singling these four men out as relatives; on that basis, all the Jews could be called relatives of Paul. Since, however, he never applies this term to all the Jews but does ascribe it to these and a few others, he clearly seems to name as his relatives people who have something in common with Timothy, Lucius, and a few others. He must, then, be basing this relationship and sharing of blood on their common descent from that paternity which he knows he shares with them: *For this reason I bow my knees before the Father, from whom every family in heaven and on earth takes its name* (Eph 3:14-15). He knows that just as there is paternity on earth, some sort of paternity is found in heaven as well. He must, therefore, know he has a relationship of heavenly parentage to those with whom he shares no earthly one. So he calls them relatives and fellow prisoners and helpers, since he shared their lot and had received with them the family identity of being born to preach the gospel and to endure the Babylonian captivity of this world.

(2) Theodoret on verse 21

Timothy, my co-worker, greets you, and Lucius, and Jason, and Sosipater, who are my relatives. Paul has remarkable co-workers; they have a famous relative. To be a co-worker is much more honorable than to be a relative. This Timothy is the one whom Paul circumcised at Lystra (Acts 16:1-3), to whom he wrote two epistles. We remember Jason from the story in Acts of the Apostles (Acts 17:1-9).

(3) Theodoret on verse 24

May the grace of our Lord Jesus Christ be with you all. Again Paul gave a share of the spiritual blessing, and he surrounded them with the grace of the Lord, like a wall as hard as steel. He both introduced and concluded his epistle with this prayer (Rom 1:7). Let us also share in it so that we may become greater than those who plot against us; so that when we are enlightened by this grace, we may travel the straight road without wandering away. By following the footprints of the Apostle, may we be worthy to see the teacher; through his prayers, may we enjoy the benevolence of the Master. May we attain to the promised good things, through the grace and love of humanity of our Lord Jesus Christ, who, together with the Father and the all-Holy Spirit, are due glory and honor, now and forever, and to the ages of ages. Amen.

Romans 16:25-27

25Now to him who is able to strengthen you according to my gospel and the preaching of Jesus Christ, according to the revelation of the mystery that was kept secret for long ages 26but is now disclosed and through the prophetic writings is made known to all nations, according to the command of the eternal God, to bring about the obedience of faith — 27to the only wise God be glory forevermore through Jesus Christ! Amen.

(1) Origen on verse 25

Now to him who is able to strengthen you according to my gospel and the preaching of Jesus Christ. . . . Paul presents two ways of strengthening those who are confirmed in the faith of the gospel: that they come to know the preaching of Paul, which is the proclamation of Jesus Christ; and that the mystery which was kept secret for long ages is revealed to them. Now the coming of Christ and his bodily presence are manifest and open, declared with suitable witnesses and supported by the prophetic writings. In this way, the decree of eternal God appeared, that through the preaching of the gospel, the nations would be called to the obedience of faith; when the mystery is revealed and the wisdom of God acknowledged, all praise and glory will be offered to the wise God alone in the ages of ages. But let us reconsider the meaning of **to him who is able to strengthen you according to my gospel and the preaching of Jesus Christ, according to the revelation of the mystery that was kept secret for long ages.** I think that these types of strengthening do not both apply to everyone. **The gospel of Paul and the preaching of Christ** certainly apply to all believers. **The revelation of the mystery that was kept secret for long ages**, however, applies not to the many called but to the chosen few, who are capable of receiving the wisdom and knowledge of God, of whom it is said: *many are called, but few are chosen* (Matt 22:14).

(2) Ambrosiaster on verses 25-27

He gives glory to God the Father, from whom are all things, praying that the powerful God might bring to fulfillment what he had begun among the Romans, confirming their souls in faith for the success of the gospel and the revelation of the mysteries hidden from the ages revealed through Christ or by Christ. The mystery hidden forever in God was made manifest in the time of Christ: that God is not alone; that from eternity the Word and the Paraclete are with God. In this truth, God has decreed that every creature will be saved through knowledge [of God]. Through the prophets, the truth of this mystery was intimated by symbols known only to the wisdom of God. God wanted the Gentiles to share in this grace, which had been hidden from the human race. God alone is wise, because all wisdom comes from God, as Solomon says, *all wisdom is from the Lord God, and it remains with God forever* (Sir 1:1). This wisdom is actually Christ, because he is from God, was always with God, and through him be glory to God forever and ever, amen.

Nothing is fulfilled without Christ, because through him are all things. When Christ is confessed, praise is given to God the Father through him, because God is known through Christ, his wisdom, in whom God saves believers. Glory therefore belongs to the Father through the Son; glory to both in the Holy Spirit, because both share the same glory.

(3) Augustine on verses 25-27

When the Apostle wrote to the Romans, he said at the end of the letter: **Now to him who is able to strengthen you according to my gospel and the proclamation of Jesus Christ, according to the revelation of the mystery that was kept secret for long ages but is now disclosed, and through the prophetic writings is made known to all the Gentiles, according to the command of the eternal God, to bring about the obedience of faith — to the only wise God, through Jesus Christ, to whom be the glory forever!** That is, everlasting glory be to God who is able to strengthen you, to the only wise God. Consider the insertion, **through Jesus Christ**. Should this be taken as, "to the only God wise through Jesus Christ," so that the only wise God is, through Jesus Christ, understood to be wise — not sharing in but generating the wisdom which is Christ Jesus? Or should it be taken not as "through Jesus Christ to the wise God" but instead, "through Jesus Christ glory to God alone wise"? It seems ambiguous. But who would dare say that God the Father becomes wise through Jesus Christ? Doubtless, God the Father is wise in his very being, and the being of the Son comes from the generating Father rather than the being of the Father coming through the generated Son. Thus it follows: "may glory be to the only wise God through Jesus Christ." Glory here is that "clear knowledge with praise," by which the triune God became known to the Gentiles. This happens **through Jesus Christ** because, to pass over other reasons, he commanded that the nations be baptized, *In the name of the Father and the Son and the Holy Spirit* (Matt 28:19), where the glory of this indivisible Trinity was most particularly revealed. God therefore, that is, the Trinity itself, is rightly called alone wise, because God alone is wise according to God's being, not according to an added or fortuitous sharing in wisdom, in the way that rational creatures are wise.

(4) Ambrosiaster on verse 28

He places Christ, through whose grace we were first created and then reformed, here at the conclusion so that he will remain in our minds. If we remember his gifts to us, he will always protect us: *Behold, I am with you always*, he says, *until the end of the age* (Matt 28:20).

Appendix 1: Authors of Works Excerpted

Ambrosiaster (probably fourth century) is a name given to an unknown early Christian writer who wrote commentaries in Latin on the thirteen letters of Paul, perhaps in Rome at the time of Pope Damasus (366-84). His commentaries were attributed to Ambrose (hence the name "Ambrosiaster"), but this attribution has been rejected by scholars since the Renaissance. His commentary on Romans has survived in three slightly different versions. Ambrosiaster is also assumed to be the author of a work called *Questions on the Old and New Testaments*.

Anonymous is used to name the unidentified author of a complete commentary on the letters of Paul (including Hebrews) which was found in a Latin manuscript in the Hungarian National Library. It seems to have been written in the late fourth century and overlaps significantly with the commentary of Pelagius.

Apollinaris (ca. 315–ca. 390) was a close associate of Athanasius of Alexandria and supporter of the Council of Nicea. He was chosen bishop of Laodicea about 360. Apollinaris developed an understanding of the union of divine and human in Christ, according to which the human mind and will were replaced by the divine. He also wrote treatises against Greek philosophers and extensive commentaries on Scripture which have been lost. His commentary on Romans survives only in fragments.

Augustine (354-430), bishop of Hippo, was the preeminent Latin theologian of the patristic period. Trained as a teacher of rhetoric, he spent many years as a Manichean before being baptized by Ambrose in Milan in 387. The immense corpus of his writings includes the autobiographical *Confessions,* the *Trinity,* his most important dogmatic work, and *The City of God,* in which he answers pagan critics of Christianity through a synthesis of philosophical, theological, and political ideas that was to become a foundational text for Western civilization. Augustine wrote commentaries on Genesis (the *Literal Commentary on Genesis*), the Psalms, the Gospel of John, Galatians, and two partial commentaries on Romans. The explanation of themes treated by Paul in Romans is central to much of his other writing and preaching.

Authors of Works Excerpted

Cyril of Alexandria (d. 444) was patriarch of Alexandria and an influential theologian who played an important role in the formulation of the classic doctrine of the person of Christ. He led opposition to the teaching of the Antiochene Nestorius, bishop of Constantinople. His writings include theological treatises, letters, and many commentaries, including one on Romans, which survives only in fragments.

Gennadius of Constantinople (d. 471) was patriarch of that city from 458 until his death. He upheld the decree of the Council of Chalcedon (451). His commentaries on Scripture, including Romans, survive only in fragments.

John Chrysostom (ca. 347-407) studied rhetoric under the pagan orator Libanius and theology under Diodore of Tarsus, head of the Christian school of Antioch. As a priest at Antioch and later bishop of Constantinople he was known especially for his high moral tone, his courage in difficult political circumstances, and his eloquence. His honorific title "Chrysostom" means "golden tongued," and it reflects his great reputation as a preacher. He preached extended series of sermons on many biblical books, including a complete explanation of Romans.

Origen of Alexandria (ca. 185-254) is the true godfather of Christian biblical scholarship and interpretation. Despite posthumous condemnations by some of his bolder theological speculations, Origen exerted an unrivaled influence on early Christian biblical interpretation not only in the eastern Christian tradition but in the West as well, through the medium of Latin translations. He wrote many commentaries and series of homilies on Old and New Testament books (e.g., on Genesis, Exodus, Leviticus, Jeremiah, Luke, and John), and apparently commented on all the Pauline epistles. Known especially for his allegorical or symbolic exegesis, Origen also concerns himself with historical and philological questions. His philological training is evident in his careful attention to the definitions of words, to shades of meaning expressed by similar phrases, and to textual variants. His commentary on Romans survives in some fragments from chapters 3–5 and in a Latin version made by Rufinus of Aquileia, in which Origen's thought seems to have been adapted to standards and needs of the late fourth-century Church.

Pelagius (born ca. 354), a British monk and leader of an ascetic movement, was active in Rome from 384 to 410. His teaching that human beings were endowed with an inalienable power to choose between good and evil was opposed by Augustine and condemned by African councils and Roman bishops. He produced a complete commentary on the letters of Paul which draws heavily on earlier commentaries. It consists mostly of brief notes and displays a particular interest in moral progress and in the power of imitating exemplary lives.

Theodoret (ca. 393–ca. 460), bishop of Cyrus in Syria (near Antioch), was educated in Antioch and defended Nestorius and Antiochene Christology against the criticisms of Cyril of Alexandria. His works include an apology that compares Christian and pagan teaching, a church history, biographies of monks, a refutations of heresies, and commentaries on many Old Testament books, in addition to a commentary on the whole of Romans.

Appendix 2: Sources of Texts Translated

1. Abbreviations of Source Titles

Bammel	Caroline P. Hammond Bammel. *Der Römerbriefkommentar des Origenes*. Vetus latina 16, 33, 34. Freiburg: Herder, 1990, 1997, 1998.
CCSL	Corpus Christianorum: Series latina. Turnhout (Belgium): Brepols, 1953ff.
CSEL	Corpus scriptorum ecclesiasticorum latinorum. Vienna, 1866ff.
Dolbeau	Francois Dolbeau. *Augustin d'Hippone: Vingt-six sermons au peuple d'Afrique*. Collection des Études Augustiniennes, série antiquité 147. Paris: Institut d'Études Augustiniennes, 1966.
Frede	Herman Josef Frede. *Ein Neuer Paulustext und Kommentar*, vol. 2. *Texte*, Vetus latina 8. Freiburg: Herder, 1974.
MA	Germain Morin, ed. *Sancti Augustini sermones post Maurinos reperti*. Miscellanea Agostiniana, vol. 1. Rome: Tipografia Poliglotta Vaticana, 1930-31.
PG	J.-P. Migne, ed. Patrologiae cursus completus: Series graeca. 161 vols. Paris, 1857-66
PL	J.-P. Migne, ed. Patrologiae cursus completus: Series latina. 221 vols. Paris, 1844-64.
PLS	A. Hamann, ed. Patrologiae latinae supplementum. Paris, 1957ff.
Pusey	P. E. Pusey. *Cyrilli Archiepiscopi Alexandrini, Fragmenta quot supersunt in Epistolam ad Romanos*. Oxford, 1872.
SC	Sources chrétiennes. Paris: Éditions du Cerf, 1948ff.
Scherer	Jean Scherer. *Le commentaire d'Origène sur Rom. III.5–V.7*. Institut Français d'Archeologie Orientale. Bibliothéque d'Étude XXVII. Cairo, 1957.
SPM	Cyrille Lambot. *Aurelius Augustinus, Sancti Aurelii Augustini sermones selecti duodeviginti*. Stromata patristica et mediaevalia 1. Utrecht: Spectrum, 1950.
Staab	Karl Staab. *Pauluskommentar aus der griechischen Kirche*, 2nd ed. Münster: Aschendorff, 1984.

Sources of Texts Translated

2. Sources of Individual Excerpts

Argument
  (1) Origen, *Commentary, Praefatio,* 1.1-2, PG 14:833-838; Bammel 1.1-2; 37.1-44.42.
  (2) John Chrysostom, *Argumentum,* PG 60:391-394.
  (3) Ambrosiaster, *Commentary, Argumentum,* CSEL 81.1:5.3–9.8.
  (4) Theodoret, *Commentary, Argumentum,* PG 82:44-48.
  (5) Augustine, *Unfinished Commentary on the Letter to the Romans,* 1, CSEL 84:145.3–146.10.
  (6) Pelagius, *Commentary, Prologus,* PLS 1:1112-1113.
  (7) Anonymous, *Commentary, Prologus,* Frede 15.1-16.46.

Romans 1:1-7
  (1) John Chrysostom, *Homily* 1.1-3, PG 60:395-399.
  (2) Origen, *Commentary,* 1.3, PG 14:845-846; Bammel 1.5; 51.18-53.43.
  (3) Augustine, *Sermon* 316.5, PL 38:1434.
  (4) Augustine, *Unfinished Commentary on the Letter to the Romans,* 3.4-5, CSEL 84:148.4-10.
  (5) Ambrosiaster, *Commentary,* 1.3, CSEL 81.1:15.8-26.
  (6) Theodoret, *Commentary,* 1.4, PG 82:52.
  (7) Origen, *Commentary,* 1.5, 7, PG 14:849, 852-853; Bammel 1.7, 9; 57.8-22, 63.2-64.18.
  (8) Augustine, *On the Predestination of the Saints,* 15.31, PL 44:982-983.
  (9) Augustine, *Unfinished Commentary on the Letter to the Romans,* 7, 11.1-2, CSEL 84:154.29–155.8, 159.6-14.

Romans 1:8-9
  (1) John Chrysostom, *Homily* 2.1, PG 60:401.
  (2) Origen, *Commentary,* 1.9, 10, PG 14:854-856; Bammel 1.11, 12; 66.11-67.22, 69.8-16.

Romans 1:10-15
  (1) John Chrysostom, *Homily* 2.2-4, PG 60:403-405.
  (2) Ambrosiaster, *Commentary,* 1.11, CSEL 81.1:27.23-29.10.
  (3) Ambrosiaster, *Commentary,* 1.13, 14, CSEL 81.1:31.9-33.2, 33.11-27.

Romans 1:16-17
  (1) Ambrosiaster, *Commentary,* 1.16, 17, CSEL 81.1:35.12-37.6, 37.13-39.9.
  (2) Origen, *Commentary,* 1.14, PG 14:861; Bammel 1.17; 79.1-11.
  (3) Theodoret, *Commentary,* 1.17, PG 82:57.
  (4) John Chrysostom, *Homily* 2.6, PG 60:409.
  (5) Augustine, *Explanations of the Psalms,* 32.2.1.4, CCSL 38:249.1-25; CSEL 93.1B: 259.1–260.23.

Romans 1:18-23
(1) Origen, *Commentary*, 1.16, 17, PG 14:861-864; Bammel 1.19; 80.5-82.30, 83.56-84.66, 84.70-79, 85.1-8, 85.14-86.28.
(2) Augustine, *Sermon* 241.1-3, PL 38:1133-1135.
(3) Anonymous, *Commentary*, 17, Frede 24.
(4) John Chrysostom, *Homily* 3.2, PG 60:412-413.
(5) Pelagius, *Commentary*, 1.19, PLS 1:1117.
(6) Ambrosiaster, *Commentary*, 1.21-22, 23, CSEL 81.1:41.30-43.20, 45.6-47.10.
(7) Augustine, *Commentary on Statements in the Letter to the Romans*, 3, CSEL 84:3.15–4.13.

Romans 1:24-27
(1) Origen, *Commentary*, 1.18, PG 14:865; Bammel 1.21; 86.1-87.15.
(2) Ambrosiaster, *Commentary*, 1.24-25, CSEL 81.1:47.11-49.26.
(3) Augustine, *On Nature and Grace*, 22.24, CSEL 60:249.11–251.10.
(4) John Chrysostom, *Homily* 4.1-2, PG 60:417-419.

Romans 1:28-32
(1) Ambrosiaster, *Commentary*, 1.28, CSEL 81.1:53.17-23.
(2) Augustine, *On the Predestination of the Saints*, 10.19, PL 44:975.
(3) Theodoret, *Commentary*, 1.29, PG 82:65.
(4) Ambrosiaster, *Commentary*, 1.32, CSEL 81.1:59.25-61.12.
(5) Origen, *Commentary*, 1.19, PG 14:870; Bammel 1.22; 94.68-95.78.

Romans 2:1-5
(1) Ambrosiaster, *Commentary*, 2.1, 2, 3, 4, 5-6, CSEL 81.1:61.13-63.12, 63.19-65.4, 65.7-16, 65.21-67.9.
(2) Pelagius, *Commentary*, 2.2-4, PLS 1:1120-1121.
(3) Origen, *Commentary*, 2.3, PG 14:874-875; Bammel 2.3; 102.1–103.26.
(4) Augustine, *Sermon* 339.3, SPM 1:114.9-35.
(5) John Chrysostom, *Homily* 5.2, PG 60:425.

Romans 2:6-11
(1) Origen, *Commentary*, 2.4, 6, 7, PG 14:878-879, 883-884, 886, 887-889; Bammel 2.4, 5; 110.136-146, 118.120–119.149, 120.161–121.171, 124.230-240, 127.280–130.350.
(2) Ambrosiaster, *Commentary*, 2.7, 8, 10, 11, CSEL 81.1:67.19-69.24, 71.11-28.
(3) Augustine, *Letter* 186.4, CSEL 57:48.6-23.
(4) John Chrysostom, *Homily* 5.4, PG 60:427.

Romans 2:12-16
(1) Ambrosiaster, *Commentary*, 2.12, 13, 14, 15, 16, CSEL 81.1:73.2-23, 75.3-77.5, 77.11-79.6.
(2) John Chrysostom, *Homily* 5.4-5, PG 60:428-429.
(3) Origen, *Commentary*, 2.8, PG 14:891-892; Bammel 2.6; 134.67-74.

Sources of Texts Translated

(4) Augustine, *On Grace and Free Will*, 3.5, PL 44:884–885.
(5) Anonymous, *Commentary*, 24; Frede 28.
(6) Origen, *Commentary*, 2.9, PG 14:892-894; Bammel 2.7; 134.1-2, 134.7–139.86.
(7) Augustine, *On the Spirit and the Letter*, 26.43–27.48, CSEL 60:196.20–197.12, 198.8-11, 198.18–202.11.
(8) Theodoret, *Commentary*, 2.15-16, PG 82:72.

Romans 2:17-24

(1) Ambrosiaster, *Commentary*, 2.18-24, CSEL 81.1:81.20-83.4, 83.11-87.23.
(2) Origen, *Commentary*, 2.11, PG 14:895-897; Bammel 2.8; 141.38–142.46, 144.90–146.126.
(3) Augustine, *On the Spirit and the Letter*, 8.13, CSEL 60:165.12–166.7.

Romans 2:25-29

(1) Origen, *Commentary*, 2.12, 13, PG 14:898-900; Bammel 2.9; 147.9–149.39, 149.51–151.85.
(2) Theodoret, *Commentary*, 2.23, PG 82:73.
(3) Ambrosiaster, *Commentary*, 2.25, CSEL 81.1:89.9-22.
(4) Ambrosiaster, *Commentary*, 2.28-29, CSEL 81.1:91.21-93.16.
(5) Augustine, *Explanations of the Psalms*, 113.1.5, CCSL 40:1638.1-14.

Romans 3:1-4

(1) Ambrosiaster, *Commentary*, 3.1-4, CSEL 81.1:93.17-97.7, 99.8-24.
(2) Origen, *Commentary*, 2.14, PG 14:916-918; Bammel 2.10; 180.90–181.110, 183.153–184.166, 184.171–185.181.
(3) Augustine, *Sermon* 143.2, PL 38:785.45–786.2.
(4) Augustine, *Explanations of the Psalms*, 91.6, CCSL 39:1283.7-24.

Romans 3:5-9

(1) Ambrosiaster, *Commentary*, 3.5-9, CSEL 81.1:101.11–105.25.
(2) John Chrysostom, *Homily* 6.5, PG 60:439.
(3) Origen, *Commentary*, 3.1, PG 14:924; Bammel 3.1; 196.76-92.
(4) Anonymous, *Commentary*, 28, Frede 30-31.
(5) Augustine, *On Grace and Free Will*, 22.44, PL 44:910.
(6) Origen, *Commentary*, 3.2, PG 14:930-931; Bammel 3.2; 207.81–209.125.

Romans 3:10-20

(1) Ambrosiaster, *Commentary*, 3.10-18, 19, 20, CSEL 81.1:107.1–111.7, 111.25–113.5, 113.10-15, 113.22–115.7, 115.13–117.9.
(2) Origen, *Commentary*, 3.6, PG 14:937-938; Bammel 3.3; 221.9–223.45.
(3) Origen, *Commentary*, 3.20, Scherer 148.8-20.
(4) Augustine, *Commentary on Statements in the Letter to the Romans*, 12, CSEL 84:6.17–7.20.
(5) Theodoret, *Commentary*, 3.20, PG 82:84.

APPENDIX 2

(6) Anonymous, *Commentary*, 31, Frede 32-33.

Romans 3:21-26
(1) Ambrosiaster, *Commentary*, 3.21, 22-26, CSEL 81.1:117.10–123.9.
(2) Augustine, *On the Spirit and the Letter*, 9.15, CSEL 60:166.23–168.9.
(3) Origen, *Commentary*, 3.7, PG 14:942, 944; Bammel 3.4; 229.37–230.59, 232.118-124.
(4) John Chrysostom, *Homily* 7.2, PG 60:443-444.
(5) Origen, *Commentary*, 3.7, 8, PG 14:945, 946; Bammel 3.4, 5; 234.154–235.170, 235.8–236.26.
(6) Theodoret, *Commentary*, 3.24-25, PG 82:84-85.

Romans 3:27-31
(1) Ambrosiaster, *Commentary*, 3.27-31, CSEL 81.1:123.11–127.2.
(2) Origen, *Commentary*, 3.9, PG 14:952-953; Bammel 3.6; 248.23–250.67.
(3) Augustine, *On Eighty-Three Varied Questions*, 76.1, CCSL 44A:218.4–220.42.
(4) John Chrysostom, *Homily* 7.4, PG 60:446-447.
(5) Origen, *Commentary*, 3.10, 11, PG 14:957-958; Bammel 3.7, 8; 256.74-82, 257.8-13, 257.19-25; 5.8; Scherer 174.11–178.5.
(6) Anonymous, *Commentary*, 35, Frede 34.
(7) Augustine, *Against Two Letters of the Pelagians*, 4.5.11, CSEL 60:532.22-27.

Romans 4:1-8
(1) Ambrosiaster, *Commentary*, 4.1-8, CSEL 81.1:127.22–133.6, 133.14–135.2.
(2) Origen, *Commentary*, 6.1, Scherer 178.9–180.20.
(3) John Chrysostom, *Homily* 8.1, PG 60:455.
(4) Augustine, *Explanations of the Psalms*, 31.2.2, CCSL 38:225.8–226.31; CSEL 93.1B:209.56–211.28.
(5) Theodoret, *Commentary*, 4.2, PG 82:88b.
(6) Augustine, *Explanations of the Psalms*, 31.2.7, CCSL 38:230.1–231.37; CSEL 93:1B:220.1–222.34.
(7) Augustine, *Commentary on Statements in the Letter to the Romans*, 15, CSEL 84:9.19-25.
(8) Augustine, *Sermon Dolbeau* 19.3 (130A); Dolbeau 157.54–158.78.
(9) Origen, *Commentary*, 4.1, PG 14:965-966; Bammel 4.1; 279.201–280.224, 281.231–282.244.
(10) Anonymous, *Commentary*, 37A, Frede 35.

Romans 4:9-12
(1) Ambrosiaster, *Commentary*, 4.9-12, CSEL 81.1:135.4–137.17.
(2) Origen, *Commentary*, 6.2, Scherer 188.4–192.3.
(3) John Chrysostom, *Homily* 8.3, PG 60:438.
(4) Augustine, *On Baptism*, 4.24.31, CSEL 51:259.8–260.9.
(5) Theodoret, *Commentary*, 4.12, PG 82:89-92.

Sources of Texts Translated

Romans 4:13-17
(1) Ambrosiaster, *Commentary*, 4.13-17, CSEL 81.1:137.18–145.12.
(2) Origen, *Commentary*, 4.3, PG 14:971-973; Bammel 4.4; 294.37-41; 294.51–297.97; 298.114-118; compare with Scherer 6.4, 196.17–204.10.
(3) Origen, *Commentary*, 4.5, PG 14:974-975, 977-978; Bammel 4.5; 299.7–300.34, 306.138-148, 307.169–308.182; compare the first segment with Scherer 6.5; 204.10–206.19.

Romans 4:18-25
(1) Ambrosiaster, *Commentary*, 4.18-25, CSEL 81.1:145.13–151.16.
(2) Origen, *Commentary*, 6.4, Scherer 212.7–214.1.
(3) Augustine, *On the Predestination of the Saints*, 10.19, PL 44:975.
(4) John Chrysostom, *Homily* 8.5, PG 60:461.
(5) Origen, *Commentary*, 4.7, PG 14:984-985; Bammel 4.7; 320.21–321.48.
(6) Augustine, *Sermon* 236.1, PL 38:1120.

Romans 5:1-5
(1) Ambrosiaster, *Commentary*, 5.1, CSEL 81.1:151.17–155.18.
(2) Origen, *Commentary*, 4.8, PG 14:989-990; Bammel 4.8; 329.46–330.66.
(3) Augustine, *Sermon* 185.3, PL 38:998.
(4) John Chrysostom, *Homily* 9.2-3, PG 60:468-470.
(5) Origen, *Commentary*, 4.9, PG 14:997; Bammel 4.9; 344.180–345.200.
(6) Augustine, *On Patience*, 17.14, CSEL 41:678.5-23, 679.15-21; *Sermon* 128.2.4, PL 38:715.
(7) Augustine, *De spiritu et littera* 2.4–3.5, CSEL 60:156.24–157.24.

Romans 5:6-11
(1) Ambrosiaster, *Commentary*, 5.6-11, CSEL 81.1:157.1–163.6.
(2) Origen, *Commentary*, 4.10, PG 14:998; Bammel 4.10; 346.17–347.41.
(3) Augustine, *Tractates on the Gospel of John*, 110.6, CCSL 36:626.1-26.
(4) John Chrysostom, *Homily* 9.3, PG 60:471-473.

Romans 5:12-14
(1) Ambrosiaster, *Commentary*, 5.12-14, CSEL 81.1:163.10–173.25, 176.30–178.18.
(2) Origen, *Commentary*, 5.1, PG 14:1009-1010, 1012-1014, 1017-1018, 1019-1020; Bammel 5.1; 366.164-166; 368.196–369.208, 373.297–374.315, 375.335–377.374, 382.482–385.530, 386.549–387.562, 387.575–388.599.
(3) Augustine, *Against Julian, an Unfinished Book*, 2.63, CSEL 85.1:209.13–210.41.
(4) Theodoret, *Commentary*, 5.12-14, PG 82:99-101.
(5) Cyril of Alexandria, *Commentary*, 5.12, PG 74:784; Pusey 182.
(6) John Chrysostom, *Homily* 10.1, PG 60:475.
(7) Augustine, *On the Merits and Forgiveness of Sins and on Infant Baptism*, 1.10.12-11.13, CSEL 60:13.8-14.25.

Romans 5:15-19

(1) Ambrosiaster, *Commentary*, 5.15-19, CSEL 81.1:179.10–185.6.
(2) John Chrysostom, *Homily* 10.1-2, PG 60:476.
(3) Augustine, *Letter* 157.3.20, CSEL 44:469.1–470.4.
(4) Augustine, *Letter* 157.3.11, CSEL 44:457.19–458.12.
(5) Origen, *Commentary*, 5.2, PG 14:1023-1025; Bammel 5.2; 395.86–398.143.
(6) Augustine, *Letter* 157.3.13, CSEL 44:460.12-19.
(7) Cyril of Alexandria, *Commentary*, 5.18-19, PG 74:788-789; Pusey 186-187.
(8) Augustine, *Against Julian*, 6.80, PL 44:871-872.
(9) John Chrysostom, *Homily* 10.3, PG 60:477-478.

Romans 5:20-21

(1) Ambrosiaster, *Commentary*, 5.20-21, CSEL 81.1:184.5-17, 185.8-27, 187.10–189.5, 188.5-20. Conflating the different versions of the text.
(2) Origen, *Commentary*, 5.6, PG 14:1032-1034; Bammel 5.6; 412.9, 413.40–414.64, 415.66, 72-80.
(3) Theodoret, *Commentary*, 5.20-21, PG 82:104.
(4) Augustine, *Letter* 157.3.16, CSEL 44:464.14–465.11.
(5) Augustine, *Letter* 157.3.17, CSEL 44:465.21–466.12.

Romans 6:1-4

(1) Ambrosiaster, *Commentary*, 6.1-3, CSEL 81.1:189.14–191.24.
(2) Origen, *Commentary*, 5.7, PG 14:1035; Bammel 5.7; 417.1–418.21.
(3) Augustine, *Enchiridion*, 52, CCSL 46:77.60-70.
(4) Origen, *Commentary*, 5.8, PG 14:1037-1039, 1041, 1042; Bammel 5.8; 422.11–423.19, 423.39–424.60, 428.129–429.146, 430.165–431.186.
(5) John Chrysostom, *Homily* 10.4, PG 60:480.
(6) Ambrosiaster, *Commentary*, 6.4, CSEL 81.1:193.11-20.
(7) Augustine, *Sermon Guelferbytana* 9.3 (229E), MA 1:468.32–469.6.

Romans 6:5-11

(1) Origen, *Commentary*, 5.9, PG 14:1043-1048; Bammel 5.9; 433.31-44, 437.110–439.149, 439.157–441.193.
(2) Ambrosiaster, *Commentary*, 6.5-6, CSEL 81.1:193.21–195.9, 195.17-23.
(3) John Chrysostom, *Homily* 11.1, PG 60:483.
(4) Augustine, *Commentary on Statements in the Letter to the Romans*, 32-34, CSEL 84:13:25-14.16.
(5) Augustine, *Against Julian*, 6.7, PL 44:824-825.
(6) Cyril of Alexandria, *Commentary*, 6.6, PG 74:796-797; Pusey 191-193.
(7) Augustine, *Against Julian, an Unfinished Book*, 2.225, CSEL 85.1:338.1–339.29.
(8) Origen, *Commentary*, 5.10, PG 14:1048-1049; Bammel 5.10; 442.25–443.43.
(9) Ambrosiaster, *Commentary*, 6.8, CSEL 81.1:197.1-12.
(10) John Chrysostom, *Homily* 11.2, PG 60:485-486.

Romans 6:12-14
(1) Origen, *Commentary*, 6.1, PG 14:1056-1057; Bammel 6.1; 457.33–458.61.
(2) Ambrosiaster, *Commentary*, 6.12-14, CSEL 81.1:199.8-21, 199.25-27, 201.5–203.1.
(3) Theodoret, *Commentary*, 6.12-13, PG 82:108-109.
(4) John Chrysostom, *Homily* 11.2-3, PG 60:486-487.
(5) Augustine, *Tractates on the Gospel of John*, 41.12, CCSL 36:364.1-21.
(6) Augustine, *On Continence*, 5.12, CSEL 41:154.20–155.5.

Romans 6:15-19
(1) Ambrosiaster, *Commentary*, 6.15-18, CSEL 81.1:203.9–205.8, 205.13–207.7.
(2) Origen, *Commentary*, 6.2, PG 14:1059; Bammel 6.2; 462.1-12.
(3) Origen, *Commentary*, 6.3, PG 14:1060; Bammel 6.3; 464.37–465.44.
(4) John Chrysostom, *Homily* 11.4-5, PG 60:489-90.
(5) Ambrosiaster, *Commentary*, 6.19, CSEL 81.1:207.12-22.
(6) Augustine, *Sermon* 159.6, PL 38:870-871.

Romans 6:20-23
(1) Origen, *Commentary*, 6.5, PG 14:1064-1065, Bammel 6.5; 473.24–474.49.
(2) Augustine, *Against Two Letters of the Pelagians*, 1.2.5, CSEL 60:426.4-28.
(3) John Chrysostom, *Homily* 12.1-2, PG 60:495-496.
(4) Origen, *Commentary*, 6.6, PG 14:1067-1068; Bammel 6.6; 480.23–481.43.
(5) Ambrosiaster, *Commentary*, 6.23, CSEL 81.1:209.23–211.13.
(6) Augustine, *Letter* 194.5.19-21, CSEL 57:190.12–193.4.

Romans 7:1-6
(1) Origen, *Commentary*, 6.7, PL 14:1070-1075; Bammel 6.7; 485.42-47, 488.100-105, 491.157–492.174, 493.183-190, 493.192–495.225.
(2) Cyril of Alexandria, *Commentary*, 7.1, PG 74:797-800; Pusey 193-194.
(3) Ambrosiaster, *Commentary* 7.2-4, 6, CSEL 81.1:213.19–217.5, 219.1-11, 17-25, 221.4-10.
(4) John Chrysostom, *Homily*, 12.2-3, PG 60:496-497.
(5) Augustine, *Commentary on Statements in the Letter to the Romans*, 36, CSEL 84:15.8-16.9.
(6) Augustine, *To Simplicianus*, 1.1.15, CCSL 44:18.251–19.270.
(7) Cyril of Alexandria, *Commentary*, 8.3, PG 74:800-801; Pusey 194-195.

Romans 7:7-13
(1) Origen, *Commentary*, 6.8-9, PL 14:1079-1084; Bammel 6.8; 498.24–500.67, 501.85–502.95, 502.101-111, 504.133-148, 505.161-166.
(2) Ambrosiaster, *Commentary*, 7.7-8, 11, 13, CSEL 81.1:223.12–225.23, 229.1-10, 229.20–231.6, 231.12-13, 231.21–233.6
(3) Apollinaris of Laodicea, *Commentary*, 7:7, Staab 63-65.
(4) John Chrysostom, *Homily* 12.4-5, PG 60:500.
(5) John Chrysostom, *Homily* 12.6, PG 60:502.

APPENDIX 2

(6) Augustine, *To Simplicianus* 1.1.2-6, CCSL 44:8.30-12.108.
(7) Augustine, *Sermon* 145.3, PL 38:792-793.

Romans 7:14-25
(1) Origen, *Commentary*, 6.9-10, PL 14:1085-1091; Bammel 6.9-10; 508.33–516.187, 518.1–519.18.
(2) Ambrosiaster, *Commentary*, 7.14, 17-18, 20, 22, 23, 24, CSEL 81.1:233.17–235.26, 237.10–239.6, 239.23–241.8, 241.17-24, 243.1-4, 12-23, 245.1-2, 25-247.5, 247.12–249.3.
(3) Cyril of Alexandria, *Commentary*, 7.15, PG 74:808-812; Pusey 202-206.
(4) Gennadius of Constantinople, *Commentary*, 7.15, Staab 372-373.
(5) John Chrysostom, *Homily*, 13.2, PG 60:509-510.
(6) Augustine, *Against Julian*, 6.23.72, PL 44:867-868.
(7) Augustine, *Against Two Letters of the Pelagians*, 1.10.17-11.23, CSEL 60:439.3–442.18, 442.21–444.5.
(8) Augustine, *Sermon* 154.17, CCSL 41Ba:99.339–101.359.

Romans 8:1-4
(1) Origen, *Commentary*, 6.11, PG 14:1091; Bammel 6.11; 519.1–520.13.
(2) Cyril of Alexandria, *Commentary*, 8.2, PG 74:816; Pusey 210-211.
(3) Origen, *Commentary*, 6.12, PG 14:1094-1095; Bammel 6.12; 525.47–526.59, 526.70-78.
(4) Cyril of Alexandria, *Commentary*, 8.3, PG 74:817-820; Pusey 211-213.
(5) Ambrosiaster, *Commentary*, 8.3-4, CSEL 81.1:255.13–257.10, 257.13–259.13.
(6) Augustine, *Sermon* 152.3-5, 7-11, CCSL 41Ba:35.49–38.115, 41.170–46.263.
(7) John Chrysostom, *Homily* 13.3, 5, PG 60:513-514.

Romans 8:5-13
(1) Ambrosiaster, *Commentary*, 8.5-7, CSEL 81.1:259.14–263.16.
(2) Augustine, *Sermon* 155.10-12, PL 38:846-847.
(3) John Chrysostom, *Homily* 13.7, PG 60:517.
(4) Origen, *Commentary*, 6.13, PG 14:1099-1100; Bammel 6.13; 533.30–534.47, 535.73–537.101.
(5) Ambrosiaster, *Commentary*, 8.10-12, CSEL 81.1:267.20–271.5.
(6) Augustine, *On the Literal Interpretation of Genesis*, 6.24.36-25.36, CSEL 28.1:197.5-24.
(7) Origen, *Commentary*, 6.14.15-52, PG 14:1101-1102; Bammel 6.14; 539.15–541.51.
(8) Augustine, *Sermon* 128.9, PL 38:717-718.

Romans 8:14-17
(1) John Chrysostom, *Homily* 14.1, PG 60:525.
(2) Origen, *Commentary*, 7.2-3, PG 14:1105-1107; Bammel 7.1; 556.70–557.89, 558.115–559.131, 560.137-145.
(3) Ambrosiaster, *Commentary*, 8.15-16, CSEL 81.1:273.19–275.11.
(4) Augustine, *Sermon* 156.15-17, CCSL 41Ba:158.374–161.418.

Sources of Texts Translated

Romans 8:18-23
(1) Origen, *Commentary*, 7.4, PG 14:1108; Bammel 7.2; 561.29–562.47.
(2) Ambrosiaster, *Commentary*, 8.19-22, CSEL 81.1:279.12–283.13.
(3) Augustine, *On Eighty-Three Varied Questions*, 67.3, CCSL 44A:167.55-66.
(4) Theodoret, *Commentary*, 8.20, PG 82:136-137.
(5) John Chrysostom, *Homily* 14.5, PG 60:529-530.
(6) Origen, *Commentary*, 7.4, PG 14:1108-1113; Bammel 7.2; 565.102–570.210.
(7) Augustine, *Explanations of the Psalms*, 125.2, CCSL 40:1845.1-22; CSEL 95.3:164.1-21.

Romans 8:24-25
(1) Ambrosiaster, *Commentary*, 8.24, CSEL 81.1:285.21–287.5.
(2) John Chrysostom, *Homily* 14.6, PG 60:532.
(3) Augustine, *Explanations of the Psalms*, 125.2, CCSL 40:1845.22-37; CSEL 95.3:164.21–165.32.

Romans 8:26-27
(1) Origen, *Commentary*, 7.6, PG 14:1119-1120; Bammel 7.4; 580.59-70.
(2) Augustine, *Letter* 194.4.16-17, CSEL 57:188.7–189.22.
(3) Cyril of Alexandria, *Commentary*, 8.26, PG 74:824-825; Pusey 218-220.
(4) John Chrysostom, *Homily* 14.7, PG 60:533.
(5) Ambrosiaster, *Commentary*, 8.27, CSEL 81.1:289.9-19.

Romans 8:28-30
(1) Cyril of Alexandria, *Commentary*, 8.28, PG 74:828; Pusey 220.
(2) Origen, *Commentary*, 7.7, PG 14:1122-1126; Bammel 7.5-6; 585.58–586.81, 587.90-107, 589.38–591.91.
(3) Ambrosiaster, *Commentary*, 8.29, CSEL 81.1:291.3-9, 291.22–293.11.
(4) Theodoret, *Commentary*, 8.29, PG 82:141.
(5) Augustine, *On Admonition and Grace*, 7.13-14, CSEL 92:1.233.1–235.26.

Romans 8:31-39
(1) Ambrosiaster, *Commentary*, 8.31, CSEL 81.1:293.12-15.
(2) Origen, *Commentary*, 7.8, PG 14:1129-1131; Bammel 7.7-8; 595.41-47, 598.20–599.42.
(3) Augustine, *Tractates on the First Letter of John*, 7.7, PL 35:2032-2033.
(4) Augustine, *Explanations of the Psalms*, 29.2.1, CCSL 38:174.35-48; CSEL 93.1B:120.32–121.44.
(5) Ambrosiaster, *Commentary*, 8.35-36, CSEL 81.1:297.9–299.19.
(6) Augustine, *Sermon Dolbeau*, 13.1, Dolbeau 90.1-26.
(7) John Chrysostom, *Homily* 15.4, PG 60:545-546.

Romans 9:1-5
(1) Ambrosiaster, *Commentary*, 9.1, CSEL 81.1:303.7-14.

APPENDIX 2

(2) Origen, *Commentary*, 7.13, PG 14:1138-1140; Bammel 7.11; 609.9–612.71, 612.80–613.113.
(3) Theodoret, *Commentary*, 9.3, PG 82:149.
(4) Ambrosiaster, *Commentary*, 9.5, CSEL 81.1:305.11-25.

Romans 9:6-13
(1) John Chrysostom, *Homily* 16.2, 4-5, PG 60:550-551, 554.
(2) Origen, *Commentary*, 7.14, PG 14:1141-1142; Bammel 7.12; 616.13-27.
(3) Ambrosiaster, *Commentary*, 9.6-7, CSEL 81.1:307.18–309.8.
(4) Origen, *Commentary*, 7.15, PG 14:1143; Bammel 7.13; 618.36–619.48.
(5) Ambrosiaster, *Commentary*, 9.9-11, CSEL 81.1:311.6–313.1, 313.10-26.
(6) Theodoret, *Commentary*, 9.9-13, PG 82:153.
(7) John Chrysostom, *Homily* 16.4, PG 60:553.
(8) Augustine, *To Simplicianus*, 1.2.3, CCSL 44:26.52-69, 27.79-28.107.
(9) Augustine, *Letter* 186.5.15–6.16, 6.21, CSEL 57:57.9-59.7, 62.4-17.

Romans 9:14-18
(1) Ambrosiaster, *Commentary*, 9.14-16, CSEL 81.1:317.25–321.7.
(2) Cyril of Alexandria, *Commentary*, 9.14-18, PG 74:833-836; Pusey 226-228.
(3) John Chrysostom, *Homily* 16.7, PG 60:558.
(4) Origen, *Commentary*, 7.16, PG 14:1145-1147; Bammel 7.14; 621.59–624.131.
(5) Augustine, *To Simplicianus*, 1.2.12-13, CCSL 44:36.318–38.378.
(6) Augustine, *Against Two Letters of the Pelagians*, 2.13, CSEL 60:473.9–474.21.

Romans 9:19-23
(1) Ambrosiaster, *Commentary*, 9.19-20, CSEL 81.1:325.27–327.13.
(2) Theodoret, *Commentary*, 9.19-20, PG 82:156-157.
(3) Origen, *Commentary*, 7.17, PG 14:1148-1149; Bammel 7.15; 627.48–628.70.
(4) Cyril of Alexandria, *Commentary*, 9.19-24, PG 74:836-841; Pusey 228-233.
(5) Origen, *Commentary*, 7.18, PG 14:1149-1151; Bammel 7.15-16; 629.8–630.28, 630.38–631.66.
(6) Ambrosiaster, *Commentary*, 9.22-23, CSEL 81.1:329.6-23.
(7) Augustine, *Letter* 194.6.22-23, 30, CSEL 57:193.5–195.2, 199.11–200.11.

Romans 9:24-29
(1) Ambrosiaster, *Commentary*, 9.25-29, CSEL 81.1:331.9–335.27.
(2) John Chrysostom, *Homily* 16.9, PG 60:562.
(3) Origen, *Commentary*, 7.19, PG 14:1154; Bammel 7.17; 635.47–636.70.
(4) Augustine, *To Simplicianus*, 1.2.19, CCSL 44:47.616–50.677.

Romans 9:30-33
(1) Ambrosiaster, *Commentary*, 9.30-31, CSEL 81.1:337.1-27.
(2) Origen, *Commentary*, 7.19, PG 14:1155; Bammel 7.17; 637.88–638.106.
(3) Ambrosiaster, *Commentary*, 9.33, CSEL 81.1:341.4-24.

Sources of Texts Translated

(4) Augustine, *Letter* 186.3.8, CSEL 57:51.8-52.7.

Romans 10:1-4
(1) Ambrosiaster, *Commentary*, 10.1-4, CSEL 81.1:343.8–345.15.
(2) Augustine, *Against Julian, an Unfinished Book,* 6.10, PL 45:1518-1519.
(3) Augustine, *Explanations of the Psalms*, 30.2.1.6, CCSL 38:195.13-26; CSEL 93.1B:152.13–153.24.
(4) Origen, *Commentary*, 8.1, PG 14:1158-1159; Bammel 8.1; 642.37–643.69.
(5) Theodoret, *Commentary*, 10.3-4, PG 82:163.
(6) Augustine, *On Grace and Free Will*, 12.24, PL 44:895.
(7) Augustine, *Against Adversaries of the Law and the Prophets*, 2.7.26, CCSL 49:111.736-751.
(8) John Chrysostom, *Homily* 17.1, PG 60:565-566.

Romans 10:5-13
(1) Origen, *Commentary*, 8.2, PG 14:1160-1161; Bammel 8.2; 645.25–646.40.
(2) Ambrosiaster, *Commentary*, 10.6-8, CSEL 81.1:345.21–347.24.
(3) Origen, *Commentary*, 8.2; PG 14:1163-1164; Bammel 8.2; 649.114–650.140.
(4) Augustine, *On the Predestination of the Saints*, 11.22, PL 44:976-977.
(5) Augustine, *Against Lying*, 9.13, CSEL 41:485.6-22.
(6) Cyril of Alexandria, *Commentary*, 10.11, PG 74:843; Pusey 237.
(7) Ambrosiaster, *Commentary*, 10.11-13, CSEL 81.1:349.11–353.7.

Romans 10:14-17
(1) Ambrosiaster, *Commentary*, 10.14-17, CSEL 81.1:353.9–355.24.
(2) Origen, *Commentary*, 8.5, PG 14:1167-1168; Bammel 8.4; 655.69–656.84.
(3) Augustine, *To Simplicianus*, 1.2.7, CCSL 44:31.199–32.215.
(4) Origen, *Commentary*, 8.6, PG 14:1171; Bammel 8.5; 661.45-55.
(5) Augustine, *On Nature and Grace*, 2.2, CSEL 60:234.7–235.6.

Romans 10:18-21
(1) Ambrosiaster, *Commentary*, 10.18-19, CSEL 81.1:355.25–359.3.
(2) John Chrysostom, *Homily* 18.1, PG 60:574.
(3) Origen, *Commentary*, 8.6, PG 14:1171-1173; Bammel 8.5; 661.56–662.73, 663.90–664.12.
(4) Origen, *Commentary*, 8.6, PG 14:1174-1175; Bammel 8.5; 666.157–667.170.
(5) John Chrysostom, *Homily* 18.2-3, PG 60:575-576.

Romans 11:1-6
(1) Ambrosiaster, *Commentary*, 11.1-6, CSEL 81.1:361.17–365.16.
(2) Augustine, *On the Gift of Perseverance*, 18.47, PL 45:1022.13-1023.11.
(3) Origen, *Commentary*, 8.6, PG 14:1175-1176; Bammel, 8.7; 667.11–668.25.
(4) John Chrysostom, *Homily* 18.4, PG 60:577.

(5) Origen, *Commentary*, 8.6, PG 14:1176-1179; Bammel 8.7; 669.45–670.66, 672.110–673.132.
(6) John Chrysostom, *Homily* 18.5, PG 60:579.
(7) Augustine, *On the Grace of Christ and Original Sin*, 1.23.24, CSEL 42:144.18-27.
(8) Cyril of Alexandria, *Commentary*, 11.6, PG 74:845; Pusey 239.

Romans 11:7-10
(1) Ambrosiaster, *Commentary*, 11.7-10, CSEL 81.1:365.17–367.7, 367.23–371.7.
(2) Augustine, *Tractates on the Gospel of John*, 53.5-6, CCSL 36:454.20–455.21.
(3) Origen, *Commentary*, 8.7, PG 14:1181-1183; Bammel 8.8; 675.67–676.85, 677.94-98, 677.110–678.115, 678.125–680.163.

Romans 11:11-12
(1) Origen, *Commentary*, 8.8, PG 14:1186-1187; Bammel 8.9; 684.71–686.115.
(2) John Chrysostom, *Homily* 19.2-3, PG 60:586-587.
(3) Augustine, *City of God*, 18.46, CCSL 48:644.13–645.50.

Romans 11:13-16
(1) Ambrosiaster, *Commentary*, 11.13, CSEL 81.1:373.11-20.
(2) John Chrysostom, *Homily* 19.3-4, PG 60:587.
(3) Origen, *Commentary*, 8.9, PG 14:1190-1191; Bammel 8.10; 691.105-116.

Romans 11:17-21
(1) Origen, *Commentary*, 8.10, PG 14:1191-1195; Bammel 8.11; 692.23–693.49, 695.82–697.121, 698.149–699.154.
(2) Ambrosiaster, *Commentary*, 11.17-21, CSEL 81.1:375.12–379.12.
(3) Augustine, *Explanations of the Psalms*, 72.2, CCSL 39:987.2-28.
(4) Theodoret, *Commentary*, 11.17-18, PG 82:176-177.

Romans 11:22-24
(1) Ambrosiaster, *Commentary*, 11.22-24, CSEL 81.1:379.13–381.17.
(2) John Chrysostom, *Homily* 19.5, PG 60:590.
(3) Augustine, *Explanations of the Psalms*, 65.5, CCSL 39:843.59–844.86.

Romans 11:25-32
(1) Augustine, *On the Predestination of the Saints*, 16.33, PL 44:983.52–985.14.
(2) Origen, *Commentary*, 8.11, PG 14:1195-1196; Bammel 8.12; 699.14–701.45.
(3) Ambrosiaster, *Commentary*, 11.25-28, CSEL 81.1:381.18–385.20.
(4) Cyril of Alexandria, *Commentary*, 11.25, PG 74:849; Pusey 242-243.
(5) Theodoret, *Commentary*, 11.25, PG 82:180.
(6) Origen, *Commentary*, 8.12, PG 14:1198-1199; Bammel 8.12; 704.1-3, 704.13–705.35.
(7) Augustine, *City of God*, 21.24, CCSL 48:793.463-485.
(8) Cyril of Alexandria, *Commentary*, 11.30, PG 74:849-852; Pusey 244.
(9) Ambrosiaster, *Commentary*, 11.30-32, CSEL 81.1:387.4–389.4.

Sources of Texts Translated

 (10) John Chrysostom, *Homily* 19.7, PG 60:592.
 (11) Theodoret, *Commentary*, 11.32, PG 82:181.

Romans 11:33-36
 (1) Ambrosiaster, *Commentary*, 11.33-36, CSEL 81.1:389.5–393.7.
 (2) Augustine, *Sermon* 26.14, CCSL 41:358.289-309.
 (3) Augustine, *On Admonition and Grace*, 8.19, CSEL 92:239.1–241.36.
 (4) Origen, *Commentary*, 8.12, PG 14:1199-1201; Bammel 8.13; 705.35–706.50, 707.63–708.82.

Romans 12:1-2
 (1) Origen, *Commentary*, 9.1, PG 14:1203-1205, 1207; Bammel 9.1; 711.21–712.38, 712.45–713.57, 714.74–715.95, 717.142–718.153.
 (2) Ambrosiaster, *Commentary*, 12.1-2, CSEL 81.1:393.18–395.10.
 (3) Augustine, *City of God*, 10.6, CCSL 47:278.1–279.39.
 (4) John Chrysostom, *Homily* 20.1-3, PG 60:595-598.
 (5) Theodoret, *Commentary*, 12.2, PG 82:186.

Romans 12:3-8
 (1) Origen, *Commentary*, 9.2-3, PG 14:1208-1209, 1211-1213, 1215-1218; Bammel 9.2-3; 719.16–721.40, 724.117–726.154, 727.1-16, 728.23-35, 731.101–733.136, 733.146–735.181.
 (2) Ambrosiaster, *Commentary*, 12.3-8, CSEL 81.1:395.15–401.18.
 (3) John Chrysostom, *Homily* 20.3, PG 60:599.
 (4) Augustine, *Letter* 185.9.42, CSEL 57:36.17-37.3.
 (5) Theodoret, *Commentary*, 12.3, PG 82:188.
 (6) John Chrysostom, *Homily* 21.1, PG 60:601-602.
 (7) Theodoret, *Commentary*, 12.7, PG 82:188-189.
 (8) John Chrysostom, *Homily* 21.1-2, PG 60:603.

Romans 12:9-13
 (1) Origen, *Commentary*, 9.4-6, 10-13, PG 14:1218-1220; Bammel 9.4-6, 10-13; 735.1–737.16, 738.1-9, 738.1–739.9.
 (2) Ambrosiaster, *Commentary*, 12.9-11, CSEL 81.1:403.1-12, 405.1-20.
 (3) John Chrysostom, *Homily* 21.3, PG 60:605.
 (4) Theodoret, *Commentary*, 12.11, PG 82:189.
 (5) Augustine, *Letter* 155.1.4, CSEL 44:434.9–435.5.
 (6) John Chrysostom, *Homily* 21.3-4, PG 60:606-607.

Romans 12:14-18
 (1) Origen, *Commentary*, 9.14-18, PG 14:1220-1222; Bammel 9.14-18; 739.1–742.9.
 (2) Augustine, *On the Lord's Sermon on the Mount*, 1.21.71-72, CCSL 35:79.1731-81.1772.
 (3) Ambrosiaster, *Commentary*, 12.15-18, CSEL 81.1:407.19–413.25.
 (4) John Chrysostom, *Homily* 22.1, PG 60:610.

(5) John Chrysostom, *Homily* 22.2, PG 60:610-611.
(6) Origen, *Commentary*, 9.19-21, PG 14:1222-1223; Bammel 9.19-21; 742.1–744.19.
(7) John Chrysostom, *Homily* 22.2, PG 60:611.
(8) Theodoret, *Commentary*, 12.18, PG 82:192.

Romans 12:19-21
(1) Origen, *Commentary*, 9.22-24, PG 14:1224-1225; Bammel 9.22-24; 744.1–747.8.
(2) Ambrosiaster, *Commentary*, 12.19-21, CSEL 81.1:415.1–417.22.
(3) Theodoret, *Commentary*, 12.19-20, PG 82:192-193.
(4) Augustine, *Commentary on Statements in the Letter to the Romans*, 71, CSEL 84:43.7-44.11.
(5) Augustine, *Sermon* 302.10, SPM 105:14-28.

Romans 13:1-7
(1) Origen, *Commentary*, 9.25-30, PG 14:1226-1230; Bammel 9.25-30; 748.1–753.3, 754.18–755.50.
(2) Ambrosiaster, *Commentary*, 13.1-7, CSEL 81.1:417.23–423.14.
(3) Augustine, *Commentary on Statements in the Letter to the Romans*, 64-66, CSEL 84:44.12-47.3.
(4) Augustine, *Against Gaudentius*, 1.19.20, CSEL 53:216.3–217.4.
(5) Theodoret, *Commentary*, 13.1-2, PG 82:193.
(6) Theodoret, *Commentary*, 13.3-4, PG 82:196.
(7) Theodoret, *Commentary*, 13.5-7, PG 82:196.
(8) John Chrysostom, *Homily* 23.1-3, PG 60:615-618.

Romans 13:8-10
(1) Origen, *Commentary*, 9.30-31, PG 14:1230-1232; Bammel 9.30-31; 755.50-57, 756.1–757.32.
(2) Ambrosiaster, *Commentary*, 13.8-10, CSEL 81.1:423.25–427.8.
(3) Augustine, *Commentary on the Letter to the Galatians*, 45, CSEL 84:119.1–120.16.
(4) John Chrysostom, *Homily* 23.3-4, PG 60:618-619.

Romans 13:11-14
(1) Origen, *Commentary*, 9.32, PG 14:1232-1233; Bammel 9.32; 758.1–760.44.
(2) Ambrosiaster, *Commentary*, 13.11-14, CSEL 81.1:427.9–433.10.
(3) John Chrysostom, *Homily* 24.1-3, PG 60:622-626.
(4) Theodoret, *Commentary*, 13.11-14, PG 82:197-200.
(5) Augustine, *Sermon* 221.4, SC 116:218.96-107.
(6) Augustine, *Sermon* 49.3, CCSL 41:616.66-93.
(7) Augustine, *Confessions*, 8.26, CCSL 27:131.18-38.
(8) Augustine, *Commentary on Statements in the Letter to the Romans*, 69, CSEL 84:47.19-48.3.

Sources of Texts Translated

Romans 14:1-4
(1) Origen, *Commentary*, 9.35-36, PG 14:1234-1237; Bammel 9.35-36; 762.7–764.39, 765.53–766.76.
(2) Augustine, *Commentary on Statements in the Letter to the Romans*, 70-71, CSEL 84:48.4-49.19.
(3) Ambrosiaster, *Commentary*, 14.2, 4, CSEL 81.1:433.25–435.10, 435.18–437.7.
(4) John Chrysostom, *Homily* 25.1, PG 60:627-629.
(5) John Chrysostom, *Homily* 25.1-2, PG 60:629-630.

Romans 14:5-6
(1) Origen, *Commentary*, 9.37-38, PG 14:1237-1238; Bammel 9.37-38; 766.1–768.26.
(2) Augustine, *Commentary on Statements in the Letter to the Romans*, 72, CSEL 84:49.20-50.13.
(3) Ambrosiaster, *Commentary*, 14.5, CSEL 81.1:437.3-11.
(4) John Chrysostom, *Homily* 25.2, PG 60:630.
(5) Theodoret, *Commentary*, 14.5, PG 82:200-201.
(6) John Chrysostom, *Homily* 25.2, PG 60:630-631.
(7) Theodoret, *Commentary*, 14.6, PG 82:201.

Romans 14:7-9
(1) Origen, *Commentary*, 9.39, PG 14:1238-1240; Bammel 9.39; 768.12–770.61.
(2) Augustine, *Explanations of the Psalms*, 114.5, CCSL 40:2091.23-33.
(3) Ambrosiaster, *Commentary*, 14.7, CSEL 81.1:437.19-24.
(4) John Chrysostom, *Homily* 25.3, PG 60:631.
(5) Ambrosiaster, *Commentary*, 14.9, CSEL 81.1:439.7-18.
(6) John Chrysostom, *Homily* 25.3, PG 60:631.

Romans 14:10-13
(1) Origen, *Commentary*, 9.41, PG 14:1241-1243, 1245; Bammel 9.41; 771.1–775.76, 778.143–779.156.
(2) Theodoret, *Commentary*, 14.10-13, PG 82:201-204.
(3) Ambrosiaster, *Commentary*, 14.11-13, CSEL 81.1:439.24–441.17.

Romans 14:14-23
(1) Origen, *Commentary*, 9.42, 10.1-5, PG 14:1246-1254; Bammel 9.42, 10.1-5; 781.47–783.85, 784.117–786.151, 786.1–789.2, 790.13–794.10, 795.16–797.52.
(2) Ambrosiaster, *Commentary*, 14.14-16, CSEL 81.1:441.18–445.15.
(3) John Chrysostom, *Homily* 26.1, PG 60:637-638.
(4) Theodoret, *Commentary*, 14.14-15, PG 82:204.
(5) John Chrysostom, *Homily* 26.1-2, PG 60:638-640.
(6) Theodoret, *Commentary*, 14.19-20, PG 82:205.
(7) Ambrosiaster, *Commentary*, 14.20, CSEL 81.1:447.22–449.16.
(8) Ambrosiaster, *Commentary*, 14.22-23, CSEL 81.1:451.7–453.11.
(9) John Chrysostom, *Homily* 26.2-3, PG 60:640.

APPENDIX 2

(10) Theodoret, *Commentary*, 14.22-23, PG 82:205-208.
(11) Augustine, *Commentary on Statements in the Letter to the Romans*, 73, CSEL 84:50.14-25.
(12) Augustine, *On Marriage and Concupiscence*, 1.3.4, CSEL 42:214.10-27.

Romans 15:1-6
(1) Origen, *Commentary*, 10.6, PG 14:1257-1261; Bammel 10.6; 797.1–800.48, 800.60–801.74, 801.77–802.109, 803.119–804.147.
(2) John Chrysostom, *Homily* 27.1-2, PG 60:645-646.
(3) Augustine, *Sermon* 76.4, PL 38:480.
(4) Ambrosiaster, *Commentary*, 15.2-4, CSEL 81.1:453.20–455.23.
(5) Origen, *Commentary*, 10.7, PG 14:1261-1262; Bammel 10.7, 804.1–806.30.

Romans 15:7-13
(1) Ambrosiaster, *Commentary*, 15.7-12, CSEL 81.1:457.15–463.23.
(2) Origen, *Commentary*, 10.7-8, PG 14:1263-1264; Bammel 10.7-8; 808.66-73, 808.1-2, 809.8-29.
(3) John Chrysostom, *Homily* 27.3-4, PG 60:647-649.
(4) Cyril of Alexandria, *Commentary*, 15.7, PG 74:853-855; Pusey 247-248.
(5) Augustine, *Sermon Morin* 7.2 (63B), MA 1:611.16–612.13.
(6) John Chrysostom, *Homily* 28.1, PG 60:650.
(7) Origen, *Commentary*, 10.9, PG 14:1265-1266; Bammel 10.9; 811.1–812.30.

Romans 15:14-22
(1) Origen, *Commentary*, 10.10-11, PG 14:1267-1268; Bammel 10.10-11; 814.30-39, 815.12-25.
(2) Origen, *Commentary*, 10.11, PG 14:1268; Bammel 10.11; 816.39-48.
(3) John Chrysostom, *Homily* 29.1-2, PG 60:655.
(4) Origen, *Commentary*, 10.12, PG 14:1270; Bammel 10.12; 817.9-15, 818.20–820.70.
(5) Ambrosiaster, *Commentary*, 15.17-20, CSEL 81.1:465.24–469.10.
(6) Ambrosiaster, *Commentary*, 15.22-23, CSEL 81.1:469.22–471.14.

Romans 15:23-29
(1) Origen, *Commentary*, 10.13, PG 14:1271; Bammel 10.13; 821.17-28.
(2) John Chrysostom, *Homily* 30.1, PG 60:661-662.
(3) Origen, *Commentary*, 10.14, PG 14:1273-1274; Bammel 10.14; 824.44–827.94.
(4) Ambrosiaster, *Commentary*, 15.27, CSEL 81.1:473.1-18.

Romans 15:30-33
(1) Origen, *Commentary*, 10.15, PG 14:1276-1277; Bammel 10.15; 829.11–831.44.
(2) Ambrosiaster, *Commentary*, 15.30-31, CSEL 81.1:475.3-10.
(3) John Chrysostom, *Homily* 30.2, PG 60:662-663.
(4) Theodoret, *Commentary*, 15.31-33, PG 82:217.
(5) Origen, *Commentary*, 10.16, PG 14:1277-1278; Bammel 10.16; 832.1-4.

Romans 16:1-2
(1) Origen, *Commentary*, 10.17, PG 14:1278; Bammel 10.17; 832.1–833.24.
(2) Theodoret, *Commentary*, 16.1-3, PG 82:217-220.
(3) Ambrosiaster, *Commentary*, 16.1-2, CSEL 81.1:477.10-22.

Romans 16:3-16
(1) John Chrysostom, *Homily* 30.2-3, PG 60:664.
(2) Ambrosiaster, *Commentary*, 16.3-4, CSEL 81.1:479.2-15.
(3) Origen, *Commentary*, 10.18-21, PG 14:1279-1280; Bammel 10.18-21; 834.20–837.15.
(4) John Chrysostom, *Homily* 31.1-2, PG 60:668-669.
(5) Ambrosiaster, *Commentary*, 6.13, CSEL 81.1:485.10-15.
(6) Origen, *Commentary*, 10.31, PG 14:1282; Bammel 10.31; 840.1–841.13.
(7) Origen, *Commentary*, 10.33, PG 14:1282-1283; Bammel 10.33; 841.1-9.
(8) John Chrysostom, *Homily* 31.3, PG 60:671.
(9) Ambrosiaster, *Commentary*, 16.16, CSEL 81.1:487.11-19.

Romans 16:17-20
(1) Origen, *Commentary*, 10.35-36, PG 14:1283-1285; Bammel 10.35-36; 843.18–846.19.
(2) John Chrysostom, *Homily* 32.1, PG 60:675-676.
(3) John Chrysostom, *Homily* 32.1, PG 60:676-677.
(4) Origen, *Commentary*, 10.37-38, PG 14:1286-1287; Bammel 10.37; 847.1–849.31, 850.1-10.
(5) John Chrysostom, *Homily* 32.1, PG 60:677.

Romans 16:21-24
(1) Origen, *Commentary*, 10.39, PG 14:1288-1289; Bammel 10.39; 850.1-2, 851.18–853.41.
(2) Theodoret, *Commentary*, 16.21, PG 82:224.
(3) Theodoret, *Commentary*, 16.24, PG 82:225.

Romans 16:25-27
(1) Origen, *Commentary*, 10.43, PG 14:1290-1291; Bammel 10.43; 855.1-2, 856.18–857.39.
(2) Ambrosiaster, *Commentary*, 16.25-27, CSEL 81.1:495.3-23.
(3) Augustine, *Against Maximinus the Arian* 2.13.2, PL 42.769.44–770.19.
(4) Ambrosiaster, *Commentary*, 16.28, CSEL 81.1:497.2-7.

Index of Names

Aaron, 373
Abednego, 320
Abraham, 3, 10-12, 14-15, 21, 24-25, 53-54, 59-60, 62-63, 78-81, 84-87, 90-101, 114-15, 130, 148, 219-24, 228, 235, 240-41, 261-63, 273-80, 304, 337, 361, 365-67, 370, 381
"Abraham, Isaac and Jacob," 21, 63, 97
Achaia, 5, 375-77, 384
Adam, 19, 78, 96, 112, 127, 129, 131, 137, 139-41, 144, 158, 162, 164, 167-68, 173-74, 181, 185-86, 194, 201, 241, 251
Adam and Eve, 96, 112, 117
Ahab, 261
Ambrosiaster, 394
Ampliatus, 382
Ancient of Days, 345
Andronicus, 382, 385
Antioch, 316
Apelles, 382
Apollinaris, 394
Apollos, 229, 383-85
Apphia, 383
Aquila, 8, 382-84
Arabs, 258
Archippus, 6
Aristobulus, 382
Asia, 382, 384
Asians, 384
Asyncritus, 383, 386
Athenians, 31
Augustine, 394
Azariah, 4

Baal, 260-61
Babylon, 311
Barbarians, 21, 23-24, 29, 60, 147, 167, 373, 382

Benjamin, 54, 260-63
Berea, 391
Boaz, 366

Caesar, 315, 317-19
Cain, 36, 68, 71, 96, 119, 129, 137, 162
Cenchreae, 3, 381-82
Cenchreans, 382
Cilicia, 316, 391
Cleopas, 194
Colossians, 6
Corinthians, 2-3, 5-6, 9, 53, 81, 119, 295, 298-300, 335, 345, 360, 376-78, 383, 388
Cornelius, 43, 92, 366
Cyprus, 3
Cyril, 395

Daniel, 6, 31, 203, 244, 318, 345
David, 13, 15, 18-19, 65, 83-85, 88-90, 94, 137, 148, 183, 200-201, 227-29, 236, 257, 265, 267-68, 279, 307, 365-66, 387
Day of Judgment, 41, 47, 109, 252
Derbe, 391

Egypt, 10-12, 60, 71, 235, 257, 283, 373
Egyptians, 31, 258, 283, 373
Elijah, 88, 260-63, 282, 292, 304
Elisha, 304
Elizabeth, 95
Encratites, 349
Enoch, 337
Epaenetus, 382, 384
Erastus, 3, 390
Esau, 11, 220, 222-23, 226-28, 234
Eve, 96, 112, 117, 137, 210, 240
Ezekiel, 6, 166, 251, 353

Index of Names

Fate, 147, 175-76
Fortune, 175-75, 308

Gaius, 3
Galatians, 6, 8, 73, 95, 148
Gaudentius, 320
Gennadius, 395
Gomorrah, 240-42
Goth, 3
Greeks, 4, 8-9, 14, 21, 23-24, 29, 41, 51-52, 65-66, 68, 73, 76, 80, 139, 167, 253, 257, 277, 283, 309, 351, 367, 373, 382

Habakkuk, 24, 74
Hadad, 389
Haggai, 6
Ham, 373
Hermas, 383, 386
Hermes, 5, 383, 386
Herod, 279
Herodion, 382

Idumeans, 258
Illyricum, 371, 373-74
Incarnation, 9, 56
Isaac, 15, 21, 63, 90-92, 95, 97, 101, 220-24, 228, 337
Isaiah, 18, 55-56, 74, 128, 165, 173, 202, 239-42, 244, 246, 251, 253-54, 256-57, 265-66, 280, 286, 307, 346, 360, 365-66, 371
Ishmael, 11, 223
Israel (people), 8, 10, 19, 42, 53, 55, 59, 63, 81, 91, 165, 197, 219-23, 234-35, 239-44, 248, 252, 256-70, 272-73, 278-83, 288-89, 304, 369, 373
Israel (person), 3, 54, 220-23, 279
Israelites, 54, 60, 217, 219, 222, 235, 239, 241-42, 257, 265-67, 279-80, 288

Jacob, 3, 21, 54, 60, 63, 97, 113, 219-24, 226-28, 255, 258, 259, 278, 281, 337, 365
James (father of Judas), 4
James (letter writer), 61, 80
James (son of Alphaeus), 4
Jason, 390-91
Jehoiachin, 4
Jeremiah, 59-60, 74, 165, 234, 311, 395
Jerusalem, 5, 204, 239, 241, 244, 254, 296, 371, 373-79
Jesse, 366, 370
Jews and Greeks, 8, 9, 24, 44, 52, 65-66, 68, 73, 76, 253, 283, 309, 351
Jezebel, 261

John Chrysostom, 395
John the Baptist, 8, 91, 94-95, 117, 119, 254, 263, 295
John the Evangelist, 8, 24, 50, 115, 134, 138, 240, 308, 315, 326, 332, 342
Jonah, 6, 15
Judas Iscariot, 166, 188-89, 211, 214, 306, 386
Judas, son of James, 4
Judea, 8, 223, 370, 378-79
Julia, 383
Julian, 118, 140
Junias, 382, 385

Laban, 113-14
Law and Prophets, 8, 42, 55-56, 72-74, 91, 119, 147, 177, 246, 285, 295, 326
Lebbaeus, 4
Levi, 115, 210
Levi (Matthew), 4
Lot, 302, 304, 337, 381
Lucius, 390-91
Luke the Evangelist, 4, 13, 15, 79, 253
Lystra, 391

Macedonia, 5, 376
Mammon, 251
Manichees, 9, 29, 186, 192
Marcion, 9
Mark the Evangelist, 4, 13
Mary, 382, 384, 385
Mary (Virgin), 17, 19, 137, 366
Matthew the Evangelist, 4, 13
Meshach, 320
Moabites, 258
Moses, 8, 11, 13-15, 46, 49, 56, 60-61, 63, 66-68, 70-71, 76, 81, 84, 92, 95-96, 112-14, 116-17, 119-22, 125, 128-29, 138-39, 147, 155-56, 162, 166-67, 170, 174, 184, 187, 219, 221, 226-28, 235, 240, 243, 248-49, 253, 256-58, 268, 283, 285, 320, 325, 350, 354, 369, 372-73

Narcissus, 382
Nazarite, 290
Nebuchadnezzar, 14, 320
Necessity, 175-76
Nereus, 383
Nero, 383
Noah, 337

Obed, 366
Olympas, 383
Onesimus, 6, 383

INDEX OF NAMES

Origen, 395

Palestine, 377
Paraclete, 335, 392
Paradise, 123, 126, 166-67, 242
Parthian, 3
Patrobas, 383, 386
Pelagians, 150, 251, 287
Pelagius, 33-34, 57, 225, 394, 395
Persis, 383
Peter, 3, 7, 43, 76, 81, 90, 106, 244, 246, 250, 252-53, 264, 315, 332-33, 348, 350, 354, 363, 387
Pharisees, 79, 243, 265-66, 307
Philemon, 6, 383
Philippians, 2, 4, 6, 340
Philologus, 383
Phlegon, 383, 386
Phoebe, 3, 381-82
Prisca (Priscilla), 8, 383-85
Pythia, 218

Quartus, 390

Rahab, 25, 257
Rebecca, 210, 212, 220, 222-24
Red Sea, 10, 12
Romans, 1, 2, 5-7, 9-10, 12, 16, 20, 22-23, 38, 270-71, 295, 298, 325, 340, 356, 364, 375-80, 382, 384, 387, 392-93
Rome (city), 5-8, 13, 16, 20-22, 259, 374-76, 378, 383-84
Rufus, 383, 386

Sabbath, 47, 49, 73, 78, 81, 240, 243, 280, 340
Samaria, 31, 261
Samaritans, 21, 314
Sarah, 3, 54, 95, 98, 220, 222-24
Satan, 2, 99, 114, 120, 128, 153, 164-65, 173, 185, 374, 387, 389, 390
Saul (King), 194, 211, 227
Saul (Paul), 3-4, 17
Scythians, 16, 29, 258
Sergius Paulus, 3
Seth, 119, 273

Shadrach, 320
Shepherd (The), 386
Shunammite, 304
Sibyl, 271
Simon the Cananean, 4
Simon (Peter), 3
Sodom, 40, 68, 96, 240-42
Solomon, 4, 31, 59, 69, 200, 203, 259, 267, 274, 297, 307, 311-12, 389-90, 392
Sosipater, 390, 391
Spain, 375
Stachys, 382
Stephen, 4, 17
Syria, 316, 395
Syrians, 8, 20, 258

Tarsus, 391
Tertius, 390
Thaddaeus, 4
Theodoret, 395
Thessalonica, 391
Thomas, 4, 255
Thracians, 16
Timothy, 3, 6, 302, 330, 389-91
Trinity, 60, 99, 214, 218, 366, 371, 393
Tryphaena, 382
Tryphosa, 382
Tychicus, 6

Urbanus, 382
Uzziah, 4

Valentinus, 9
Valley of Jehoshaphat, 345
Wisdom (personified), 125, 209, 236
Word of God, 17, 209, 214, 218, 224, 294, 296, 335, 348, 350, 369, 372, 374, 377, 387, 392

"Zebedee, sons of," 3
Zechariah, 95
Zedekiah, 4
Zephaniah, 6
Zion, 244, 278, 281

Index of Subjects

Abraham, 222, 276-77
    children of, 62, 221-22, 240, 261, 365
    father of all, 90-93, 95
Adam
    all sinned in, 112, 118-19, 121-22, 126-27, 226, 237
    and Christ, 112, 115, 117-27
    sin of, 114-24, 120, 194
Almsgiving, 296-303
Apostles, 254, 257-58, 282, 290, 374, 385
Astrology, 191

Baptism, 174, 194, 197, 224, 328
    of Christ, 133-39, 148, 156-57
    and circumcision, 58-59, 92, 367
    and the Holy Spirit, 99, 183
    and resurrection, 135-36
    as ritual, 134
    sin and, 85, 89, 99, 133, 137, 139, 186, 213, 328
Barbarians and Greeks, 10-11, 24
Blasphemy, 56-57
Blessing, 304
Boasting, 84-87, 103, 105, 109, 373
Body, 144-45, 177-78
    of Christ, 117, 136-37, 294-99, 369
    of death, 174, 181
    defects, 290, 292
    of glory, 181
    mortal, 142-44, 179, 194-95
    passions of, 139, 143-45, 148, 160-61, 330-31, 333
    of sin, 136-39, 174

Calling, 210-12, 230-32, 254, 259
    of apostles, 2-4, 14, 16
    of nations, 3
    of saints, 2, 14

Children (of God), 44, 110, 115, 150, 248, 365
    adopted, 25, 99, 219, 222, 239-42, 262, 275
    and baptism, 60, 85, 94, 194
    and the Spirit, 105, 196-203, 207
Christ, 14, 19, 324, 329-31
    and Abraham, 222, 240-41, 369-70
    and Adam, 112, 115, 117-27, 140
    burial of, 134
    and the church, 117, 136, 203, 294-99, 369
    conception of, 5, 15, 18, 188
    and the cross, 142, 258-59
    and the curse, 77, 91, 126, 139-40
    death of, 108, 110, 115, 136-41, 157, 341-43
    descent of to the dead, 343
    and devil, 63, 74, 185-86, 240, 250, 280, 343
    as divine and human, 17-19, 112, 253
    divinity of, 15, 18, 220
    dying for, 341-43
    faith of, 75
    and light, 328
    as Lord, 342
    as mediator, 19, 103, 136-41, 153, 157, 214
    miracles of, 3, 15, 18
    and Mosaic Law, 46, 55, 261
    and patriarchs, 55, 253
    as physician, 192
    as predestined, 6, 18-19
    as priest, 21
    prophecies about, 11-12, 15
    as redeemer, 99, 240, 342-44, 353-54, 369
    as rejected, 11-12, 244, 246, 256, 363-64, 369
    resurrection of, 15, 18, 341-42
    as root, 273
    as sacrifice, 77, 184, 189, 292
    and sin, 188-89, 317
    and Spirit, 15, 165

INDEX OF SUBJECTS

suffering of, 18
sustaining the weak, 362-63, 365
church, 239, 241, 268, 275, 324
   as body of Christ, 117, 294-99, 369
   as bride of Christ, 136, 203
   gifts of, 294-97, 299
   and nations, 370, 383-84, 392-93
Circumcision, 59-60, 367, 391-92
   and faith, 90-92
   of flesh and heart, 3, 56, 58-60, 90-92, 365
   and justification, 84, 90, 92-93, 95
   and Mosaic law, 60, 95
   as required, 10, 91, 95
Compassion, 296-98
Concupiscence, 72, 142
Confession (of faith), 252
Conscience, 50, 54, 67, 129, 218, 317-18, 321-22
   and food, 340-41, 347-48, 350-58
Consent, 143, 147, 170, 178-81
Consolation, 306
Continence, 290
Conversion, 89
Covetousness, 34, 162-64, 167
Creation, 13-16, 20, 200-204
Cross, 139-40, 142, 258-59
Curse, 77, 91, 126, 218-21, 306

Death, 240
   of Christ, 104, 108, 110, 256
   first, 113-14, 148, 151-52
   natural, 110, 117
   reign of, 113-17, 119-22, 125, 136-41, 148, 151
   second, 24, 99, 113-14, 143, 158, 174
   and sin, 113, 115, 117-20, 126, 152-53, 175
   to sin, 136-41, 148, 151, 159
   spiritual, 97, 148, 151-52
   spread of, 118, 119, 159
Delight and fear, 148-49, 181
Devil, 307, 330, 368-69, 389-90
   and Christ, 185-86
   and law, 164, 166, 284
   power of, 143, 173
   and sin, 158, 164, 173, 185
   and sinners, 74, 164, 174, 186, 268-69, 280, 317
   works of, 24, 151, 166
Discerning good and evil, 9, 41, 50, 71
Disciple, 193, 368-69, 383

Equality, 3, 11, 16, 47, 231, 272
Election, 212-13, 222, 226, 231, 261-62, 279
   and merits, 223-25, 258, 279
Encouragement, 360-61

Endurance, 103, 105
Envy, 20, 34-36, 74, 300, 308, 329
   devil and, 99, 128, 151, 164
   of the Jews, 266, 270, 274, 280
Eternal life, 42-44, 69, 126-29, 141, 150-53, 165, 183, 195, 291
Evil, 36, 41-42, 192, 235, 311-13
Evildoers, 38-39, 52, 113
Exhortation, 296-97, 299

Faith, 253-54, 295, 299
   of Abraham, 53, 98, 222
   affirms implausible, 98-99, 100, 103, 191, 250, 252
   credulity, 352
   of Gentiles, 11, 222
   as gift of God, 45, 97, 103, 251, 255, 296, 298
   justifying, 70, 242, 250, 347, 351-58
   living by, 24-26, 242, 273
   and Mosaic law, 9, 55, 73, 81-82, 243, 246
   reconciling, 103-5
   rewarded, 84, 86, 98
   and righteousness of God, 24-25
   saving, 23, 25, 46, 103, 242, 254-55
   weak and strong, 334-38, 352, 357, 362
   and works, 247
Fasting, 339-41
Fear, 21, 57, 111, 197, 236, 250, 318
Fidelity, 24, 63, 64
Flesh, 161, 179, 191-92
   desires of, 129, 144, 168, 172, 179-80, 183-84, 190-95
   destroyed sin, 141, 189-90
   goodness of, 173-74
   living according to, 1, 156, 190, 194-96
Flesh of sin, 174, 183, 185, 187-88
Flesh and spirit, 161, 172, 175, 186, 190-93, 195
   and peace, 104, 186
Food, 334-38, 340-41, 346-57
   and idolatry, 226-28, 261, 336, 350
Foreknowledge (divine), 22, 100, 200, 223, 229-30, 237, 239
   and election, 16-17, 209-11, 222, 226-28, 261
Foreshadowing, 158, 186-87, 222, 238, 291
Forgiveness, 9, 66, 147, 150, 158, 185-87, 238, 291
   and faith, 84-85, 253, 284
Free will, 150, 174, 229
   choice, 107, 144, 165, 175-76, 178, 272-73, 277, 281
   determinism, 1, 175-76, 228, 233-34, 238, 272-73
   and faith, 246, 256, 281
   performance of, 171, 184

Index of Subjects

Futility, 30-31, 200-203

Gentiles, 268-77, 365-66, 373, 377, 383
Glory, future, 44, 199-200
Gentleness, 6, 9, 172, 195, 302, 306, 326
Gospel, 11
   delay of, 2, 9, 14, 22
Governance (church), 297
Governance (divine), 21, 27, 70, 164-65, 229-30, 233-36, 273, 321
   denied, 35, 38, 128, 164
   and human action, 229-30, 268-71, 274, 278-84
   unsearchable, 286-88
Governance (human), 315-23
Grace, 7, 146, 178-79, 390
   and faith, 246, 251-52, 255
   and free choice, 230, 231, 251-52, 259, 264, 280
   and good works, 71, 130, 224-25, 145, 221
   gratuitous, 10, 20, 99, 147, 151-52, 225-26, 238, 262-65, 286, 295
   and law, 146
   merits of, 67, 147
   as persuasive, 15, 294-96
   precedes works, 71, 130, 224-26, 230
   reign of, 122, 125, 128-30, 145
   and sin, 121-29, 146, 150, 238
Gratitude, 7, 8, 20

Habit, 171, 183
Handing over, 214
Hardening, 230, 235, 238, 266-67, 270-71, 275-76, 280
Hatred, 195, 301
Hell, 73-74, 99, 113, 122, 151-52, 158, 174, 186, 250
Holiness, 15, 16, 150, 290
Holy Spirit, 183, 196-97, 206-7
   as gift, 193-98, 208, 302-3
   living by, 185-86, 188, 195-96, 302-3
   as pledge, 103, 105, 198-99
   and righteousness, 165-66
Honor, 44
Hope, 98, 100, 103, 105, 150, 205, 303
Hospitality, 304, 381, 383-84
Humility, 297-98, 305, 326
Hypocrisy, 19, 38, 56-57, 228

Idolatry, 10-12, 17-19, 26-27, 33, 46, 235, 306, 336
Idols, 15, 17, 26, 29, 31
Ignorance, 17, 49
Image of God, 14, 27, 209-11, 290
Impurity, 32-33, 251, 290, 301
Incarnation, 5, 9, 55-56

Infidelity, 24, 62, 64, 66, 70
   of Jews, 62-64, 74, 268-74, 288
Inheritance, 94-95, 97, 197-99
Innocence, 108-9
Intention, 149, 170-72
Intercession, 17, 213
Israel, 10
   spiritual and carnal, 3, 53, 272
   true and false, 239, 265-66

Jealousy, 259, 266, 277
Jews, 56, 60, 76, 270-71, 278
   belief and unbelief of, 261, 270, 274, 277-78, 281-82
   as elect, 221, 261, 269-70, 279
   as jealous, 257, 259, 266, 270, 277
Jews and Gentiles, 10-12, 74
   joined, 10, 198, 242, 366-67, 370
   mutual service of, 269-75, 278-83
   as saved, 239-42, 252-53, 269-75
   as sinners, 8-9, 55, 242
Judgment (divine), 41, 43, 47, 265-67, 344-47
   delayed, 38-39, 41, 44
   impartial, 38-39, 43-45, 231-32, 266-67, 287
Judgment (human), 336-37, 344-45
Justice (divine), 225-26, 226-38, 266-67, 287
   and mercy, 285, 288
Justice (human), 95, 169, 287, 307
Justification, 78-81, 84-89, 91-93, 95, 224-25
   in Christ, 78, 80, 109

Kiss, 386-87
Knowledge (divine), 210, 234
Knowledge (human), 66, 75, 339-40
   of God, 9, 11, 13-15, 27-30

Languages, 103
Law, 174, 316
   dead to, 155, 157, 159-60
   death of, 155, 157, 159-60
   of death, 158, 183
   and divine will, 42, 163, 165, 168, 170, 176
   of faith, 96, 158
   of flesh, 171, 174, 184
   on heart, 51-53, 165
   letter and spirit of, 3, 50, 58, 67, 349
   of love, 21-22
   in members, 96, 129, 156, 171-72, 187
   of mind, 96, 156, 172, 174, 187
   reign of, 160-61, 178-80
   and righteousness, 70, 130, 146, 160, 162-63, 167

INDEX OF SUBJECTS

and sin, 71-72, 120, 128, 130, 146, 160-63, 166-68, 184, 187
of sin, 96, 118, 126, 172, 174, 180, 183-87
of Spirit, 58, 183-84, 187, 243
types of, 48, 67, 70-71, 96, 243
of works, 84-85, 96
Law (Mosaic), 3, 174, 184, 187, 189, 219, 332
abbreviated, 8, 240
abolished, 8, 78, 155-56, 240, 247-48
and Christ, 46, 55-56, 60, 73, 248-50, 261
and faith, 81, 94, 243, 265
and Gentiles, 46, 66, 284-85
and Jews, 11, 12
letter and spirit of, 170
natural law, 50, 67, 128, 130, 166-67
and rituals, 47, 94, 240, 242, 280
and Roman Christians, 8-9
and sin, 164, 167
and transgression, 96, 165, 167, 187
and wrath, 94, 96, 165
Law (natural), 113, 170
accuses, 67-68, 70-71, 75, 95-96, 162-63
approved, 170-71, 179
and faith, 47, 146-47, 243
human law, 317-18, 320, 322-23
and judgment, 8-9, 46, 47-50, 53, 70-71, 116
on heart, 51-52, 113, 129, 162, 174, 184-85, 317-18
parts of, 53, 70-71, 113, 116
and sin, 62, 128
Law (Paradisal), 166-68
Life (eternal), 11, 143, 150-52
Light and darkness, 327-28, 331-32
Love, 106-7, 149, 169
of enemies, 305-6, 310-12, 325, 368-69
of God, 106-7, 169, 247, 291, 300-301, 325-26
of neighbor, 301-2, 324-26
and obedience, 8-9, 21
of sinners, 301, 309
Love (Christ), 215-16
Love (divine), 103-6, 110-11, 298
Lust, 171-72, 178-81

Manna, 10-11
Marriage, 290, 383
Martyrdom, 192, 290, 383
Mercy, 237-38, 283, 291
and ministry, 291, 296-97, 300
Merits, 150-53, 255, 281-82
Mind, 145, 174, 183
Ministers, 8, 381-82
Miracles, 10, 23, 217, 254, 373-74
Money, 376

Mortality, 142-43, 200-201, 204, 291

Nature, 50, 53, 255-56

Obedience, 130, 173, 187, 213, 291, 302, 322, 387-89
of Christ, 118, 121-27, 353, 355-56
Obstacle
to neighbor, 346, 348, 350-51, 353, 355-56
Olive
grafting of, 53
Oracle, 63, 303

Passion, 170-72, 176, 329
Paternity, 391
Patience (divine), 39-41, 77, 229-30, 236-37, 276
Paul, 2-5, 14-19
authorship of, 2-8, 13
Peace, 254, 307-10, 350, 354, 371, 380
and struggle, 44, 104-5
Penance, 195
Perseverance, 287
Philosophers, 28
Poverty, 40, 292-93, 330-33, 362, 375-77
Prayer, 206-8, 290, 348, 378-79, 390-91
Preaching, 253-57, 294, 299, 373-75
Predestination, 18-19, 100
foreknowledge, 17, 209, 222, 226-28, 261-62
gratuitous, 19-20, 211-12, 262
Presence (divine), 6-7, 27, 209-12
Presumption, 40
Pride, 55, 86, 92, 130, 299, 303, 305-9, 357
in merits, 10, 40, 153
Promises (divine), 11, 94-95, 100, 221, 224, 367
Prophecy, 267-68, 295-97, 299, 306
Prophets, 2, 4, 17
Propitiation, 77
Prudence, 296
Punishment
delay of, 236-37, 276
nonremedial, 33-36, 246, 19-21
remedial, 111, 236, 267
of sin, 17-19, 42, 111, 169
Purpose (divine), 209, 212, 222-23, 232, 234-35

Red Sea, 10, 12
Redemption
as exchange, 76-77, 157-58
Rejoicing, 305, 308
Remnant (of Israel), 239-42, 262-63, 279, 281-82
Renewal (of life), 134-35
Resurrection, 101, 137-38, 195
of Christ, 101

Index of Subjects

Revenge, 309-11
Reward, 42-43, 251, 261, 328, 332
Righteousness, 108-9, 143, 150
   before humans, 84-86, 143, 247, 250, 265
   of law, 184, 187
Righteousness (divine), 67, 75, 76
   of Christ, 73, 243-44, 247, 249
   gratuitous, 24-25, 87
   and law, 24, 73, 246-47
   promises of, 24, 62-63, 73-74, 246
Righteousness (human), 48, 70, 123
   and faith, 10, 12, 60, 84-85, 87-88, 243-44, 248-50, 265
   gratuitous, 52, 74-75, 147, 151-53, 244, 247-48
   and law, 10, 243, 248, 265
   and works, 46, 99, 244, 250-51, 265
Rulers, 318-23

Sacrifice, 77, 290-92
   by priest, 21, 291-92
   and sin, 137, 184, 189, 291
   and victim, 289-92, 372-73
Saints, 11, 22, 106, 290-92, 301-2, 377
Salvation
   economy of, 15, 74, 205-6, 240
Scripture, 5, 267-68, 271, 334-36, 339, 361, 364
Servant, 1, 14, 21, 22
   of God, 146-48, 301-3
   of sin, 146-47, 150
Servile status, 223
Sexual desire, 34
Sin, 19, 22, 85, 113, 164, 171, 213, 286
   body of, 136-40
   condemned, 184-86, 188-90
   and death, 144, 149-52, 163
   dying to, 132-34, 136-42, 149-50, 157-58, 160
   and flesh, 174
   justifies God, 13, 65, 132-33
   and law, 116, 162-68
   living to, 19-21, 133-34, 157
   original, 121, 125, 173-74, 183-84, 238
   reign of, 128-30, 142-45, 149-51, 170-74, 174, 177, 180
   universal, 13, 66, 69-70, 73, 238
Sin of Adam, 112-13, 119, 168
   and death, 121-23, 125-27
   as universal, 122-23, 126, 173, 237
   and weakness, 173
Soul, 137, 139, 202-3, 315, 327
Spirit (human), 196, 199, 207-8, 315
Strengthening, 392
Suffering
   as temporary, 103-5, 111-12, 199-200, 303

Taxes, 317-18, 321, 323
Teaching, 107
   as ministry, 296-97, 299
Transgression, 168
   of Adam, 114, 117
   and law, 96, 114, 116, 160
   as sin, 160, 167-68, 187
Trinity, 20, 366, 390, 393
Truth, 218
   suppressed, 12, 26, 28, 32

Unbelief, 11, 253
Underworld, 114
Unity (Christian), 22, 364, 367-70, 388

Vengeance, 44
Victory, 216
Virgin, 210, 290
Vocation, 2-4, 14, 16

Weak and strong, 360-63, 370
Will (divine), 209, 290, 292-93, 343
Willing (human), 71, 171, 183, 209
Wisdom (divine), 191-92, 290, 392-93
Wisdom (worldly), 23, 191, 258, 305, 10, 13
Women ministers, 381-86
Works, 46, 52, 57-58, 71, 87-89, 264, 327-28
   of faith, 63
   of law, 11, 263-64
World, 269
Worship, 289
Wrath, 310-11
   of God, 26, 29, 44, 231-38

Index of Scripture References

HEBREW BIBLE

Genesis
1:31	337, 356
2:17	187
2:24	34
3:8	251
3:19	201
4:1	137, 210
4:8	36
4:13	71, 162
6:3	193
8:21	119
12:7	241
15:5	98
15:6	83, 98
15:16	40, 53, 84
17:4	93
17:5	3, 100
17:15	3
18:3	304
18:10	220, 222
20:4-5	54
21:12	220
22:1-13	15
22:18	53, 130, 222, 365, 370
24:16	210
25:1-6	223
25:23	220, 226
31:30	114
31:32	113
32:30	221
35:1	3
39:20	70
40	113
40:1-3	70
42:21	71
42:22	54
49:8	55

Exodus
2:11	113
3:6	21
3:14	97
4:21	230
6:2-3	253
9:16	162, 226
12	15
17:11-13	15
18:4	149
20:3-17	324
20:13	324
20:17	161
21:15	116
24:7	128
32:10	369
32:25-29	228
32:32	219, 369
33:19	226

Leviticus
4	290
4:3	189
4:3-4	189
4:4	189
11:4	352
11:29	94
12:28	137
15:31	9
19:18	307, 324, 325

Numbers
21:9	15
24:17	365

Deuteronomy
5:21	161
6:13	112
9:28	221
10:16	60
21:23	138
24:13	126
25:4	361
27:26	265
29:29	86, 337
30:12	249, 250
30:14	242, 249, 250
32:7	372
32:8-9	219, 269
32:35	310
32:43	366
33:9	210

Joshua
1:2	14
2:1-6	25
2:10	257
6:17-25	25
24:2	114

Judges
20:18	55

1 Samuel
10:10	194

2 Samuel
12:24-25	4

1 Kings
2	389
12:28	31
15:26	117

Index of Scripture References

19:10	260
19:18	260

2 Kings
15:1-7	4
15:32-34	4
25:7	4
25:27	4

2 Chronicles
25:4	126

Job
14:4-5	136
31:33	71

Psalms
2:1	306
2:8	94
2:11	331
6:8	110
14:3	119
16:5	199
18:43-45	370
19:1	29, 257
19:3-4	258
19:4	19, 256
21:19	306
22:26	57
23:6	152
26:5	387
31:19	236, 283
32:1	85, 148
32:1-2	85, 90
32:2	85, 90
32:9	49
33:1	25, 26
34:3	57
36:4	49
36:6	267
36:11	130
37:23	130
37:27	58
38:6	200
41:4	53, 130
43:3	116
44:22	3, 215
44:25	137
44:26	116
45:2	19
50:10	193
50:18	309
51:1	130
51:4	65, 71
51:5	137, 183
52:8	273
55:8	286
59:10	152
59:10-11	271
59:11	260, 271
66:3	277, 278
67:19	117
69:6	359
69:22	306
69:22-23	270
72:7	371
73:28	291
76:1	239
79:6	49
85:10	104
85:11	104
94:10	1
102:26	201, 202
103:4	152
105:15	14
105:27	373
109:7	213, 352
109:9	306
111:5	213
114:2	60
115:11	64
117:22	198
119:29	130, 187
119:40	130
119:91	14
119:133	130, 145
120:3-4	313
120:6	307
127:1	229
132:11	365
144:5	116
145:14	336
147:20	57

Proverbs
1:6	2
1:7	69
3:16	75
3:27	297-298
3:34	307
8:35	246
13:24	236
14:14	322
19:25	237
23:1	268
23:14-15	236
24:17	274
25:21-22	310
27:2	360
28:27	297

Ecclesiastes
1:2	200
1:2-3	201
5:4	39
5:7	39
7:16	311

Isaiah
1:26	321
3:4	321
5:14	120
5:20	387
5:21	307
6:10	246
9:9	361
7:9	153
7:14	18
8:20	128
10:22	270
10:22-23	239
11:10	366
28:16	244, 249, 251
40:2	296
40:5	194
40:13	286
42:14	38
43:10	346
44:6	346
45:9	232
45:13	267
45:14-15	55
45:23	346
47:14-15	311
50:1	173
51:6	202
52:5	54, 56
52:7	253, 254, 257
52:15	361
53:1	253
53:4	155, 360
53:11	155
55:21	346
56:7	74
59:21	165
61:1	385
65:2	256, 259
66:2	326

Jeremiah
3:15	321
4:4	59, 60, 365
9:26	59
12:10	269
18:2-10	235
24:6	276

INDEX OF SCRIPTURE REFERENCES

25:9	14
26:2	295
31:33	53
31:33-34	166
31:34	74

Ezekiel

18:4	97, 143, 151, 163, 194
33:10	40
33:12	353
36:27	252

Daniel

2:34-35	244
3:29	320
3:86 (LXX)	50
4:14	318
7:9-10	345
7:10	345
10:13	203

Hosea

2:7	380

Joel

1:5	176
2:32	249, 253
3:2	345
3:12	345
3:14	345

Habakkuk

2:4	23, 74, 85, 153, 265

Zechariah

12:2	239

Malachi

1:2-3	220, 223, 226
1:6	197, 317
3:6	62

NEW TESTAMENT

Matthew

1:21	14
3:7	263
3:9	263
3:17	56
4:10	112
5:3	299, 377
5:4	305
5:7	378
5:11-12	103
5:16	309, 361
5:20	307
5:43	307
5:45	38
5:46	368
6:9	52, 198
6:9-10	207
7:5	307
7:7	5
7:12	50, 177, 305
7:15	388
7:18	149
7:23	177, 181, 209
8:10	63
8:11-12	63
8:22	148
9:9	4
9:11	361
9:12	368
9:21	247
10:3-4	4
10:6	270
10:19-20	165
10:20	206, 207
10:21	213
10:28	148
10:32	110
10:38	193
11:14-15	263
11:21	306
11:23	306
11:25	366
11:29	326
11:29-30	148
11:30	242
12:27	47
12:33	149, 273
12:36	345
12:39	15
12:42	59
13:13	256
13:17	14
15:10-20	336
15:11	348
15:19	348
15:24	10, 269, 369
15:26	10, 269
16:16	363
16:17	3
17:5	350
17:11	282
17:27	317
18:19	364
18:20	364
19:21	333
19:28	197
20:13-15	232
20:15	232
20:28	365
20:41	379
21:42	198
21:43	239
22:9	269
22:13	328
22:14	210, 212, 230, 231, 279, 392
22:21	315, 317, 318
22:24	319
22:30	349
22:32	148
22:37	326
22:37-39	326
22:38-41	269
22:39	326
22:42-46	268
23:8	336
24:40-41	51
25:21	316
25:42	317
26:41	194
27:40	259, 363
27:42	259, 363
27:50	141
27:52-53	117
28:19	125, 393
28:20	215, 393

Mark

2:11	192
2:28	81
3:16-17	3
3:18	4
8:35	218
10:18	110
10:45	369

Luke

1:17	263
1:31	14
1:35	137
1:36	183
2:29	152, 254
3:6	194
4:18	19, 385
5:27	4
6:15-16	4
6:45	313
7:37-39	79
7:39	361
7:47	130

Index of Scripture References

7:48-50	79	4:19	20	20:22	193
8:3	386	4:20	326	20:29	255
8:10	15	4:22	376	21:15	7
8:11	240	4:23	21		
8:12	173	5:1	86	**Acts**	2, 3, 193
8:45	370	5:18	86	2:3-11	103
9:48	56	5:21	390	3:6	315, 377
10:1	385	5:22	197, 213	3:15	387
10:1-20	211	5:23	109	3:17	246
10:16	289	5:26	390	3:23	253
10:20	305	5:39	76	4:10	244
10:29	52	5:43	281	4:12	90
10:29-37	324	5:45	268	4:16	216
10:33-34	87	5:46	63, 81, 240	4:24	364
11:52	266	6:29	88, 335	4:24-28	279
12:46	50	6:38	363	4:30	364
12:47	49	6:44	209	5:15	348
12:48	49	6:60-71	211	5:28-29	316
14:11	307	7:48	226	5:29	315
15:4	259	8:28	15	8:2	383
15:8	259	8:34	113	9:4	17
16:8	388	8:36	150	10:5	354
16:16	8, 91, 117, 119, 295	8:44	64	10:13	350
16:23	114	8:56	14, 101	10:14	350
16:29	119	10:16	263	10:15	350
17:5	97	10:17-18	188	10:34-35	43
18:1	253	10:20	265	10:36	253
18:14	274	10:21	265	11–12	92
19:10	45	10:27	263	11:18	366
21:28	327	11:50	218	13:6-12	3
23:39-43	92	12:24	241	13:9	4
23:42	78	12:34	268	13:46	269, 270
23:43	78, 242	12:39	266	14:12	5
24:32	194	12:39-40	246	15:24	316
		12:40	266	16:1-3	391
John		12:47	269	16:3	302
1:1	97	13:18	263	16:14	15
1:3	253	13:34	302	16:17	218
1:5	254	13:35	368	16:18	218
1:9	2	14:6	42	17:1-9	391
1:12	150	14:9	221	17:28	32
1:14	214	14:30	188, 317	18:3	383
1:16	153	14:31	188	18:26	383, 384, 385
1:29	94, 188	15:5	329	19:12	348
1:45	46	15:13	214, 383	19:20	15
2:19	15	15:14	329	21:24	302
3:2	138, 332	16:9	64	23:3	306
3:5	43	16:12-13	335		
3:8	24	16:18	265	**Romans**	
3:16	369	17:3	249	1:7	391
3:18	43	17:12	261	1:11	6
3:21	50	17:18	365	1:13	375
3:30	81	17:21	106, 367	1:13-14	373
4:2	134	17:24	197	1:14-15	7
4:8	106	19:15	282	1:16	24, 52, 270

INDEX OF SCRIPTURE REFERENCES

Ref	Page	Ref	Page	Ref	Page
1:16-17	51	7:1	167, 176	11:6	52
1:17	153, 166	7:4	167	11:7	262, 279
1:18	32	7:7	187	11:8	280
1:18-20	43	7:8	178	11:9-10	270
1:21	43	7:8-9	116	11:11	276
1:22	33	7:9	68, 71, 178	11:11-12	280
1:23	33	7:11	178, 187	11:13	47
1:28-31	34	7:12	189	11:16	236
1:29	137	7:12-13	178	11:17	53
2:4-6	230	7:13	178, 181	11:25	286
2:5-6	310	7:18	184	11:25-26	91
2:6	40	7:22	187	11:33	67, 76, 238, 267
2:8-13	51	7:22-23	96	11:35	390
2:10	52	7:23	118, 129, 187	12:3	45
2:11	52, 287	7:24	137	12:11	64
2:12	120, 268	7:25	145, 187	12:19	309
2:14	147	8:1	180	13:2	84
2:14-15	184	8:2	180	13:10	130
2:15	72, 218	8:3	116, 137, 139, 140, 189	13:14	195
2:28-29	367	8:7	161	14:1-2	6
2:29	56	8:8	161	14:18	112
3:2	42, 267	8:10	329	15:14	7
3:4	67	8:11	160	15:15-16	7
3:8	141	8:12	63	15:25-26	5
3:9	129	8:13	251	16:1	3
3:20	75	8:14	196, 251	16:23	3
3:23	64, 87	8:23	179, 181		
3:24	52	8:27	209	**1 Corinthians**	
3:26	88	8:29	16, 18	1:13	88
3:27	96, 297-98	8:29-30	222	1:14	3
3:28	52	8:30	283	1:18	9
4:3	92	8:34	329	1:21	258
4:4	225, 265	8:35	219	1:24	125
4:5	67	8:35–9:1	3	1:30	76
4:15	72, 129, 167	8:38-39	3, 220	1:31	45, 104, 373
4:24	282	9:3	221	2:8	278
5:5	45, 130	9:11-12	212	2:9	207
5:12	102, 126, 187, 226	9:13	255	2:11	50
5:13	68	9:14	238, 267	2:14	196
5:14	102, 122, 123, 125, 168	9:15	226	2:15	335
5:18	186	9:19	203	3:2	335
5:19	124	9:32	246	3:6	229
5:20	72, 120, 133, 156, 160	10:3	305	3:7	229
6:1	142	10:3-4	244	3:13	345
6:1-2	147	10:4	250	3:16	290
6:2-4	152	10:8-10	242	3:21-22	134
6:3	139	10:10	141	4:5	345
6:4	141, 251, 329, 341	10:12	336	4:7	45, 75, 153, 273
6:5	135, 139, 329	10:15	257	4:10	244
6:7	130, 159	10:18	19	4:12	304
6:12	133	10:19-20	262	4:14	204
6:12-14	156	10:21	262	5:1-2	337
6:13	291, 293, 342	11:5	279	5:5	2, 165
6:17-18	14	11:5-6	212, 225	6:12	339
6:23	87	11:5-7	242	6:13	352

Index of Scripture References

6:16	142
6:17	97, 142, 301
7:1	6
7:15	309
7:16	385
7:29	301
8:6	301
8:8	354
9:9-10	361
9:16	16
9:20-21	349
9:22	170, 360
9:27	2, 3, 16, 173
10:11	361
10:23	339
10:31	331, 352
10:32	309, 351
10:33	349, 360, 363
12:3	350
12:7	295
12:8	1
12:9	97
12:11	295
12:26	306, 369
12:27	136
12:31	295
13:1-3	299
13:3	368
13:4	247
13:7	106
13:9	371
13:10	81
13:13	100
14:1	295
14:3	295
14:20	388
14:24-25	295
14:32	208
15:10	5, 16, 19, 171, 264
15:21	118
15:21-22	181
15:22	115, 127
15:25	319
15:26	151
15:44	179
15:53	181, 332
15:55	115, 181
15:56	115, 160
16:4	5
16:15	384
16:19	383

2 Corinthians

1:1	17
1:12	50
2:8	2
2:15	97
2:17	55
3:3	53, 129, 162
3:6	58, 63
3:7	81, 160, 248
3:11	219
3:13	248
3:13-16	245
3:15	119
3:18	135
4:8-10	2
4:10	134, 142, 290
4:12	141
4:16	135, 202
4:17-18	199
5:4	203
5:6	203
5:7	107
5:9-10	345
5:10	43
5:19	116
5:20	329, 371
5:20-21	188
5:21	181, 189
7:10	195, 305
8:9	362
9:2	5
9:6	300
9:7	300
10:17	45
11:2	203, 329
11:3	340
11:6	7, 184
11:10	218
11:26-27	16
11:28-29	296
12:7	153
13:3	189
13:4	268

Galatians

1:9	340
1:10	309, 360, 361
2:20	134, 214, 329
2:21	256
3:11	153
3:13	73, 91, 219
3:16	240, 241, 279
3:21-22	120
3:24	81
3:28	383
4:1	81, 85
4:1-3	197
4:6	207
4:19	204
4:22	361
4:26	254
5:2	91
5:4	95
5:6	45, 211
5:15	326
5:17	142, 161, 162
5:22	195
5:24	139, 148
6:1	362, 377
6:1-2	306
6:2	360, 369
6:8	333
6:14	176

Ephesians

1:23	329
2:4	353
2:6	135, 137
2:8	287
2:9	45
2:12	19
2:14	198, 369, 380
2:15	369
2:20	10
3:14-15	391
3:16-17	329
4:3	369
4:8	117, 225
4:32	360
5:2	189
5:8	192, 332
5:13	345
5:16	301, 302
5:25	362
5:27	136
5:32	117
6:6	320
6:12	173, 378

Philippians

1:7	4
1:23-24	203
1:29	97
2:6	185
2:6-7	361
2:6-8	305
2:7	362
2:8-9	197
2:10	220
2:12-13	230
2:13	165
3:2	340
3:3	58

3:5	67	4:1-3	352	4:10	264
3:9	24, 244	4:4-5	348		
3:10-11	2	5:2	385	**2 Peter**	
3:12-13	2	5:10	385	1:2	264
3:13-14	2	5:23	330	1:4	106
3:15	2			1:19	332, 333
3:19	21, 60, 176	**2 Timothy**		3:9	39
3:20-21	211	1:7	106		
3:21	137, 197	1:9	212	**1 John**	
4:7	380	2:19	209, 210	1:1	97
4:22	6	2:20-21	233	3:2	138, 332
		4:6	6	3:8	24
Colossians		4:6-8	203	3:21	50
1:13	106	4:7	225, 378	4:2	134
1:15	209, 273	4:7-8	225	4:8	106
1:16	27	4:14	306	4:19	20
2:11-12	367	4:15	389	4:20	326
2:15	116, 155, 185	4:20	3	5:1	86
2:20-23	6			5:18	86
2:21	56	**Philemon**			
3:1	138	1-2	383	**Revelation**	
3:4	324	2	6	4:8	342
3:5	142, 148	9	6	5:3	240
4:6	302			13:8	115
4:7	6	**Hebrews**			
4:17	6	1:14	203		
		3:1	19	**APOCRYPHA**	
1 Thessalonians		4:12	296		
2:16	282	4:15	247	**Wisdom of Solomon**	
2:18	374	5:14	335	1:2	259
4:3	291	6:5	97	2:24	151
4:9-10	5	7:9-10	115	4:11	287
5:5	332	8:3	21	9:15	203
5:19	303	10:38	153	10:1	125
		11:1	250	11:25	110
2 Thessalonians		11:31	25	13:9	31
1:7-8	49	12:2	362	15:17	31
2:8	281	13:24	6		
2:10-11	281			**Sirach**	
3:6	389	**James**		1:1	392
		1:17	153, 286	1:14	197
1 Timothy		2:17	59, 247	7:36	213
1:5	301	2:20	79	10:12	305
1:8	168	2:26	247	15:14	320
1:9-10	316	4:3	207	30:24	291
1:19	210	5:12	170		
2:4	97, 320			**Baruch**	
2:5	19, 53	**1 Peter**		4:4	42
2:7	225	1:18-19	76		
2:12	385	2:22	136, 188	**Bel and the Dragon**	
2:14	168	3:19	152	23-27	31
2:15	385	4:6	250		

www.ingramcontent.com/pod-product-compliance
Lightning Source LLC
Chambersburg PA
CBHW080722300426
44114CB00019B/2457